Internet Innovators

Internet Innovators

The Editors of Salem Press

SALEM PRESS
A Division of EBSCO Publishing

Ipswich, Massachusetts

GREY HOUSE PUBLISHING

Library of Congress Cataloging-in-Publication Data

Internet innovators / the editors of Salem Press.
    pages cm
  Includes bibliographical references and index.
  ISBN 978-1-4298-3807-8 (hardcover)
 1. Computer engineers--Biography. 2. Women computer engineers--Biography. 3. Internet industry. I. Salem Press.
  TK7885.2.I58 2013
  338.7'610046780922--dc23

2012045267

ebook ISBN: 978-1-4298-3808-5

Contents

PUBLISHER'S NOTE

Internet Innovators profiles the most innovative and influential individuals in the development of computer technology and the evolution of the Internet, many who have never been covered in any Salem Press set before. From the genesis of the World Wide Web in 1989 as a way to organize and manage data to the founding of the world's largest Internet retailer, Amazon.com, in 1994, to the first documented tweet in 2006, the history of the Internet is immeasurably rich, with milestones that have revolutionized our society. This new title examines those individuals most responsible for the technology and strategies behind the Internet today, from the pioneering community of engineers and intellectuals who worked to realize a vision of shared networks and research, to the dot-com founders and leaders driving business and commerce today.

SCOPE OF COVERAGE

Internet Innovators features more than 120 biographies of individuals who have had a significant influence on the development and evolution of the Internet, with an emphasis on dot-com founders and leaders. Each essay has been written specifically for this set; biographies represent a strong, global, cross-gender focus, and each biography offers a sidebar focusing on the company, organization, online service, or website with which that individual is most often associated. Among the editors' criteria for inclusion in the set was an individual's historical significance, whether through their respective company's influence in the Internet world or their role in the development and evolution of the Internet itself; his or her relevance to academic curriculum; and his or her appeal to high school and undergraduate students and general readers.

ESSAY LENGTH AND FORMAT

Each essay is approximately 2,000 words in length and displays standard reference top matter offering easy access to the following biographical information:

- The name by which the subject is best known.
- A succinct description of each individual's nationality and occupation.
- The most complete dates of birth and death, followed by the most precise locations of those events available.

- The areas of achievement, including primary field and specialty, with which the subject is often most closely identified. This latter is an all-encompassing categorical list and includes: mathematics and logic; physics and engineering; computer software; computer hardware; computer programming; security; Internet; management, executives, and investors; marketing; commerce; social media; content and data; applications; news and entertainment; and ethics and policy.
- The primary company or organization with which the individual has been associated in a meaningful way.
- A synopsis of the individual's historical importance in relation to computer technology and the evolution of the Internet, indicating why the person is or should be studied today.

Each essay concludes with a byline for the contributing writer. The bodies of the essays are divided into the following parts:

- Early Life provides facts about the individual's upbringing. Where little is known about the person's early life, historical context is provided.
- Life's Work, the heart of the article, consists of a straightforward, generally chronological account of how the individual gained recognition in his or her chosen primary field (applied science; computer science; business and commerce; and Internet), emphasizing the most significant endeavors and achievements—and failures—of the figure's life and career.
- Personal Information provides closing remarks on the person, including post–achievement activities or positions, family life, and topics of general interest.

Each essay also includes an annotated Further Reading section that provides a starting point for additional research.

SPECIAL FEATURES

Several features distinguish this series as a whole from other biographical reference works. The back matter includes the following aids, appendices, and indexes:

vii

- Timeline: presents a comprehensive time line of milestone events that represent a concise history of the Internet, both theoretical and commercial in scope.
- General Bibliography: offers an extensive list of resources relevant to the study of the history of computer technology and the Internet.
- Biographical Directory: an annotated and concise listing of those individuals featured in the volume.
- Category Index: profiles figures by area of primary field or specialty.
- Company Index: lists the individuals associated or affiliated with a company or organization, in many capacities.
- Index: provides a comprehensive index including people, scientific and computer-related concepts and discoveries, technologies, terms, principles, and other topics of discussion.

Other features include:

- Sidebars: A highlight of this publication and key feature of every essay, the sidebars describe the company, organization, online service, or website for which each profiled person is best known. Sidebars also describe why the company was influential in the Internet world.
- Images: More than eighty illustrations appear with the essays.

CONTRIBUTORS

Salem Press would like to extend its appreciation to all involved in the development and production of this work. The essays have been written and signed by writers and scholars of history, the sciences, and other disciplines related to the essays' topics.

CONTRIBUTORS

Sonya Alexander

Geoffrey R. Archer

Jean Béhue

Joe Bogdan

Sarah Boslaugh

Marcella Bush Trevino

Abby Dress

Ellen Elder

Shayna Hargraves

Jason A. Helfer

Sabine H. Hoffmann

Steve Jones

Bill Kte'pi

Vytautas Malesh

Shari Parsons Miller

Trish Popovitch

Wylene Rholetter

Elizabeth Rholetter Purdy

Tom J. Sanders

Stephen T. Schroth

Robert N. Stacy

John Walsh

Andrew J. Waskey

Rachel Wexelbaum

Gavin Wilk

Internet Innovators

A

Jay Adelson

CEO of Digg

Born: September 7, 1970; Detroit, Michigan
Died: -
Primary Field: Internet
Specialty: Social media
Primary Company/Organization: Digg

Introduction

One of the founders and the first chief executive officer (CEO) of the social news website Digg, Jay Adelson started with Netcom, one of the first wide-scale Internet providers, and was among the industry representatives called to testify before the U.S. House of Representatives' Homeland Security Subcommittee on Cybersecurity, Infrastructure Protection, and Security Technologies on the role of the private sector in securing the Internet. After leaving Digg in 2010, he became the CEO of SimpleGeo, Inc., a position he held for less than a year before the company was purchased by Urban Airship. He continues to serve as an adviser for SimpleGeo.

Early Life

Jay Steven Adelson was born on September 7, 1970, in Detroit, Michigan, and grew up in the suburb of Southfield. His parents, Sheldon and Elaine Adelson, were schoolteachers during his early childhood; then his father inherited a small electric supply store in Detroit that he strove to build into a sustainable business. His parents lost both the business and their house during a recession that hit Detroit hard in the late 1980s. Adelson has acknowledged that this experience shaped his fiscal philosophy and his belief that it is important to grow a business slowly to the point of sustainability, rather than chase billions in income.

In 1988, Adelson graduated from Cranbrook Schools, a private college preparatory school located in Bloomfield Hills, Michigan. That autumn he enrolled in Boston University, graduating in 1992 with a degree in film and broadcasting, having minored in computer science. After graduation, Adelson moved to San Rafael, California, because he had an unpaid internship as a sound engineer at Skywalker Sound. To earn money,

Jay Adelson.

Adelson relied on his college minor to land temporary tech jobs. He had a friend who was working with Netcom, and when he was offered a job with the company in 1993, Adelson took it.

LIFE'S WORK

Begun in nearby San Jose in 1988, Netcom was a startup put together by Bob Rieger and Bill Gitow to provide dial-up shell accounts to college students who wanted to be able to access their universities' networks when off campus. Shell accounts are accounts on remote servers that provide a command-line interface to a "shell," that is, software built around something, in this case the network connection. Shell accounts were more common before the World Wide Web became popular, because their interface is text-only; web access was available beginning in 1992 through a text-only browser called Lynx, and other services could be accessed through programs like Telnet (or its more secure cousin SSH), FTP (for "file transfer protocol," to transfer files to and from servers), Pine (an e-mail client), tin or trn (newsgroup clients), IRC (for "Internet relay chat," a group chat program), or talk (an instant-messaging program). Netcom also provided e-mail accounts to its customers, with an @netcom.com address.

Although the academic and scientific communities formed the traditional user base of the Internet when Netcom began, the company soon expanded its customer base and found that the demand for Internet access was higher than expected. Service extended beyond the academic community, and soon beyond the San Francisco area. The staff was expanded, and a Windows program called NetCruiser was developed to provide a graphical user interface (GUI) with the Internet service provided, in lieu or in addition to the command-line interface of the shell account. T1 accounts (faster-speed Internet access through dedicated lines, such as cable) were soon offered. In late 1995, toward the end of Adelson's tenure, the company expanded into Canada as it grew to become the world's largest Internet service provider (ISP) with the largest territory of coverage.

Adelson was hired as part of the staff expansion, initially as an installation coordinator. He soon became the director of network operations and was responsible for Netcom's network. He was in charge of the network at the time that hacker Kevin Mitnick was tracked down by computer security expert Tsutomu Shimomura and journalist John Markoff, after Mitnick used Netcom's network to access Shimomura's computer illegally, leading to an arrest that inspired a film and several

books. Netcom also made the news during Adelson's tenure when the ISP was sued for copyright infringement for providing service to a an electronic bulletin board system (BBS) that hosted documents alleged to infringe on the copyright held by the Church of Scientology, part of Scientology's ongoing effort to control access to its internal documents and prevent leaks onto the Internet.

Adelson left Netcom toward the end of 1996, shortly after getting married, and was hired by the Digital Equipment Corporation (DEC). He joined the team at DEC's Network System Laboratory that was developing the Palo Alto Internet Exchange (PAIX). PAIX is an Internet exchange point, part of the neutral Internet infrastructure used by ISPs to send traffic back and forth between their networks. PAIX was eventually spun off into PAIX, Inc., renamed the Peering and Internet Exchange, acquired by AboveNet, and sold to Switch and Data when AboveNet declared bankruptcy; Switch and Data was acquired by Equinix (which Adelson founded) in 2010. Adelson worked both on scaling the exchange point's operations to Internet traffic and building its data center.

Adelson left DEC along with his supervisor, Albert M. Avery IV, to found Equinix, Inc. in the summer of 1998. As chief technology officer and cofounder, Adelson continued in the same kind of work he had performed at the Network System Laboratory, responsible for the company's Internet exchange points and data centers as well as its research and development and patent generation. Although it was his technical expertise that he contributed to the venture, he proved instrumental in funding as well, raising capital in several private equity rounds prior to Equinix's August 2000 initial public offering (IPO); it is listed as EQIX on NASDAQ. The Equinix business model was to provide data centers to meet the demands of a rapidly growing Internet, and the IPO in the midst of the dot-com boom raised nearly $300 million. Like PAIX, the Internet exchanges provided by Equinix were network-neutral, meaning that no network received favorable treatment. When the bubble burst, Equinix was one of the survivors, and it bought up, at a discount, many of the surplus data centers left behind as dot-com businesses failed. It was able to prosper when many other companies in the industry were disappearing, and it was the best-performing stock on the NASDAQ from 2003 to 2004.

During this period, Adelson testified before the U.S. House of Representatives' Homeland Security Subcommittee on Cybersecurity, Infrastructure Protection, and

Affiliation: Digg

The social news site Digg was founded after Kevin Rose, host of Tech TV's *The Screen Savers* (the predecessor to G4's *Attack of the Show*) met Equinix founder Jay Adelson while interviewing him. Digg began in February 2005, with the collaboration of Adelson (the first CEO), Rose, Owen Byrne, and Ron Gorodetzky. The site's initial design was developed by Dan Ries.

Digg allows users to share and recommend content on the web, with a focus on news. Members vote on shared content, using a system familiar from Slashdot, Reddit, and other sites: A given page shared with the site may be voted up (a "digg") or voted down (a "bury"). The front page displays currently popular and trending content, which is constantly in flux as users read and respond to content and share new links. Changes to the website in the first year included adding categories for stories (technology, science, world and business, videos, entertainment, gaming), the capacity for users to build a friends list and keep track of their friends' stories, and improvements to the interface. Popularity grew steadily, and, like Slashdot, Reddit, and other sites, Digg experienced spikes in traffic resulting from a story becoming popular. One of Digg's primary merits was its ability to focus a spotlight on something on the Internet that might otherwise go unnoticed by most, so that audiences no longer had to rely as heavily on the news "curation" of traditional media.

The impact of user votes on the site inevitably led to attempts to game the system. There were several known attempts, uncovered by sting operations, to upvote stories for cash (with the implied threat of a downvote if no payment were made—a sort of protection racket). There was also the explicit, openly conducted Bury Brigade, which responded to the popularity of Ron Paul among Digg users—social news users in the United States long having included a vocal libertarian contingent—by downvoting every Paul story submitted in an attempt to bury any mention of him. Digg's popularity led to a high ranking on Google's PageRank, meaning that "digged" stories would feature prominently in Google search results—providing a clear financial motivation for abuses of the system.

Around the height of the site's fame, Google attempted to purchase Digg for $200 million but eventually walked away from the table without completing the deal. Digg was considered one of the ripest websites for purchase, and other deals were entertained, but by the end of the year, then-CEO Adelson announced that the company was not for sale. Fox News, Microsoft, and Yahoo! had been among the suitors. Over time, the shine may have left the apple, although hits remained high, with about 20 million visitors per month; Digg never developed the level of mainstream awareness that Facebook or Twitter did, and its niche competitor, Reddit, began to attract mainstream media attention because of several high-profile news stories and the celebrity involvement in AMA/IAMA threads. In 2010, the site had to lay off more than a third of its staff, and Adelson left after disagreements with Rose and others.

Google's AdSense was originally used to provide ads, the source of Digg's revenue, but in 2007 the company switched to Microsoft's ad service.

In 2012, Digg went through significant changes. Although it was widely reported that the site was sold for a paltry $500,000—an extremely low amount relative to both the market for popular websites and the previous offers that had been made—this price, paid by Betaworks, was only for the website, technology, and Digg brand. Patents developed under Adelson were sold to LinkedIn for an additional $4 million, and staff were transferred to *The Washington Post* for $12 million. The total was still a far cry from the $200 million once bandied about, but that reflected the financial realities of the intervening years as much as anything else.

On July 31, 2012, a new version of Digg launched, based in part on user surveys collected through Betaworks' RethinkDigg.com. The new site integrated better with social media (the site had been integrated with Facebook Connect since 2009 and offered an iPhone app, although a previously offered Android app was no longer available with the relaunch), featured a more image-heavy design, and was built around an editorially centered front page.

Security Technologies and worked extensively with the government in its inquiries into the nature of cyberspace threats and vulnerabilities. The work reportedly exhausted him. He and his family moved to New York in 2004 and commuted back and forth for five years between New York and San Francisco, where he founded Revision3 and Digg. In 2009, he moved back to California.

Equinix grew into a company with more than one thousand employees, a growth attributed to its flexibility and efficiency in creating "ecosystems" for different types of business customers, including an ecosystem of data centers and related services for the prosperous financial industry, designed to meet its needs. The company took advantage of the surplus of postboom data centers and used many of them for data colocation, the off-site storage of data for businesses like Microsoft, Google, and major banks. The boom in cloud computing has been a boon to Equinix, and Google uses Equinix data centers to back up much of its cloud for safekeeping. In addition to offering simple data storage, Equinix allows companies to outsource their information technology functions.

Adelson left Equinix in October 2005, a few months after starting the privately held companies Digg (in February) and Revision3 (in March). Digg was a social news website designed by Dan Ries for Adelson, Kevin Rose, Owen Byrne, and Ron Gorodetzky. Rose and Adelson had met when Rose was interviewing Adelson for TechTV's *Screen Savers* show (which, following TechTV's merger with G4, became *Attack of the Show*), and Rose put up the initial investment in Digg while Adelson acted as CEO, provided mentorship based on his experiences with Equinix, and raised a round of venture capital, after which he left Equinix to focus on the two start-ups full time. The offices were established in San Francisco despite Adelson's continuing to live in New York.

Adelson also became CEO and chairman of the board of Revision3, cofounded with Rose, Gorodetzky, Dan Huard, David Prager, and Keith Harrison. The name of the company refers to the third "revision" of television delivery, of which broadcast and cable were the first and second. Revision3 was founded to produce and distribute special-interest television shows (reflecting the increasingly narrow audience of any given show over the course of television history, from the age of three networks to the present day's diminished ratings expectations) for the web. Most of the employees were former TechTV employees Adelson met through Rose. Revision3 series had much in common with *Screen Savers*, as well as with the podcasts that were becoming popular. The flagship series, begun in July 2005, was *Diggnation*, hosted by Rose and Alex Albrecht (previous hosts of the *Screen Savers*), discussing stories from Digg. "Diggnation" had originally been proposed as the name for Digg.

Adelson stepped down as CEO in 2007 but continued serving as chairman of the board and hosts the *Ask Jay* show, answering viewer questions. Recent Revision3 initiatives include a partnership with Gawker Media to produce video podcasts associated with the site, including the *Lifehacker* show and io9's *We Come from the Future* and the popular cooking show *Epic Meal Time*. In 2012, Revision3 remained a small, privately held company.

Adelson left Digg in April 2010 over disagreements about the direction of the site, which by then had experienced a decline in popularity. In November 2010, he became the CEO of SimpleGeo, Inc., replacing cofounder Matt Galligan; Galligan had founded the company with former Digg lead architect Joseph Stump, whom Adelson had advised. The company provides location-aware services to mobile app developers. Adelson became an adviser to the company in 2011 after it was acquired by Urban Airship.

Today Adelson is on the board of Revision3, SimpleGo, and 3Crowd Technologies; he also serves as a consultant to start-ups. His clients tend to be entrepreneurs and individuals who have recently become CEOs.

Personal Life

In 1994, while working for Netcom, Adelson met Brenda Shea. They were married in June 1996 and have three children and a cat named Watson. Unlike many individuals associated with the dot-com boom, Adelson has never made accumulating a fortune his goal. He has said that his career choices are guided by the long-term effect of his work and his desire to pursue projects about which he feels passionate. In 2008 he was named to *Time* magazine's list of the 100 Most Influential People in the world.

Bill Kte'pi

Further Reading
Grossman, Lev. "The 2008 *Time* 100: Builders and Titans—Jay Adelson." *Time* 5 May 2008: n. pag. Print. A profile of Adelson during Digg's peak.
Lacy, Sarah. *Once You're Lucky, Twice You're Good: The Rebirth of Silicon Valley and the Rise of Web 2.0.* New York: Gotham, 2008. Print. Lacy's Silicon Valley history includes a chapter on Adelson in the early twenty-first century.
Rafferty, Brian. "Jay Adelson: 2009 *Time* 100 Finalist." *Time* May 2009: n. pag. Print. Brief profile of Adelson a year after his first appearance in the *Time* 100, noting that the shine was gone from Digg's apple.
Sarno, David. "Digg Gets $28.7M Boost, Plans to Double Size, Go Global." *Los Angeles Times* 23 Sept. 2008: n. pag. Print. Coverage of Digg's rise from the company's peak period.

TOM ANDERSON

Cofounder of Myspace

Born: November 8, 1970; Los Angeles, California
Died: -
Primary Field: Internet
Specialty: Social media
Primary Company/Organization: Myspace

INTRODUCTION

The cofounder of Myspace in 2003, Tom Anderson was for years the face of social media, his account being added as a friend by default to any new user on Myspace—making his profile photo possibly the most-viewed face on the Internet, at least in North America, during that time. Although Myspace was neither the first social network nor in the end the biggest success, it was the first success, and introduced most of the general public to the idea of online social networking.

EARLY LIFE

Thomas Anderson was born on November 8, 1970, in Los Angeles, California. As a teenager, he was a hacker known as yLord Flathead and was raided by the Federal Bureau of Investigation (FBI) after breaching Chase Manhattan Bank's network. He attended the University of California, at both Berkeley and Los Angeles. While attending film school at UCLA, he joined digital storage firm XDrive as a product tester, later becoming a copywriter. When XDrive went bankrupt in 2001, he and coworker Chris DeWolfe founded a direct marketing company, ResponseBase. ResponseBase was sold to eUniverse in 2002, bringing the two into contact with Brad Greenspan. Greenspan had founded eUniverse, a marketing company, in 1998 and survived the bursting of the dot-com bubble.

LIFE'S WORK

Anderson, DeWolfe, and Greenspan founded Myspace in 2003 as a division of eUniverse. DeWolfe had previously written a proposal for a social network while at UCLA and was responsible for the prominence of music on the site. Anderson, who was put in charge of product development, also instituted the policy that allowed users to use fictional names, in contrast with Friendster, then the most popular social network.

Anderson became the public face of the site. His account was added as a friend to every new user's account by default, although they could remove him if they wished. He was often recognized on the street as the site grew in prominence. Although always present at the celebrity-filled company parties and events, Anderson was known as a workaholic behind the scenes, staying at work late as a matter of routine or logging on from home.

Myspace became an enormous success. Anderson was made president of eUniverse, now called Intermix Media, and in 2005 Intermix was sold to News Corp. (owner of Fox News and *The Wall Street Journal*) for $580 million. The main aim of the sale was to acquire Myspace—the cost was more than recouped when News Corp. made a $900 million deal with Google to make Google the single search engine of Myspace. Anderson continued to work on Myspace, but as many entrepreneurs find after buyouts, he found that he now answered to a larger and more involved hierarchy and that his decision-making ability was constrained by needing to account for his actions to other people. Anderson had hands-on involvement with the Myspace 2.0 redesign in 2008, adding and enhancing video features

Tom Anderson.

Affiliation: Myspace

Myspace was not the first social network, but it was the first to become a huge success and the first to popularize the idea of social media and come to the attention of the Internet novices in the general public. It was founded when Tom Anderson and Chris DeWolfe met Brad Greenspan, the head of eUniverse (later Intermix Media), the company that had just bought out their marketing company in 2002.

Myspace premiered the next year. Anderson, who became head of product development and the public face of the company (wholly owned by Intermix), was dissatisfied with Friendster, the largest extant social network. DeWolfe implemented some ideas he had developed during college project while at the University of California, Los Angeles, and brought a focus on music, which remains the site's most distinctive feature.

In 2005, Intermix Media was bought for $580 million by News Corp., Rupert Murdoch's corporation, which also owns *The Wall Street Journal*, Fox Television, and the 20th Century Fox film studio. The purpose of the Intermix purchase was simply to acquire Myspace, and while some thought the price was too high, within a year Myspace was worth at least $1 billion.

One of the strengths of Myspace was its use by bands, from the arena-touring to the unsigned. Bands that established a Myspace page (for free if they were unsigned) could host MP3 files of their music on it, with a built-in streaming player and the possibility of allowing downloads. For young, struggling bands, this was an enormous boon: They did not need to pay for server space or worry about bandwidth issues to encourage fans and potential fans to check out their music; all they had to do was agree to let Myspace users add their songs (with attribution) to their profile pages and allow other promotional uses. Even once Myspace began to decline, it continued to be a strong base for music; it was, for example, the launching pad for Lily Allen's career.

Little by little, Myspace was overtaken by Facebook, which exceeded its user base in 2008 and went on to become the subject of the Oscar-winning movie *The Social Network*, several lawsuits, and the default Internet destination for a large chunk of the online demographic. Part of the reason for Myspace's decline was its association with news stories about pedophiliac predators and pornography; Myspace had little control over

content and ineffective spam filters relative to Facebook. Meanwhile, sites like Twitter, while offering comparatively few features relative to the richness of profiles at Facebook and Myspace, nevertheless prospered because their leanness suited them to the growing use of smart phone apps to interact with the Internet—part of the growing "post-PC" Internet. In 2009, when founder DeWolfe stepped down as CEO to become a strategic adviser—as Anderson had already left the Intermix presidency to do likewise—he was replaced with a former Facebook executive, Owen Van Natta.

The shift from Myspace to Facebook was not universal or uniform. In 2007, researcher danah boyd (she deliberately lowercases her name) noted a class difference between Facebook-using teenagers and Myspace-using teenagers. Middle- and upper-class teens, especially teenagers expecting to attend college, were for the most part either switching to Facebook from Myspace or, if young enough to be creating their first social media profile, choosing Facebook over Myspace. Teenagers from poorer backgrounds, teenagers with parents who had not attended college, and teenagers who identified with certain subcultures were more likely to choose or remain with Myspace. That Facebook had originated as a social network for college students may have played a role in this. A major exception, ethnicity-based rather than class-based, was the tendency of Latino teenagers to use Myspace regardless of economic background and collegiate aspirations. Thus the Myspace demographic was shifting, at least in the United States, and it was less affluent and less WASPy. Boyd also noted that teenagers who had more than one social media profile were more likely than adults to differentiate those profiles—they would use a different profile photo for each and perhaps list different interests, whereas adults were likeliest to use identical information on every profile they actively maintained.

While its peak had passed, Myspace continued to develop, with a new design referred to internally as Myspace 2.0. Features were added to allow users to watch streaming television (featuring licensed content from News Corp.'s holdings), while music and photo-sharing features were refined and expanded. The overall aesthetic of Myspace was made cleaner and brought forward, away from the chaotic black screens and

Affiliation: Myspace (continued)

blinking text of the early social web. Support for apps was added, as well as compatibility with Twitter.

In 2011, News Corp. announced its readiness to sell Myspace, hoping to get $100 million for it—less than a fifth of what it had paid, although that money had long been earned back. After several months of enter- taining offers, Myspace was sold to Specific Media for $35 million, with News Corp. retaining a small stake in the company's shares. Many of the games once hosted on Myspace by developers like Zynga (which also develop Facebook and mobile games) have been closed.

(with licensed content from News Corp. and its Fox television and 20th Century Fox holdings), music, pho- to sharing, and integration with Twitter, while cleaning up the physical look and feel of the site to something more streamlined and functional. The business side did not seem to appeal to him as much, and when he was replaced as president in 2009, he seemed content in his "ambassador" role—although he has not seemed to have much involvement with the company since.

Since 2010, the default friend on Myspace has been a nonpersonal profile called Today on Myspace rather than Tom Anderson. In 2012, Anderson's profile page displayed the same profile photo (and about fifteen thousand others) and directed users to send him a mes- sage if they had questions or want to suggest a feature. As of 2012, however, his most recent Myspace blog en- try was from 2009.

Although Anderson always downplayed the sig- nificance of Facebook, he has made his admiration of Google+ known. In his view, Google+ realized much of what he had hoped Myspace would become, incorporat- ing a social overlay that would draw users into as much of the Internet experience as possible.

Anderson's web page describes him as retired and traveling the world. In summer 2012, he became an ad- viser to the Los Angeles start-up RocketFrog Interactive, developers of Facebook games. RocketFrog's business model combines games and ads; the prizes won in games like poker and blackjack are provided by sponsors who also pay to display their brand on game objects.

PERSONAL LIFE

Anderson remains active on social media sites, with hun- dreds of thousands of followers on Twitter and active Facebook and Google+ accounts. According to his own Myspace profile, he is a fan of the young Michael Jack- son and the Jackson 5, Teenage Fanclub, and the Beatles, and he names as his heroes his favorite authors: Friedrich Nietzsche, George Orwell, and Laurens van der Post.

Bill Kte'pi

FURTHER READING

Angwin, Julia. "Putting Your Best Faces Forward." *Wall Street Journal* 29 Mar. 2009. Print. An article on the then-nascent rise of Facebook and its impact on Myspace.

---. *Stealing Myspace: The Battle to Control the Most Popular Website in America*. New York: Random House, 2009. Print. An account of Myspace's peak, examining both the online culture and the impact of the company in the business world.

boyd, danah. *It's Complicated: The Social Lives of Net- worked Teens*. New Haven: Yale UP, forthcoming. Print. Boyd's in-depth look at teenagers online, in- cluding Myspace.

---. *Zephoria.org*. The website of danah boyd, senior researcher at Microsoft Research, is the single best resource, online or off, for scholarly writing on social networks and youth Internet culture. In- cludes access to her blog, her professional biog- raphy, a list of publications, and from there other resources.

From Myspace to My Place: The Men's Guide to Snag- ging Women Online. New York: Flyness, 2008. Print. A pick-up guide to Myspace, demonstrating (in conjunction with Kendall's *Rewired*) the ver- satility of Myspace's appeal. From the publisher of later pick-up guides to Twitter and other social media.

Kendall, Peggy. *Rewired: Youth Ministry in an Age of IM and Myspace*. Valley Forge: Judson, 2007. Print. Another examination of the effect of social media on youth, in this case with an emphasis on ministry efforts, from the publishing arm of the American Baptist Churches.

Winograd, Morley, and Michael D. Hais. *Millennial Makeover: Myspace, YouTube, and the Future of American Politics*. New Brunswick: Rutgers UP, 2008. Print. The impact of social media on Ameri- can politics, especially in the lead-up to the 2008 election.

MARC ANDREESSEN

Cofounder of Netscape

Born: July 9, 1971; Cedar Falls, Iowa
Died: -
Primary Field: Computer science
Specialty: Computer software
Primary Company/Organization: Netscape Communications

INTRODUCTION

Mark Andreessen led the team that created Mosaic, the first graphical web browser, in the early 1990s, and soon afterward he cofounded Netscape Communications to commercialize this revolutionary innovation, opening the use of the Internet to millions of people around the world. He went on to found companies that pioneered cloud computing, social media, e-commerce, and many other Internet-related applications taken for granted today. He also cofounded Andreessen Horowitz in Silicion Valley, a venture capital firm investing in emerging products that have the potential to transform society through information technology. His opinions and forecasts are widely sought today, and he serves on the boards of a number of major technology companies.

EARLY LIFE

Marc Lowell Andreessen was born on July 9, 1979, in Cedar Falls, Iowa, and was raised in the rural town of New Lisbon, Wisconsin, from the age of two. His mother, Patricia, worked for the Land's End clothing company as a customer service representative, and his father, Lowell, was sales manager of a seed and farm supply company. Marc and his brother Jeff grew up in a middle-class household, neither rich nor poor. Andreessen did not like living in such a rural setting and was not interested in being a farmer or factory worker, which was the norm in his community. He did not have much in common with others his age. He was interested in mathematics and science and proved to be a bright and accomplished student; some, however, regarded him as arrogant.

When Marc was eleven, after learning about computer programming from books in his school library, he asked his parents to buy him an early microcomputer from RadioShack. He was fascinated by the computer's possibilities and displayed a clear gift for programming. During his teenage years, this enthusiasm for computers turned into passion to study computer science in college.

As a National Merit Scholar and after graduating at the top of his high school class, he had the opportunity to leave rural Wisconsin and attend his choice of the best colleges in the country.

LIFE'S WORK

In 1989, Andreessen entered the University of Illinois at Urbana-Champaign. In 1992, he got a part-time job working in a government-funded research lab at the university known as the National Center for Supercomputing Applications (NCSA). This job provided an opportunity to work with powerful computers and computer networks, since the university was part of the Advanced Research Projects Agency Network (ARPANET), a computer network between major research universities funded by the U.S. government and a precursor to the Internet. Working at NCSA allowed Andreessen to witness the birth of the World Wide Web after Tim Berners-Lee introduced it in 1991 as a means for connecting computers around the world. Not the same thing as the Internet, the web is a system of documents, linked

Marc Andreessen.

by means of hypertext, that are accessed via the Internet. Using the Internet at that time required advanced computer skills. Andreessen saw the need for a simpler method for people to navigate the it.

In the autumn of 1992, less than a year after the web had been introduced, Andreessen led a team of fellow students in developing the first truly graphical user interface (GUI), which allowed web navigation by point-and-click commands. Working day and night, he and his team produced the first version of the new web browser they call Mosaic and made it available in January 1993. On March 13, 1993, Andreessen posted a free version of the Mosaic browser on the Internet for anyone to download. With 2 million downloads in its first year, Mosaic was successful because of its simplicity in integrating innovations that simplified browsing, such as bookmarks, hyperlinks, the creation of a browsing history, and the integration of images with text via "tags" to create the linkages.

After graduating, Andreessen started to work for a technology company in California when Jim Clark, a well-known Silicon Valley entrepreneur, contacted him about starting a web venture. In March 1994, they decided to enhance the Mosaic browser as a commercial product. Clark provided $4 million in start-up funding to form Mosaic Communications Company (MCC), and they proceeded to recruit most of the programmers who had worked on development of Mosaic at NCSA. By October 1994, Andreessen and his team had their new browser ready and offered it as a free download on the Internet. This led to conflict with NCSA, which was licensing the original Mosaic browser to other software companies to modify and market. While MCC claimed that its browser was based on completely new programming, a settlement was reached in December 1994 whereby MCC paid an undisclosed fee to NCSA and agreed to change its name. Thus, MCC became Netscape Communications Corporation (NCC), and its browser was renamed Netscape Navigator.

Netscape Navigator was an immediate success, sometimes described as the web's "big bang" moment. Netscape's business model involved charging businesses for copies of the browser software but making it easily available to noncommercial users. This model allowed Netscape to generate revenue and quickly expand use of Navigator in the marketplace, ultimately reaching a 75 percent penetration of the market by 1996. By late 1995, Navigator had 2 million users, making Netscape the fastest-growing software company in the industry and the prototype for the dot-com boom of the late

1990s. An initial public offering in August 1995 was overwhelmingly successful; by the end of 1995, NCC revenues exceeded $100 million and the company's stock value had soared to an estimated $2.9 billion. Andreessen's shares were worth an estimated $55–$60 million.

This success provoked intense competition. Netscape's fiercest competitor was Microsoft, where executives realized that its Windows operating system and its Microsoft Office Suite of applications needed to be compatible with the web. In a major shift in strategy, Microsoft acquired an enhanced a web browser and named it Internet Explorer (IE). It was based on the original NCSA Mosaic. Microsoft bundled IE into its market-dominant Windows 95 operating system, essentially giving it away to all of its customers who purchased the program either prepackage on a personal computer or as a stand-alone program. As IE's market share increased in 1996, Navigators plunged. Netscape alleged that Microsoft was rigging its Windows operating system to place IE at an advantage and to place competing browsers at a disadvantage and hence effectively force customers to use IE. These charges led to the U.S. Department of Justice to launch an antitrust investigation and to bring suit against Microsoft in *United States v. Microsoft*. The Supreme Court found in 2001 that some of Microsoft's practices were illegal; a settlement was ultimately reached.

This early episode in the so-called browser wars ultimately led to the demise of Netscape. As Microsoft continued to improve new releases of IE and push its use through its bundling strategy, Navigator development stalled and NCC began to lose money. Andreessen faced downsizing NCC to cut costs as revenues plunged. By 1998, the dot-com bubble was expanding and the stock values of competitors such as Yahoo! and America Online (AOL) were exploding while NCC stock was dropping. This led to sale of NCC to AOL in March 1999 for $4.2 billion; Navigator was later abandoned.

Andreessen worked for AOL for a few months, then left with several colleagues to form a new web services company call Loudcloud. Loudcloud was a web-hosting service that used cloud computing by a network of computers to help companies establish websites faster and at lower cost via software that automated website development, operation, and maintenance and supported e-commerce. From its launch in October 1999, Loudcloud grew rapidly, providing web hosting for a ballooning list of well-known companies through 2000. It had a successful initial public offering in March

Affiliation: Netscape

In early 1994, after graduating from college, Marc Andreessen was contacted by Jim Clark about forming an Internet start-up company. Clark was becoming bored as CEO of Silicon Graphics, the computer company he had started in the early 1980s, and was aware of Andreessen's success in creating the Mosaic web browser while in college. They decided that a new version of the Mosaic browser, written from scratch to incorporate a number of innovative enhancements, could be a successful commercial product. They hired many of the original programmers who had worked on Mosaic, and Clark provided $4 million in initial funding. After resolving a licensing dispute in December 1994, they renamed their new venture Netscape Communications Company (NCC) and their new browser Netscape Navigator. It was immediately successful, ultimately garnering 75 percent market share by 1996. A highly successful initial stock offering was made in 1995 and the value of the stock soared to some $2.9 billion. However, this success attracted a number of competitors—chief of which was Microsoft, which decided to offer its own browser, Internet Explorer, bundled with the market-dominant Windows 95 operating system. With Microsoft giving its browser away and using allegedly unfair marketing practices, Netscape went into decline, losing market share and revenue until it was ultimately sold to America Online (AOL) in March 1999 for $4.2 billion. Although Microsoft underwent litigation for violating the Sherman Antitrust Act, Navigator ultimately was abandoned as a product by AOL.

2001, when the dot-com bubble was bursting for many Internet start-ups. Loudcloud was soon caught up in the bust, however, as demand declined for dot-com hosting and server network hardware and software economics changed. In August 2002, the Internet services portion of the company was sold to Electronic Data Services and the remaining portion of the company was renamed Opsware and refocused on developing and selling software to manage large server networks. Hewlett-Packard purchased Opsware in September 2007 for $1.6 billion.

Andreessen went on to pioneer many other web ventures. He cofounded Ning, Inc., in 2004 to provide web services to social networking sites and later sold it in 2011 to Glam Media. He invested in a number of other technology companies, including Digg (web archiving), Twitter (social media), Groupon (online cupons), and Instagram (photo sharing). On July 5, 2009, Andreessen joined with his longtime friend and fellow investor Ben Horowitz to form the venture capital firm of Andreessen Horowitz to work with entrepreneurs on commercializing transformative advances in information technology. In September 2009, Andreessen Howrowitz invested in Skype Limited (a web-based video communications company), and in 2010 they invested in Kno (a digital education platform) and Airbrnb (a social media company focusing on real estate exchange). Andreessen Horowitz is actively engaged in providing advice and early funding to a host of new web-based enterprises.

PERSONAL LIFE

Andreessen was married to Laura Arrillaga, the daughter of Silicon Valley real estate billionaire John Arrillaga, in the summer of 2006. Laura founded the Silicon Valley Social Ventures Fund, a "venture philanthropy" that is modeled on venture capital funds to provide both expertise and investment to build the capabilities of nonprofit organizations. She holds a master's in business administration from Stanford Business School and a graduate degree in education and has served on the faculty at Stanford University. She is also president of the Marc and Laura Andreessen Foundation and serves on the boards of numerous other charitable organizations. The Andreessens reside near Stanford University in the San Francisco Bay area.

Forbes magazine estimated Andreessen's net worth in 2012 at approximately $600 million. He remains actively engaged in transforming society through information technology, serving on the boards of leading Silicon Valley companies such as eBay, Facebook, Hewlett-Packard, and the many companies in which his venture capital firm invests. Andreessen has said that he believes that "software is eating the world," meaning that as broadband Internet becomes more ubiquitous, cloud computing more powerful, and smartphones more globally adopted, software will continue to change the world as a transformative force for human progress.

Tom J. Sanders

FURTHER READING

Clark, Jim. *Netscape Time: The Making of the Billion Dollar Start-Up That Took on Microsoft.* New York: St. Martin's, 1999. Print. The engrossing inside story of how Clark and Andreessen conceived and started Netscape and the obstacles they faced in competing with Microsoft that ultimately led to the company's demise.

Cusumano, Michael A., and David B. Yoffie. *Competing on Internet Time: Lessons from Netscape and Its Battle with Microsoft*. New York: St. Martin's, 1998. Print. Focuses on management lessons that can be learned from studying Netscape's competition with Microsoft.

Lacey, Sarah. *Once You're Lucky, Twice You're Good: The Rebirth of Silicon Valley and the Rise of Web 2.0*. New York: Gotham, 2008. Print. Engaging story of the entrepreneurs who rebuilt Silicon Valley After the dot-com bubble of 2000 and how technology development and venture creation have changed.

Livingston, Jessica. *Founders at Work: Stories of Startups' Early Days*. New York: Springer, 2008. Print.

Collects more than thirty interviews with contemporaries of Andreessen who provide insights on the challenges they faced with the development and commercialization of their widely known products.

Payment, Simone. *Marc Andreessen and Jim Clark: The Founders of Netscape*. New York: Rosen, 2006. Print. Short, readable, and straightforward history of the cofounders of Netscape and the company, with numerous pictures and key facts clearly identified. The introduction is particularly good for students.

Quittner, Joshua, and Michelle Slatalla. *Speeding the Net: The Inside Story of Netscape, How It Challenged Microsoft and Changed the World*. New York: Atlantic Monthly, 1998. Print. Excellent chronology of the creation of the world's first graphical browser and first purely Internet-based company, with detailed information on what happened and its implications.

ANONYMOUS

Hacking and activist group

Born: 2003
Died: -
Primary Field: Computer science
Specialty: Security
Primary Company/Organization: Anonymous

INTRODUCTION

Computer hacking has become increasingly political and ideological. The term hacktivism, *for example, has been coined to refer hacking that is motivated by a conviction that access to online information should be free and open; hacktivists may engage in crashing websites and publishing sensitive information online. The online network of hactivists known as Anonymous, with thousands of members and no official leadership, is variously viewed as either heroes or cyber criminals and is the best known of all hacking groups. Membership in Anonymous, as in most computer hacking groups, is intentionally loose, with members entering and leaving at will. However, a group of highly skilled and particularly active members form the core and are responsible for the online* Anonymous Security Starter Handbook, *a how-to book for novice hackers. Members of Anonymous come from all walks of life and include high school and college students, journalists, office workers, software developers, and information technology experts as well as corporate spies, members of the mob, and ordinary con artists. The group's motto is "We are Anonymous. We are legion. We do not forgive. We do not forget. Expect us." The overall purpose of Anonymous, according to members, is to empower the public. High-profile targets have included Senator Joe Lieberman, the Church of Scientology, Post Finance Bank of Switzerland, MasterCard, Visa, PayPal, and Amazon. A threatened attack against the North Atlantic Treaty Organization (NATO) was never carried out, nor was a threat against the Federal Reserve. In the latter case, Anonymous posted a video on YouTube, charging the Federal Reserve with "crimes against humanity." In response to increased threats, officials around the globe have engaged in organized manhunts for members of Anonymous and other hacking groups, with the result that a number of arrests have been carried out in both North America and Europe.*

EARLY LIFE

Anonymous was created in 2003 from the website 4chan.com, a chat room where users signed in as "anonymous" to discuss and plan computer hacking activities. In the early days, the website was heavily associated

11

with pornography, particularly with "dirty jokes." The explosion of online communities has provided members and potential members with easy access to one another and facilitates the planning of activities. Anonymous gained notoriety in 2009 as a result of Operation Payback, an attack waged against corporate giants that included MasterCard, Visa, Amazon, and PayPal, after those organizations had canceled the accounts of WikiLeaks in response to that website's publishing of classified diplomatic cables. Lulz Security (LulzSec), a splinter group, was allegedly behind the attack on the Public Broadcasting Service (PBS) program *Frontline*, which reported on the WikiLeaks scandal. Before the attacks, Anonymous widely publicized their intentions. Using the open source application Low Orbit Ion Cannon (LOIC), thousands of volunteers helped to launch the denial-of-service attacks.

Since the attacks resulting from the WikiLeaks scandal, Anonymous has focused on what it identifies as anticensorship activities. This focus has led to subsequent attacks on government sites in Egypt and Tunisia, during which Anonymous stated that they were opening up citizen access to government information. The group also resorted to physical tactics by ordering large amounts of pizza to be delivered to the embassies of both countries.

Members of Anonymous do not always support the activities of other members. For instance, when an individual claiming to be a member of Anonymous posted an online video in August 2011 that threatened to "kill" Facebook on November 5, other members stated that it was a hoax. Information subsequently surfaced suggesting that such an attack had been planned but later discarded.

LIFE'S WORK

The year 2011 was a banner year for computer hackers, and one of the most successful hacking activities undertaken by Anonymous occurred early in the year when five members of the group managed to bring down the security firm of HBGary Federal and its client, the law firm of Hunton and Williams. Anonymous's vendetta was a response to an announcement by Aaron Barr, chief executive officer (CEO) of HBGary Federal, to a suspected member that he was planning to reveal the names and addresses of members of Anonymous at an upcoming computer security conference before releasing them to authorities. Anonymous responded by hacking the firm's computers, changing all employee passwords, and stealing seventy thousand e-mail messages.

Damaging e-mails were posted online, and Barr was subsequently forced to resign.

The most public Anonymous activity of 2011 was to launch the Occupy Wall Street protests that began in New York and spread globally. During protests, the Guy Fawkes masks made popular by the film *V for Vendetta* (2005) served the dual purpose of ensuring anonymity and making a political statement. Perpetrated through the Internet, the Occupy Wall Street movement was intended to call attention to corporate greed and the increasing gap between the rich and poor in the United States. During the protests, Anonymous threatened to "erase" the New York Stock Exchange.

Affiliation: Computer Hacking

The incidence of computer hacking has been steadily rising since the 1990s, but experts disagree over whether there are actually more electronic crimes being committed or the increase is due to more cases being reported. Governments around the world have tightened requirements under which hacking must be reported to authorities. According to the U.S. Government Accountability Office, reports of hacking that occurred in the United States between 2005 and 2010 increased by 60 percent, with a total of 4,776 hacks being reported in 2010 alone. Some estimates suggest that more than 70 percent of websites in the United States have been hacked. Around the world, government agents have recruited individuals known as "white hat" hackers to help them catch the most destructive members of hacking groups. A former hacker working with the Federal Bureau of Investigation was instrumental in the arrests of several members of Anonymous, and white hats played a major role in bringing down LulzSec.

The most frequent targets of hacking groups are government agencies, banks, large corporations, and popular websites. The most common intention of hackers is to steal sensitive data such as credit card information, but the most notorious hacking groups, which include Anonymous, are not interested in stealing money. They are more likely to deposit malware, steal data for public consumption, or engage in retaliatory hacking. When Anonymous and other groups attack public targets, the media pay attention. It is believed that this attention, in turn, can lead to increased incidents of hacking and adds to the mystique of the hactivists.

Considered more malevolent than any other hacking group, LulzSec, which stands for "laughing out loud at security," is believed to be a splinter group of disenchanted Anonymous members. Before it was brought down, LulzSec was so well organized that the group had its own public relations office. Successful hacking attacks targeted the Federal Bureau of Investigation (FBI), the Central Intelligence Agency (CIA), the U.S. Senate, the Serious Organized Crime Agency of the United Kingdom, Fox.com, PBS, Citigroup, and Sony. LulzSec members tweeted that they had joined Anonymous in Operation Anti-Security to steal and leak information online. The splinter group became so troublesome within the hacking community that other hackers cooperated with authorities in bringing it down.

The hacking activity that disrupted the lives of the most people in 2011 was the hacking of Sony Corporation's PlayStation Network, which resulted in the entire network being offline for twenty-eight days beginning on April 20. Hackers gained access to credit card numbers, passwords, and game activity, and they deprived PlayStation Network members of access to the PlayStation Store and the ability to play online games from the PlayStation 3. Once it was discovered that hackers had intentionally left behind a file labeled "Anonymous," both outraged PlayStation users and the media were quick to blame Anonymous for the crime. The group denied involvement, but Spanish authorities subsequently arrested several hackers who claimed to be members of Anonymous. PlayStation Network was back in service in early June at a cost of $173 million. Even after Sony completely remodeled its security measures and restored service, LulzSec hacked into ten thousand Sony websites, bragging about the feat on Twitter. By contrast, when other hackers attacked Sega's website, LulzSec announced that it would help to locate the perpetrators.

In March 2012, Anonymous announced that it had hacked the Vatican's website as reprisal for "corrupt" and "retrograde" activities. Anonymous was accused of hacking *Time* magazine's website and rigging the votes so that the group came in first place on the reader's poll of the 100 Most Influential People of 2012, recording 395,793 votes. In the published list, Anonymous ranked thirty-sixth. Anonymous also intercepted an FBI conference call about investigations into the group's activities and posted it online.

Other activities in 2012 included ongoing attacks against Arab dictators. Anonymous accused President Bashar al-Assad of Syria of slaughtering seventeen hundred Syrians and hacked the government website, encouraging Syrians to overthrow the Assad regime. Anonymous also published the e-mail passwords of government officials in Bahrain, Egypt, Morocco, and Jordan. Anonymous has also developed so-called care packages that contained instructions for hackers with details on how to cover up hacking tracks. When members of Food Not Bombs were arrested in Florida for feeding the homeless in violation of local ordinances, Anonymous launched an attack on the Florida Chamber of Commerce.

PERSONAL LIFE

Traditionally, few names have been attached to members of Anonymous, because members tend to work behind the scenes, often using assumed names. Some members' names became public in 2011, however, as the result of a number of high-profile arrests in several countries. Many of the hackers arrested were young and relatively inexperienced; older, more experienced hackers probably were astute enough to cover their tracks. Some security experts argue that releasing details of arrests serves to attract other hackers and gives groups the publicity they crave instead of acting as a deterrent to additional hacking activities.

In June 2011, Spanish police arrested three males suspected of being at the core of Anonymous activities. The group responded to the arrests by crashing the website of the Spanish police. Later in the month, Turkish authorities arrested thirty-two others who were believed to be active members of Anonymous. On July 19, twenty-one alleged hackers associated with Anonymous were arrested in the United States, Great Britain, and the Netherlands. Sixteen of those were accused of taking part in the WikiLeaks attacks. In the fall, Scottish authorities arrested Jake Davis, eighteen, who was accused of hacking the CIA, Rupert Murdoch's media empire, the British police, and the *Sun* newspaper.

In August 2011, Hector Xavier Monsegur of New York, who helped to found LulzSec in May 2011, was charged with taking part in the WikiLeaks attacks; hacking the governments of Tunisia, Algeria, Zimbabwe, and Yemen; and stealing personal data of potential *X-Factor* contestants. His subsequent cooperation with the FBI led to the arrests of four other members of LulzSec: Jack Davis of the Shetland Islands, Ryan Ackroyd of England, and Darren Martyn and Donncha O'Cearrbhail of Ireland. O'Cearrbhail was also charged with intercepting the FBI conference call that appeared online.

Elizabeth Rholetter Purdy

FURTHER READING

"An Anonymous Foe: Hackers Hit Big Companies, the IMF and the Headlines." *Economist* 399.8738 (2011): 67–68. Print. Covers the activities of Anonymous and reports on arrests of suspected hackers. Contains illustrations and charts.

Clayton, Mark. "Hacker Arrests: Why Anonymous Might Not Be So Anonymous." *Christian Science Monitor* 21 July 2011: n. pag. Print. Article deals with the arrests of members of Anonymous.

Dysart, Joe. "Hactivists." *ABA Journal* 97.12 (2011): 40–46. Print. Detailed examination of Anonymous and its role in the hactivist community. Illustrated.

Iltan, Cigdem. "Moving Targets." *Maclean's* 124. 33/34 (2011): 63. Print. Focuses on recent activities of Anonymous. Illustrated.

Laurie, Penny. "Rise of the Digital Natives." *Nation* 293.18 (2011): 20–22. Print. Examines the rise in computer hacking, focusing on groups such as Anonymous. Illustrated.

Murphy, Samantha. "The Heart of a Hacker." *New Scientist* 211.2820 (2011): n. pag. Print. Focus is on LulzSec, a splinter group of Anonymous.

Saporito, Bill. "Hack Attack." *Time* 178.1 (2011): 50–55. Print. Overview of the current status of political hacking, with a focus on the activities of LulzSec, the offshoot of Anonymous. Illustrated.

MARCO ARMENT

Cofounder of Tumblr

Born: June 11, 1982; Columbus, Ohio
Died: -
Primary Field: Internet
Specialty: Social media
Primary Company/Organization: Tumblr

INTRODUCTION

During two weeks in 2006, Marco Arment helped David Karp in the creation of the blogging platform Tumblr. By combining the best of online social networking and the Web 2.0 revolution, Arment and Karp were able to provide users with a simple platform for self-expression. Arment's work on Tumblr and his later project Instapaper reflect the developer's desire for efficiency in the Internet age.

EARLY LIFE

Marco Arment was born in Columbus, Ohio, on June 11, 1982. His mother Catherine lives in Bexley, Ohio. Arment attended Allegheny College in Meadville, Pennsylvania. He graduated in 2004 with an undergraduate degree in computer science. During his college career, Arment was a member of the Phi Delta Theta fraternity. He was also a member of the Association for Computing Machinery (ACM). After graduation, Arment worked for Vivisimo in Pittsburgh as a developer. His friend and web design consultant David Karp asked him to help with a two-week project he was working on between paid jobs.

LIFE'S WORK

Karp was in between clients for his web design consultancy business, so he and Arment decided to work on creating a simple, clean Web 2.0 blogging platform for

Marco Arment.

those interested in sharing ideas but not wanting to become professional bloggers. It took two weeks to create a beta version of Tumblr.

The name of the platform and subsequent company comes from the concept of the tumble log. A tumble log is a stream-of-consciousness microblog post. The idea of being able to produce web content without much work was growing as a moneymaking idea in the mid-2000s. Tumblr did not invent the tumble log (it was created by Christian Neukirchen on March 27, 2005), but Arment and Karp developed the concept. In doing so, they combined the short post of the social networking platform with the self-expression of the traditional blog post. The basic Tumblr tool was finished in October 2006 but would not go public until April 27, 2007.

It was not long before the site became a hit among computer professionals and bloggers. By the end of the first two weeks of public beta testing, Tumblr had attracted seventy-five thousand users. The Tumblr code was very pliable, allowing users to manipulate it to suit their needs. Unlike traditional blogging platforms, which require adherence to a set template, Tumblr allows users to change and reshape that template to personalize their space. Users can share content without having to establish an electronic relationship with other users, as is the case with traditional social networking sites.

The most notable difference between the Tumblr platform and the traditional blogging platform was the absence of the blank, white virtual paper of the text box. Instead, Arment and Karp decided to go with a few simple oversized buttons at the top of the user's home page that provided ease of posting, uploading, and pasting content from other bloggers. Tumblr thus provided a blogging platform for people who did not have the energy or time to devote themselves to a one of the preset themes provided by the free version of, say, a Wordpress.com blog. Arment and cocreator Karp wanted to provide efficiency for the busy person but at the same time share ideas and build an online community. Karp sees Tumblr users as an "engaged community." Tumblr is not just a place to post a short blog and disappear. Tumblr allows users to share content and ideas, get to know folks with similar interests, and spend quality personal time on the computer.

The features of Tumblr are the main reasons for its ever-growing user base. Unlike many Web 2.0 platforms, Tumblr is specifically designed to make it easier for the layperson to produce web content. Being able to cut and paste another user's blog post with the click of a button (located on the user's dashboard), a feature added in May 2007, was the icing on the cake; Tumblr began to soar.

It was costing Karp and Arment $5,000 per month to keep the platform going, and they did not want to lose users by adding a price tag. In October 2008, Tumblr cofounder Karp raised capital for Tumblr by selling 25 percent of the company to venture capital firms. This provided development revenue that allowed Tumblr to remain a free service.

By January 2010, Tumblr hosted seven million individual blogs. As use of the website increased, so did the need for capital; the first sale simply was not enough. Cofounder Karp visited Silicon Valley several times to secure funding. He was successful, and the company was valued at around $100 million by the third year of its existence. Karp and Arment were clever about those from whom they accepted money, preferring to work with experienced, cyber-savvy individuals, including the former chief executive officer of Mozilla, the well-known Virgin owner Richard Branson. Their strategy paid off. Tumblr benefited from both advice and investment capital.

Trying to avoid user fees and viral advertising, Karp and Arment developed several design applications for Tumblr that users could buy at the Apple iStore and use on their Tumblr home pages. This made it possible to retain users but still make some revenue. Both Karp and Arment admit that their goal was not to create a hugely profitable online business but to give Internet users a space to grow a community and share their thoughts.

In a 2011 study, Tumblr was ranked among the fastest-growing blogging platforms on the web. It was also ranked least reliable, having the most downtime of any similar site. Some connect the unreliability of Tumblr with its massive user base. Nonetheless, Tumblr was valued at $800 million by September of 2011.

By then, Arment had announced his resignation from Tumblr (on September 21, 2010). He explained his reasons on his personal blog, Marco.org. It seems the rapid growth of Tumblr and the needs of the users meant the company needed a "technical manager," a position that Arment did not feel qualified to hold. For four years, he acted as community manager and lead developer for Tumblr. As the site's popularity increased, Arment found himself moving away from what he really wanted to do. He decided instead to devote his time to his own project, known as Instapaper.

Instapaper began in late 2007 when Arment wanted to take items he saw online while at work and read

Affiliation: Tumblr

Tumblr is a blogging platform that was founded on February 17, 2007, by David Karp and Marco Arment. It is a New York–based company that began when its founders took two weeks to create a beta version of the site. Arment and Karp created the site without any capital or funding. Tumblr provides an online community platform for users to share their thoughts on the arts, life, and society. Tumblr users can post their own short blog posts (tumble logs), comprising one or two paragraphs. The website encourages the use of a variety of media: video clips, photographs, graphics, and of course text. More than 40 percent of Tumblr's content is photographic.

A mix of social networking and Web 2.0, Tumblr allows for short blogs geared toward self-expression rather than the editorial content that dominates many other blogging platforms. Tumblr is a moral blogging platform that hopes to inspire its users to be socially responsible when in the virtual world. The tumble logs are set up so users have the ability copy and paste other people's Tumblr posts on their own page to stimulate dialogue among users as well as save time.

As of 2012, Tumblr hosted approximately 70 million blogs, had a more than one hundred employees, and had offices in both New York and Virginia.

them during his train commute to and from home. A train commute makes using a mobile device very difficult and browsing the Web impossible or extremely frustrating. Arment hated wasting time and wanted to transfer the material he should not be reading during the workday to the time when he had little or no Internet connection. Arment created one of the earliest smartphone applications when he devised Instapaper. His app was accepted by the Apple store on the second official day because of an overload of application submissions on August 26, 2008.

Instapaper was created in a single day. Arment decided to keep it to himself for several months, using it daily and making minor improvements that allowed him to transfer data from his personal computer to his iPhone in a legible format. The improved app became the basis for the Instapaper software and platform. Arment posted a link to his blog so people could download the app for their own use a few months after the initial tweaking. It was an instant success.

Profitable since 2008, Instapaper and the idea of saving web content to peruse later proved popular, and many companies brought out their own version of Arment's iPhone application. Where Arment charges $5 for his application, his competition is providing the same service free of charge. Arment told a reporter that he needed to focus on growing his customer base and improving his product so people would still choose Instapaper over the free generic versions.

PERSONAL LIFE

In his spare time, Arment writes on his personal blog Marco.org and enjoys podcasting. He listens to music while working. A huge fan of Apple products, Arment spends his time developing his Instapaper application and researching future iPhone app ideas. He is a member of the advisory board for Stack Overflow, LLC, a website that provides free assistance to computer programmers.

Trish Popovitch

FURTHER READING

Arment, Marco. "Instapaper Founder Marco Arment's Journey from Bagel Jockey to Publishing Pioneer." Interview by Lydia Dishman. *Fast Company* 1 Nov. 2012. Web. 7 Aug 2012. Interview with Arment where he discusses both Tumblr and Instapaper. Short article that manages to provide a sense of Arment's work ethic and approach to business management.

---. "Job Transition." *Marco.org*. 21 Sept. 2010. Web. 12 Aug. 2012. Arment's unofficial resignation post regarding his decision to leave his position as lead developer at Tumblr and devote his time to his own product, Instapaper.

Boutin, Paul. "Tumblr Makes Blogging Blissfully Easy." *New York Times* 13 Mar. 2009. Web. 7 Aug. 2012. Short blog post that praises the Tumblr website. Discusses the idea of tumble logs and the ease of using the blogging platform.

Cheshire, Tom. "Tumbling on Success: How Tumblr's David Karp Built a £500 Million Empire." *Wired* 2 Feb. 2012: n. pag. Print. Details on how Tumblr played a role in the Occupy Wall Street movement. Explains how Tumblr was founded and provides facts on the company's market value.

Darlin, Damon. "Feel Free to Read This Later, on Your Phone." *New York Times* 12 Dec. 2010. Web. 7 Aug. 2012. Details the services of Instapaper and the use of readers to review web content when offline. Refers to Instapaper as a "personalized magazine." Discusses RSS feeds and self-editing the web.

Emerson, Ramona. "Tumblr Ranked 'Least Reliable' Blogging Platform: Study." *Huffington Post*. 19 Dec. 2011. Web. 8 Aug. 2012. Brief article sharing the results of a blogging platform study that found Tumblr to have the most downtime of all the blogging platform sites.

Karp, David. "Would You Take a Tumblr with This Man?" Interview by Doree Shafrir. *New York Ob-*

server 15 Jan. 2008. Web. 7 Aug. 2012. Tumblr co-founder Karp mentions the origins of Tumblr and provides observations on the future of social networking and user-generated content.

Tsotsis, Alexia. "Marco Arment Leaves Tumblr to Devote Himself to Instapaper." *TechCrunch Magazine* 21 Sept. 2012. Web. 7 Aug. 2012. Discusses Arment's decision to devote his time to his solo project, the smart phone application Instapaper. Also mentions the issue of copyright in regard to apps.

JEFF ARNOLD

Founder of WebMD

Born: December 30, 1969; Dallas, Texas
Died: -
Primary Field: Internet
Specialty: Content and data
Primary Company/Organization: WebMD

INTRODUCTION

Jeff Arnold engineered his knowledge of marketing medical equipment into creating the website WebMD, which became one of the Internet's most often visited sites for medical information. Arnold has operated on the principle of buying out competitors and making them part of his team; he has purchased ten competitors and brought them into the fold. Arnold's goal for WebMD was to make it the link among the different facets of the medical industry, providing consumer access to doctors, pharmacists, drug companies, and insurance companies. After leaving WebMD, Arnold helped found other successful websites, including HowStuffWorks, LidRock, and Sharecare.com. He has continued to demonstrate a unique ability to develop ideas, persuade investors of their profitability, and deliver on his promises. In 1999, Fortune *named him as one of the richest Americans under the age of forty.*

EARLY LIFE

Jeffrey T. Arnold was born in Dallas, Texas, on December 30, 1969, into a middle-class family; he is one of five children. The family moved to Georgia when Arnold was still a child, and he was raised there. He met his future wife, Meg Nichols, who lived in the Atlanta area, when they were both students at the University of Georgia in Athens. In 1983, while majoring in speech

communications, he dropped out of school to work as a pharmaceutical salesman. He told relatives that he planned to be a billionaire by the time he was thirty.

In 1994, at the age of twenty-four, with a $25,000 investment from his wife's family, Jeff and Meg Arnold founded Quality Diagnostic Services (QDS), a company that gathered data from heart monitors. The Arnolds both worked from their apartment, manning a toll-free

Jeff Arnold.

telephone line and using a fax machine to submit patient data to physicians. Under Arnold's guidance, QDS grew into one of the most profitable cardiac arrhythmia monitoring companies in the United States.

In 1998, Arnold sold QDS to Matria Healthcare, also based in Atlanta, for $2.5 million. He used that money to found WebMD. Even with limited credentials, Arnold was able to persuade high-profile partners to invest in his new site. He talked Microsoft into investing $250 million, DuPont into investing $220 million, and News Corporation into investing $100 million (which gave that company 11 percent of WebMD's stock). Within a year, WebMD's value had reached $20 billion.

LIFE'S WORK

Arnold's formula in founding WebMD was to entice consumers searching for Internet-based health information to the site to buy health-related products from WebMD's partners. Arnold believed that the site could ultimately be used by patients making doctors' appointments, filling prescriptions, and ordering lab tests online. However, physicians were initially dubious about trusting sensitive information to the Internet and were reluctant to fall in line.

The success of WebMD derived instead from Arnold's skill in signing up companies with established reputations to align themselves with the site. He convinced the drugstore chain CVS to sign on as the official pharmacy for the site. Humana, a health care provider, also signed on with the goal of making drug information available to all of a patient's doctors, thereby cutting down on chances of dangerous drug interactions. From the beginning, WebMD was designed to be user-friendly, providing for search by either keywords or questions. Users were also able to identify possible health conditions by using a symptom checker. Separate sections of the site were devoted to issues such as health news, drugs, wellness, parenting, teens, and pets.

In November 1999, Arnold bought out WebMD's chief rival, Healtheon, and the company became Healtheon/WebMD. Healtheon, which was later dropped from the company name, had been founded by Jim Clark, a Silicon Valley engineer, who was convinced that he could create the perfect method for automating health care activities. In February 14, 2000, Arnold expanded the company further by acquiring CareInsite and its parent company, Medical Manager Corporation (MMC), for a reported $5.4 billion in stocks. MMC was the chief management software provider for 185,000 physicians, On February 16, for a price of $312 million,

Arnold added OnHealth Network to WebMD's expanded holdings. Because OnHealth placed an emphasis on wellness, it added a new element to WebMD, which was more focused on identifying diseases and their treatments. The new acquisitions placed WebMD in a position to move from third place to first place among Internet health sites. Despite this, WebMD was not showing a profit, and critics continued to raise concerns about privacy rights and content reliability.

In 2000, Arnold announced that he had negotiated a billion-dollar deal with Rupert Murdoch for WebMD to provide health-related information to Fox and other Murdoch enterprises. However, investors were becoming concerned that Arnold had taken on too much too fast. As stock in dot-coms plummeted, WebMD stock dropped from $70 per share to $10 per share. Arnold resigned from the company, salvaging $100 million of his personal fortune by selling off his company stock.

In 1998, Marshall Brain had created HowStuffWorks as an online encyclopedia to explain the rationale behind the workings of everything from lightbulbs to hybrid automobiles. Arnold invested in HowStuffWorks in 2001 and purchased the American portion of the company via his investment company, Convex Group, in 2002 for $2 million. He subsequently launched an investment campaign that generated close to $1 million. With Arnold as chief executive officer (CEO), the site continued to gain in popularity. In May 2007, it drew 1.5 million unique visitors and had climbed to 10.5 million by the end of the year. Arnold sold HowStuffWorks to Discovery in 2007 for $250 million, and Discovery Channel launched a HowStuffWorks television program the following summer. Arnold continued to serve as chief digital architect of HowStuffWorks' Curiosity Project (curiosity.com) until the end of 2011.

In January 2001, in a partnership with Eric Gleacher, Arnold established the Convex Group, which John Helyar of *Fortune* described as "a combination turbo charged vulture fund and souped-up web-navigation delivery engine." Arnold manages his own investments through the Convex Group, which also claims investors such as Time Warner and Cox Communications. The search engine was designed chiefly for use by advertisers.

In January 2003, Jeff Arnold founded LidRock as a means of selling CDs by artists such as Britney Spears, Black Eyed Peas, Ashanti, Jessica Simpson, and Elvis Presley. The CDs were packaged in the lids of soft drinks sold at fast-food stores, theme parks, and movie theaters. He managed to sign up Universal Studios,

Affiliation: WebMD

When Jeff Arnold founded WebMD in 1998, the company had only sixty employees. WebMD produced annual sales of $75,000 that first year. It was the first Internet site to succeed at providing generally reliable information to both consumers and members of the medical profession. Arnold convinced Billy Payne, the organizer of the Atlanta 1996 Summer Olympics, to serve as vice president of WebMD.

Despite Arnold's high hopes for the company, some investors felt that it did not live up to its potential. A number of partners ended their relationship with the site because they believed that WebMD had reneged on promises of exclusive partnerships. By 1999, Arnold owned only 22 percent of the company's stock, and his shares were worth $2.58 billion. However, WebMD suffered a serious setback in the midst of spiraling failures of dot-com companies.

Despite its failures and flaws, Arnold had established WebMD with a solid business plan, which allowed it to continue to flourish after his departure in 2000. Arnold no longer has any connection with the company and has sold all his shares. By 2001, WebMD had five thousand employees and was generating annual sales of almost a billion dollars. By 2007, the site's market capitalization was estimated at $3.3 billion.

NASCAR, and the BP convenience stores chain as a way of reaching teenagers, his target audience. Within a year, LidRock had sold 10 million CDs. In May 2004, LidRock added full-length movies to the line. For a cost of $4, users could play purchased movies for up to sixty hours after they were removed from lids.

By the fall of 2010, Jeff Arnold was back in the business of providing medical information via the Internet as chairman and CEO of Shareware.com, an interactive website that is able to answer more than a million health-related questions. Other interactive features include the ability to set up user pages on the site and to become "friends" with physicians connected to the site, which gives users added access to ongoing health news and information. The success of the project was virtually assured through affiliations with media giants that included Oprah Winfrey's Harpo Studios, the Oprah Winfrey Network, HSW International, Sony, and Discovery. Winfrey's protégé Dr. Mehmet Oz, a cardiac

surgeon and the host of the *Dr. Oz Show*, was recruited, and Arnold also signed up a huge roster of hospitals, physicians, and other health care professionals, including the Cleveland Clinic, Johns Hopkins Hospital, and New York–Presbyterian Hospital. Other partners included organizations ranging from the American Association of Retired Persons (AARP) and the American Red Cross to the American Diabetes Association and the American Heart Association.

Arnold's critics have challenged the wisdom of having partners such as Colgate-Palmolive, Pfizer, Johnson and Johnson, and Walgreens as paid affiliates on Sharecare.com. Arnold has responded to the criticism by citing data indicating that brand answers are accessed just as often as those provided by medical experts. In January 2012, Sharecare.com purchased the rights to *The Little Blue Book*, a major reference tool for physicians.

Arnold also owns the star rating service and travel guide series Forbes Travel Guide (formerly Mobil Travel Guide), which he licensed to *Forbes* in 2009 and for which he serves as chairman.

PERSONAL LIFE

In 1998, Arnold's newfound success allowed him to purchase a home in Buckhead, an upscale area of Atlanta, for $4 million. The mansion, previously owned by Prince Faisal of Saudi Arabia, had also been used in publicity shots for *Gone with the Wind* (1939). When the house was destroyed by fire in October 2000, Arnold rebuilt it on the same site. Arnold also enjoys lavish entertaining in both the private and professional realms. In 2000, he hired Elton John, who also has a home in the Atlanta area, to provide entertainment for a Super Bowl party. When trying to convince Microsoft to invest in WebMD, Arnold flew an entire team from Seattle to the Masters Golf Tournament in Augusta, Georgia. After the merger with Healtheon, he took five friends to golf school.

Elizabeth Rholetter Purdy

FURTHER READING

Burke, Monte. "Pop Music." *Forbes* 173.1 (2004): n. pag. Forbes.com. Web. 1 May 2012. Examines Arnold's entry into the field of entertainment through LidRock.

Carrns, Ann. "Young Atlantan Makes Billions with WebMD." *Wall Street Journal* 21 May 1999. Print. Profile of Arnold's life and career.

Elliott, Stuart. "Web Site to Offer Health Advice, Some of It from Marketers." *New York Times* 7 Oct. 2010.

Print. Profiles Sharecare.com and the controversy over using marketer-generated material.

Helyar, John. "Jeff Arnold, Founder of WebMD, Could Be the Poster Boy for the Internet Bubble." *Fortune* 5 Mar. 2001. Web. CNN.com. 1 May 2012. Profile of Arnold, focusing on his charisma and persuasiveness.

Moukheiber, Zina. "WebMD Founder Jeff Arnold Stages Comeback with New Health Site." *Forbes* 22 Oct. 2010. Web. Forbes.com. 1 May 2012. Profile of Arnold's career and the founding of Sharecare. com.

Pack, Thomas. "Sharecare: Getting a Healthy Prognosis." *Information Today* 28.1 (2011): n. pag. Print.

Examination of Arnold's role in Sharecare. Illustrated.

Sherrid, Pamela. "The Microsoft of Medical Web Sites." *U.S. News and World Report* 128.8 28 Feb. 2000. Print. Traces the role of Jeff Arnold in engineering the rise of WebMD. Illustrated.

Stelter, Brian. "Online Encyclopedia Gets New Push from Discovery." *New York Times* 30 June 2008. Print. Profiles Jeff Arnold's career, focusing on his tenure at HowStuffWorks.

Warner, Melanie. "The Young and the Loaded." *Fortune* 140.6 (1999): n. pag. CNN.com. Web. 1 May 2012. Surveys the forty richest Americans under age forty at the time, including Arnold.

J. MICHAEL ARRINGTON

Founder of TechCrunch

Born: March 13, 1970; Huntington Beach, California
Died: -
Primary Field: Internet
Specialty: Commerce
Primary Company/Organization: TechCrunch

INTRODUCTION
J. Michael Arrington is an influential technology blogger and venture capitalist. A former corporate attorney, Arrington has a hard-hitting, take-no-prisoners writing style that has catapulted some Silicon Valley start-ups and sunk others. Although often under fire or a subject of derision for his brash manner and outspokenness, he is nonetheless considered one of the most prominent technology personalities and a major power broker. The companies in which he has invested have for the most part done well, and his buoyancy and knack for honing in on cutting-edge start-ups are major components of that success.

EARLY LIFE
J. Michael Arrington was born on March 13, 1970, and grew up in Orange County, California, and in Surrey, England. He attended the University of California, Berkeley, then transferred after his freshman year to Claremont McKenna College, a private liberal arts college east of Los Angeles, where earned his bachelor's degree in economics in 1992. In 1995, he obtained a juris doctor degree from Stanford University.

Arrington had an entrepreneurial spirit early in life. During college, he gave his neighbors competition in the recycling arena. They had been taking their empty beer cans and bottles to a local Latino family, until

J. Michael Arrington.

Arrington infiltrated the exchange and collared the market for himself.

After earning his law degree, Arrington worked for a few years at Wilson Sonsini Goodrich and Rosati, and O'Melveny and Myers, where he dealt solely with technology companies. Some of his clients included Netscape, Pixar, Apple, and Idealab. The Internet was just starting to boom. Arrington deserted corporate and securities law and got involved in the dot-com world. Even though he was involved with two auspicious Internet companies, RealNames and Achex, he did not make any huge financial gains with them. He went on to take an active role at a Carlyle-backed start-up in London, founded and ran two companies in Canada (Zip.ca and Pool.com), was chief operating officer to Kleiner Perkins Caufield and Byers–backed company Razorgator, and consulted with various other companies, including SnapNames and Verisign. In addition to TechCrunch, he founded Edgeio and was a member of its board of directors.

LIFE'S WORK

Following the dot-com bust, Arrington took a year off, then returned to work. In 2005, he was inspired by American software developer, entrepreneur, and writer Dave overall done Winer and started writing about Silicon Valley and start-ups as a hobby. His writing was in sharp, plain English, and he would intersperse images to break up the text. He made the tech world and its goings-on accessible to everyone. Backed by Archimedes Ventures, he and Keith Teare started producing what would be known as TechCrunch. It garnered a large following quickly because of Arrington's intense writing style, insider knowledge, and business strategy. TechCrunch involved not only blogs but also events. The company won a reputation for throwing fabulous parties at Arrington's Atherton home, and through these soirées Arrington got on the inside track regarding what was happening in Silicon Valley. The social networking that took place at these parties, which started in August 2005, encouraged the growth of the blog's readership. Arrington had also anticipated another surge in the tech industry and developed a band of influential allies that included Robert Scoble as well as Winer. He was astute enough to notice a rising trend in investments, so by the time Tim O'Reilly, founder and chief executive officer (CEO) of O'Reilly Media, dropped the term *Web 2.0*, Arrington was already entrenched in the second tech boom. His access to venture capitalists as a corporate attorney and his experience in the investing trenches as an entrepreneur gave him the upper hand and added to his writing a credibility that others did not necessarily have. He had built a solid reputation with heavy hitters in Silicon Valley, and that cachet followed him to his Technorati blog.

Soon, Arrington became one of the most powerful people on the Internet, but not without stepping on a few toes. Frequently involved in controversy, the serial entrepreneur butted heads with many of his peers, all the while putting his money where his mouth was by constantly investing. Daylife, Dogster, Omnidrive, DanceJam, and Seesmic were some of the companies he supported. He also extended his Crunch base with CrunchGear, CrunchMobile, and CrunchBoard. Touching on the live arena, he formed a partnership with Jason Calacanis (blogger and founder of Silicon Alley, Weblogs, Inc., and Mahaho) to mount the TechCrunch 20 conference, a successful conference for start-ups that evolved into TC40 and TC50. Arrington and Calacanis went their separate ways on TC50, doing separate conferences, but not without Calacanis's claiming that Arrington had stiffed him. Arrington started TechCruch Disrupt in San Francisco, and Calacanis produced the Launch Conference. Both have been successful.

A man of many talents and with a keen eye for innovative technology, Arrington launched a project in 2008 with Fusion Garage to develop a $200 tablet, the CrunchPad. However, after several prototypes, Arrington claimed the company had cut him out of the process. When the tablet went on the market, it fizzled. Arrington has an ongoing lawsuit with the company. During this time, animosity started to grow between Arrington and consumer electronics blog Engadget because, contending that what Engadget was publishing about his relationship and falling out with Fusion Garage was incorrect. This animosity would grow and come into play later in Arrington's career.

As TechCrunch's popularity grew, Arrington, who was already brash, grew more menacing in his articles and demeanor. He started getting death threats in the summer of 2008 and reported these to the police, then went to Hawaii until the air cleared. His relationships with certain colleagues remained contentious. On June 6, 2009, he had a falling out with radio personality and tech reporter Leo Laporte on the Gillmor Gang after accusing him of giving a positive review on the Palm Pre in exchange for a five-day evaluation unit. Laporte was enraged that his journalistic integrity had been questioned and stormed off the stage where this exchange took place. Arrington and Laporte apologized to each other the same day, but not long afterward, the Gillmor

Affiliation: TechCrunch

TechCrunch was first published on June 11, 2005, founded by serial entrepreneur and technology revivalist J. Michael Arrington. This website offers the latest technology news and analysis, including reports on start-ups, websites, and products. The blog averaged nearly five posts every two days in its first year: 879 posts.

Since its inception, TechCrunch's network has grown into several popular sites and programs. Some of these affiliated websites include CrunchBase, Crunchboard, TechCrunch TV, TechCrunch IT, Elevator Pitches, international TechCrunch sites (Europe, Japan, and France), InviteShare, and Gillmor Gang.

In 2010, the company was involved in a bribery scandal. Daniel Brusilovsky, a seventeen-year-old part-time employee, accepted a MacBook Air from a start-up in exchange for writing a post about them. Arrington fired him and removed his posts from the site.

Two earlier sites that merged with TechCrunch are MobileCrunch and CrunchGear. They have mounted several one-day events—including Tech-Crunch London's GeeknRolla and TechCrunch Disrupt—as well as the annual TechCrunch50 in San Francisco. They were also the founding host of The Crunchies. In 2012, TechCrunch had an estimated 1,628,000 feed subscribers.

Gang was removed from the TWiT network. In the same year, Arrington was leaving a business conference in Munich and someone walked up to him and spat in his face. Although Arrington was accustomed to being insulted in public, he expressed his outrage about this incident in a blog post. He decided to make Seattle his part-time home in 2010.

In September 2010, AOL's CEO Tim Armstrong announced that the company had purchased Tech-Crunch for undisclosed amount, which was projected to be between $25 and $40 million. Despite Arrington's declaration that he would have a long-lasting relationship AOL, that was not to be. He immediately claimed his independence from the company by engaging in a gratuitous war with Engadget, an old wound that he reopened. He targeted the editors with public criticism, to which editor Joshua Topolsky promptly responded on Tumblr, temporarily diffusing the situation.

Arrington tempered his irascible behavior toward Engadget and returned to investing, starting up venture

capital firm CrunchFund in 2011 with former college mate and venture capitalist Patrick Gallagher and MG Siegler. There were immediate concerns that this would present a conflict of interest, since Arrington was still contributing to TechCrunch. Arianna Huffington told *The New York Times* that Arrington no longer had editorial responsibilites with the site and that he was an unpaid blogger. Arrington walked away from AOL and TechCrunch at that point, although he kept the $8 million investment that AOL had contributed to Crunch-Fund. A venture capital company, CrunchFund finances information technology companies at any stage but prefers seed or early-stage investments.

PERSONAL LIFE

In 2012, Arrington was single with no children, leading a private personal life. His extremely long work hours have often interfered with his cultivating a personal life. He once dated a Miss Universe contestant from Denmark and was in a long-term relationship of four years, until he started TechCrunch, where his devotion to the tech world interfered with his relationship. From 2007 to 2008, he was in an on-again/off-again relationship with Silicon Valley heiress Meghan Asha, which eventually faded. In 2009, on April Fool's Day, TechCrunch ran an article asking women to submit information to be considered to go on a Ustreamed dinner date with Arrington. Some did not realize this was a joke and eagerly submitted their photos. Arrington recently invested in the social dating network theComplete.me; he has noted that online dating is stagnant area in need of disruption. He is also an avid animal activist.

Sonya Alexander

FURTHER READING

Cringely, Robert X. *Accidental Empires: How the Boys of Silicon Valley Make Their Millions, Battle Foreign Competition and Still Can't Get a Date*. New York: HarperBusiness, 1996. Print. An exploration of geekdom's finest and the building the computer industry empire.

Kaplan, David A. *The Silicon Boys and Their Valley of Dreams*. New York: Morrow, 1999. Print. A look at the ways Silicon Valley rivals Washington, D.C., and Hollywood in the realms of celebrity, money, and success.

Kenney, Martin. *Understanding Silicon Valley: The Anatomy of an Entrepreneurial Region*. Stanford: Stanford UP, 2000. Print. An analysis of what makes Silicon Valley so productive and a hub of technological advancement.

Siegler, MG. *You're Damn Right I'm a Fanboy: MG Siegler on Apple, Google, Startup Culture and Jackasses on the Internet*. Hyperink, 2012. Digital.

CrunchFund partner and TechCrunch columnist makes observations about Silicon Valley.

JULIAN ASSANGE

Founder of WikiLeaks

Born: July 3, 1971; Townsville, Queensland, Australia
Died: -
Primary Field: Internet
Specialty: Ethics and policy
Primary Company/Organization: WikiLeaks

INTRODUCTION

Australian computer programmer, journalist, publisher, and activist Julian Assange's career has been shaped by his beliefs in transparency and the freedom of information. He entered the computer field as a hacker at age sixteen. After arrest and prosecution, he turned his talents to the rapidly growing Internet, helping the 1993 development of one of Australia's first public Internet service providers, the Suburbia Public Access Network. He also developed a number of free computer software programs. Assange achieved widespread recognition in 2006 as the founder and public spokesman for the website WikiLeaks, which used Internet technology to enter leaked or hacked secret and classified information into the public domain. The site sparked enormous public debate over Internet posting ethics and censorship after it released approximately ninety thousand classified documents related to the U.S. military records regarding the war in Afghanistan, known collectively as the Afghan War Diary, in 2010.

EARLY LIFE

Julian Paul Assange was born in Townsville, Queensland, Australia on July 3, 1971. Assange himself once claimed to come from a blended background that included Scottish, Irish, Taiwanese, and French ancestry. He credits Australian architect John Shipton as his biological father. Shipton had no contact with Assange until the latter was twenty-five years old. His stepfather was Australian theater director Richard Brett Assange, whom his mother, Christine Ann Hawkins, married when he was only one year old. Assange's mother raised him. She had numerous marriages and moved more than thirty times during Assange's childhood. He attended Goolmangar Primary

School in New South Wales from 1979 to 1983 among shorter stints at numerous other schools and periods of home schooling. Assange later attended the University of Melbourne and the University of Canberra from 2002 to 2005, studying for a bachelor of science degree before dropping out. His main fields of study were mathematics and physics. His departure was reportedly partly in protest over his belief that student research was being used for military purposes.

In 1987, when he was a teenager, Assange began operating as a computer hacker by the name of Mendax. He chose the name based on the Latin phrase *splendide mendax*, which means "nobly untruthful." He and his mother were living outside Melbourne, Australia, at the time. He joined other hackers to form the International

Julian Assange.

Subversives. The group operated under a computer hacking code of ethics, including such policies as not damaging hacked computer systems, not changing system information unnecessarily, and sharing any information gathered.

The Australian Federal Police (AFP) began investigating the group, and Assange was caught hacking into the master terminal of the Canadian telecommunications corporation Nortel in 1991. He was charged for this and numerous other hacking crimes, facing thirty-one counts in the Australian court system. Six charges were eventually dropped, and Assange pleaded guilty

---

Affiliation: WikiLeaks

Julian Assange founded the Internet website WikiLeaks in 2006. WikiLeaks enters secret documents and classified information into the public domain by posting them on the Internet. Assange, whose personal beliefs include the belief that total transparency of information is in the public interest, also emerged as the website's public face and spokesman. The site's main server is located in Sweden, a nation that has enacted legislative protection for whistle-blowers.

WikeLeaks' goal is to use the publicizing of information and new technological documents such as the Internet to end illegitimate governmental practices. Site workers also believe that leaks leave unjust governments more vulnerable to those who wish to replace them and will encourage more open government systems in their wake. Most of the site's information is obtained from sources, although computer hacking is also employed.

WikiLeaks' first published document was the 2006 posting of a Somali Islamic Courts Union decision of questionable authenticity, which advocated the execution of government officials. Other notable posts have included evidence of Kenyan extrajudicial killings; U.S. procedures for the treatment of detainees at Guantánamo Bay, Cuba; manuals from the Church of Scientology; and a video of a 2007 U.S. helicopter strike in Iraq that killed a number of civilians and several journalists. WikiLeaks' most noteworthy publication was the 2010 posting of the Afghan War Diary, the collective title for thousands of classified U.S. military records involving the war in Afghanistan.

---

to the remaining charges in 1995. A lack of evidence of malicious intent induced the judge to sentence Assange to pay only a small amount in damages.

LIFE'S WORK

Assange began his legal career in the computer and information technology field in the 1990s, first turning his attention to the rapidly growing Internet field. He played a role in the 1993 founding of the Suburbia Public Access Network in Australia, one of the country's first public Internet service providers. During this period, he also developed free computer software and programming, including Strobe, Surfraw, the Linux Rubberhose deniable encryption system, and the Usenet caching software NNTPCache.

Assange's most famous career milestone was the 2006 founding of the website WikiLeaks to support his belief in the importance of the free exchange of information. He believed that freedom of information through leaking sensitive information into the public domain would bring an end to illegitimate government and organizational practices. WikiLeaks followed in the footsteps of the earlier intelligence leak website Cryptome, run by New York architect John Young. Assange designed WikiLeaks to advance his mission of achieving transparency in journalism.

Although WikiLeaks relies mostly on sources to provide information, Assange has admitted that the site's workers, including him, have also relied on computer hacking to obtain information. Assange has called himself the website's editor in chief, with final approval over all posted documents. He has used WikiLeaks' success, in terms of the amount of information posted, as a rebuke of more traditional sources of journalism for their failure to publish suppressed information. Assange and many WikiLeaks workers believe that such leaks weaken secretive governments and organizations, paving the way for their ouster and replacement by more open governments and organizations.

WikiLeaks' first published document, a Somali Islamic Courts Union decision of questionable authenticity advocating the execution of government officials, carried a disclaimer warning of its potential basis in a U.S. intelligence community trick. The site has also exposed extrajudicial killings in the African nation of Kenya through its publication of a 2008 report by the Kenya National Commission on Human Rights titled *The Cry of Blood: Extra-Judicial Killings and Disappearances*. The 2010 release of a 2007 incident in which a U.S. helicopter attack killed a number of civilians and several journalists in Baghdad, Iraq, achieved widespread renown as the Collateral Murder video. Assange had been involved in the online posting while staying temporarily in a safe house in Iceland nicknamed the Bunker.

WikiLeaks' most noted achievement was the publication of approximately ninety thousand classified U.S. military documents from 2006 to 2010 regarding the war in Afghanistan. WikiLeaks published these documents, known collectively as the Afghan War Diary, in 2010. Many detailed the role of the Pakistani Inter-Service Intelligence Agency (ISI) in aiding al-Qaeda and the Taliban and fueling the Taliban insurgency against U.S. troops in Afghanistan. Criticisms have included the unfiltered and unqualified nature of the leaked data and the potential of providing false data in hopes of a monetary or other form of reward or a hidden agenda.

Assange served house arrest in Norfolk, England, from December 2010 to June 2012 under a European Arrest Warrant. He had served more than a week in prison before being freed on bail. The warrant was related to charges of sex crimes involving the alleged rape and assault of two women in separate incidents in Sweden. Assange claimed the encounters were consensual and appealed his extradition to Sweden, fearing that the U.S. government was behind the measure to gain time to build a case against him in that country for his WikiLeaks activity.

Assange filed to trademark his name in Europe for the purposes of public speaking, reporting, journalism, publishing, education, and entertainment in 2011. He worked with WikiLeaks to produce a politically based weekly talk show entitled *The World Tomorrow* while serving his house arrest. WikiLeaks ananounced the show in 2012, and the first episode was broadcast online later that year. The first guest was Muslim militant organization Hezbollah's leader Hassan Nasrallah. Assange also sought and in August 2012 was granted political asylum in Ecuador through that country's London embassy, where he fled to avoid extradition.

Assange found both himself and WikiLeaks in financial difficulty. In 2010, he sold the publishing rights to his proposed autobiography to the publishing firm Canongate, receiving more than £1 million. The book, ghostwritten by Andrew O'Hagan, was nonetheless published without his consent in 2011. Meanwhile, WikiLeaks has endured censorship, filtering, and suppression of its submission system in various countries and has been unavailable at times. Such censorship has inspired protests among WikiLeaks supporters. In 2010,

computer hacker collectives known as Anonymous and LulzSec launched a cyberattack on Visa, MasterCard, and PayPal sites to protest their actions against WikiLeaks. The use of hacking as a form of political protest has become widely known as hacktivism or the "global cyber insurgency." The controversial website has also prompted discussions as to whether or not Assange is a journalist.

Assange has described himself as a cynic who loves intellectual fights. He is the author of several essays and articles outlining his overall philosophy in using the Internet to promote transparency and freedom of information for the public good. He is listed as a researcher for the 1997 book *Underground: Tales of Hacking, Madness and Obsession on the Electronic Frontier*, which details the work of his early computer hacking organization, the International Subversives. Supporters have referred to him as "the Robin Hood of hacking."

PERSONAL LIFE

Assange was married in either 1988 or 1989. The couple had one son, resulting in a lengthy and bitter custody battle when the couple divorced. The experience drove Assange's formation of Parent Inquiry into Child Protection, an activist organization dedicated to the facilitation of access to custody-related legal records. Assange had a daughter through a subsequent relationship.

Assange has lived a nomadic existence since beginning WikiLeaks in 2006. He has stayed in Kenya, Tanzania, Egypt, France, Germany, and Iceland. He has appeared at various conferences and symposiums on computers, hacking, communication, freedom of information, and investigative journalism in Germany, Austria, Spain, Denmark, Norway, Australia, Belgium, and the United States. He has not revealed much personal information, including a confirmation of his birth date, age, or any permanent address.

Assange emerged as the public spokesman for WikiLeaks. His numerous awards have included the Amnesty International UK Media Award (2009), the Sam Adams Award (2010), the Sydney Peace Foundation of the University of Sydney Gold Medal (2011), and the Martha Gellhorn Prize for Journalism (2011). He was selected *Time* magazine's Readers' Choice Man of the Year for 2010 and nominated for the Nobel Peace Prize in 2011. His work has been recognized for its use of computer and Internet technology to pursue governmental and journalistic transparency, freedom of information, and human rights.

Marcella Bush Trevino

FURTHER READING

Assange, Julian. *Julian Assange: The Unauthorized Biography*. Edinburgh: Canongate, 2011. Print. A biographical overview of the life and career of the notoriously elusive WikiLeaks founder, including the convictions that led to his founding of the controversial website.

Assange, Julian, and Suelette Dreyfus. *Underground: Tales of Hacking, Madness and Obsession on the Electronic Frontier*. Edinburgh: Canongate, 2011. Print. Detailed account of the work of the computer hacking collective known as the International Subversives, of which Assange was a member known as Mendax.

Domscheit-Berg, Danial, Tina Klopp, and Jefferson S. Chase. *Inside WikiLeaks: My Time with Julian Assange at the World's Most Dangerous Website*. New York: Crown, 2011. Print. Provides an inside view of the website's evolution and finances as well as its inner workings, including worker tensions, from the point-of-view of a former employee.

Leigh, David, Luke Harding, Edward Pilkington, Robert Booth, and Charles Arthur. *WikiLeaks: Inside Julian Assange's War on Secrecy*. New York: Public Affairs, 2011. Print. Discusses both the history and potential future of the website as well as its impact on the fields of global politics and freedom of information.

B

MITCHELL BAKER

Chair of the Mozilla Foundation

Born: June 7, 1957; Berkeley, California
Died: -
Primary Field: Internet
Specialty: Applications
Primary Company/Organization: Mozilla Corporation

INTRODUCTION

Answering to the self-chosen title Chief Lizard Wrangler at the Mozilla Foundation and Mozilla Corporation,

Mitchell Baker.

Mitchell Baker has remained committed to offering open source tools for Internet development. She stands out in the field of Internet technology because 98 percent of its members are male. Baker is so committed to her job that she continued working as a volunteer when parent company AOL downsized Mozilla in 2001. In 2005, Time magazine named Baker on its annual list of 100 Most Influential People. An unabashed liberal, Baker is well known in technology circles for her asymmetrical red hairstyle, which has been compared to the well-known Firefox logo. (Although rumor has it that the comparison is intentional, Baker insists that her distinctive hairdo preceded the introduction of the logo.) At her husband's urging, Baker conquered her fears and followed through on a desire to become an amateur trapeze artist. She has a lifelong interest in Asia, where she has studied and traveled extensively, and she speaks Mandarin Chinese. Baker maintains a blog (blog.lizardwrangler.com) to keep the public abreast of activities at Mozilla.

EARLY LIFE

Winifred Mitchell Baker was born on June 7, 1957, in Berkeley, California. Although few facts about her early life are available, it is known that she grew up in the Berkeley area and attended high school in Oakland, California, where she opted to spend her senior year working at the Oakland Zoo. While attending college at the University of California–Berkeley, Baker spent a year in Communist China studying at Peking University (later Beijing University). Baker completed her bachelor's degree in Asian studies in 1979. In 1987, she received a law degree from Berkeley's Boalt School of Law. Before beginning her first job, Baker returned to

Asia for a year and was forced to undergo rabies treatment after being bitten by a dog in Tibet.

Baker spent the years between 1990 and 1993 working with high-profile technology clients at Fenwick and West, a nationally known law firm based in Mountain View, California. She then accepted a position as associate general counsel on Sun Microsystems' legal team, becoming part of the Netscape team in November 1994. At Netscape, Baker's chief responsibility lay in working with intellectual property rights. Pursuing her interest in legal technology, she established the Tech Group as a subgroup within the legal department. Almost immediately following her rise to head the company in 1998, Netscape was purchased by AOL for $4.2 billion.

LIFE'S WORK

During what became known as first browser wars, Microsoft's Internet Explorer (IE) rose to the top of the browser market, garnering the lion's share of users. The computer giant also managed to survive a federal antitrust suit, *United States v. Microsoft* (filed in 1998 and settled in 2001), in which it was charged with attempting to monopolize the browser market by bundling IE with its Windows operating system. As a result, interest in Netscape's Communicator (a suite of Internet tools that included the Navigator web browser), Microsoft's chief competitor and a motivating force behind the antitrust lawsuit, continued to dwindle. In 1998, the decision was made to make Netscape Communicator's code open source, and Baker was assigned the responsibility for writing the license in language that allowed developers to benefit from the code without claiming proprietary interests in the product. As Netscape disappeared from the scene, a number of employees gravitated to the Mozilla Foundation, which had been created to manage continued development of the open source product.

Thus, Mozilla began life as a start-up with only seventy employees and a host of volunteers. The name is reported to have been derived from the phrase "Mosaic killer," which pays homage to Mosaic, the first Internet browser. Scorning the corporate image and giving away its browser for free, Mozilla soon rose to the position of Microsoft's chief competitor.

By February 1999, Baker had become known as Chief Lizard Wrangler and general manager of the Mozilla Corporation, where she served as general spokesperson and troubleshooter as well as policy arbitrator. At Mozilla, Baker came into her own, developing a unique management style that has been copied by other technology companies. Baker prefers working

---

Affiliation: Mozilla Corporation

Headquartered in Mountain View, California, Mozilla, the owner of the popular Firefox web browser, has been dubbed "the Burger King to Microsoft's Internet Explorer" by Mozilla's Mitchell Baker. Because, as of 2012, it was solidly in second place, the open sourced browser worked hard under Baker's guidance to deliver a quality way of surfing the Internet, promising security, stability, and innovation that devotees claim is unequaled by Microsoft's Internet Explorer, Google's Chrome, or any other Internet browser. In August 2012, Mozilla announced that downloads for its popular add-ons had reached the 3 billion mark. Allowing users to personalize Firefox while improving performance, the most popular add-ons at the time were identified as Adblock Plus, Video Download Helper, Firebug, Grease Monkey, Download Status Bar, NoScript, Personas Plus, and Down Them All.

Personally, Baker's favorite add-on is Personas, which allows users to personalize their browsers with such themes as Harry Potter, Spider Man, anime favorites, art, or nature images. Baker also promotes the use of the Ubiquity add-on, which saves users time by allowing them to send information directly from the Firefox browser. Popular applications, including Songbird, an open source music program similar to Apple's iTunes, and Joost, a web video channel, have also been generated by using Firefox's free code. Some Mozilla applications have been sold to for-profit companies such as eBay, which purchased StumbleUpon for $75 million, and Yahoo, which bought a bookmarking tool for $15 million.

---

with small groups that come up with ideas that are then dispersed to larger groups before being put into practice. Siobhan O'Mahony of Harvard Business School, who has become an expert on Baker's management style, has expressed great admiration for it; she predicts that Baker has established the standard management model for technology companies of the future.

In 1998, AOL purchased Netscape in a stock-for-stock deal. In 2001, the parent company began laying off workers, and Baker's job was eliminated. However, Baker continued to fulfill her duties as a volunteer at Mozilla until 2002, when she was hired by the Open Source Applications Foundation, which agreed to subsidize her work at Mozilla by paying her a portion of her former salary. In April of that year, Blake Ross and David Hyatt developed Mozilla 2.0, which was released as a suite of applications that included a browser, e-mail and chat capabilities, bulletin boards, and website development tools. The browser introduced the concept of tabs as a replacement for opening individual web pages in separate windows. The release of the Phoenix browser subsequently improved the Mozilla browser with the addition of the add-ons that would eventually become one of Mozilla Firefox's biggest draws. Unimpressed with the development, AOL displayed a lack of foresight by negotiating a deal with Microsoft and firing Mozilla's developers.

AOL's actions aroused the interest of other developers, who were convinced that Microsoft was violating antitrust laws. Mitchell Kapor, the founder of Lotus, a major Microsoft competitor, invested $300,000. Developers from IBM, Sun Microsystems, and Red Hat were assigned to work with Mozilla, and even AOL agreed to invest $2 million to create the not-for-profit Mozilla Foundation in 2003 with Baker as president.

The Mozilla browser was officially renamed Firefox in 2004, after briefly being known as Firebird. From the beginning, Firefox was noted for its ability to fend off hackers and viruses more successfully than Microsoft's Internet Explorer, which had become known for its vulnerability to hackers and spammers. Mozilla volunteers flooded blogs and websites, promoting the new browser. They also chipped in $30 each to finance a two-page ad for Firefox in *The New York Times*. The result of the volunteer efforts was that 10 million copies were downloaded in the first month after its release. Volunteers continue to form the backbone of Mozilla's workforce, and they promote Firefox by placing the famous logo on everything from their faces to weather balloons and highway overpasses. In 2006, some of them even cosponsored a Firefox crop circle that was 220 feet in diameter, placing it in an oat field in Amity, Oregon.

By the beginning of 2005, Baker was back to working full time at Mozilla, becoming chief executive officer (CEO) of the newly established for-profit Mozilla Corporation, which generates funds to underwrite the work of the foundation, while continuing her work at the Mozilla Foundation. That year, the number of Mozilla volunteers rose to 100,000 (it would swell to 200,000 by 2007), and downloads of Firefox averaged 250,000 per day. Mozilla was also claiming 8 percent of the market, and its share continued to rise. By 2006, the Mozilla Corporation was reporting $70 million in revenue, most of which was generated from links placed on Google and Yahoo! Within a year, Firefox was reporting 120 million users speaking more than fifty languages, and its market share had climbed to 13 percent.

Although Mozilla is headquartered adjacent to Google in Mountain View, California, Mozilla's emphasis on keeping its product free has led the company to continue to eschew a corporate lifestyle. The company's headquarters have been compared to a ski lodge or military barracks. Instead of the expensive automobiles that fill its neighbor's parking lot, the transportation of Mozilla's employees and volunteers reflects their modest lifestyles. Subsidiaries of Mozilla are located in Toronto, Tokyo, and Paris.

In January 2008, as the Mozilla Corporation continued to grow, Baker opted to devote her full attention to the Mozilla Foundation and gave up her position as CEO of the Mozilla Corporation. That year, Mozilla released Firefox 3.0, including an application designed for use on mobile phones. Within a single day, 10.7 million users had downloaded the browser. By 2012, Firefox was up to version 14.0.1, and Mozilla was reporting that it had claimed almost a fourth of the Internet browser market share.

PERSONAL LIFE

Dedicated to open source sharing of Internet development tools and the concept of providing quality products that are offered to the public at no charge, Baker was heavily involved in the ongoing antitrust battle against Microsoft. Under her leadership, Mozilla has joined the European Commission and a host of technology companies that strongly object to Microsoft's bundling its Internet Explorer within its Windows software, ensuring its dominance of the Internet browsing market. Baker insists that Microsoft's behavior is both illegal and monopolistic.

Baker's contributions to Internet development have been recognized by a number of organizations. In 2009, she was awarded the Women of Vision Award by the prestigious Anita Borg Institute. The following year, Baker was honored with the Aenne Burda Award for Creative Leadership and Frost and Sullivan's Growth, Innovation, and Leadership Award. In 2012, Baker was named to the Internet Hall of Fame by the Internet Society. Baker is also an active participant in the Innovator Program, run by the Henry Ford Museums. She lives in San Jose, California, with her husband, Casey Dunn. The couple have one son.

Elizabeth Rholetter Purdy

FURTHER READING

Andreessen, Marc. "Mitchell Baker." *Time* 165.16 (2005): n. pag. Print. Highlights Baker's accomplishments by profiling her as one of the magazine's most influential people of the year. Illustrated.

Freedman, David H. "Mitchell Baker and the Firefox Paradox." *Inc.* 29.2 (2007): 104–11. Print. Profile of Mozilla, with a focus on Baker's role in the success of the company.

Hardy, Quentin. "Web Warrior." *Forbes* 180.9 (2007): 60–64. Print. Traces the rise of Mozilla Firefox amid stiff competition.

LaVallee, Andrew. "Questions for Mitchell Baker, Mozilla Chairman." *Wall Street Journal* 4 Mar. 2009. Print. Question/answer session with Baker.

Mellor, Paul. "Mozilla Joins EC in Microsoft Suite." *Computer World* 43.7 (2009): n. pag. Print. Discusses Mozilla's role in the new antitrust suit against Microsoft.

Singel, Ryan. "Mozilla's Mitchell Baker on Being the Alternate to Microsoft, Google, and Apple." *Wired* 7 May 2012: n. pag. Print. Overview of Baker's career, with a focus on her time at Mozilla.

PAUL BARAN

Developer of the Internet and researcher at RAND Corporation

Born: April 29, 1926; Grodno, Second Polish Republic (now in Belarus)
Died: March 26, 2011; Palo Alto, California
Primary Field: Internet
Specialty: Applications
Primary Company/Organization: RAND Corporation

INTRODUCTION

Paul Baran's research suggested a distributed network as a strategy for building communications systems that could survive serious infrastructural damage (specifically a nuclear attack), and when the Internet ancestor ARPANET was created, it was with that goal in mind. Baran also developed a key form of data transmission for networks, packet switching, which helped make the Internet feasible.

EARLY LIFE

Paul Baran was born the youngest child of a Jewish family in Grodno, Poland (now part of Belarus), on April 29, 1926, and immigrated with his family to Boston in 1928. When Paul was still young, his family relocated to Philadelphia, where he delivered groceries in the neighborhood from a small store his father, Morris, ran. He studied electrical engineering at the Drexel Institute of Technology (now Drexel University), graduating in 1949. His first serious work was for the Eckert-Mauchly Computer Corporation (EMCC), formed by the designers of the Electronic Numerical Integrator and Computer (ENIAC). EMCC had recently built the Universal Automatic Computer (UNIVAC), an ambitious

improvement on ENIAC that used magnetic tape for memory storage and was employed to tabulate the 1950 U.S. Census.

After marrying in 1955, Baran relocated to Los Angeles, where he worked on radar systems at Hughes Aircraft while attending night classes at the University

Paul Baran.

of California to earn his master's degree. His graduate adviser later commented that Baran was his first student to investigate the patentability of his thesis—a sign that he was not just a theorist but interested in immediately engaging with the practical applications of his field. In 1959, once he had earned his master's of science in engineering, he began work at the nonprofit RAND Corporation in the mathematics division's computer science department.

LIFE'S WORK

During the late 1950s and early 1960s, much of the public was focused on the space race as a manifestation of Cold War tensions. The threat of nuclear attack, however, was also a grave concern in the wake of the U.S. deployment of the first atomic bombs at the end of World War II and the development of the hydrogen bomb. With the threat of increasing stockpiles of nuclear weapons by the world's two superpowers, the United States and the Soviet Union, Baran focused on the problem of dealing with the aftermath of a possible nuclear attack, working under contract to the Air Force through RAND. Long-distance communication networks were still young: The first coast-to-coast telephone call had been placed in 1915, only fifty years earlier, and the greatest teledensity was found in the parts of the country most likely to be struck in a nuclear attack. Like electricity, telephone lines had not become commonplace in much of rural America until the 1930s, only a generation earlier. The technology involved in the nation's long-distance communication was also rather primitive in many respects: Touch-tone signaling had not yet been introduced, outages were a regular occurrence in severe weather, and cellular phone technology had been proposed but remained undeveloped. In short, a nuclear attack or any other serious attack on the nation's infrastructure would make an organized response and even basic continuity of government difficult if not impossible. As a result, retaliation would be more difficult, and without the threat of retaliation, the country would be more vulnerable. The doctrine of mutually assured destruction (MAD) was widely accepted: As long as each side was too intimidated by retaliation to launch a strike, peace could be assured through this deterrent effect; however, MAD worked only if that retaliatory capacity would survive a nuclear strike.

Designing a communications network that could survive at least that first strike would ensure continuity of government and a retaliatory capability because of the still-functioning command-and-control systems.

For Baran, digital computers seemed to promise the solution, yet they were still quite new: ENIAC itself had been only the second electronic digital computer, and computers were still used principally for intensive computation and manipulation of numeric data for research; they were not synonymous with communications systems, as they are today; indeed, it is Baran's work that led to that alignment. Baran's colleagues did not always follow his reasoning, so he was inspired to write a critical series of technical papers, defending his ideas and forcing him to define and develop them more rigorously. Key to understanding Baran's solution to the problem of ensuring that communications networks could survive an attack is the metaphor of the human brain, which is not destroyed by damage to a single part and which is capable of resuming functions by working around the damaged portion. Baran wanted a network that would work the same way: a network that would function with whatever surviving parts (nodes) it possessed.

This idea ran counter to the model of the time: Communications networks were discussed in terms of centralization. A centralized network is one in which all nodes connect to a hub that routes data back and forth among them. This makes it easy to add new nodes, up to the capacity of the hub, but the health of the network depends on the health of the hub. A decentralized hub solves this problem; in a decentralized system, destroying one hub destroys only part of the network. Baran's idea was to develop a hubless network—that is, a distributed network, in which nodes were connected not to hubs that moderated traffic but to each other. Although a node might be stranded if enough of its neighboring nodes were destroyed, the network as a whole could survive significant damage without losing its communication capabilities.

Originally Baran approached AT&T with the idea, but decision makers at that company insisted his idea was unworkable, despite repeated pitches from Baran. Ultimately, the distributed network was developed by the Defense Department's Advanced Research Projects Agency (ARPA). Although it originally connected only four nodes, one of the important innovations of ARPANET over previous computer networks was that it was heterogeneous; computers did not have to be compatible with one another in order to be compatible with the network. ARPANET went into development in 1967, incorporating both the distributed network idea and Baran's packet-switching methodology.

Packet switching is Baran's second major contribution to the Internet: a method of delivering data

Affiliation: RAND Corporation

The RAND (originally Research and Development) Corporation was founded in 1948 as a nonprofit think tank providing the American government and military with research and analysis. It was established by the Douglas Aircraft Company as the Cold War began in the years following World War II. Its first project, while still a division of Douglas in 1946, was the ambitious preliminary design of an experimental world-circling spaceship, proposing an orbital satellite program.

RAND was deeply involved in providing intellectual and philosophical guidance on American military strategy and foreign policy, especially during the Cold War era. The think tank's work in game theory introduced the concept of mutually assured destruction (MAD), whereby the repercussions of a military retaliation were predicted to motivate each side of the Cold War to avoid a first strike. However, the peace promised by MAD required that each side retain retaliatory capability. Paul Baran's work on a distributed network, which later became the early Internet, originated as a way to guarantee the continuity of the nation's communications networks and control of strategic command in the event of a nuclear attack or similar infrastructural damage.

RAND's work has ranged in focus from foreign policy to corporate governance to the military use of war games to an in-depth health insurance study in the late 1970s and the publication of *A Million Random Digits with 100,000 Normal Deviates*—a book-length random number table, seemingly an oddity, but actually of critical value between the 1940s and 1960s in statistics, experimental sciences, and cryptography. Later, computerized random number generators replaced this table.

across a network by reducing the original package into bundles for transmission. Baran called the bundles of data "message blocks," which were sent across the network and reassembled at the node of their destination to form the original package of data. Because communications networks transmit data in bursts rather than in a continuous stream, packets are an especially efficient means of transmission. Baran's proposal was to use nodes that would automatically route packages as they were received, whenever bandwidth was available— taking advantage of the pauses between those bursts.

Advanced computers (at least advanced by the standards of the time) could monitor network activity in order to maximize efficiency in packet routing, sending packets to nodes that had the bandwidth capacity to deal with them—an approach called "dynamic routing." Simultaneous with Baran's work, British computer scientist Donald Davies proposed a similar system using the term *packets*, which became the accepted label.

Although Baran's network ideas originated in considering the nuclear attack problem, he advocated numerous applications for them. In particular, in 1966 he presented a paper on the future of marketing to the American Marketing Association, describing—before ARPANET even began development—something very similar to online shopping. He envisioned customers at home using their television sets to interact with different stores.

By the time of ARPANET's first demonstration in 1969, Baran had left RAND to cofound the Institute for the Future in 1968. The nonprofit research group focused on another intriguing and difficult problem: the science of long-term forecasts. Baran continued to consult on ARPANET's work. Originally intended for researchers to share information, ARPANET quickly became a communication network used for just about anything those with access to it could imagine. Not just researchers but also college students were granted access through their universities' computer departments, and as computers became more common, so did net users. ARPANET split off from its military component in 1983 and was renamed the Internet in 1989, around the time that modem speeds were becoming fast enough for home use of the Internet to be feasible over normal telephone lines. Because there was initially no need to install a new infrastructure or dedicated high-speed lines used to connect professional servers, general use of the Internet via the World Wide Web quickly spread among the public.

Baran was always quick to point out that the modern Internet was the result of not one or two innovations but the hard work of hundreds of people—an emergent invention. Nonetheless, his vision and practical development of both distributed networking and packet switching place him in the vanguard of those now considered responsible for creating the Internet.

PERSONAL LIFE

Baran married Evelyn Murphy in 1955. They had one son, David. After Evelyn's death in 2007, he dated and later lived with Ruth Rothman, although they did not marry. He died on March 26, 2011, of complications from lung cancer.

Bill Kte'pi

FURTHER READING

Abbate, Janet. *Inventing the Internet*. Cambridge: MIT, 2000. Print. A history of the Internet with a focus on ARPA, including a discussion of Baran's packet-switching technology.

Hafner, Katie. *Where Wizards Stay Up Late: The Origins of the Internet*. New York: Simon, 1998. Print. Although old enough to be noticeably incomplete now, this history of the Internet nevertheless provides thorough coverage of its origins and early years.

Lima, Manuel. *Visual Complexity: Mapping Patterns of Information*. Princeton: Princeton Architectural Press, 2011. Print. Visualizations of data, including Baran's distributed network.

Salus, Peter H., ed. *The ARPANET Sourcebook: The Unpublished Foundations of the Internet*. New York: Peer to Peer Communications, 2008. Print. Assembles primary sources related to the ARPANET project.

Wu, Tim. *The Master Switch: The Rise and Fall of Information Empires*. New York: Vintage, 2011. Print. An analytical look at the Internet and its role in history.

JOHN PERRY BARLOW

Cofounder of the Electronic Frontier Foundation

Born: October 3, 1947; Cora, Sublette County, Wyoming
Died: -
Primary Field: Internet
Specialty: Ethics and policy
Primary Company/Organization: Electronic Frontier Foundation

INTRODUCTION

John Perry Barlow has been one of the most influential political thinkers of the Internet society. Over the course of a career when he has been simultaneously lyricist, lobbyist, essayist, and consultant, he has never ceased to use his communication skills for protecting the constitutional rights of American "netizens." A man of both ideas and action, Barlow helped found the Electronic Frontier Foundation. Widely acclaimed for his visionary insights, he has been a source of inspiration for a generation of political thinkers specializing in new technologies.

EARLY LIFE

John Perry Barlow was born to a family of politicians on October 3, 1947, in Cora, Wyoming. The grandson of a Sublette County founder on his mother's side and the son of a Republican state legislator, he grew up in the middle of a 22,000-acre ranch and developed a passion for wide-open spaces.

As a teenager, Barlow and his friends were looking for ways to break the routine of life in a small town, when his father sent him off to the Fountain Military Academy in Colorado Springs, where he met Bob Weir, another rebellious teen, who would become a lifelong friend. With Weir playing the guitar and Barlow writing poetry, the two teenagers spent all their free time together. When Weir was expelled from the academy,

John Perry Barlow.

Barlow immediately denounced an injustice and threatened to quit to show solidarity with his friend. He was persuaded to stay, however, and graduated in 1965.

Barlow enrolled at Wesleyan University, leaving his native region for the East coast. While studying comparative religion, he took advantage of his academic years to explore new intellectual horizons and became a friend of psychologist and LSD advocate Timothy Leary. In 1967, he reconnected with his old friend Weir, who had helped formed a music band the Grateful Dead. They discovered that they still shared similar political views and a vision of the world, which departed from social conventions. In 1969, Barlow graduated and left the continent for an initiatory journey in India.

LIFE'S WORK

With his father's health declining, Barlow put an end to his student life in 1970. He returned to the family ranch and took over its administration. There he met his future wife, a former classmate. Animated by his political convictions, Barlow embraced the fate of the family, engaging himself in the political life of his region. He notably served Dick Cheney as his Wyoming campaign coordinator during Cheney's 1978 congressional campaign and worked on a number of environmental issues, notably to pass the Wyoming Wilderness Act in 1984.

Given his political activism, Barlow was offered the chance to transform his ideas into action and to share them with the rest of the world. After clashing with Grateful Dead lyricist Bob Hunter, Barlow's old friend Weir asked him to write lyrics for the Grateful Dead. Barlow wrote "Mexicali Blues," launching a string of more than twenty-five songs on which he and Weir would collaborate for the one of the most iconic bands of the 1960s, 1970s, and 1980s.

Traveling with the rest of the band from one concert venue to another, Barlow enjoyed an active social life and found a new way to extend his spectrum of relationships. Barlow's ranch quickly became a center of intellectual and social life, hosting celebrities such as Marlon Brando and John F. Kennedy, Jr.

In 1987, Barlow bought a computer to help with managing the ranch, just one year before he left the countryside for a two-bedroom house in Pinedale. At a moment when cyberspace was turning into a consensual reality in the Silicon Valley, and with a strong presence of Deadheads (fans of the Grateful Dead) online, he joined the Whole Earth 'Lectronic Link (WELL), a leading virtual community. With the possibility getting

> ## Affiliation: Electronic Frontier Foundation
>
> The Electronic Frontier Foundation was created in June 1990 by John Perry Barlow and Mitch Kapor in reaction to a large operation orchestrated by the U.S. Secret Service against alleged hackers. With the support of Internet entrepreneurs, Barlow launched the foundation with the goal of protecting constitutional rights in the burgeoning Internet age.
>
> With the government preparing to amend the 1934 Communications Act, the EFF lobbied to uphold the speech rights protected by the First Amendment, opening an office in Washington, D.C., in 1993. After the Telecommunications Act was signed into law on February 8, 1996, the EFF joined the American Civil Liberties Union and seventeen other not-for-profit organizations in an action against the Communications Decency Act.
>
> In 1998, in response to the Data Encryption Standard (DES), the EFF released the Deep Crack, a machine designed to decrypt encrypted messages by testing every possible key (known as a brute-force cyberattack) and thus reveal how easily government secrets and other sensitive information could be stolen by malicious entities; EFF's goal was to show that the DES was inadequate. Strongly attached to the values of sharing and innovating on the Internet, the EFF also supported inventors of peer-to-peer systems in the war against regulation, including Music City in 2001, Morpheus in 2002, and Grokster in 2003. In 2012, the EFF headquarters moved to San Francisco, in the Silicon Valley.

in touch with the rest of the world, he became an active member and an enthusiast of the cyberspace culture.

Having lost the race for a state senate seat in 1989, Barlow had a rare opportunity to play a leading role on the political scene just one year later. In May 1990, the Secret Service launched a nationwide operation against alleged hackers and an agent of the Federal Bureau of Investigation (FBI) questioned Barlow about his connections with the hacker community NuPrometheus. Barlow noticed the confusion of the federal administration about computers and networks and realized that freedom of speech could be endangered in emerging information networks. A few days later, Barlow was contacted by Mitch Kapor, the inventor of the spreadsheet program Lotus 1-2-3. Together, they asked for advice from one of the New York's most distinguished constitutional law firms, which encouraged them to create a foundation. In June 1990, Barlow left a message for the WELL community, announcing his intention to create the Electronic Frontier Foundation (EFF) to "fund, conduct, and support legal efforts to demonstrate that the Secret Service has exercised prior restraint on publications, limited free speech, conducted improper seizure of equipment and data, used undue force, and generally conducted itself in a fashion which is arbitrary, oppressive, and unconstitutional." This generated publicity, earning Barlow access to major figures in the computer industry and to the financial support of John Gilmore and Steve Wozniak, among others.

While supporting the case of *Steve Jackson Games, Inc. v. United States Secret Service*, Barlow started to open the eyes of the American public to the threats that could be posed to freedom of speech in the Internet information society by writing a number of essays aimed at sharing the vision of cyberspace, using media as diverse as *Mondo 2000*, *Communications of the ACM*, *The New York Times*, and *Time* magazine. In 1993, he also contributed to the launch of *Wired*, a magazine dedicated to new technology.

Barlow thus threw himself into the battle for the defense of freedom on networks. At a moment when amending the Communications Act of 1934 was on the agenda of the Clinton administration, the EFF's offices moved from Kapor's Kapor Enterprises to Washington, D.C., and a new team was formed. By 1994, Barlow's ideas had become more popular. Not only was he supported by a new generation of Internet users, but his vision of the economy was being seconded by supporters. By declaring that the era of "the economy of ideas" had arrived, he made a major contribution to the constitution of the so-called New Economy by a number of unconventional economists and experts.

In January 1996, the Telecommunications Act was passed, and on February 8, 1996, President Bill Clinton signed it. Contrary to the EFF's expectations, it introduced a Communications Decency Act, aiming at regulating Internet indecency and obscenity. Barlow immediately saw this as a restriction on free speech and a violation of the First Amendment of the U.S. Constitution. He responded by writing "A Declaration of the Independence of Cyberspace," which was widely circulated on the Internet. The EFF joined the American Civil Liberties Union (ACLU) and seventeen other nonprofit organizations in a legal action against the Communications Decency Act. In June 1996, a panel

of federal judges ruled in favor of the ACLU. A year later, on June 26, 1997, the judgment was upheld by the Supreme Court.

With the Internet economy booming, Barlow's influence grew. During this period, he consulted for companies such as Apple and Microsoft and served on the advisory boards of different organizations. He traveled the world, especially the Southern Hemisphere, sharing his vision of an interconnected world freely sharing information. A Fellow at Harvard University's Berkman Center for Internet and Society since May 1998, he has been a source of inspiration for a new generation of political thinkers. Echoing his message, his disciple Lawrence Lessig wrote *The Future of Ideas: The Fate of the Commons in a Connected World*.

PERSONAL LIFE

Barlow married Elaine Parker, an old school friend, in 1977. Together, they had three daughters. Another high school friend, Bob Weir, was the founder of the Grateful Dead, and Barlow wrote more than twenty-five songs for that group during the 1970s and the 1980s, occasionally traveling with the other band members and meeting other artists, including actor Marlon Brando.

Until 1988, Barlow lived with Elaine and their three daughters at the family ranch, in Cora, Wyoming; they separated in 1992. After he sold the ranch, Barlow moved to a two-bedroom house in Pinedale, only three doors from Elaine and his daughters. In 1992, he met Cynthia Horner, a twenty-seven-year-old psychiatrist, with whom he lived in New York. In April 1994, Horner died from an undiagnosed heart ailment, leaving Barlow deeply affected; he received thousands of condolences via e-mail, and he would later confess that he had lost his greatest love.

Barlow eventually returned to Pinedale, where he retired. While enjoying life in the West, he continued to travel and to offer his expertise for those who could benefit from it. More than ever, he is a citizen of the world.

Jean Béhue

FURTHER READING

Barnes, Barry. *Everything I know About Business I Learned from the Grateful Dead: The Ten Most Innovative Lessons from a Long, Strange Trip*. New York: Business Plus, 2011. Print. The business side of the Grateful Dead music band, with an afterword by Barlow.

Lessig, Lawrence. *The Future of Ideas: The Fate of the Commons in a Connected World*. New York: Vintage, 2002. Print. A popular essay that extends Barlow's views to the Internet regulation debate.

Morozov, Evgeny. *The Net Delusion: The Dark Side of Internet Freedom.* New York: PublicAffairs, 2011. Print. An argumentative essay that counterbalances the ideas promoted by Barlow and the EFF.

Morrison, Aimée H. "An Impossible Future: John Perry Barlow's Declaration of the Independence of Cyberspace." *New Media and Society* 11.1–2 (2009):

53–71. Print. A discussion of the widely circulated essay that Barlow wrote in reaction to the enactment of the Telecommunications Act.

Sterling, Bruce. *The Hacker Crackdown: Law and Disorder on the Electronic Frontier.* New York: Bantam, 1993. Print. A tale of the nationwide raid operated by the U.S. Secret Service against hackers, with an insight on the creation of the EFF.

CAROL A. BARTZ

Former CEO of Yahoo!

Born: August 28, 1948; Winona, Minnesota
Died: -
Primary Field: Business and commerce
Specialty: Management, executives, and investors
Primary Company/Organization: Yahoo!

INTRODUCTION

Carol A. Bartz is an American business executive who served as chief executive officer (CEO) of Yahoo, an Internet corporation best known for its web portal and directory of websites, from 2009 to 2011, when she was fired amid a storm of media exchanges. She was among the nation's best paid CEOs, with a compensation package that totaled more than $75 million for her brief tenure at Yahoo! Earlier (1992–2006) she was the CEO of Autodesk, Inc., where more than doubled the company's revenue and transformed it from a little-known creator of computer-aided design software into the world's leading supplier of design software used in buildings, automobiles, and movie animation.

EARLY LIFE

Carol Ann Bartz was born on August 28, 1948, in Winona, Minnesota. Her mother died when Bartz was eight and her younger brother Jim was two. For four years after her mother's death, she and her brother lived with their father, who worked at a feed mill for $40 per week and never hesitated to reinforce discipline with a belt. When Bartz was twelve, she and Jim went to live with their grandparents on their farm near Alma, Wisconsin. Bartz flourished under their love and support. Her grandmother was especially influential in teaching her to be a strong, independent woman, capable of completing whatever job needed to be done. Although Bartz

showed an early aptitude for science and mathematics, she was far from the stereotypical nerdy girl. In high school, she was a majorette, a cheerleader, student body president, and homecoming queen; she was also the only girl in her physics and advanced algebra classes.

She still found time to work in the bank where her Sunday-school teacher was president, eventually earning seventy-five cents an hour as a teller. Her employers helped her get a scholarship to attend William Woods

Carol A. Bartz.

College in Fulton, Missouri, at that time an elite, private institution for women. Working in the cafeteria serving food to her wealthy classmates taught her humility, but it was her enrollment in a computer class at a neighboring all-male school that changed her life. There that she began to think that her love of mathematics could lead to careers other than teaching. She transferred to the University of Wisconsin at Madison to study computer science. Working as a cocktail waitress in a local supper club, she learned the importance of remembering details about her regular customers, a lesson that served her well later when she worked in marketing. After graduating with an honors degree in computer science, she sold automated banking services briefly and then worked for four years at the 3M Company, where she was the only woman in a sales division of three hundred men. She was employed in product-line and sales management by Digital Equipment Corporation (DEC) before she moved to Sun Microsystems in 1983.

LIFE'S WORK

Bartz started at Sun as a customer marketing manager, but within a year she became marketing vice president. She then served as vice president of customer service until mid-1990, when she was promoted to vice president of worldwide field operations. Bartz helped triple the division's sales. In 1992, her final year with Sun, the company's worldwide revenues increased from $2.6 billion to $3.6 billion.

Bartz's achievements at Sun made her a top candidate for the position vacated by the departure of Alvar J. Green, the president, chairman, and CEO of Autodesk, in 1992. Autodesk was a major player in the computer-assisted design (CAD) software industry, but growth was minimal and profits were falling when Bartz was named CEO. As if the challenge were not great enough, on her first day on the job she was diagnosed with breast cancer. She had a radical mastectomy and TRAM flap surgery to rebuild the breast with abdominal tissue, but she worked from her hospital bed and returned to work two weeks earlier than her doctors advised, full time, continuing on the job through seven months of chemotherapy.

Bartz soon proved not only that she was tough but also that she was skillful at balancing business acumen with a vision for the technology. Smart acquisitions and new product development protected the company's base while extending its reach. In 1996, the company created Kinetix, an animation division. By 2006, Autodesk was a different company from the one Bartz had taken on

seven years earlier. In 1991, Autodesk had catered to a niche market by offering software that made it possible for engineers, architects, contractors, and others to produce powerful models on relatively inexpensive personal computers. In 2006, the company had diversified into broader markets, and its growth had earned it a place on *Business Week*'s list of the fifty best-performing large companies. Revenue, which was about $275 million in 1991, exceeded $1.5 billion in 2006. Profits reached $315 million the same year, up from $47 million in 2003.

At the age of fifty-seven, Bartz took stock. The transformation of Autodesk had been successful. Her husband had retired, and the man she had been training as her replacement was being courted by other companies. On January 17, 2006, she announced that she would step down as CEO on May 1, remaining to chair the board. She spent the next few years relaxing in Hawaii, volunteering with charities, and serving on the boards of Autodesk, Cisco, Intel, and NetApp. However, the less stressful life had grown dull by 2008, and when Yahoo! cofounder Jerry Yang came calling, Bartz was willing to listen. She became chief executive of Yahoo! in January 2009.

From the beginning of her tenure at Yahoo, Bartz was under pressure to manage a turnaround far more complex than the situation she had faced at Autodesk. Even critics concede that she made some right moves. Under her leadership, Yahoo! hired dozens of editorial employees and bought Associated Content, a freelance news site, allowing the company to focus on the plan to make Yahoo! a hub for news, sports, finance, and entertainment. E-mail and instant messaging, popular Yahoo! products, were high priorities. The new CEO also cut costs, eliminating some services and outsourcing others that were not a good fit for the more focused Yahoo! The cost-cutting helped the company double its operating income to $748 million, exceeding a goal of $630 million set by the board and garnering Bartz a $2.2 million bonus in 2010.

Despite all these changes, Bartz was unable to increase Yahoo!'s advertising revenue significantly, even with an audience that was one of the largest on the web. The celebrated agreement with Microsoft in 2009 that outsourced Yahoo!'s search business to Microsoft failed to live up to its promise, and by 2012 the partnership was rumored to be on the verge of dissolution. The stock remained flat, Yahoo! missed revenue targets, and Bartz was attracting more press for her salty language than for delivering good news to shareholders. Pressure from

Affiliation: Yahoo!

Yahoo! is a digital media company that began in 1994 as the book-mark lists of David Filo and Jerry Yang, both Stanford University graduate students in electrical engineering. The site quickly attracted a growing audience. Filo and Yang incorporated the business in 1995 and began selling advertising space on the website. Traffic on the site increased at such a rate that the two left graduate school and in 1996 mounted a public offering for a multimillion-dollar corporation. That year, the company went international, launching Yahoo! Europe and Yahoo! Japan. Growth continued at a rapid pace throughout the 1990s. No longer merely a list, the site had become a web portal. New acquisitions allowed the company to increase the diversity of its offerings. Soon news, stock prices, entertainment, and other information were added to the search engine and e-mail services.

Yahoo! stocks closed at a high of $118.75 per share on January 3, 2000. Although that high hit a dismal low the next year, when the dot-com bubble burst, the audience continued to expand, as did the advertisements. The company's dominance in online news, sports, and entertainment seemed unassailable. However, as Google, Apple, Facebook, and Twitter emerged and reshaped online communication and commerce, Yahoo! began to flounder. Improving existing services such as the popular Yahoo! Mail, Yahoo! Messaging, and Yahoo! Groups did little to halt the loss of advertising dollars that were increasingly awarded to Google, with its customer search information, and Facebook, with its community connections. Adding Flickr, a video-sharing service, in 2008 and a partnership with ABC News in 2011 created audience appeal but failed to attract advertisers. Carol Bartz, who held the CEO's office from January 2009 to September 2011, was fired when she failed to change the company's direction. As of 2012, Yahoo! has had four CEOs after Bartz, two of them as interims until a new leader could be found. The third, Scott Thompson, was hired from eBay's PayPal in January 2012 as Bartz's successor but left the company in May 2012 amid accusations of discrepancies in his academic credentials. After a career at Google, Marissa Mayer took the helm on July 17, 2012.

major investors increased, and employees gave their leader a grim 33 percent approval rating. On September 6, 2011, after thirty months at the helm of Yahoo, Bartz was fired. Company chairman Roy Bostock delivered the news to the CEO by telephone. She resigned from Yahoo!'s board of directors on September 9, 2011.

Media gleefully had reported Bartz's early memo to her new Yahoo! team to fire any employee who leaked company secrets (the language she used was much more emphatic and colorful). Now news outlets just as eagerly reported the drama surrounding her firing, from the graceless cell phone call to Bartz's reference to the company's board members as "doofuses" to the Yahoo! stock jump of more than 6 percent in afterhours trading following the announcement of her termination. Ironically, the rise in stock prices increased the value of Bartz's severance package of more than $11 million in cash and stock. Less than a year after Yahoo! rejected her leadership, Bartz advised audiences in her frequent speeches to graduates and others to accept failure and remain open to new challenges.

PERSONAL LIFE

Bartz is married to William G. Marr, a retired Sun Microsystems executive. They live in Atherton, California, and are the parents of three adult children: Bill, Meredith, and Layne. She is an avid gardener, a passion she shared with the grandmother who brought her up. Through half a dozen moves around the country, from the Midwest to Atlanta to Boston to California, she has transported plants she was nurturing, from bearded irises to heirloom tomatoes. Other hobbies include golf and tennis.

Personal experience has made Bartz an advocate for women's health issues. A survivor of breast cancer, she has served on the board of the National Breast Cancer Research Foundation. As a woman with daughters, she is also interested in educational issues concerning girls and has advocated for separate classes or schools for boys and girls. Bartz was inducted into the Women in Technology International Hall of Fame in 1997, received the Augusta Ada Lovelace Award from the Association for Women in Computing in 2003, and was named to the most powerful women lists of both *Forbes* (2004 and 2005) and *Fortune* (2005).

Wylene Rholetter

FURTHER READING

Fortt, Jon. "Yahoo's Taskmaster." *Fortune* 27 Apr. 2009: 80–84. Print. The article considers the results of Bartz's willingness to make difficult choices and the actions she took during her first months as CEO of Yahoo! Color photographs and one graph.

Hardy, Quentin. "Carol Bartz." *Forbes* 7 Sept. 2009: 84–88. Print. The article analyzes the pressures on Bartz as CEO of Yahoo! to remake the company and reports on the Microsoft deal and why it intensified the pressures.

Lacy, Sarah. "Just Don't Call It Retirement." *Businessweek* 6 Mar. 2006: 66–68. Print. The article reports on the retirement of Bartz as CEO of Autodesk and provides an overview of her career generally and her fourteen years at Autodesk specifically. Includes praise for Bartz from John Chambers, chief executive of Cisco Systems. Photographs.

Malone, Michael S. "Carol Bartz." *Betting It All: The Entrepreneurs of Technology*. New York: Wiley, 2001. 108–21. Print. The book looks at the successes and failures of sixteen American entrepreneurs associated with technology companies, including the wealth they attained and the challenges they faced. Carol Bartz is among them.

"One Tough Yahoo!" *Economist* 17 Jan. 2009: 66. Print. The article looks at the appointment of Bartz as CEO of Yahoo! Details include her record with other companies, with particular attention given to her years at Autodesk.

TIM BERNERS-LEE

Inventor of the World Wide Web and director of the World Wide Web Consortium

Born: June 8, 1955; London, England
Died: -
Primary Field: Computer science
Specialty: Internet
Primary Company/Organization: European Organization for Nuclear Research

INTRODUCTION

Like those of many innovators, Tim Berners-Lee's career has been one of collaboration. Very few, however, can claim such a high degree of individual responsibility for a major accomplishment as he can in developing the World Wide Web. Working as a Fellow at the European Organization for Nuclear Research (Conseille Européen pour la Recherche Nucléaire, or CERN), he created a means by which large amounts of technical and scientific information could be stored, accessed, and freely shared by a large community. This system, which in its early years was used exclusively at CERN, became available on the Internet and has changed nearly every aspect of life in social, economic, political, and cultural spheres of activity. In addition to his continuing efforts to advance the technology of the web, he has been active in advocating its value in improving life on a global basis. He has created the World Wide Web Foundation in order to determine how the web can improve people's lives and has consistently supported practices and technologies that will maintain free access to information and exchange unhindered by governments or commercial organizations.

EARLY LIFE

Born in London, England, on June 8, 1955, Tim Berners-Lee was one of four children. His parents, Conway Berners-Lee and Mary Woods, were both mathematicians and involved in early computer development. In 1973, he began studies at Queen's College, Oxford

Tim Berners-Lee.

University. He was, for a time, suspended as punishment for his hacking into the Oxford computer system. He graduated in 1976 with a degree in physics.

His first position was at Plessey Telecommunications, where he stayed until 1978 (the year he married his first wife) to work for D. G. Nash. At Nash, he wrote computer programs to support printing documents and developed a computer operating system. In 1980, Berners-Lee worked for six months as a consulting contractor for CERN. While there, he began a project to find ways to store information.

In 1980, the concept of hypertext—accessing text by clicking links embedded in another text—already existed, having been developed by Ted Nelson and Douglas Engelbart in the early 1960s. Building on what was known at the time, Berners-Lee began to work on a hypertext system that would make communication among CERN's staff and scientists easier and more effective. That increased access was necessary; the amount of research and the size of the research and development teams were growing, and success of CERN activities required rapid and complete accessibility.

Berners-Lee left CERN in 1980 and worked for Image Computer Systems, where he remained until 1984. While there, he gained experience in programming for computer networks. In 1984, Berners-Lee returned as a Fellow at CERN and began the work that would result in the World Wide Web.

Life's Work

When Berners-Lee returned to CERN, he was able to work on some of the concepts he had explored and experimented with a few years before, when he was a contractor. His original ideas of creating the ability to share large amounts of complex information, his work on hypertext to expand communication abilities, and his recent experience working on computer networks combined to place him in a position to begin what would be his most important project.

In 1989, Berners-Lee proposed a hypertext project with the intent of creating a collection of CERN documents that could be linked and then easily accessed by researchers. In the following year, using a NeXTStep computer (manufactured by NeXT, the company Steve Jobs created after leaving Apple in 1985), Berners-Lee and Robert Cailliau placed the information on a server (the NeXTStep computer). Berners-Lee then accessed it from the same machine and was able to read it and access additional data using hypertext links. To be able to navigate to, and access, that information, Berners-Lee

developed a software tool called a browser. The World Wide Web, as it would be called, was used exclusively on an internal basis at CERN until 1991. In August, the world's first website was created and the web became available on the larger Internet. That first web page described the World Wide Web, how it worked, how pages could be created and managed, and the web's objectives.

Over the next two years, as the web was used more widely, substantial modifications were made to the software components that made it operate. These elements were improved on a continuing basis and included creating web page addresses (uniform resource locators, or URLs) and the hypertext transfer (or transmission) protocol (HTTP) that made communications among users at different computers and access to information residing on distant computers possible. In addition, the manner of creating, organizing, and formatting web pages was further developed through the modifications made to hypertext markup language (HTML), a language based in part on the already existing standardized general markup language (SGML).

Berners-Lee was not only an innovator, however, recognizing that something as immense as the World Wide Web would be able to work only if innovations and technologies were held to rigid standards such as existed in other technical fields. Since the early 1990s, he has been director of the World Wide Web Consortium (W3C). This organization, headquartered at the Massachusetts Institute of Technology, combines both academic and commercial organizations and acts as the web standards organization. Berners-Lee has stated that one of the objectives of the web should be that, regardless of where an individual is or what kind of equipment (hardware or software) he or she uses, the user should be able to access the same information in both substance and appearance.

In addition to monitoring technical aspects of the web's growth and development, W3C functions to advance ideas and standards that essentially emerged from Berners-Lee's outlook. At W3C, the standards are based on open systems. Nothing is dependent on proprietary or licensed technologies or information.

Just as important as technical developments is the nature of the web itself and how independent it is from external enmities. Berners-Lee's comment about any user anywhere being able to access the same information is not just a technical operating goal. The ability of users to access information freely, without government or commercial interference, is essential to the democratic and open nature of the web, as he envisions it. His

Affiliation: European Organization for Nuclear Research

The European Organization for Nuclear Research, located in Geneva, Switzerland, is a center for high-energy physics research. While it is particularly famous currently for its research on particle physics—including confirmation of the existence of the Higgs boson (the so-called God particle) using the Large Hadron Collider (LHC)—CERN has existed as a research organization supported by an advanced laboratory since 1952. It was formed in that year under the name Conseille Européen pour la Recherche Nucléaire. Although it was renamed in 1954, it retained the acronym CERN, under which it continues to operate. Originally the cooperative effort of scientists from twelve nations, it comprises twenty member countries, each with a vote, that now form the organization. There are observer nations, and research is performed and supported on a worldwide basis. The original purpose of CERN was to focus on research in nuclear physics but over the years the emphasis changed to researching particle physics. CERN members include the Nobel Prize laureates in physics (1984 and 1992).

Employing approximately twenty-four hundred individuals at its main facility, CERN is organized into several departments, including Physics, Information Technology, Beams, Technology, Finance, and Procurement. The nature of CERN's work is based on a distributed organization. While a great deal of research and experimentation take place in Geneva (to include operations such as the LHC), there is a great deal of interaction among colleagues who are scattered across the globe. The need to communicate results and queries required an effective communications network, and the World Wide Web was developed to support that requirement.

work with the British government (starting in 2009) has shown just how a conflict of those ideals with government interests could affect open and free access. Britain's official map-making agency, the Ordnance Survey, has opposed to to some cartographic information, for example. W3C also opposes another type of restriction: the censorship of searches that Google performed (and stopped doing in 2010).

Since 2009, in addition to directing W3C, Berners-Lee has been director of the World Wide Web Foundation, an organization that seeks to explore how the web can best be used to further humanitarian causes.

PERSONAL LIFE

Berners-Lee has been married twice and has two children. He has received honorary degrees from several universities: Harvard, Oxford, Lancaster University, the University of Manchester, Columbia, and the Parsons School of Design among them. He is an Honorary Fellow of the Society for Technical Communication. Other honors include the Order of the British Empire (OBE), the Charles Babbage Award, a MacArthur Fellowship, the Mikhail Gorbachev Award, and Charles Stark Draper Prize. In 2002, he shared the Prince of Asturias Award with Larry Roberts, Robert Kahn, and Vinton Cerf, whose work on developing the ARPANET led to the eventual development of the Internet. In 1995, Berners-Lee received the Software System Award from the Association for Computing Machinery (ACM) in conjunction with his collaborator on the development of the web, Robert Cailliau.

Berners-Lee was knighted in 2004 by Queen Elizabeth II, is a Foreign Associate of the National Academy of Science, and in 2012 was inducted into the Internet Hall of Fame.

Robert N. Stacy

FURTHER READING

Berners-Lee, T. J. "Long Live the Web: A Call for Continued Open Standards and Neutrality." *Scientific American* 22 (2010): n. pag. Print. In this article, Berners-Lee discusses both the democratic and open-information origins of the Internet and the threats to those characteristics. Citing governments, social networking sites, and even Internet providers as agencies that can and sometimes do restrict access to information, Berners-Lee makes a plea to retain the openness and neutrality of the web.

---, et al. "World-Wide Web: Information Universe." *Electronic Publishing: Research, Applications and Policy* Apr. 1992: n. pag. Print. Two years after developing and then accessing the web page, Berners-Lee describes the design considerations and technologies involved as well as the purpose of the World Wide Web and its objectives.

---, and Mark Fischetti. *Weaving the Web: The Original Design and Ultimate Destiny of the World Wide Web*. San Francisco: Harper, 1999. Print. Berners-Lee's account of how the World Wide Web was developed in response to the needs of exchanging information at CERN as well as its development and potential as seen in 1999.

Gillies, James, and Robert Cailliau. *How the Web Was Born*. Oxford: Oxford UP, 2000. Print. An account of the creation of the World Wide Web by Berners-Lee's prime collaborator, Robert Cailliau.

Shadbolt, Nigel, and Tim Berners-Lee. "Web Science: Studying the Internet to Protect Our Future." *Scientific American* 299.4 (2008): 76. Print. Berners-Lee briefly traces how developments on the web have led to other developments (for example, e-mail, instant messaging, and social networking) and how a recent web science research initiative has been created not only to identify new possibilities but also to ensure that the Internet's openness is maintained.

GARRY BETTY

Former President and CEO of EarthLink

Born: March 4, 1957; Huntsville, Alabama
Died: January 2, 2007; Atlanta, Georgia
Primary Field: Computer science
Specialty: Internet
Primary Company/Organization: EarthLink

INTRODUCTION

Garry Betty's role as chief executive officer (CEO) of EarthLink dramatically transformed the Internet service provider from a floundering start-up to a global telecommunications giant. By embracing new technologies, partnering with the right people, and constantly expanding the company's reach, Betty laid a foundation for the way Internet-based companies did business. Competitive, soft-spoken, but ever-adaptable, he was always a force to be reckoned with, refusing to allow stock prices or his competitors to get the better of his can-do attitude.

EARLY LIFE

Charles Garrett "Garry" Betty was born on March 4, 1957, to Bobbie and Charles Betty in Huntsville, Alabama. He grew up in Columbus, Georgia, with his sister Rena. The children were raised with a strict southern conservative background and attended the local Baptist church. Betty graduated from the Georgia Institute of Technology in 1979 with a degree in chemical engineering. He paid for his own college tuition by selling aluminum siding. A photographic memory was probably one of the reasons that Betty graduated after only three and a half years of school.

Betty received his first taste of corporate life as an executive for computer giant IBM. After a stint at Hayes, a modem company, he moved on to work for Digital Communications Associates. In 1989, the company went public, and Betty became the youngest CEO of a company on the New York Stock Exchange.

Both of Betty's parents dealt with disabilities during their lives. Betty's father had a speech impediment and became a speech pathologist. His mother suffered from rickets as a child and struggled to walk her entire life. Betty's childhood was a source of strength and determination; he grew into a competitive, intelligent fighter who refused to back down.

LIFE'S WORK

Despite being the first Internet service provider to offer unlimited access at a set monthly fee, EarthLink was not doing well. Betty seemed like the right man to save it, and he became CEO in 1996, only two years after the company came into existence. In March 1994, surfer and child prodigy Sky Dayton had founded the company. A Scientologist, Dayton had used L. Ron Hubbard's teachings to manage the company and had nearly run it into the ground. The first thing Betty did when he took the reins was to establish more traditional business management practices. He then coordinated a merger with EarthLink's main competitor, MindSpring, which immediately improve the firm's value and added customers. Betty took the company from near bankruptcy to the world's second-largest provider of Internet services, bested only by America Online.

Early in 1997, EarthLink became a publicly traded company—one of the first Internet-based companies to do so. In the lead-up to the dot-com collapse, EarthLink remained a major player in telecommunications because Betty refused to give up. As the twenty-first century dawned, however, EarthLink began to lose customers to broadband service providers. In 2001, Betty expanded broadband services to 10 percent of the company's customers and refocused the company on providing good customer service. For EarthLink, this meant solid connections, great technical support services, and partnering with major players in the world of online content, such as Amazon and Disney. Betty decided the company should provide services such as assigning domain names and website hosting, and he pushed the company to take advantage of the emerging open access of the Internet, whereby infrastructure could be supplied by one company and services by another.

In 2005, EarthLink faced ever-growing competition from the providers of the latest broadband technology. It still had five million dial-up subscribers, but because it did not own the phone lines, telecommunication companies were refusing to host EarthLink's services, wanting to provide their established customers with the faster broadband service. EarthLink as a result was beginning to stagnate: The company stock had fallen from $60 to $7 per share.

Betty proposed some major changes in the hope of keeping the company afloat. He decided that the company need both to embrace and to compete with broadband, offering more services to its customers. Those services included manufacturing cell phones (Helio), offering commercial Wi-Fi and "line-powered voice" as

Garry Betty.

an alternative to telecommunication company Internet phone bundling. It was an expensive risk. The technology and directional change cost EarthLink millions.

In January 2005, EarthLink's Helio cell phone, a joint venture with Korean company SK Telecom, was born. Betty chose Dayton to run this branch of Dayton's own company. The company was unfortunately short-lived and discontinued on May 25, 2010. Betty, who died in 2007, would never know that his effort to expand EarthLink into cell phones was not successful. The company did manage to gain market share in the landline business, however, offering it as a security blanket in uncertain times.

By providing customers with mobile wireless service they could use within their city limits, Betty thought he had found a niche that EarthLink could exploit to stay solvent if the Helio phone did not perform. By creating the infrastructure for the citywide projects, Betty realized that EarthLink's Internet services would no longer have to rely on the phone companies in order to exist. Betty scored major contracts with large cities such as Philadelphia and Anaheim, cornering the market in municipal wireless networks.

Acquisition of companies that provided technology solutions became a major focus for EarthLink in the new millennium. Between 2006 and 2011, EarthLink purchase eight different companies to help it stay on the cutting edge. The acquisitions provided security, data platforms, voice technology, cloud technology, research and support centers, and data carriers and communication networks. The acquisitions meant EarthLink could provide its customers with the services they required without having to restructure the company completely. By 2012, EarthLink had divided itself into two main sections—Business Services and Consumer Services— branching out while still remain focused. In 2011, the company reported $1.3 billion in annual revenue and more than three thousand employees.

As EarthLink adapted and changed with the market, it saw continued success. Betty was integral to saving EarthLink from poor management and stagnation. His personality, business acumen, and overall desire to improve made Betty instrumental in transforming EarthLink into the telecommunications giant it is today.

PERSONAL LIFE

In his spare time, Betty enjoyed collecting first-edition books and running. On November 21, 2006, however, Betty was forced to take a leave of absence from his role as CEO of EarthLink. He was diagnosed with an

Affiliation: EarthLink

Sky Dayton began the dial-up Internet service provider (ISP) EarthLink in 1994 as the ISP industry began to take off. It was not long, however, before the company floundered under the weight of ever-growing competition. Garry Betty took over the day-to-day running of EarthLink in 1996. EarthLink was one of the first Internet-based businesses to go public, which it did in January 1997. At one point, it was the second-largest provider of Internet service in the world. It managed to survive the dot-com crash, when so many other ISPs disappeared. Through mergers, acquisitions, and a constant search for ways to improve, Betty managed to turn the company around and break into the world of broadband and wireless. In 2004, EarthLink became the first ISP to provide customers with a voice and Internet alternative to broadband.

After Betty died in 2007, Rolla Huff was named CEO. Company founder Dayton retired that year. Despite executive changes, EarthLink managed to maintain the momentum that Betty had started. In 2011, it purchased a portion of Synergy Global Solutions to improve their customer services and logical solutions so the company could provide cloud hosting services. The move reflected EarthLink's tradition of continual expansion and self-improvement in the face of the ever-changing world of technology and telecommunications.

aggressive form of adrenal cortical cancer. He never returned to work. Betty passed away from heart problems connected to his illness on January 2, 2007. He left behind his wife, Kathy, and his niece and nephews, who lived with him. He was forty-nine years old. Kathy, with the help of Betty before he died, began a foundation in her husband's name to help other families dealing with the genetic mutations that lead to cancer.

During his career, Betty received numerous accolades from the business community. While at IBM, Betty received his first professional accolade, the President's Excellence Award, in 1982. It was only three years after he graduated from college. In 2001, he received the Los Angeles Chamber of Commerce's annual Technology Leadership Award. He was named one of the Most Influential Atlantans by the *Atlanta Business Chronicle* in 2004. He was inducted into the Technology Hall of Fame in Georgia in 2005. He sat on boards

for several companies and organizations, including the Georgia Tech Board of Trustees Foundation and the Carter Center Board of Councilors.

Trish Popovitch

FURTHER READING

Armstrong, Larry. "The Mac of Internet Providers." *Business Week* 15 Dec. 1997. Web. 7 Aug. 2012. Shares the beginnings of EarthLink and the business choices of the company founder Sky Dayton. Includes statistical information and introduces Betty as the company's new chief executive officer.

Bertola, David. "Synergy Sells Portion of Business to EarthLink." *Buffalo Business First* 27 Oct. 2011. Web. 8 Aug. 2012. Details the acquisition of Synergy Global by EarthLink for $5 million. Provides some details about Synergy and why EarthLink made the strategic purchase.

Betty, Garry. "Going Faster." Interview by Steven Levy. *Newsweek* 26 June 2006: n. pag. Print. An interview with Betty that focuses on the end of dial-up and the emergence of broadband technology. Mentions competition between EarthLink and AOL.

"EarthLink CEO Passes Away at Age 49." *Fortune* 3 Jan. 2007. Web. 7 Aug. 2012. Tells the tale of Betty's passing, including details of his professional career and accolades. Explains that Mike Lunsford temporarily took over the role of chief executive officer.

"EarthLink's Corporate History." *EarthLink.net*. 2012. Web. 7 Aug. 2012. A corporate history of Earth-Link, including details of the time prior to the merger of EarthLink and MindSpring as well as information regarding products and executives in chronological order.

Granelli, James S. "EarthLink Aims to Be Provider of Services Beyond Dial-Up Internet." *Los Angeles Times* 20 Feb. 2006. Web. 8 Aug. 2012. Provides details on Betty's ideas to save the company from further decline by expanding the business to city-wide wireless networks. Discusses stock prices, Time Warner Cable, and AOL.

Keegan, Paul. "The ISP Is Dead. Long Live the ISP." *Business 2.0* 7.11 (2006): n. pag. Web. 8 Aug. 2012. Interview with Betty that provides a graph and several color photos. Discusses the changes EarthLink intends to implement to compete with the growing broadband market.

Wooley, Scott. "Tommorowland." *Forbes* 3 Jul. 2006. Web. 7 Aug. 2012. Details the wireless project in Anaheim, California. Explains how the new wireless system works and what it means to Internet users and EarthLink as a company.

Yang, Jia Lynn. "It's Broadband. It's Wireless. It's Cheap." *Fortune* 26 Apr. 2006. Web. 7 Aug. 2012. Explains EarthLink's transition into the municipal wireless world, including projects in San Francisco and Philadelphia. Details the partnership with Google as well as the effect of wireless on the American consumer.

JEFF BEZOS

Founder and CEO of Amazon

Born: January 12, 1964; Albuquerque, New Mexico
Died: -
Primary Field: Internet
Specialty: Commerce
Primary Company/Organization: Amazon

INTRODUCTION

Jeff Bezos is the founder and chief executive officer (CEO) of Amazon, among the earliest and most respected Internet entrepreneurs. He turned Amazon into a billion-dollar business that has gone far beyond the books that were its first products. Throughout Amazon's meteoric rise, Bezos has maintained an emphasis on offering a wide selection of products, keeping prices competitive, and ensuring fast delivery. Calling himself a "change junkie," he has never been afraid to take chances and has been guided by his own intuitive grasp of what customers want. Publishers Weekly *selected Bezos as its Person of the Year in 2008, the same year in which Amazon introduced its Kindle e-reader. In 2009,* Time *magazine chose Bezos as its Person of the Year and* Media Week *named him Marketer of the Year. Calling him a "technological seer,"* The Economist *suggested that Bezos may be the heir to Steve Jobs as the industry's chief visionary. Bezos's financial success has allowed him to pursue one of his childhood dreams, founding Blue Origin, a company that builds private spacecraft. Among powerful pioneering Internet companies with histories similar to Amazon's—such as eBay, Yahoo, and Google—Amazon is the only one that is still headed by its founder, who owns more than 88 percent of company's stock.*

EARLY LIFE

Jeffrey Preston Jorgensen was born on January 12, 1964, in Albuquerque, New Mexico, to a teenage mother, Jacklyn Gise Jorgensen, and Ted Jorgensen. His parents separated when he was only a year old. When he was four, his mother married Cuban-born Miguel

(Mike) Bezos, who worked as a petroleum engineer for Exxon, and he adopted Jeff. The family subsequently moved to Houston. As a youngster, Bezos spent much of his time on his maternal grandfather's 25,000-acre farm, the Lazy G, in Cotulla, Texas. His grandfather, Lawrence Preston Gise, was also the regional director of the Atomic Energy Commission. Bezos participated in the gifted program at River Oaks Elementary School, where he was first exposed to computers.

In 1978, the Bezos family, which also included siblings Christina and Mark, moved to the upscale Palmetto district of Miami, where Bezos was able to pursue his love of computers and dreamed of becoming an astronaut. He graduated from Palmetto High School in 1982

Jeff Bezos.

as valedictorian. By that time, he had already started his own business, an educational children's summer camp that he called the Dream Institute.

He entered Princeton University in 1982 with the intention of majoring in theoretical physics but switched to computer science and electrical engineering, graduating summa cum laude in 1986. At Princeton, he met his future wife, Mackenzie Tuttle, who became a fiction writer. At their wedding reception, the couple arranged for adult outdoor playtime that included water balloons.

LIFE'S WORK

In 1994, Jeff Bezos was earning a six-figure salary as senior vice president at D. E. Shaw, a New York financial trading company, when he began researching possible products for his own Internet firm. Believing that there was a ready-made market for books in the early days of the Internet, Bezos undertook to learn everything he could about the bookselling business. Jeff and Mackenzie Bezos moved to Seattle to gain access to book publishers and the technological knowledge of Silicon Valley, running the company from their home. Bezos raised $1 million from investors and $300,000 from his family. He chose the name Amazon because he equated the unlimited potential of the company with the mighty Amazon River.

Bezos officially launched Amazon on July 16, 1995. With only two additional employees and three large computers, Amazon initially depended on word-of-mouth advertising. The site generated $12,438 in profits the first week. By December, sales had climbed to $540,000, and the company's customer base had expanded to 50 states and 45 countries. As the company grew, Bezos assigned workers to small teams, adhering to his personal rule that teams should be small enough to be fed by two pizzas. These teams of five to seven people subsequently generated features that have become synonymous with Amazon, including the animated "gold box" that identifies special deals on the company's home page, the search-inside-the box method of searching books' full text, and the patented one-click checkout.

In 1996, the bookstore chain Barnes and Noble launched a rival website, and detractors predicted that it would put Amazon out of business. After generating $15.7 million in sales in 1996, Bezos took Amazon public in 1997. By 1998, Amazon had expanded to selling a range of products and had become known as "the world's largest book store." As dot-coms continued to crumble throughout the decade, Amazon's stock

fell from $100 to $6, but Bezos refused to lose faith in the company. At the turn of the century, Amazon was plagued by high workforce turnover and a devastating financial report issued by Lehman Brothers. Ultimately, however, Bezos's faith proved to be well founded. By 2003, Amazon was recording close to $7 billion in sales and $400 million in earnings. As stock rose to $50 per share, Amazon's total worth was estimated at $21 billion.

In 2005, Amazon purchased BookSurge and a French e-book company, Mobi-Pocket. The following year, Amazon acquired Brilliance Audio. In 2008, acquisitions included Audible Books, Abe Books (which added a number of online book sites to the Amazon stable), and Shelfari (a book-based social networking site). That year, Amazon introduced its first e-reader, the Kindle, which quickly sold out. With more than 200,000 digital books available, sales comprised 10 percent of all units sold that year. In 2009, Amazon reported $24 billion in annual revenue, of which nearly $6 billion was in books and media; Barnes and Noble, its nearest rival, had posted only $4.52 billion the year before, and competitors such as Borders/Waldenbooks lagged far behind. Subsequently, Amazon acquired Lexcylce and Toucho, gaining access to improved e-reader technologies.

While still a long way from catching up to Apple's dominance of the digital music market through iPod and the iTunes products available at its web-based Apple Store, Amazon steadily gained digital music customers, rising to the number-two position in 2011. The previous year, Amazon had introduced its cloud drive service, which has the capability of streaming music from any device connected to the Internet.

By 2011, Amazon was recording total revenues of $48 billion. A large portion of those profits could be attributed to the release of the Kindle Fire that November, which added color to the e-reader and successfully competed with other readers and, with its lower price point, the more expensive Apple tablet, the iPad. Learning a lesson from the shortage experienced by the original Kindle, Amazon was prepared for the success of the Kindle Fire, selling almost four million units during the 2011 holiday season with what had become Amazon's best-selling product. Weighing only 14.6 ounces and offering Wi-Fi capability and a fast dual-core processor, the Kindle Fire was capable of displaying 16 million colors. It used Whispersync technology to allow users to maintain book progress across Kindle devices. Amazon integrated the Kindle Fire with its online book and

Affiliation: Amazon

By the early twenty-first century, Amazon had become a household name, selling everything from books and DVDs to clothing and household items. After taking three years to develop the Kindle, Amazon introduced its e-reader in 2008. The Kindle sold out in less than six hours, and customers were forced to wait months for it to become available again. Over the course of the year, estimates for the sale of the Kindle rose to five hundred thousand units and climbed to an estimated million units in 2009. Bezos refused to release exact numbers, but it was no secret that the Kindle became Amazon's top-selling product. It also led the list of most-gifted products.

Promising downloads in "less than 60 seconds," an entire Kindle library of digitalized books was offered. Bezos pledged to ultimately offer every book ever published in digital format. Originally, the Kindle sold for an expensive $359, but Bezos insisted that Amazon would not cut costs by placing advertising inside books, as Google had done. In 2009, the Kindle was generating 48 percent of the sales of print book sales sold on Amazon. By 2011, it had surpassed print book sales. The sale of e-content has allowed Amazon to decrease the price of the Kindle and keep it competitive with other e-readers and tablets.

Updated models of the Kindle have kept Amazon's customer base growing and have offered added storage, additional battery life, Wi-Fi capability, and a touch screen. Introduced in late 2011, the Kindle Fire was Amazon's version of the tablet computer, offering a plethora of applications, including a free "app of the day" and web access. In 2012, Kindle prices ranged from a low of $79 for a basic Kindle e-reader to $199 for the Kindle Fire, and thousands of e-titles were being added to the Amazon store every week.

application stores and provided instant streaming of its own movies and television shows via Amazon Prime or individual rentals. It also provided free applications for streaming subscription services such as Netflix and Hulu Plus.

While device storage on the Kindle Fire was limited to 8 gigabytes, Amazon offered free storage through its cloud service. When some customers complained about the device's limited battery life (seven or eight hours), Bezos suggested that customers also purchase a traditional Kindle, which offers one to two months of battery life. Amazon negotiated deals to stream its movies and television shows through the PlayStation 3 and Xbox 360 gaming consoles and offered free Kindle applications for use on devices such as the BlackBerry, the Android, the iPad, the iPhone, and the iPod Touch.

Amazon has not been without its critics, and some of the harshest critics have been book publishers who accuse Amazon of forging a monopoly in the publishing industry. Tensions with publishers heightened in the early twenty-first century over the rising number of authors who negotiated deals with Amazon to self-publish digitally, bypassing traditional publishers.

PERSONAL LIFE

Known for his jeans and blue button-down shirts, Bezos has been labeled a "super geek" who makes decisions by examining all sides of an issue by enumerating and prioritizing relevant points. He has remained adamant that Amazon will never build a chain of retail brick-and-mortar stores, as Apple has done. His prioritization of good customer relations has allowed Amazon to maintain a loyal base of customers.

Publishing companies were outraged when Amazon opted to allow readers to review books and make those reviews available to potential customers. Bezos countered complaints by insisting that customers have the right to see what others think of a book before they buy it. Bezos has never been afraid of controversy. Despite naysayers, he stuck by decisions to provide free shipping on qualified orders of more than $25, offer third-party sales through Amazon, and display used items alongside new products.

Slightly more than a decade after its founding, Amazon had thousands of employees and was headquartered high on a hill in Seattle. The company was housed in a former hospital run by the Veterans Administration. In 2010, Amazon began moving onto a new campus in the section of Seattle known as South Lake Union. When completed in 2013, the campus will contain 2 million square feet and twelve separate buildings, including 100,000 square feet of retail stores and restaurants at street level.

The Bezos family, which includes four children, live in a $100 million home on Lake Washington with Microsoft cofounder Bill Gates as a neighbor. Bezos's personal wealth is estimated at more than $19.1 billion, and he and his wife have dedicated a significant amount of that wealth to philanthropic endeavors, including a $10 million gift to Seattle's Museum of History and Industry to establish the Center for Innovation and a $15 million award to Princeton University to build a bioscience unit at the Princeton Neuroscience Institute.

Elizabeth Rholetter Purdy

FURTHER READING

Brandt, Richard L. *One Click: Jeff Bezos and the Rise of Amazon.com*. New York: Penguin, 2011. Print. Detailed examination of the founding and rise of Amazon and of the influence of Bezos on e-commerce. Illustrated.

Christman, Ed. "Jeff Bezos." *Billboard* 124.2 (2012): n. pag. Print. Looks at additions to Amazon's services.

Deutschman, Alan. "Inside the Mind of Jeff Bezos." *Fast Company* 85 (2004): 52–58. Print. Follows the founding of Amazon and Bezos's career.

Milliot, Jim. "PW's Person of the Year: Jeff Bezos." *Publishers Weekly* 49.24/25 (2008): 24–25. Print. Profiles Bezos and chronicles the rise of Amazon.

Morrissey, Brian. "Marketer of the Year: Jeff Bezos." *Media Week* 19.32 (2009): n. pag. Print. Examines Bezos as an Internet visionary, focusing on the introduction of the Kindle.

Scally, Robert D. *Jeff Bezos: Founder of Amazon and the Kindle*. Greensboro: Morgan Reynolds, 2012. Print. Part of the Great Business Leaders series for young adults, this book profiles Bezos and Amazon. Illustrated.

"Taking the Long View." *The Economist* 402.8774 (2012): 23–24. Print. Profiles Bezos and makes comparisons between him and Steve Jobs.

Treanor, Ted. "Amazon: Love Them? Hate Them? Let's Follow the Money." *Publishing Research Quarterly* 26.2 (2010): 119–28. Print. Traces the financial success of Amazon and compares that success to that of other online booksellers.

DAVID BOHNETT

Cofounder of GeoCities

Born: August 2, 1956; Chicago, Illinois
Died: -
Primary Field: Internet
Specialty: Commerce
Primary Company/Organization: GeoCities

INTRODUCTION

David Bohnett is an entrepreneur who cofounded the free web hosting service GeoCities, founded the Los Angeles venture capital firm Baroda Ventures, and has been involved in many other online ventures, including OVGuide.com, Wireimage.com, and Xdrive.com. While remaining active as a technology entrepreneur, he has become a noted philanthropist and patron of the arts. His Bohnett Foundation has provided more than $40 million in funding to a variety of arts, educational, and civic programs, as well as gay and lesbian causes.

EARLY LIFE

David Bohnett was born in Chicago and had an early interest in electronics, including ham radio, a hobby that allowed him to communicate with other people around the world. This interest would be reflected in the development of GeoCities, the company most identified with

David Bohnett.

him. Bohnett received his bachelor's degree in business administration in 1978 from the Marshall School of Business of the University of Southern California, and he earned his master's degree in business administration (concentrating in finance) from the University of Michigan in 1980.

LIFE'S WORK

Bohnett began his professional career working for Andersen Consulting, the consulting wing of the major accounting firm Arthur Andersen (later Accenture). From 1988 to 1990, he was the chief financial officer for Essential Software, which merged with Goals Systems; Bohnett served as Goal Systems' director of product marketing from 1990 to 1994.

GeoCities began as an Internet service provider (ISP), originally called Beverly Hills Internet (BHI) because of its location in Beverly Hills, California. Bohnett has described the genesis of the company as a sort of "do it yourself" project built on a Sun workstation in Bohnett's dining room table; he and collaborator John Rezner did all the early work for the program, including writing the code, creating web pages, and answering e-mails. One of Bohnett's early coups was attracting widespread attention in 1995 when he established a live video feed on the company's web page, showing the corner of Hollywood and Vine in the Beverly Hills neighborhood. Bohnett's interest in establishing a sense of place was also reflected in the names of the home pages on BHI, such as RodeoDrive, SunsetStrip, and WallStreet (all named after real geographic locations). Bohnett often referred to users of GeoCities as homesteaders or residents, strengthening the geographical analogy between physical and virtual communities.

The guiding principle for GeoCities was to create virtual communities through digital "neighborhoods" within which users could create their own web pages for free. GeoCities provided templates through its Personal Home Page Generator to make it easy for nonspecialist users to create web pages, a concept that proved extremely popular and has since been imitated by many other companies. The virtual communities were organized around common interests; for instance, WallStreet for those interested in investments, Athens for those interested in philosophy, and Heartland for those interested in parenting and pets.

In 1995, as the business was growing rapidly, Bohnett moved GeoCities to an office in Beverly Hills, and the name GeoCities was adopted in November 1995; at the time, GeoCities had 10,000 members, and

number that increased to 135,000 by the end of the year and to more than 1 million by 1997. In 1998, Bohnett moved GeoCities again, to a location in the Los Angeles suburb Marina Del Ray. The staff of GeoCities grew rapidly to accommodate the number of subscribers; by 1999, it employed more than 250 people. Bohnett was the president and chief executive officer (CEO) of GeoCities (and later of Yahoo! GeoCities) from 1994 to 1998; Thomas R. Evans, formerly the publisher of *U.S. News and World Report*, took over as CEO in the spring of 1998. The same year, Bohnett founded Baroda Ventures, a venture capital firm focusing on early-stage investments in the digital media, Internet, mobile, SaaS (software as a service), and related industries, and in companies based in Los Angeles.

GeoCities became a public company in August 1998, at the height of the dot-com bubble. At the time of its initial public offering (IPO), it was an immensely successful company with more than 17 million pages and 2.1 million residents and experienced more than 14.8 unique visits per month, while its closest rival, Tripod, had about 1.8 million members and 2.7 million pages. GeoCities' stock opened at $17 per share and closed at $34 per share. Less than a year later, in January 1999, Yahoo! purchased GeoCities for $4.6 billion in stock. Most of GeoCities' revenue by then came from banner advertising, with a smaller amount derived from partnerships with companies such as Amazon.com, which shared some of the revenue from sales generated by referrals from GeoCities.

At about the same time that GeoCities held its IPO, it became the first Internet company charged with violating the privacy of its members. The charges related to GeoCities' practice of collecting demographic and interest information from new members, claiming it would not share the information without permission while in fact selling it to third-party advertisers who used it to send targeted advertising to members. On August 13, 1998, GeoCities signed a consent decree with the Federal Trade Commission (FTC) stating that it did not admit wrongdoing would create a stringent set of guidelines guarding user privacy; the incident did not interfere with the IPO.

Although GeoCities had a large number of users, monetizing those users (creating revenue from them) proved to be a more difficult problem; in fact, GeoCities is sometimes cited as a demonstration of the fact that having large numbers of users does not guarantee that a website will prove profitable, and more specifically that displaying advertising to a large volume of users does

Affiliation: GeoCities

David Bohnett created GeoCities, a hugely successful website that emphasized the web as a means to create communities of people bound by common interests rather than physical location. GeoCities was also a pioneer in providing easy-to-use software (the Personal Home Page Generator) to create web pages, encouraging nonspecialist users to become creators rather than simply consumers of Internet content. Bohnett drew heavily on familiar concepts of physical geography, such as neighborhoods, to encourage users (called "residents") to think of themselves as members of communities.

GeoCities also incorporated a number of different uses for the Internet into a single site, including a headline news service, free e-mail and home pages, targeted mailing list creation (people signing up for the site were asked if they wanted to receive messages about particular topics as well as from specific advertisers), and online shopping. GeoCities monetized visitors primarily through the sale of banner advertising but also through revenue from online sales generated by merchants (for example, CD-Now, Surplus Direct, and Amazon) through the site. In 1999 Yahoo! purchased GeoCities (changing the name to Yahoo! GeoCities), and ten years later the company announced that the site would be closed after sites offering similar services had proliferated.

broadcaster. Bohnett is the chairman of the board for the Los Angeles Philharmonic Association, a trustee for the Los Angeles County Museum of Art, and a trustee for the American Foundation for AIDS Research (AMFAR). He is chair of the David Bohnett Foundation, an organization that has provided funding to many political, social, and arts organizations and causes. Through the Foundation, Bohnett has helped create and fund more than sixty Bohnett CyberCenters, providing Internet access to local gay and lesbian community organizations and thus providing members of those organizations and their guests with the ability to use the Internet without feeling they are being scrutinized. Other causes supported by the Bohnett Fund include the Fund for Los Angeles; leadership programs at several universities, including Harvard and the University of Michigan; various initiatives to reduce gun violence; animal protection organizations; and various initiatives to increase voter registration and support voter rights. In 2011, the Bohnett Foundation gave more than $5.6 million to various causes, including the American Civil Liberties Union's Foundation of Southern California, Affordable Living for the Aging, the American Foundation for Equal Rights, the American Society for the Prevention of Cruelty to Animals, the Center for Great Apes (in Wachula, Florida), the Empire State Pride Agenda Foundation, the Gay and Lesbian Community Center of Baltimore, the Los Angeles Museum of Art, and the Women's Guild of the Cedars-Sinai Medical Center.

Sarah Boslaugh

not guarantee sales. In addition, the personal and creative aspects of GeoCities declined after Bohnett sold the company, and other ventures began offering similar services to users, increasing competition for the same market. In April 2009, Yahoo! announced that the U.S. GeoCities services would cease in October of that year, although GeoCities would continue operations in Japan; at the time of this announcement, an estimated 38 million GeoCities accounts existed around the world.

PERSONAL LIFE
Bohnett is an out gay man who has devoted much of his time and finances to philanthropy (he reportedly gained about $300 million in the GeoCities IPO). Bohnett has credited his former partner Rand Schrader (who died in 1993), a municipal court judge and AIDS activist in Los Angeles, with demonstrating to him the importance of taking a stand on issues of personal importance. As of 2012, Bohnett's partner was Tom Gregory, a writer and

FURTHER READING
Hiltzik, Michael. "Internet Pioneer Pushes Social Change Through Investing, Activism." *Los Angeles Times* 29 Nov. 2011: n. pag. Print. A news article about Bohnett, focusing on his transition from Internet entrepreneur to philanthropist, as well as the need for philanthropists to focus on political concerns (for example, the effort to defeat California's Proposition 8 in 2008) in addition to more traditional, charitable concerns.

Lehoczky, Etelka. "Cyber Center Stage." *The Advocate* 26 Oct. 2004: 49. Print. Feature article about Bohnett's charitable activities, with particular focus on his creation of the LGBT CyberCenters and his giving to other gay and lesbian causes, including the Gay and Lesbian Victory Fund, the Sexual Orientation in the News Program at the University of Southern California, and the Servicemembers Legal Defense Network (to aid men and women serving in the military who have been targeted because of their sexual preference or perceived sexual preference).

Lunau, Kate. "Lessons from GeoCities' Death." *Maclean's* 122.34 (2009): 29. Print. A journalistic account of the rise and fall of GeoCities, with comments on the website's initial innovativeness and why it failed to remain viable later in its history.

Nagourney, Adam, and Brooks Barnes. "Gay Marriage Effort Attracts a Novel Group of Donors." *New York Times* 23 Mar. 2012. Print. A news article on the effort to establish a constitutional right to mar-

riage for same-sex couples in the United States, with particular emphasis on the range of individuals (including Bohnett) involved in these efforts.

Roberts, Mary Lou. "Case Study: Geocities (A) and (B)." *Journal of Interactive Marketing* 14.1 (2000): 60–72. Print. A straightforward presentation of the history of GeoCities, intended for college students; Roberts includes discussion of the Federal Trade Commission's charges of privacy violation against GeoCities as well as a more general discussion of the company's business model and general characteristics.

ANDREW BREITBART

Founder of Breitbart.com

Born: February 1, 1969; Los Angeles, California
Died: March 1, 2012; Los Angeles, California
Primary Field: Internet
Specialty: News and entertainment
Primary Company/Organization: Breitbart.com

INTRODUCTION

Andrew Breitbart was a driving force behind the alternative media movement, which recognized and harnessed the power of the Internet to engage the masses and drive political change. He spent his early career working with Matt Drudge to create one of the world's most influential political news aggregation sites, The Drudge Report, *which provides ready and direct access to content from all types of news channels all over the world. Breitbart went on to cofound the equally influential* Huffington Post *but left almost immediately when it became a forum for the liberal left. In 2005, Breitbart created his own online community for the political right under the umbrella of Breitbart.com. His sites—Breitbart.tv, Big Hollywood, Big Government, Big Journalism, and Big Peace— went beyond directing or hosting media traffic. They also served as channels to present breaking news that challenged what Breitbart believed to be the liberal establishment and leftist popular culture. Individuals and organizations have been toppled by the Breitbart. com franchise, which continues to pursue its controversial agenda even after the death of its founder in March 2012.*

EARLY LIFE

Andrew Breitbart was born to a Jewish mother and an Irish father on February 1, 1969, in Los Angeles, California. His birth parents gave him up, and he was adopted as an infant by successful restaurateur Gerald Breitbart and

Andrew Breitbart.

51

his bank executive wife, Arlene. Andrew grew up in the Breitbart home in Brentwood, California, and was raised as a secular Jew along with his adopted younger sister, Tracy.

Breitbart attended the prestigious Carlthorp School in Santa Monica, California, for his elementary education before enrolling in the private Brentwood School in Los Angeles, California, to complete his secondary education. He was not a typical straight-A Brentwood student bent on an Ivy League future. He got average grades and spent his time pulling pranks aimed at entertaining his fellow students and subverting the school's upper-crust establishment.

Upon graduation from Brentwood School, a lifelong resident of Los Angeles, left his home state and moved to New Orleans, Louisiana, to attend college at Tulane University. He relished the freedom and became immersed in the college party scene. He joined the Delta Tau Delta fraternity and by his own account spent much of his time at Tulane engaged in excessive consumption of alcohol, experimentation with drugs, and gambling. Despite his focus on extracurricular activities, Breitbart graduated from Tulane University in 1991 with a bachelor of arts degree in American studies.

After receiving his degree, Breitbart moved back to Los Angeles and floated in and out of menial jobs. He worked as a waiter, a delivery man, and a low-level movie production worker. A lack of direction had him searching for focus. His search took him briefly to Austin, Texas. However, it was not until he began listening to Rush Limbaugh and like-minded conservatives on the radio that he finally found his motivation. He embraced a philosophy of resolute conservativism and set his sights on ridding the country of what he considered to be a debilitating liberalism that was spreading throughout the United States. He felt that rampant liberalism was being driven by the mindsets and messages of the country's powerful media companies, so he targeted his efforts on that industry. He recognized that the Internet would be the most potent weapon in his conservative campaign.

Life's Work

In 1995, Breitbart contacted Matt Drudge, the founder and force behind the conservative *Drudge Report*, and asked if he could be of assistance. Breitbart began working for Drudge both in creating content and behind the scenes. For the next decade, Breitbart helped Drudge transform the once gossip-based electronic newsletter into one of the most prominent and powerful web-based aggregation sites for the world's political news. Breitbart believed that by using the Internet to deliver news directly to the public, *The Drudge Report* could circumvent what he considered to be liberally biased reporting by established media channels. A single link from *The Drudge Report* could expose any story from any newsroom around the globe in an instant to hundreds of thousands of readers anywhere.

Drudge introduced Breitbart to Arianna Huffington, at the time a right-wing author and analyst. Breitbart began working with Huffington as a researcher and web expert. When the mainstream media published the presence of Drudge and Huffington at the embezzlement trial of Susan McDougal (significant because she was a former business associate of President Bill Clinton), Breitbart had an epiphany about the power he and his colleagues held over the media.

Breitbart decided he wanted to have a bigger voice. In 2004, he coauthored a book along with journalist Mark Ebner titled *Hollywood, Interrupted*. It was a scathing commentary on the state of Hollywood celebrity. Around the same time, Huffington contacted Breitbart to help create *The Huffington Post*. Breitbart envisioned the site as a bipartisan blog that would complement *The Drudge Report*. By then, however, Huffington's ideology had swung to the left. She and the other site cofounders—Internet entrepreneur Jonah Peretti and media businessman Ken Lerer—decided that they wanted to give the site a more liberal bent. The site launched in May 2005 as a hosted forum for liberal discussion. Breitbart quickly became dissatisfied and left the project. However, his experiences at *The Huffington Post* had given him the opportunity to build a site from the ground up and had helped him realize that if *The Huffington Post* could create an online gathering place for the liberal left, he could do the same for the conservative right.

Later that year, Breitbart launched Breitbart.com. He used the conservative news and commentary site to break high-impact stories, especially those that exposed or riled his liberal foes. The site attracted more than 2.5 million readers in its first month, helped largely by links to the site from the by-then-well-established *Drudge Report*. By November, Breitbart had partnered with two business owners—Brian Cartmell and Brad Hillstrom—to form Gen Ads. The venture had the exclusive rights to display banner ads on Breitbart.com, but distrust and disatisfaction led to the dissolution of the partnership within three months.

In the years that followed, Breitbart launched several other sites under the Breitbart brand's umbrella.

Affiliation: Breitbart.com

Andrew Breitbart launched Breitbart.com in 2005 as a complement to the conservative *Drudge Report* and as a counterpoint to the liberal *Huffington Post*. Earlier in his career, Breitbart had helped develop *The Drudge Report* into a leading news aggregation site with conservative leanings. He also helped launch *The Huffington Post* before it transformed into a hosted forum catering to progressives and the political left. Entering new territory, Breitbart.com emerged as an aggressive news hound determined to expose what Breitbart considered to be the fallacies and failings of the nation's liberal influencers: namely, government, Hollywood, and the mainstream media.

Between 2005 and 2010, Breitbart expanded his franchise to include dedicated sites focused on key target groups. For example, he launched Breitbart.tv in 2007 to showcase and blog about political videos. In 2008, Big Hollywood.com was created to spotlight what Breitbart perceived to be rampant liberalism among Hollywood celebrities. Big Government.com followed in 2009, targeting the political arena, and Big Journalism.com was launched in 2010 to expose what Breitbart deemed to be the left-leaning bias of the popular press. Later that year, Big Peace.com appeared, casting a conservative light on foreign policy and national security.

The Breitbart sites have been ranked by Technorati as among the hundred most influential alternative media channels. The Big Government site rocked the political establishment in 2009 when it posted an undercover video showing alleged misdeeds by the Association of Community Organizations for Reform Now (ACORN), which led to the dissolution of the agency. The Breitbart franchise also broke the "Weinergate" story, exposing the alleged sexual indiscretions of former congressman Anthony Weiner (D–New York) on Big Journalism.com, leading to Weiner's resignation.

After Breitbart's sudden death in March 2012, Breitbart.com and its affiliated sites continued to pursue the controversial philosophy and practices of their founder.

Political video blog Breitbart.tv debuted in 2007. The next year, Breitbart launched the first site in his "Big" franchise. It started with Big Hollywood.com in 2008 as a tool to showcase what Breitbart believed was the liberal hold Hollywood has on popular culture. Big Government.com followed in 2009 to put the spotlight on the government's liberal leanings, as perceived by Breitbart. In 2010, Big Journalism.com was born to bring attention to what Breitbart emphatically believed was the left-leaning bias of the popular press. Later that year, Breitbart launched Big Peace.com to address international news, foreign policy, and national security from a conservative perspective.

When it launched in 2009, the fledgling Big Government site featured an undercover video revealing alleged improprieties that led to the defunding and downfall of the Association of Community Organizations for Reform Now, better known as ACORN. The next year, another video on Breitbart's sites forced the temporary dismissal of U.S. Department of Agriculture official Shirley Sherrod. In 2011, Breitbart's Big Journalism site posted an explicit photograph and broke the story of sexual indiscretions by Congressman Anthony Weiner, Democrat from New York. The story forced Weiner's resignation from office one month later, in June. Only two months earlier, Breitbart's second book, *Righteous Indignation: Excuse Me While I Save the World,* was published. It was ranked on *The New York Times* bestseller list.

Breitbart's sites have been listed among the top hundred most influential new-media sites as ranked by Technorati. Even after Breitbart's death, his alternative media empire continued his legacy of targeted-assault journalism. In May 2012, Breitbart.com posted a 1991 booklet from President Barack Obama's former literary agency, indicating that the president was born overseas in Kenya rather than in the U.S. Hawaiian Islands, as has been publicly stated and verified.

PERSONAL LIFE

Breitbart met his wife, Susannah, through a mutual friend during a night out at a karaoke bar when he was a college student in 1988. However, the couple did not begin dating until they met again in 1992. The Breitbarts wed in 1997 in a backyard ceremony at the Venice Canals home of the bride's father, actor Orson Bean. They welcomed their first son, Samson, two years later and their first daughter, Mia, two years after that. Their son Charlie was born after a four-year interval, and William followed two years later. The family of six lived in Westwood, California.

Shortly after midnight on March 1, 2012, Breitbart collapsed on a sidewalk not far from his house during a late-night walk. A witness called paramedics, who attempted to revive Breitbart at the scene. He was rushed to Ronald Reagan UCLA Medical Center in Los Angeles, located nearby, but all attempts to save him failed and he was pronounced dead at the age of forty-three. An autopsy revealed that Breitbart had died of natural causes as a result of heart failure. The stress on his heart stemmed from coronary disease and an enlarged heart that had begun causing symptoms a year earlier.

Shari Parsons Miller

FURTHER READING

Breitbart, Andrew. *Righteous Indignation: Excuse Me While I Save the World!* New York: Grand Central, 2011. Print. Breitbart discusses the key issues facing Americans, his affiliation with the Tea Party movement, and his philosophy of exposing and attacking liberal news. He talks about his early career and how he launched his conservative websites.

Breitbart, Andrew, and Mark Ebner. *Hollywood Interrupted: Insanity Chic in Babylon; The Case Against Celebrity.* New York: Wiley, 2005. Print. Highlights the underpinnings of the Hollywood entertainment scene, emphasizing celebrity perspectives, experiences, failings, political jockeying, and general hypocrisies.

"Breitbart Tells Tea Partiers: 'We Are The Majority in This Country.'" *Human Events* 66.8 (2010): 3. Web. 12 Aug. 2012. An excerpt from a speech given by Breitbart at the Tea Party convention in Nashville, Tennessee, on February 6, 2010.

Dobuzinskis, Alex. "Conservative Activist Andrew Breitbart Dead at 43." 1 Mar. 2012. *Reuters.* Web. 12 Aug. 2012. Provides a brief overview of Breitbart's career, medical history, and the circumstances of his sudden death.

Friedersdorf, Conor. "Andrew Breitbart's Legacy: Credit and Blame Where It's Due." *The Atlantic* 8 Mar. 2012. Web. 12 Aug. 2012. Isaacson gleans information from more than forty interviews of Jobs, friends, relatives, and competitors. Presents a comprehensive perspective on Breitbart's professional achievements, shortcomings, and legacy in the wake of the Internet entrepreneur's sudden death.

Jonsson, Patrik. "Andrew Breitbart, a 'Happy Warrior,' Rallied the Right and Vexed the Left." *Christian Science Monitor* Mar. 2012: n.pag. Web. 12 Aug. 2012. Provides an overview of Breitbart as a controversial Internet mogul who created a community of conservatism on the web to provide a united and potent voice against the liberal establishment.

Oney, Steve. "Citizen Breitbart." *Time* 175.13 (2010): 34–37. Web. 12 Aug. 2012. Presents a profile of Breitbart's political alliances, conservative websites, media reporting of the ACORN scandal, and escalating public popularity.

Rosen, Rebecca. "What Andrew Breitbart Got About the Internet." *The Atlantic* 1 Mar. 2012. Web. 12 Aug. 2012. Discusses Breitbart's understanding and harnessing of the power of the Internet to inform and influence.

SERGEY BRIN

Cofounder of Google

Born: August 21, 1973; Moscow, Russia
Died: -
Primary Field: Internet
Specialty: Applications
Primary Company/Organization: Google

INTRODUCTION

Sergey Brin cofounded Google, the leading Internet search engine, with Larry Page; the company has since expanded into many other Internet services, including e-mail, cartography, shopping, blogging, and social networking. Brin and Page are also noted for their emphasis on articulating a corporate philosophy based on making the world a better place and helping people to access information freely.

EARLY LIFE

Sergey Brin was born to a Jewish family in Moscow, Russia (then part of the Soviet Union), in 1973; his father was a professor of mathematics. The family fled the country in 1979 to escape anti-Semitism and settled in Maryland, where Brin's father held a post at the University of Maryland. Brin attended the Miskan Torah Hebrew School and the Pain Branch Montessori School, then Eleanor Roosevelt High School in Greenbelt, Maryland. He began programming at age nine, on a

Sergey Brin.

Commodore 64 computer that his father had given him. He began studying mathematics at the University of Maryland at age fifteen and dropped out of high school after his junior year to enroll full time in the university. Brin earned his bachelor's degree in mathematics and computer science from the University of Maryland in 1993 and won a National Science Foundation Fellowship. He began studies for a Ph.D. in computer science at Stanford in 1993, where in 1995 he met future collaborator Page.

LIFE'S WORK

While at Stanford, Brin and Page developed a project called BackRub, initially as a class asignment. BackRub was a new kind of search engine that analyzed the number of backlinks connecting one web page to another; they analyzed this information to evaluate the usefulness of the different pages, with the logic that pages with more links were probably more useful. Brin and Page operated BackRub on the Stanford servers for a year but ran into trouble with the university because of the amount of bandwidth it required.

It was already clear that an efficient search engine would be a useful product, because the rapid growth of the Internet (including an estimated 25 million web pages by the late 1990s) meant that users needed a way to locate the best and most relevant information without getting sidetracked by minimally helpful or irrelevant web pages. Brin and Page tried to sell their idea to existing search engine companies such as Excite and Infoseek, then decided to develop the search engine on their own. Both left Stanford in 1998 and moved their computer equipment into a friend's garage, while living in rented rooms in Menlo Park, California.

The name Google refers to a very large number called a *googol* (written as the digit 1 followed by 100 zeros), in reference to the large number of web pages on the Internet; the domain name was registered as google.com because the website *googol.com* had already been taken. The company Google, Inc., was incorporated on September 7, 1998; it would attract $25 million in venture capital by June 1999.

The google.com website is noted for its simplicity; initially this was because of the founders' lack of expertise in creating websites but was retained as a design feature because of its efficiency. However, the algorithm PageRank, which powers Google searches, is extremely sophisticated, searching an index of the World Wide Web rather than the web pages themselves. The index (which included more than 3 billion web pages by 2001) is created by so-called web crawlers, which follow links on the web to catalog web pages; PageRank analyzes the index in a manner similar to a popularity contest, in which a link from one page to another is interpreted as a "vote" and links from pages with many links to them (more popular pages) count more than links from pages with few links to them.

Google received more than 18 million queries per day in 2000, becoming the default search provider for Yahoo! in the same year. In May of 2000, Google was released in ten foreign languages, and by September fifteen languages were offered, including Chinese, Japanese, and Korean. By 2002, number of languages had grown to seventy-two, including the Klingon (the language of a species featured in the television franchise *Star Trek*). In December 2000, the plug-in Google Toolbar was released, allowing users to conduct Google searches without visiting the company's home page. A final innovation that year was AdWords, a program that displayed targeted advertising (sponsored links) to companies selling products related to the keywords in an individual user's searches. The AdWords system was creating more than $600 million in annual revenue for Google by 2003.

Because of the growing dominance of Google as a search engine and the importance of being near the

Affiliation: Google

Google is the dominant search engine on the Internet, with about 85 percent of the market in the United States as of 2012, and is involved in many other enterprises, including e-mail, word-processing and spreadsheet software, document-sharing programs, and cloud-based storage. Google also acquired YouTube, the leading video-sharing site on the Internet, in 2006, and is involved in an effort to digitize all the books in the world (although that effort has been hampered by lawsuits charging copyright infringement); by September 2012, Google had scanned more than 20 million books in thirty-five languages. Despite the company's continual expansion into new activities, however, Google founders Sergey Brin and Larry Page have taken pains to articulate their core values. This was evident in an unusual open letter Brin and Page published before Google's initial public offering (IPO) in 2004, articulating their goal of having a positive effect on the world and providing free and unbiased access to information.

The Dutch auction process used for Google's IPO was another statement of Brin and Page's desire to do things differently—they bypassed the investment banks, allowing anyone offering at least the minimum price per share to participate, and set a minimum purchase requirement of only five shares. Google's website also contains an articulation of the company's values, including how it balances the demands of making money with its ethical principles. In October 2008, Google released a proposal, Clean Energy 2030, to reduce oil use by cars by 40 percent in the United States by 2030. On a lighter note, Page and Brin are famous for their annual April Fool's jokes: In 2002, for instance, they announced that Google was powered by pigeons; in 2004, they announced that they were opening a research facility on the Moon; in 2006, they announced a dating product, Google Romance; and in 2010, Google temporarily changed its name to Topeka.

top of search results (studies have shown that most users do not look at more than one page of results), other companies developed programs and strategies to "game the system" and improve their ranking on Google; in response, Brin and Page have continually refined the Google algorithm; they have also developed a blacklist to block sites that abuse the search process.

In 2001, Eric Schmidt joined Google as the company's chairman and chief executive officer; Brin became president of technology at this time, and Page became president of products. In the same year, Google created Google Groups, after purchasing the Deja News Research Service (an archive of Usenet messages), and created test versions of Froogle (a search engine for shopping) and Google News (a service that searches the web for news stories). In December 2003, the company launched Google Print, which included small excerpts from books in search results. In 2004, Google created Gmail (a free e-mail service), Google SMS (a short message service), and Google Desktop Search.

In April 2004, Google announced the date of its initial public offering (IPO) and stated that the IPO would be conducted as a Dutch auction, with anyone allowed to bid for stock. The auction began on April 13, 2004, and ended five days later. Stock prices dropped from more than $120 per share to about $85 over the course of the auction, generating less money than anticipated; however, on the first day of trading on the NASDAQ, share prices surged to almost $110.

Since the IPO, Google has continued to innovate and expand, following principles articulated by Brin and Page in 2004: They focus 70 percent of their resources on their core business of the Google search engine, 20 percent on ancillary services such as e-mail, and the remaining 10 percent on innovation. Innovations in 2005 included Google Maps, Blogger Mobile, institutional access for Google Scholar (so users can locate journals in their home libraries), Google Earth (a mapping service using satellite imagery and search capabilities), and Google Analytics. In 2006, Google launched Google Calendar, Google Trends (an application to visualize chronological changes in the popularity of searches), and Google Checkout (for online purchases); the company also acquired YouTube that year. In 2007, Google added traffic information to Google Maps for thirty cities and Street View in five cities. By May 2008, Google Translate was available in twenty-three languages (which had grown to more than sixty by 2012), and in August 2009 Google Street View expanded to Japan and Australia. Google Voice was launched in 2009, as was the venture capital fund Google Ventures, the Google Translator Kit, Google Dashboard, and the surveillance tool Flu Trends. In 2010, Google launched a new indexing system, Caffeine.

PERSONAL LIFE

Brin is married to Anne Wojcicki, a biologist and cofounder (with Linda Avey) of the biotechnology company

23andMe, which sells rapid genetic testing services; Wojcicki's garage in Menlo Park was Google's first work space after Brin and Page left Stanford. Brin and Wojcicki have one child, a son.

Sarah Boslaugh

FURTHER READING

Auletta, Ken. "The Search Party." *New Yorker* 83.43 (2008): 30–37. Print. An article on the history and growth of Google, its approach to business, its image among its competitors, and the working relationships among the company's founders, Brin and Page, and its chief executive officer, Eric Schmidt.

Brin, Sergey, and Larry Page. "Letter from the Founders: 'An Owner's Manual for Google Shareholders.'" *New York Times* (2004): n. pag. Print. An open letter written on the occasion of Google's IPO, emphasizing the company's goals of continuing to serve end users, to have a positive effect on the world, and to maintain a long-term focus even if that meant passing up short-term gains. Also explains Google's rationale for selling the IPO shares through an auction.

Byrne, John A. "The 12 Greatest Entrepreneurs of Our Time and What You Can Learn from Them." *For-tune* 165.5 (2012): 68–86. Print. Magazine article about innovative entrepreneurs and their approaches to their work. Brin and Page are noted for their continued investment in research and development ($11.8 billion in 2009–11), their efforts to remain innovative, and their allocation of effort following the 70-20-10 rule (70 percent to core efforts, 20 percent to expansion and adjacent efforts, and 10 percent for truly out-of-the-box ideas).

Lowe, Janet. *Google Speaks: Secrets of the World's Greatest Billionaire Entrepreneurs, Sergey Brin and Larry Page*. Hoboken: Wiley, 2009. Print. Popular history of Google and its founders, Brin and Page, written in a conversational style and emphasizing the personalities of the two principal subjects as well as their accomplishments.

Vise, David A., and Mark Malseed. *The Google Story*. Updated ed. New York: Bantam Dell, 2008. Print. Journalistic history of Google, emphasizing the unique qualities of both the product and its founders, and the transformative influence it has had on modern life; the lead author is a Pulitzer Prize–winning reporter and senior adviser to a private equity firm.

TINA BROWN

Cofounder and editor-in-chief of *The Daily Beast*

Born: November 21, 1953; Maidenhead, England
Died: -
Primary Field: Internet
Specialty: News and entertainment
Primary Company/Organization: *The Daily Beast*

INTRODUCTION

Tina Brown parlayed a successful career in print media, notably at Vanity Fair *and* The New Yorker, *into leading roles with the website* TheDailyBeast.com *and* Newsweek *magazine. Noteworthy for her ability to find content that is wildly popular with the reading public, Brown has sometimes been accused of relying on sensational and low brow material. A member of the Magazine Editors' Hall of Fame, Brown has been able to translate her success in traditional media to new platforms, providing a model for other media conglomerates seeking to make a profit with web-based publications.*

EARLY LIFE

Christina Hambley Brown was born on November 21, 1953, in Maidenhead, England, the daughter of film producer George Hambley Brown and Bettina Iris Mary Kohr, a former assistant to the actor Sir Laurence Olivier. Brown has an older brother, Christopher. She grew up in the Thames River village of Little Marlow and was educated in boarding schools. Her father achieved some success in the film industry, including producing five movies starring Margaret Rutherford that were based on Agatha Christie's novels. Brown has described herself as "lively" as a child, often engaging in behaviors that resulted in the approbation of school authorities. Expelled from three different schools, she was frequently punished for her irreverent attitude and noncompliance with school rules. Brown nevertheless excelled at school and entered St. Anne's College at Oxford University when she was seventeen years old.

Tina Brown.

At Oxford, Brown studied English literature, ultimately graduating with a bachelor's degree. A polished and insightful writer even as an undergraduate, Brown wrote for Oxford's literary journal, *Isis*, and had work published with the left-wing British cultural and political magazine *The New Statesman* while still enrolled as a student. While writing for the *Isis*, Brown was able to interview a variety of authors and celebrities, including actor Dudley Moore and journalist Auberon Waugh, the son of novelist Evelyn Waugh. Brown's attempts as a dramatist met with some success: A play she wrote while at Oxford won a student competition run by *The Sunday Times*, and a later effort was produced by the Royal Academy of Dramatic Art. After graduating from Oxford in 1973, Brown turned immediately to free-lance journalism and used Waugh's influence to advance her writing career.

A weekly column Brown wrote for the literary humor magazine *Punch* helped her to win the Catherine Pakenham Award, given annually to the best journalist under the age of twenty-five. In 1978, Australian Gary Bogard hired the then twenty-five-year-old Brown to edit a small magazine he had purchased, the *Tatler*. Although little known when Brown assumed her

editorship, *Tatler* was soon transformed into a slick, glossy magazine. Believing that the public often purchased magazines from newsstands based on the appearance of the cover, Brown hired top photographers, such as Norman Parkinson and David Bailey, and prominently displayed their work on *Tatler*'s cover. Using her old friend Waugh as a resource, Brown solicited articles by writers such as Julian Barnes, Dennis Potter, and Waugh himself, thereby increasing the profile of the magazine. During this time, Brown frequently wrote for *Tatler* herself and discovered that issues of the magazine containing articles about Princess Diana always led to increased sales at the newsstands. Brown's changes were successful: The *Tatler*'s readership increased fourfold, and the publication garnered critical acclaim as well. After Bogard sold the *Tatler* to publishing giant Condé Nast in 1982, Brown resigned as editor and returned to writing. After a year, however, Condé Nast was able to lure her to the United States to edit its troubled publication *Vanity Fair*.

LIFE'S WORK

Condé Nast had resurrected *Vanity Fair*, which had been popular in the 1920s, in March 1983. Inaugural editor Richard Locke lasted only three months at the helm before he was replaced by Leo Lerman, but this change had little effect on *Vanity Fair*'s sales. With monthly sales of 200,000 and only twelve pages of advertising per issue, the magazine was failing. Brown's transformation of the *Tatler* led Condé Nast's chief executive officer (CEO), in a last-ditch effort to save *Vanity Fair*, to hire Brown as a contributing editor to assist with a turnaround. Named editor-in-chief on January 1, 1984, Brown quickly made changes to improve the magazine's circulation.

Considering *Vanity Fair* dull, Brown set about to transform it, using many of the techniques she had earlier tried at the *Tatler*. She hired television producer Dominick Dunne to write a true-crime report about the trial of his daughter's murderer (she was killed in 1982. Titled "Justice: A Father's Account of the Trial of His Daughter's Killer," the piece was highly successful and launched Dunne on a long-lasting and lucrative writing career. To produce more eye-catching covers, Brown encouraged photographers to be creative and to present images that had not been seen before. To that end, Harry Benson captured an image of Ronald and Nancy Reagan dancing at a White House reception and Helmut Newton created a portrait of accused murderer Claus von Bülow with his mistress. Brown herself wrote about Britain's Princess Diana, discovering that issues with her image on the cover dramatically spiked sales. Brown also changed the editorial policies of the magazine, combining stories focusing on foreign affairs and political matters with stories about celebrities and true-crime accounts. These changes proved effective, and *Vanity Fair*'s circulation soared.

Under Brown's stewardship, *Vanity Fair*'s monthly sales increased from 200,000 to 1.2 million copies. Advertising pages increased to more than 1,400 by 1991, and circulation revenues were reputed to top $20 million per issue. Brown's strategy of using eye-catching covers paid off: *Vanity Fair* sold 55 percent of issues sent to newsstands, well above the industrywide average of 42 percent. Brown's efforts were also successful critically: The magazine won four National Magazine Awards under her editorship, including a 1989 prize for overall excellence. In 1992, Condé Nast asked Brown if she would move to *Vanity Fair*'s sister publication, *The New Yorker*. She agreed to do so and edited that magazine through 1998. Although the announcement of her editorship was met with skepticism by some, Brown was credited with making *The New Yorker* more relevant while maintaining its values and quality. She increased the magazine's use of photographs, color, and coverage of topical interests. *The New Yorker*'s sales base increased slightly during Brown's tenure, from approximately 650,000 in 1992 to more than 800,000 in 1997, with newsstand sales increasing 145 percent. Under Brown, *The New Yorker* won multiple awards for excellence, including four George Polk Awards, ten National Magazine Awards, and five Overseas Press Club Awards.

In 1998, Brown left Condé Nast to join a new media company funded by Miramax Films and the Hearst Corporation. In this position, Brown launched the monthly magazine *Talk*, which reached sales of more than 670,000 per month before shutting down in 2002, and a publishing imprint, Miramax Books, which published many best sellers.

After a brief foray into broadcasting for MSNBC and writing a best seller, *The Diana Chronicles*, about Princess Diana, Brown in 2008 joined forces with Barry Diller's InterActiveCorp (IAC) to launch *The Daily Beast*, an online magazine that combines journalism with links to other news sources. *The Daily Beast* quickly became one of the top fifty Internet sites and received a warm reception from writers who had previously been unwilling to write for an online publication. In 2010, *The Daily Beast* announced that it was merging with *Newsweek* magazine to form the News

---

Affiliation: *The Daily Beast*

While many print-based newspapers and magazines established a presence on the Internet soon after it became popular, many traditional publishers struggled to find a way to make money doing so. While news aggregation sites—those that provide links to other published websites—were popular, many original content providers that tried to charge to view their content found this unsuccessful. When seeking to rely on advertising revenue, these same content providers found that many advertisers preferred to spend money on aggregation sites, which drew greater traffic. Brown changed much of this with *The Daily Beast*, which combines both aggregation of other news sources with original journalism.

Brown's reputation as an editor with well-regarded print publications such as Vanity Fair, *The New Yorker*, and *Talk* has encouraged many authors to publish with *The Daily Beast* who had never done so before. The well-known writers and public figures who have published with *The Daily Beast* include Tony Blair, Christopher Buckley, Howard Kurtz, Mark McKinnon, Michael Medved, Gerald Posner, Condoleezza Rice, Michael Tomasky, and Scott Turow. Such content led *The Daily Beast* to be immediately successful, and by 2009 the site was logging more than 3 million unique visitors per month and generating significant advertising revenue.

The Daily Beast has used consistent and familiar sections to build readership, such as "Cheat Sheet" (brief summaries of articles from other sites), "Book Beast" (book reviews), and "Sexy Beast" (entertainment and fashion news). Since *Newsweek*'s merger with *The Daily Beast* in November 2010, the weekly newsmagazine has begun to include a section called "Perspectives," which reviews content from the website from the previous week.

---

week Daily Beast Company, with Brown to serve as editor of both publications.

PERSONAL LIFE

From birth, Brown was comfortable dealing with actors, performers, writers, and other celebrities she met as a result of her father's connections within the British film industry. Not only was Brown able to make many connections that would serve her well later in her career; she also had a keen understanding of the public's fascination with celebrities and those who surround them. Brown also developed a keen sense of the visual due to her frequent viewing of films.

Throughout her time at Oxford, Brown considered a career as a serious writer, working to develop her skills as a playwright and dating novelist Martin Amis. In 1973, the editor of *The Sunday Times*, Harold Evans, was given some of Brown's writings, which led to her receiving freelance assignments from various editors at the newspaper. After a relationship developed between Brown and Evans, Brown sought to maintain the appearance of impartiality in her writing and resigned from *The Sunday Times* to write instead for the rival *Sunday Telegraph*. Brown married Evans in 1981 at the East Hampton home of longtime *Washington Post* executive editor Ben Bradlee. Brown and Evans have two children, George, born in 1986, and Isabel, born in 1990. After Evans was knighted by Queen Elizabeth II in 2004 for his services to journalism, Brown automatically became Lady Evans (although she seldom goes by that title).

Brown has long worked as an advocate for women, and in 2010 she partnered with Diane von Furstenberg, Vital Voices Global Partnership, and the United Nations Foundation to sponsor the first annual Women in the World Summit. The summit focused on an array of issues facing women, including education, equal rights, literacy, global challenges, human slavery, and access to health care. Drawing a host of celebrities, the summit was attended by Madeleine Albright, Cherie Blair, Hillary Clinton, and Meryl Streep, among others.

Stephen T. Schroth and Jason A. Helfer

FURTHER READING

Bachrach, J. *Tina and Harry Come to America: Tina Brown, Harry Evans, and the Uses of Power.* New York: Free Press, 2001. Print. Critical look at Brown's editorships at *Vanity Fair* and *The New Yorker*, and how Brown and Evans used social connections, an understanding of corporate America, and ambition to get to the top.

Brooks, D. *Bobos in Paradise: The New Upper Class and How They Got There.* New York: Simon, 2000. Print. Examines how a new group of "bourgeois bohemians" have affected education, commerce, politics, and other areas of life in the information age.

Brown, Tina. *The Diana Chronicles.* New York: Doubleday, 2007. Print. Brown's biography of Princess Diana also casts light on Brown's insights into media as well as her writing style, methods, and priorities.

Byers, Dylan. "Tina Brown, Media Darling." *Brandweek* 52.8 (2011). Print. Brown as editor of *The Daily Beast* and *Newsweek* has been successful in garnering publicity as a journalist but less successful in other ventures, including her faile experiment as a talk show host and losses associated with *The Daily Beast*.

Florida, R. *The Rise of the Creative Class: And How It's Transforming Work, Leisure, Community, and Everyday Life.* New York: Basic, 2003. Print. Explores the growing role of creativity in the economy and how those who are able to tap into the public's choices and attitudes, such as Brown, are successful in a variety of contexts.

STEWART BUTTERFIELD

Cofounder of Flickr

Born: March 21, 1973; Lund, British Columbia
Died: -
Primary Field: Internet
Specialty: Content and data
Primary Company/Organization: Flickr

INTRODUCTION
Stewart Butterfield is one of the pioneers of the Canadian technology evolution. His desire for nonviolent online communities that foster communication and sharing is a hallmark of his life's work. After he helped solidify the concept of Web 2.0 and image sharing online, *Butterfield returned to the programming life. Whether through his work in online video games or his revolutionary photo-sharing platforms, Butterfield has proven the importance of user-driven content. By providing Flickr users with the site features they need to store and share their images with the world, Butterfield's platform has changed the way people think about photo sharing.*

EARLY LIFE
Daniel Stewart Butterfield was born in Lund, British Columbia, on March 21, 1973. He studied philosophy in college, earning a bachelor's degree in philosophy

from the University of Victoria in Canada. He earned a master's in philosophy from the University of Cambridge in England. He began his career as a computer programmer in Vancouver, working with several large corporations, including Sears and HSBC. In those early years, Butterfield provided design consultancy services for several big names, including *The Economist* magazine and the Canadian Broadcasting Company.

Butterfield's parents ran their own real estate agency in Vancouver, modeling a married couple who could successfully run a business together. Butterfield met Caterina Fake, the future cofounder of Flickr, in San Francisco in 2000. Despite Fake's initial refusal to date Butterfield, the two eventually got together, marrying in June 2001. Before that, however, they began a company called Ludicorp.

LIFE'S WORK

Butterfield and Fake founded Ludicorp in 2002. The company was meant to be a video game maker; the first game released for beta testing *Game Neverending*, reflecting the vision of the new company. The role-playing game was online and interactive, allowing users to chat with one another and even share their own uploaded photographs. Many view Butterfield's desire to

Stewart Butterfield.

create a virtual role-playing platform as growing out of his childhood, when role-playing games such as *Dungeons and Dragons* were extremely popular. By moving such games to the Internet, many companies had been successful. In the beginning, however, that was not the case for Ludicorp.

Ludicorp struggled to develop *Game Neverending* for about a year. In 2003, money grew tight. The couple had to mortgage their home to keep the company afloat. Butterfield began to wonder about the time and money being invested in the video-gaming project. One day, during a particularly bad bout of flu, Butterfield decided to ditch *Game Neverending* and focus on the photo-sharing aspect of the game, which was proving popular with users.

The decision to change Ludicorp's focus was not welcomed by the employees of the young company. The game designers and code programmers wanted to continue the project they had started. An initial vote resulted in a stalemate. After some dialog, a coder was convinced to vote in favor of Butterfield's idea. He broke the stalemate. Flickr became the focus of Ludicorp despite an unenthusiastic and small staff. At the time, only one of the employees was receiving a paycheck; the rest were friends who worked without payment. Finally, a loan request was approved, and Ludicorp had some money to move forward with the Flickr idea.

Ludicorp expanded its photo-sharing application into a platform that allowed folks to upload their personal photos, providing a limited amount of free online storage space. The new photo-sharing platform was called Flickr, at the suggestion of a friend. Ludicorp wanted to call it Flicker with an *e*, but that domain name was already spoken for, and the owner refused to sell the name.

Flickr officially opened for business in February 2004. Butterfield's image-sharing platform offered both free services and premium membership features to paying subscribers. This provided revenue and increased the number of users rapidly. The programmers and game designers of Ludicorp began to focus on making the website more user-friendly. They added features, such as tagging, that allowed the users to attach certain words to their image so it could be found in a search. Bloggers were able to post images directly from Flickr to a blog, increasing the start-up photo site's popularity. Flickr allowed users to upload images for free. It also allowed members to place a "creative commons" tag on their images so they could be reposted around the Internet.

From its launch, Flickr grew users and content every day. Because the website's members were responsible for developing all the content, Ludicorp was free to continue to develop the platform. It was not long before the social aspect of Flickr flourished. Both amateur and professional photographers began to enjoy not only the thousands of images on the site but also the sense of community their shared interest fostered. After a year of operation, Flickr had 1.5 million registered users.

The burgeoning website made a bleep on the radar of Internet giant Yahoo, Inc. At the time Flickr came into existence, Yahoo! already offered its own image-sharing platform. However, the Yahoo! image site lacked the features that made Flickr easy for users and popular among photographers. Yahoo! wanted to buy Ludicorp so it could substitute Flickr for its own lackluster image platform (which it would eventually do on September 20, 2007).

In 2005, there were fourteen thousand images being posted to Flickr every hour. The site made more than $4 billion in revenue by end of 2005. The first time Butterfield and Fake met with Yahoo! to discuss the future, they also had a meeting with Google later in the day. Despite a not very successful first meeting, Ludicorp met with Yahoo, not Google, six months later to continue discussions, and Ludicorp was ultimately sold to Yahoo! The programming and code for the online community and photo-sharing site was transferred from Canada to the United States. This legally made Flickr an American website. Butterfield and Fake continued to run the company for Yahoo! after the sale. They moved to the company headquarters in San Jose, California.

Butterfield admitted in an interview that he sold the company to Yahoo! because he was worried about another dot-com crash. If he had retained the company even a few months longer, the $35 million he did receive would have been pocket change in comparison to the profits that were on the horizon. Butterfield left Yahoo! and Flickr on July 12, 2008. The cofounder of one of the web's most popular image-sharing sites decided to leave California and return to Vancouver to help develop the growing city's technology culture.

PERSONAL LIFE

Butterfield and Fake have one daughter together, Sonnet, who was born in 2007. The marriage lasted nine years and the couple divorced in 2010. After leaving Flickr, Butterfield moved back to Canada and began another online gaming start-up, Tiny Speck, Inc., in 2009. The idea was to provide online gaming with an alternative to the

---

Affiliation: Flickr

Stewart Butterfield met Caterina Fake in 2000. They began the gaming company Ludicorp in 2002, developing an online game that offered a real-time photo-sharing application. The company's revenues began to dwindle, however. Butterfield, during an illness, decided that Ludicorp should focus on image sharing and hosting rather than creating games. Flickr was launched in February 2002 and was successful from the start. By the end of its first year in operation, the site had more than 1.5 million registered users. From its inception, Flickr was a major force in the Web 2.0 evolution, providing professional photographers and bloggers with user-generated content that could be reposted elsewhere.

Internet giant Yahoo! decided to purchase Flickr, along with its parent company Ludicorp, in July 2005 for $35 million. Butterfield and Fake continued with the company. They transferred their code from Vancouver to San Jose, California, turning Flickr from a Canadian to an American concern.

On April 9, 2008, video uploading was added to Flickr. In May 2009, the official White House photographer used Flickr to share government photos, vastly increasing users and content. Stewart Butterfield left Yahoo! on July 12, 2008, to found an online gaming start-up company, Tiny Speck.

The Flickr website has had issues with censorship, copyright, and privacy laws at home and abroad. However, none of these problems has prevented continued success for the company. In 2011, there were rumors that Yahoo! would close Flickr down as competition from social networking sites increased. Yahoo! denied the rumors, and as of 2012 the site continued to operate, attracting professional photographers, bloggers, and photo fans from across the globe.

---

violent video games that currently dominated the web. He wanted to provide a richer game-playing experience to adults in comparison to the games on social networking sites. The name of Butterfield's latest online gaming world is *Glitch*. *Glitch* offers a creation story, a purpose, and time travel. As of 2012, the game was in the beta-testing phase.

Butterfield is a professional speaker, providing presentations to corporate clients. He and Fake won the Webby Award for Special Achievement in 2005. He also acts as a judge for the creators of the Webby Awards, sponsored by the International Academy of Digital Arts and Sciences. Butterfield received a Chrysler design award in 2001. He has appeared on the cover of *Time* and *Newsweek* magazines. In 2005, he was named one of the TR35 (*Technology Review*'s "35 innovators under 35," an annual list thirty-five top innovators under the age of thirty-five) when he was thirty-two.

Trish Popovitch

FURTHER READING

Chatterjee, Pia. "Making Beautiful Startups Together." *Business 2.0* 12 Sept. 2007. Web. 7 Aug. 2012. Discusses married couples who started their companies together and were successful. Butterfield and Wake are featured. Provides some background on Flickr and the working relationship between the couple.

Farrelly, Glen. "Top 15 Canadians in Digital Media." *Backbone* 20 Nov. 2011. Web. 8 Aug. 2012. Short biography of Butterfield explaining how Flickr improved online photo sharing with RSS feeds and other features. Includes a little on Butterfield's time and role with Flickr.

Fitzgerald, Michael. "How We Did It." *Inc.* 1 Dec. 2006. Web. 7 Aug. 2012. Interview with both Butterfield and Caterina Fake about the founding of Flickr. Provides insight into each of the cofounder's personalities.

Kopytoff, Verne G. "At Flickr, Fending Off Rumors and Facebook." *New York Times* 30 Jan. 2011. Web. 8 Aug. 2012. Discusses the rumor of Yahoo! closing down Flickr. Provides details of the Yahoo! Flickr relationship and mentions some of the newer features of the site.

Massachusetts Institute of Technology. "Annual List of the 35 Innovators under 35." *Technology Review* 2005. Web. 8 Aug. 2012. Provides a photograph of Butterfield at the age of thirty-two and details his nomination to the 2005 list of thirty-five innovators under the age of thirty-five.

"President Stewart Butterfield." 2005. *Ludicorp.com.* Web. 8 Aug. 2012. Provides details of Butterfield's appointment as a judge for the International Academy of Digital Arts and Sciences. Mentions his winning of the Chrysler design award back in 2001.

Scalza, Remy. "The Philosopher Game King." *BC Business* 7 Feb. 2011. Web. 7 Aug. 2012. Details Butterfield's gaming exploits after leaving Yahoo! with a focus on his new company Tiny Speck and the game *Glitch.* Shares something of his business approach.

Schonfeld, Erick. "The Flickrization of Yahoo!" *Business 2.0* 1 Dec. 2005. Web. 7 Aug. 2012. Written after the sale of Flickr to Yahoo, provides details on how Flickr transformed Yahoo!'s approach to online image hosting and social networking, as well as facts about the website's users and the purchase.

DRIES BUYTAERT

Founder of Drupal

Born: November 19, 1978; Wilrijk (now Antwerp), Belgium
Died: -
Primary Field: Internet
Specialty: Content and data
Primary Company/Organization: Drupal and Acquia

INTRODUCTION

Dries Buytaert created the Drupal open source content management system (CMS) and platform in 2000 while attending university in his native country of Belgium. The system powers approximately 1 million websites across the globe—including such significant and disparate sites as those for the National Aeronautics and Space Administration (NASA), Twitter, and eBay. In 2006, Buytaert cofounded the Drupal Association, a not-for-profit organization dedicated to promoting Drupal. A year later, in 2007, he cofounded Acquia, ranked by Forbes *in 2011 as one of the Top 100 Most Promising Companies. Acquia is a for-profit enterprise designed to help companies leverage Drupal's technology, reach, and value through complementary products, services, and support. In 2008, Buytaert cofounded Mollom, a web service that helps sites filter the quality of content contributions and stop website spam. Buytaert holds a Ph.D. in computer science and engineering and has been recognized as a leading technology entrepreneur and innovator.*

EARLY LIFE

Dries Buytaert is a native of Belgium. He was born in a town called Wilrijk, now part of the city of Antwerp, on November 19, 1978. By the time he was six years old, he was already programming. His first job, however, was not in the computer science realm. While still attending high school, Buytaert joined the workforce as a cook, making hamburgers for a fast-food franchise called Quick. Thankful that his parents had committed to paying for his college tuition, books, and other essential university expenses, Buytaert was able to use his paychecks to purchase technology devices and other items for his entertainment.

Once he became a computer science student at the University of Antwerp, he left the fast-food franchise and joined a start-up Internet service provider named Planet Internet. He managed the company's technical service desk and helped with external sales via telemarketing. This job gave him unlimited high-speed Internet access, and he used his earnings to buy more technology gadgets. Such extensive access was a luxurious perq at the time, and Buytaert took advantage of the opportunity to learn all he could about the Internet.

LIFE'S WORK

While wrapping up his final year of studies at the University of Antwerp in 1999, Buytaert began to explore web development using computer-generated imagery, PHP server-side scripting, and the MySQL open source relational database management system. At about the same time, his student dormitory was clamoring for an internal messaging system to help communicate and manage student activities. Buytaert decided to solve the problem by creating a user-friendly message board that he hosted on the university's local area network. Upon his graduation the following year—magna cum laude with a degree in computer science—Buytaert had developed the internal electronic bulletin board system into an external news and discussion site and posted it to the Internet at Drop.org. The site was supposed to be named Dorpje.org (in Dutch, *dorpje* means "little village"), but Buytaert typed the registration incorrectly and ended up with the name Drop.org.

Buytaert spent the next year experimenting with new features, such as content rating, and new technologies, such as Really Simple Syndication (RSS) feeds. During that time, Drop.org attracted a great deal of consumer interest. User feedback and suggestions began pouring in. Rather than becoming swamped under the pressure to respond to the vast and growing input, Buytaert

Dries Buytaert.

decided instead to release the software behind the site as an open source program in order to let users experiment with making their own improvements.

Buytaert officially released Drupal 1.0.0 as open source technology on January 15, 2001. Drupal.org followed a few months later, in April. The site enables users to download the Drupal software free of charge and build their own websites using a simple framework that can be customized with the addition of specific modules.

Within only a few years, Drupal had attracted hundreds of thousands of users throughout the world. Buytaert realized that there was a need to establish an organization that would be responsible for ensuring the continued organic growth of the Drupal framework as its user base grew. Toward that end, he cofounded the nonprofit Drupal Association in 2007, along with longtime Drupal collaborators Dries Knapen and Steven Wittens. The organization handles details associated with Drupal's community web-hosting infrastructure and marketing and promotion efforts.

Those promotional efforts have helped Drupal attract nearly 800,000 contributors in more than two hundred countries. Drupal's soaring success provided Buytaert with cachet in the technology industry, but the software was free and thus his achievement did little to pad his wallet. That changed in 2007, when he and Pingtel founder Jay Batson secured $7 million in venture capital and cofounded Acquia in Boston, Massachusetts. The company provides technical support services and products such as prepackaged software combinations designed to speed and simplify Drupal execution and management in the fast-changing open source environment. Buytaert is the firm's chief technology officer. He relocated to Boston with his family in 2010 to reduce his transatlantic travel miles and the amount of time spent away from his burgeoning start-up. Acquia experienced rapid growth in its first few years, with some $38 million in venture capital funding and more than two hundred employees as of March 2012.

Another demand on Buytaert's time is Mollom, a start-up he cofounded in 2008 with college friend Benjamin Schrauwen. The company was created on the idea that the credibility of websites powered by open source technology could eventually be diminished without certain controls available to help site publishers evaluate content quality and restrict unwanted content such as spam. Mollom is a web tool designed specifically to meet that need for open source publishers. It is available via Mollom.com and as part of Acquia's site support offerings as well.

In addition to managing his own companies, Buytaert serves as an adviser to the Oregon State University's Open Source Lab, cloud-scale visualization solutions provider Akiban Technologies, and mobile application management services provider Apperian. Buytaert, who received a Ph.D. in computer science and engineering from Ghent University in Belgium in 2008, has also coauthored numerous technology articles for U.S. and European publications and has spoken to audiences at major industry symposia around the world. He was recognized by Business Insider as one of the 50 Most Powerful People in Enterprise Technology in 2012.

PERSONAL LIFE

In 2006, Buytaert married a biotechnology research scientist. The couple have two young children, Axl and Stan. Until 2008, Buytaert and his family resided in Antwerp, Belgium. The family moved to the United States in 2010 for a limited stay in Boston while Buytaert focused his efforts on Acquia from the company's New England headquarters. The family planned to return to life in Belgium to enable the children to begin their education in Europe and his wife to resume her research position at Flanders Institute of Technology. In their free

---

Affiliation: Drupal and Acquia

Drupal is a free open source web publishing platform that enables users to create their own customized websites rapidly and easily. An example of what is known as a content management system (CMS), it was created in 2000 by Dries Buytaert when he was a computer science student at the University of Antwerp. Since then, Drupal has garnered tens of thousands of active contributors across the globe. It is the framework behind approximately 2 percent of all websites on the Internet, including those for Harvard, NBC, and Sony Music.

In 2007, Buytaert and others founded the Drupal Association as a nonprofit organization to support Drupal's advancement through effective promotion. A year later, Buytaert cofounded Acquia as a commercial enterprise based in Boston, Massachusetts, with the purpose of providing products and technical support to optimize Drupal's ease of use and customer value. Among Acquia's customers is Whitehouse.gov. In 2011, *Forbes* ranked Acquia as one of America's Top 100 Most Promising Companies.

---

time, they enjoy hiking together and visiting parks and zoos. Buytaert likes photography and often brings his camera along.

Buytaert has received numerous awards for his contributions to enterprise technology. Among them are the 2012 Entrepreneur of the Year Award for New England from Ernst and Young, CIO of the Year 2012 by the *Boston Business Journal*, and 2012 CIO of the Year by Mass High Tech in the Emerging Technology category. He also received the CIOnet Innovation Award in 2009, was named as one of the Top 5 Most Influential People in Open Source by MindTouch in 2009, and was ranked among the top young innovators by both MIT and *Businessweek* in 2008.

Shari Parsons Miller

FURTHER READING

Andrews, Jeremy. "An In-Depth Interview with Dries Buytaert, Drupal Founder." *CMS Wire* 11 May 2011. Web. 12 Aug. 2012. Presents a discussion with Buytaert on this personal background and the launch and evolution of Drupal and Acquia.

Chavan, Abhijeet. "Migrating to Drupal." *Linux Journal* 151 (2006): 60–65. Web. 12 Aug. 2012. Provides an overview of Drupal as an open source, online collaboration tool for facilitating content management by a wide range of websites and portals.

Dearing, George. "Who Was That Masked Dot?" *Informationweek* 1177 (2008): 24. Web. 12 Aug. 2012. Discusses the commercialization of the open source content management platform, Drupal, via a suite of services being offered by newly funded Acquia.

Druckman, Katherine. "Linuxjournal.Com—under the Hood." *Linux Journal* 197 (2010): 14. Web. 12 Aug. 2012. Highlights the modules of Drupal that support LinuxJournal.com, including the views and views attach modules, the flag module, the content construction kit module, and the Mollom module, responsible for eliminating junk mail.

Hubble, Ann, Deborah A. Murphy, and Susan Chesley Perry. "From Static and Stale to Dynamic and Collaborative: The Drupal Difference." *Information Technology and Libraries* 30.4 (2011): 190–97. Web. 12 Aug. 2012. Discusses the decision of the University of California, Santa Cruz, Library to abandon its HTML-based website in favor of a database-driven website using Drupal's open source content management system.

Shirky, Clay. "Dries Buytaert, 29." *Technology Review* 111.5 (2008): 54–55. Web. 12 Aug. 2012. Discusses the impact Buytaert's free Drupal content management system has had on the U.S. information technology industry by enabling rapid and simple website customization without loss of site capability or stability.

OWEN BYRNE

Cofounder of Digg

Born: 1965; Halifax, Nova Scotia, Canada
Died: -
Primary Field: Internet
Specialty: Social media
Primary Company/Organization: Digg

INTRODUCTION

A cofounder of Digg, Owen Byrne was an experienced software engineer who prepared the PHP code for the social news site while assisting Kevin Rose and other partners in organizing the business. He is also a web engineer for GazeHawk, a company that develops eye-tracking services using webcams rather than specialized peripherals, which was purchased by Facebook in March 2012.

EARLY LIFE

Owen Byrne was born in 1965 in Halifax, Nova Scotia. Byrne graduated from Saint Mary's in 1986 with a bachelor's degree in computer science, and after working for ASL Environmental Science as a systems programmer for four years, he returned to school to earn his master's in business administration from Dalhousie University in 1994. He worked in tech support for Dalhousie's Faculty of Medicine from 1990 to 1992.

After school, Byrne worked as an adviser for Enercon Engineering and Consulting (1994–95) before taking a position as a software developer for the Halifax *Chronicle-Herald* in 1994, a position he held for six

Owen Byrne.

years, working concurrently the first two years as a test preparation instructor for Kaplan Test Prep. He attended graduate school at the University of Manitoba while working for the *Chronicle-Herald*, completing all the

requirements for a Ph.D. in management and operations research except the dissertation. From 2001 to 2004, he was a self-employed web developer; he was hired by TechTV's Kevin Rose to develop the code for a new site

Affiliation: Digg

The social news site Digg was founded after Kevin Rose, host of Tech TV's *The Screen Savers* (the predecessor to G4's *Attack of the Show*) met Equinix founder Jay Adelson while interviewing him. Digg began in February 2005, with the collaboration of Adelson (the first CEO), Rose, Owen Byrne, and Ron Gorodetzky. The site's initial design was developed by Dan Ries.

Digg allows users to share and recommend content on the web, with a focus on news. Members vote on shared content, using a system familiar from Slashdot, Reddit, and other sites: A given page shared with the site may be voted up (a "digg") or voted down (a "bury"). The front page displays currently popular and trending content, which is constantly in flux as users read and respond to content and share new links. Changes to the website in the first year included adding categories for stories (technology, science, world and business, videos, entertainment, gaming), the capacity for users to build a friends list and keep track of their friends' stories, and improvements to the interface. Popularity grew steadily, and, like Slashdot, Reddit, and other sites, Digg experienced spikes in traffic resulting from a story becoming popular. One of Digg's primary merits was its ability to focus a spotlight on something on the Internet that might otherwise go unnoticed by most, so that audiences no longer had to rely as heavily on the news "curation" of traditional media.

The impact of user votes on the site inevitably led to attempts to game the system. There were several known attempts, uncovered by sting operations, to upvote stories for cash (with the implied threat of a downvote if no payment were made—a sort of protection racket). There was also the explicit, openly conducted Bury Brigade, which responded to the popularity of Ron Paul among Digg users—social news users in the United States long having included a vocal libertarian contingent—by downvoting every Paul story submitted in an attempt to bury any mention of him. Digg's popularity led to a high ranking on Google's PageRank, meaning that "digged" stories would feature prominently in Google search results—providing a clear financial motivation for abuses of the system.

Around the height of the site's fame, Google attempted to purchase Digg for $200 million but eventually walked away from the table without completing the deal. Digg was considered one of the ripest websites for purchase, and other deals were entertained, but by the end of the year, then-CEO Adelson announced that the company was not for sale. Fox News, Microsoft, and Yahoo! had been among the suitors. Over time, the shine may have left the apple, although hits remained high, with about 20 million visitors per month; Digg never developed the level of mainstream awareness that Facebook or Twitter did, and its niche competitor, Reddit, began to attract mainstream media attention because of several high-profile news stories and the celebrity involvement in AMA/IAMA threads. In 2010, the site had to lay off more than a third of its staff, and Adelson left after disagreements with Rose and others.

Google's AdSense was originally used to provide ads, the source of Digg's revenue, but in 2007 the company switched to Microsoft's ad service.

In 2012, Digg went through significant changes. Although it was widely reported that the site was sold for a paltry $500,000—an extremely low amount relative to both the market for popular websites and the previous offers that had been made—this price, paid by Betaworks, was only for the website, technology, and Digg brand. Patents developed under Adelson were sold to LinkedIn for an additional $4 million, and staff were transferred to *The Washington Post* for $12 million. The total was still a far cry from the $200 million once bandied about, but that reflected the financial realities of the intervening years as much as anything else.

On July 31, 2012, a new version of Digg launched, based in part on user surveys collected through Betaworks' RethinkDigg.com. The new site integrated better with social media (the site had been integrated with Facebook Connect since 2009 and offered an iPhone app, although a previously offered Android app was no longer available with the relaunch), featured a more image-heavy design, and was built around an editorially centered front page.

called Digg (the domain name dig.com was taken by Disney), which would be a news site with a social networking element.

Life's Work

Although urban legend has it that Digg founder Rose hired Byrne via the freelance project listings site Elance for $200, Byrne was actually an equity contributor to the site, which was constructed in 2004 before the company organized in February 2005 and became a full-time job a few months later, when Rose left his TechTV hosting job.

Byrne was instrumental in getting the site off the ground, and Digg grew quickly in popularity, but when Jay Adelson came on board as chief executive officer (CEO) and the staff expanded, the site was redesigned from the ground up by Tim Ellis, Steve Williams, and Eli White, while Ron Gorodetzky developed a search engine and the HTTP architecture. Until 2005, Byrne remained the primary technical decision maker and had input into strategy, operations, and customer support.

Digg prospered quickly. Even before Byrne, as senior software engineer, handed over the reins of the site design to the new staff, it was one of the top 500 sites in the world, and Alexa ranked it as high as fifty-fifth in world traffic. It filled a niche similar to that filled by Slashdot (already a dinosaur, having been founded in 1997) and Reddit (established the same year as Digg): It was a social news site that, whether by design or in response to the demographics of heavy Internet users, appealed largely to "geeks" (albeit not necessarily the *Star Trek*–quoting science fiction fans portrayed in popular culture): detail-oriented, cerebral, pragmatic, and well-read engineers, linguists, and scientists. Any registered user could submit any link (typically to a news story, although not necessarily to a professional news source). Other users voted on links, with votes in favor counted as "diggs" (as in "I dig your link, it's really cool") and votes against counted as "buries." The result—the key to Digg in a nutshell—was a constantly shifting series of lists of ranked stories. The more people used Digg, the more robust the system of voting would be. (By extension, a story's popularity on Digg could lead to its server being overwhelmed by the traffic, as had been the case with "slashdotted" sites for years.)

Digg's success happened, in Ernest Hemingway's words, "gradually, then suddenly." The site was almost constantly tweaked in its first year, as Rose and others transitioned from other jobs to working on Digg nearly full time. (Rose, Adelson, and some of the other Digg staff were also involved with the web TV start-up Revision3, begun at the same time and occupying some of their attention.) Adelson raised considerable venture capital. Like Twitter later, the site became a recognizable brand name even while it was still occupied with defining that brand. As with many Internet start-ups, even after the dot-com bubble had burst, established companies—including Google, Microsoft, and Yahoo!—began to make offers to buy Digg. No agreement was reached, however, and the allure of the brand faded. Interestingly, one of the factors affecting the perception that Digg's popularity was going to fade was the introduction of Yahoo!'s Buzz, a social news site that Yahoo! rolled out when it was unable to acquire Digg; as it turned out, Buzz remained such a nonentity in social media that Google had no qualms naming its social networking tool Google Buzz two years later, before Yahoo! Buzz was even formally discontinued.

Byrne left Digg in October 2007, three years after he had come on board, right around the height of its fame. Since then, he has worked for Expedia (July 2008–May 2010, as senior manager of Travelpod Labs) and Astrum Solar (2010, as director of information technology), and he was director of engineering for GazeHawk (April 2011–April 2012), a company that offered eye-tracking services using webcams and paid volunteers to track the areas of a web page to which the viewer's attention was drawn. GazeHawk was bought out by Facebook. In April 2012, Byrne began working for Reputation.com as senior software engineer.

Personal Life

Byrne lives in the San Francisco Bay Area. He occasionally blogs about his experiences at Digg, including a disclaimer for legal safety, but he has been clear that the possibility of legal reprisals prevents him from being too open and specific. He is an avid photographer (with photos featured in several magazines) and marathon runner, and he is an active member of the public-speaking group Toastmasters International.

Bill Kte'pi

Further Reading

Jenkins, Henry. *Confronting the Challenges of Participatory Culture: Media Education for the 21st Century*. Cambridge: MIT, 2009. Print. Examines social media, new forms of creative expression, and their impact on media studies.

Qualman, Erik. *Socialnomics: How Social Media Transforms the Way We Live and Do Business*. New York: Wiley, 2010. Print. Examines the impact of social media on the business world.

Sarno, David. "Digg Gets $28.7M Boost, Plans to Double Size, Go Global." *Los Angeles Times* 23 Sept. 2008: n. pag. Print. Coverage of Digg's rise from the company's peak period.

C

ROBERT CAILLIAU

Cocreator of the World Wide Web

Born: January 26, 1947; Tongeren, Belgium
Died: -
Primary Field: Computer science
Specialty: Internet
Primary Company/Organization: World Wide Web

INTRODUCTION

Robert Cailliau is a Belgian-born engineer and computer scientist who, independently of Tim Berners-Lee, proposed a project to develop a hypertext system at the European Organization for Nuclear Research (Conseille Européen pour la Recherche Nucléaire, or CERN), also known as the European Laboratory for Particle Physics. The project resulted in the World Wide Web. In 1990, Cailliau joined Berners-Lee as a partner in his attempt to win approval for the Berners-Lee proposal. Cailliau rewrote the project proposal, lobbied management for funding, and collaborated with Berners-Lee on papers and presentations. In 1992, Cailliau produced Samba, the first web browser, for the Apple Macintosh. He was instrumental in the push to secure approval of the document that allowed CERN to place the web technology in the public domain in 1993. He is also a founding member and past chairman of the International World Wide Web Conference Committee.

EARLY LIFE

Robert Cailliau was born January 26, 1947, in Tongeren, Belgium. His ancestors have lived in Flanders, the northern part of Belgium, since early in the seventeenth century. His parents moved the family to Antwerp in 1958. Cailliau attended school in Antwerp from the time he was eleven until he graduated in 1964. He

then attended the University of Ghent, where he received a degree in electrical and mechanical engineering, the equivalent of a master's in science, in 1969. After graduation, he continued his association with the University of Ghent, working at the Laboratory of Mechanical Engineering. His work there inspired him to learn more about computers, and he left for the United

Robert Cailliau.

States. He spent nine months at the University of Michigan in Ann Arbor, obtaining a master's degree in computer, information, and control engineering.

When he returned to Belgium, he worked at the Laboratory of Control and Hybrid Computation, where he helped develop software for the hybrid computer. About this time, he paid his first visit to CERN in Geneva, Switzerland. From this point, his ambition was to work on a CERN project, but Belgium required a year of military service of all able-bodied males. Completing his military service took priority. He was stationed at the Royal Military Academy and initially assigned to infirmary duty. However, he was soon transferred to the School of War, where he spent the remainder of his term of service in the computer center maintaining a large troop-movement simulation program, which he compared to SimCity with text data only. He wrote Fortran programs for the simulation, but during that time he also learned ALGOL 68, a computer language he found poetic.

LIFE'S WORK
With his military service behind him, Cailliau was free to pursue his dream of working at CERN. He received a fellowship in 1974 to work in the proton synchrotron division on an improvement program for the control systems of the accelerator complex. When the fellowship ended, he was hired and began working on document markup and formatting. In 1975, he designed and implemented a widely used document markup and formatting system. From 1987 to 1989, he ran CERN's Office Computing Systems group. In 1987, he moved to the Data Handling Division. Restructuring within CERN led to another move two years later, this time to the Electronic and Computing for Physics Division.

As early as 1974, Cailliau had introduced to CERN a system that allowed the easy transfer of documents, code, and files. Before he met Berners-Lee in 1989, Cailliau was already using Hypercard, an Apple programming environment that could be used to create custom applications. Cards could be linked to one another, like hypertext links on the web. He was working on his own proposal to develop a hypertext system for CERN when he met Berners-Lee, whose own hypertext proposal was further along than Cailliau's. Enthusiastic about the possibilities of combining hypertext and networking, Cailliau began working with Berners-Lee. Cailliau is often identified as coinventor of the web, but both men have made clear that the specifications for universal document identifiers (later known as uniform

resource locators, or URLs), the hypertext language, the protocol, and the code of the original implementation were the work of Berners-Lee.

Some have called Cailliau an evangelist for the web; others describe his role as that of a manager. CERN calls him the number-one advocate of Berners-Lee's proposal. However, everyone, including Berners-Lee, agrees that Cailliau's role was essential to the success of the project. He rewrote Berners-Lee's proposal to make it more specific and likelier to appeal to an administrator. He had been a group leader for several years at this point and possessed knowledge of CERN's hierarchy that Berners-Lee lacked. Cailliau himself views his contribution primarily as a securer of resources. On a minimal budget, he found computers, offices, and people. He pleaded with management for young programmers who were at CERN for a year as part of the Technical Student Program, and he succeeded in getting a fair number assigned to the web project. Some of the students went on to do work that earned them a place in web history, including Henrik Frystyk Nielsen, who helped to create hypertext transfer protocol (HTTP).

Understanding that CERN was a physics laboratory and, as such, unlikely to devote major resources to the web, Cailliau began to contact other groups with an interest in informatics. He forged ties with the European Commission, the executive branch of the European Union; France's National Institute for Research in Computer Science and Control (known by its French acronym INRIA); and the Fraunhofer Society, Germany's application-oriented research institution. It was also Cailliau who devoted time and energy to persuading CERN's management to give the World Wide Web (WWW) technology away without requiring royalties, a task that took eighteen months, six of them requiring Cailliau's working with the CERN legal service to prepare the document that put the web technology into the public domain on April 30, 1993.

In May 1994, Cailliau organized the first International WWW Conference, which was held at CERN. More than six hundred web enthusiasts showed up for the conference; CERN could accommodate only four hundred of them. By the second WWW conference, held in Chicago in October 1994, eighteen hundred people showed up, five hundred more than could be admitted. Also in 1994, Cailliau cofounded the International WWW Conference Committee (IW3C2), the group that became responsible for organizing the international conferences that provided a forum focused on the development of the web, the standardization of its

Affiliation: World Wide Web

In March 1989, Tim Berners-Lee, an English physicist, with the European Organization for Nuclear Research (CERN) in Geneva, Switzerland, wrote a proposal showing how information could be transferred over the Internet using hypertext. Despite the enthusiasm of his immediate superior, the proposal failed to capture the support of CERN administrators. A year later, Robert Cailliau, a Belgian engineer and computer scientist employed in a different division of CERN, read Berners-Lee's proposal and found it to be more advanced, and with greater potential, than his own hypertext project. He became Berners-Lee's strongest advocate, rewriting the proposal to make it more specific and using language more likely to appeal to administrators. The combination of Berners-Lee's innovative technology and Cailliau's managerial and public relations skills gave birth to what the two agreed to call the World Wide Web. Within a month after the proposal was approved, Berners-Lee had the first server and the first browser-editor ready. On August 6, 1991, the first website was available.

The web was still a long way from fulfilling its creators' vision of a universal common information space where a hypertext link could make available countless texts. However, by 1994 the First International World Wide Web Conference, organized by Cailliau, attracted a crowd of six hundred, and the number of servers had increased to 250. Less than six months later, the Second International WWW Conference in Chicago had triple the attendance numbers, and twenty-five hundred servers were operating. In the summer of 1994, Berners-Lee founded the World Wide Web Consortium, an international community committed to developing web standards. In 1995, there were more than seventy thousand servers, and by then the World Wide Web was generally (if erroneously) equated with the Internet—an indication of how broad and far-reaching the web was regarded to be. What had begun as a way for a group of physicists to communicate with one another about their work was growing in unpredictable ways and at an unprecedented rate, moving far beyond scientific and academic communities. In 2012, the web contained more than 40 billion pages, and more than 2 billion users accessed their choice of those pages through public computers in schools and libraries, desktop and laptop personal computers, smart phones, e-readers, and other devices.

technologies, and its impact on society and culture. That year, he persuaded the European Commission that the web was a learning tool and started the Web for Schools project. Cailliau continued as a member of IW3C2 through 2004.

Cailliau retired from CERN in 2007 after thirty-two years of service. During those years, he variously worked on control engineering, user interfaces, text processing, administrative computing support, and hypertexts. He ended his CERN career as head of CERN's External Communications, part of the Directory Services Unit, where his duties included looking after CERN's Intranet and Web presence. Cailliau continues to speak on the web and web-related issues.

PERSONAL LIFE

Cailliau is a neurological rarity: He has synaesthesia, a condition in which two or more senses are linked. In his case, letters have colors. He finds the disorder sometimes useful in spell checking, because his eye can detect errors in the color patterns of words. His synaesthesia played a role when he designed the historical logo of the World Wide Web (WWW), three superimposed Ws, which were

green not to signal green technology (as might be assumed) but because Cailliau sees the letter W as green.

When Cailliau has been asked to consider changes in the web in the more than two decades since he helped to develop it, he has expressed mixed reactions. He approves of blogging, finding the practice close to the idea that he and Berners-Lee had at the beginning of the web as a means whereby anyone can create original content. He has concerns about the inability to control one's data on social media sites and admits to avoiding them for that reason.

Wylene Rholetter

FURTHER READING

Berners-Lee, Tim, et al. "The World Wide Web." *Communications of the ACM* 37.8 (1994): 76–82. Print. This article appears in a special issue of the journal. Berners-Lee and four of the scientists who worked on the World Wide Web Project with him, including Robert Cailliau, explain the computer network called the World Wide Web and how to use it. Includes two color photographs, one diagram, one chart, and one graph.

Brun, René, Frederioco Carminati, and Giuliana Galli Carminati, eds. *From the Web to the Grid and Beyond: Computing Paradigms Driven by High-Energy Physics*. New York: Springer, 2012. Print. A scholarly account of the history of experimental high-energy physics (HEP), covering topics such as programming languages, software engineering, large databases, the web, grid and cloud computing, and intellectual property regulations. The article is rich with information but is most accessible to an audience with a basic understanding of physics and computer science.

Gillies, James, and Robert Cailliau. *How the Web Was Born: The Story of the World Wide Web*. New York: Oxford UP, 2000. Print. Cailliau's account of the creation of the World Wide Web, written with Gilles, a professional science writer. The prose is lucid, the tone engaging, and the information interesting to a general audience—made more so by a useful time line. Also includes photographs, charts, acronyms, bibliography, and source notes.

Marchant, Joanna. "Out of the Shadows." *New Scientist* 167.2253 (2000): 41–43. Print. This article is based on an interview with Cailliau conducted just as his book on the creation of the web was launching. He describes his role in the process and shares his vision of the future of the web.

Zimmer, Ben. "Web." *The New York Times Magazine* 14 Nov. 2010: MM34. Print. The author, a linguist and lexicographer, considers the choice that Berners-Lee and Cailliau made for the name of their system to share hyperlinked information and how their choice of the name World Wide Web has affected the lexicon.

ELISA CAMAHORT PAGE

Cofounder and COO of BlogHer

Born: April 4 (year unknown); California
Died: -
Primary Field: Internet
Specialty: Social media
Primary Company/Organization: BlogHer

INTRODUCTION

Elisa Camahort Page is the groundbreaking chief operating officer (CEO) of BlogHer, one of the largest social networking organizations focused specifically on women. Before cofounding BlogHer in 2005 with Jory Des Jardins and Lisa Stone, Camahort Page ran Worker Bees, a marketing consultancy that integrated social media with corporate marketing strategies. Camahort Page has been influential in encouraging women to take part in technology, to use the Internet for communication, and to create a financially sound model that allows her large-scale blog to thrive.

EARLY LIFE

Elisa Camahort Page was born in the Bay Area of California. She has commented that her mother was one of her role models, because her mother made a successful career in the corporate world, becoming the first woman to act as vice president of her company. Camahort Page worked in Silicon Valley for seventeen years before founding BlogHer and credits several workplace mentors with helping her understand the technical side of the high-tech business. She worked primarily in marketing before founding BlogHer, running the marketing consultancy Worker Bees and working as senior director of product marketing at Terayon Communication Systems.

LIFE'S WORK

Camahort is the founder and chief operating officer of BlogHer, a company she cofounded with Jory Des Jardins and Lisa Stone in 2005. BlogHer is an online community that had approximately twenty-five hundred member blogs by October 2010. It is organized into categories such as Blogging and Social Media, Family, Feminism, Health, News and Politics, Style, and Tech. The website also includes BlogHer TV (videos) and an online book club where readers post questions relating to the books and others comment on them. As of April 2012, an estimated 14 million women visited the BlogHer site monthly. The associated BlogHer conference, which grew from three hundred attendees in 2005 to more than five thousand in 2011, is the world's largest conference for women social media leaders. BlogHer is supported by advertising and sponsorships, and it achieved revenues in eight figures for both 2010 and 2011.

Elise Camahort Page.

Camahort Page is a frequent public speaker and has presented keynote addresses on conferences such as South by Southwest (SXSW) Interactive, MediaBistro Circus, and New Communications Forum. She has received many honors: She has been named (along with cofounders Des Jardins and Stone) three times (in 2008, 2009, and 2010) as among the most influential women in technology by *Fast Company*, a progressive business media publication and website. Camahort Page, Des Jardins, and Stone were also named to the Ernst and Young Winning Women Class of 2011 and were jointly awarded the PepsiCo Women's Inspiration Award in 2011. In 2008, Page, Des Jardins, and Stone were given the Anita Borg Institute Social Impact Award.

The purpose of BlogHer's conference and other events is to bring together women who are involved or who would like to become involved in blogging. There are no restrictions on who may attend; no particular level of experience or skill is required, and about 10 to 15 percent of the attendees at a typical annual conference are male. The most recent annual conference was held in August 2012 in New York City and included a variety of sessions, social events, and speeches. Some of the programs at BlogHer 2012 were geared toward instruction in technical aspects of blogging and the Internet (such

as HTML coding, podcasting, screen design, and search engine optimization), some toward marketing (such as turning blog entries into publishable books and articles and drawing attention to one's blog), and some toward using blogs for particular purposes (garnering support for a political cause or health promotion, for example). Two special programs were presented on the first day of the conference: Health Minder Day covered issues related to caregiving, health promotion and advocacy, and maintaining a balanced life, and Pathfinder Day covered issues related to using blogs for different purposes, including as a business, to create change, as a media company, and as a path to writing and publishing a book.

President Barack Obama addressed the gathering by live video; conference organizers say they also approached former Massachusetts governor Mitt Romney, the Republican nominee for the upcoming presidential election, who declined to participate. Obama's talk was seen by conference organizers as recognition of the influence of BlogHer, and of blogs in general, on the political process, as well as the importance of women in the electorate. In his talk, Obama specifically addressed women's concerns in the upcoming election, including access to contraception and health care, as well as the importance of women providing strong role models and having their voices heard on the Internet and elsewhere.

Because of the size and success of BlogHer, it is often discussed in connection with general Internet issues, such as the 2009 U.S. Federal Trade Commission ruling that bloggers who discuss or review products on their blogs must disclose any material connections they may have with the producer of a product they discuss; this ruling interprets such discussions on a blog as endorsement, and failure to comply can result in fines of up to $11,000. Although this may sound like reasonable consumer protection rule, some charge that it amounts to a restriction of free speech, because many bloggers are amateurs not well versed in communications laws; were a few such nonprofessionasls to be assessed large fines, others might well be discouraged from participating in online communications in fear that they might violate some other law with which they were not familiar. In addition, some point out that the availability of free products and other in-kind merchandise has encouraged many women to become involved in blogging, a sphere previously dominated by men; some argue that receiving free products is the way most bloggers are compensated for their work, because they do not receive wages or salaries, and thus the availability of free products facilitates online communications.

Affiliation: BlogHer

Elisa Camahort Page is one of three cofounders of BlogHer, a massive social communications company. BlogHer consists of three main parts: the BlogHer conferences, the world's largest social media conference for women; the BlogHer Publishing Network, hosting more than twenty-five hundred blogs by women; and BlogHer.Com, an Internet guide to news and trends of interest to women. As of 2012, BlogHer had offices in Silicon Valley (California) and New York City, employed more than fifty people, and received venture capital from Azure Capital Partners, Comcast Interactive Capital, and Venrock. Camahort Page has emphasized fostering communication among visitors to BlogHer, maintaining a civil and respectful tone, and including a broad range of points of view both on the website and at the annual conference. *Forbes* named BlogHer one of its Top 100 Websites for Women in 2010, 2011, and 2012, and BlogHer was also named to the AlwaysOn OnMedia Top 100 for 2011 and the Global 250 for 2010 and 2011.

BlogHer held its first conference in 2005, with the purpose of bringing together women bloggers so they could connect with one another in person and creating opportunities for them to pursue economic opportunities, gain greater exposure, learn, and form stronger communities. BlogHer emphasizes that although the focus of the conference is on women bloggers, anyone at any level of experience can attend, and the event is not restricted to women; in fact, about 10 to 15 percent of attendees in any given year are men. The 2012 conference was held in New York City on August 2–4 and attended by more than five thousand participants. Besides offering workshops to increase participants' technical skills—for example, how to write HTML code and how to use search engine optimization (SEO) to increase the visibility of a blog—topics covered at the conference including using blogging as a means of self-expression, blogging to effect political change, blogging as a business, and blogging as a means to begin or further one's career as a published writer of books and magazine articles.

BlogHer has also proven to be a lightning rod for issues important to women. For instance, sponsorship of the August 2010 BlogHer conference by two Nestlé product lines, Stouffer's frozen foods and Butterfinger candy, drew the wrath of some breastfeeding advocates; Nestlé has been subject to a consumer boycott since 1977 based on issues surrounding the infant formula it has marketed in developing countries. Some women boycotted the 2010 conference, and others made political gestures such as making charitable contributions to organizations focused on mother and child health and welfare.

Camahort Page is a founding member of the Society for New Communications Research, a nonprofit 501(c)3 foundation, which studies new media and its effects on business and society.

PERSONAL LIFE

Camahort Page is married to a software developer and lives in San Jose, California. She is a member of the board of directors of the 42nd Street Moon Theatre in San Francisco, a company that specializes in producing both classic and little-known musical comedies. She also serves on the board of advisers for the Anita Borg institute for Women and Technology, an organization dedicated to increasing the positive impact of technology on women and women's impact on technology; she is on the programming advisory committee for SXSW Interactive, an annual conference in Austin, Texas; and she is on the advisory board for Food on the Table, a website and mobile app designed to help families plan and organize food shopping as well as cook and serve healthy meals.

Sarah Boslaugh

FURTHER READING

Cross, Mary. *Bloggerati, Twitterati: How Blogs and Twitter are Transforming Popular Culture*. Westport: Praeger, 2011. Print. An examination of the influence of the digital revolution on human behavior, as well as the demographics of the users of different types of Internet services, including blogs and Twitter.

Funk, Tom. *Social Media Playback for Business: Reaching Your Online Community with Twitter, Facebook, LinkedIn, and More*. Westport: Praeger, 2011. Print. A book written for business people just starting to get into social media, written by a long-time website developer, marketing manager, and e-commerce veteran. BlogHer is cited as an example of a successful blog reaching a targeted population segment.

Marcus, Jake Aryeh. *Mothering* 162 (2010): 37. Print. An article about the controversy surrounding the BlogHer conference held in August 2010. One of the conference sponsors was Nestlé, manufacturer of, among other things, infant formula, and has been severely criticized in the past for promoting the use of infant formula in developing countries rather than encouraging women to breastfeed their infants.

Walker, Rob. "Monetizing Motherhood." *New York Times* 22 (2010): 30. Print. A journalistic account of the 2010 BlogHer conference, with particular focus on the potential effects on BlogHer and other blogging sites of the Federal Trade Commission guidelines requiring bloggers to disclose any "material connections" (for example, receiving products for free) that they may have with products reviewed or discussed on their blogs.

Steve Case

Cofounder and former CEO of America Online

Born: August 21, 1958; Honolulu, Hawaii
Died: -
Primary Field: Internet
Specialty: Commerce
Primary Company/Organization: America Online

Introduction
In 1990, only 15 percent of American households owned home computers. Over the next seven years, computer ownership climbed, and time spent computing more than tripled. The so-called Super Information Highway promised by the Internet was difficult for some individuals to navigate. With America Online (AOL), Steve Case gave new computer users a tool for entering the world of technology. A service provider, social network, and Internet browser, AOL became one of the most respected names in the computing industry. After negotiating the merger of AOL with Time Warner, Case left the company in 2003 to devote his time to Revolution, a venture firm that manages his network of health care and media investments, and to the Case Foundation. He and wife Jean have signed the Giving Pledge, through which American billionaires promise to give away at least half of their fortunes within their lifetimes. In 2008, Modern Healthcare named Case the most powerful American in the field of health care.

Early Life
Stephen McConnell Case was born in Honolulu, Hawaii, on August 21, 1958. His father, Daniel, a lawyer, and his mother, Carol, an elementary-school teacher, had also been born in Hawaii. One of four children, Case was particularly close to his brother Dan, and the two brothers established their own business, Case

Enterprises. With Steve running the business end and Dan serving as front man, they sold greeting cards and seeds and managed a paper route. Steve attended Punahou School, a private school where he served as the editor of the newspaper, *Ka Punahou*. He also wrote music reviews and articles for *Youth Unlimited*. He graduated in 1976.

At Williams College in Williamstown, Massachusetts, Case started his own band and worked as a disc

Steve Case.

jockey. Although he enjoyed political science classes, he did not like the computer science classes, which required him to use punch cards. Case graduated with a bachelor of arts in political science in 1980. That year, he began marketing hair care products as an assistant brands manager in the marketing department of Procter & Gamble. He left in 1982 to take a job in Wichita, Kansas, in new development at Pizza Hut. In his spare time, he built a Kaypro computer, and he and a friend established a marketing consulting company.

LIFE'S WORK

Case's brother Dan grew up to become an investment banker with Hambrecht and Quist. When Dan invited Steve to attend the Consumer Electronics Show in Las Vegas in 1983, Case met William von Meister, the developer of The Source, an interactive computer resource used by Atari gaming consoles. Case signed on as a consultant for von Meister at Control Video and ultimately became a full-time employee. Atari's fortune faltered as more sophisticated gaming consoles reached the market. By that time, Jim Kimsey, a Control Video executive, had already begun grooming Case to take over the company. Case began marketing interactive services to IBM, Commodore, Apple, and Tandy, but Apple opted to launch its own service and withdrew from the fold.

In 1985, Steve Case cofounded the company that became known as America Online, forging what could be salvaged from Control Video into Quantum Computer Services, using his computer skills and technical know-how to create the user-friendly interface and his marketing skills to sell the product to the public. He launched a direct-mail campaign (the AOL setup CD would become ubiquitous in people's mailboxes). With Case as chief executive officer (CEO) and Kimsey as chairman of the board, the company became America Online, Inc., in 1991. The following year, AOL became the first Internet company to be publicly traded, selling at $184 per share and raising $66 million. Case used the money to grow AOL. However, AOL was still in third place, trailing both CompuServe (the first major online service) and Prodigy. By 1994, however, AOL had gone global and was claiming a million subscribers.

At the same time that AOL was on its way to becoming the best-known name in the field of Internet service providers, Microsoft, under the guidance of Bill Gates, was turning Windows into the most popular operating system in the world. Gates allegedly offered to buy 20 percent of AOL in 1993 but was turned down. Instead, AOL began purchasing other companies, acquiring Advanced Network Services and Book Link Technologies in 1994. The subscriber base grew from 600,000 in early 1994 to more than 1 million by March 1995. In August, Microsoft introduced Windows 95, which included the web browser Internet Explorer. Instead of competing, the two giants made a deal to promote each other. By 1997, AOL had 17 million subscribers, and Case was chairman of the board. AOL acquired its rival, CompuServe, in 1998 and purchased the Internet browser Netscape the following year.

In 2000, AOL had 32 million subscribers. That year, Case led AOL into a merger with the venerable Time Warner in what became known as the largest and in American history. For $164 million in cash and stock, AOL shareholders gained a majority interest in the new company. However, Case agreed to step down as CEO while remaining with AOL Time Warner as chairman of the board of directors. Gerald Levin of Time Warner served as CEO. When the merger was completed, the company was valued at $290 billion. In addition to the AOL subscription base, the combined media conglomerate comprised thirty-five magazines, the Little, Brown publishing company, television channels (including HBO, CNN, and TBS), and a host of film and television properties. Projected earnings for AOL Time Warner included $8.07 billion from films, $6.88 billion from the Internet, $4.7 billion from publishing rights, and $3.08 billion from music rights. Both Disney and Microsoft opposed the merger, claiming that it gave AOL Time Warner a media monopoly. The Federal Trade Commission based its approval of the merger on the sharing of company technologies.

In 2002, AOL reported a subscriber base of 27 million. By that time, however, the focus of the Internet was changing, and cable modems and digital subscriber line (DSL) connections were making dial-up access obsolete. AOL membership steadily declined, and stock in the merged company fell by 75 percent. Ultimately, the company lost nearly $100 billion, making it the largest loss ever reported in a single year in the United States. Both the Securities Exchange Commission (SEC) and the Department of Justice launched investigations into the company's accounting practices. The company ultimately paid $360 million as a result of the SEC investigation and spent another $3 billion settling various lawsuits filed by shareholders. Case left AOL Time Warner in 2003.

In 2010, Time Warner divested itself of AOL, putting the erstwhile Internet giant up for public trading. On its own again, AOL set out to reestablish itself as an advertising business and the owner of a number of online communities that include Engadget, a technology blog; WalletPop, a personal finance website; and Slashfood, a food website. In only a short while, AOL began showing a small profit.

Personal Life

Case married Joanne Barker, whom he had met while attending Williams College, in 1985, in her hometown of Rumson, New Jersey. After having three children, they divorced in 1996. He married Jean Villaneuva, a former AOL executive, in 1998 in a ceremony presided over by the Reverend Billy Graham. The combined Case family, which includes four daughters and one son, live in McLean, Virginia, in the childhood home of Jackie Kennedy Onassis. Case is still heavily invested in his home state of Hawaii, and he donated $10 million to Punahou School to build a new junior high named after his parents. By 2011, Case's net worth was estimated at $1.5 billion.

In 1997, Case founded the Case Foundation, which focuses on promoting technology, health care, and community development to underserved groups, particularly children and youths. Jean heads the foundation. In 2000, Case and his brother Dan established Accelerate Brain Cancer Cure (ABC2) to promote research on brain cancer. The brothers had a personal reason for establishing ABC2: Dan Case had been diagnosed with brain cancer; he died in 2002.

In 2005, with a $250 million investment, Case founded the Washington, D.C.–based Revolution, which is made up of twelve separate companies networked under the umbrellas of Revolution Growth, Revolution Ventures, Revolution Health, and Revolution Places. Revolution Money was sold to American Express in 2009. Revolution Growth invests in fast-growing companies that include Zipcar, Living Social, and Exclusive Resorts. Revolution Ventures invests in technology companies that are on their way up. Revolution Health comprises both websites and offline partnerships dealing with all aspects of health care. One of those partnerships is with Walmart and concerns the establishment of Red Clinics, onsite clinics that offer alternatives to lengthy and expensive trips to emergency rooms. Revolution Places invests in real estate and hospitality businesses such as Grove Farms and Maui Land and Pineapple.

Living in the Washington, D.C., area allows Case to maintain his interest in politics. In 2011, President Barack Obama appointed him to head the Startup America Partnership. Case also serves on the President's

Affiliation: America Online

In the 1990s, computer use in the United States grew from 200,000 to 20 million. In the early days, the Internet was generally accessed by a computer modem connected to a telephone line, using what came to be known as dial-up service. Under the guidance of Steve Case, America Online became the top service provider for accessing the online world.

Through its colorful and user-friendly interface, which owed much to the popular Macintosh user interface, America Online offered a one-stop online community for e-mail, chat rooms, bulletin boards, instant messaging, downloading software, keeping up with news and sports, planning trips, and shopping. Users could also link to the rest of the Internet through the AOL browser. When accessing America Online, users were greeted with a friendly, "You've got mail." The phrase became so interwoven with popular culture that it was used as the title of a romantic comedy in 1998. starring Tom Hanks and Meg Ryan as business rivals who fall in love through e-mail exchanges the Internet.

However, there were a number of problems with AOL. Telephone lines were often busy, preventing subscribers from gaining access. Modem speeds were slow, which meant that downloading was often a time-consuming activity. Since customers paid a flat rate of $9.95 for only five hours of online time and $2.95 for each additional hour, slow speeds resulted in increased fees. In response to a class action lawsuit, AOL in 1996 instituted a flat-rate plan of $19.95 a month with no limits on online time.

Council on Jobs and Competitiveness. He has made a number of appearances on CNBC's *Squawk Box* to discuss the activities of both groups.

Elizabeth Rholetter Purdy

Further Reading

Bulik, Beth Snyder. "Steve Case, a Man with a Medical Mission." *Advertising Age* 79.11 (2008): n. pag. Print. Focuses on Case's career after leaving AOL Time Warner.

Munk, Nina. *Fools Rush In: Steve Case, Jerry Levin, and the Unmaking of AOL Time Warner*. New York: HarperCollins, 2004. Print. Follows the AOL Time Warner merger, focusing on the damage it did to Time Warner's reputation. Illustrated.

"Parted from Time Warner, AOL Posts a Small Profit." *New York Times*, 3 Feb. 2010. Print. Account of AOL after the break from Time Warner.

Plosker, George R. "How Do We Get Here from There? Entrepreneur Steve Case Talks about Early Online Days." *Information Today* 22.5 (2005): 22–28. Print. Profile of Case, including his career and his philanthropic activities.

Sloan, Allan. "Don't Blame It All on Steve Case." *Newsweek* 139.14 (2002): 47. Print. Offers a defense of Case's role in the AOL Time Warner merger.

Stives, Steve. "The (R)evolution of Steve Case." *Fortune* 152.10 (2005): 88–96. Print. A profile of Case's Revolution networks.

Swisher, Karen. *AOL.com: How Steve Case Beat Bill Gates, Nailed the Netheads, and Made Millions in the War for the Web*. New York: Times, 1998. Print. Traces the life of Case, the founding of AOL, and the early battle for the Internet. Includes illustrations and index.

---, and Lisa Dickey. *There Must Be a Pony in Here Somewhere: The AOL Time Warner Debacle and the Quest for a Digital Future*. New York: Crown Business, 2003. Print. Unflattering portrait of AOL and the notorious merger. Illustrated.

CATHERINE M. CASSERLY

CEO of Creative Commons

Born: Date and place unknown
Died: -
Primary Field: Internet
Specialty: Ethics and policy
Primary Company/Organization: Creative Commons

INTRODUCTION

Catherine M. Casserly is the chief executive officer (CEO) of Creative Commons, a nonprofit organization with the purpose of simplifying the legal, free exchange of knowledge and culture in the new digital environment created by the Internet. Since 2001, Casserly has been involved with the open source movement. As a program consultant at the William and Flora Hewlett Foundation, she was instrumental in the $1 million grant by that foundation that helped to establish Creative Commons in 2001. She was directing the Open Educational Resources program of the Carnegie Foundation for the Advancement of Teaching when she was elected to the Creative Commons board of directors in 2010. In March 2011, she succeeded Joi Ito as the nonprofit's CEO.

EARLY LIFE

Catherine M. Casserly received a bachelor's degree in mathematics from Boston College and a Ph.D. in the economics of education from Stanford University. After college, she participated in an international volunteer program. Through this program, she taught mathematics to students in middle school and high school in Kingston, Jamaica. She worked for the Walter S. Johnson Foundation, a California nonprofit that funds education, leadership, and economic development programs for youth and families. She served as a program officer for evaluation and was responsible for improving the

Catherine M. Casserly.

efficacy of education, school-to-career, and youth development grants. She also tutored in a high-security prison and served as a trustee for the San Mateo County Board of Education from 1997 to 2000.

Casserly worked as a policy analyst for SRI International, directing and participating in research projects related to the quality of education and training services targeting economically disadvantaged youth and adults. In 2001, she joined the William and Flora Hewlett Foundation as a program consultant with the education program. In that position, she was primarily responsible for technology-based grants in the area of open content. She became director of the foundation's Open Educational Resources initiative. As director, she managed investments totaling more than $100 million. In April 2009, she was named the first full-time senior partner at the Carnegie Foundation for the Advancement of Teaching. Her responsibilities at the Carnegie Foundation included new program initiatives and managing the strategic direction of Carnegie's work in open

educational resources. With the extended Carnegie team she launched a continuous performance improvement system to create alternative mathematics pathways for community college students.

LIFE'S WORK
In January 2010, Casserly was elected to the board of directors of Creative Commons, a nonprofit organization that promotes the sharing of intellectual works and provides licenses whereby owners can share their art, music, photographs, research, and other work within existing copyright laws. A decade of work at the William and Flora Hewlett Foundation and the Carnegie Foundation had established her as an advocate of open educational resources (OER). These are teaching, learning, and research resources that reside in the public domain or have been released under an intellectual-property license that permits their free use or repurposing by others. Such resources include full courses, course materials, modules, textbooks,

---

Affiliation: Creative Commons

Creative Commons is a nonprofit organization with the purpose of simplifying the legal, free exchange of knowledge and culture in the new digital environment created by the Internet. The organization was established in 2001 with the support of the Center for the Public Domain, the John D. and Catherine T. MacArthur Foundation, and the William and Flora Hewlett Foundation. Recognizing that the owners of creative works generally were forced to choose between the "all rights reserved" model of full copyright and the surrender of all rights by placing works in the public domain, Creative Commons set out to provide options that would encourage the sharing of materials for use and collaborative reuse while reserving some rights for the original creators. In 2002, the organization released its first licenses. By the next year, approximately 1 million licenses were in use. By 2012, more than 400 million Creative Commons–licensed works were available on the Internet, from music and photographs to research findings, full-length novels, and complete college courses.

The six Creative Commons licenses allow the creators to specify the limits under which their work can be used. All six are combinations of four fundamental provisions: attribution (BY), which requires that the author of the work be acknowledged by anyone who uses the work in any way; noncommercial (NC), which

allows for reuse but specifies that the resulting work cannot be used to make money; no derivatives (ND), which permits redistribution but forbids alteration of the original work; and share alike (SA), which requires that any derivative work be licensed in exactly the same way as the original.

Creative Commons is based in the United States, but it is global in its reach. More than one hundred affiliates work in more than seventy countries, from Argentina to Vietnam, to support and promote Creative Commons' activities. Flickr was among the first online communities to incorporate Creative Commons' licensing options, and by 2012 more than 200 million images on the site fell under Creative Commons licenses. Perhaps more surprising has been the adoption of Creative Commons licensing by commercial enterprises. In 2003, Cory Doctorow became the first writer to use a Creative Commons license to release a freely sharable e-book version of a commercially released novel, *Down and Out in the Magic Kingdom*, the same day it became available in stores. The rock group Nine Inch Nails released their Grammy-nominated Ghosts I–IV under a Creative Commons BY, NC, SA license in 2008. Both Doctorow and Nine Inch Nails followed their initial releases with the release of other Creative Commons–licensed material.

streaming videos, tests, software, and any other tools, materials, and techniques used to support access to knowledge or that have an impact on teaching, learning, and research. As program officer at the Hewlett Foundation, which funded Creative Commons from its inception, Casserly has been involved with the organization at some level from its beginning. Serving on the Creative Commons board offered her an opportunity to use her experience in the OER movement worldwide. She received the President's Award for OpenCourseWare Excellence for her work in developing the open educational resources program at the Hewlett Foundation in March 2011. That month, she was named CEO of Creative Commons.

As CEO, Casserly speaks frequently at conferences, addressing the topic of open resources and explaining opening licensing. She argues that the infrastructure provided by Creative Commons is critical in promoting innovation and collaboration, particularly within the context of education. In June 2011, the Association of Educational Publishers and Creative Commons announced a partnership to improve search results online through the creation of a metadata framework specifically for learning resources. Casserly expects that the framework will enable educators and students to more efficiently and effectively and discover the resources they need, including those they can reuse under Creative Commons' licensing. This partnership marks the first joint effort by traditional content companies and free, open content sites.

During her tenure as CEO of Creative Commons, Casserly has seen more than four million YouTube videos made available for use through the Creative Commons' attribution license, which essentially allows the videos to be edited and changed for use in other projects as long as the original creator is credited. By the end of 2011, Flickr hosted more than 2 million photographs licensed by Creative Commons.

PERSONAL LIFE

Casserly has served on the board of directors of Startl, a social enterprise committed to accelerating the growth of digital innovations for all levels of education, and Peer-2-Peer University, a grassroots open education project. She has also served on advisory committees for MIT OpenCourseWare and the University of the

People. The latter awarded her an honorary doctorate in 2012.

Wylene Rholetter

FURTHER READING

Bitton, Miriam. "Modernizing Copyright Law." *Texas Intellectual Property Law Journal* 20.1 (2011): 65–114. *Academic Search Premier*. Web. 24 May 2012. The article examines copyright law in the United States in 2011. Among the topics discussed are the increase in piracy of copyrighted material and the regulation of Creative Commons licenses.

Casserly, Catherine M., and Marshall S. Smith. "Revolutionizing Education through Innovation: Can Openness Transform Teaching and Learning?" *Opening Up Education: The Collective Advancement of Education through Open Technology, Open Content, and Open Knowledge*. Ed. Toru Iiyoshi and M. S. Vijay Kumer. Cambridge: MIT, 2008. 261–76. Print. In this collection of essays by leaders in open education, Casserly and Smith describe the open education work funded by the William and Flora Hewlett Foundation.

Gordon-Murnane, Laura. "Creative Commons: Copyright Tools for the 21st Century." *Online* 34.1 (2010): 18–21. *Academic Search Premier*. Web. 24 May 2012. Describes Creative Commons licenses and discusses the protection they provide in the 21st century, the changing content of public domain, and the potential problems libraries may experience.

"Interest in Open Educational Resources Grows." *Electronic Education Report* 15.19 (2008): 1–4. *Academic Search Premier*. Web. 24 May 2012. Focuses on recent revisions to copyright law in the United States and the ways the Internet has affected the use, reuse, and distribution of digital content. Also looks at how Creative Commons initiated a new kind of copyright protection.

Smith, Marshall S., and Catherine M. Casserly. "The Promise of Open Educational Resources." *Change* 38.5 (2006): 8–17. *Academic Search Premier*. Web. 24 May 2012. Defines open educational sources and looks at the increased interest in such sources in the United States. Casserly, representing the William and Flora Hewlett Foundation, comments on open textbooks and their effects on cost and quality.

VINTON CERF

Developer of the Internet

Born: June 23, 1943; New Haven, Connecticut
Died: -
Primary Field: Internet
Specialty: Applications
Primary Company/Organization: Defense Advanced
    Research Projects Agency

INTRODUCTION

Acknowledged as one of the fathers of the Internet,
Vinton Cerf was involved both with the development
of the transmission-control protocol/Internet protocol
(TCP/IP) used by the Internet and other networks and
with the first Internet-compatible commercial e-mail.
Additionally, he helped form and eventually chaired
the Internet Corporation for Assigned Names and
Numbers (ICANN), which coordinates Internet domain
names, IP addresses, name servers, and registries, and
he has worked as an executive for Google since 2005.

EARLY LIFE

Vinton Gray "Vint" Cerf was born in New Haven, Connecticut, on June 23, 1943, the son of aerospace executive Vinton Thurston Cerf and Muriel Gray. He attended
Stanford University, earning a bachelor's degree in
mathematics, and the University of California at Los
Angeles (UCLA), earning his master of science degree
in 1970 and his doctorate in 1972. Between his undergraduate and graduate studies, he worked for IBM as
part of the team that developed QUIKTRAN, an offshoot of IBM's Fortran programming language.

As a graduate student at UCLA, Cerf met Robert
E. Kahn, with whom he now shares the title of "father
of the Internet." Cerf and Kahn both worked on ARPA-
NET, the Defense Department's precursor to the Internet, while at UCLA. Kahn was tasked with working on
its architecture, while Cerf helped develop its communications protocol, the network control protocol (NCP),
and was part of Leonard Kleinrock's team connecting
ARPANET's first two nodes. NCP created connections
between ARPANET computers using the ARPANET
host-to-host protocol, which set the procedures for uni-
directional data streams, and the initial connection protocol, which established procedures for bidirectional
streams between processes. Specific applications for file
transfers and electronic mail were built on top of Cerf's
NCP.

LIFE'S WORK

After earning his doctorate at UCLA, Cerf returned
to Stanford to teach in 1972. As an assistant professor, he worked with Kahn again, designing the TCP/
IP for the Defense Department. The Defense Advanced
Research Projects Agency (DARPA) had begun ARPA-
NET, a distributed network that would eventually develop into the Internet, in 1969 and remained interested
in developing data transmission methodologies. Kahn
had taken a job with DARPA's Information Processing
Techniques Office at the same time that Cerf accepted
the Stanford position, and the following year Cerf was
invited to work on the generation of network protocols
to succeed NCP.

In the first few months during which Cerf and Kahn
worked out the broad strokes of what they wanted from
the new protocol: a protocol that put the burden of reliability on the individual hosts rather than on the network (as with NCP) and that used an internetwork protocol that would render irrelevant differences between
network protocols, allowing for a vast expansion of

Vinton Cerf.

ARPANET. Because this new set of protocols was rigorously simple and focused on data transmission and routing—the direction of packets of data traveling through the network, by and through a computer called a router (Cerf and Kahn called it a gateway)—the protocols could be used to connect any network to DARPA without compatibility conflicts.

In 1974, Cerf finished the TCP, the foundation for the suite of protocols commonly called TCP/IP now, or the Internet protocol suite. TCP provides the transport layer of the network, where host-to-host communication transpires, whereas the link layer consists of the communication among the nodes of a local network and the application layer on top of all the network layers handles protocol for specific applications such as web browsers and e-mail. Versions of the TCP/IP were developed for different hardware by various university research teams, and various TCP/IP demonstrations and tests were conducted throughout the rest of the decade. On January 1, 1983—ARPANET's "flag day" (the industry term for a sizable switchover of software or protocols)—ARPANET converted over to TCP/IP. The protocol was promoted much more aggressively than NCP had been, in part because of its strengths and in part because of the changes to the computer industry over the previous decade. The first annual Interop conference was held in 1985 to promote TCP/IP in the interest of network interoperability; attendees at Interop I included IBM and Digital Equipment Corporation (DEC), two of the largest computer manufacturers of the time. Both adopted TCP/IP as their standard, abandoning the network protocols they had developed internally. The widespread adoption of TCP/IP was similar to that of Fortran, the programming language originally developed for IBM computers, which was useful enough and popular enough that competing manufacturers adopted it in place of their own internally developed languages.

By TCP/IP's flag day, Cerf had finished his work with DARPA, which he had left Stanford to join in 1976. He left DARPA in 1982 for a vice presidency of architecture and technology at MCI Digital Information Services. As vice president, he directed the engineering team that created MCI Mail, the first commercial e-mail service connected to the Internet. MCI Mail was introduced in 1983, the same year the Internet migrated to TCP/IP, and the service was offered for another twenty years. Users of MCI Mail could send e-mails to other MCI Mail users, telex machines (teletypewriters

that transmitted text messages across telephone lines, both a precursor to and eventually replaced by today's e-mail), and even postal addresses. MCI Mail services would print out messages sent to postal addresses and mail them at a fee of $1 to $2 per page. For an extra fee, postal mail could be sent overnight or within a four-hour window, if the destination was in one of several major cities (including Honolulu and Brussels briefly, and Washington, D.C., where the service was first introduced). A message sent by four-hour delivery was printed out at an MCI facility in the city of its destination rather than traveling through the mail. In the early 1980s, the appeal of the postal component of the service was the quality of printing offered, at a time when laser printers were new and would for years remain unaffordable for anyone with only moderate printing needs. More affordable dot-matrix printers, in comparison, were too low-resolution to be appropriate for formal business use.

MCI Mail also added the ability to send faxes and soon allowed users to send e-mail to non-MCI addresses. First compatibility was offered with the X.400 protocol, which included about twenty-five different e-mail services that were introduced in MCI Mail's wake; then full Internet access was available with mcimail.com addresses.

Cerf left MCI in 1986 to work for the Corporation for National Research Initiatives, before returning to MCI in 1994, where he stayed until 2005 and was instrumental in helping the company capitalize on the growing popularity of the Internet and the dot-com boom.

In 1999, Cerf joined the board of the Internet Corporation for Assigned Names and Numbers (ICANN), where he remained until 2007. He had been instrumental in forming the Los Angeles–based nonprofit, which took over certain Internet-related tasks from the federal government, mainly those pertaining to IP addresses, regional Internet registries, domain-name space, and root name servers. As chair of ICANN, Cerf developed the Domain Name System (DNS) policy; during his watch new top-level domains—including .eu, .asia, and .cat—were introduced.

Since 2005, Cerf has worked as Google's chief Internet evangelist (and a vice president), and has enjoyed a good deal of public exposure as one of the nation's most prominent futurists, delivering talks on the future of television, artificial intelligence, conservation, and the further development of Internet protocols.

Affiliation: MCI

MCI began as Microwave Communications, Inc., on October 3, 1963. Initially the company built microwave relay stations that allowed communication between two-way radios used by truckers along Route 66, between Chicago and St Louis. Further communication services were planned for business customers as an alternative to the expensive services offered by AT&T.

MCI's expansions were delayed by AT&T's rule prohibiting private two-way radio connections to a telephone network, a rule struck down by the Federal Communications Commission in 1968, now allowing non-AT&T companies meeting the right technical standards to connect to the telephone network and ending AT&T's monopoly on that technology. MCI responded by planning a nationwide microwave relay system, with AT&T fighting its attempts to be licensed every step of the way. AT&T's efforts slowed MCI but not stop it.

At the time, AT&T had a monopoly on telephone service, which the federal government had permitted. MCI eventually relocated its headquarters to Washington, D.C., because of the need for frequent meetings with legislators, regulators, and industry lobbyists. It filed an antitrust suit against AT&T in 1974, which resulted in the breakup of Ma Bell (AT&T, based on its former name American Bell Telephone Company, had been known) into the "baby Bells," smaller regional companies. AT&T's monopoly was ended, and other companies were now able to compete. MCI quickly became the second-largest long-distance carrier in the country, not only opening the industry to competition but also pioneering many forms of that communication, such as the Friends and Family loyalty program (as an incentive for customers to leave AT&T or Sprint) and the 1-800-COLLECT dial-around service.

In addition to phone services, MCI pioneered commercial telecommunications applications, including MCI Mail, offered in 1983 to customers with modems, allowing them to send e-mails, telex messages, faxes, or postal mail printed out and mailed at MCI Mail printing centers. MCI was the first company to apply for a license to offer satellite-based communications, which it used to launch the Comsat Corporation, a joint venture with Lockheed. It also was the first to use single-mode fiber-optic cable in its telecommunications networks.

A 1980s partnership with the academic community led to the National Science Foundation Network (NSF-NET), a TCP/IP-using computer network using MCI's high-speed connections and university computers under the oversight of the National Science Foundation. This was the missing link between ARPANET and the modern Internet, and the MCI network became part of the global Internet backbone.

MCI was bought by WorldCom in 1998, and in 2006 its corporate descendant was purchased by Verizon Communications, becoming the Verizon Business division.

PERSONAL LIFE

Cerf married his wife, Sigrid, in 1966. The couple have two children, David and Bennett Cerf (not to be confused with the late Random House publisher), and enjoy cooking and wine tasting. Cerf is hard of hearing and has been active in advocacy for the deaf and hard-of-hearing community; his activities have included supporting funding for computers to assist hearing-impaired students.

Cerf has received sixteen honorary degrees from institutions in ten countries, honors from numerous foreign countries (including Sweden and Japan), the National Medal of Technology (1997), and the Presidential Medal of Freedom (2005).

Bill Kte'pi

FURTHER READING

British Computing Society. *Leaders in Computing*. London: BCS, 2011. Print. A collection of interviews, including a lengthy one with Cerf.

Ceruzzi, Paul E. *Computing: A Concise History*. 2nd ed. Cambridge: MIT, 2012. Print. A broad overview of Internet history, including Cerf's contributions.

Hafner, Katie. *Where Wizards Stay Up Late: The Origins of the Internet*. New York: Simon, 1998. Print. An early history of the Internet, with good coverage of its origins and antecedents, including Cerf's involvement both at DARPA and MCI.

Wu, Tim. *The Master Switch: The Rise and Fall of Information Empires*. New York: Vintage, 2011. Print. An account of the Internet's rise from a broad historical perspective.

STEVEN CHEN

Cofounder and former CTO of YouTube

Born: August, 1978; Taipei, Taiwan
Died: -
Primary Field: Computer science
Specialty: Internet
Primary Company/Organization: YouTube

INTRODUCTION

Steven Chen, a former PayPal employee, cofounded YouTube with his partners Chad Hurley and Jawed Karim in 2005. Since its inception, YouTube has become the most popular video-sharing site on the Internet and the third most popular website in the world, following Google and Facebook. In 2006, Chen sold YouTube to Google and has since founded AVOS Systems, which owns the popular bookmarking site Delicious.com (formerly del.icio.us) and in 2012 was launching a new online magazine publication site, Zeen.com.

EARLY LIFE

Born in Taipei, Taiwan, in August 1978, Steven Chen immigrated to the United States with his parents when he was fifteen years old. The Chen family settled in suburban Chicago, Illinois, and Steven finished his secondary education at both John Hersey High School in Arlington Heights and the Illinois Mathematics and Science Academy. He was a talented student who earned money after school working at a local 7-11 store. After graduation, he attended college at the University of Illinois at Urbana-Champaign, where he studied computer science until his classmate, PayPal cofounder Max Levchin, offered him a job at the fledgling e-payment site.

LIFE'S WORK

Chen worked at PayPal as a software developer from 1999 until 2005. At PayPal, Chen served primarily as a programmer, and had a reputation for delivering code quickly, though usually by taking unorthodox shortcuts, which, while effective, caused confusion among his peers. For the last two years of his career at PayPal, Chen worked to launch PayPal in China, and eventually left the company in 2005.

In 2005, Chen, along with partners Chad Hurley and Jawed Karim, started YouTube.com with an $11.5 million venture capital grant from Sequoia Capital. The popular and often repeated version of the website's conception begins with a dinner party in Chen's San Francisco apartment (though Chen has stated that the popular story is probably a slightly romantic and marketable exaggeration). The guests took a number of videos at the event but had no easy way to share them in the same way that people were able to share photographs through sites such as Myspace and Flickr.

This discussion led to an exploration of video-sharing and hosting technologies. Ultimately, the trio decided that Adobe Flash was the optimal file format and that the site would be coded in HTM15. While designing and coding the site, Chen briefly worked at the then-fledgling Facebook as a senior software engineer, but he left within a few months to pursue YouTube full time. YouTube operated as an open beta beginning in April 2005 and formally launched in November of 2005. Initially, Chen and his cofounders paid for the venture with their own credit cards, but prior contacts at PayPal connected Chen and his partners with investors at Sequoia Capital, a prominent tech investing firm, which seeded the venture with $3.5 million to cover start-up costs.

Steven Chen.

The website was immediately popular. Users appreciated the extremely simple user interface, diverse content, and peer-review community. This popularity engendered another round of capital funding from Sequoia in April 2006, when the firm put up another $8 million.

For all its popularity, the website has struggled for profitability, in large because of the founders' resistance to intrusive advertising. Chen has rejected so-called pre-roll advertising (advertisements that load in-window before the user can play a selected video) as intrusive and unwelcome; only reluctantly did he accede (in January 2006) to the introduction of any ads at all—and then only out of financial necessity.

Within one year, more than one million videos had been posted to YouTube, and sixty-five thousand were being uploaded every day. Although the site was undeniably successful as an Internet entity, this success led to numerous copyright issues, notably in February 2006, when users began uploading the popular but copyrighted *Saturday Night Live* digital short "Lazy Sunday." This resulted in an informal take-down request from NBC (the company that produces *Saturday Night Live*), with which Chen and YouTube complied. YouTube does not prescreen content, but it does go beyond the requirements of the Digital Millennium Copyright Act compliance by stating in the site's upload instructions that users should not post pirated or otherwise copyright-infringing videos.

In October 2006, the Ohio machinery company Universal Tube and Rollform Equipment Corporation initiated a lawsuit against YouTube. The popularity of YouTube was causing unwelcome surplus traffic to Universal's website, the similarly named utube.com. The conflict was settled in 2007, when Universal changed its domain to utubeonline.com and withdrew its opposition with the U.S. Patent and Trademark Office.

Chen and cofounder Hurley sold YouTube to Google for $1.65 billion, making Chen a multimillionaire virtually overnight. Chen was also employed by Google as chief technology officer of the site he created, which allowed him to maintain some control over the direction and technology of the site as it evolved.

After Google's purchase of YouTube, copyright liability became a pressing concern for the now consolidated company. Numerous copyright infringement lawsuits were filed by major media production companies, including Lions Gate Entertainment and Viacom, resulting in YouTube's being compelled to limit user-uploaded videos to those with a duration of no more than ten minutes; this limit was later relaxed to fifteen minutes. Chen oversaw this implementation and contributed to the creation of several marketing and publication

---

Affiliation: YouTube

Founded in 2005 by Steven Chen, Chad Hurley, and Jawed Karim (three former PayPal employees), YouTube quickly became the Internet's most popular video-sharing site: In 2011, the website had more than one trillion views, and users watched more than eight billion hours of video every month. The website utilizes Adobe Flash to display its content and is the third most popular website on the Internet, following only Google and Facebook.

YouTube initially started as a user-based media-sharing site but has since been embraced by major media and content producers such as the television networks NBC, CBS, and ABC; by music labels such as Sony, Warner Music Group, and Universal Music Group; and by countless other small media production companies that run their own video series, or "channels," on the site.

When YouTube originally debuted, users could upload unlimited content, but this changed in 2006, when analysis revealed that users were posting unlicensed copies of movies and television shows to the site. This resulted in a ten-minute length restriction, which was raised to fifteen minutes in July 2010. Trusted users may be invited to upload videos up to twelve hours in length upon account confirmation.

Although highly successful, the site has not been without its controversies: notably, ongoing disputes concerning intellectual property and copyright infringement and controversial or prohibited material. YouTube is blocked or censored, or has been blocked or censored, in a number of countries, including Morocco, Thailand, Iran, Pakistan, and most infamously China (which has issued an outright ban of the site for all Chinese users).

In 2006, Chen (along with YouTube cofounder and business partner Hurley) sold YouTube to the search engine company Google for $1.65 billion in stock. Under Google, YouTube continues to be the most popular video site on the Internet and the third most popular website of all time. According to a 2008 *New York Times* report, YouTube consumes more bandwidth in one year than the entire Internet did in 2000.

partnerships with large media firms that began uploading copyrighted content on approved terms.

Chen stayed on as chief technology officer of YouTube until 2008 but continued to work with Google until 2009 in various capacities. Although he still consults with the search giant, he founded a new company with YouTube cofounder Hurley, AVOS Systems, in 2011. He also purchased Tap 11, a social analytics company in May 2011. One month later, Chen's AVOS purchased the long-running bookmarking site Delicious (formerly del.icio.us) from search engine provider Yahoo! Delicious had been floundering under Yahoo, losing visitors and struggling to find a purpose. Chen expressed an interest in the site's potential, which led to the buyout.

Chen continues at the helm of AVOS Systems and is in the process of revitalizing Delicious. The company is also in the process of launching Zeen.com, an online magazine production site, and in 2011 AVOS launched MeiWei.fm, a Chinese-language sister site to Delicious, which allows East Asian users to bookmark and share content.

In April 2012, Chen and AVOS systems secured Series A funding from a number of investors and venture capitalists, including Innovation Works, Madrone Capital, and Google Ventures (which Chen helped to found). Chen maintains an office at AVOS's U.S. headquarters in San Mateo, California, although the company also has offices in Dunedin, New Zealand, and Beijing, China. Chen has described AVOS as a development laboratory, a space in which he and Hurley can freely explore new projects and possibilities.

PERSONAL LIFE

Chen Lives in San Francisco, California, and continues to oversee operations at his start-up company, AVOS Systems. He has received numerous nominations and honors: He was named one of *Business 2.0*'s 50 Most Influential People one of *GQ* magazine's men of the year in 2006, as well as one of *Fortune* magazine's most powerful people in business.

Vytautas Malesh

FURTHER READING

AVOS Systems. "Home Page." 2011. Web. 1 Aug. 2012. The home page of Steven Chen's start-up, AVOS systems, describing the company's mission statement, funding history, and new projects.

Cloud, John. "The YouTube Gurus." *Time* 25 Dec. 2006: n. pag. Web. 30 July 2012. Time magazine's lengthy profile of YouTube cocreators Chen and Hurley covers both men's education and professional histories and includes brief personality descriptions and speculation on the future of YouTube after the Google buyout.

Grossman, Lev. "The People's Network." *Time International* (Canada edition): n. pag. 13 Nov. 2006: 42–45. Print. 31 July 2012. Grossman analyzes the factors that made YouTube a success: Web2.0 socialization, a popular fatigue with "top-down culture," and a collective need for a visually stimulating creative outlet.

Levy, Steven. "Now on GooTube: The Price Is Right." *Newsweek* 23 Oct. 2006. Print. This article analyzes Google's purchase of YouTube in the context of a profitability outlook and with regard to ongoing copyright disputes between Google/YouTube and media conglomerates such as CBS, Universal, and Sony.

Miles, Beckett. "Chad Hurley and Steven Chen." *Time International* (Canada edition) 14 May 2007: 86. Print. 31 July 2012. A short writeup penned by the creator of the YouTube sensation "Lonelygirl15," which concisely describes the impact of YouTube on popular culture.

Smalera, Paul. "YouTube Cofounder Quits CTO Post: No One Notices." *BusinessInsider.com* 30 June 2009: n. pag. Web. 1 Aug. 2012. This brief article makes mention of Chen's departure from YouTube, clarifying that Chen's departure did not create a formal vacancy and linking to the Chen portions of Chen and Hurley's Google buyout announcement.

"Steve Chen and Chad Hurley." *Encyclopedia of World Biographies*. Advameg, Inc. Web. 31 July 2012. A thorough biography of YouTube cofounders Chen and Hurley from 1978 to 2006, including information on education, early life, and the founding and sale of YouTube.com.

"YouTube Co-founder Steve Chen Leaves Company but Remains with Google." *International Business Times.com* 30 June 2009: n. pag. Web. 30 July 2012. This short article describes Chen's departure from YouTube and is noteworthy for embedding Chen and Hurley's video announcement regarding the sale of YouTube to Google in 2006.

"YouTube.com Site Info." *Alexa*. Amazon.com. Web. 1 Aug. 2012. This is web page shows current and live-updated traffic and usage statistics for YouTube.com.

"YouTube's Chad Hurley and Steven Chen Bookmark Delicious." *Forbes* 27 Apr. 2011: 65. Print. A *Forbes* magazine article (also available at Forbes.com) announcing the purchase of bookmarking site Delicious by Chen's company AVOS Systems.

DAVID CLARK

Former chairman of the Internet Architecture Board

Born: April 7, 1944; Concord, Massachusetts
Died: -
Primary Field: Internet
Specialty: Ethics and policy
Primary Company/Organization: Internet Architecture Board

INTRODUCTION

In the twenty-first century, David Clark is considered one of the Internet's elder statesmen. The former chief protocol architect of the Internet, he headed the Internet Architecture Board for most of the 1980s, overseeing the transitional period after the early days of the Defense Advanced Research Projects Agency (DARPA) and before the inception of the World Wide Web.

EARLY LIFE

David Dana Clark was born on April 7, 1944, in Concord, Massachusetts. He attended Swarthmore College, graduating with distinction in 1966 with a bachelor of science degree in electrical engineering. In 1969, he earned a master's degree in electrical engineering and computer science from the Massachusetts Institute of Technology (MIT). Four years later, he earned a doctoral degree in electrical engineering and computer science from MIT. His thesis was titled "An Input/Output Architecture for Virtual Memory Computer Systems."

During his graduate studies, Clark worked on the Multics project, which was a time-sharing operating system that is perhaps most famous as something of a precursor to Unix. It was initially the product of a joint venture between MIT, General Electric (GE), and Bell Laboratories (Bell Labs); Bell Labs pulled out in 1969, and the Bell Labs programmers who had been working on Multics switched their attention to a new operating system that became Unix, retaining some of the Multics conventions but none of its basic design. Multics, in fact, was intended as a commercial endeavor for GE, which wanted to offer a computing-power utility similar to other utilities, such as water, electricity, and gas; a computing-power utility would supply rented time on a powerful computer accessed remotely. From today's perspective, that GE was interested in spending years developing this plan says something about how abruptly the personal computer revolution began: Barely a decade after Multics started, the notion of marketing com-

puter time was superseded by the purchase of personal computers that would become more powerful than envisioned at the time. The computing-power utility model would never become a successful commercial operation, and Multics would be put to different uses. The work on Multics was sophisticated, however, and it introduced the first hierarchical file system. It was also the first major operating system designed with security in mind.

After finishing his Ph.D., Clark continued to work at MIT in the Laboratory for Computer Science, which today is the MIT Computer Science and Artificial Intelligence Laboratory. He joined the TCP development team in 1975.

LIFE'S WORK

TCP stands for transmission-control protocol, which along with the Internet protocol forms the TCP/IP suite, the core protocols of the Internet. TCP is used by e-mail, the World Wide Web, and file transfer programs—the applications that function on the transport layer of the

David Clark.

Internet (while IP is the communications protocol, routing packets from network to network). TCP works with IP, detecting problems such as lost, improperly ordered, and duplicated packets (data in the form of sequences of octets, preceded by a header describing the destination).

In a 1981 paper that he wrote with Jerome H. Saltzer and David P. Reed, Clark defined the end-to-end principle, which is the principle that communications protocol operations should be defined at the end points of the communications system. Internet architecture soon adopted the principle.

From 1981 to 1989, Clark served as the Internet's chief protocol architect and chaired the Internet Activities Board, predecessor to the Internet Architecture Board (IAB). The IAB is the steering committee that guides the development of Internet protocols. After his term as chair ended, he was the first head of the Internet Research Task Force (IRTF), a body of the IAB charged with long-term research issues (as opposed to the older Internet Engineering Task Force (IETF), which concerns itself with shorter-term issues such as developing Internet standards).

In 1991, Clark resigned from the IAB to pursue the advanced research that has occupied him since. He has performed considerable research in support for very large, very fast networks and methods to support real-time Internet traffic. He has also focused on the coming "post-PC" era and networking issues concerning mobile Internet-enabled devices, Internet-enabled appliances, and embedded computers. In his work with protocol overhead, he has helped develop a new set of protocol organization principles for high-performance systems.

Clark is also known for his talks on the future of the Internet. He has raised concerns about Internet security and the necessity of the redesign of the Internet's architecture. The variety and quantity of Internet applications have increased to a degree utterly unlike any foreseen by its designers, and as various technologies such as wireless devices and peer-to-peer protocols were developed, their developers incorporated patches and workarounds to make them possible. Incremental changes and home-brewed solutions have been wrought on what is now an old architecture. This ad hoc growth has resulted in an increasing amount of resources being spent patching holes instead of moving forward. What was once a relatively simple if decentralized communications technology has become convoluted and, in Clark's view, increasingly fragile. He has called for a rethinking of the Internet's basic architecture, with a view toward

---

Affiliation: Internet Architecture Board

The Internet Architecture Board (IAB) oversees the development of the protocols of the Internet. It began as the Internet Configuration Board in 1979, and was created by the U.S. Defense Department's Defense Advanced Research Projects Agency (DARPA). It has been renamed several times: to the Internet Advisory Board in 1984, the Internet Activities Board in 1986, and the Internet Architecture Board in 1992. The 1992 renaming was part of a transition to making the Internet an intergovernmental entity rather than a tool solely of the American government, and concurrent with that renaming was the founding of the nonprofit Internet Society (ISOC), headquartered in Geneva, Switzerland, and Washington, D.C., with chapters throughout the world. ISOC provides a forum for collaboration and discussion among Internet-concerned organizations and to promote the Internet and its evolution; IAB oversees ISOC.

IAB is charged with oversight of the Internet's architecture; managing the Request for Comments (RFC) series; overseeing the development of Internet standards; administering the Internet Engineering Task Force (IETF) protocol parameter values in collaboration with the Internet Corporation for Assigned Names and Numbers; guiding ISOC; confirming the IETF chair and Internet Engineering Steering Group (IESG) area directors; and selecting the chair to the Internet Research Task Force (IRTF). There are two special task forces: the IRTF, which focuses on long-term issues, and the IETF, which deals with short-term issues and the development of standards. The IRTF includes the RFC editor, who edits the requests for comments series.

David Clark was the first chairman of the IAB, serving until 1989 and succeeded by Vint Cerf (1989–91), Lyman Chapin (1991–93), Christian Huitema (1993–95), Brian Carpenter (1995–2000), John Klensin (2000–02), Leslie Daigle (2002–07), Olaf Kolkman (2007–11), and Bernard Aboba (as of 2011).

---

actual implementation, not merely impressive hypothetical designs. In 2006, Clark was a vocal advocate of the National Science Foundation's plan to do just that. Redesigning the architecture could incorporate what is now known about Internet traffic, prepare for scaling in ways the original designers were not in a position to do, and perhaps offer better protection from botnets, spam, viruses, and distributed denial-of-service attacks.

Clark identified four goals for the new design: security, including a way of authenticating both users and computers; protocols, such as better routing agreements between Internet service providers so that everyone benefits from a more efficient Internet; instrumentation, the requirement that every component of the Internet be able to report problems to an administrator; and mobility, specifically the assignment of IP addresses to mobile devices of all sorts in order to ensure network security.

Clark has also pointed out a compelling truth about the Internet in the twenty-first century: The rise of video, both streaming and downloaded, will change everything. In the United States, flat-fee Internet service billing quickly became the standard for nonbusiness customers. That model has survived long enough that the public is accustomed to it, but it was adopted when most forms of Internet usage were roughly equal in their resource consumption; even early exceptions to the flat-fee model, after all, charged by the hour, not by the byte. While BitTorrent and other file-sharing programs created a class of resource-intensive users, they have remained a small, if impactful, portion of the demographic. Video files, however, are much larger even than audio files and moreover have become mainstream; indeed, Netflix streaming movies, Hulu, and YouTube are popular among even "light" users of the Internet, who may access little else. As much as it is painful to accept and unpopular for service providers to admit, the "all-you-can-eat" pricing model has become untenable.

Clark has worked as a consultant for a number of companies, including Openroute, Inc. (1984–99), Bellcore (1994–95), MCI (1994–96), Time Warner Cable (1997–98), and Hewlett-Packard Labs (1997–99), and he has served on the advisory committees of Nexabit (1988–99), Broadband Access Systems (1999–2000), AT&T (1999–2001), Invisible Worlds (1998–2001), Chiaro Networks (starting in 2000), and Telcordia (starting in 1998). He is a previous chairman of the Computer Science and Telecommunications Board of the National Academies. He is a fellow of both the Institute of Electrical and Electronics Engineers (IEEE) and the Association for Computing Machinery (ACM).

Today, Clark is a senior research scientist at the MIT Computer Science and Artificial Intelligence Laboratory, leading the Advanced Network Architecture group. He is also the codirector of the MIT Communications Futures Program and the networking series editor for Morgan Kaufmann Publishers. Clark has said that the primary benefit of the Internet is its ability to connect people and to connect people to information. He believes that the primary Internet issue concerns how to police and control the bad elements on the Internet without impeding or impairing the good elements.

PERSONAL LIFE
Clark is a Monty Python fan. His sense of fun may be reflected in the fact that a colleague once hung a sign on the door of his office, identifying it as the office of Albus Dumbledore, the Hogwarts headmaster and wise sage of the Harry Potter novels. The Oxford Internet Institute presented Clark with its Lifetime Achievement Award in 2011.

Bill Kte'pi

FURTHER READING
Carpenter, Brian, ed. *Charter of the Internet Architecture Board.* RFC 2850. N.p.: The Internet Society, 2000. Web. Internet Engineering Task Force. 12 July 2012. The central document of the IAB, setting out the committee's rules and responsibilities.

Clark, David. "An Input/Output Architecture for Virtual Memory Computer Systems." Ph.D. dissertation, Project MAC Technical Report 117, Jan. 1974. Print. Clark's dissertation on memory architecture.

---. "The Internet Is Broken." Interview by David Talbot. *Technology Review* Dec. 2005/Jan. 2006: n. pag. Print. Clark discusses his views on the problems with twenty-first century Internet architecture.

---. "A Taxonomy of Internet Telephony Applications." *Telephony, the Internet, and the Media.* Ed. J. Mackie-Mason and D. Waterman. Mahwah: Erlbaum, 1999. Print. Clark's chapter outlining classifications of telephony applications for the Internet, many of which have become commonplace.

---, Karen Sollins, John Wroclawski, and Ted Faber. *Addressing Reality: An Architectural Response to Real-World Demands on the Evolving Internet.* ACM's Special Interest Group on Data Communication (SIGCOMM) 2003 Workshops, August 25 and 27, 2003. *Daedalus* 140.4 (2011). Print. A special issue devoted to cyberpsace security and privacy, guest edited by Clark.

McKnight, L. W., W. Lehr, and D. D. Clark, eds. *Internet Telephony.* Cambridge: MIT, 2001. Print. Covers the integration of voice and data services for students and professionals.

JAMES H. CLARK

Cofounder of Netscape

Born: March 23, 1944; Plainview, Texas
Died: -
Primary Field: Computer science
Specialty: Internet
Primary Company/Organization: Netscape Communications

INTRODUCTION

James H. Clark is a legendary Silicon Valley technology innovator and entrepreneur. He used his research on computer graphics as an engineering professor at Stanford University to develop powerful new computer chips to render three-dimensional computer images in real time and thus has been dubbed by some as the "father of computer graphics." He founded Silicon Graphics, Inc. (SGI) in the early 1980s to commercialize this technology and thereby revolutionized visual production of movies, videos, and scientific imaging. In the mid-1990s, he left SGI and partnered with Marc Andreessen to found Netscape Communications to commercialize a graphical web browser. Netscape Navigator, as it was ultimately called, simplified use of the Internet with a graphical point-and-click interface that helped launch the Internet revolution. Clark also pioneered the Silicion Valley venture capital model that became the hallmark of the dot-com boom of the late 1990s. Clark went on to invest in a cadre of new web start-ups, such as myCFO, Shutterfly, and Healtheon, which he merged with WebMD in the early 2000s to create one of the most widely visited health information portals on the web. Clark has become a legend in Silicon Valley and a billionaire because of his technological prescience in recognizing promising new technical advances and his entrepreneurial skills in commercializing them.

EARLY LIFE

James H. Clark was born on March 23, 1944, in Plainview, Texas, and had a difficult childhood that included an alcoholic father, the divorce of his parents when he was fourteen, and abject poverty thereafter as his mother struggled to support the family. Clark was recognized as bright, with an excellent memory, but he did not do well in school. Ongoing behavioral problems ultimately led to his suspension in his junior year, which prompted him to drop out and join the Navy at age sixteen, with his mother's consent. After basic training, he was sent to sea for nine months doing menial chores that he hated; however, he was subsequently given a test that indicated he had an aptitude for mathematics. This led to his teaching math to new recruits in New Orleans and to his attending Tulane University at night, despite his lack of a high school diploma. Clark earned enough credits while in the Navy that, upon discharge, he was able to enroll in the University of New Orleans and earn both bachelor's and master's degrees in physics in the late 1960s. He then went to the University of Utah to earn a Ph.D. in computer science in 1974.

LIFE'S WORK

On completing his doctoral work, Clark did research at the New York Institute of Technology's Computer Graphics Lab, which pioneered three-dimensional (3-D) computer imaging. Clark also served as a faculty member at the University of California at Santa Cruz (1974–78) and then moved to Stanford University as a faculty member (1979–82) in their engineering

James H. Clark.

program. As a researcher, Clark specialized in how to accelerate display of 3-D images with computer hardware and software. His breakthrough development was called the Geometry Engine, an early computer chip that could greatly speed rendering of 3-D images in real time. Commercializing this technology led to founding his first company, Silicon Graphics, Inc. (SGI), in 1982 to produce powerful computer workstations that took advantage of his new chip. Because of this superior technology, SGI was able to dominate top-tier Hollywood graphic effects in movies and thereby command premium pricing and margins in this lucrative market. By the early 1990s, SGI sales had reached $550 million. Also, by this time Clark felt increasingly at odds with the more conservative SGI board and chief executive officer (CEO)—to the point that he finally quit the company and sold his stock in 1994.

Before leaving SGI, Clark had met with a brilliant young computer scientist named Marc Andreessen, who had recently relocated to Silicon Valley after finishing college in computer science at a branch of the University of Illinois. While working at the National Center for Supercomputing Applications (NCSA) at the college, Andreessen led a team that developed the NCSA Mosaic web browser, the first graphical user interface (GUI) for accessing content on the recently developed World Wide Web. This simple point-and-click browser made it practical for millions of people around the world to use the Internet. In March 1994, Clark and Andreessen decided to create a substantially enhanced version of Mosaic in a new software company they founded called Mosaic Communications Company (MCC). Clark invested several million dollars and raised other investment capital to finance the start-up, while Andreessen gathered most of the team who wrote the original Mosaic browser to develop the enhanced version. Within a few months, they had a completely new and much more sophisticated browser that was made available for download on the Internet in October 1994.

MCC's enhanced Mosaic was an immediate hit, with some million users by 1995. However, this success led to legal issues with NCSA, which was still licensing use of the original Mosaic browser to other companies. In the settlement that was ultimately reached, MCC paid NCSA an undisclosed sum to resolve the infringement claim, and MCC agreed to change the name of both the company and the product. Thus, MCC became Netscape Communications Company (NCC), and the enhanced browser was renamed Netscape Navigator.

Affiliation: Silicon Graphics

James H. Clark is sometimes called the "father of computer graphics" because of his founding of Silicon Graphics, Inc. (SGI) in 1982 to commercialize new technology he had developed as an electrical engineering professor at Stanford University. Clark's Geometry Engine was a new device that made possible rapid display of graphic images in three dimensions, similar to what had been possible only with powerful supercomputers until that time. Surprisingly, the sophisticated SGI workstations, originally intended for scientific and engineering use, were quickly adopted by Hollywood to create special effects in movies like *Terminator 2* and *Jurassic Park* and for fully animated feature films like *Toy Story*. SGI became a public company in 1986 and began a series of acquisitions of related technology companies, many of which proved to be poor investments, such as Cray Research, that made supercomputers when this market was declining. SGI found it increasingly difficult to sell its proprietary operating system in competition with more general-purpose systems and microprocessors that were less expensive. By 1997, SGI was losing money and seemed incapable of tapping the booming Internet market of the late 1990s. Clark resigned and sold his stock in 1994 because of friction with a conservative SGI board and CEO, and other executives and engineers also began to leave for new Silicon Valley ventures. SGI sought to forge alliances with Microsoft and Intel in the late 1990s to integrate with their software and hardware and spun off its chip division, MIPs Technologies, in 2000. SGI filed for bankruptcy on April 1, 2009, and its name and most assets were acquired by Rackable Systems in May 2009.

In addition to pioneering browser software, Clark pioneered a new business model at Netscape that would become the blueprint for the explosion of Internet start-ups in the so called dot-com boom of the mid- to late 1990s. This model involved selling software to companies but practically giving it away to users. The approach allowed Netscape to generate an early stream of revenue and grow market share with users quickly, making the company a potentially attractive investment. As a result, Netscape generated some $100 million in revenue by 1995 and ultimately reached 75 percent market share in

1996. A second entrepreneurial innovation was to sell shares of stock in the company before it became profitable through an initial public offering (IPO) in 1995, which earned an estimated $2 billion return for Clark and became the model for other Internet start-ups in the dot-com boom.

The success of Netscape attracted the attention of many potential competitors, chief of which was Microsoft Corporation, which produced the dominant Windows operating system and MS Office suite of applications. Microsoft had been reluctant to incorporate a web browser into its product portfolio until it saw the overwhelming success of Netscape Navigator. Realizing the browser could threaten its market dominance, Microsoft purchased a modified version of NCSA Mosaic and rebranded it as MS Internet Explorer (IE), which it then bundled with its Windows operating system, essentially giving integrated browser software to its customers. It was also alleged by Netscape and other competitors that Microsoft used its market power to force companies to adopt IE and actually programmed Windows to run better with IE than with other browsers. As a result, Netscape's sales plunged to the point that the company was sold to America Online in March 1999 for $4.2 billion; Navigator was later abandoned by AOL. Clark pursued legal action against Microsoft, which led the U.S. government to bring antitrust action against Microsoft (*United States v. Microsoft*) that forced changes in its business practices.

Clark moved on to create other information technology ventures. In 1996, he founded Healtheon to streamline the handling of health care information and generate substantial operating economies in transaction processing for health care providers and insurers. Actual performance of the company never achieved his vision, and when a competitor called WebMD, backed by Microsoft, emerged with a similar business plan, Clark proactively sought consolidation of the companies to avoid a replay of his Netscape experience. As a result, Healtheon was merged into WebMD in 1999, creating the leading health information portal on the Internet, with Clark as a major investor. In 1999, Clark backed the launch of myCFO, a wealth management firm that focused on managing investments for many of Silicon Valley's technology entrepreneurs. This firm was sold in 2002, and thereafter Clark invested in a number of other information technology, financial services, construction/development, and biotechnology firms. As of March 2012, Clark's estimated net worth was $1 billion, had he ranked at 416 on *Forbes'* list of billionaires in America, with significant stakes noted in Apple, Facebook, and Twitter.

PERSONAL LIFE

Clark has been married four times and has three children. He married Australian model and actress Kristy Hinze in 2009, and they have a daughter, born in 2011. There was some critical press coverage at the time because Clark is thirty-six years her senior. Hinze is an active environmentalist and is known for her efforts in ocean preservation. Clark was a major financial backer of a 2009 Academy Award–winning film, *The Cove*, which documented harmful practices in the Japanese dolphin hunting industry.

Clark has been an active philanthropist since earning his fortune. Examples of his contributions include $90 million (as of 2001) to a center for biomedical engineering named in his honor at Stanford University, where he taught; $30 million to Tulane University, where he was a student; and contributions to various wildlife, environmental, and cultural causes. Clark is also an active collector of art, with a highly regarded collection of works by Impressionist painters including Pablo Picasso, Claude Monet, Henri Matisse, and Vincent van Gogh. In addition, he is a notable wine collector, with reputed holdings of some forty thousand bottles. He is also a yacht enthusiast, owning several vessels; he built the largest computer-controlled yacht in the world and has spent as much as half a year sailing.

Tom J. Sanders

FURTHER READING

Clark, Jim. *Netscape Time: The Making of the Billion Dollar Start-up That Took on Microsoft*. New York: St. Martin's, 1999. Print. Engrossing inside story of how Clark and Andreessen conceived and executed start-up of Netscape and the obstacles they faced competing with Microsoft that ultimately led to demise of the company.

Cusumano, Michael A., and David B. Yoffie. *Competing on Internet Time: Lessons from Netscape and Its Battle with Microsoft*. New York: St. Martin's, 1998. Print. Focuses on management lessons that can be learned from studying Netscape's competition with Microsoft.

Lacey, Sarah. *Once You're Lucky, Twice You're Good: The Rebirth of Silicon Valley and the Rise of Web 2.0*. New York: Gotham, 2008. Print. Engaging story of the entrepreneurs who rebuilt Silicon Valley after the dot-com bubble of 2000 and how tech development and venture creation have changed.

Lewis, Michael L. *The New New Thing: A Silicon Valley Story*. New York: Norton, 1999. Print. In-depth look at Silicon Valley through the eyes of Clark as the serial entrepreneur who created three billion-dollar companies.

Livingston, Jessica. *Founders at Work: Stories of Start-ups' Early Days*. New York: Springer, 2008. Print. More than thirty interviews with contemporaries of Clark who provide insights into the challenges they faced with the development and commercialization of their widely known products.

Payment, Simone. *Marc Andreessen and Jim Clark: The Founders of Netscape*. New York: Rosen, 2006. Print. Short, readable, and straightforward information about the cofounders of Netscape and the company with numerous pictures and key facts clearly identified. A particularly good introduction for students.

Quittner, Joshua, and Michelle Slatalla. *Speeding the Net: The Inside Story of Netscape, How It Challenged Microsoft and Changed the World*. New York: Atlantic Monthly Press, 1998. Print. Excellent chronology of the creation of the world's first graphical browser and first pure web company with detailed information on what happened and its implications.

BRAM COHEN

Cofounder of BitTorrent

Born: October 12, 1975; New York, New York
Died: -
Primary Field: Internet
Specialty: Applications
Primary Company/Organization: BitTorrent

INTRODUCTION

The father of BitTorrent, Bram Cohen developed a peer-to-peer file-sharing protocol (and wrote its first client program in Python), which has since taken up nearly half of the Internet's traffic. What BitTorrent offered was not a single service or site, such as Napster and previous peer-to-peer file-sharing programs, but a protocol to be used by programs to distribute "torrents" of data, bit by bit. Cohen founded BitTorrent, Inc., to continue to support the program, which has become the most successful peer-to-peer file-sharing program. He was recognized in 2005 as an influential business leader, named to Technology Review*'s TR35 (thirty-five innovators under age thirty-five) and* Time *magazine's 100 Most Influential People.*

EARLY LIFE

Bram Cohen was born on October 12, 1975, in New York City. The son of a computer scientist and a teacher, he grew up on the upper West Side and attended Stuyvesant High School. A mathematics prodigy who competed in the USA Mathematical Olympiad, he became interested in computer programming early, beginning on the household's Timex Sinclair computer, an early personal computer.

Cohen attended the State University of New York at Buffalo but dropped out during the dot-com boom to work for several start-ups in succession, the most significant of which was Evil Geniuses for a Better Tomorrow. Jim McCoy had founded that company to develop Mojo Nation, a digital cash system that used encrypted data. The venture reflected its place in geek culture: The company's name was taken from Steve Jackson Games' *Illuminati* card game (which was inspired in part by Robert Anton Wilson's *Illuminatus!* books of counterculture conspiracy theory fiction), while Mojo Nation reflected the influence of Hakim Bey, who had written about eighteenth-century pirate culture and "temporary autonomous zones." Bey's writing had barely preceded the 1990s rise of the Internet, and the counterculture embraced the idea of the Internet as a virtual space where these autonomous zones, rather than the communes and new sovereignties that Bey had envisioned, could be created. Although Mojo Nation was funded by venture capital, its intent was to create an open source marketplace, one protected by encryption, in which virtual cash (mojo) was used to buy and sell services.

Mojo Nation was developed and launched during the heyday of Napster and the popularity of decentralized peer-to-peer file sharing, and it used similar principles. The space required by Mojo Nation to operate was scattered across users' computers; in return for renting part of their computing resources (memory, processing, and so on) in order to keep the network running, each user received a payment in mojo. That mojo could then be exchanged with other users in return for whatever was on offer. The essential engine of the Mojo Nation economy was in broad strokes the same as that which drives real-world economies: A central authority creates and distributes money, the value of which fluctuates in response to its supply and the economic activity to which it is put to use. McCoy had a utopian vision according to which the system would encourage people to share and to pay the artists and other copyright holders who had created the works being distributed through the system; he thought it would change the Internet entirely and would be protected from obsolescence in a way Napster and its cohorts (such as Gnutella and Kazaa) were not. What particularly interested Cohen, though, was the way Mojo Nation handled file transfers: breaking up large files into small, encrypted pieces in order to limit the bandwidth of its transfers and minimize the system's impact on any given user's computer. This method of file transfer was key to the system's scalability.

Bram Cohen.

Cohen left Mojo Nation in 2001, inspired to create a new project: BitTorrent. He spent nine months writing it, during what he has called his "starving artist period."

LIFE'S WORK

Cohen announced BitTorrent, a new file-sharing program, at the first CodeCon conference, organized by Cohen and his roommate, privacy advocate and Anonymizer systems engineer Len Sassaman. The first CodeCon was held in 2002 at San Francisco's DNA Lounge; it continued to be held every year until 2009, focusing on developers presenting technologies in development.

It took a few years to refine the BitTorrent protocol, and after the CodeCon presentation, Cohen distributed free pornography with the protocol in order to encourage beta testers to sign up. Cohen briefly worked for Valve Software—developing the digital distribution system Steam—in 2003, but in 2004 he started BitTorrent, Inc., with Ross Cohen (his brother) and Ashwin Navin.

BitTorrent was designed as a peer-to-peer file-sharing protocol to distribute data over Internet connections. Numerous client programs have been developed to use BitTorrent; Cohen wrote both the protocol and the first client program (also called BitTorrent). While previous peer-to-peer programs exchange a file from one peer to another, BitTorrent was designed to handle downloads from multiple sources of the same file—even from other users who are in the process of downloading it and do not yet have a complete copy. (Users sharing complete copies are called "seeds"; continuing to provide access to a downloaded file is "seeding.") Provided users continued to seed anything they downloaded, the most popular files (the files in greatest demand) would also be the fastest to download, since they would have the greatest number of available copies and the most users sharing them.

While various torrent servers offer copyright-infringing material—which has led to some notorious site shutdowns and arrests, including those of The Pirate Bay and Demonoid—the official BitTorrent website has an agreement with the Motion Picture Association of America (MPAA) dating from 2005, according to which no illegal material will be listed and the site will adhere to the procedures of the Digital Millennium Copyright Act. Despite this cooperation with Hollywood, Cohen has been straightforward in his dissatisfaction with the conventional media distribution model and his hope to "kill off television" (that is, the traditional broadcast model), already threatened legitimately by time-deferred viewing

Affiliation: BitTorrent

Less than a decade after its introduction, the BitTorrent protocol accounts for almost half of all Internet traffic. Even in 2005—four years after its introduction—the Internet-analysis firm CacheLogic reported that BitTorrent accounted for a third of the Internet's traffic. Perhaps only streaming video has so quickly claimed such a large a portion of traffic—and for that matter, arguably only the popularity of streaming video services such as Hulu and Netflix, offering movies and television programs, can account for BitTorrent's consuming only half the Internet's traffic. The protocol was developed by Bram Cohen in 2001 and is maintained by BitTorrent, Inc. BitTorrent addressed one of the fundamental challenges that has faced the Internet since its early days: the task of transferring large files (where "large" has scaled over time, in accordance to technological advances) efficiently and without the inconvenience of continually restarting failed transfers. The fundamentals of peer-to-peer file sharing had already been pioneered and popularized by Napster, which made the act of sharing files a passive one; unlike many previous forms of file transfers, with BitTorrent the user from whom the file was downloaded did not need to be present to initiate or agree to the transfer but could passively host files and open a program that would allow others to initiate downloads. This alone was a considerable advance over the software available to most users who were not operating servers.

The BitTorrent protocol was inspired in part by Cohen's work on Mojo Nation, a digital cash economy and file-sharing platform that stored pieces of files on users' computers, as in cloud computing, with the storage burden shifted to the client side. BitTorrent similarly shifts some of the burden to the client side. Rather than creating file transfers between two peers, as Napster did, with BitTorrent the file may be downloaded from any of the connected users who have a copy and have agreed to share it—and critically, the BitTorrent client programs download from multiple source copies simultaneously. The fact that BitTorrent allows users who are still downloading to be downloaded from in turn—that incomplete copies of a file are still used as sources for other downloaders—is key to BitTorrent's efficiency, because this eases the load from the server (or from seeds). The moment a user begins downloading, every bit of data downloaded reduces the demand on the seed, and thus the more users are downloading, the faster the file can be downloaded—which is the reverse of the situation experienced in traditional downloading-from-server scenarios.

Mojo Nation encouraged sharing by compensating users for their computing resources with mojo, a digital cash that was then spent on downloaded files. BitTorrent sites (although this is not formally encoded by the protocol) have developed a different incentive: Users are incentivized through various means to maintain a reasonable ratio of bytes uploaded to bytes downloaded, which encourages them to continue seeding files they have successfully downloaded, since this is a passive, resource-light method of increasing their bytes-uploaded count.

BitTorrent arrived at just the right time, as MP3 files were becoming, if not passé, no longer the amazing novelty they had been; with streaming video becoming more common, video, not audio, was the medium of the moment. BitTorrent was much better suited for transferring video files (which are much larger than audio files); even a half-hour video was several times larger than a high-quality MP3 of an entire music album. Of course, BitTorrent's adroitness at handling large files made it well suited to the copyright-infringing transfer of movies, television shows, software, and other files—and it became common, surprisingly quickly, to find television shows available by torrent within hours of their airing and full DVD downloads available the week of release if not sooner—but BitTorrent, Inc., which Cohen founded with his brother Ross and business partner Ashwin Navin in 2004, made an alliance with the MPAA, a move predecessors such as Napster had been unable or unwilling to do. While BitTorrent, Inc., could do nothing to stop the use of its software for illegal purposes, the official BitTorrent site complies with the requirements of the Digital Millennium Copyright Act. BitTorrent is often used as the official means of distribution for legitimate files, from movies to software, and allows files to be released from individuals or companies that cannot afford the resources to offer it for direct download from a server. One well-known example early in BitTorrent's history, in 2003, was the open source Red Hat Linux 9 operating system; Red Hat's servers crashed under the demand of downloaders when the operating system was released, but once a copy was made available via BitTorrent, 21.15 terabytes of data were exchanged over three days, an amount of traffic that would have cost as much as $50,000 in bandwidth through conventional means but, with BitTorrent, never exceeded the amount of traffic allowed by the host's $99 server rental fee.

Affiliation: BitTorrent (continued)

The Red Hat release demonstrated that BitTorrent had arrived at exactly the right time, when the Internet was on the verge of suffering from its own growth. It prevented the stifling that could have occurred, and enabled sharing that simply could not have happened otherwise, such as when graduate student Gary Lerhaupt convinced the filmmakers behind the Fox News exposé *Outfoxed* to let him release it as a torrent file; fifteen hundred people downloaded it, at a cost to Lerhaupt of $4.

The BitTorrent protocol is always being developed. Recent changes have included a shift to delay-based congestion control in 2012, in order to be friendlier to the limitations of the transmission-control protocol (TCP) and those of the routers that provide the Internet with its infrastructure—and in order to consume less bandwidth to address the common problem of users who are unable to use BitTorrent (or use it effectively) at the same time as resource-intensive applications such as *World of Warcraft* and other massively multiplayer online role-playing games.

BitTorrent, Inc., supports BitTorrent, Codeville (a distributed revision control system developed by the Cohen brothers), BitTorrent DNA (a "disruptively effective" content delivery technology to reduce bandwidth costs to websites), and the BitTorrent Device Partners program for hardware and software companies manufacturing Internet-enabled consumer electronics. Bram Cohen remains cofounder and chief scientist of BitTorrent (as well as cofounder of related projects CodeCon and Codeville) and serves on the board of directors. The remaining board members are CEO Eric Klinker, previously of Internap and Excite@Home; David Chao, cofounder and general partner of DCM; Ping Li, general partner of Accel; and John J. Cadeddu, managing director of DAG Ventures. The rest of the management team is chief strategist and executive vice president of marketing Shahi Ghanem, previously of STL and DivX; vice president of data science Simon Morris, previously of Openwave; vice president of engineering Ilan Shamir, previously of Check Point Software Technologies and SideTalk, Inc.; vice president of finance and operations Claude Tolbert, previously of Covad Communications; and vice president of marketing and business development Ro Choy, formerly of Formspring.

---

like that offered by Hulu, Netflix, DVDs, DVRs, and on-demand cable services, and illegitimately by copyright-infringing file sharing. The successor to BitTorrent, in Cohen's view, will be a similar peer-to-peer distribution system (which some have called "peercasting") that supplants over-the-air and cable broadcasting.

Cohen also did some of the design work on his brother Ross's Codeville, a Python-written distributed revision control system. Revision control systems manage changes to bodies of data, such as programs, websites, and documents.

PERSONAL LIFE

Cohen and his wife, Jenna, have three children. He continues to be interested in mathematics and regularly delves into recreational mathematics and related topics on his blog, as well as discussing programming issues and engineering problems. His hobbies include origami, juggling, and puzzles.

Cohen is self-diagnosed with Asperger syndrome, an autism spectrum disorder. He has expressed the belief that his condition contributed to social difficulties in his adolescence, which in turn encouraged his computer programming by focusing his attention away from the social sphere. He is sometimes uncomfortable in everyday social situations and admits to a tendency to lecture at length, without concern for his audience's interest level or ability to follow his train of thought. The disorder also led to difficulties in his early work life, when he would undiplomatically criticize the business plan or other elements of his employers. Asperger syndrome is somewhat more common in Silicon Valley than elsewhere, however, and the disorder has not proven an obstacle in his running BitTorrent, Inc.

Bill Kte'pi

FURTHER READING

Aigrain, Philippe. *Sharing: Culture and Economy in the Internet Age*. Amsterdam: Amsterdam UP, 2012. Print. Considers BitTorrent as one of several technologies enabling the sharing of information and media, and the effects thereof on culture.

Botsman, Rachel, and Roo Rogers. *What's Mine Is Yours: The Rose of Collaborative Consumption*. New York: HarperCollins, 2012. Print. Botsman and Rogers do not address BitTorrent by name—nor many other file-sharing technologies, perhaps fearing sounding dated—but discuss in depth the role of the Internet in sharing and collaboration.

Gold, Lorna. *The Sharing Economy: Solidarity Networks Transforming Globalization.* Burlington: Ashgate, 2004. Print. BitTorrent and sharing applications in the context of globalization.

Roth, Daniel. "Torrential Reign." *Fortune* 31 Oct. 2005: n. pag. Print. An article on the alliance between the MPAA and BitTorrent, Inc., which in retrospect was probably instrumental in the company's long-term success.

Thompson, Clive. "The BitTorrent Effect." *Wired* 13.1 (2005): n. pag. Print. An in-depth, technically informed profile of BitTorrent and the spike in movie piracy.

Ron Conway

Angel investor

Born: 1951; San Francisco, California
Died: -
Primary Field: Business and commerce
Specialty: Management, executives, and investors
Primary Company/Organization: SV Angel

Introduction

Ron Conway is an angel investor—typically a wealthy individual who invests money (typically amounts from $20,000 up) in high-potential start-up firms, often as a source of initial funding before venture capitalists become involved. He has invested in almost every major Internet start-up since the 1980s, including Google, Facebook, PayPal, and Yelp. He is also well known for saving distressed young companies from certain failure by tapping his extensive network of capital sources. In 2005, Conway left Angel Investors LP, the fund he founded in 1998, to launch SV Angel. SV Angel is a venture capital fund that provides investment support to young companies primarily in the technology sectors that cannot secure funding through traditional investment channels. To many observers, Silicon Valley would not be the same without Conway and his unrivaled track record of investment volume and success.

Early Life

Ron Conway grew up in the San Francisco Bay Area during the 1950s. His father was a top executive at a shipping company called American President Lines. His mother raised the couple's twelve children: six boys and six girls. Conway and his twin brother were the sixth in birth order, making them the middle children. The entire family regularly attended church services at nearby Nativity Church in Menlo Park, California. Together, the Conways the entire last pew as well as some of the

standing-room overflow space behind. Conway attended Catholic schools in both San Francisco and Atherton, California. He received average grades and thus was not an exceptional. Upon graduating from high school, he enrolled in community college, then transferred to San Jose State University, where he earned a bachelor's degree in political science.

Conway's first professional job was with National Semiconductor in Santa Clara, California, where he held several marketing positions. He moved through the company echelons and by 1979 was ready to launch his own

Ron Conway.

company. That firm, Altos Computer Systems, was one of the earliest manufacturers of multiuser computers. Within three years of cofounding the company, Conway took it public and instantly became a multimillionaire.

LIFE'S WORK

As the president and chief executive officer (CEO) of Altos Computer Systems, Conway orchestrated a successful initial public offering (IPO) of Altos stock in 1982. The deal garnered him his first millions. He continued to lead Altos until 1990. At that time, he took the helm of Personal Training Systems, a leading multimedia desktop training firm. He stepped down as the company's president and CEO in 1995. Conway then made the transition to angel investing, which involves putting up one's own money to back emerging companies in need of funds.

In 1998, Conway formed a fund designed specifically for angel investing. He aptly named it Angel Investors LP. He would serve as the fund's managing partner until 2005. By investing a small stake in high-potential enterprises before venture capitalists recognize a start-up's potential value, Conway has helped hundreds of companies gain contacts, credibility, and success. For example, without Conway, there may not have been a Google or a PayPal. The two companies are characteristic of the types of business enterprises that pique Conway's investing interest and characterize the level of success achieved by many of his beneficiaries.

In 2001, however, the successes of both Google and PayPal was uncertain. Both firms were starting to implode, which would have meant significant losses for Conway financially as well as in terms of his credibility. An IPO of PayPal stock in 2002 turned things around. Google followed with an IPO in 2004. As a very early investor in both companies, Conway recouped his initial losses and was once again firmly in the black on both counts. The experience confirmed his belief in his investment approach: Take the risk to get in early with promising start-ups, and reap high rewards.

When he emerged on the other side of the potential declines of Google and PayPal, Conway found himself facing more competition from other investors, who by then had recognized the potential of Internet start-ups, which required relatively small amounts of seed money but had the potential to generate substantial gains. By that time, however, Conway had found a more specific niche: Web 2.0. He quickly became one of the biggest financial backers for social media–focused start-ups, including Ning, Rock You, and Yammer. Using that strategy, Conway again saw significant successes. By 2010,

---

Affiliation: SV Angel

Silicon Valley–based SV Angel is a micro venture capital fund that provides mentorship and capital to fledgling start-ups in the technology sector that are either too small or too risky to lure funding from ordinary venture capital funds or everyday lenders. It was founded in 2005 by angel investor Ron Conway, who serves as special partner. Since 2007, the fund has been managed by former Google business development leader David Lee, who serves as SV Angel's managing member.

SV Angel invests relatively small amounts of money from its estimated $40 million fund in promising enterprises that are involved in the Internet, e-commerce, mobile, media, and other information technology sectors. SV Angel receives its funding primarily through external investors and limited partnerships. As of November 2011, SV Angel reported 290 companies in its active portfolio. Among the well-known firms on that list are Digg, Flixster, Foursquare, and ZocDoc.

---

more than thirty of the companies in Conway's portfolio had been acquired by industry leaders. One of the notable sales involved Amazon's purchase of online shoe retailer Zappos, a Conway-backed company.

Conway has earned a reputation for predicting winners, but that has not always been the case. For instance, Conway invested in a podcasting company named Odeo that was being run by entrepreneur Evan Williams. When Odeo failed, Williams returned to Conway the money he had invested in the start-up. Rather than reinvesting the funds right away on the next suitor in line, Conway set them aside and resolved to use the money to fund the next start-up that Williams wanted to launch. True to his word, Conway held onto the money until Williams approached him with another start-up idea: Twitter. According to Twitter cofounder Biz Stone, Conway did more than help the project get off the ground financially; he also helped the entrepreneurs locate office space and introduced them to key players in the industry.

Providing that type of service is exactly why Conway founded SV Angel. SV Angel is an investor-supported fund that has been providing financial support and business development advice to technology start-ups that might otherwise fall under the radar of traditional investors and lenders. From 2005, when Conway cofounded the fund, through the end of 2011, SV Angel grew its portfolio to nearly three hundred companies—many notable, some still emerging.

In addition to SV Angel, Conway founded several other enterprises, including content registration firm SNOCAP in 2003 and advertising solutions provider Anchor Intelligence in 2006. He has also shared his expertise and experience as an adviser or board member with a significant number of technology companies: Associated Content, Backflip, Plaxo, and ViTrue, to name a few.

PERSONAL LIFE

Conway is active in supporting his community. He cofounded the UCLA Venture Capital Fund to provide investments that benefit the University of California, Los Angeles. He also serves on the university's development committee. For several years, from 1999 to 2002, Conway was a member of the DAPER Venture Capital Fund, which benefits the Stanford University athletic department. He also chairs the development committee of the Ronald McDonald House and the Packard Children's Hospital in Stanford, California. He is on the development committees of St. Francis High School, Sacred Heart Schools, and the University of California, San Francisco, Medical Center. Conway was the driving force behind the San Francisco Citizens Initiative for Technology and Innovation (sfciti.com) in early 2012; the initiative seeks to generate sustained civic support by leveraging the power of the city's technology sector.

Conway and his wife, Gayle, live in San Francisco and have three grown sons: Ronny, Danny, and Topher. Topher serves as a partner at SV Angel.

Shari Parsons Miller

FURTHER READING

Brush, Candida G., Linda F. Edelman, and Tatiana S. Manolova. "Ready for Funding? Entrepreneurial Ventures and the Pursuit of Angel Financing." *Venture Capital* 14.2–3 (2012): 111–29. Print. Examines the readiness of start-up firms to accept funding by angel investors based on a study of 332 firms that sought investment from a prominent angel group between 2007 and 2008.

Geron, Tomio. "Ron Conway's Data on What Makes Successful Entrepreneurs." *Forbes* 23 May 2011: 34. Print. Talks about a survey of U.S. start-up companies conducted by SV Angel partners David Lee and Conway; finds that having a cofounder is an important component of success.

Helft, Miguel. "The Silicon Valley Startup's Best Friend." *Fortune* 165.3 (2012): 90–102. Print. Discusses angel investor Conway's investment strategy, operational structure, investor recruitment practices, and industry connections in technology, media, and profession sports.

Payne, William H., and Matthew J. MacArty. "The Anatomy of an Angel Investing Network: Tech Coast Angels." *Venture Capital* 4.4 (2002): 331–36. Print. Provides an overview of the recipient selection process for Tech Coast Angels, an alliance of three angel investor networks in California.

Sarasvathy, Saras D., et al. "Prediction and Control under Uncertainty: Outcomes in Angel Investing." *Journal of Business Venturing* 24.2 (2009): 116–33. Print. Discusses the predictive strategies used by angel investors and highlights results of a study that found nonpredictive strategies to be more successful.

"Where Angels Will Tread." *The Economist* 17 Nov. 2011. Print. Presents angel investor Conway's perspective on where today's entrepreneurial start-ups will create the next generation of billion-dollar companies.

STEPHEN CROCKER

Inventor of Requests for Comments

Born: October 15, 1944; Pasadena, California
Died: -
Primary Field: Computer science
Specialty: Computer hardware
Primary Company/Organization: Internet Corporation for Assigned Names and Numbers

INTRODUCTION

Since the 1960s, Steve Crocker has been involved with nearly every major American body overseeing the Internet, including the Advanced Research Projects Agency (ARPA), the Internet Engineering Task Force, the Internet Architecture Board, and the Internet

Society. In 2012 he was chair of the board of the Internet Corporation for Assigned Names and Numbers (ICANN). One of the fathers of the Internet, he has received awards for his early work on the general architecture of the Internet, development of the community that has continued to work on networks, and the Request for Comments series, which he assumed was merely a temporary series of notes.

EARLY LIFE

Steve Crocker was born on October 15, 1944, in Pasadena, California, and grew up mainly in Los Angeles. He had some experience with computers while in high school, and after graduating in 1961, he got a job programming computers. Crocker attended the University of California at Los Angeles (UCLA), earning his bachelor's degree with a concentration in mathematics (1968) and his doctoral degree with a concentration in computer science (1977).

Throughout college, Crocker devoted considerable time to programming for both work and fun. While a graduate student, he worked on the team that developed the protocols used by ARPANET, the network funded by the U.S. Department of Defense that evolved into today's Internet. His most significant contribution was the

Stephen Crocker.

requests for comments (RFCs) that helped shaped the network. Crocker was part of the small group of UCLA researchers who attempted to send the first message between nodes on the ARPANET on October 29, 1969. They were trying to send a message from UCLA to Stanford Research Institute. The system famously crashed. He also taught a computer programming course for the IBM 7094 mainframe computer that was offered to high school teachers and students. The class was an effort to accelerate the spread of computer programming education at the high school level.

In the 1960s, Crocker attended graduate school at the Massachusetts Institute of Technology (MIT) for a brief period, working on a chess program in the MIT Artificial Intelligence Laboratory, before transferring back to UCLA to finish his Ph.D.

LIFE'S WORK

Crocker remained intimately involved with the formation and development of the Internet after graduate school. He was a program manager at ARPA and involved in the creation of its Network Working Group, the forerunner of the Internet Engineering Task Force (IETF), which develops Internet standards. He was also a member of the Internet Architecture Board (IAB), which oversees the development of the Internet, and the Internet Society (ISOC), the international nonprofit organization that oversees Internet standards and policy. Today ISOC copyrights all IETF requests for comments.

One of Crocker's most important contributions was the invention of the Request for Comments series (RFCs), in 1969. RFCs are memoranda drafted by computer scientists as published discourse on matters pertaining to the Internet—especially research, methods, etiquette, and other issues (Crocker notes that RFCs are the source of the Internet's rules, formal and unwritten). Those adopted by the IETF become Internet standards. Crocker wrote the first RFCs to keep track of and circulate notes on ARPANET as it was developed. At the time of RFC 1, ARPANET consisted of a network of four computers: at UCLA, the Stanford Research Institute, the University of California at Santa Barbara, and the University of Utah at Salt Lake City. Graduate students from all four institutes—the Network Working Group—had been meeting informally when possible, in order to discuss ARPANET issues and what could be done with the network. In 1969, they decided to begin writing down notes from their discussions, in order to circulate them for comment from other interested parties, and Crocker drafted the first such document. The

Affiliation: Internet Corporation for Assigned Names and Numbers

Internet Corporation for Assigned Names and Numbers (ICANN) was founded on September 18, 1998, as part of the ongoing transition as the American government gave up control of the Internet and passed it on to various international and nonprofit bodies. ICANN was created in response to a green paper issued by the National Telecommunications and Information Administration, "A Proposal to Improve the Technical Management of Internet Names and Addresses." The Internet's Domain Name System, previously under control of the government even years after the development of the Internet had been handed over to the Internet Architecture Board (IAB), was privatized on the recommendations of the paper. It is a nonprofit corporation.

In establishing ICANN, the government mandated that ICANN be consensus-driven and democratic. The founding chairwoman was Esther Dyson, the daughter of mathematician Freeman Dyson. The younger Dyson—a journalist, economist, and philanthropist—remained chair until 2000. She also served on ICANN's reform committee beginning in 2004.

Several supporting organizations and advisory committees deal with specific areas of policy. The Address Supporting Organization, made up of representatives from the Regional Internet Registries, deals with policy concerning Internet protocol (IP) addresses, while the Country Code Names Supporting Organization handles country-code top-level domain policy and the Generic Names Supporting Organization deals with generic top-level domains. Generic top-level domains—top-level domains that are not associated with country codes, infrastructure top-level domains, or testing top-level domains—include .com, .info, .net, and .org (the core group). The domains .edu, .gov, .int, and .mil were originally considered generic but are now considered sponsored, since they are restricted to specific registrants sponsored by designated agencies. In 2008, ICANN voted to expand the list of generic top-level domains (GTLDs), and in 2011 it voted to end restrictions on GTLDs, allowing groups to apply for specific domain names (such as .starbucks, .ipad, .bank, or .romney). The first such domains were expected to go live in 2013, after the first round of applications had been approved. Esther Dyson was vocal in her opposition to the plan, as was the Coalition for Responsible Internet Domain Oversight.

Although it is young, there have been several attempts to reform ICANN, or perhaps an ongoing attempt at reform that has not ended. It is difficult, for instance, to see ICANN as the consensus-driven organization described in its initial mandate. In 2002, the At-Large Advisory Committee (ALAC) was created as an advocate for Internet users, but it is safe to say that most Internet users are unaware of the mechanisms by which representatives of the ALAC are elected—each Regional At-Large Organization (RALO) appoints two members, and each RALO is in turn made up of "at-large structures," the ICANN term for Internet user groups it has accredited. Even then, the ALAC rarely uses its limited statutory authority to influence ICANN policy, instead issuing advisory statements. To be fair, the number of ALSes has grown steadily. ICANN also holds public meetings.

One of the most important things ICANN has done is establish the Uniform Dispute Resolution Policy, in collaboration with the World Intellectual Property Organization, for resolving disputes about domain name ownership (as in a case, for example, where Peter Plum might own plum.com and is sued by a television manufacturer named Plum that owned a trademark or service mark on "plum"). Simpler disputes might involve a case wherein a person registers bluecars.com in an attempt to sell it at a profit to Blue Cars Incorporated but can demonstrate no legitimate interest in the domain beyond that—a case of what (in American law) is considered cybersquatting.

There is speculation that the United Nations, or rather a body it creates, may subsume the responsibilities of ICANN. The Internet Governance Forum was created by the United Nations in 2006, for instance, to consult on Internet policy. It is unknown if it will assume ICANN's policy-making responsibilities at some future date.

first RFC had to be photocopied and circulated by mail; later RFCs were, of course, posted to the Internet.

RFCs serve many purposes. They preserve knowledge, they open discussions, and they explain and define the workings of the Internet, both technical and cultural; a great education can be yielded by reading the RFCs, imparting most if not all of the same information as a college course. Modern RFCs are rarely actual requests for comments and must be vetted before publication. They are preceded by working documents called Internet Drafts (I-Ds), which are works in progress published by the IETF; I-Ds in some ways are the actual successors to the original RFCs, as they are written in a less formal style. They are considered inherently obsolete after six months and are not intended to be used as reference documents. RFCs are held to a higher standard.

In 2007, the IETF defined streams (categories) of RFCs, with different editors responsible for each. These streams have since been refined, with specific standards defined for each, and include an IETF stream of RFCs from within the IETF or sponsored by an IETF area director; the IAB's stream; the stream of the Internet Research Task Force (IRTF); and the Independent Submission stream. These streams were defined in RFC 4844.

Each RFC is designated a number, which never changes, and a status indicating its relevance to Internet standards: informational, experimental (generally for proposals that, if they work or are adopted, are promoted to the "standards track" status), best current practice (consisting of official rules, with a fuzzy line dividing it from the standards track), standards track (RFCs intended to become Internet standards), historic (documents no longer relevant to the current Internet because of obsolescence or other factors), and unknown (which applies only to some old RFCs). There are a great many terms with official meaning to RFCs, defined in previous RFCs.

As serious and formal as the RFC process is compared to the days of the Network Working Group, it retains one exception from those days: the April Fools RFC, a humorous RFC issued on most April Fools Days. The grandfather of the April Fools' Day RFCs is RFC 527—from June, not April, 1973—which parodied Lewis Carroll's poem "Jabberwocky" with "ARPAWOCKY." Other April Fools' Day RFCs have described a protocol for using homing pigeons to transmit IP packets, an analysis of the infinite monkey theorem, the use of semaphore signaling to transmit IP data, and other particularly jokes best appreciated by engineers.

In 1994, Crocker cofounded CyberCash, Inc., and served as its chief technology officer. CyberCash was an online payment system for e-commerce, developing electronic wallet software and credit card payment processing software. CyberCrash was one of the victims of the Y2K (millennial) bug—problems occasioned by format for dates used by many computers and software prior to the twenty-first century, which were often based on only a two-digit place for the year—which resulted in credit card payments being recorded twice in their system. It filed for bankruptcy a year later and was acquired by Verisign, which in 2005 was acquired by PayPal, now the leading online payment system.

Crocker later founded the DSL-based ISP Executive DSL (1998) and Longitude Systems (1999). In 2002, he cofounded Shinkuro, from the Japanese word for "synchronize," with Jeffrey Kay. A private company based in Washington, D.C., Shinkuro is a research and development company focused on information sharing and developing file-sharing software.

Crocker chaired ICANN's Security and Stability Advisory Committee from its inception in 2002 until 2010. In 2011, he was elected Chairman of the ICANN board. He was Institute of Electrical and Electronics Engineers' Internet Award in 2002.

PERSONAL LIFE

Howard Sobel, Crocker's stepfather, introduced him to sailing, and Crocker enjoyed it so much that he quickly bought his own boat. His brother David, who has been involved with Internet issues since the Internet's inception, is perhaps best known for his work standardizing e-mail. In 2012, Crocker remained active in Internet issues. He and his wife, Beth, have two children, Melissa and Andrew.

Bill Kte'pi

FURTHER READING

Abbate, Janet. *Inventing the Internet*. Cambridge: MIT, 2000. Print. An Internet history with a focus on ARPA and early innovators.

Crocker, Stephen. "Oral History Interview with Stephen Crocker." 24 Oct. 1991. Charles Babbage Institute. Web. 12 Aug. 2012. Part of the Charles Babbage Institute's oral history project documenting the computer and Internet industries.

Hafner, Katie. *Where Wizards Stay Up Late: The Origins of the Internet*. New York: Simon, 1998. Print. A history of the Internet. Although old enough to be noticeably incomplete now, it is nevertheless thorough in its coverage of the Internet's origins and early days.

Wu, Tim. *The Master Switch: The Rise and Fall of Information Empires*. New York: Vintage, 2011. Print. An analytical look at the Internet and its role in history.

D

SKY DAYTON

Founder of EarthLink

Born: August 8, 1971; New York, New York
Died: -
Primary Field: Business and commerce
Specialty: Management, executives, and investors
Primary Company/Organization: EarthLink

INTRODUCTION

Entrepreneur Sky Dayton, at twenty-three, was already the owner of two successful Los Angeles coffeehouses when he founded EarthLink, an Internet service provider, in 1994. A millionaire by age twenty-six, he went on to cofound eCompanies, an Internet start-up incubator; Boingo, a Wi-Fi software and service provider; and Helio, a mobile virtual network operator for the youth market. He is also is a member of the Warren Bennis Leadership Circle of the Center for Public Leadership at the Kennedy School at Harvard University

EARLY LIFE

Sky Dylan Dayton was born August 8, 1971, in New York City. His father is a sculptor, and his mother is a poet. The couple moved to Los Angeles when Dayton was a toddler, and it was in that city that Dayton grew up. His grandfather, an IBM Research Fellow, introduced him to computers when Dayton was nine. He was voted "most likely to succeed" in his fourth-grade class. A window-cleaning business he started when he was still in elementary school signaled his entrepreneurial spirit. He made a few dollars cleaning the windows of his family's apartment but soon realized that his income would increase of he washed more windows. After he distributed flyers under the doors of neighbors, his first business proved successful.

His parents, both Scientologists, sent him to the Delphian School, a boarding school in Sheridan, Oregon, based on the teachings of L. Ron Hubbard, founder of Scientology. He dreamed of being an animator and during an internship helped create the Elephant Man skeleton used in the video of Michael Jackson's *Leave Me Alone*. In 1988, when his application to the California Institute for the Arts was denied, he decided on a

Sky Dayton.

business career. He lied about his computer skills to get a job in the graphics department of a Burbank advertising firm; three months later, was head of the department. He then moved on to work at a larger ad agency, Mednick and Associates, until he was eighteen.

In 1990, he and a friend opened a coffeehouse, Café Mocha. Six months later, the coffeehouse, with its poetry readings and discussion salons, had become a popular West Hollywood gathering place frequented by the likes of Quentin Tarantino and featured on MTV. Dayton opened a second coffeehouse, Joe. In 1992, he started a computer graphics firm and targeted the entertainment industry. Soon his clients included Fox Television, Disney, Columbia, Sony Pictures, and Warner Bros. By twenty-one, he had established three successful businesses.

LIFE'S WORK

In the early 1990s, Dayton wanted to get online. He searched a week for an Internet service provider (ISP) and spent eighty hours trying to set up a working Internet connection after he had chosen one. Deciding there had to be a more effective way, he created a business plan for an ISP. It took him more than a year, but he eventually raised $100,000 from investors. EarthLink was formally incorporated in March 1994, and the first customer signed in July. The company started in a six-hundred-square-foot office in Pasadena, California. It was filled with used furniture; the services ran on ten 14.4 modems, two used Sun workstations, and a two-line phone, one for sales and one for technical support. However, less than a year later, Dayton introduced EarthLink Software, giving customers one of the easiest and most direct routes to the Internet.

EarthLink was still a local business at this point, but in August 1995 the company signed a contract that changed that status. Dayton signed with UUNET Technologies, a company that was already providing Internet backbones for America Online (AOL), AT&T, and Microsoft, and became a national company providing Internet service in nearly one hundred cities. Three months later, EarthLink began offering a flat usage fee, a rare move at a time when AOL, the giant in the ISP forest, was still charging by the hour. Also in 1995, Microsoft agreed to include EarthLink on the Windows 95 desktop.

EarthLink was also establishing a reputation as a customer-friendly company that offered friendly, competent customer service twenty-four hours per day, seven days per week. At a time when Internet usage was exploding, Dayton understood the connection between

retention of customers and profitability for his company. In 1999, eight hundred of EarthLink's thirteen hundred employees were supplying technical support.

Dayton's strategies were working. EarthLink was retaining satisfied customers, adding new ones, and becoming the fastest-growing independent ISP in the United States. In October 1997, the company had more than 200,000 customers; less than a year later, that number had almost doubled. In February 1998, a deal EarthLink struck with the long-distance company Sprint added another 130,000 customers and gave the growing ISP $24 million in cash and another $100 million in credit. In August of the same year, Apple Computer announced that it had chosen EarthLink as its ISP for the one-month free Internet access that would be provided with the purchase of each new iMac. By the end of the decade, EarthLink had 1.5 million customers.

In September 1999, the news of a $4 billion merger between EarthLink and another ISP, MindSpring, broke. The merger was completed in February 2000. The new company took the name EarthLink, but company headquarters would be in Atlanta, MindSpring's home base. The move not only allowed the new EarthLink to jump ahead of Internet access providers CompuServe, Microsoft Network, AT&T WorldNet, and NetZero with its free Internet access offer; it also made Dayton's company the country's number-two ISP, behind AOL. After the merger, Dayton stepped down as acting chief executive officer (CEO) but remained a company director.

Dayton and Jake Winebaum, who headed Disney's Internet businesses, had been talking for years about starting a business together. In June 1999, they founded eCompanies, an idea company that would launch other companies. They had no difficulty raising capital. Within two months, they had raised $130 million from investors, who included both EarthLink and Disney. However, most of their start-ups performed poorly. The exception, Business.com, a business search engine and web directory that proved moderately successful, was nevertheless a subject of mockery because of the exorbitant amount (reportedly $7.5 million) that Dayton had paid a cybersquatter for the domain name.

Just as frustration with ISPs led Dayton into EarthLink, frustration with wireless connections led him into his next venture. He founded Boingo in December 2001. Boingo aggregated Wi-Fi "hot spots" into one access point for subscribers. Dayton's $15 million budget was insignificant in comparison to the high dollar capital he and Winebaum had raised for eCompanies, but it was enough for him to provide short-range, high-speed

Affiliation: EarthLink

EarthLink is a U.S. company that provides Internet protocol (IP) infrastructure and services to individual customers and integrated communications and related services to businesses, enterprise organizations, and communications carriers. The company's headquarters are in Atlanta and its business operates primarily in the United States. EarthLink was founded in 1994 by Sky Dayton. A year later, EarthLink introduced the world's first open and direct Internet access software. That year, a contract with UUNET Technologies allowed EarthLink to become a national company, serving customers in nearly one hundred cities. In 1997, the company went public on NASDAQ. MindSpring Enterprises and EarthLink merged in 2000, creating the second-largest Internet service provider in the United States.

A decade later, EarthLink introduced its EarthLink Business division, signaling a new emphasis on information technology and network and communication services for businesses. Also in 2010, in line with the newly intensified business focus, EarthLink acquired Deltacom, a telecom service provider with thirty-two thousand small and mid-sized business customers, along with enterprise, government agency, and wholesale customers. In 2011, STS Telecom, a privately held business providing voice, data, and Internet services to small and medium-sized business customers in Florida and Georgia, became another EarthLink acquisition. EarthLink has been divided into two distinct entities under one company since 2012: EarthLink Businesses Services and EarthLink Consumer services. As of 2012, the company provided services to more than 150,000 businesses and more than one million consumers.

Wi-Fi connections in airports (including some in Texas and California), hotels (including some in the Hilton, Marriott, and Sheraton chains), cafés, and other places people were likely to seek Wi-Fi connections. The subscription service was set up with a cut going to the hot spot. By January 31, 2002, there were four hundred such places in the network. When the company went public in 2011, the network had almost nineteen thousand hot spots in the United States alone and thousands more globally. The company is now one of the largest Wi-Fi networks in the world.

In 2004, on a visit to Korea, Dayton became aware of cell phones on which people were listening to music, watching videos, and playing games. In 2005, Dayton became CEO of Helio, a joint venture of EarthLink and SK Telecom, Korea's leading wireless carrier, to bring these phones and the services they require to the United States, targeting the large youth market and other early adopters of the latest technology. He resigned as chairman of EarthLink when he accepted the CEO position, although he remained as a director. Virgin Mobile USA acquired Helio in 2008.

PERSONAL LIFE

Almost as well known for his love of surfing and snowboarding as for his entrepreneurship, Dayton first took surfing lessons in 1998. He was immediately hooked on the sport. He has been known to steal away from work to surf in Malibu, the Channel Islands, and Santa Barbara and admits to owning six Channel Island boards. He has also surfed in Fiji and Baja. Surfparks, a company that has developed wave-riding facilities in Florida and California, asked Dayton to serve as adviser, which he did. However, he is still a purist and prefers the real thing. He started snowboarding in the early 1990s, but he wrote on his blog in 2010 that after fifteen years of snowboarding, he was switching to skiing. He is a member of the board of trustees of the U.S. Ski and Snowboard Team.

Dayton is married to science-fiction novelist and screenwriter Arwen Elys Dayton. Like her husband, she is a Scientologist who attended the Delphian School. The couple have three children: a son, born in 2001, and two daughters, born in 2002 and 2006.

Wylene Rholetter

FURTHER READING

Ankeny, Jason. "Sky Dayton's Next Big Thing (Again)." *Wireless Review* Mar. 2005: 44–49. Print. Describes the beginnings of the partnership between the Korean company SK and EarthLink that eventually became Helios. It discusses Dayton's role and why he was the best choice for CEO.

Caulfield, Brian. "Sky Dayton." *Internet World*. 1 Apr. 2000: 94–98. Print. An interview with Sky Dayton. He answers questions about EarthLink and eCompanies and talks about his role as a venture capitalist and what he thinks about his competition. Photographs.

Lee, Alfred. "Connecting: Boingo Wireless Chairman Sky Dayton Cites Communication as a Guiding Factor in His Artistic Pursuits and His Internet Business Career." *Los Angeles Business Journal* 31 May 2010: 12–13. Print. Reports on Dayton's views on the importance of communication and the role it has played in various aspects of his life. Includes biographical details.

"News of the Week: Sky Dayton of Helio LLC Will Step Down." *Los Angeles Business Journal* 4 Feb. 2008: 4. Print. An announcement of Dayton's departure as CEO of Helios, providing a brief professional history of Dayton.

O'Shea, Dan. "Sky Dayton Is Smarter than You, Richer than You and Younger than You. (But He's Very Sorry about That.)." *Wireless Review* 1 Apr. 2002: 48–57. Print. The article profiles Dayton, focusing on his role as CEO of Boingo Wireless as well as information about his character and personality. It also discusses his plans for the company.

SUSAN L. DECKER

Former President of Yahoo!

Born: June 28, 1962; Denver, Colorado
Died: -
Primary Field: Business and commerce
Specialty: Management, executives, and investors
Primary Company/Organization: Yahoo!

INTRODUCTION

Susan L. Decker has served as a role model for women who want to be successful in their careers without giving up the right to have a family. She is best known for her tenure (2000–09) at Yahoo, where she began as chief financial officer and ultimately became president of the company in 2007. During that time, she was the second most highly paid female business executive in the United States. She grew the company's the advertising base, making key acquisitions and focusing on maintaining transparency with Wall Street. When the economic downturn and a takeover bid from Microsoft led to a difficult period for the company, chief executive officer (CEO) Jerry Yang was replaced in 2009 with an external candidate, Carol Bartz, leading to Decker's resignation from Yahoo! in 2009. Her business acumen and her ability to get along well with others have made her a top choice of company heads such as Steve Jobs, Warren Buffet, and Craig R. Barrett when looking for individuals to serve on their boards.

EARLY LIFE

Susan Lynne "Sue" Decker was born on June 28, 1962, in Denver, Colorado, where she was raised. She attended Tufts University, earning a bachelor's degree in computer science and economics in 1984. After receiving an MBA from Harvard Business School in 1986, Decker signed on as a media analyst with Donaldson, Lufkin, and Jenrette.

Decker remained with Donaldson, Lufkin, and Jenrette for fourteen years, becoming an equity research analyst. In 1996, she was assigned the task of reporting on Yahoo! Her lengthy report on the new company was so well received that it became a case study at the Stanford School of Business. In 1998, she became the global

Susan L. Decker.

Affiliation: Yahoo!

Based in Sunnyvale, California, Yahoo! was founded by Jerry Yang and David Filo in 1994 while they were still Ph.D. students at Stanford University. The name was devised as an acronym of the phrase "yet another hierarchical officious oracle." For most of Yahoo!'s history, Yang and Filo left managing the company to experienced professionals. In 2007, however, Yang became CEO upon the departure of Terry Semel, who had previously been a Hollywood studio head.

For many Internet users around the world, Yahoo! has served as their entry to the Internet. With Yahoo! as their home page, millions of users regularly check their e-mail and special interest groups, read the news, keep up with the stock market, and follow notable events in the worlds of entertainment and sports. Millions of others use Yahoo! as their search engine of choice, which provides Yahoo!'s advertisers with a large base of potential customers.

Yahoo! was incorporated in 1995. On April 12 of the following year, the company went public, with trading opening at $13 per share. By the end of the day, Yahoo! stock had climbed to $33 per share. In 1996, Yahoo! began running "Do You Yahoo?" ads on television, which became synonymous with the company's success. By November 1997, Yahoo! was being visited by 2.5 million users per month in the United States alone. By 2000, the company was worth $1 billion.

With the rise of Google in the late 1990s, Yahoo! eventually took a backseat to that search-engine behemoth. However, Yahoo! remains the second most widely used search engine, followed by Microsoft's Bing.

director of equity research. Part of her job involved managing media, advertising, and publishing stocks.

LIFE'S WORK

After becoming friends with Yahoo! executives, Decker was in an excellent position to be considered for the post of Yahoo!'s chief financial officer under Terry Semel in 2000. Decker worked well with Semel, who was considered one of the top executives in the United States. They decided to purchase key Internet content in areas such as search, music, jobs, and personals that could be seamlessly integrated into the overall Yahoo! community. By 2002, Decker was also serving as executive vice president of finance and administration, which placed her in charge of human resources, facilities, and investment relations. In 2004, Yahoo!'s net income came close to quadrupling, rising to $840 million. However, as the situation at Yahoo! worsened during the downward slide of the dot-coms, Yahoo!'s revenue plunged 40 percent, precipitating a flurry of top-level departures.

When Decker had come on board, Yahoo! had been outsourcing its searches to Google, but she understood the importance of search engines in promoting advertising, and she brought the search function back home to Yahoo! In 2003, Yahoo! introduced an improved search engine. Decker also worked to expand Yahoo, acquiring almost thirty companies, including Kekkoo SA, a Parisian shopping site; Inktomi; Overture; Hot Jobs; and the music site LAUNCH. In 2007, Decker negotiated Yahoo!'s acquisition of Right Media, an online publisher that merged advertising transactions with publishers and networks by allowing advertisers to bid on advertising space. The acquisition was criticized, since it was carried out in stages, with the first 20 percent purchased in October 2006 and the final 80 percent acquired in April 2007 for an additional $680 million.

Decker's strategy for improving Yahoo's financial status was largely dependent on protecting the features that generated the most revenue for the company: content brands, mail services, personals, and services for small businesses. By 2006, Google had become an Internet company to be reckoned with, and it had become Yahoo!'s chief rival. As a result, Yahoo! instituted a major reorganization plan. Decker became executive vice president of the Advertiser and Publisher Group while still serving as chief financial officer. At the time, Yahoo! was attracting 500 million visitors every month.

Under Decker's guidance, Yahoo! had become one of the top sellers of Internet advertising and was running its own ads on other sites, such as eBay, Comcast, and newspaper sites. Decker's professional rivalry with Google did not extend to personal relationships, and she became good friends with Sheryl Sandberg, who was a senior executive at Google at the time. The two women had met through Sandberg's husband, David, a former head of Yahoo! Music.

By 2007, Yahoo! was reporting $751 million in profits and $6.4 billion in sales. However, with a market value of $162.8 billion as compared to Yahoo!'s $36.5 billion, Google continued to outpace Yahoo! Social networking sites such as Facebook and Myspace were also giving Yahoo! stiff competition, and Yahoo! missed out on deals that would have allowed it to sell ads on those sites. Instead, Facebook partnered with Microsoft, and Google inked a deal with Myspace. By that time, Yahoo!'s employment base had grown to twelve thousand, and morale was often low, since the company was seen as too bureaucratic.

In 2007, in the midst of Yahoo!'s financial woes, Decker became president while Yahoo! cofounder Jerry Yang served as CEO. As Yahoo!'s situation became grave, the company faced a Microsoft takeover. Decker was adamant about resisting Microsoft's $44.6 billion offer to buy out Yahoo, but her decision was seen as a mistake by many both inside and outside the Yahoo! circle. Efforts to solve financial problems by partnering with Google failed to win approval from the federal government because of antitrust considerations. When Decker failed to negotiate a buyout of the popular video site YouTube, which was eventually bought by Google, and missed a short window of opportunity to purchase Facebook, her failures were seen as major mistakes.

Yahoo!'s board of directors hired Heidrick and Struggles, an executive recruitment firm, to look for a replacement for Yang when he was ousted as CEO. When Yang was forced out of Yahoo, Decker fully expected to be named CEO and was generally considered the most qualified person for the job. Instead, the board hired an outsider, Carol Bartz, who was well known in Silicon Valley. Decker stepped down on January 13, 2009, when she was passed over for the position. Despite financial problems, her time at Yahoo! had proved profitable for the company, with revenues growing from $1 billion in 2000 to more than $7 billion at her departure. Bartz's tenure would prove to be unsuccessful: In April 2009, the same month in which Decker's resignation became effective, Bartz accused a number of employees of not doing their jobs and instituted a series of layoffs. When she, in turn, was ousted in 2011, only a third of Yahoo! employees expressed approval of her job performance.

After leaving Yahoo, Decker accepted a position as entrepreneur in residence at her alma mater, Harvard Business School. In 2010, she was honored with the Alumni Achievement Award, the highest form of recognition offered by Harvard Business School. Subsequently, Decker became a private investment consultant. She has always been much sought after as a member of boards of companies, including Pixar, Costco, Berkshire Hathaway, Intel, and LegalZoom. She is also a trustee of the charity Save the Children.

PERSONAL LIFE

While attending Harvard Business School, Decker met Michael Dovey. They married in 1992. At the age of thirty, with $13 million in the bank, Dovey, an investment banker, gave up a $1.5 million annual salary at Montgomery Securities to retire.

Decker's personal life became a major news story when she and Dovey became involved in protracted divorce proceedings. Beginning in 2007, their battles for child custody and control of $71 million in real estate, cash, stocks, and other assets were drawn out over a five-year period. Divorce papers reflected the lavish lifestyle enjoyed by the high-power couple, who owned a five-bedroom home in San Francisco Bay, a $6 million condo in Laguna Beach, two condos in Lake Tahoe, land in Napa Valley, a private jet, two sailboats, five motorcycles, and a $260,000 golf club membership. A private agreement finally reached in 2012 was dubbed the "Treaty of Versailles" by the media. It resulted in the sale of real estate, with profits divided, and the establishment of large trust funds for the three children produced by the marriage. An avid skier and hiker, Decker settled with her three children in Marin County.

Elizabeth Rholetter Purdy

FURTHER READING

Breslau, Karen, et al. "Big Thinkers for Big Business." *Newsweek* 145.24 (2005): 49–60. Print. Profile of Decker as an important name of the year in the business world. Illustrated.

Christopher, L. Carol. "Yahoo! Raises Online Ad Ante with Purchase of Right Media." *Seybold Report* 7.10 (2007): 2–3. Print. Examines Yahoo!'s acquisition of online publisher Right Media.

Heffes, Ellen M. "Something to Yahoo! About: An Internet Winner." *Financial Executive* 20.3 (2004): 32–36. Print. Profile of Yahoo!

Helft, Miguel. "Can She Turn Yahoo! into, Well, Google?" *New York Times*, 1 July 2007: B1+. Print. Profile of Yahoo! and examination of Decker's overall career. Includes chart.

Kim, Cherry. "On the Record: Yahoo!'s Susan Decker." *CFO* 21.12 (2005): n. pag. Print. Traces Decker's success at Yahoo! and her philosophy as chief financial officer.

Kopytoff, Verne. "Yahoo!'s Embattled CEO to Step Down." *San Francisco Chronicle* 18 Nov. 2008: A-1. Print. Profiles Yang's tenure at Yahoo! and addresses the issue of his replacement.

Pachal, Peter. "How Carol Bartz Blew It as Yahoo! CEO." *PC Magazine* 30.10 (2011): n. pag. Print. Examines Yahoo! after Decker was passed over for CEO and exited the company.

Schack, Justin. "Susan Decker: Yahoo!" *Institutional Investor* (Americas edition) 39.2 (2005): n. pag. Print. Traces Decker's career and her rise to president of Yahoo!

JORY DES JARDINS

Cofounder and president of Strategic Alliances at BlogHer

Born: 1972?; Evanston, Illinois
Died: -
Primary Field: Internet
Specialty: Social media
Primary Company/Organization: BlogHer

INTRODUCTION

Jory Des Jardins, together with new media entrepreneurs Elisa Camahort Page and Lisa Stone, cofounded BlogHer in 2005. She leads the company's partnership initiatives as president of Strategic Alliances. Her leadership in that capacity has helped BlogHer develop unique and potent strategic relationships that make it easier for women across the globe to communicate and find information and products. Before BlogHer's conferences, publishing platform, and online community, women were only a footnote in the male-dominated blogosphere. Thanks to BlogHer, all tech-saavy women, from social media entrepreneurs to stay-at-home moms, have a voice that can be heard worldwide.

EARLY LIFE

Jory Des Jardins was raised in Evanston, Illinois, a Lake Michigan community about thirty minutes' drive north of Chicago. She once blogged that her childhood home had a fluorescent basement in hues of orange, pink, and yellow and was filled with Beanie Babies from her mother's extensive collection.

Des Jardins was not a risk taker in her early years, despite her creative nature. She was a solid student and adhered to all the norms and rules. She dreamed of being a television news anchor or a TV talk show host. In the days before media communications programs were widely offered by institutions of higher education, Des Jardins chose the next closest major—English literature—when she became a student at the University of Illinois at Urbana-Champaign.

Des Jardins received bachelor of arts degree in English literature from the university and then relocated to New York. She did not find steady work as an editor. She expected to follow the traditional career path of working her way up through the ranks of an organization over time. However, she found the process to be slow and unfulfilling. She abandoned and returned to corporate life several times before finally deciding to venture out on her own. At one point, she was offered a contract to write a book. While most aspiring authors would have jumped at the chance, Des Jardins declined the offer. Making that decision helped her realize that she wanted (and owed it to herself) to be passionate about whatever she decided to do, which at the time did not entail writing a book. A chance meeting with some California entrepreneurs, however, was the

Jory Des Jardins.

spark she was looking for; she packed up and moved to the West Coast.

LIFE'S WORK

Des Jardins moved to California to join a start-up run by acquaintances she had met in New York. The company survived for less than three years but gave her insight into entrepreneurship and what she wanted her own future to be. She stayed in California and started blogging. To pay the bills, she took on consulting jobs to help businesses like Pluck and Rojo launch their own syndicated blogs and began writing articles for the business magazine *Fast Company*.

While attending a blog conference, Des Jardins connected with early professional blogger Elisa Camahort Page, who in turn introduced her to online community consultant Lisa Stone. The three discussed the lack of female representation at the conference and decided to host a conference of their own that would be dedicated specifically to women bloggers. The first BlogHer conference was held in 2005 and attracted three hundred women.

To help attendees and other interested women stay in touch, Des Jardins and her partners began a blog using Typepad for hosting and publishing. Within a year, the blog had gained such popularity that Camahort Page, Des Jardins, and Stone decided to leave their day jobs and launch BlogHer as a limited liability company in 2006. Around the same time, they moved their blog onto the Drupal platform in order to enhance the site's design and functionality. The same year, the cofounders developed an advertising and publishing network designed to facilitate and promote women's blogging, both personal and professional. They also enhanced their annual conferences with sponsorship from industry giants such as Procter & Gamble and Johnson and Johnson, as well as guests speakers, who have included such notables as the president of the United States.

In her role as BlogHer's president of Strategic Alliances, Des Jardins has helped the company develop critical partnerships with Fortune 1000 companies across the United States who are seeking to connect with influential bloggers as a way to promote and market their products and services within the context of social media.

Des Jardins also serves as a consultant to Fortune 500 companies that need assistance maneuvering through the social media universe. Through her training and advice, she helps companies build messaging models and campaigns that will expand the reach of their brands and have an impact on the blogging community. In addition, Des Jardins represents BlogHer on the

---

Affiliation: BlogHer

BlogHer is a media company created in 2005 by entrepreneurs Elisa Camahort Page, Jory Des Jardins, and Lisa Stone in response to the realization that female bloggers were getting lost in the expanding blogosphere. BlogHer.com is an online community that enables women to share information and advice relevant to them as professionals, wives, mothers, and sisters. As of April 2012, the site was attracting approximately 40 million unique users per month.

In addition to providing women with and online forum for communication, BlogHer hosts an annual social media conference for women, the largest of its kind in the world. The 2012 BlogHer Conference, held in New York in August, featured an address by President Barack Obama.

BlogHer also operates a massive publishing network, featuring some three thousand high-quality blogs written exclusively by women. BlogHer is supported by more than fifty employees at offices in New York and Silicon Valley and by funding from Azure Capital Partners, Comcast Interactive Capital, and Venrock.

---

board of directors of the Interactive Advertising Bureau and is an advisory board member for FeedBlitz and Juno Baby. She serves as BlogHer's representative through public speaking engagements, performing as a keynote speaker or panelist at important U.S. and international industry events, such as BlogWorld Expo, the Marketing to Moms Conference, ad:tech Chicago, Web 2.0, South by Southwest (SXSW) Interactive, Girls in Tech, and the Monaco (Monte Carlo) Media Forum.

In less than a decade of business, BlogHer has seen its revenue soar to eight figures, its conference participation rate explode into the thousands, its advertising network achieving top-tier distribution status, and the utilization of its BlogHer.com community approaching half a billion hits per month.

Despite the dramatic and swift success of BlogHer, Des Jardins continues to draw from her editorial roots by writing on women's issues and contributing regularly to online and print publications. Her work has appeared in *Fast Company*, *Good Housekeeping*, *Sports Illustrated for Women*, *The New York Times*, the *San Francisco Chronicle Magazine*, *USA Today Magazine*, and *Working Woman*. She also posts frequently to BlogHer on the topics of entrepreneurship and career advancement.

As a way to remain connected within her own physical community, Des Jardins partnered with Camahort Page and a few other local women to found a networking group for women in the Silicon Valley. The organization, called the Silicon Valley Supper Club, enables women in all stages of their careers to connect with and support one another with everything from job leads to reading recommendations.

PERSONAL LIFE

Des Jardins continues to serve as a media consultant and write for prominent publications on topics related to women's business. She also manages From Here to Autonomy, her personal blog, at jorydesjardins.com.

She was included in Ernst and Young's Winning Women Class of 2011. That year, she and her BlogHer cofounders Camahort Page and Stone were jointly awarded the PepsiCo Women's Inspiration Award. She was a semifinalist for Ernst and Young's 2010 Entrepreneur of the Year Award. *Fast Company* named her as one of the most influential women in social media and technology in 2008, 2009, and 2010, and *Forbes* magazine identified her as one of the seven most power individuals in new media in 2009. She was also the recipient of the Anita Borg Institute's Social Impact Award in 2008.

In her free time, Des Jardins likes to power-walk while listening to music. She married landscape designer Jesse Markman in 2006. The couple live in the San Francisco Bay Area with their two-year-old daughter, Olive, and a cat named Ginger. A second daughter was born in 2012.

Shari Parsons Miller

FURTHER READING

Des Jardins, Jory. "Business Blogging for Beginners." *Fast Company* 97 (2005): 28. Print. Provides advice for establishing customer networks via a business blog, including blogging style, etiquette, linking, and tracking.

---. "I Am Woman (I Think)." *Fast Company* 94 (2005): 25–26. Print. The article gives an overview of the experiences Des Jardins has had in a business climate dominated by men.

---. "A Reality Check." *Business 2.0* 8.1 (2007): 115. Print. Talks about how the book *The Artist's Way at Work: Riding the Dragon* helped Des Jardins during the development of her career, teaching her the importance of working a job that reflects who she is as a person.

---. "When Blogs Go Bad." *Inc.* 27.11 (2005): 44–45. Print. Highlights the shortcomings associated with blogging for business purposes in the United States.

"Study: 3 in 4 Online Women Are Active Social Media Users." *Public Relations Tactics* 17.5 (2010): 10. Print. Reports on findings from the BlogHer-iVillage 2010 Social Media Matters Study, which concluded that 73 percent of female Internet users are active in social media and engage with top social media platforms such as Facebook, Twitter, and blogs.

Swartz, Jon. "The New Faces of Tech." *USA Today* 5 June 2012: n. pag. Print. Discusses how young female technology entrepreneurs and executives are changing the face of the traditionally male-dominated Silicon Valley.

Viveiros, Beth Negus. "Picking Up Chicks." *Chief Marketer* 2.5 (2010): 41–42. Print. Describes how BlogHer views female users of social media as a separate marketing segment and how some companies are capitalizing on the site's targeted community to promote and sell their products.

CHRIS DEWOLFE

Cofounder of Myspace

Born: 1966; Portland, Oregon
Died: -
Primary Field: Internet
Specialty: Social media
Primary Company/Organization: Myspace

INTRODUCTION

Chris DeWolfe was the cofounder of the first globally successful social networking site, Myspace. For years it dominated the Internet as the place to be for cyber-active teenagers. It engaged a marketing strategy that

*took affiliate marketing and social data storage to a
new level, largely thanks to DeWolfe, with his background in the world of finance, marketing, and Internet
start-ups. He used this experience to assist in the creation of an Internet phenomenon that took the world by
storm—so much so that traditional media king Rupert
Murdoch bought Myspace. The success of Myspace
solidified DeWolfe's place in social networking history,
despite Facebook's later dominance.*

EARLY LIFE

Chris DeWolfe was born in 1966 in Portland, Oregon.
His father, Fred, wrote history books; his mother, Bri-
gitte, taught college German. The younger of two boys
(with an older brother, Andrew), DeWolfe was fortunate
to grow up in a reasonably affluent household and was
considered popular during high school. Known for his
athleticism, especially his skills in basketball, he graduated from high school in 1984.

DeWolfe moved to Seattle to attend the University
of Washington, from which he graduated with a degree
in finance in 1988. After spending a few years in San
Francisco, he completed a two-year master's of business administration program, graduating from the University of Southern California in 1997. While attending

Chris De Wolfe.

business school, DeWolfe developed a social networking site plan he called Sitegeist (a play on the German
word for "spirit of the times," *Zeitgeist*). This school
project would eventually provide the foundational logistics for Myspace.

After graduating from college, DeWolfe moved to
Pasadena with his future wife, Lorraine Hitselberger.
He worked in the credit department of the First Bank
of Beverly Hills. In 1999, DeWolfe quit his bank job
for a position as the head of marketing for the Internet
start-up XDrive. XDrive was a data storage service that
offered Internet users online storage. XDrive felt the
full brunt of the bursting dot-com bubble, however, and
DeWolfe found himself without a job in March 2001.

LIFE'S WORK

After his time with XDrive came to an end, DeWolfe
decided to begin his own start-up business, Response-
Base, an e-mail marketing company. Former copywriter
for XDrive Tom Anderson became one of DeWolfe's
early collaborators in the new venture.

The website Myspace was one of DeWolfe's first
clients for his new company, which he announced to
the world through a press release on June 20, 2001. At
that time, Myspace was an online data storage site not
dissimilar to XDrive. Myspace was struggling to stay
afloat as Internet shares crashed on Wall Street.

DeWolfe decided to purchase the domain name
Myspace when the company that owned the website
went bankrupt. He paid $5,000 for the name. It would
be some time before he did much with the company's
domain name, however. He had a reputation in the online world for creating spam marketing. Anderson was
known for his interest in online pornography sites. Neither was considered a major player in the online world.

As their company established itself, it moved away
from e-mail spam marketing to virtual newsletters and
online books. This moved ResponseBase from e-mail
marketing to the world of e-commerce, immediately improving the company's reputation. Profits continued to
increase, and e-commerce entrepreneurs began to take
notice.

ResponseBase came to the attention of eUniverse—
a growing online company managing several websites
and expanding at a time when many online companies
were shrinking—and its owner, Brad Greenspan. ResponseBase was constantly improving, and Greenspan
was interested: After his offer to buy the company using eUniverse stock was rejected, Greenspan purchased
ResponseBase for $3.3 million. Under eUniverse's

tutelage, ResponseBase continued to perform well and saw a major climb in corporate profits.

In 2003, Friendster was a popular online social networking site that enjoyed a broad subscriber base. The idea of offering storage space combined with online chat was proving profitable and had low costs. DeWolfe approached his partners about creating a site similar to Friendster but better, using the domain name he had purchased in 2001, Myspace. Despite the reservations his partner expressed about the strangeness of the domain name, they launched the site on August 15, 2003. As Internet access improved across the United States, so did the popularity of Myspace.

Affiliation: Myspace

Tom Anderson was a laid-off copywriter when finance and marketing major Chris DeWolfe asked him to work for his start-up company ResponseBase in 2001. ResponseBase was an e-mail marketing business. DeWolfe had purchased the domain name Myspace after one of his e-mail marketing clients went bankrupt. He paid $5,000 for the domain name, which two years later he and Anderson would relaunch as the world's go-to source for online music, information about new bands, and fan-to-fan communication. Myspace catered to those involved or interested in the entertainment world, but it also attracted an entire generation of teenagers to its data storage options, page personalization capabilities, and social networking features. The site grew exponentially, seeing 70 million unique users by the end of 2005. Myspace became a phenomenon: It was the seventh most popular site in the world in 2006, and the parent company's cofounders, Anderson and DeWolfe, made *Time* magazine's Top 100 list that year. The website was also the first globally successful social networking site, although membership peaked as Facebook began to dominate the market in 2009.

Myspace was sold to Rupert Murdoch's company News Corp. in 2005 for $580 million. In 2008, Myspace had 117 million unique users and was ranked the top social networking site in the world. DeWolfe stepped down as CEO in 2009, and News Corp. sold Myspace in 2011 for $35 million to pop star Justin Timberlake and the company Specific Media. The site remains popular with musicians and still showcase's new albums for established artists.

In its early days, Myspace was a platform for musicians to showcase their latest albums, deliver their music to the public without having to negotiate a deal with a recording company, and communicate with fans on a deeper level through feedback and song comments. Both DeWolfe and Anderson had musical aspirations, and relaunching the site as a place for musicians made sense for those goals as well. The site did a good job promoting new bands and attracted significant numbers of Generation Y users. Soon, Myspace began doing double duty as a music storage website and a social networking hub.

Myspace grew its reputation for online music and online chat. User stats continued to improve, and the world of social networking began to dominate the market. In 2006, Myspace was the seventh most popular website in the entire world. After some issues occurred with eUniverse, the parent company became Intermix Media. In July 2005, the popularity, profitability, and mass-media appeal of Myspace eventually piqued the interest of traditional media mogul Rupert Murdoch. Murdoch's News Corp. dominated the television news industry but had yet to find a firm footing online. Myspace seemed like the perfect acquisition.

After the cofounders sold Myspace to Murdoch in 2005 for $580 million, DeWolfe became the chief executive officer (CEO) and Tom Anderson became the president. Between 2005 and 2008, Myspace saw record web traffic, often beating online giants such as Google. Despite the fact that Myspace surpassed Facebook in user stats in 2009, DeWolfe decided to step down as CEO to pursue other business interests.

In 2011, News Corp. sold Myspace for $35 million to music artist Justin Timberlake and Specific Media. Myspace still promotes bands and offers users a place to share their music and comment on their favorite songs, but was largely superseded by Facebook as the most popular social networking site.

PERSONAL LIFE

After graduating from college, DeWolfe married Lorraine Hitselberger in 1997, whom he had met in business school. The couple moved to Pasadena, California. The marriage appeared to have been an unhappy one from the beginning. DeWolfe began divorce proceedings in 2007 and a long and difficult litigation began, including a restraining order against DeWolfe and proceedings with the Department of Family Services regarding the couple's only daughter, although few details of the case were released.

After leaving Myspace, DeWolfe began devoting his time to social gaming, game development, and gaming applications. In 2010, along with Colin Digiaro and Aber Whitcomb, DeWolfe bought the social gaming site MindJolt, which already had an established user base. It enjoys 20 million active monthly users and continues to expand. It has offered DeWolfe the chance to use his work experience and his mistakes to create a solid on-line gaming business. MindJolt provides online games and gaming apps for smart phones. DeWolfe has also devoted his attention to creating social gaming apps, including one for the American Humane Society.

DeWolfe sits on the board of the Los Angles County Museum of Art. In 2012, he joined the board of the creative marketing firm Talenthouse. He lives in Los Angeles, California.

Trish Popovitch

FURTHER READING

Anguin, Julia. *Stealing Myspace: The Battle to Control the Most Popular Website in America.* New York: Random House, 2009. Print. A mixture of facts and author interpretation of the events leading up to the purchase of Myspace by Rupert Murdoch. Often considered the "tell all" book of Myspace.

Collier, Anne, and Larry Magid. *Myspace Unraveled: A Parent's Guide to Teen Social Networking.* Berkeley: Peachpit, 2007. Print. Shows parents how to set up Myspace page, monitor their children, presents the basic components of social networking and provides background on how the website operates.

Foo, Sharin. "Time's Top 100: Tom Anderson and Chris DeWolfe." *Time* 8 May 2006. Web. 25 July 2012. Myspace founders Tom Anderson and DeWolfe make number 23 on Time's Top 100 for 2006. Discusses Rupert Murdoch's purchase of Myspace.

Keen, Andrew. *The Cult of the Amateur: How Blogs, Myspace, YouTube, and the Rest of Today's User-Generated Media Are Destroying Our Economy, Our Culture, and Our Values.* New York: Crown, 2008. Print. Looks at the downside of the social media phenomenon and addresses the negative associations with Myspace regarding privacy and teen safety, fears addressed publicly by Myspace parents, adding to the controversy of the site.

Kozlowski, Lori. "New Life: How Myspace Spawned a Start-up Ecosystem." *Forbes* 15 May 2012. Web. 25 July 2012. Explains how Myspace pioneered change in the social networking world and the ability of one company, no matter how successful, to lay the foundation of change in the business world.

Lusted, Marcia Amidon. *Social Networking: My Space, Facebook and Twitter.* Edina: ABDO, 2011. E-book. An easy-to-read history of Myspace and how the company changed over time. Discusses the phenomenon of social networking and Myspace's role in establishing the trend.

Nakashima, Ryan. "Chris DeWolfe, Myspace Cofounder, to Step Down." *Huffington Post* 23 Apr. 2009. Web. 25 July 2012. Explains DeWolfe's reasons for leaving the company. Provides some background information on the company and its cofounders.

Rusli, Evelyn. "A Myspace Founder Builds Again, Buying Gaming Companies." *New York Times* 18 Apr. 2011. Web. 25 July 2012. Discusses DeWolfe's involvement with the gaming company MindJolt and its many gaming platforms and acquisitions. Contrasts DeWolfe's success and profitability with Myspace with his choices in the online gaming world.

Vincent, Francis. *Myspace for Musicians: The Comprehensive Guide to Marketing Your Music.* Boston: Cengage, 2011. Print. Shows how Myspace remained an effective portal for musical entertainment and musicians even after the ascendancy of Facebook. Gives detailed instructions on how to use Myspace to further music-based careers.

WILLIAM DING

Founder of NetEase

Born: 1972?; Fenghua, Ningbo Prefecture, Zhejiang Province, People's Republic of China
Died: -
Primary Field: Internet
Specialty: Applications

Primary Company/Organization: NetEase

INTRODUCTION
William Ding changed the state of the Chinese Internet industry with the founding and evolution of NetEase.

115

When he launched the company in 1997, most of China's immense population did not have easy or affordable access to the Internet. Ding revolutionized the market by creating an online portal that gave anyone in China free access to e-mail and the Internet. Building on the success of the portal NetEase.com, Ding expanded the business into new segments with innovative technologies. In the process, he created many "firsts" within China's Internet industry, including the country's first online auction (which paved the way for e-commerce applications) and the first Chinese-language search engine and online community. NetEase became China's leading Internet portal and community and made Ding one of the world's wealthiest entrepreneurs. With the inclusion in its portfolio of online multiuser computer games, NetEase and Ding continued to blaze trails in China's Internet frontier.

EARLY LIFE

William Ding was born as Ding Lei in the small and ancient city of Fenghua in Zhejiang Province on China's southeast coast. The city is best known as the hometown of political and military leader Chiang Kai-shek. Despite growing up in the region, Ding was more impressed by revolutionary science and technology than

William Ding.

military might. As a child, Ding counted among his heroes Albert Einstein and Thomas Alva Edison. By his early teens, Ding had become fascinated with electronics and was able to assemble his own transistor radios. He envisioned himself one day being an exceptional mechanical engineer.

Ding attended Chengdu Institute of Radio Engineering, China's first institution of higher education dedicated to electronic and information science and technology. During his four years at the school (now known as the University of Electronic Science and Technology of China) Ding was an eager and inquisitive student, but he was also fiercely independent. He approached things his own way, whether it was the question he posed or the methods he used to study. He earned high grades and spent his free time perusing the school library's enormous collection of books on information technology and electronics. He has reflected on his days at the school—and the time spent in its grand library—as among his most cherished. Ding did not spend all his time with books, however. He was creating and developing his own software by the time he graduated with a bachelor's degree in communication technology in 1993.

LIFE'S WORK

Ding began his professional career as a technical engineer working for China Telecom's branch in Ningbo Prefecture. He left that position in 1995, after two years, relocating to the country's third-largest city, Guangzhou, in southern China. There he accepted a high-paying position as a project manager and technical support engineer at the China offices of U.S.-based software company Sybase. He stayed with Sybase for only one year before departing in 1996 to join Guangzhou Feijie Company as a systems analyst. Ding again left after a year. This time, however, he did not put down roots with another existing enterprise. Instead, he created his own.

Ding founded NetEase in May 1997 in Beijing as an Internet portal specifically designed for users in mainland China. By then, he had realized two things: first, that the Internet represented the future of information technology, and second, that the majority of the mainland Chinese population either did not have or were unlikely to use their disposable income to pay for Internet service. Ding, a lifelong believer in the importance of setting goals and seizing opportunities, decided to take a calculated risk. He launched Netease.com to provide every user with free e-mail and a personal website. His peers called him crazy, saying he would never be able to make money with his model of free access. In fact, his own brother declined to join the fledgling firm for fear of imminent disaster. Ding held fast to his belief that the volume of traffic generated by the site would attract paying advertisers.

Ding's gamble paid off. After only three years of operation, NetEase.com was experiencing some 6 million page views daily. The substantial success of Ding's unorthodox endeavor started attracting investors, and it was not long before the company had financial backing from several of the leading financial giants of the time, including the bank ING and Goldman Sachs. Spurred by his company's early wins and newly acquired fiscal support, Ding, as chief executive officer (CEO), began expanding the business. He added China's first personalized information service, the first Chinese-language search engine, and his country's first online auction site. The latter required some ingenuity once it became evident that most of China's population did not have credit cards to pay for items online. Ding solved the problem with the inclusion of a cash-on-delivery option for online purchasers. That move opened the door for e-commerce in China, not only demonstrating the colossal demand among the Chinese population for diverse merchandise and value (not available via the country's brick-and-mortar retail stores) but also providing a model and means to help businesses tap a massive and widely scattered national market.

In April 2000, Ding stepped down as NetEase's CEO, becoming the company's chief technology officer. The move was designed to enable him to focus on technology and product innovation rather than on the daily operations of managing the business. In both capacities, he faced strict challenges in the form of Chinese government regulations restricting and censoring content, defining user privacy policies, and regulating public offerings by corporations. NetEase became public company.

In 2001, NetEase faced a crisis amid rumors that it had misreported its finances. Its stock price plunged on threats of delisting, but NetEase pulled through, and by the next year its stock was soaring. In March, Ding became chief architect of NetEase.com, which was ranked among the most-visited Internet sites in the world. Ding held the chief architect position until November 2005, when he returned to the top spot as the company's CEO.

Since returning to the helm, Ding has developed NetEase into one of China's largest and most successful companies for massively multiplayer online role-playing games (MMORPGs). In 2009, NetEase entered

---

Affiliation: NetEase

NetEase is an Internet technology company founded in Beijing, China, by William Ding (Ding Lei) in 1997. It was the first company of its kind in China and pioneered the development of the country's Internet market through innovative products, services, and technologies. It operates through several China-based affiliates—Guangzhou NetEase, Guangyitong Advertising, and Shanghai EaseNet—to provide an interactive online community for China's population. Specifically, NetEase offers Chinese-language content and services, massively multiplayer online role-playing games, free Internet portal and e-mail services, advertising and e-commerce platforms, and wireless value-added offerings (such as instant messaging, microblogs, news content, community forums, and music and photo applications).

After beginning with only $60,000 in seed money, NetEase had a market capitalization of more than $6 billion in the first quarter of 2012. The majority of its revenue is generated from its online games, including its license for Activision Blizzard, Inc.'s hugely popular *World of Warcraft* games and its own NetEase-developed popular game products *Tianxia II* and *Heroes of Tang Dynasty*.

---

into a lucrative licensing agreement with Irvine, California–based Blizzard Entertainment to bring the U.S. gaming company's hugely successful *World of Warcraft* to audiences in mainland China. Under the agreement, the two companies also launched several other games, which have been well received. In March 2012, NetEase and Blizzard extended the agreement to continue their partnership for an additional three years. That was good news for NetEase. The company's online game operations accounted for the biggest share of the company's millions of dollars in revenue. It was also good news for Ding, who held 45 percent of NetEase's stock.

In 2003, Ding was recognized as being China's wealthiest individual. Since then, he has consistently appeared on the *Forbes* lists of the world's richest billionaires. With a net worth of $2.8 billion as of March 2012, Ding ranked a 418 among world billionaires and 17 among China's billionaires.

PERSONAL LIFE
In addition to leading NetEase, Ding has become involved with two decidedly low-tech ventures: a pig farm

and a winery. Both enterprises resulted from Ding's negative personal experiences: one at a Chinese fondue restaurant and the other while purchasing a bottle of wine that proved to have expired. The first incident prompted Ding to invest in an 800-square-kilometer pig farm in China's rural countryside and launch an agriculture division of NetEase. As a result of the second incident, Ding used his own money to partner with some friends in the purchase of a château in Zhejiang Province near his hometown in Ningbo Prefecture. The purpose of the château was to serve as the base for the operation of a wine importation business.

While those ventures have garnered Ding some unusual attention, he has also earned public kudos for his work with NetEase. In 2004, he was honored with the Wharton Infosys Business Transformation Award for his innovative utilization of information technology, and in 2000 he was nominated for the prestigious Internet World Asia Industry Award in the category Internet Visionary of the Year.

Shari Parsons Miller

FURTHER READING

"Behind the Great Firewall." *Advertising Age* 82.24 (2011): 12. Web. 12 July 2012. Discusses the Internet industry in China, with detailed consideration given to Chinese companies—such as Baidu, Renren, and Youku—that are similar to the U.S. Internet and social media companies that the Chinese government has banned from the market.

Ewing, Richard Daniel. "China's Online Video Game Wars." *China Business Review* July/Aug. 2007: 45+. Web. 12 July 2012. Discusses China's emergence as a key battleground for foreign investors seeking to tap its more than $1 billion market, which is growing rapidly and on track to become a world gaming leader.

Gold, Donald H. "NetEase Beats Estimates, and Stock Hits New High." *Investors Business Daily* 18 May 2012: B04. Web. 12 July 2012. Highlights NetEase's financial results for the first quarter or 2012 and identifies the company as one that investors should keep watch of for continued high performance.

Hoogewerf, Rupert. "The Taint of Original Sin." *Asiamoney* (2003): 6–7. Web. 12 July 2012. Provides a discussion of the challenges faced by trailblazing Chinese technology entrepreneurs Ding of NetEase, Chen Tianqiao of Shanda, and Charles Zhang Chaoyang of Sohu amid the country's significant income disparity and intensifying global competition.

"Is Real-Name Registration Necessary for Micro-Blogs?" *Beijing Review* 55.5 (2012): 28–30. Web. 12 July 2012. Talks about the impact of Chinese government regulation requiring Internet companies with microblogging services to require accurate personal data upon registration, a practice some believe will limit use and lead to service provider losses.

Yoon, Taesik. "Buy at a High?" *Forbes* 8 June 2012. Web. 12 July 2012. Recommends investing in the robust and rising stocks of Chinese Internet service provider and online gaming powerhouse NetEase, which is benefiting from increased Internet access and income levels throughout China.

Zhang, Jun. "China's Dynamic Industrial Sector: The Internet Industry." *Eurasian Geography and Economics* 49.5 (2008): 549–68. Web. 12 July 2012. Presents an analysis of China's Internet industry, paying particular attention to inequitable access on a regional basis, exacerbated by an uneven endowment of both industrial and entrepreneurial resources.

JACK DORSEY

Founder of Twitter

Born: November 19, 1976; St. Louis, Missouri
Died: -
Primary Field: Internet
Specialty: Social media
Primary Company/Organization: Twitter

INTRODUCTION

Entrepreneur and computer programmer Jack Dorsey is best known as the creator of Twitter, a microblogging tool that uses messages of 140 characters or fewer to share news and other information with followers.

At first disregarded by many as a trivial service for the egotistical, Twitter gained respect as groups and individuals used it as a platform for political, social, and increasingly commercial agendas. Between Twitter and Square, a platform to accept debit or credit-card payments via smart phones, Dorsey has helped generate $10 billion in market value. He has been hailed by the press as a modern Thomas Edison and the next Steve Jobs.

EARLY LIFE

Jack Dorsey was born on November 19, 1976, in St. Louis, Missouri, and grew up in the city, the oldest of three sons born to Tim and Marcia Dorsey. His father was an engineer, and his mother owned a coffee shop in an era before the Starbucks chain. By the time he was eight, Dorsey was fascinated with maps of cities and covered the walls of his small bedroom with maps from magazines and gas stations. A shy, skinny boy, he liked walking through the city, his curiosity excited by all the sights. He was particularly interested in the trains, taxis, and police cars that moved around the city and spent hours with his younger brother Danny videotaping moving trains. When his father brought home the family's first computer, an IBM PC Jr., Jack found another

Jack Dorsey.

fascination. He could now design his own maps using a graphics program. At fourteen, listening to police and ambulance radio frequencies, he developed an interest in real-time physical information transfer. He taught himself programming, and at fifteen, still a student at Bishop DuBorg High School, he was working as a programmer, writing dispatch software that some taxicab companies still use.

After high school, Dorsey attended the University of Missouri at Rolla (now the Missouri University of Science and Technology) briefly, but he left to write code for a dispatch software company in New York. After another try at college life, this time at New York University, he moved to Oakland, California, and in 2000 started a company that offered his dispatch software through the Internet. It was while he was running this company that an idea came to him: combining dispatch software with instant messaging. When he heard that Odeo (a company that enabled the creation, recording, and sharing of podcasts) was hiring programmers, he applied and signed a three-week trial contract. Meanwhile, wanting a backup plan in case programming proved unsatisfying, he enrolled at a fashion class at Apparel Arts, a trade school in San Francisco, and began designing and sewing clothes.

LIFE'S WORK

When Apple incorporated a directory of podcasts into iTunes, Odeo had to find a new direction. Odeo cofounder Evan Williams asked his staff for ideas, and Dorsey offered his concept of combining dispatch software with instant messaging. Reactions were mixed, but Dorsey began working on his idea with others. A number of people contributed to the project, then called "twttr," but agreement that all the work was based on Dorsey's original idea is unanimous. Dorsey sent the first message, or "tweet," on March 21, 2006, and four months later, on July 15, Odeo officially launched Twitter for the public. Initially the service it did not generate much buzz, but in March 2007, at the South by Southwest (SXSW) music and digital conference in Austin, Texas, thousands of conferees, attracted by Twitter's demonstration display, began tweeting about conference events and the best parties. At the time, Twitter normally carried about twenty thousand messages per day. The figure rose to sixty thousand during the conference.

Williams bought Odeo from its investors, and in late 2006 he, Twitter cofounder Biz Stone, and Dorsey founded Obvious Corporation, a company designed to be a start-up incubator with Twitter as its first project.

Affiliation: Twitter

Twitter, Inc., is a free online social media service that allows subscribers to send and receive text messages of 140 characters or less, called "tweets," through the Twitter website using both conventional computers and compatible mobile devices. Initially it was the idea of Jack Dorsey, a programmer at the podcasting company Odeo. After Apple's iTunes added a podcasting directory, Odeo needed a new direction. Dorsey offered his idea of a service that combined texting with dispatching, and within weeks he and a few others had created a prototype. Launched in its full-scale public version on July 15, 2006, the service was named when a dictionary search yielded the word "twitter" with its remarkably apt definitions: "a short burst of inconsequential information" and "chirps from birds." In October 2006, Evan Williams, a cofounder of Odeo, bought out the company's shareholders, and he, Dorsey, Biz Stone, and several other Odeo employees founded Obvious Corporation with all the assets of Odeo, including Twitter.

In March 2007, a Twitter demonstration at the South by Southwest (SXSW) music and digital conference in Austin, Texas, captured the interest of the tech-savvy crowd. Twitter's daily usage surged to sixty thousand tweets daily, three times its usual number. A year later, subscriptions to the service had increased tenfold. In 2008, presidential candidate Barack Obama tweeted his thanks to forty thousand followers who had helped carry him to victory. In 2009, the U.S. government called, requesting that Twitter maintenance be delayed so that the world could learn of Iranian voters' protest against election results. Tweets provided the only unblocked source of news from the country.

Twitter announced an $800 million funding deal in 2011, reportedly the largest venture capital deal in history. By 2012, the number of subscribers had reached half a billion, and Twitter was being used to promote not only tweets but also trends and marketing for name brands such as McDonald's and Pepsi, which increased advertising revenue substantially.

The next year, Twitter was spun off as a separate company with Dorsey as chief executive officer (CEO). Catapulted from being one of the group to being in charge left Dorsey uneasy. Since many of Twitter's employees had moved from the failed Odeo, morale was low. Dorsey felt that the company belonged to the older, more experienced Williams and was reluctant to advance his own ideas. Pressure was intensified by the speed at which Twitter was growing. By 2008, the company had 5 million users. According to some sources, tension between Dorsey and Williams had increased to the degree that they were hardly speaking to each other. In October, Dorsey was ousted as CEO and Williams took over. Dorsey remained as company chairman, but he was no longer an employee of Twitter, the company built on a product he had conceived. The normally private Dorsey has admitted that his dismissal was painful.

A few months after he left Twitter, Dorsey was in St. Louis visiting his parents for the Christmas holiday. He had a chance encounter with Jim McKelvey, an entrepreneur turned glassblower, for whom a fifteen-year-old Dorsey had written CD-ROM software. Dorsey and McKelvey decided they wanted to work together again. In February 2009, McKelvey called and shared with Dorsey the story of a lost sale. McKelvey had been unable to complete the sale of a $3,000 glass faucet because he could not process credit card payments from his studio. Both Dorsey and McKelvey were using iPhones at the time of the conversation, and Dorsey began wondering whether, with that technology readily available, it would be feasible to process credit cards using a smart phone. Within a month, McKelvey had built a magnetic reader through which cards could be swiped. Dorsey had written the software for the server to process the payments, and Tristan O'Tierney, who wrote the Twinkle application for Tapulous, a Disney subsidiary, wrote the iPhone app. On December 1, 2009, Dorsey tweeted to announce the birth of a new company, Square, Inc., a service that allows any individual or small business to accept payment by credit card using a mobile phone. Once again, Dorsey was a cofounder and a CEO.

Twitter continued to grow. U.S. presidential candidates Barack Obama and John McCain had demonstrated that the service could be an effective campaign tool in 2008, and the presidential election that year showed that the service could also be a weapon against tyranny. Iranian Twitter users tweeted live updates of the thousands protesting the victory claimed by incumbent Mahmoud Ahmadinejad after the Iranian government blocked text messaging and satellite feeds of foreign news coverage. By 2010, Twitter had more than 105 million users, who together tweeted some 55 million times a day.

Inside the company, however, the situation was troubled. In October 2010, Williams was replaced as CEO by Dick Costolo, the company's chief operating officer. By his own account, Williams chose to leave, but several other sources say that the board asked him to leave. In March 2011, rumors began to circulate that Dorsey, who had remained chairman of the board, would be resuming a more active role at Twitter. He had privately expressed regret that he had not been part of Twitter's recent growth and dissatisfaction with the company's recent product design and inattention to users' needs. On March 28, CEO Costolo tweeted that Dorsey would return as executive chairman in charge of product development. Dorsey's own tweet added that he would also continue as CEO of Square. On March 29, Williams announced, after a four months' vacation, that he would not be returning to Twitter in a management role.

PERSONAL LIFE

Dorsey is a paradox. A wealthy man whose personal fortune has been estimated in excess of $300 million, he gave away the software he wrote as shareware for years. A techie since he was in elementary school, he is also an admirer of ballet with an avowed appreciation for its coordination and discipline. Perhaps not coincidentally, he had a serious relationship was with Sofiane Sylve, a principal dancer with the San Francisco Ballet. A CEO of one successful company and board chairman and head of product development in another, he sports a black, nine-inch tattoo in the shape of a thick *S* that runs along his left forearm. He says it represents his interests in math, music, and anatomy.

Dorsey is also a lover of cities. It was curiosity about his home city that propelled him into technology. Although he own an automobile (his first, a BMW M3), he spends a great deal of time walking in a fourteen-block area of San Francisco where his office at Square and his office at Twitter are located less than half a mile apart and his loft apartment is just around the corner from his office at Square. He dreams of becoming mayor of New York City and is serious enough about that ambition to have discussed his goal with Mayor Michael Bloomberg. Dorsey has said that thinking about cities keeps him energized.

Wylene Rholetter

FURTHER READING

Hempel, Jessi. "Trouble@Twitter." *Fortune* 2 May 2011: 66–76. Print. Examines the internal politics of Twitter that led to Dorsey's return to an active role in the company in 2011. Compares Twitter to rival social network company Facebook and analyzes Twitter's failure to turn popularity into profits.

Johnson, Steven. "How Twitter Will Change the Way We Live (in 140 Characters or Less)." *Time* 5 June 2009: 32–37. Print. Examines Twitter as a cultural phenomenon and offers an explanation of why Twitter is needed and its effects on users' connections to those in their social network.

Kirkpatrick, David. "Twitter Was Act One." *Vanity Fair* Apr. 2011: 170–71. Print. A detailed profile of Dorsey from his childhood as a shy boy obsessed with city maps through his Twitter years to his current ambitions for Square, the company he cofounded in 2009 after his dismissal as CEO of Twitter.

Miller, Claire Cain. "Two of Twitter's Founders Exchange Roles." *New York Times* 29 Mar. 2011: 12. Print. Reports on the changes the relationships of Dorsey and Williams withTwitter. Looks at the two men as cofounders and then examines the shifts as Dorsey was forced out as CEO, was replaced by Williams, and ultimately returned to active involvement with the company.

Smith, Chris, and Marcie McGrata. *Twitter: Jack Dorsey, Biz Stone, and Evan Williams*. Greensboro: Morgan Reynolds, 2011. Print. Covers the early lives of the three founders of Twitter. Discusses Dorsey's early fascination with city maps and computer programming and the interest Williams and Stone had in blogging that led to their careers. Traces the development of Twitter and the roles each founder played. Aimed at young adults, this source nonetheless contains a wealth of information that anyone interested in Twitter or its founders will find useful.

MATT DRUDGE

Founder of *The Drudge Report*

Born: October 27, 1966; Takoma Park, Maryland
Died: -
Primary Field: Internet

Specialty: News and entertainment
Primary Company/Organization: *The Drudge Report*

INTRODUCTION

Matt Drudge is the creator and editor of the eponymous website The Drudge Report. *Although the website is reviled by some, the self-proclaimed antigovernment libertarian created one of the more popular sites by offering aggregation of news found elsewhere as well as some original stories. Drudge includes links to sites from across the political spectrum and has developed a reputation for sometimes breaking news stories before large news organizations do so.*

EARLY LIFE

Matthew Nathan "Matt" Drudge was born on October 27, 1966, in Takoma Park, Maryland, a suburb of Washington, D.C. Drudge's father, Robert, was a social worker, and his mother, who went by several first names and who changed her surname from Kudish to Drudge to Star, worked at one point for Senator Edward Kennedy until she had to resign to address mental health problems. Drudge's parents, whom he has described as Reform Jewish Democrats, divorced when he was six. Drudge lived with his mother after his parents' divorce and was relatively unpopular in school, forming few friendships. Drudge attended Northwood High School in Rockville, Maryland, where he earned his diploma in 1984, ranking 341st in his class of 355.

After high school, Drudge moved around a great deal, living in New York City for a time. He held a variety of different jobs during this period. He worked during the 1980s as a telemarketer for Time-Life Books, as a clerk at a 7-Eleven convenience store, at a McDonald's restaurant, and as a stocker at a grocery store. In 1989, Drudge relocated to his father's hometown, Los Angeles, where he worked as a clerk and later manager at the gift shop at CBS Television City, located in the Fairfax district. While there, he became accustomed to hearing rumors about the entertainment industry and lived in a small Hollywood apartment. By 1994, Drudge's father had expressed concerns about his son's lack of ambition and purchased him a desktop computer in an attempt to provide him with some direction. With this machine and dial-up Internet access, Drudge began *The Drudge Report* as an e-mail that he sent to a few friends and later posted to a Usenet forum.

LIFE'S WORK

Early editions of *The Drudge Report* focused on providing gossip and opinion related to the entertainment industry. Drudge used his access to gossip regarding ratings, cancellations, and other media information before it became publicly known. He also sometimes included political gossip, which proved of interest to many of his readers. Because they enjoyed *The Drudge Report*, they forwarded it to friends, who in turn were added to Drudge's subscription list. By 1995, *The Drudge Report* had more than a thousand subscribers, all of whom received the publication by e-mail.

Drudge began to attract national attention in 1996, when he identified Republican presidential nominee Bob Dole's choice of vice presidential running mate as Jack Kemp before any of the mainstream media had done so. As a result of this scoop, *The Drudge Report*'s popularity soared, and by 1997 more than eighty-five thousand subscribed to Drudge's e-mail service. Beginning in 1997, Drudge also started to make *The Drudge Report* available over the World Wide Web, which greatly expanded his audience. *The Drudge Report*'s real breakthrough, however, came about as a result of the scandal involving White House intern Monica Lewinsky. A reporter for *Newsweek* magazine, Michael Isikoff, had learned of reports that President Bill Clinton had engaged in an inappropriate relationship with twenty-three-year-old. *Newsweek* was prepared to publish the story on January 17, 1998, but decided not to

Matt Dudge.

do so at the eleventh hour. *The Drudge Report* first reported on the Lewinsky story on January 18, 1998, beating its closest rival, *The Washington Post*, which did not break the story until January 21. This scoop generated a great deal of positive press for *The Drudge Report*, and the website became popular, especially with more conservative readers. Drudge became known for including information on his website that the mainstream media will not include, such as exit poll information while the polls are still open.

The Drudge Report's design has seen few modifications or upgrades since its debut and consists of a headline and photograph above the title and three columns below, mostly links to stories in other publications, against a plain white background. Drudge uses a red font for stories he considers especially important, and for breaking news—such as that involving a U.S. Supreme Court opinion on a controversial issue or the death of a major celebrity—a flashing blue and red light appears at the top of the screen. *The Drudge Report* includes advertisements that generate revenue for Drudge, estimated to be approximately $3,500 per day, nearly $1.3 million per year. Drudge runs *The Drudge Report* with an extremely small staff, usually employing only one or two assistants.

The Drudge Report is estimated to be among the top hundred websites visited daily in the United States, and it is among the top 400 globally. The website generates approximately 3 million visits per day and is especially popular with political insiders, such as congressional staffers. This popularity is due in part to *The Drudge Report*'s continuing ability to break stories and cover accounts that the mainstream media have traditionally been reluctant to cover. Examples of content that has generated attention for *The Drudge Report* include claims of the Swift Boat Veterans for Truth (which worked to discredit candidate John Kerry) during the 2004 U.S. presidential elections, unflattering photographs of President Barack Obama, and reports on the deployment of Britain's Prince Harry in Afghanistan. *The Drudge Report*'s style of publishing stories without verifying information according to the rules of journalism has caused controversy, especially when errors occur. For example, Drudge's site published a story on a CNN reporter allegedly heckling Republican senators during a news conference, even though video clips showed no such behavior on the part of the reporter.

Drudge understands that the public is fascinated by tabloid-style stories, and as a result *The Drudge Report* covers topics such as the cancer risks of cell phones and

---

Affiliation: *The Drudge Report*

Growing from an e-mail circulating gossip about the entertainment industry, *The Drudge Report* has grown into one of the more popular websites on the Internet. Although mostly an aggregator of news generated by other sources, *The Drudge Report* does occasionally break original news stories, often originating from tips provided by political insiders to Matt Drudge. While initially seen as a conservative site, *The Drudge Report* is now viewed as more libertarian and has supporters from both of the major political parties.

The Drudge Report is a fairly simple-looking website that contains links to selected news stories chosen by editor Drudge. Favorite themes include those stories related to politics, finance, and foreign affairs, but it also offers many links to reports of celebrity misdeeds and film box-office results. Although *The Drudge Report* is often criticized by members of the mainstream media, such exemplars of journalism as *The New York Times* have advertised on Drudge's website.

The Drudge Report has used a series of exclusives to build a reputation as a place to go for breaking news on the Internet. Unconstrained by practices and procedures that demand sources be vetted and rumors confirmed, Drudge is unafraid to put up stories that other media sources will not and indeed is unapologetic about publishing rumors that later turn out to be untrue. The popularity of *The Drudge Report* has even led some mainstream media outlets to relax policies and procedures in order to be able to compete with Drudge. In that sense, *The Drudge Report* has been both emblematic and in the vanguard of the evolution of journalism and new media in the Internet age.

---

celebrity misdeeds alongside war reports and economic news. Some have compared Drudge to a performance artist, insofar as he balances the public's need for conflicting yet complimentary types of information. Well aware of the power of the Internet, Drudge seeks to feed the public's appetite for almost instant information, especially when other outlets cautiously avoid disclosing unconfirmed reports. Accused early in his career of having a predisposition for mounting dirty attacks, Drudge has become more reluctant to run stories involving the domestic peccadilloes of elected officials. Although Drudge is the bane of many in the media, he has been invited to address the National Press Club, granting a form of legitimacy not just to *The Drudge Report* but also to bloggers and other web-based news sources. Although controversial, Drudge has stated that his populist approach to the national leaders and events has made the process of news gathering more egalitarian and open. Certainly, *The Drudge Report* has met a demand for quick and sometimes edgy news.

Drudge has also worked to extend his reach by appearing in different media, including radio, broadcast television, and cable news channels. These attempts have met with mixed results. Drudge had a program on the Fox News Channel in 1998 and 1999, but this program was ended by mutual consent after a dispute about content. A book, *Drudge Manifesto*, was published in 2000 and appeared on the *New York Times'* best-seller list. Drudge next appeared on a weekly talk radio show, also known as *The Drudge Report*, which was syndicated by Premiere Radio Networks. Although this program enjoyed some success, Drudge decided to end it in 2007 in order to concentrate on his website.

PERSONAL LIFE

Drudge lived for years in Southern California, putting together *The Drudge Report* in his one-bedroom Hollywood apartment. Moving to Miami, Florida, he sought the lower tax rates enjoyed by residents of that state and purchased a home on Rivo Alto Island and a condominium in the Four Seasons Hotel. He has never married and is known to have few friends, save for other political commentators, often those who are seen as politically conservative, such as Ann Coulter and Rush Limbaugh, but also liberals such as Camille Paglia.

When Drudge was seventeen, he was arrested for making a series of annoying telephone calls and was briefly sent to live with his father on Maryland's eastern shore. Drudge enjoyed playing video games in arcades as a teenager and had a paper route delivering the now defunct *Washington Star*. Known to like cats, he at one time adopted a stray, which he named "Cat."

Drudge enjoys traveling and has done so extensively: in Argentina, England, Germany, and Israel among other destinations. A longtime owner of a Corvette, he has stated that the car is his one indulgence. Suffering from a receding hairline since high school, Drudge often is pictured wearing a hat. While his public persona is combative and aggressive, those who know him in private life say that he is quiet, shy, and sweet natured. He has long admired individuals such as Rupert Murdoch and Andy Warhol, whom he respects for having invented their own career genres.

Stephen T. Schroth and Jason A. Helfer

FURTHER READING

Drudge, Matt, with Julia Phillips. *Drudge Manifesto*. New York: NAL Trade/Penguin, 2000. Print. An account in which Drudge sets forth his beliefs, experiences, and perspectives on the news media, government, and other issues.

Farnsworth, S. J., and S. R. Lichter. *The Nightly News Nightmare: Media Coverage of U.S. Presidential Elections 1988-2008*. 3rd ed. Lanham: Rowman, 2010. Print. Reviews inaccuracies and errors present in national networks' coverage of presidential elections, suggesting that new-media blunders might be more the norm than many would like to admit.

Mann, T. E., and N. J. Ornstein. *It's Even Worse than It Looks: How the American Constitutional System Collided with the New Politics of Extremism*. New York: Basic, 2012. Print. An accounting of how the polarization of American politics since the 1980s has resulted in the market for, among other things, news sources that appeal to those sharing a particular point of view.

Tewksbury, D., and J. Rittenberg. *News on the Internet: Information and Citizenship in the 21st Century*. New York: Oxford UP, 2012. Print. Examines how news-related Internet sites have altered the process of news gathering, resulting in the segmentation of the news audience.

E

ERIC ELDRED

Cofounder of Creative Commons

Born: 1943; Florida
Died: -
Primary Field: Internet
Specialty: Ethics and policy
Primary Company/Organization: Creative Commons

INTRODUCTION

Eric Eldred has been a computer engineer, analyst, and computer systems administrator at various times in his career. His most significant efforts, however, have not been in any technical specialty but in the legal and economic realms, to expand public access and the list of works in the public domain. Running his own organization, Eldritch Press, to make works in the public domain available over the World Wide Web, he has been restricted by the provisions of the Copyright Term Extension Act (also known as the Sonny Bono Act), which extended the time that authors and their estates—both personal and corporate copyrights—are in effect. The result was Eldred's attempt, through the Supreme Court case Eldred v. Ashcroft *(2003), to overturn the copyright extensions and challenge the constitutional power of Congress to extend copyrights.*

EARLY LIFE

Eric Eldred was born in 1943 in Florida and attended Harvard University, graduating in 1966. Shortly afterward, he began working at Massachusetts General Hospital as a respiratory therapist, a term of his status as a conscientious objector during the Vietnam War era. He stayed at the hospital until 1987.

While working at the hospital, Eldred became interested in computers, eventually returning to Harvard (through its extension school) to study programming and technical writing. During the late 1980s and the early 1990s, he worked in various companies in computer industry and along the Route 128 beltway, including Apollo Computer, the Cahners publishing company, and the Government Services Division of Wang Computer. His jobs involved engineering, analysis, writing, and computer systems administration.

Eric Eldred.

Among his activities before his Supreme Court battle, Eldred worked for Project Gutenberg, scanning public domain texts that were then uploaded to Project Gutenberg's website. Eldred next started his own publishing house, Eldritch Press, which made public domain texts available on the Internet. The server for Eldritch Press was located in his home, and he was involved in every step of the process of making texts available for public access. One of Eldred's major projects for his publishing house was to upload all of the works of Nathaniel Hawthorne. (In addition to his other pursuits, Eldred is an independent scholar specializing in Hawthorne and his works.)

In the late 1990s, Eldred wanted to make a set of poems by Robert Frost, published as *New Hampshire* (1923), freely available to the public. It was this

projected initiative that brought Eldred into direct conflict with copyright law, which had been amended to extend copyrights beyond the term of the 1976 law. The result would be a case brought before the Supreme Court, *Eldred v. Ashcroft*, in an effort to bring literary (and other) works into the public domain.

LIFE'S WORK

In 1998, the Copyright Term Extension Act was passed by both houses of Congress. Commonly referred to as the Sonny Bono Act, the law made significant modifications to copyright terms that had been legislated in 1976. Under the terms of the new law, copyright protection for intellectual property would run for seventy years beyond the death of the author or creator, an extension of twenty years. For corporate copyrights (such as those held by Disney or film studios), the copyright protection was extended from seventy-five years to 120 years after the time of creation or ninety-five years from the time of release or publication, whichever came first.

Although the new act protected authors and corporations, it adversely affected those who wanted to expand the body of works considered in the public domain. Organizations that made works freely available over the Internet—such as Archive.org, Project Gutenberg, and the Eldritch Press—would not, therefore, be able to scan, upload, and distribute materials created after 1923 (the baseline year for determining public domain) until 2019.

As a result, in January 1999, Eldred launched a lawsuit, *Eldred v. Reno* (Janet Reno was then attorney general of the United States). The case named the current attorney general of the United States as a representative of the U.S. government; the case would later become known as *Eldred v. Ashcroft* (John Ashcroft succeeded Reno as attorney general). In 2002 *Eldred vs. Ashcroft* went before the Supreme Court for a hearing.

Eldred's lawyer was Lawrence Lessig. Lessig's area of specialization involved cases in which loosened constraints resulting from new technologies came into conflict with legislation enacted before the technologies came into existence. One of the major issues in this conflict, copyright law, was one of his area of specialization. In addition, Lessig had a thorough academic background, teaching at Stanford, Harvard, and the University of Chicago.

Although Eldred brought the case, he was not alone. He was joined by several organizations, including Dover Publishing (which specializes in reprints of older works in the public domain), the Higginson Book Company, and two publishers of sheet music. Legal support from

Affiliation: Creative Commons

Creative Commons began it operations in 2001. Eric Eldred was a cofounder, as was Lawrence Lessig, who represented Eldred in *Eldred vs. Ashcroft*. A nonprofit organization, Creative Commons defines its mission as enabling "the sharing and use of creativity and knowledge through free legal tools."

Creative Commons is best known for its licensing program, which began with its 1.0 version the year after it was founded. Currently the Creative Commons license is in a draft 4.0 version. The licenses, which do not replace copyrights but supplement them, allow the licensees to grant limited rights to others to use their material free of charge for specified purposes. When a copyright is held, the law allows the copyright holder to reserve all rights. Creative Commons licenses (of which there were six versions as of 2012) allow various limited rights to others. The purpose is to allow freedom to use research or other intellectual property for other creative or research purposes while protecting the core rights of the creator. In 2009, more than 350 million works were registered with Creative Commons licenses. These licensed works included not only text but also films and videos (in 2012 there were 4 million videos on YouTube that the creators had licensed under Creative Commons).

International in scope, Creative Commons has affiliates in most countries and has supported other efforts, such as petitioning the U.S. government to make all publicly funded scientific research freely available to the public.

Harvard's Berkman Center for Internet and Society was present during the hearing. On the side of the defense was the U.S. government, supported by several parties with substantial interests at stake. First, there was the Walt Disney Company; because it was the foremost supporter of the copyright extension, the law was sometimes known as the "Mickey Mouse Protection Act." The Motion Picture Association of America (then run by Jack Valenti, a former aide to President Lyndon Johnson), the Recording Industry Association of America (RIAA), and the American Society of Composers, Authors and Publishers (ASCAP), joined as well.

Lessig's argument was based on the definition of constitutional powers. Congress, Lessig argued, had acted unconstitutionally by extending the time limits granted to copyright holders. Lessig also argued that copyright extensions should be seen as a restriction on free speech as defined in the First Amendment to the Constitution. The government argued that the Constitution specifically stated that Congress could create the terms of copyright for a limited time but did not specify what that time limitation might be. In any event, there was nothing in the Constitution to prohibit Congress from making any changes to existing copyright laws. The government also argued that the case had earlier been upheld in appellate courts. (The fact that lower appellate courts had upheld this view had seemed to many to guarantee that the case would never be heard in the Supreme Court, and the fact that the high court accepted the case had surprised many observers.)

In January 2003, the Supreme Court handed down its decision, by a 7–2 majority, that Congress had acted within its constitutional rights to extend the copyright time limits. The dissenters in the Court did not question that Congress could extend copyrights but that extensions would deprive Americans of free access to creative works.

Eldred no longer performs all of the system administration tasks for Eldritch Press, which were taken over by ibiblio, "the public's digital archive," an organization based at the University of North Carolina at Chapel Hill.

PERSONAL LIFE

Eldred is divorced and has three daughters (triplets). In 2002, Eldred began his Internet Bookmobile program, traveling to various locations, especially schools and libraries, to make it possible for people to own their own free copies of public domain books. In 2004, Eldred attempted to print and distribute free copies of *Walden* at Walden Pond. Because he did not have a permit, he was forced to stop the printing and distribution by the State

Park management. After gaining legal assistance from the Berkman Center at Harvard, he returned the following year to distribute free copies. His Internet Bookmobile, which eventually traveled across the country from Boston to San Francisco, had two purposes. The first was to bring attention to the issues surrounding public domain books. The other was to educate librarians and teachers concerning the use of technology to make information available to wider audiences.

Eldred was one of the founders of Creative Commons, an organization that works to bring issues concerning public access and the public domain to the attention of the public as well as to devise and help manage a licensing process whereby individuals who create works can allow limited access to their works as part of the copyright process.

Robert N. Stacy

FURTHER READING

Biegel, Stuart. *Beyond Our Control? Confronting the Limits of Our Legal System in the Age of Cyberspace.* Cambridge: MIT, 2001. Print. A detailed discussion of technical and legal issues concerning open access with discussions of the significance of *Eldred v. Ashcroft.*

Bollier, David. *Viral Spiral: How the Commoners Built a Digital Republic of Their Own.* New York: New Press, 2008. Print. A history of Creative Commons: its origins and accomplishments in developing flexible licenses to provide limited rights to the public.

Clark, Drew. "A Mickey Mouse Copyright Law?" *National Journal* 34.41 (2002): 2990. Web. 25 July 2012. A discussion of the Sonny Bono Act, the protection of the Disney copyright, and the case of *Eldred v. Ashcroft.*

Posner, Richard A. "The Constitutionality of the Copyright Term Extension Act: Economics, Politics, Law, and Judicial Technique in *Eldred v. Ashcroft.*" *Supreme Court Review* 2003 (2003): 143–62. Print. A discussion of the *Eldred v. Ashcroft* case from the perspective of intellectual property law, economics, constitutional policy, and judicial method. Earlier in his career, Eldred's lawyer, Lawrence Lessig, had clerked for Posner.

Schwartz, Paul M., and William Michael Treanor. "Eldred and Lochner: Copyright Term Extension and Intellectual Property as Constitutional Property." *Yale Law Journal* 112.8 (2003): 2331–14. Print. *Eldred v. Ashcroft* was based on the legal argument that Congress did not have the constitutional right to extend the length of copyright protection. This article surveys the constitutional arguments behind the case.

F

CATERINA FAKE

Cofounder of Flickr

Born: June 13, 1969; Pittsburgh, Pennsylvania
Died: -
Primary Field: Internet
Specialty: Social media
Primary Company/Organization: Flickr

INTRODUCTION

Caterina Fake developed online communities where people could share art, photography, and writing and chat about common interests. Her Internet start-ups Flickr and Hunch gained the attention of Yahoo! and eBay, earning her millions. Today, Fake is seen as a role model for women interested in Internet entrepreneurship. Her abilities to think outside the box, focus on a goal, and collaborate with others on creative projects have played key roles in her success.

EARLY LIFE

Caterina Fake was born to an American father and a Filipina mother on June 13, 1969, in a wealthy suburb of Pittsburgh, Pennsylvania. Fake's father, Peter, a retired insurance executive with a master's degree in English literature, shared his love of learning and sense of wonder with his daughter. Some of Fake's earliest memories involve playing word games, collecting seashells and butterflies, and learning about astronomy with her father.

Fake's leadership potential was evident as early as kindergarten, when one day she decided to go to school without shoes and successfully persuaded her classmates to throw their own shoes out the window. She was a highly intelligent, studious girl who spent many afternoons checking out books from the public library.

Curious and driven, Fake did best in classes where she could design her own program for learning. During her high school years, she skipped many classes but did all of the assigned reading, often outsmarting her teachers by asking them unanswerable questions.

Following in her father's footsteps, Fake decided to study English literature, graduating from Vassar College in 1991 with a bachelor's degree in English.

Caterina Fake.

She appreciated the professors who challenged her to think and work hard. During her college years, she also worked at the Women's Studio Workshop in Rosendale, New York, where she created art and handmade books.

LIFE'S WORK

Fake's original career plans involved art and writing, but she was drawn to the Internet for its potential to connect similarly minded people with common interests from around the world. The experience of creating and sharing art and literature in an alternative space inspired Fake to develop analogous online environments. She taught herself programming code in hypertext markup language (HTML) over the course of several months at her sister's house.

In the 1990s, Fake started her online career as a lead designer at the web-development agency Organic Online. There, she worked on the first websites and online ventures for Fortune 500 companies such as McDonald's, Kimberly-Clark, Colgate-Palmolive, Levi's, and Nike. After that, Fake became art director of the new Internet site Salon.com, which was heavily involved in the development of online community, social software, and personal publishing. In 1997, she took a job managing the community forums of Netscape. She also worked as creative director of Yellowball, an online space that enabled people to collaborate in the creation of stories and animations.

Fake's career as an Internet entrepreneur took off when she met Canadian web developer Stewart Butterfield online in 2001. Fake lived in San Francisco at the time, and Butterfield lived in Canada; they fell in love and began a long-distance relationship. During their courting phase, Butterfield suggested to Fake that they start a company together. In 2002, the two founded Ludicorp (from *ludis*, the Latin word for "play"). The goal of Ludicorp was to build a better platform for real-time online interaction. Their corporate philosophy, based on a passage from Charles Spinosa's *Disclosing New Worlds: Entrepreneurship, Democratic Action and the Cultivation of Solidarity* (1997), involved working for the enjoyment of the game and producing identities that people would care about.

Initially, Ludicorp developed a massively multiplayer online role-playing game (MMORPG) called *Game Neverending*, which included instant messaging. In 2004, they added a new feature: a chat environment with photo sharing. Fake and Butterfield discovered that the beta testers actually enjoyed sharing photos and chatting about them on the site more than they did the game itself. Based on user reactions and the fact that Ludicorp was running out of money, Fake and Butterfield designed a new site called Flickr, which became one of the world's most popular photo-sharing websites. In 2005, Flickr was acquired by Yahoo! and became part of the core of so-called Web 2.0 sites, integrating features such as social networking, tagging, and algorithms that surfaced the most popular content.

After the Flickr acquisition, Fake took a job overseeing the technology development group at Yahoo! The group was known for its Hack Yahoo! program, a stimulus to foster innovation and creativity. Under Fake's leadership, the group also created Brickhouse, a rapid-development environment for new products. Fake resigned from Yahoo! on June 13, 2008. While business partner Butterfield penned a long, bizarre resignation letter to Yahoo, Fake's reasons for her resignation remain unknown.

In August 2008, Fake joined the board of directors of Creative Commons. As a creator of media-sharing sites, Fake had embraced Creative Commons' open-content licensing to encourage users to make their work available through Flickr and other sites. In keeping with her creative philosophy, Fake believes that Creative Commons licensing encourages creativity by freeing ideas from legal constraints.

In 2009, Fake cofounded the website Hunch with entrepreneur Chris Dixon. Hunch builds the "taste graph" of the Internet, intended to connect every user on the Internet to every entity based on his or her affinity for that entity. Hunch launched in June 2009 and was acquired in November 2011 by eBay for an estimated $80 million. In the same year, Fake started a new site called 2bkco. While as of May 2012 the 2bkco did not reveal the mission or activities of the company, 2bkco created Pinwheel, a social site where people can leave notes, annotations, tips, and photos for other users at designated locations. Fake envisions Pinwheel as a community rather than a business. While Pinwheel has received tens of thousands of e-mail requests to join, the company adds user registrations in a slow, staggered manner in order to establish a dedicated and engaged user community. According to Fake, social sites should grow because users find them valuable and then recommend them to friends.

Fake invests in ventures that appeal to her personally. She was an early investor in Etsy, a social and commercial site for artists and craftspeople, and has served on Etsy's board since 2011. She is also a founding partner in Founder Collective, a seed-stage

Affiliations: Flickr, Hunch, 2bkco, and Pinwheel

Caterina Fake and Stewart Butterfield developed Ludicorp in 2002, planning to launch a massive online role-playing game that would include social features such as instant messaging and photo sharing. While the role-playing game never got past the beta stage, Fake and Butterfield took its most popular feature, photo sharing, and built a new social photo-sharing site called Flickr in 2004. After its massive growth in one year, Yahoo! purchased Flickr in March 2005 for $35 million.

In 2009, Fake and entrepreneur Chris Dixon cofounded the website Hunch, designed to map Internet users to various entities based on their interests and affinities. Hunch launched in June 2009 and was acquired in November 2011 by eBay for an estimated $80 million.

Also in 2009, Fake started up a new Internet company called 2bkco. 2bkco developed Pinwheel, a social site where people can leave notes and photographs for other users at designated locations. Investors Redpoint Ventures, SV Angel, and the Obvious Corporation (run by Twitter founders Evan Williams and Biz Stone) put an initial $9.5 million into the venture and serve on the Pinwheel board of directors. Fake has said that she sees Pinwheel as a community rather than a business. As of May 2012, Pinwheel was still in its private beta verson; a mobile app version was also available.

venture capital fund organized by entrepreneurs that advises many start-ups and new businesses. Fake believes that if people choose a problem to solve, pick a good market, and are ambitious and hardworking, they will not fail. She chooses to back young entrepreneurs because she is conscious of the many people who helped her on her way up and wants to return the favor. For this reason, Fake also makes time to advise her alma mater, Vassar College, on social media and digitization projects. In addition, she participates in women-in-technology organizations such as the Forum for Women Entrepreneurs, maintains a group blog with other women in technology, and is working on getting women more speaking engagements at industry conferences.

PERSONAL LIFE

Fake married Flickr cofounder Stewart Butterfield in 2001; the two separated in 2010. They had one daughter, Sonnet, in 2007. Fake homeschools her daughter and has argued eloquently in support of the homeschooling movement and how it improves the socialization of children. She is an avid reader who enjoys discussing literature, making and sharing art, and traveling. Most of all, she enjoys activities that bring people together, such as making crafts, playing board games, and brainstorming, with or without beer.

Fake has been widely recognized for her work as an Internet entrepreneur. In 2005, she was named one of *Businessweek*'s Best Leaders, *Forbes*' eGang, and Fast Company's Fast 50; the following year, she appeared in *Time* magazine's list of 100 Most Influential People and was featured on the cover of *Newsweek*. In May 2009, she received an honorary doctorate from the Rhode Island School of Design. Fake divides her time between New York City and San Francisco.

Rachel Wexelbaum

FURTHER READING

Fake, Caterina. "Caterina Fake: Cofounder, Flickr." Interview by Jessica Livingston. *Founders at Work: Stories of Startups' Early Days*. New York: Springer, 2008. Print. Discusses Fake's work with Butterfield on their development of Flickr.

---. "One on One: Caterina Fake, Flickr and Hunch." Interview by Nick Bilton. *New York Times* 6 Oct. 2010. Web. 4 May 2012. Presents an overview of Fake's career and social media sites Flickr, Hunch, and Etsy.

Katayama, Lisa. "Meet Our Board Members: Caterina Fake." 8 Dec. 2010. Creative Commons. Web. 4 May 2012. Provides Fake's philosophy on copyright and stimulating creativity through sharing work.

Rao, Leena. "More Details on Caterina Fake's New Startup, Pinwheel: A Mobile Flickr for Places (Ish)." 16 Feb. 2012. TechCrunch. Web. 4 May 2012. The history of Pinwheel and instructions on how to use the site.

Spragins, Ellyn, ed. "Caterina Fake: Founder of Flickr." *If I'd Known Then: Women in Their 20s and 30s Write Letters to Their Younger Selves*. Philadelphia: Da Capo, 2008. Print. Focuses on Fake's childhood and adolescence.

JOHN FANNING

Cofounder of Napster

Born: December 21, 1963; Boston, Massachusetts
Died: -
Primary Field: Internet
Specialty: Social media
Primary Company/Organization: Napster

INTRODUCTION

John Fanning is a somewhat controversial figure who is both credited and chastised for his role in the founding and fall of the Internet-based peer-to-peer music-sharing company, Napster. He cofounded the company with his nephew, Shawn Fanning, in 1999. As owner of a 70 percent stake in Napster, John Fanning maintained control of the company as its chief executive officer (CEO) and chairman of the board of directors. At first hailed as a revolutionary new way to distribute music, Napster soon became the target of media and recording industry giants claiming copyright infringement and illegal distribution. Fanning ultimately lost the legal battles and the company but continues to be recognized as an Internet industry pioneer. In addition to his role in the original Napster in the area of distributed aggregation of content, Fanning has been involved with Internet innovations such as client-server game play, Voice over Internet Protocol for audio chat, and auto-upgrading/authentication as part of his own startup firms, NetGames, NetMovies, and NetCapital.

EARLY LIFE

John Fanning grew up in Rockland, Massachusetts, a working-class town approximately twenty miles south of Boston. He and his seven siblings lived with their parents in a three-bedroom house and were constantly on the brink of poverty.

When Fanning was fourteen years old, his older brother, Eddie, graduated from high school. To celebrate, the Irish family threw a big party for the entire neighborhood and hired a local band to provide live music. Fanning solicited all the attendees with a hat to collect money for the band's fee. He ended up with several thousands of dollars in profit thanks to the massive crowd. The experience ignited in Fanning a passion for entrepreneurism.

The following year, Fanning joined the carpentry program at South Shore Vocational Technical High School in southeast Massachusetts. During that time,

his family moved to nearby Brockton and his older sister, Colleen, discovered she was pregnant. The baby's father abandoned her, and Fanning would eventually go on to become a sort of father figure to Colleen's son, Shawn.

After high school, John Fanning enrolled in the Economics program at Boston College. However, he left the program before completing his degree when an opportunity arose for him to purchase a beleaguered computer company called Cambridge Automation from a friend on credit. While that company ultimately failed, the experience gave Fanning valuable knowledge and the drive to create his own company. He moved to Hull on the Nantasket Peninsula of Massachusetts Bay and in 1993 secured investor backing of some $500,000, tapped the programming expertise of several students from Carnegie-Mellon University—including chess Grandmaster Roman Dzindzichashvili—and founded an Internet chess service company called Chess.net.

LIFE'S WORK

Chess.net became a haven for Fanning's nephew, Shawn. He would spend his summers learning about computers from the company's programming team. By the time Shawn entered Boston's Northeastern University, he was already an accomplished programmer with a knack for hacking. During his freshman year, Shawn developed an MP3 digital music file sharing program that he called Napster in honor of his school nickname. He would work on the program at the Chess.net offices on weekends and his uncle soon became intrigued by the concept and its considerable potential. John Fanning recognized that his nephew's program offered a revolutionary new way of distributing information, enabling individuals to share their own content with one another via a global information index and their own computers. With the elder Fanning's support, Shawn dropped out of college to focus full time on Napster from the Chess.net offices. Shawn's tech-saavy hacker friends Jason Ritter and Sean Parker soon joined the project. Within months, in mid-1999, John Fanning surprised his nephew by incorporating Napster as a company. He persuaded his nephew to sign over a 70 percent share in the enterprise to him based on his contention that the company would be able to attract necessary investors only if an experienced business leader was running the company.

John Fanning.

John Fanning began to woo investors while Shawn Fanning launched a test version of Napster among thirty of his friends. Within just a few days, word of the revolutionary new music-sharing service had spread like wildfire across the Internet, with fifteen thousand users downloading the program within the first week. Napster's initial success enabled John Fanning to secure the company's first external investor. Venture capitalist and software executive Yosi Amram invested $250,000 in the fledgling firm. In exchange, he stipulated that the company relocate to his own stomping ground in northern California and that he be given the right to name new company management. Fanning agreed and in September 1999 the company moved to San Mateo, California. John Fanning was named chairman of the board.

Almost immediately the company encountered problems. By the end of 1999, usage became so strong among college students that many schools began to block the service in order to avoid clogging their servers with bandwidth from Napster-related file transfers. At about the same time, the music industry had started to notice Napster. The Recording Industry Association of America called a meeting with Napster's Amram-appointed CEO, Eileen Richardson, asking the company to cease operations until copyright infringement allegations could be addressed. Richardson refused and in December 1999 the company found itself at the center of a heated legal battle with the country's major recording labels and media companies.

While some of Napster's leadership favored a settlement, John Fanning did not and worked to delay settlement talks until he could round up more funding, which he felt would bolster Napster's credibility and influence at the bargaining table. However, Fanning, Richardson, and Napster's board of directors spent too much time arguing the details, and several opportunities from interested big-league venture capital firms fell by the wayside. Other opportunities to save Napster were missed as a result of disorganization among the company's top management and poor pitches to potential investors by Fanning, who tried to bundle investment in his own start-up Internet firms into a Napster bailout package.

Napster and Fanning got a reprieve in May 2000, when Hummer Winblad Venture Partners invested $15 million in the company and took control, ousting Amram and Richardson but keeping Fanning on the board. Fanning was soon forced out, however, and by July the company found itself facing a federal court order to cease operations. An appeals court ruling stayed the injunction almost immediately, giving Napster enough time to secure a $50 million loan from German publisher Bertelsmann in an effort to establish a more traditional commercial music service. Hopes of a Napster revival were short-lived: In February 2001, the company was ordered to stop permitting the sharing of copyrighted material on its website. Napster attempted to comply with the order but fell short. By this time, John Fanning had sold some of his 70 percent stake in the company, earning himself half a million dollars while the company he cofounded with his nephew faltered. Napster voluntarily shut down its site on July 1, 2001. A year later, Napster filed for Chapter 11 bankruptcy protection to avoid a takeover by Bertelsmann. The following year, in November 2002, digital media company Roxio purchased the Napster name and intellectual property for $5 million. A new version of Napster went live in 2003, armed with appropriate licensing agreements and new leadership, which did not include John Fanning.

After leaving Napster, Fanning focused his efforts on his other Internet ventures: online gaming software company NetGames (which owns Chess.net), boutique venture capital and private equity firm NetCapital, and online movie site NetMovies (in partnership with Blockbuster). In November 2011, Fanning also joined the advisory board of business-to-business cloud commerce solutions company, Savtira Corporation, as an expert in the areas of streaming, distribution of content aggregation, and video on demand. In addition, Fanning holds patents for Real Time Search Engine and Use Sensitive Distribution of Data Files Between Users.

PERSONAL LIFE

John Fanning located his nephew's biological father via an Internet search when Shawn was seventeen years old. He approached his sister with the information. With her permission, Fanning helped orchestrate an in-person reunion between father and son that sparked a lasting relationship between the two men.

Apart from family and finance, Fanning is a man of varied interests. In addition to his appreciation for music, movies, and chess, Fanning is an avid player of the massively multiplayer online role-playing game *World of Warcraft*. He is also a dedicated supporter of the Boston Red Sox baseball team and New England Patriots football club. In addition, Fanning is a renowned poker player. He placed eighth in the world during the 2004 World Poker Tour, winning more than $200,000 for his efforts. The following year, he won more than €11,000 and secured the twenty-first spot during the 2005 European Poker Tour in Monte Carlo. In 2012, he was living in his home on the South Shore of Massachusetts in the waterfront community of Blackrock Beach.

Shari Parsons Miller

FURTHER READING

Gorman, Linda. "Copyright Protection and the Quality Of Recorded Music Since Napster." n.d. *NBER Digest*. Web. 25 Sept. 2012. Discusses whether the quality of music is affected by technology, using Napster to represent technological change and critics' retrospective lists of the best music, radio airplay, and sales of music as indices to evaluate the quality of new music. Concludes that the quality of new music has not declined since Napster.

Himelstein, Linda, and Tom Lowry. "The Sound at Napster: Tick, Tick, Tick...." *Businessweek* 3777 (2002): 73. Web. 25 Sept. 2012. Highlights the legal dispute between Napster board members John Fanning, John Hummer, and Hank Barry and how it could influence a proposed buyout deal with Bertelsmann.

Menn, Joseph. *All the Rave: The Rise and Fall of Shawn Fanning's Napster*. New York: Crown Business, 2003. Print. Provides an account of Napster's evolution and initial demise, addressing John Fanning's behind-the-scenes role in the company and highlighting some of Napster's visionary strides that altered the shape of the music distribution industry and some of the debilitating business decisions that led to the company's downfall.

Navissi, Farshid, Vic Naiker, and Stewart Upson. "Securities Price Effects of Napster-Related Events." *Journal Of Accounting, Auditing and Finance* 20.2 (2005): 167–83. Web. 25 Sept. 2012. Positions Napster as a surrogate for Internet piracy and examines the effects of eleven key Napster-related events on the equity value of companies in the U.S. music industry. Findings suggest that events that increased the effectiveness of Napster as a distribution system improved the stock prices of the music firms, whereas events that jeopardized Napster's survival resulted in reduced stock prices of the music firms.

Rodrigues, Rodrigo, and Peter Druschel. "Peer-to-Peer Systems." *Communications of the ACM* 53.10 (2010): 72–82. Web. 25 Sept. 2012. Provides an overview of peer-to-peer computing, with an em-

---

Affiliation: Napster

Napster launched in 1999 as the brainchild of a young computer science student named Shawn Fanning. With the help of his uncle, John Fanning, the innovative file-sharing program became the core of an enterprise that would transform the way individuals use the Internet.

Napster was a free downloadable program that converted individual computers into servers that enabled sharing of MP3 music files across the Internet. Rather than employing a traditional central server to store all music files, Napster instead became the distribution medium. Users could log onto the site, search for music by artist or title, and then download their selection directly from another logged-in user's hard drive. Napster was an instant success, attracting some 60 million users at its peak. It also attracted the attention of recording companies. With a battle cry of "copyright infringement" the key players in the recording and music industries launched an assault on Napster that would ultimately lead to its demise in just two years.

Napster relaunched in 2003 as a property of Roxio. Napster was purchased by Best Buy in 2008 and became part of online music store subscription service Rhapsody in 2011.

phasis on its usefulness as a mechanism for making services such as music and data sharing easier to deploy. Highlights both the advantages and the disadvantages of having no centralized control or dedicated infrastructure and describes the move of peer-to-peer computing into the area of commercial content distribution.

Seff, Jonathan. "My Time with Napster." *Macworld* 28.6 (2011): 70. Web. 25 Sept. 2012. Presents both the positive and the negative experiences the writer experienced regarding Napster during his one-year subscription to the company's streaming music service.

SHAWN FANNING

Cofounder of Napster

Born: November 22, 1980; Brockton, Massachusetts
Died: -
Primary Field: Internet
Specialty: Social media
Primary Company/Organization: Napster

INTRODUCTION

Shawn Fanning is a pioneer of peer-to-peer technologies and social networks. After releasing Napster, a revolutionary software application enabling Internet users to exchange music files, he launched various projects aimed at enhancing social interactions on networks. A computer programmer, entrepreneur, and angel investor, he has helped shape the digital society with ventures such as SNOCAP, Rupture, Path.com, and Airtime.

EARLY LIFE

Shawn Fanning was born on November 22, 1980, and was raised by his mother, Coleen, in the Boston area. Despite financial difficulties at home, he demonstrated some talent at school and emerged as a good basketball player. His friends gave him the nickname Napster in reference to his short, nappy hair.

His uncle, John Fanning, who watched over his nephew, played the role of a substitute father. While seeing Shawn regularly and offering him guidance, he bought him his first computer, an Apple Macintosh. Shawn quickly became obsessed with programming and networking via Internet relay chat (IRC). He worked during the summers at his uncle's company, NetGames, a platform for playing chess online. He also became friends with Sean Parker and Jordan Ritter, two other teenage computer enthusiasts, who lived respectively in Virginia and California. Animated by his passion to explore and learn, Fanning taught himself how to program

in the Unix environment. In 1998, after graduating from high school, he enrolled at Northeastern University on a scholarship.

LIFE'S WORK

The year Fanning arrived at the university coincided with the breakthrough of the MP3 format for compressing CD-quality music into digital files. However, despite the rise of the Internet, it was still difficult to share MP3 files online. Around the end of 1998, Shawn got an idea to solve the problem, and he embarked on the creation of

Shawn Fanning.

a music-file-sharing platform, with his two IRC friends Parker and Ritter. Immersing himself in his project, he increasingly skipped classes at the university.

After some months, Shawn's project had taken form, and in May 1999 his uncle, John, who had sensed the opportunity, encouraged him to incorporate a company. With years of experience in the high-tech sector, his uncle persuaded Shawn to let him run the company and to assign 70 percent of the business to him. In June, Shawn distributed a test version of his program to a handful of friends he had met on the IRC. The success was immediate, and dozens of copies quickly circulated on Internet forums, enabling any Internet user to share music easily and freely. After some improvements, the so-called Napster service was officially launched in September 1999.

Quickly identified by venture capitalists as the next Internet's "killer app" (application), Napster, Inc., was approached by angel investor Yosi Amram. In exchange for $2 million, he obtained the nomination of experienced manager Eileen Richardson as chief executive and the relocation of Napster's team to San Mateo, California.

With a rapidly growing number of potential customers exchanging music files freely and building libraries of songs without any consideration for copyright owners, it did not take long for the Recording Industry Association of America (RIAA) to sue the company. In December 1999, a complaint was filed for "contributory and vicarious copyright infringement." A few months later, Metallica, the heavy metal group, backed the RIAA. In July 2000, a federal judge ruled against Napster and ordered the closing of the service. However, with the victory of website MP3.com against the RIAA in mind, Napster had good reason to appeal against the decision. Moreover, use of the Napster service was at the same time skyrocketing.

Despite the serious blow to Napster's reputation, the immediate effect of the trial was a fantastic increase in the success of its service. One year after it was launched, Napster had 4 million users worldwide. It was becoming a global brand. This led Hummer Winblad Venture Partners to enter the capital with $65 million, with the idea of developing a commercial service. Some months later, with the support of German publishing conglomerate Bertelsmann, owner of the BMG label, the future looked bright. In October 2000, twenty-year-old Shawn Fanning was featured on the cover of *Time* magazine. He was identified as the rising star of the so-called new economy.

The situation did not go as expected, however. The Napster team proved unable to control the traffic of copyrighted materials on its network. As a consequence, when the first judgment was confirmed by the court of appeals, in February 2001, the only solution was to negotiate with the principals or shut down the servers. After more than a year of litigation, on July 11, 2001, the service was closed. The service had been able to attract more than 50 million unique users.

Far from putting an end to the exchange of music files, the closing of Napster was synonymous with the opening of a new era, full of new possibilities as well as new fears. New technical systems were made available on the Internet that allowed exchanging files of any kind without appealing to servers. These totally virtual systems, which eventually became the bane of copyright owners, were soon united under the banner of peer-to-peer systems.

After Napster filed for bankruptcy protection, Roxio paid $5 million for the company's name and its intellectual property. Shawn Fanning briefly served as a paid consultant. Sensing the need of copyright owners, in 2003 he and former Napster's chief architect Jordan Mendelson founded SNOCAP, aiming at protecting digital rights. With the support of influential angel investor Ron Conway, they developed a system used by new entrants into the digital economy, including Sony-BMG and Myspace. However, with people using peer-to-peer systems, the digital music market did not really take off, and the company never really grew up. In April 2008, the company was sold to Imeem, Inc., a social networking company. At that time, Shawn had already embarked on a new project.

Exchanging digital files quickly proved to be part of a larger need for social interactions on networks. Recognizing this, Shawn launched Rupture in 2006. At the moment when his former counterpart, Parker, had launched himself into the Facebook adventure, his solution offered enhanced communication between members of global multiplayer online role-playing game *World of Warcraft*. A few months later, his technology was acquired by *World of Warcraft* operators Electronic Arts for $15 million. He and his team kept working for the company until November 2009, when he invested in a new project.

In 2010, former Facebook executive Dave Morin joined with Fanning to create a social networking–enabled photo-sharing and messaging site, Path.com. Capitalizing on the Facebook experience, the duo wanted to help people enhance existing relationships; thus,

Affiliation: Napster

Napster began as a way of solving the problem of exchanging MP3 music files through networks. With the support of Internet pals Sean Parker and Jordan Ritter, nineteen-year-old Shawn Fanning released his software application in June 1999, when the company was incorporated under the name of Napster. Shawn's uncle, John Fanning, a pioneer in the Internet economy, took control of the company.

Because Napster offered the extraordinary possibility of downloading music from a huge library of songs for free, the service experienced dramatic success. After having conquered university campuses, it quickly became one of Internet users' favorite applications. This situation alarmed copyright owners, whose intellectual property was being acquired for free, and in the fall of 1999, the Recording Industry Association of America (RIAA) sued Napster for contributory and vicarious copyright infringement. Despite legal uncertainties, the court ruled against Napster in July 2000, and the judgment was confirmed by a court of appeals in February 2001.

Thus, despite attempts to launch a commercial service and the support of angel investors, the company found itself unable to control its users and the service was closed in July 2001. With more than 50 million users worldwide, the service had become a global brand, and therefore the company's name was sold for $5 million. Since its closing, Napster has been acknowledged as the pioneer of peer-to-peer systems and in the vanguard of the social networking revolution.

Path.com limits each user's social network to fifty close friends. With millions of dollars injected by angel investors, including longtime friend Conway, the service was launched in 2011.

In parallel, Fanning imagined Supyo, a live video social networking service, which has been compared to the Chatroulette service, a digital jukebox of human interactions. Envisioning the future evolution of social networks and with the idea of helping people build new relationships rather than reinforce old ones, Fanning decided to reunite with old friend and Facebook founding president Parker. This service of the former Napster pals came to be known as Airtime.

In only ten years, Fanning not only saw the fruition of the peer-to-peer revolution but also launched a range of services, all focused on improving social interactions in the digital society. More than ever, he appears to be at the core of a promising online ecosystem.

Personal Life

After moving with his Napster pals to the Bay Area in the summer of 1999, Fanning settled in Mountain View, California. In 2002, he adopted his fifteen-year-old brother and offered to move him to the West coast. He is married with a child, a daughter.

With the success, as well as controversy, surrounding Napster, Fanning has been in the limelight since the age of twenty. Not only was he identified by the Massachusetts Institute of Technology's *Technology Review* as one of the TR35 (thirty-five top innovators under age thirty-five) in 2002; he has also appeared on various magazine covers since this period, including *Time* magazine. In 2012, he was about to appear in the documentary *Downloaded*, which tells the story of the birth and growth of the digital society.

Jean Béhue

Further Reading

Alderman, John. *Sonic Boom: Napster, MP3, and the New Pioneers of Music*. Cambridge: Perseus, 2001. Print. The dazzling success of Napster put into perspective, with an enthusiastic vision of the future evolution of the music market.

Benkler, Yaochaï. *The Wealth of Networks: How Social Production Transforms Markets and Freedom*. New Haven: Yale UP, 2006. Print. An influential essay on the way social networks allegedly reconfigure the laws of economy.

Brafman, Ori, and Rod A. Beckstrom. *The Starfish and the Rider: The Unstoppable Power of Leaderless Organizations*. New York: Trade Paperback, 2008. Print. A plea in favor of self-organizing communities enabled by peer-to-peer technologies and social networks.

Giblin, Rebecca. *Code Wars: 10 Years of P2P Software Litigation*. Northampton: Edward Elgar, 2011. Print. A book that summarizes a decade of complex debates relative to the legal basis of the digital society.

Menn, Joseph. *All the Rave: The Rise and Fall of Shawn Fanning's Napster*. New York: Crown, 2003. Print. How the music industry finally beheaded hydra-headed monster Napster, with a focus on the role played by Shawn's uncle John Fanning.

Oram, Andrew. *Peer-to-Peer: Harnessing the Power of Disruptive Technologies*. Sebastopol: O'Reilly, 2001. Print. A plea for the technology invented by Fanning, improved for creating totally virtual networks, and used by a whole generation of Internet users.

Palfrey, John, and Urs Gasser. *Born Digital: Understanding the First Generation of Digital Natives*. New York: Basic, 2010. Print. The digital world through the eyes of newborns, and a perspective on a generation gap.

JAKE FEINLER

Manager at the Network Information Center, Stanford Research Institute

Born: March 2, 1931; Wheeling, West Virginia
Died: -
Primary Field: Computer science
Specialty: Internet
Primary Company/Organization: Stanford Research Institute

INTRODUCTION

Jake Feinler is an Internet and information scientist who worked at the Stanford Research Institute (SRI), where she managed the Network Information Center (NIC) for the Advanced Research Projects Agency Network (ARPANET) and then the Defense Data Network (DDN),

which were the first packet-switching networks that allowed scientists to share resources among universities. Over time, this system evolved into the Internet. Feinler's group was also responsible for the Internet's Domain Name System (DNS). From 1989 to 1996, Feinler worked at the National Aeronautics and Space Administration's Ames Research Center. In 2010, she published a history of the NIC. Feinler was inducted into the Internet Hall of Fame as an Internet "pioneer" in 2012.

EARLY LIFE

Elizabeth Jocelyn "Jake" Feinler was born in Wheeling, West Virginia, on March 2, 1931. Her stepfather worked at a steel mill and her mother was a homemaker. She had a sister and a half brother. At first interested in art, she attended college in Cincinnati on an advertising design scholarship; there she planned to work for a semester at an advertising firm. However, impatient that this was not allowed in her freshman year, she transferred to West Liberty State College in West Virginia, where she became interested in chemistry. She was the first person in her family to attend college.

LIFE'S WORK

Feinler finished course work toward a Ph.D. in biochemistry at Purdue University in West Lafayette, Indiana. As a graduate student short of money, Feinler took off a year in 1957 and worked for Chemical Abstracts Service (CAS) in Columbus, Ohio. While at CAS, Feinler discovered her interest in and aptitude for manipulating data and compiling data research. CAS was then compiling the *Fifth Decennial Index*, an index the world's chemical compounds developed during the past hundred years. It was one of the biggest information projects in the world at the time. Feinler served as its assistant editor.

Feinler grew up in the mid-twentieth century, a time of scientific advancement (Sputnik, the Russian

Jake Feinler.

satellite, was launched in 1957). Feinler became interested in science when there were not many women in scientific fields, let alone information technology. Feinler heard about Stanford Research Institute (SRI) in Menlo Park, California (now SRI International) at Columbus meetings of the American Chemical Society. In 1960, she contacted SRI about a job. She had just made plans to tour Europe for a month with a friend when SRI hired her. After a month abroad, Feinler returned to the United States and moved to Menlo Park, an affluent region in the San Francisco Bay Area, where she settled in 1966.

In 1972, Feinler worked in the Literature Research section of the Information Resource Center (IRC) of what was then SRI's library. There she created the *Handbook of Psychopharmacology* and the *Chemical Process Economics Handbook*. That year, Douglas Engelbart—the innovative networking pioneer and inventor of the multiuser oN-Line System (NLS) and graphical user interface (GUI) devices such as the computer mouse—recruited her to join his Augmentation Research Center (ARC). ARC was sponsored by the Office of the U.S. Defense Advanced Research Projects Agency, or DARPA (originally ARPA).

Engelbart's team was busy working on ARPA's cutting-edge ARPANET, a packet-switching experiment. This experiment created the first computer-to-computer transmission of text messages for ARPANET when it successfully communicated with a computer at the University of California at Los Angeles (UCLA). Engelbart chose Feinler to compose the much-needed *Resource Handbook for the Internet* to accompany the ARPANET at the 1972 International Computer Communication Conference (ICCC) in Washington, D.C. Engelbart thought Feinler best qualified for the job, although neither was clear what such a handbook entailed. The group successfully demonstrated the ARPANET at the conference.

In 1974, Feinler became principal investigator at SRI's Network Information Center (NIC). In an interview describing her time working with Engelbart, Feinler compared herself—dressed professionally in a skirt and blouse—to Engelbart's group, which she described as a group of Birkenstock-wearing, long-haired students she had first observed rolling a strange device around on a desk with their eyes glued to a television screen; the device turned out to be a groundbreaking input device now known as the computer mouse.

Feinler and Engelbart worked together for years. Feinler's NIC team provided user services, whereas

Engelbart's ARC team conducted the research. These user services included identifying the first links to online documents using ARC's NLS system; making available reference services to network users via telephone and physical mail; maintaining a "white pages" directory of interested or involved personnel; maintaining a resource handbook (a "yellow pages" listing all available services); and providing a protocol handbook.

In 1975, the Defense Communication Agency (DCA) took over and split the ARPANET into research and military networks. The DCA used the name Defense Data Network (DDN) for the military portion. Feinler and the NIC stayed as part of SRI.

In 1978, Feinler worked with Steve Crocker, Jon Postel, and Joyce Reynolds of the Network Working Group (NWG) to establish a technical manual for the ARPANET. As the network grew, NIC registered names, allowed access control across terminals, provided billing and audit information, and initiated a number of requests for comments (RFCs). In 1974, Feinler's team had installed a simple text format for names of servers that they revised several times. The Domain Name System was then implemented to assign authority and names to such servers, and by 1979 Feinler's team was responsible for developing and assigning the now familiar top-level domain names, including .mil, .gov, .edu, .org, and .com.

In 1982, an Internet protocol was defined by Ken Harrenstien and Vic White, both of Feinler's group, which provided access to an online directory of people, WHOIS. In 1983, ARPANET was converted to transmission-control protocol/Internet protocol (TCP/IP) format and became the Internet.

When Feinler retired from the NIC in 1989, she had worked as its principal investigator from 1974 to 1985 and as its director from 1985 to 1989. In 1989, Feinler joined the National Aeronautics and Space Administration (NASA) at Ames Research Center, where she worked as a networks requirements manager and helped develop guidelines for managing the NASA Science Internet (NSI).

Over her career, Feinler conscientiously preserved a massive amount of archival information related to the Internet's evolution, once even saving papers off the floor before they could be thrown away. Upon retiring from SRI, Feinler donated an extensive collection of archives (which had filled two garages) to the Computer History Museum in Mountain View, California, where she worked as a volunteer organizing her material. According to the museum's newsletter, Feinler runs the

Volunteer Steering Committee as if the museum were a Silicon Valley start-up.

PERSONAL LIFE

"Jake" Feinler got her nickname from her older sister, Mary Lou. It was common to have two first names at the time, and Feinler was nicknamed Betty Jo, short for Elizabeth Jocelyn. However, Mary Lou, only two at the time, mispronounced her name as "Baby Jake." To Feinler's delight, the "Baby" was later dropped, although "Jake" stuck.

Feinler enjoys sewing and has a collection of 350 pin cushions from around the world, having first complained that she did not like sticking pins in tomatoes. She also enjoys painting watercolors and listening to

opera. She has a witty, keen sense of humor and a knack for storytelling. To emphasize how tedious research was before the advent of the Internet, she tells of thumbing through enormous volumes of abstracts and skimming printed articles manually. Once she scoured volumes of information to locate the composition for walrus milk in order to save a baby walrus. Today, such feats could be accomplished with a few quick clicks.

Feinler continues to volunteer at the Computer History Museum. Summarizing the Internet's legacy, she has said that what was once an amazing experiment is no longer an experiment, but the greatest technological achievement of our time.

Ellen Elder

Affiliation: Stanford Research Institute

The Stanford Research Institute, now SRI International, is a nonprofit research institute located in Menlo Park, California. It was created by trustees at nearby Stanford University in 1946 to foster economic development. It is divided into five specialty divisions: the Engineering + Systems Group, the Policy Division, the Information + Computing Science division, SRI Biosciences, and the Physical Sciences division.

Now one of the largest contract research centers in the world, SRI's most famous alumnus is Douglas Engelbart, who founded SRI's Augmentation Research Center (ARC) and designed early human-computer interaction through the graphical user interface (GUI), including the development of the multiuser oN-Line System (NLS), which featured early versions of hypertext and bitmapped displays. In 1969, the world's first four-node computer network, ARPANET—the Advanced Research Projects Agency Network—was established when SRI researchers successfully transmitted a text message to a computer at the University of California at Los Angeles (UCLA), although the first three-way internetworked transmission did not occur until 1977.

Other notable SRI discoveries were led by Elizabeth "Jake" Feinler, who directed SRI's Network Information Center (NIC) and the team who created the Domain Name System (DNS). SRI, which was funded by Defense Advanced Research Projects Agency (DARPA), split from Stanford in 1970 and became known as SRI International in 1977.

FURTHER READING

Braman, Sandra. "The Framing Years: Policy Fundamentals in the Internet Design Process." *Information Society* 27.5 (2011): 295–310. Print. Focuses on social policy issues surrounding the logistics of a communications network, from privacy and intellectual property rights through the definition of common carriage and environmental problems, with a focus on 1969–79.

Feinler, Elizabeth. "Elizabeth Jocelyn Feinler, an Oral History." Interview by Jane Abbate. *IEEE Global History Network.* 2002. Web. 12 July 2012. Interview describing Feinler's long career at SRI and the transition of the Internet from military to commercial use.

---. "Host Tables, Top-Level Domain Names and the Origin of Dot.com." *IEEE Annals of the History of Computing* 32.3 (2011): 83–89. Print. Anecdotal article that describes the organizations and people involved in the early efforts at naming and addressing server hosts, in particular the transition to the Domain Name System (DNS) and the origin of top-level domains (TLDs).

---. "The Network Information Center and Its Archives." *IEEE Annals of the History of Computing* 33.3 (2010): 74–79. Print. Describes how the NIC (which Feinler directed) exchanged information, how early business was carried out on the Internet, and how it is archived today.

Lukasik, Stephen. "Why the ARPANET Was Built." *IEEE Annals of the History of Computing* 33.3 (2011): 4–21. Print. A who, what, where, when, and how of the ARPANET: Discusses J. C. R. Licklider and the dedication of computer scientists, engineers, and graduate students in the creation of ARPANET.

BARBARA J. FELDMAN

Founder of Surfnetkids

Born: June 3, 1953; Bethel Park, Pennsylvania
Died: -
Primary Field: Internet
Specialty: Content and data
Primary Company/Organization: Surfnetkids

INTRODUCTION

Barbara J. Feldman is the owner and founder of Surfnetkids.com, Inc., an online publishing company that creates educational content for parents, teachers, families, and children. Feldman created Surfnetkids in 1996 as an archive for her nationally syndicated weekly newspaper advice column Surfing the Net with Kids. *Feldman has more than sixty websites, including FreeKidsColoring.com and JokesByKids.com. She is an expert in building audiences for advertising-supported content sites and promoting them for educational uses on the Internet. A former computer consultant and programmer, she is also a newsletter publisher, shareware author, and self-proclaimed "websurfer surpreme." She blogs at barbara.feldman.com.*

EARLY LIFE

Barbara J. Feldman was born June 3, 1953, in Bethel Park, Pennsylvania. She became interested in computers while in her teens and pursued that interest in college. In 1976, she graduated cum laude from the University of California at Irvine with a bachelor's degree in information and computer science. In the mid-1990s, Feldman, a mother of two, became aware of the web browser Mosaic. She realized that the browser would allow the Internet to become a limitless educational resource. That realization led to her syndicated newspaper column, *Surfing the Net with Kids*. In this column, Feldman addresses a different topic each week and offers the best educational sites for children on that topic. She launched her first website in 1996 to share the results of her exploration of the educational possibilities of the web.

LIFE'S WORK

Feldman has worked as a computer consultant, computer programmer, original equipment manufacturer (OEM) computer sales representative, newsletter publisher, shareware author, and "mommy blogger." A self-described computer nerd, she worked as a programmer for Varian Data Machines and Sperry-Univac and as an independent consultant for small businesses in need of database applications.

Feldman's expertise is in educational uses of the Internet and monetizing online content, but her background in business consultation also allowed her to create websites that offer information for those interested in the technical, marketing, or business side of publishing.

In 1996, Feldman had been writing her successful weekly newspaper column *Surfing the Net with Kids* for one year. Her aim was to help parents and educators navigate the many circuitous channels of the then-burgeoning Internet. The column's popularity, along with Feldman's background in information technology, led her to launch her first website, Surfnetkids.com, in 1992. Today it is the most popular of Feldman's nearly sixty websites. The umbrella site, Feldman Publishing, also serves as a distribution point for her e-books. The sites attract more than 1.1 million visitors per month.

Surfnetkids is an educational content-based website that includes website reviews, educational games, newsletters, widgets, and other tools and information

Barbara J. Feldman.

geared toward children and parents. It is divided into nine sections: Calendar, Games, Free, Fun, Parents, Shopping, Teachers, Top Ten, and Topics. Several sections—such as the free kids' games and the website reviews newsletter—are free. The site's Printables Club is a membership-only service that offers downloadable educational material that promotes technological integration in the classroom. There is also a link to child-friendly videos.

Other online educational reading and writing materials available through Feldman's websites include the Chapter-a-Day project, in which book segments are e-mailed as newsletters to increase readership of a book; by the end of two weeks, a reader will have read the first few chapters and will then be prompted to purchase the entire book. There is also a page that teaches children how to write and publish their own book reviews and suggestions for online virtual "field trips."

Feldman's sites also include forums that discuss issues of online safety such as whether certain websites are suitable for children and ways to regulate Internet usage by children and students. Feldman enforces one steadfast rule for parents of budding Internet users: Do not allow a computer with Internet access to be located in a room where doors can be closed, such as children's bedrooms. She also recommends that parents periodically check their children's browser histories. Feldman encourages her readers to suggest topics for her to address, provide feedback, and ask questions.

Feldman has written a booklet about the Internet for parents, which she provides royalty-free to website subscribers for reprinting and distribution. She is an advocate for getting more girls interested in math and science, and she maintains a popular blog at barbarafeldman.com. It offers an "Internet Tip of the Week," such as highlighting websites that are useful for educational searches and guidelines on how to manage passwords and automate document processing. She has made a living writing online since the creation of Surfnetkids.

PERSONAL LIFE

Feldman's husband, Howard, a nationally recognized expert on alarm systems and president of Pioneer Security Services, a commercial and residential security company headquartered in San Diego. They live in Solana Beach, California, with an assortment of pets. They have two grown children; Feldman has blogged about her experiences growing accustomed to an empty nest and helping her mother cope with dementia.

Ellen Elder

Affiliation: Surfnetkids

Surfnetkids, Inc. is a content-based website that promotes educational material for children, parents, and educators. It was founded by owner Barbara J. Feldman in 1996 after the success of her weekly nationally syndicated advice column *Surfing the Nets with Kids*. Surfnetkids.com is the flagship website and includes freekidscoloring.com and jokesbykids.com. Surfnetkids includes a library of free reference material and educational projects, including a calendar and holiday events, educational games and projects, links to and reviews of useful educational websites, and user feedback and recommendations. The website also offers pages reserved for members, where parents and educators can access useful information, such as educational handouts. Surfnetkids and its related sixty websites attract more than 1.1 million visitors each month.

FURTHER READING

Descy, Don E. "Keeping Kids Safe Online." *TechTrends: Linking Research and Practice to Improve Learning* 50.5 (2006): 3–4. Print. This brief article provides information on how caregivers and educators can keep children safe while surfing the Internet, particularly from harmful sites and predators. It provides names of software programs equipped for safe searching tools.

Dodge, Autumn M., Nahid Husain, and Nell K. Duke. "Connected Kids? K-2 Children's Use and Understanding of the Internet." *Language Arts* 89.2 (2011): 86–98. Print. This article reports on the findings of a study about K–2 schoolchildren's use and understanding of the Internet and its safe use in teaching and education in the United States.

"Info on Internet." *Editor and Publisher* 129.39 (1996): 34. Print. A review of Feldman's nationally syndicated column that highlights its usefulness for parents and Feldman's free booklet on safe Internet surfing.

Ybarra, Michelle L., et al. "Associations Between Blocking, Monitoring and Filtering Software on the Home Computer and Youth-Reported Unwanted Exposure to Sexual Material Online." *Child Abuse and Neglect* 33.12 (2009): 857–69. Print. An academic article that examines the relationship between the use of preventive software on home computers and unwanted exposure to sexual material online, based on a national youth survey conducted in 2005. Discusses the Children's Internet Protection Act, passed by Congress in 2000.

DAVID FILO

Cofounder of Yahoo!

Born: April 20, 1966; Madison, Wisconsin
Died: -
Primary Field: Internet
Specialty: Content and data
Primary Company/Organization: Yahoo!

INTRODUCTION

While he was pursuing a Ph.D. in electrical engineering at Stanford University, David Filo cofounded the Internet directory that soon became Yahoo, Inc. Famously working for a salary of only $1 per year, he has retained a technical role and as of 2012 was still Yahoo!'s largest single shareholder. Perennially listed as a billionaire high-tech entrepreneur, he is not fond of publicity and maintains a very private life, working diligently behind the scenes to support the world-renowned business that he cocreated in a trailer in 1994.

EARLY LIFE

David Filo was born to Jerry and Carol Filo on April 20, 1966, in Madison, Wisconsin. When he was six years

David Filo.

old, his family moved to Moss Bluff, Louisiana, a suburb of Lake Charles, Louisiana. There they lived a partially communal life in an alternative community. His father, an architect, and his mother, an accountant, shared a kitchen and garden chores with six other families. After graduating from Sam Houston High School, Filo matriculated to Tulane University, where he earned a bachelor's degree in computer engineering in 1988. His studies at Tulane were made possible by a dean's honor scholarship. Following Tulane, Filo decided to continue his computer studies at Stanford University. He earned a master's degree in electrical engineering from Stanford in 1990 and began work on a doctoral degree in the same subject. However, he left Stanford to concentrate on Yahoo! and never earned his doctorate. During a panel discussion held by the London newspaper *The Guardian* in 2007, Filo remarked that initially he did not view what he was doing (focusing on Yahoo!) as a business. He was spending so much time on the lists of websites that would become Yahoo! that he had to choose between continuing to work toward his doctorate and focusing on the Yahoo! project. In the early days of Yahoo, Netscape let Filo and cofounder Jerry Yang use a bit of their rack space at their data center. When asked whom in technology he most admired, Filo named Steve Jobs, citing Apple's culture of innovation, design, and savvy marketing. Interestingly, Filo also admitted during the panel discussion that he believed that he and Yang had grossly underestimated the business potential Yahoo! presented and consequently had made some bad short-term decisions.

LIFE'S WORK

Filo met Yang when they were both pursuing doctoral degrees in electrical engineering at Stanford. They shared a makeshift office in a campus trailer. There they worked together on electrical engineering research, publishing at least one academic paper together. Fascinated by the nascent World Wide Web, Filo and Yang sought a website that listed all websites then in existence. They wanted something like a telephone book for the Web and when could not find one decided to build it themselves. Both had accumulated lists of websites that they liked, so the natural next step was to combine their efforts and produce a guide to navigating the Internet.

"Jerry and Dave's Guide to the World Wide Web" was launched in the February 1994. As their list of

Affiliation: Yahoo!

Sergey Brin and Larry Page, cofounders of Google, were not the first two Internet billionaires whose business was born in a makeshift office. In 1994, two other Stanford students, David Filo and Jerry Yang, were working out of the electrical engineering Ph.D. students' office trailer on the Stanford University campus. At the dawn of consumer awareness of the World Wide Web, after seeking and failing to locate a reference guide to places on the Internet, they cofounded the index of websites that later became known as Yahoo!

Something like a virtual telephone book, Yahoo! organized all known websites into categories and subcategories. Yahoo! was a portal, a place where regular people started their Internet session. Quickly this unique and very useful index attracted a cultlike following. Through word of mouth, that growing usage snowballed into a great deal of Internet traffic. When that occurred, Stanford's servers felt the strain and File and Yang were asked to move their project off of Stanford's servers. Befriending Marc Andreessen of Netscape yielded a temporary hosting solution that kept the site alive and growing.

In 1995, Filo and Yang met another key businessperson, Randy Adams, who ran the Internet Shopping Network. Adams saw the promise in their product and brought them to meet Mike Moritz of the powerful Sequoia Capital venture firm. "Jerry and Dave's Guide to the World Wide Web" was renamed Yahoo, an acronym that stands for "yet another hierarchical officious oracle" as well as a word that connotes youthful rebelliousness and energy. Sequoia led an investment that culminated in a very lucrative initial public offering (IPO) in 1996.

As the dot-com boom crescendoed at the end of the 1990s, the Yahoo! brand name, website, and associated yodel used in marketing campaigns became familiar to hundreds of millions worldwide. Popular products included Yahoo! Mail and Yahoo! Finance.

The tide turned in 2001 when, for the first but certainly not the last time, Yahoo! laid off hundreds of employees. Jerry Yang was seen crying at the related analyst's call. Tim Koogle, Yahoo!'s first chief executive officer (CEO), was replaced by Terry Semel, whose background was in Hollywood entertainment.

Strong competition in the most lucrative vertical markets—like search, e-mail, auctions, shopping, and classified ads—demonstrated emphatically that in the new millennium Yahoo! would no longer be all things to all users. Leadership turnover, myriad priorities, and problematic decisions regarding mergers and acquisitions have all been blamed for exacerbating this fall from grace. Following the scandalous ousting of its fourth CEO inside a single calendar year, in June 2012 Yahoo! thirty-seven-year-old engineer Marissa Mayer took the reins. She brought with her fifteen years of experience as an engineer at Google.

---

websites grew, it became unwieldy and had to be organized into categories. When the categories grew too large, they were broken into subcategories. This became the basis of Yahoo!'s hierarchical design. By this time, after consulting a dictionary, Filo and Yang had also renamed their guide Yahoo!—both as an acronym for "yet another hierarchical officious oracle" and for the dictionary meaning of the term *yahoo* (which Yang especially liked): a rude, unsophisticated, somewhat wild person (or in this ease, entity).

By the autumn of 1994, the site had its one-millionth hit. The response to the guide was so strong that Filo and Yang chose to leave school and devote themselves to their endeavor. Initially the web browser company Netscape allowed them to use some of its computers to access lines in exchange for plugging Netscape on their site. In March 1995, Filo and Wang incorporated their business and met with venture capitalists from Silicon Valley. They accepted $2 million in financing from Sequoia Capital in April 1995.

After Yahoo!'s lucrative 1996 initial public offering (IPO), personality differences between Yahoo!'s cofounders became apparent. Although both Filo and Yang made business cards that announced their titles as Chief Yahoo, Filo's more reserved demeanor seemed at odds with the exclamation point. Typically barefoot and clad in khaki shorts and an old silkscreened white T-shirt, Filo gave the impression that he is much more comfortable in a room full of servers than a room full of reporters or *Wall Street* stock analysts. For many years, the more extroverted Yang was the face of the company, whereas Filo was rarely spotted by the media.

Since its early days, rumors have circulated about buyers interested in Yahoo, including America Online and Microsoft. Filo, Yang, and the board have repeatedly rejected any offers. However, in 2011, Yang wanted to take Yahoo, then worth $20 billion, off the public markets. He failed to persuade Filo and the Yahoo! board, and the company remains public. In 2012, the more gregarious Yang resigned and sold all his stock in the company.

In 1993, Filo was known in the company as the Chief Yahoo; today the company website describes him rather generically as a "technologist"—notably, neither chief technology officer nor chief information officer. He is, however, credited for building Yahoo! into one of the world's most heavily visited websites.

This personal preference for a low-profile work life has not stopped Filo from amassing a fortune that is estimated to exceed $1 billion. Thus, he is regularly listed in magazines' "top" lists of high-net-worth individuals. This social and financial standing is still closely tied to Yahoo!'s stock price, as Filo still holds more Yahoo! equity than anyone else in the world. Although today Google dominates the market among Internet service providers, considering that the project that became Yahoo! started as a way for the founders to keep track of favorite websites (and avoid working on their doctoral dissertations), the business is a remarkable success.

PERSONAL LIFE

Filo is married to Angela Buenning Filo, a teacher and photographer from East Palo Alto; they dated thirteen years before marrying. Together they have one child. While not a recluse, Filo is intensely private. Predictably, information on his personal life is sparse. It is known that Filo donated $30 million to the engineering faculty at his alma mater Tulane University in 2005. Together with Yang, he has also endowed a $2 million professorship at Stanford.

Geoffrey R. Archer

FURTHER READING

Himelstein, Linda, Heather Green, Richard Siklos, and Catherine Yang. "Yahoo! The Company. The Strategy. The Stock." *Business Week* 7 Sept. 1998: n. pag. Print. Intended for a general business audience, this article profiles Yahoo! in its heyday.

Lardner, James. "Search No Further." *U.S. News and World Report* 18 May 1998: 49–53. Print. Describes the Internet start-up with the crazy stock price as being run by nonetheless sane people.

Moritz, Michael. "TechCrunch40: Michael Moritz Interviews Marc Andreessen, David Filo, and Chad Hurley." 17 Sept. 2007. *AllThingsD*. Web. 6 Aug. 2012. Interviews with three Internet pioneers at the conference.

Sherman, Josepha. *Jerry Yang and David Filo (Techies)*. Brookfield, CT: 21st Century, 2001. Print. Written for a younger audience, this eighty-page double biography gives an account of the early years of Yahoo!

Weston, Michael R. *Jerry Yang and David Filo: The Founders of Yahoo!* New York: Rosen, 2006. Print. These 112 pages are meant to inspire juveniles and young adults to accomplish great things.

HEATHER PERRAM FRANK

Former executive director at America Online

Born: 1959; Washington, D.C.
Died: -
Primary Field: Internet
Specialty: News and entertainment
Primary Company/Organization: America Online

INTRODUCTION

Heather Perram Frank is a writer, editor, blogger, media consultant, and editor-in-chief of USA Today*'s* Weekend *magazine. Her experience includes extensive media production at* The Huffington Post *and at the popular Internet service provider and media production company America Online.*

EARLY LIFE

Heather Perram Frank was born in Washington, D.C., in 1959, the daughter of Anthony and Shirley Perram. She earned a bachelor's degree from Newcomb College at Tulane University in New Orleans, Louisiana, in 1981. She began her career as the general manager for New Media for WHERE Magazines, a position she held until joining America Online (AOL) in 1997.

LIFE'S WORK

Frank worked with AOL from 1997 until 2003, serving first as a senior editor developing pop-culture-themed programming and content, then as a group programming director. In all her positions at AOL, she managed web content teams to coordinate AOL programming with breaking events, and she was a media spokesperson for the programming department.

In 2005, after leaving AOL, Frank assumed the role of editor in chief of the Women's Lifestyle and Parenting Group for Meredith Corporation. There, she managed the content teams that produced web translations of traditional women's magazines such as *Ladies' Home Journal*, *Family Circle*, and *Fitness*. After 2007, she was employed by Revolution Health as a content editor, verifying the accuracy and validity of information prepublication, driving page views, and increasing and retaining readership.

In August 2008, Frank founded Jump Strategies, a media consultancy firm. The firm specialized in attracting female audiences to media ventures, such as websites and magazines. She ceased the company's operations in 2010.

In 2010, Frank joined the popular newspaper *USA Today* as general manager of the "Your Life" health and lifestyle section. Shortly thereafter, she was appointed vice president of vertical development for the same paper and was promoted to editor in chief of *USA Today*'s *Weekend* magazine in January 2012. In that year she became owner of two trademarks, MEHAB and WEHAB, both listed as representing personal development firms.

Heather Perram Frank.

PERSONAL LIFE

Frank lives in Washington, D.C., with her husband, physician and author Justin Frank. She has served on the board of the Sitar Arts Center, an after-school arts program in Washington, and is a member of the organization's leadership council. She is also a member of the Washington Area Women's Foundation, which strives to ensure that economically vulnerable girls and women have the financial resources they need to flourish. She continues to write actively, posting as Missinformation on Twitter.

Vytautas Malesh

FURTHER READING

"America, Online!" Sept. 1995. *Wired*. Web. 10 Aug. 2012. Describing the rise of Internet giant AOL, this exhaustive article examines the company's business model, technologies, and history.

"AOL Buys *Huffington Post*: The Beginning of the End?" 7 Feb. 2011. *The Guardian*. Web. 8 August 2012. This article takes a pessimistic view of the acquisition of *The Huffington Post* by America Online, as well as a critical view of AOL's previous business practices and acquisitions.

AOL.com. "About AOL." n.d. Web. 8 Aug. 2012. This "about" page is America Online's own account of its history, business practices, and principles.

Frank, Heather Perram. "Creating Your New Blog." 2012. *Montclair.edu*. Web. 8 Aug. 2012. Frank wrote this how-to article as a project for her company, Jump Strategies, offering advice on blog authorship.

"Heather Frank." n.d. *Huffingtonpost.com*. Web. 8 Aug. 2012. Interested readers can go through an archive of Heather Perram Frank's blog articles for *The Huffington Post*, written between 2005 and 2009.

"Heather Perram." n.d. *Spoke.com*. Web. 9 Aug. 2012. A biographical sketch accompanied by a photograph and detailing some of Frank's career and education.

"Heather Perram Frank." n.d. *LinkedIn.com*. Web. 10 Aug. 2012. Frank's actual LinkedIn.com profile details her career in some depth, beginning with her time at Where media and running through to her current position with *USA Today*.

"Heather Perram Frank Named Vice President of Vertical Development for USA Today." 23 Sept. 2010. *Bloomberg.com*. Web. 8 Aug. 2012. A press release detailing Frank's promotion to the position of vice president of vertical development in 2010. Mentions her time at AOL and provides a brief description of the *USA Today* newspaper brand.

Affiliation: America Online

In 1981, the Atari 2600 was the undisputed king of the video game consoles, although its simple graphics and elementary gameplay were a far cry from today's platforms. However, the 2600 did, in some cases, have a component that modern gamers would find familiar: online play. That online play was provided by Control Video Corporation, which would over the next decade grow up to become one of the world's largest Internet conglomerates, America Online.

Control Video Corporation produced a product called Gameline, which allowed Atari 2600 owners to play remotely over telephone lines. That company also produced Quantum-Link for the Commodore 64; this product was unique because it used a graphical user interface, or GUI, which was exceedingly rare at the time (today all interfaces are GUI and it is taken for granted).

In 1989, Control Video Corporation changed its name to America Online, or AOL, and offered something akin to a bulletin board service; customers used modems and the telephone lines to "dial up" or connect to an AOL server, where they could chat, play games, and explore interactive fiction.

AOL's competitors were CompuServe (the first major online service) and Prodigy. These companies, and other small start-ups, competed for the fledgling online communication market for a few years until 1993, when America Online became the breakaway favorite of a new generation of Internet users. That year saw the introduction of the Mosaic web browser. Realizing that World Wide Web, and not Telnet or FTP (for "file transfer protocol"), would be the way the world communicated on the Internet, AOL integrated web browsing into its so-called "walled garden" application suite (a collection of branded applications and filters used to deliver online and proprietary online content).

In the mid-1990s, AOL launched the feature for which it would arguably become most famous: the chat room. Chat rooms allowed multiple users to send text messages, which would be displayed on a single public screen. Chat rooms emerged for every possible interest in arts, education, science, technology, and pop culture.

AOL was also famous for its aggressive marketing strategy; it was one of the only Internet service providers (or ISPs) to advertise on national television. It was also one of the first ISPs to give away free trials of its service by sending free samples of its software (30-day start-up CDs) by direct mail to millions of potential subscribers' homes and businesses.

The remainder of the 1990s saw exponential growth in Internet usage, and AOL remained America's most popular ISP for most of that time, becoming a giant in the telecommunications industry. In the mid-1990s, AOL partnered with the National Education Association to produce educational online content, but perhaps the most significant partnership, for both AOL and the Internet business community as a whole, was its acquisition of media giant Time Warner in 2000.

In the early 2000s, AOL found its market share threatened by telecommunications competitors such as AT&T, Comcast, and Cox Communications, which were beginning to offer low-cost high-speed connections to existing cable and telephony customers. AOL began giving its ISP service away for free while still offering its "walled garden" content model in the form of chat rooms, e-mail, and a branded portal, but the company's reign was ending. An unfortunate series of mergers throughout the first decade of the twenty-first century cost AOL an inestimable fortune, even as its user base dwindled to a fraction of its peak 30 million users.

In 2009, AOL was spun off from Time Warner and left to operate again as an independent corporation. AOL merged with *The Huffington Post*, exemplifying its new mission as a content and media creation company. This new paradigm permeated the corporate structure such that in 2010, AOL cut off access to its once iconic chat rooms. Although America Online is now better known for managing a host of media sites, including *The Huffington Post*, Engadget, and TechCrunch, its importance to the online revolution of the 1990s and early 2000s cannot be understated. The company and the brand remain iconic, and AOL remains one of the longest-enduring technology companies in the world.

JANUS FRIIS

Cofounder of Skype and Kazaa

Born: June 26, 1976; Copenhagen, Denmark
Died: -
Primary Field: Computer science
Specialty: Internet
Primary Company/Organization: Skype

INTRODUCTION

Janus Friis is the cofounder of two of the Internet's most popular and influential technology products: Kazaa, a file-sharing service designed to operate on the FastTrack protocol, and Skype, an Internet telecommunications suite. Friis maintains an active interest in the ownership of Skype and has also cofounded Joltid, which devleops online marketing technologies, the commercial music network Altnet, and the online music and video-streaming sites Rdio and Vdio.

EARLY LIFE

Janus Friis was born in Copenhagen, Denmark, on June 26, 1976. He attended public school but dropped out of high school at the age of sixteen, first to travel through India and then to pursue a career in technology development. He has no further formal education. He began working for the Danish cybersecurity firm Cybercity in 1996. He then worked for the company Tele2, where he met Kazaa and Skype cofounder Niklas Zennström. The two began working together immediately and established a close professional and personal relationship. Friis stayed in Zennström's apartment for a short time in order to coordinate the efforts that would lead to Kazaa and Skype within a few years.

LIFE'S WORK

While working as a technological consultant and analyst for the European telecom provider Tele2, Friis and coworker Zennström began to create Kazaa (formerly styled as KaZaA), a peer-to-peer file-sharing network utilizing the FastTrack protocol (which Friis had helped to create) in 2000. By 2001, Friis had quit Tele2 and was preparing to launch Kazaa.

Kazaa enjoyed immediate success, thanks in part to the decline of Napster, which was at the time suffering from a ongoing litigation brought by entertainment industry associations such as the Recording Industry Association of America (RIAA) and the Motion Picture Association of America (MPAA), along with a host of

media companies and conglomerates, which charged that Napster was participating in copyright violations.

Kazaa immediately found itself in a similar situation, so the creators of the utility sold the property to Sharman Networks, based in Australia, to control, own, and protect the property. Friis and Zennström sold Kazaa to Sharman Networks for approximately $600,000.

In response to litigation regarding copyright infringement claims, Friis attempted to placate representatives of the entertainment industry by creating Altnet, a pay-for-play online streaming service meant to coordinate with Kazaa in such a way that Kazaa users could listen to a portion of a song and then pay to enjoy it in its entirety. This tack ultimately proved unsuccessful, and Friis and Zennström began distancing themselves from normal operations.

In the meantime, litigation persisted. The Kazaa organization spanned three countries (Friis in Denmark, Zennström in Sweden, and the development offices in Estonia), and the need for communication was constant. International telephone fees threatened to overwhelm

Janus Friis.

Affiliation: Skype

While Janus Friis and Niklas Zennström did not invent Voice over Internet Protocol (VoIP), they gave the world what is arguably the first truly useful, easy, and convenient implementation of the technology in their groundbreaking product Skype. Friis and Zennström created Skype in 2003 while phasing out of their operations at Kazaa, the peer-to-peer file-sharing network. Skype required users to create individual account IDs, verified by an e-mail address, but was otherwise very similar in technology and execution to VoiP applications that preceded it.

Friis has acknowledged that a key component in Skype's success was timing. Previously, computer users were predominantly bound to dial-up connections, meaning that users connected to the Internet via phone line. The intermediary step of connecting a computer to the Internet to be able to talk over those same lines was superfluous. The increasing popularity of broadband connections meant that users stayed connected constantly (as opposed to dialing up) and had

the bandwidth to communicate over IP channels. From its inception, Skype was meant to exemplify geographically neutral communication—a phone call from New York to New Jersey was, technologically speaking for the users' part, identical to a call from New York to New Delhi.

Skype was immediately successful, and as a result, Friis and Zennström sold the company to eBay in 2005 for $2.6 billion. Both men remained with the company after its sale, serving as executives and as lead developers. In January 2006, Skype introduced video chat service. Skype users could communicate not only via text and instant messaging, as they had done before, but also through video conferencing, providing all users had webcams.

In 2011, Skype was sold again, this time to Microsoft, for $8.5 billion, making it Microsoft's most expensive acquisition to date. Skype remains the preeminent VoiP suite, with an exponentially greater user base than competitors like Google Talk, Mumble, and SIP.

---

the company, so a need for easy-to-use and affordable Voice over Internet Protocol (VoIP) communication emerged.

In 2003, Friis and Zennström debuted Skype. Originally intended as an interoffice, intracompany communication platform, the application saw an open beta release in August of that year. Skype proved to be immensely popular, and Friis devoted himself to Skype full time. The website soon had millions of users: By 2005, this one applicaton would account for 2.9 percent of the international call market share, and by 2010 that figure had climbed to 13 percent.

In 2005, Friis sold Skype to eBay, but he and Zennström remained active in the company's operations, helping with the introduction of text messaging and later video telecommunications. However, despite the profitability of the sale for Skype, Friis and Sharman were forced to pay $100 million to various record labels and entertainment companies for numerous copyright infringement claims.

Friis was named one of *Time* magazine's 100 Most Influential People in 2006 for his work on the Skype platform. In that year he also won the Danish IT-Prisen (IT prize) in commemoration of his creation. He also received the Wharton Infosys Business Transformation Award.

Also in 2006, Friis, along with longtime partner Zennström, began plotting (and hiring programmers to produce) Joost, an online application that attempted to do for television what Skype was doing for telecommunications. The ad-supported application launched in 2007 with a number of unique features, key among which was design synergy with Sony's PlayStation 3 gaming console; users of the PlayStation 3 would be able to use native features of the console (such as its "X button" functionality) to navigate video options efficiently. Joost was not as popular as Skype or Kazaa, and consequently it was less successful. In 2009, Friis and Zennström announced that they would discontinue its operation.

While Friis was shuttering Joost, he found himself in another legal confrontation, this time with Joltid, the company that produced the peer-to-peer architecture upon which Skype ran. This dispute was settled out of court in November 2009, allowing Skype to continue business operations without interruption and granting Friis a 14 percent stake in Index Ventures, the company that owned the original peer-to-peer architecture.

Skype operations continued normally, and the company's VoiP and international calling market share grew apace. In May 2011, Microsoft purchased Skype for $8.5 billion. Friis and Zennström received $780 million each.

Friis continues to work with Zennström to produce new peer-to-peer web products. His latest offerings include Vdio, a streaming video service similar to Netflix available in the United Kingdom, and Rdio, a subscriber-based, ad-free music service launched in 2010 and available in the United States, the United Kingdom, Brazil, Australia, New Zealand, and a few other countries.

PERSONAL LIFE

In part because of the vigorous litigation associated with his professional life, Friis is known to keep a low profile. He has expressed an affinity for cold-water swimming and is constantly traveling to meet professional obligations in Scandinavia, Australia, the United States, and the United Kingdom. He has been romantically linked to Christina Knudsen, the daughter of actor Roger Moore.

Vytautas Malesh

FURTHER READING

Caplan, Jeremy. "50,000 TV Channels! The Skype Guys Strike Again." *Time* 12 Mar. 2007: 52–54. Print. A curiously optimistic article that explains the concept, business model, and legal peculiarities for Friis's first major (and ultimately unsuccessful) post-Skype venture, Joost.

Friis, Janus. "Janus Friis." Interview by Anthony Bruno. *Billboard* 16 Oct. 2010: 8. Print. In this interview, Friis opines on the nature of Internet services, including commentary on Kazaa and Skype, and discusses the role of Rdio in the online music landscape.

Geron, Tomio. "Rdio Looks for Distribution with Verizon, Echo Nest Deals." *Forbes* 4 May 2011: 40. Print. Rdio, a relatively new start-up from Kazaa founders Friis and Niklas Zennström, has found recent success in its mobile platform adaptations. This article focuses on the integration of that mobile platform with wireless carrier Verizon and surveys the potential for market share for Rdio.

Maney, Kevin. "Skype: The Inside Story of the Boffo $8.5 Billion Deal." *Fortune* 25 July 2011: 125–28. Print. Delivers a point-by-point breakdown of Microsoft's 2011 purchase of Skype and attempts to analyze the potential for profit in that venture. Includes contextual background on the product's founding, a study of why Skype was not profitable for earlier purchaser eBay, and a final opinion on what Microsoft will have to do with its new, expensive acquisition.

Martinsen, Bent. "Why Were Janus Friis and Niklas Zennström successful with Kazaa and Skype?" *Ebbemunk.dk* 2006. Web. 5 Aug. 2012. An exhaustive website covering every stage of the development of Kazaa and Skype. Analysis runs year by year and includes numerous quotations of website creators Friis and Niklas Zennström. Also includes a contextual breakdown of the success of both sites, referencing necessary conditions and product demand. Provides an extensive list of external sources.

McCrea, Bridget. "Skype Takes Students Where No School Bus Can Go." *The Journal, Transforming Education through Technology* June–July 2012: 18. Print. Exemplifies some of the possibilities of Friis's Skype platform, particularly from an educational perspective. Recounts the experiences of several students and teachers in coordinating classroom activities by using Skype, and provides tips for teachers and students looking to use Skype for similar activities.

Roth, Daniel. "Catch Us if You Can." *Fortune* 9 Feb. 2004: 64–74. Print. This lengthy and informal interview/op-ed intermixes personal profiles and descriptions of both Friis and Zennström in the early days of Skype, post-Kazaa. This article blends interview paraphrase with analysis of the legal and business aspects of the men's activities circa 2001–04.

G

Gail F. Goodman

Chairman, president, and CEO Constant Contact

Born: 1960; place unknown
Died: -
Primary Field: Business and commerce
Specialty: Marketing
Primary Company/Organization: Constant Contact

INTRODUCTION

Gail F. Goodman is chairman, president, and chief executive officer (CEO) of the e-mail marketing company Constant Contact, Inc., based in Waltham, Massachusetts, and founded in 1998. A small business expert and visionary, Goodman revolutionized the way that small businesses and organizations effectively maintain relationships with their customers, clients, and members through e-mail and othering marketing campaigns. Constant Contact provides small businesses with e-mail marketing, event marketing, social media marketing, and online survey tools and has become an industry leader in online marketing, used by more than 450,000 small organizations worldwide and earning more than $174 million in revenue. In 2007, it became a publicly traded company.

EARLY LIFE

Gail F. Goodman was born in 1960, the youngest of four children. She earned a bachelor of arts degree from the University of Pennsylvania and a master's of business administration form the Tuck School of Business at Dartmouth College in 1987.

LIFE'S WORK

Goodman launched Constant Contact, Inc. (formerly known as Roving Software) in April of 1998. In starting this business, she was aware that small companies were strapped for time and needed an affordable and easy way to maintain a loyal customer base. She devised Constant Contact as an online marketing tool to help small businesses, associations, and nonprofits with their e-mail marketing, particularly with permission-based e-mail and stopping spam. The goal was to help entrepreneurs connect with their customers, clients, and

Gail F. Goodman.

members through the most efficient online marketing tools: e-mail marketing, online surveys, event marketing, social media, and "deal tools" such as coupons. Other tools included personal coaching and support, guidance in creating professional-looking e-mail newsletters, and access to the latest industry information and education for entrepreneurs to learn about e-mail marketing.

Goodman's business philosophy is that entrepreneurs should maintain a useful dialogue with their customers, with a goal of building successful, lasting customer relationships and referrals. Because this strategy is more likely to be used by small businesses, Goodman's geared her software toward these companies, and 70 percent of Constant Contact's clients have fewer than ten employees. Goodman broke new ground not only by reinventing ways entrepreneurs and their employees could target customers but also by providing this means of communication in an affordable program that is easy to learn and well supported. For example, Goodman provided her Constant Contact clients with live customer support at rates or $15 or $30 per month, a step virtually unheard of in electronic marketing at the time.

Goodman's expertise in electronic marketing is reflected in her product. For example, Constant Contact assures its clients high e-mail deliverability rates due to strong partnerships with Internet service providers (ISPs), a no-tolerance spam policy, and a leadership role in organizations such as the Email Sender and Provider Coalition (ESPC). Goodman works with the ESPC on Project Lumos, a project oriented toward finding an industrywide spam solution. Today, Constant Contact has some five hundred thousand customers worldwide. After going public on the NASDAQ exchange in 2007, Constant Contact expanded into other areas, including social network marketing campaigns.

Constant Contact has experienced some shortfalls, with less successful showings in door-to-door sales and radio endorsement. Goodman has steered Constant Contact toward coupon-based "deal" marketing in its SaveLocal project, competing with rival companies Groupon and LivingSocial. SaveLocal charges business customers between $1 and $3 per coupon. With such strategies, Constant Contact has grown steadily under Goodman, including acquisitions. Companies acquired by Constant Contact in 2012 included CardStar, a mobile loyalty and location-based service platform, for which Constant Contact paid an undisclosed amount, and SinglePlatform, a web designer for which Constant Contact is reported to have paid up to $100 million.

Affiliation: Constant Contact

Constant Contact, Inc., was founded in 1998 by chairman, president, and chief executive officer Gail F. Goodman. The company helps small businesses create and grow loyal customer bases through electronic marketing campaigns that generate repeat business and referrals.

Constant Contact's trademark formula for "engagement marketing" works marketing campaigns that use e-mail, social media, events, local deals, and online surveys. Clients include more than half a million small businesses, nonprofits, and associations worldwide. Particularly geared toward small companies (70 percent of whom have fewer than ten employees), Constant Contact provides entrepreneurs and their employees with an easy and affordable way to build successful, lasting customer relationships. The company offers a free "KnowHow" service, which includes seminars, personal coaching, and award-winning product support.

In 2007, Constant Contact became a publicly traded company. It is headquartered in Waltham, Massachusetts, and has offices there and in Loveland, Colorado; Delray Beach, Florida; San Francisco, California; New York, New York; and London, England. In 2011, Constant Contact purchased customer relationship management (CRM) start-up Bantam Live for $15 million. In 2012, Constant Contact purchased CardStar, a mobile loyalty and location-based service platform, for an undisclosed amount. That year it also purchased SinglePlatform Corporation, a website that helps businesses design their online storefronts, for a total acquisition price nearing $100 million.

Constant Contact was ranked number 153 on Deloitte's 2009 Technology Fast 500. Goodman remains chairman of the board at Constant Contact.

PERSONAL LIFE

Goodman is married to Dave Swindell and lives in Acton, Massachusetts. She is a member of the board of trustees of the Massachusetts Technology Leadership Council and a member of the board of directors of the Service Corps of Retired Executives (SCORE).

In 2001, Goodman was inducted into the MITX Innovation Hall of Fame and named one of Boston's Top 30 Innovators by the *Boston Globe*. She was the

2008 New England Regional winner of the Ernst and Young Entrepreneur of the Year award. In 2009, she was named Executive of the Year at the American Business Awards, and her company Constant Contact was ranked Best Overall Company at the 2009, 2010, and 2011 American Business Awards.

In 2012, Goodman published *Engagement Marketing: How Small Business Wins in a Socially Connected World*. She speaks frequently at industry events about "engagement marketing," her formula for developing and tracking effective small business strategies through online tools. However, not all of Goodman's successful strategies are founded in online technology; much of her small business knowledge begins with the visionary expertise she developed in business school. For example, one marketing tool that she emphasizes is teamwork. Goodman theorizes that even a mediocre strategy can win if executed perfectly, whereas a perfect strategy will suffer if executed poorly.

Ellen Elder

FURTHER READING

Freedman, David H. "A Groupon Alternative Aims to Offer Small Businesses a Better Deal." *New York Times* 15 Mar. 2012: B5. Print. An interview with Goodman that details how her company, Constant Contact, offers small businesses online help in building, managing, and creating marketing campaigns around customer e-mail lists.

Goodman, Gail F. *Engagement Marketing: How Small Business Wins in a Socially Connected World*. Hoboken: Wiley, 2012. Print. A definitive small business guide filled with practical advice based on the author's experience helping thousands of small businesses to increase repeat sales through e-mail outreach.

Goodman, Gail F. "'Tis the Season." *Entrepreneur* 34.11 (2006): 22. Print. Interview with Goodman that offers tips for holiday marketing trends and etiquette; also points to free shipping as the marketing method to which consumers respond most positively.

RON GORODETZKY

Cofounder of Digg

Born: Date unknown; Los Angeles, California
Died: -
Primary Field: Internet
Specialty: Social media
Primary Company/Organization: Digg

INTRODUCTION

Ron Gorodetzky was one of the first employees of Digg, hired by founder Kevin Rose to develop much of the code and architecture for the social news-sharing site for which Owen Byrne had written the PHP script. Gorodetzky was instrumental in developing many of the features and site changes that Digg adopted in its early years, as it became one of the most popular sites on the Internet— fifty-fifth in Alexa's global rankings—and was pursued by larger companies. He remained with the site as it declined (to 215th in Alexa's 2012 ratings) and as a new version was rolled out, before founding the Fflick movie recommendation site, which was purchased by Google.

EARLY LIFE

Ron Gorodetzky grew up in Los Angeles and studied computer engineering at the University of California at San Diego. He became a computer consultant working in Silicon Valley. When cable network TechTV was bought by Comcast and merged with its network G4, relocating to Los Angeles, Gorodetzky took an internship, teaching new staff and crew members how to use various technologies. Through this internship, he met Kevin Rose, host of Tech TV/G4's *The Screen Savers* (which later became *Attack of the Show*). Rose hired him in late 2004 to help with the programming and administration of a site Rose and others were putting together called Digg.

LIFE'S WORK

Digg was one of two start-ups Rose founded with Jay Adelson, the chief executive officer (CEO) of data server and Internet business services provider Equinix, whom Rose had met while interviewing him for TechTV. The original ad-free version of Digg was designed by Dan Ries. Software engineer Owen Byrne was hired to write the site's PHP scripts, and Gorodetzky was hired to revamp and maintain the site, becoming principally responsible for the HTTP architecture as well as developing a search engine that remained in use for years. Digg formally organized as a company in early 2005, with Gorodetzky as one of its core employees, and the start-up soon became a full-time pursuit, with Adelson leaving Equinix and Rose leaving his hosting job at TechTV. A new staff was hired to augment, refine, and replace Byrne's code, and Gorodetzky remained on staff as essentially the lead operations architect. Ads were soon added to generate revenue, first using Google's service and later Microsoft's.

The second start-up, Revision3, was founded to produce Internet-distributed television shows for niche audiences. Godoretzky was cofounder and director of technology.

As a social news site, Digg was a contemporary of the similar (but then little-known) site Reddit and the elder dinosaur of the niche, Slashdot. Registered users could submit links (typically news items, though not necessarily from formal news sources), and other users voted on them, positively (a "digg") or negatively (a "bury"). "Digg" was the term chosen to signify approval in reference to "I dig(g) that story you posted"; the double *g* was necessary because the domain name dig.com was already in use by Disney. The name Diggnation or Dignation had been proposed but rejected as too long and was instead used for a Revision3 show

Ron Gorodetzky.

in which Rose and his cohost discussed popular stories from Digg. Digg was also featured on Rose's TechTV show *The Screen Savers* (predecessor to G4's *Attack of the Show*) before Rose left to work on Digg full time.

Digg combined elements of social networks and news sites. The ability for a user to create a "friends list" was soon added, making it easy to monitor the stories uploaded by other users the user knew or trusted as sources. Stories were also categorized, encouraging browsing, and users were able to flag a story as spam, notifying moderators to remove it, which countered the natural tendency for social media spammers and bots to target Digg as it became more popular. (Interestingly, the science category was the least frequently spammed category, by a considerable margin.) The community at Digg developed its own traditions, habits, and quirks, which influenced the nature of the stories that received the most votes, leading to a number of cases of fraudulent behavior as users accepted cash to "digg" stories and provide them with publicity. Essentially the same type of reward-for-endorsement exchange would survive in today's social media landscape, where users can "like" a business's Facebook page for above-board, noncash incentives.

At the height of its popularity, Digg was ranked fifty-fifth on Alexa's global traffic ratings. Although its revenue in 2008 was only about $8 million, numerous established companies attempted to purchase it. Offers from Google ($200 million) and Current (presumably comparable) are public knowledge; offers from Microsoft and Yahoo, among others, were rumored but never official. Rather than entertain courters, the company, at Rose and Adelson's direction, opted to keep the firm privately held. Byrne left around this time, in late 2007, and later implied difficulties behind the scenes.

Adelson left in 2010 after a reported disagreement with Rose over the direction of the company. Gorodetzky worked on the site overhaul already in progress at the time of Adelson's departure, which changed not only the interface but also the site's underlying architecture, including switching to a new distributed database system. The redesign was greeted with hostility by a vocal contingent of the user base. That, along with the increased popularity of Reddit and the increasing tendency of social networking sites Facebook, Twitter, and Tumblr to encourage link sharing and for sites to include buttons to enable that (alongside Digg's button), contributed to Digg's decline.

Gorodetzky too left both Digg and Revision3 in 2010, to cofound Fflick, of which he became chief

---

Affiliation: Digg

The social news site Digg was founded after Kevin Rose, host of Tech TV's *The Screen Savers* (the predecessor to G4's *Attack of the Show*) met Equinix founder Jay Adelson while interviewing him. Digg began in February 2005, with the collaboration of Adelson (the first CEO), Rose, Owen Byrne, and Ron Gorodetzky. The site's initial design was developed by Dan Ries.

Digg allows users to share and recommend content on the web, with a focus on news. Members vote on shared content, using a system familiar from Slashdot, Reddit, and other sites: A given page shared with the site may be voted up (a "digg") or voted down (a "bury"). The front page displays currently popular and trending content, which is constantly in flux as users read and respond to content and share new links. Changes to the website in the first year included adding categories for stories (technology, science, world and business, videos, entertainment, gaming), the capacity for users to build a friends list and keep track of their friends' stories, and improvements to the interface. Popularity grew steadily, and, like Slashdot, Reddit, and other sites, Digg experienced spikes in traffic resulting from a story becoming popular. One of Digg's primary merits was its ability to focus a spotlight on something on the Internet that might otherwise go unnoticed by most, so that audiences no longer had to rely as heavily on the news "curation" of traditional media.

The impact of user votes on the site inevitably led to attempts to game the system. There were several known attempts, uncovered by sting operations, to upvote stories for cash (with the implied threat of a downvote if no payment were made—a sort of protection racket). There was also the explicit, openly conducted Bury Brigade, which responded to the popularity of Ron Paul among Digg users—social news users in the United States long having included a vocal libertarian contingent—by downvoting every Paul story submitted in an attempt to bury any mention of him. Digg's popularity led to a high ranking on Google's PageRank, meaning that "digged" stories would feature prominently in Google search results—providing a clear financial motivation for abuses of the system.

Around the height of the site's fame, Google attempted to purchase Digg for $200 million but eventually walked away from the table without completing the deal. Digg was considered one of the ripest websites for purchase, and other deals were entertained, but by the end of the year, then-CEO Adelson announced that the company was not for sale. Fox News, Microsoft, and Yahoo! had been among the suitors. Over time, the shine may have left the apple, although hits remained high, with about 20 million visitors per month; Digg never developed the level of mainstream awareness that Facebook or Twitter did, and its niche competitor, Reddit, began to attract mainstream media attention because of several high-profile news stories and the celebrity involvement in AMA/IAMA threads. In 2010, the site had to lay off more than a third of its staff, and Adelson left after disagreements with Rose and others.

Google's AdSense was originally used to provide ads, the source of Digg's revenue, but in 2007 the company switched to Microsoft's ad service.

In 2012, Digg went through significant changes. Although it was widely reported that the site was sold for a paltry $500,000—an extremely low amount relative to both the market for popular websites and the previous offers that had been made—this price, paid by Betaworks, was only for the website, technology, and Digg brand. Patents developed under Adelson were sold to LinkedIn for an additional $4 million, and staff were transferred to *The Washington Post* for $12 million. The total was still a far cry from the $200 million once bandied about, but that reflected the financial realities of the intervening years as much as anything else.

On July 31, 2012, a new version of Digg launched, based in part on user surveys collected through Betaworks' RethinkDigg.com. The new site integrated better with social media (the site had been integrated with Facebook Connect since 2009 and offered an iPhone app, although a previously offered Android app was no longer available with the relaunch), featured a more image-heavy design, and was built around an editorially centered front page.

---

technology officer, with three other former Digg employees: Dav Zimak, Kurt Wilms, and Marc Hemeon. Fflick was similar to a social news site but more focused than Digg: It aggregated tweets about movies, functioning as a crowd-sourced movie review site while allowing users to add movies to Netflix queues or purchase tickets. Rather than competing with existing social networks, the site was designed as, in essence, an overlay on top of them, while offering a more personalized and informal sort of movie review than those of Rotten Tomatoes or Metacritic—one that could generate movie recommendations, much like the recommendation engines of Netflix, Amazon, or Goodreads. Fflick launched in August 2010 and the following year was acquired by YouTube, itself owned by Google. Gorodetzky and the rest of the Fflick team were folded into a team of engineers working to improve Google+, Google's social network, by emphasizing the aspects Facebook and other social networks could not hope to replicate—namely, Google's many other services. Gorodetzky became part of a team redesigning elements of YouTube in order to integrate them with Google+. Early elements of integration included the ability to start Google+ Hangouts in YouTube and live video streaming in Google+.

PERSONAL LIFE

Gorodetzky had a cameo as "Robot Consultant" in the straight-to-video sequel *American Pie: Band Camp*. (His sister, Karen Gorodetzky, was a production supervisor on the film and now works as a line producer on MTV's *Teen Wolf* series.) Gorodetzky is an aficionado of skydiving, a hobby he shares with former Digg colleague Rose.

Bill Kte'pi

FURTHER READING

Jenkins, Henry. *Confronting the Challenges of Participatory Culture: Media Education for the 21st Century*. Cambridge: MIT, 2009. Print. Examines social media, new forms of creative expression, and their impact on media studies.

Qualman, Erik. *Socialnomics: How Social Media Transforms the Way We Live and Do Business*. New York: Wiley, 2010. Print. Examines the impact of social media on the business world.

Sarno, David. "Digg Gets $28.7M Boost, Plans to Double Size, Go Global." *Los Angeles Times* 23 Sept. 2008: n. pag. Print. Coverage of Digg's rise from the company's peak period.

BRAD GREENSPAN

Cofounder of Myspace

Born: 1976; Los Angeles, California
Died: -
Primary Field: Internet
Specialty: Social media
Primary Company/Organization: Myspace

INTRODUCTION

Considered a "boy wonder" among Internet entrepreneurs, Brad Greenspan started both eUniverse and Myspace. Myspace especially became an exceptional success, but by the time of its $580 million sale to News Corp., Greenspan had left the business after an accounting scandal.

EARLY LIFE

Brad Greenspan was born in Los Angeles in 1976. When he was thirteen, he orchestrated his first big deal: collecting money and buying fireworks for his syndicate of friends. He managed to cajole his mother, Judith Guilfoyle, into signing for the package of fireworks; unfortunately, his mother's opposition to bottle-rocket battles in the backyard meant the deal would not be repeated. He attended the Menlo School, an independent college preparatory school in Atherton, California. After graduation, Greenspan enrolled at the University of California at Los Angeles (UCLA), graduating in 1997 with a double major in political science and business.

In 1996, Greenspan founded his first company, a merchant bank called Palisades Capital, Inc., from his dormitory room. Within three years, he had raised more than $55 million for three publicly traded companies. Using his profits from Palisades, he began the work on what would become eUniverse, an Internet marketing company, in 1998. His intent was to create a public Internet company. Greenspan took the company public in 1999 and managed to survive the burst of the dot-com bubble.

LIFE'S WORK

In 2002, eUniverse acquired a marketing company called ResponseBase, and its two partners, Tom Anderson and Chris DeWolfe, joined Greenspan's staff. In time, after discussing the social network Friendster and Anderson's dissatisfaction with some aspects of it, they persuaded Greenspan to start a social network

Brad Greenspan.

using eUniverse's servers. It launched ten days later, in August 2003, using Adobe's ColdFusion web development platform. Some of the ideas for the site, especially its focus on music, came from DeWolfe; he also came up with the name. DeWolfe had bought a domain name in 2002 that he had intended to use for an online data storage site like his former employer XDrive, but that plan was never realized, because he and Anderson had taken their start-up in a different direction. It struck him that the name would be suitable for a social network, at the same time saving some money by using a domain he already owned. Myspace was born.

Greenspan held contests to see who could sign up the most users to Myspace in order to build the user base quickly. The first users were his employees at eUniverse; the next wave came from eUniverse's large body of users and subscribers; from there, it spread by word of mouth as the partners' friends signed up. Greenspan hired Toan Nguyen as an architect for the site; he built a website that, as the user base increased, would scale better than the initial architecture would allow.

It was Greenspan's idea to offer Myspace free of charge. The others came to him with the notion that if Myspace improved on Friendster and charged money for

its service, they might do very good business. Greenspan, however, believed the site needed to be free to use for it to gain in popularity and prosper. Myspace's rise to fame has essentially ensured that subsequent social networks have needed to be free as well.

Myspace greatly eclipsed Friendster and popularized the notion of social media. Teenagers in particular were drawn to the ability to create and manipulate an identity online: Myspace (unlike Friendster or Facebook and Google+ later) did not require the use of a real name. Users were also attracted by the presence of many bands, both famous and unsigned, on the site, with free music for streaming and download. Revenue came through advertising and marketing. As Myspace became popular, large media corporations realized that it might be better to buy it than to create their own social networks to compete with it, and Rupert Murdoch's company News Corp. (owner of Fox Broadcasting, 20th Century Fox, and *The Wall Street Journal*) won a bidding war for Intermix Media (as eUniverse was now known), which included Myspace, for $580 million. News Corp. subsequently expanded Myspace to numerous other countries.

Greenspan had left the company by that point. At the end of 2003, accounting problems had halted the trade of eUniverse stock and prompted an investigation by the Securities and Exchange Commission. Greenspan then stepped down as chief executive officer. He was also named in a case brought by New York attorney general Eliot Spitzer, alleging that eUniverse had disseminated spyware. Greenspan retained much of his stake in the company, though, and owned 10 percent of it when the News Corp. sale (which he opposed) was made. Shortly after, he attempted a takeover bid of *The Wall Street Journal*, but his bid failed in 2007.

Greenspan continued to oppose News Corp. after the sale, publishing reports on a website that alleged that Myspace had been undervalued ($327 million of the $580 million sale represented the supposed value of Myspace). He stipulated that because Myspace should have been valued at $20 billion, Intermix shareholders, of whom he was one, had been defrauded. The lawsuit he filed was dismissed.

Greenspan later founded the social network company LiveUniverse, the Asian Internet company Broadwebasia, and the Borba line of health products. An attempt to buy Answers Corp., the owner of Answers.com, was unsuccessful. His business endeavors also include Big Fish Games (gaming), Fluid Music (music), and Draths (clean technology).

Affiliation: Myspace

Myspace was not the first social network, but it was the first to become a huge success and the first to popularize the idea of social media and come to the attention of the Internet novices in the general public. It was founded when Tom Anderson and Chris DeWolfe met Brad Greenspan, the head of eUniverse (later Intermix Media), the company that had just bought out their marketing company in 2002.

Myspace premiered the next year. Anderson, who became head of product development and the public face of the company (wholly owned by Intermix), was dissatisfied with Friendster, the largest extant social network. DeWolfe implemented some ideas he had developed during college project while at the University of California, Los Angeles, and brought a focus on music, which remains the site's most distinctive feature.

In 2005, Intermix Media was bought for $580 million by News Corp., Rupert Murdoch's corporation, which also owns *The Wall Street Journal*, Fox Television, and the 20th Century Fox film studio. The purpose of the Intermix purchase was simply to acquire Myspace, and while some thought the price was too high, within a year Myspace was worth at least $1 billion.

One of the strengths of Myspace was its use by bands, from the arena-touring to the unsigned. Bands that established a Myspace page (for free if they were unsigned) could host MP3 files of their music on it, with a built-in streaming player and the possibility of allowing downloads. For young, struggling bands, this was an enormous boon: They did not need to pay for server space or worry about bandwidth issues to encourage fans and potential fans to check out their music; all they had to do was agree to let Myspace users add their songs (with attribution) to their profile pages and allow other promotional uses. Even once Myspace began to decline, it continued to be a strong base for music; it was, for example, the launching pad for Lily Allen's career.

Little by little, Myspace was overtaken by Facebook, which exceeded its user base in 2008 and went on to become the subject of the Oscar-winning movie *The Social Network*, several lawsuits, and the default Internet destination for a large chunk of the online demographic. Part of the reason for Myspace's decline was its association with news stories about pedophiliac predators and pornography; Myspace had little control over content and ineffective spam filters relative to Facebook. Meanwhile, sites like Twitter, while offering comparatively few features relative to the richness of profiles at Facebook and Myspace, nevertheless prospered because their leanness suited them to the growing use of smart phone apps to interact with the Internet—part of the growing "post-PC" Internet. In 2009, when founder DeWolfe stepped down as CEO to become a strategic adviser—as Anderson had already left the Intermix presidency to do likewise—he was replaced with a former Facebook executive, Owen Van Natta.

The shift from Myspace to Facebook was not universal or uniform. In 2007, researcher danah boyd (she deliberately lowercases her name) noted a class difference between Facebook-using teenagers and Myspace-using teenagers. Middle- and upper-class teens, especially teenagers expecting to attend college, were for the most part either switching to Facebook from Myspace or, if young enough to be creating their first social media profile, choosing Facebook over Myspace. Teenagers from poorer backgrounds, teenagers with parents who had not attended college, and teenagers who identified with certain subcultures were more likely to choose or remain with Myspace. That Facebook had originated as a social network for college students may have played a role in this. A major exception, ethnicity-based rather than class-based, was the tendency of Latino teenagers to use Myspace regardless of economic background and collegiate aspirations. Thus the Myspace demographic was shifting, at least in the United States, and it was less affluent and less WASPy. Boyd also noted that teenagers who had more than one social media profile were more likely than adults to differentiate those profiles—they would use a different profile photo for each and perhaps list different interests, whereas adults were likeliest to use identical information on every profile they actively maintained.

While its peak had passed, Myspace continued to develop, with a new design referred to internally as Myspace 2.0. Features were added to allow users to watch streaming television (featuring licensed content from News Corp.'s holdings), while music and photo-sharing features were refined and expanded. The overall aesthetic of Myspace was made cleaner and brought forward, away from the chaotic black screens and

Affiliation: Myspace (continued)

blinking text of the early social web. Support for apps was added, as well as compatibility with Twitter.

In 2011, News Corp. announced its readiness to sell Myspace, hoping to get $100 million for it—less than a fifth of what it had paid, although that money had long been earned back. After several months of entertain-

ing offers, Myspace was sold to Specific Media for $35 million, with News Corp. retaining a small stake in the company's shares. Many of the games once hosted on Myspace by developers like Zynga (which also develop Facebook and mobile games) have been closed.

PERSONAL LIFE

Greenspan is active in politics and charitable work. His net worth is approximately $20 million.

Bill Kte'pi

FURTHER READING

Angwin, Julia. "Putting Your Best Faces Forward." *Wall Street Journal* 29 Mar. 2009: n. pag. Print. An article on the rise of Facebook and its impact on Myspace.

Angwin, Julia. *Stealing MySpace: The Battle to Control the Most Popular Website in America.* New York: Random House, 2009. Print. An account of Myspace's peak, examining both the online culture and the impact of the company in the business world.

Flyness. *From Myspace to My Place: The Men's Guide to Snagging Women Online.* New York: Flyness, 2008. Print. A pick-up guide to Myspace, demonstrating (in conjunction with Kendall, below) the versatility of Myspace's appeal; from the publisher of later pick-up guides to Twitter and other social media.

Kendall, Peggy. *Rewired: Youth Ministry in an Age of IM and Myspace.* Valley Forge: Judson, 2007. Print. Another examination of the effect of social media on youth, in this case with an emphasis on ministry efforts, from the publishing arm of the American Baptist Churches.

Winograd, Morley, and Michael D. Hais. *Millennial Makeover: MySpace, YouTube, and the Future of American Politics.* New Brunswick: Rutgers UP, 2008. Print. Examines the impact of social media on American politics, especially in the period leading up to the 2008 election.

H

HEATHER HARDE

Former CEO of TechCrunch

Born: Date and place unknown
Died: -
Primary Field: Internet
Specialty: News and entertainment
Primary Company/Organization: TechCrunch

INTRODUCTION
For five years, Heather Harde ran the most successful and most popular technology news site on the Internet. As general manager of the top technology blog on the web, TechCrunch, Harde increased traffic, diversified the brand, and ensured that the blog provided the very latest in technology and start-up news. In her role as vice chairman of a San Francisco–based technology innovation organization, Harde inspires women in technology while having a significant impact on perceptions of media and technology.

EARLY LIFE
Heather Harde graduated from Mount Holyoke College in 1991 and earned a master's degree in business administration from Harvard Business School in 1996. After completing her education, she began her career as an investment banker for Brown Brothers Harriman and Co. She discovered an interest in media and soon left the world of banking, working for Showtime Networks, News American Marketing, ASkyB, and then Fox Interactive Media, owned by News Corp. During her ten years with News Corp., Harde was involved in the relationship between technology and media. She helped secure $1.3 billion in new acquisitions for Fox and proved a capable and popular executive. When J. Michael Arrington, founder of TechCrunch, realized his

company was about to explode in popularity, he thought Harde the right person to have by his side.

LIFE'S WORK
After a decade working for the Internet branch of Rupert Murdoch's media empire, Arrington recruited Harde to run the day-to-day business of TechCrunch by growing its sales team and managing the company.

Heather Harde.

159

Harde was not easily lured away from her job with Fox Media, but on March 17, 2007, Arrington officially announced Harde's hiring on his blog.

TechCrunch had published its first blog post on June 11, 2005. At the time, Arrington had considered his blogging on technology news as little more than a hobby. With a background in start-ups, initial public offerings (IPOs), and Internet law, Arrington was in a unique position to learn the latest news from the new technology businesses around Silicon Valley. New businesses would feed him information and tips, and Arrington would in turn post the tips and his research on his blog, creating a virtual newspaper for the latest tech business news. It was not long before he attracted subscribers to his RSS feed. A well-researched and well-formatted tech news blog was unheard of at the time and filled a gap in the online business revolution.

It was not long before the simple blog posts became a business for Arrington, forcing him to hire staff and move the operation out of his house. The company moved from Palo Alto (Silicon Valley) to San Francisco in June of 2010. As the company expanded, so did the range of branded products. TechCrunch went from a simple blog to a multifaceted online empire. Under the direction of Harde, TechCrunch developed CrunchBase, The Crunchies, and the Disrupt conferences.

CrunchBase is one of the main subsidiaries of the TechCrunch blog. Started in 2007, CrunchBase is an online database of who's who in the world of technology. It lists individual investors as well as companies and websites. It focuses on those in the world of venture capital, entrepreneurs, and notable tech executives. Entries provide biographical information and chronologies for people and companies. A section titled Milestones lists notable achievements, from professional accolades to hirings. Although TechCrunch hosts the database and provides must of its information, CrunchBase operates on a open source basis and thus is available for the public to edit. This helps keeps the information up to date, allowing companies to correct their own profiles. The accuracy and completeness of the information on CrunchBase have made it a popular and accepted authority on new technology businesses and the people invest in them.

Harde was very involved in the development of the Disrupt conferences, appealing to both affluent blog readers and the many companies featured on Crunch-Base. Disrupt is a series of conferences that highlight the best in new technology and design as well as introduce new tech start-ups to the world. The conferences have been held in New York, Tokyo, and San Francisco,

attracting large crowds and a steady stream of entrance-fee revenue. Many new companies attend Disrupt to gain exposure and locate investors among the other attendees. Presentations by the executives at TechCrunch, including Harde and Arrington, are often the highlight of the conference schedule.

The Crunchies are a set of technology awards, bestowed annually in January in San Francisco and first developed by TechCrunch in 2007. The Internet community is allowed to vote and nominate firms and individuals for the Crunchies. The awards celebrate start-ups, venture capital firms, and new ideas and leaders in the world of technology.

From the beginning of Harde's tenure with TechCrunch, the company began to flourish and expand past all expectations. In 2010, Arrington decided to sell his company to America Online (AOL) to increase TechCrunch's online presence as well as the sites' technology news offerings. The company was valued at $10 million and sold for at least $25 million.

After AOL acquired the TechCrunch family of websites, Arrington resigned as editor of the blog. Editing had been the only role he kept for himself after he had hired Harde to run the company. In September 2011, it was announced that Arrington would devote his time to the $20 million venture capital fund Crunch-Fund. He would still be working for AOL but not for the TechCrunch blog. This period was a complicated time for TechCrunch as it clashed with new owner AOL over the differences between traditional journalism models and adapting employees and business perceptions for the web audience. Arrington argued that during the AOL acquisition it was decided that TechCrunch would retain its editorial independence, the very thing that made it so successful, and demanded that AOL return control of the company back to the shareholders. AOL representatives, including Arrington's official boss, Arianna Huffington of *The Huffington Post*, publicly stated that Arrington had nothing to do with the running of Tech-Crunch. Confusion and disappointment permeated the employees and contributors to the many websites involved in the acquisition and subsequent overhaul.

Harde was another casualty of the clash between TechCrunch and AOL. A few interoffice e-mails asking for recognition of several members of the AOL family resulted in more conflict between staff and editors. Harde, like many employees involved, felt the growing stress in the office and finally announced her resignation from all of her AOL-related endeavors, specifically TechCrunch, on December 16, 2011.

Affiliation: TechCrunch

J. Michael Arrington began writing a blog entitled TechCrunch in 2005. The first blog post went out on June 11, 2005. It was the height of the Web 2.0 evolution, and Arrington capitalized on both his timing and his contacts, as well as his experience in start-up companies, to create one of the most popular blogs on the Internet. A former Silicon Valley lawyer, Arrington did his research, combined journalism with quality advertising space, and created a tech news leader online.

In 2006, TechCrunch saw massive jumps in popularity and revenue, and Arrington needed help. He decided to hire News Corp. executive Heather Harde. At this time, TechCrunch was still operating out of Arrington's house. The need for a capable general manager was apparent. Harde is considered one of the main players behind the unprecedented success of TechCrunch.

As of 2012, TechCrunch enjoyed 37 million views and 12 million established users. Arrington grew the technology blog into a $10 million company before bowing out. TechCrunch was sold to America Online (AOL) in 2010 for $25 million (although some sources put the purchase price closer to $40 million). Arrington stepped down as CEO at that time. Friction between AOL, TechCrunch, and *The Huffington Post* made for some major changes at the company, including Harde's resignation as CEO and the departure of many writers and contributors from the AOL network. The TechCrunch brand, however, survived the storm and remains one of the most popular tech news sites in the world.

TechCrunch sponsors the Crunchies, annual technology awards, as well as the popular technology database CrunchBase. Recent additions to the TechCrunch group of websites include Disrupt, a popular technology conference.

PERSONAL LIFE

After leaving TechCrunch, Harde stated in her LinkedIn profile that she was "gainfully unemployed with negative stress." In February 2012, she took a public role in a start-up civic group in San Francisco called the San Francisco Citizens Initiative for Technology and Innovation. As the vice chairman of the tech-based advocacy group, Harde planned to promote the interests of the tech community within the city in terms of employment, legislation, and education.

Harde was a popular leader at TechCrunch and received the 2011 TechFellows award for Best General Manager. In 2011, *Fast Company* magazine named her as one of the most influential women in technology. MizWhiz inducted Harde into its Technology Hall of Fame in 2011 as a Media Mogul.

Harde keeps her private and professional lives separate and can be considered one of the most popular workaholics in the tech news business.

Trish Popovitch

FURTHER READING

Arrington, Michael. "Welcome to TechCrunch Heather." *TechCrunch* 17 Mar. 2007. Web. 24 Aug. 2012. Arrington discusses his decision to hire Harde as the chief executive officer of TechCrunch. Provides an overview of her professional background and what he hopes she will bring to the company.

Bercovici, Jeff. "TechCrunch CEO Reported Out After Clashing with HuffPost-ers." *Forbes* 17 Nov. 2011. Web. 24 Aug. 2012. Discusses Harde's resignation from TechCrunch and her issues with the *Huffington Post* editor. Explains that several resignations have taken place at AOL and TechCrunch since the takeover.

Boyd, E. B. "Most Influential Women in Technology: Heather Harde Vice President. TechCrunch." *Fast Company* 2011. Web. 21 Aug. 2012. Explains Harde's decision to join the TechCrunch team, her management skills, and what she felt need to be accomplished at TechCrunch to keep it on top of the blogosphere.

Harde, Heather. *CrunchBase*. 2012. Web. 24 Aug. 2012. Provides details of Harde's professional and educational background as well as a portrait photograph. Includes a work history as well as links to other articles that mention Harde.

Ovide, Shira. "Exactly What Is Tech Crunch Worth?" *Wall Street Journal* 28 Sept. 2010. Web. 24 Aug. 2012. Discusses the acquisition of TechCrunch by AOL and the value of the TechCrunch websites. Includes portions of the original press release announcing the purchase.

"San Francisco Tech Leaders Launch sf.citi." *Cloud Times*. 13 Jan. 2012. Web. 24 Aug. 2012. Discusses Harde's involvement in a new San Francisco–based civic advocacy group led by technology leaders.

Explains Harde's partnership with the city mayor and Ron Conway.

Sloan, Paul, and Paul Kaihla. "Blogging for Dollars." *Business 2.0* 1 Sept. 2006. Web. 24 Aug. 2012. Discusses the profitability of well-written blogs combined with affiliate marketing, using TechCrunch as an example. Explains how the Web 2.0 evolution has changed the face of virtual commerce.

Sweney, Mark. "AOL Buys TechCrunch." *The Guardian* 29 Sept. 2010. Web. 24 Aug. 2012. Discusses AOL's acquisition of TechCrunch and the possible fallout from the purchase, including the future of Michael Arrington. Includes portrait photograph of Arrington.

Welch, Liz. "The Way I Work: Michael Arrington of TechCrunch." *Inc.* 1 Oct. 2010. Web. 24 Aug. 2012. Arrington explains his working methods and business management perspectives. Details his workday and approach to his staff, and discusses the future of his company.

MICHAEL S. HART

Founder of Project Gutenberg

Born: March 8, 1947; Tacoma, Washington
Died: September 6, 2011; Urbana, Illinois
Primary Field: Internet
Specialty: Content and data
Primary Company/Organization: Project Gutenberg

INTRODUCTION

Michael S. Hart is best known for his invention of electronic books and for founding Project Gutenberg. With access to substantial computing power at the University of Illinois at Urbana-Champaign and inspired by a free printed copy of the U.S. Declaration of Independence, he began typing the text of the declaration into a computer and transmitting it to other users on July 4, 1971. He added many other public-domain texts to that first one over the next forty years. Project Gutenberg, named for the fifteenth-century German printer Johannes Gutenberg, whose movable-type printing press is considered to have inaugurated the age of print, was the first and largest single collection of free electronic books available on the Internet. Hart also devoted four decades to championing the open source movement, which he helped to start. In 2006, he cofounded the World eBook Fair.

EARLY LIFE

Michael Stern Hart was born on March 8, 1947, in Tacoma, Washington. His father was an accountant and his mother, a cryptanalyst during World War II, worked as a business manager for an upscale women's store. The family lived in Tacoma until Hart was eleven, when they moved to Urbana, Illinois, where both his parents pursued advanced degrees. In 1958, they found jobs at the University of Illinois in Urbana, where his father taught Shakespeare and his mother taught mathematics. Hart, an Eagle Scout, was interested in intellectual pursuits from an early age. He began attending lectures at the university while he was still a high school student. When he officially enrolled in college, he studied chemical engineering but dropped out because he did not like his classes. He was drafted into the U.S. Army

Michael S. Hart.

during the Vietnam War. After he completed his military service, he returned to school and completed a course of individual study on human-machine interfaces. He earned a bachelor of science degree in 1973.

Hart was a street musician in San Francisco for a time. Operating under the same philosophy that later guided his most famous project, he gave his music away, believing that it should be free to all who could appreciate it. He was also an inveterate tinkerer, acquiring hands-on experience with radio, stereo, and video equipment, as well as computers.

LIFE'S WORK

Hart was still a student at the University of Illinois at Urbana-Champaign, where he spent much of his time with the engineers in charge of the university's mainframe computer, when he began the project with which he would be identified for the rest of his life. The engineers gave him a nearly inexhaustible amount of computer time. Reckoning its worth at $100 million, Hart felt duty-bound to do something significant with that gift. On July 4, 1971, on the occasion of the nation's independence day, he had been handed a copy of the Declaration of Independence at his local grocery store, and when he was searching for something to do with his computer time, he found in his backpack that copy printed on imitation parchment. Inspired, he began typing the words into a fifty-year-old teletype machine.

Warned that sending his text via e-mail could crash the system, he sent a message to approximately one hundred people on the network informing them that they could download the text. Six of them did. Hart was encouraged, and over the following years he added the Gettysburg Address, the Constitution, and the individual books of the King James version of the Bible, all of them laboriously typed by Hart himself. Not many people noticed, but he was excited by the accessibility and permanence of these digital texts. Once he had typed the text into the computer, it was available from then on to anyone with a computer and modem who wanted to read it. An unlikely revolutionary, a guerrilla fighter with books as his weapons and a vision of world changes in his head, Hart called his work Project Gutenberg. Just as Johannes Gutenberg's printing press in the fifteenth century had put books in the hands of those could not previously afford them and exposed them to ideas that shifted their worldview, Hart hoped to see his project cause book prices to fall and literacy and education rates to increase. His stated mission was "to break down the bars of ignorance and illiteracy."

Only twenty-three computers in the United States were online in 1971, and computer memory was small by today's standards. However, Hart, who had seen radios go from the size of a large piece of furniture to handheld devices running on transistors, believed that computers would similarly shrink in size over the coming years. He also thought that the greatest value created by computers would be the storage and retrieval of library materials. At the end of the first decade, Project Gutenberg had 100 books in its collection. By 1997, Hart had personally typed in 313 books. That year, a colleague at the University of Illinois PC user group, Mark Zinzow, helped him set up a mailing list to publicize his project and ask for volunteers. By the end of the year, the archive held about 1,600 titles.

As it became possible to scan rather than type the texts, the number of volunteers assisting in the project increased. By the mid-1990s, when the Internet grew substantially in popularity, hundreds of volunteers in many countries were working on the project. Although Hart was still adding books himself, more and more of his time was consumed in coordinating the project. In August 1997, Project Gutenberg released its thousandth book, Dante's *Divine Comedy* (in Italian, its original language). Less than two years later, the number of books had doubled. By 2011, Project Gutenberg could boast 33,000 books, accumulating at a rate of 200 per month, with translations into sixty languages—all made available for free.

Despite the advances in technology, Hart insisted on using the original 7-bit ASCII for all the e-texts generated by Project Gutenberg. He was determined that Project Gutenberg's offerings be readable on the systems of any era. A change in file format would have provided more attractive formatting features (such as italics, boldfacing, tab stops, font selections, extracts, and page representations), but Hart's concern was ensuring the broadest possible readership. Project Gutenberg texts can be read easily by any machine, operating system or software, including on a mobile phone and an e-book reader.

Hart was also a fierce champion of open access programs, and he objected to proprietary displays, the requirement of special software, and anything but the simplest connections. He also thought existing copyright laws were an unnecessary obstacle to open access. He vehemently opposed the Copyright Term Extension Act, passed in 1998. The act, sponsored by the California congressman and former pop singer Sonny Bono, removed one million e-books from the public domain

Affiliation: Project Gutenberg

On July 4, 1971, Michael S. Hart, an undergraduate at the University of Illinois in Urbana, uploaded a copy of the Declaration of Independence that he had typed into the university's mainframe computer, and Project Gutenberg—named for the fifteenth-century German printer whose movable-type printing press led to the widespread availability of printed books and other documents—was born. Six people read that first e-text. In 2008, Project Gutenberg, the world's first and now oldest digital library, averaged more than three million downloads monthly from the twenty-five thousand digitalized books in its collection.

Hart, who devoted his life to the project, worked alone for seventeen years before a few volunteers joined his cause in 1997. With the increased availability of the Internet and the wide availability of scanners, even more people volunteered. In 2000, Charles Franks launched Distributed Proofreaders, with the sole purpose of digitizing books in the public domain for Project Gutenberg. By 2008, fifty-two thousand volunteers were proofreading the digitalized texts, most in increments of one page per day. All texts are written in the "Plain Vanilla" (7-bit) ASCII text to ensure the widest availability across various computer platforms for the longest period.

Today the work continues: Each book is scanned, converted to text, and proofread twice, each time by a different person. Project Gutenberg maintains a 99.5 percent accuracy rate, the same standard as that set by the Library of Congress. In 2001, Project Gutenberg Australia was launched. Since then, Project Gutenberg sites have been launched in Europe, Canada, Portugal, the Philippines, Taiwan, Luxembourg, and Russia.

by extending their copyrights by twenty years. Under U.S. law, the average copyright now lasts for 95.5 years. Lawrence Lessig, then a law professor at Stanford University (later at Harvard), talked with Hart about participating in a constitutional challenge to the law, but the conversation convinced Lessig that Hart was too much of a visionary for such an effort. In 2003, in a decision handed down in the case of *Eldred v. Ashcroft*, the Supreme Court upheld the constitutionality of the Copyright Term Extension Act.

Project Gutenberg's original audience of six, who had read his copy of the Declaration of Independence in 1971, expanded beyond even Hart's expectations. Gutenberg Australia, Canada, Europe, and others were adding to the corpus. In 2007, Project Gutenberg's e-texts were included (with multilingual versions) on the platform for One Laptop Per Child (a nonprofit program offering inexpensive laptops to children in developing countries), as well as in hundreds of other free e-book collections worldwide. The works fall into three basic categories: light literature such as James Barrie's *Peter Pan* (one of the earliest works added to the list), "heavy" literature such as Herman Melville's *Moby Dick*, and reference works such as dictionaries. Most of these works are in the public domain. A few are still under copyright protection, but the authors or their estates have granted similar unrestricted rights of use.

In 2006, Hart cofounded the World eBook Fair. Project Gutenberg and the World eBook Library collaborated in a monthlong celebration of the e-book. Beginning July 4, the day Hart generated the first e-book, free public access was provided to a growing number of e-books. In the first year, about three hundred thousand e-books, including light and heavy reading and reference works, were available. In 2011, the number had increased to 6.5 million e-books plus offerings in other media, such as music, movies, and artwork, with more than one hundred libraries participating worldwide.

PERSONAL LIFE

Hart lived a frugal life. He supported himself in the early years by repairing high-fidelity stereos. He worked as an adjunct professor. In later years, he often did not bother to pick up his monthly salary. He lived without a cell phone, and the computer hardware he used to oversee the project to which he devoted his life was a decade old. He used home remedies rather than seeking professional medical care. When home repairs or automobile malfunctions occurred, he did the repairs himself. He was married briefly, but he lived alone for most of his life, surrounded by pillars of books, from which he frequently selected one to send home with a friend. He particularly liked Hermann Hesse's *Siddhartha*, and he had a fondness for Romanian poetry.

He died on September 6, 2011, in his home in Urbana, Illinois. He was survived by his mother, Alice Hart, of Belvoir, Virginia, and a brother, Bennett Hart, of Manassas, Virginia. His legacy survives as Project Gutenberg continues to add to its archives.

Wylene Rholetter

FURTHER READING

Grimes, William. "Michael Hart, a Pioneer of E-Books, Dies at 64." *New York Times* 9 Sept. 2011: A21. Print. The article is an obituary that summarizes the Hart's life and recognizes him as founder of Project Gutenberg, the world's oldest and largest collection of e-books.

Jensen, Michael Jon. "For 40 Years, Michael Hart Defined the Landscape of Digital Publishing." *Chronicle of Higher Education* 23 Sept. 2011: A27. Print. The article presents a memorial to Hart, offering an overview of his personal life and focusing on the development of Project Gutenberg.

Lake, Susan E. L. "Electronic Books for the 21st century." *Library Media Connection* 21.6 (2003): 53–55. Print. The article reports on the Hart's development of the website for Project Gutenberg and discusses the purpose of the project and its uses. Color photographs.

Quint, Barbara. "O! Pioneers!" *Searcher* 19.9 (2011): 4–6. Print. The article examines the qualities of a pioneer and uses Hart, founder of Project Gutenberg, as an example of one who possessed the vision, work ethic, and communication skills required of a true pioneer.

Weller, Sam T. "2,000 World Classics on Line." *UNESCO Courier* 52.6 (1999): 45. Print. Focuses on Project Gutenberg as an innovation in preserving the world's literary heritage. Includes the history of the project, biographical details about Hart, and Hart's vision of the future of e-books. Includes a color photograph.

REED HASTINGS

Founder of Netflix

Born: October 8, 1960; Boston, Massachusetts
Died: -
Primary Field: Internet
Specialty: Commerce
Primary Company/Organization: Netflix

INTRODUCTION

Reed Hastings cofounded Netflix, the world's most popular DVD-by-mail service, with Marc Randolph in 1998. Netflix has since transformed the movie rental business: Brick-and-mortar competitors have downsized or gone out of business (although Blockbuster attempted a similar DVD-by-mail service for a time). Netflix's streaming service on the Internet helped drive the popularity of streaming video, which in turn greatly increased the bandwidth usage of the average Internet customer and drove the need for more robust infrastructure and higher-bandwidth connections. Despite notable missteps, Netflix's success has endured, transforming itself from a well-known novelty to a true force in the entertainment industry to one that has further balkanized the television audience and affected movie ticket sales.

EARLY LIFE

Wilmot Reed Hastings, Jr., was born on October 8, 1960, in Boston, Massachusetts. His father, W. R. Hastings, Sr., was an attorney who later served in Department of Health, Education, and Welfare during the presidency of

Reed Hastings.

165

Richard M. Nixon. Hastings attended high school in the affluent Boston suburb of Cambridge, at the Buckingham Browne and Nichols private day school, which had just been created through the merger of the Buckingham School with Browne and Nichols. After graduating in 1978, Hastings majored in mathematics at Bowdoin College in Brunswick, Maine, winning two mathematics department prizes and graduating with his bachelor's degree in 1983.

Hastings underwent Marine Corps officer training during summers while in college, but he requested permission to leave when he felt he was a poor fit. He spent his time after college in the Peace Corps instead, teaching mathematics in Swaziland from 1983 to 1985. Turned down at the Massachusetts Institute of Technology (MIT), he attended graduate school at Stanford University, earning a master's degree in computer science in 1988. After graduate school, he briefly worked for Adaptive Technology until founding Pure Software in 1991. The company initially developed troubleshooting software packages but grew quickly, and Hastings found he had difficulty managing it and was ill prepared for the business world. The business went through a series of mergers, first with Atria Software in 1996 and then an acquisition by Rational Software in 1997. Although Hastings was made chief technical officer of the merged company, he soon left. His next business venture was Netflix, which began in 1998.

LIFE'S WORK

Hastings has said that the idea for Netflix came to him when he was obligated to pay a late fee upon returning a movie to a video store. The core concept of Netflix is its flat-fee pricing. Customers are charged a specific fee on a monthly by means of a debit from an account (a credit card) for their participation in the Netflix service. Hastings compares the model to a membership fee at a gym, which is the same regardless of how much a customer uses the service. The nature of that service, however, has evolved and continues to evolve. Initially, it was limited to DVD rentals by mail. Small, thin, flat, and light, DVDs could be mailed inexpensively in special envelopes so that customers were not charged separately for shipping the discs back to Netflix's distribution center; when Netflix became especially popular, the Post Office responded by developing specific techniques for processing its easy-to-spot red rental envelopes.

While the lack of late fees benefited customers who were only occasional movie watchers or might not have

a chance to watch a movie right away—busy people who knew they wanted to watch the movies they had rented as soon as they had time but were not sure when that time would be—other features benefited hard-core movie fans, particularly as studios capitalized on the superior quality of the DVD over the videocassette and released special editions of movies, curated collections like the Criterion Collection, and other products for movie buffs. Netflix's online queue functions like a combination wish list and shopping cart: Movies may be queued at any time, the queue may be reordered at any time, and movies are sent in order as availability allows. Despite a five-hundred-movie limit, this allows fans to build wish lists of films they want to see without risking that they will forget the name of a movie that was recommended to them.

While Pure floundered because of Hastings's inexperience in business management, Netflix benefited from his concern for corporate culture. His goal was to grow the company without growing it into something unmanageable, which Pure had become. Salaries are a little higher than is common, and at the same time so are severance packages. The first incentivizes prospective employees; the latter keeps managers from being too reluctant to fire employees who are not a good fit. Employees are also given the choice of taking their compensation in cash or stock options. The personal talk that Hastings gave each new employee was eventually recorded as a PowerPoint presentation and posted online (by Hastings) in 2009 in an effort to keep the company's policies transparent.

Hastings made two major missteps in the second decade of the twenty-first century. The first, in July 2011, was his handling of the announcement that Netflix would begin charging for streaming video. It had originally been offered as a free feature that accompanied subscriptions, with a limit on the number of hours each customer could stream. The limit was removed, and people began to treat the free extra as part of the service they were paying for—which meant that they wanted the bugs eliminated and more options added. This cost money—especially since, unlike DVDs, streaming video rights were not a finite, countable commodity. Negotiating the cost of a thousand DVDs was easier for movie studios to manage than negotiating the cost of letting an unknown number of people (whether ten, a thousand, or 10 million could not be tracked) stream a movie. For that reason, streaming rights were typically contracted for a finite amount of time and required frequent renegotiations. The Hastings solution

Affiliation: Netflix

Netflix is a movie rental company that began in 1997 as a DVD-by-mail company based in Los Gatos, California. It has since expanded to numerous other countries, primarily by offering streaming video. About 90 percent of Netflix customers, however, are in the United States. The popularity of Netflix, as first DVD players and later broadband Internet accounts became more common, has been a significant force in the entertainment industry.

DVDs presented numerous advantages over videotape cassettes, many of which were pertinent to Netflix's business mode: Because they were smaller and lighter-weight, shipping them to customers was a fairly inexpensive proposition for a large company with a sufficient profit margin, so Netflix did not charge shipping fees to its customers, which were instead built into the company's operating expenses (similar to magazine subscriptions). Moreover, because DVDs were fairly durable, they were unlikely to be damaged in transit, and because they did not need to be rewound, the labor cost of processing returns was a fraction of what it would have been in an identical service for videocassettes. From a customer perspective, the advantages were numerous as well. Netflix's online catalog of movies facilitated leisurely browsing of available titles, and the Netflix user community—a feature that has been removed or downplayed in recent years—made for more informed choices. The use of a rental queue, from which movies would be sent (as available) in the order the customer queued them, automated the rental experience rather than requiring users to search through the catalog again for each rental instance. The company charged no late fees, instead charging a flat fee per month for as many DVDs as the customer managed to rent and return; the number of DVDs allowed out at one time was defined by the customer's rental plan, which in turn determined the monthly fee. That monthly fee was charged automatically every month to a credit card and thus did not require the processing of invoices or depend on timely payment of a bill.

Netflix soon expanded from DVDs to offer streaming video as well. Initially, the hours of streaming video available were limited by the customer's pricing plan, although there was no extra charge for streaming.

Later, streaming was made unlimited. Under the current pricing plan, after a disastrous attempt to separate streaming and DVDs into separate companies, Netflix offers streaming-only, DVD-only, and DVD-and-streaming plans, with the latter two categories tiered according to the number of DVDs. There is an additional charge for Blu-ray rentals. HD-DVD was briefly supported, but no longer. CEO and cofounder Reed Hastings has made it clear that he believes streaming to be the future of the company.

Studies have shown that more than half of streaming hours are spent watching television shows rather than movies. While a large part of this consists of people watching shows no longer on the air or catching up on episodes in series they might have intended to follow on broadcast or cable television, Netflix and similar streaming services, such as Hulu, have contributed to the trend of "cutting the cord." So-called cord cutters remain ardent "television" watchers via streaming services but cancel their subscriptions to cable. Because business models of television networks, production studios, and affiliate stations are still dependent on ratings—and on the impact of those ratings on the cost charged for advertising time—this trend has had a negative impact on the television industry, where once-mighty networks such as CBS, NBC, and ABC now struggle to survive. Furthermore, the fact that such a large share of revenue is generated by advertising rather than the sale of DVDs or streaming rights is the very thing that keeps the cost of DVDs and streaming low; were television able to abandon its dependence on advertising and cable subscriptions overnight, it would need to charge so much for DVDs that cord-cutting would no longer be an option.

Another significant change has been Netflix's video-recommendation system. While engines at services such Amazon, which generate basic product recommendations based on purchase history (by reporting data such as"customers who bought" *Two-Lane Blacktop* also bought *Le Samourai*), serve to drive sales by informing customers of products they might not otherwise be aware of or purchase, Netflix has no such incentive: Barring factors such as the variable cost of individual titles, Netflix makes the same amount of money no matter which movies customers watch,

---

Affiliation: Netflix (continued)

because of the flat-fee structure. Despite this, in order to improve customer satisfaction and cultivate customers' interest in movies, Netflix offered a $1 million prize in 2006 to any developer who could beat its recommendation algorithm by better than 10 percent. The prize was eventually awarded in 2009—and yet the popularity of streaming video has changed the recommendation situation considerably. While the DVD recommendation algorithm could depend only on rental history and data (which might indicate little about interest) such as the length of time a customer keeps a movie, the company has access to much more information about streaming habits, including whether or not a movie is watched in one sitting or is paused and restarted frequently, how far into the movie a rating is made, and whether a customer watches ten minutes of a movie and then abandons it (indicating dislike). A recommendation algorithm has not yet been developed to take full advantage of the depth of behavioral information now available.

The availability of recent movies on Netflix, often only months after their theatrical run, has combined with other factors (notably the worldwide financial crisis) to reduce attendance at movie theaters. This in turn has caused movie studios to, first, focus more of their attention on "tentpole" blockbuster releases, movies in which significant marketing expenditures create manufactured demand (such that the audience feels they need to see the movie in order to participate in a cultural watershed moment), and, second, to develop film exhibition technologies that encourage theater attendance by offering features in theaters that are unavailable at home. Studios in the 1950s were the first to rely heavily on three-dimensional features in order to compete with the free entertainment available at home on television; twenty-first century studios have turned back to that toolbox, adding a surcharge for three-dimensional movies as well as for those shown on 48fps film (as with Peter Jackson's *The Hobbit*) or on IMAX screens.

---

was to treat streaming as a service: to both improve it and charge for it. However, stock values dropped as the service's power users fumed that their cost would increase by more than half as much.

Two months later, Netflix announced that it would split its services between two companies, spinning its DVD rental service off as Qwikster. Customers were outraged and mocked the new company's name, and stock prices plunged again. The company reversed its decision in a matter of weeks, but the public image of Netflix, and especially its stock, had been tarnished far worse than it had been by an earlier class-action suit filed by subscribers whose rentals had been "throttled" because of their rapid use.

PERSONAL LIFE

Hastings is married, with two children. He is active in education reform, particularly the funding of charter schools. He also serves on the board of directors of

Microsoft, meeting with the other directors four times per year.

Bill Kte'pi

FURTHER READING

Anderson, Chris. *The Long Tail: Why the Future of Business Is Selling Less of More.* New York: Hyperion, 2006. Print. The editor of *Wired* examines trends in the technology business.

Goldfayn, Alex L. *Evangelist Marketing: What Apple, Amazon, and Netflix Understand about Their Customers.* Dallas: BenBella, 2012. Print. A look at the marketing techniques of the e-commerce giants.

Kaplan, Saul. *The Business Model Innovation Factory: How to Stay Relevant When the World Is Changing.* New York: Wiley, 2012. Print. Netflix serves as an example of innovation in an existing field; coverage includes the way it triumphed over older, established Blockbuster.

SHANI HIGGINS

CEO of Technorati

Born: 1973; place unknown
Died: -
Primary Field: Internet
Specialty: News and entertainment
Primary Company/Organization: Technorati

INTRODUCTION

After working for a number of investment, software, and publishing firms, Shani Higgins was hired to head day-to-day operations at Technorati, Inc., the company behind the Technorati.com blog search engine. Higgins launched Technorati Media, the world's largest social media advertising network, as well as Technorati's private advertising exchange. She also arranged the company's first content acquisitions, acquiring the blogs and staff of Blogcritics and the Silicon Valley Moms Group. In 2011, she became the company's third chief executive officer (CEO).

EARLY LIFE

Shani Higgins-Levine was born in 1973, the daughter of an agent of the Federal Bureau of Investigation and now former naval officer William F. Higgins and Wendy Higgins. Her mother was a teacher and then a real estate agent. The family eventually included six children. Shani attended Rutgers University, earning a bachelor of arts degree in communications with a double minor in art history and economics.

In 1996, Higgins became director of partner services and director of commerce market development for Infoseek/Go Network. Three years later, she became vice president of business development for SmartPlanet (Ziff Davis). Her next position was as a venture capitalist for the Benedek Investment Group in New York City. She was vice president for business development for Tacit Software before being hired by Technorati, Inc., in 2007. Technorati is today the parent company of the Technorati Media ad network, the Technorati.com blog search engine and directory, the Blogcritics site, and the AdEngage advertising platform.

LIFE'S WORK

Higgins headed Technorati's strategy and day-to-day operations, focusing on business development. The company doubled its revenue and by 2010 became profitable. Higgins oversaw the launch of Technorati Media, which became the world's largest social media advertising network, covering more than three thousand sites.

Higgins oversaw two critical acquisitions: those of Blogcritics in 2008 and of SV Moms in 2010. SV Moms (the Silicon Valley Moms Group) was a blogging network of about two hundred women and mothers founded in 2006. After the Technorati acquisition, SV Moms cofounder Jill Asher became the editorial director of both Technorati.com and Blogcritics, while SV Moms editors Akemi Bourgeois and Vanessa Druckman were made editors of the new Technorati Women Channel, absorbing the SV Moms blogs and other Technorati blogs by women on parenting, food, fitness, style, and household finances.

Blogcritics was founded in 2002 as a self-described "sinister cabal of superior writers": an online magazine with fifty members contributing blog entries to the online magazine. Anyone was allowed to contribute, and the number of contributors rose to the thousands. After being acquired by Technorati, Blogcritics founders Eric Olsen and Phillip Winn became full-time Technorati employees, although Olsen stepped down in 2010.

Shani Higgins.

Affiliation: Technorati

Technorati, Inc., is an Internet social media services company consisting of Technorati.com, the world's largest search engine for blogs; Technorati Media, an advertising network for blogs and social media; the self-service advertising platform AdEngage; and the Blogcritics webzine, which the company calls a "journalism 3.0 site."

The popularity and prevalence of blogs rose steadily over the first decade of the twenty-first century, with most magazines, many large newspapers, and other media outlets adding blogs to their other content, in addition to the "unaffiliated" professional or hobbyist blogger. By 2010, the overwhelming majority, more than three-quarters, of American Internet users read at least one blog on a regular basis: Blogs had become mainstream reading material. Many argued that bloggers wielded more influence on the reading public than the major newspapers, particularly given the decline of print journalism and the contraction of newspaper staffs across the country. What is commonly called "social media" now, encompassing both blogging and social networks like Facebook and Twitter, was then often referred to as "conversational media," which underscored the importance of the comments sections in blogs and of the tendency of blogs to write responses to one another; indeed, it is not trivializing them to point out that some blogs do little else other than write commentary on other blogs, such is the information-richness of the modern blogosphere.

In response, Technorati was formed, beginning with a search engine to help users find blogs in areas in which they are interested. Dave Sifry, an entrepreneur and open source advocate who had previously cofounded the twenty-four-hour Linux tech support service Linuxcare, founded Technorati, freely admitting that it was an "ego project"—he was building something that he himself wanted to use, a search engine he wished existed. Software engineer Tantek Celik (of Microsoft, formerly of Sun Microsystems, Oracle, and Apple) served as chief technologist. Celik wrote the Election 2004 section of the Technorati site, featuring blog coverage of the U.S. presidential election (and gubernatorial and congressional elections). In interviews, Sifry regularly touted the importance of blogs to serious readers and the idea of blogs as leading indicators. Technorati's focus on Election 2004 coverage reflected this core tenet of the site, that blogs included not only disposable fluff or personal journals but also up-to-the-minute, in-the-moment journalism that conventional news media could not provide.

By 2006, Technorati was tracking 27.7 million blogs and noted that there were approximately 75,000 new blogs added daily. Numerous mechanisms had had to be put in place in order to prevent blogs from gaming the system in order to spam search results or manipulate rankings through link farming. Sifry also promoted the practice of bloggers pinging Technorati when updating their blogs; while this helped make Technorati's results better, he appealed to bloggers' egos by pointing out that it was the best way to guarantee that a blogger got credit for being the first to say something.

Much of the focus on the site at the time was on political blogging, corporate news blogging, and tech blogging, but that changed as Technorati acquired content for the first time. Blogcritics was its first acquisition, in 2008. Founded in 2002, the site published blog entries from anyone who contributed—having been founded with an initial roster of fifty bloggers—although all content was approved by editors first. The editorial control had given it a reputation for quality reflected by several awards and its use by Google News and Yahoo! News as news sources. At the time of its acquisition, it was visited by approximately 1 million unique visitors per month. Blogcritics' founder, Eric Olsen, and lead developer, Phillip Winn, were made Technorati employees. Key to the acquisition was the assurance that blogs controlled by Technorati would not be given favorable treatment in rankings or search results.

The Silicon Valley Moms Group, SV Moms, a network of female bloggers in the Silicon Valley, was acquired in 2010, and its cofounder Jill Asher became Technorati's editorial director. The SV Moms blogs were folded into the newly created Technorati Women Channel, along with a number of other blogs by women about various topics.

Since 2004, Technorati has published an annual "State of the Blogosphere" address, which in 2007 was streamed live by Sifry. The 2011 address, delivered by chief executive officer Shani Higgins, identified the predominant new trend as the entrepeneur-blogger—

Affiliation: Technorati (continued)
a (usually) small business owner using a blog to promote that business. Higgins noted that internal surveys revealed that the biggest influence on bloggers' content was other bloggers and that bloggers were increasingly concerned with remaining transparent in their relationships with any products they promoted. Facebook and Twitter were the primary sources of blog traffic, with Digg in a serious decline.

Higgins was also in charge of the development and launch of Technorati's private exchange, which went live in April 2011. A private exchange is an advertising network that lets online publishers like Technorati sell advertising space directly to advertisers, rather than going through a middleman. This generally leads to greater revenues for the company and lower costs for the advertiser, offering more direct control over the advertising inventory. Usually these arrangements are used in addition to third-party advertising networks (like those offered by Microsoft and Google, among many others), but publishers that want to retain total control over advertising inventory and its suitability for their audience may rely exclusively on a private exchange. Technorati's private exchange is run on AppNexus and automates real-time bidding for advertisers and a customizable dashboard for publishers on the Technorati network.

Higgins was promoted to CEO of Technorati in 2011. Exiting CEO and new executive chairman Rich Jalichandra credited her oversight of the day-to-day business over the previous three years for the company's success. By 2011, Technorati had become the third-largest social media property behind Facebook and Twitter.

Not long after being promoted to CEO, Higgins was the subject of controversy at the annual PR Summit Conference in San Francisco. While speaking about some of the results of Technorati's annual blogger survey, which forms the basis of the "State of the Blogosphere" address that Technorati executives have delivered since 2004, Higgins remarked that paid posts—posts for which a blogger is compensated, especially by a brand or company featured in the post—were no longer stigmatized. Transparency had become of increasing concern: The Federal Trade Commission (FTC) regulations required that bloggers who received free samples to review products reveal that compensation, and this had led to an increasing desire on the part of bloggers to make their relationships to any brands clear and aboveboard. Higgins drew a line between this and her statement. Concern for transparency, after all, did not mean an aversion to paid posts, only the need to identify them explicitly as such. Others in the blogging community expressed concern that this kind of thinking could lead to blogs being turned into grassroots advertising.

Higgins has noted the increase in female bloggers and in personal blogging, as well as the more aggressive targeting of bloggers by brands looking for promotion—although the amount of free material sent to bloggers in the mere hope of a mention online has declined since the 2008 financial crisis. She sees blogging increasingly as one part of a larger social media strategy, particularly as more bloggers maintain presences on Twitter and even Tumblr in addition to their blogs—and may, on top of that, have a Facebook or Google+ page for their blog. Blogging has thus become less about a single site and more about a social media identity represented by a cluster of overlapping activities and outputs. Communication among bloggers is important for the same reason.

PERSONAL LIFE

Higgins is married and lives in San Francisco; she and her husband have one child. She is a fan of the Korean barbecue food truck Seoul on Wheels.

Bill Kte'pi

FURTHER READING

Jenkins, Henry. *Confronting the Challenges of Participatory Culture: Media Education for the 21st Century*. Cambridge: MIT, 2009. Print. Examines social media, new forms of creative expression, and their impact on media studies.

Qualman, Erik. *Socialnomics: How Social Media Transforms the Way We Live and Do Business*. New York: Wiley, 2010. Print. The impact of social media on the business world.

Rosenberg, Scott. *Say Everything: How Blogging Began, What It's Becoming, and Why It Matters*. New York: Broadway, 2010. Print. A history of blogging by a journalist and Salon.com cofounder, without the hype, misconceptions, or fast-money tips of similar books.

REID HOFFMAN

Executive chairman and cofounder of LinkedIn

Born: August 5, 1967; Stanford, California
Died: -
Primary Field: Internet
Specialty: Social media
Primary Company/Organization: LinkedIn

INTRODUCTION

Reid Hoffman is a risk taker whose visionary viewpoint has helped shape the way the world does business. From the start, Hoffman knew that he wanted to make a difference on a global scale. He recognized that the Internet was the best means to that end and focused his efforts on employing technology to connect and empower individuals everywhere. He cofounded LinkedIn as a forum for online networking and sharing of information among professionals and would-be entrepreneurs. Today, LinkedIn is the world's largest professional networking site. With the success of LinkedIn, Hoffman has used his influence and affluence to help other entrepreneurs realize their dreams: as a partner at venture capital firm Greylock Partners, as a board member for various technology companies, as a philanthropist supporting not-for-profit enterprises, and as a coauthor of a book on the role and realities of entrepreneurship.

EARLY LIFE

Reid Garrett Hoffman grew up in Berkeley, California, as the only child of two free-thinking lawyers, Deanna Ruth Rutter and William Parker Hoffman, Jr. From a very early age, Hoffman participated in his parents' ethics discussions and activism—a foundation that shaped his goals and career.

At twelve, Hoffman got his first job as an editor for Chaosium, a local publisher of role-playing games, after hand-delivering a critique of one of the company's game guides. The publisher recognized the value in some of Hoffman's points and asked him to review another guide in exchange for payment.

By the age of fourteen, Hoffman was unchallenged at school and decided on his own to apply for a spot at the independent Putney School, a private boarding school in Vermont. He was accepted and persuaded his parents to let him attend. Hoffman graduated from the Putney School in 1985 and went on to study symbolic systems—a combination of artificial intelligence and cognitive science—at Stanford University, receiving a bachelor of science degree in 1990. Next, Hoffman traveled to England as a Marshall scholar. He studied at Oxford University and received a master of arts in philosophy in 1993. Initially, Hoffman wanted to become an academician as a means of influencing broad discussion and bringing world-changing ideas to fruition. However, by the time he left Oxford, he had concluded that intellectuals have less influence than entrepreneurs, and he shifted his focus to the business world—specifically, the online business world.

LIFE'S WORK

After completing his studies in England, Hoffman returned to California. Almost immediately he networked his way into a job with Apple Computer's user-experience group. After two years learning the ropes on the design side, he moved to Fujitsu to become more educated about the product management end of the business. By 1997, Hoffman felt ready to set out on his own. He formed a team of friends and former coworkers,

Reid Hoffman.

raised the required start-up capital, and launched Social-Net.com. The online dating site had some growing pains due to its reliance on print publication partnerships. Hoffman's differences with the company's board of directors did not help. He decided to leave SocialNet.com in 1999, shortly before the company was purchased by match.com.

Rather than launch another company, Hoffman was persuaded to join the management team of a fledgling company named PayPal at the request of his friend and PayPal cofounder, Peter Thiel. Hoffman had held a seat on PayPal's board of directors since the company's launch a few years earlier, but it was not until January 2000 that he became a full-time employee responsible for external relations involving corporate development, payment infrastructure, and government, legal, and international affairs. Hoffman had become executive vice president of the company by the time PayPal was purchased by eBay in 2002.

During an interview appearing in, *Inc.* in 2009, Hoffman told Mark Lacter that during his tenure at PayPal, he had become aware of how the Internet was transforming individuals into their own small businesses, creating a need for new tools to manage each person's brand, business, and career. He thought he could provide a solution. Once again, Hoffman recruited his peers and former coworkers, gathered funds, and launched a company. The new company, LinkedIn, was established in December 2002 to facilitate online professional networking and information sharing. The site went live online in May 2003. It attracted some forty-five hundred members in its first month and had grown to more than 160 million members worldwide as of March 2012. That, coupled with LinkedIn's hugely successful initial public offering on May 20, 2011, gained for Hoffman a reputation as a man with the golden touch.

While providing strategic leadership to LinkedIn as the company's executive chairman, Hoffman joined Greylock Partners in 2009. The company works with small businesses that need support to bring their big ideas to the marketplace. Hoffman's focus is on helping high-potential companies in the segments he knows best: consumer Internet enterprises, Web 2.0, mobile, social gaming, e-commerce, online payments, on-demand software, and social networks. Several such companies in Greylock's portfolio are Facebook, Pandora, DropBox, Groupon, and, of course, LinkedIn. As a representative of Greylock, Hoffman sits on the boards of directors for several companies, including Airbnb, Edmodo, shopkick, and Wrapp. In addition, he serves independently on the boards of directors at Mozilla, Kiva.org, Zynga, and QuestBridge.

Hoffman contributes financially to budding start-ups and nonprofits and speaks publicly about entrepreneurship. He does more than offer insightful advice, however. He puts his money where his mouth is, having invested funds in more than eighty burgeoning technology companies that he believes have great potential to influence business and communication. Among the enterprises that have benefited from Hoffman's backing are Facebook, Flickr, and Digg. He has also put his financial support behind many nonprofit organizations, including Donors Choose, Endeavor Foundation, and Kiva.org. He is passionate about the mission of Kiva.org, a not-for-profit that connects impoverished peoples with philanthropists willing to provide microloans as start-up money to create self-reliant, socially responsible businesses. For Hoffman, Kiva.org embodies his belief in the power of social media as a tool to link people willing to invest in themselves with resources that empower them to do so.

In fact, that concept is central to Hoffman's book *The Start-up of You: Adapt to the Future, Invest in Yourself, and Transform Your Career,* coauthored with fellow entrepreneur and writer Ben Casnocha. Published by Crown Business in February 2012, the book emphasizes the need for individuals to embrace entrepreneurship in their daily lives, modeling their perspectives and behaviors as if they were small businesses. The key, according to Hoffman and Casnocha, is for each of us to adapt proactively to change and create our own opportunities for success. Thus, the theory goes, we will add value to ourselves and to society.

PERSONAL LIFE

Hoffman is married to his college sweetheart, Michelle Yee. The couple met during Hoffman's Stanford University days and were eventually wed in a quiet ceremony before a justice of the peace and three witnesses. They live in California and had no children as of early 2012.

Hoffman and Yee have made a point to reserve Saturday nights for themselves and, if time permits, Sunday afternoons as well. Hoffman also tries to squeeze in an hour of down time for himself each night to unwind before he goes to bed. He likes reading, watching movies, and playing the strategic board game Settlers of Catan.

Hoffman has the respect and admiration of virtually everyone in the technology industry. He is considered to be a fearless visionary, a staunch supporter of entrepreneurial practices and principles, and a generous

Affiliation: LinkedIn

Reid Hoffman conceptualized and cofounded LinkedIn in December 2002. The driving concept behind the company was interconnectedness and facilitating the exchange of ideas among and between individuals and businesses. With LinkedIn as their tool, Hoffman hoped individuals would become more proactive in shaping their own careers, more entrepreneurial in their behavior, and more aware of their social responsibilities.

Based on those notions, LinkedIn was formed. It was designed to provide an environment that enables people to expand their opportunities by enlarging their sphere of access and influence through professional contacts and relevant information and resources. This was a visionary model at the time, and its success helped lay the groundwork for other social media behemoths, such as Facebook and Twitter.

LinkedIn has become the largest online professional network in the world, with more than 160 million members in some 200 countries. Hoffman continues to lead the company as executive chairman.

philanthropist dedicated to driving positive societal change. He has also garnered a reputation as an approachable, open, and honest individual.

Shari Parsons Miller

FURTHER READING

Breitbarth, Wayne. *The Power Formula for LinkedIn Success: Kick-Start Your Business, Brand, and Job Search*. Austin: Greenleaf, 2011. Print. Explains how to harness the full potential of LinkedIn for business advancement and success, including tips on sustaining connections, developing an individual brand, and creating beneficial business opportunities.

Casnocha, Ben, and Reid Hoffman. *The Start-up of You: Adapt to the Future, Invest in Yourself, and Transform Your Career*. New York: Crown, 2012. Print. Positions each individual as his or her own small business and provides tips on how to use entrepreneurial principles to propel one's career and enhance one's influence and impact.

Hoffman, Reid. "How I Did It." *Inc.* 1 May 2009: n. pag. Print. Hoffman talks about his early influences and career, the rationale behind and creation of LinkedIn, his management style, and the opportunities of LinkedIn for businesses.

---. "Interview with Reid Hoffman." *Venture Capital* 50.1 (2010): 2. Print. Interview with LinkedIn's cofounder in which he discusses social media as a tool for social change and the ways in which open source projects are shaping identities and society.

"Reid Hoffman: Mr. LinkedIn." *Financial Times* 17 Mar. 2002. Web. A discussion of Hoffman's social networking philosophy that is centered on the power of broad connections that can be tapped to enhance professional success.

"Reid Hoffman: The Network Philosopher." *Wired* Apr. 2012: n. pag. Print. An overview of the evolution of Hoffman's career, from adolescent achiever to would-be academic and philosopher to technology visionary and social networking guru.

MEG HOURIHAN

Cofounder of Pyra Labs

Born: 1973; Boston, Massachusetts
Died: -
Primary Field: Internet
Specialty: Applications
Primary Company/Organization: Pyra Labs

INTRODUCTION

Meg Hourihan is the cofounder of Pyra Labs, which created the popular weblog software Blogger, a free web-based tool that introduced a simple means of launching a personal website, the blog. Blogger was later bought by Google. An innovative entrepreneur and pioneer blogger, Hourihan writes the award-winning blog Megnut.com and was one of Technology Review's TR35 ("35 innovators under 35") and one of PC Magazine's People of the Year in 2004. Along with Blogger cocreators Paul Bausch and Matthew Haughey, Hourihan published the book We Blog: Publishing

Online with Weblogs in 2002. She frequently speaks on the subject of blogs and young women entrepreneurs.

EARLY LIFE

Meg Hourihan was born in 1973 in Boston, Massachusetts, where she grew up. She became interested in technology at a young age. She attended Tufts University and majored in English, then worked at a consulting firm before cofounding Pyra Labs.

LIFE'S WORK

In January 1999, at the height of the dot-com bubble, Hourihan founded Pyra Labs in San Francisco with fellow pioneer web designer, blog creator, and then boyfriend Evan Williams. (Williams later became widely known for developing Twitter.) Paul Bausch, one of Williams's friends from high school, later joined. The team's initial goal was to create a web-based tool that would help project managers share information with co-workers. Their first project was a web tool called Pyra, which combined a project manager, contact manager, and to-do list. The team later repurposed Pyra into the in-house tool Blogger, which was made public in August 1999. Blogger was a free, web-based tool that allowed users to create and promote their own websites. Hourihan, with her background in English, was interested in creating the blog as a tool that was attractive to the nontech crowd. She recognized that the Internet was becoming an increasingly popular venue for expression for all users across web and that blogs could be the primary vehicle. Before Blogger, web users who wanted to create a weblog had to be fluent in HTML coding and rent server space. Blogger's team capitalized on the creation of a simple interface to promote usability, and Pyra hosted the web space for free. Hourihan began her blog in May 1999. In the early 2000s there were barely 100 blogs; today, the blogosphere includes more than 100 million, with many boasting thousands of visits each day.

Initial coding for Blogger was done by Williams and Matthew Haughey, who went on to found MetaFilter. At first free of charge, Blogger met difficulty when its funds dried up in 2001, less than a year after the NASDAQ dive that heralded the dot-com bust in April 2000. This end of the initial Internet boom that challenged the still-nascent means of subsidizing online personal websites, and the question of how to subsidize them was a driving force in their evolution. Initially, Pyra survived the plunge of Internet start-ups through venture capitalist investors and with help from

Meg Hourihan.

Hourihan's parents, but Pyra needed a steady stream of revenue for the long term.

Pyra Labs and Williams were revolutionary in asking their blogger users for funds, but as the tech bubble burst and Blogger depleted its funds, the company's five employees, including Hourihan, walked out. Williams ran the company alone until he was able to garner the support of Trellix creator Dan Bricklin, who invested in it after becoming aware of Blogger's situation and did not want to see the groundbreaking blogging tool disappear.

By June 2001, Blogger had started making money by charging for added features. As the popularity of Blogger across the blogosphere increased, advertisers provided the main revenue, and in 2002 Blogger underwent a major overhaul and in its expanded form was licensed to large global companies such as Globo.com in Brazil. Advance Publications, an American media company, also invested in Blogger.

Hourihan and other pioneer blog users theorized early that the nature of blogging was influenced by the events of September 2001, which increased the capabilities of the blogosphere for nonjournalist civilians to share political thoughts and reactions to global news from across the political spectrum. Still today, Hourihan is adamant that blogging is more about the lives of

Affiliation: Pyra Labs

Meg Hourihan cofounded Pyra Labs with fellow web pioneer Evan Williams in San Francisco in 1999. The company's first project was Pyra, which aimed to create a web-based tool that would assist in project management. Pyra consisted of a project manager, contact manager, and to-do list. The team later repurposed Pyra into the in-house tool Blogger, which was made public in August 1999. Coding was done by Williams and Matthew Haughey (who went on to found MetaFilter). Blogger's weblog services made it easy for users to post content, articles, and links to photographs and other blogs. At first free of charge, Blogger met difficulty when its funds were exhausted in 2001. Pyra was revolutionary in asking its blogger users for funds, but ultimately most of the company, including Hourihan, walked out. Williams ran the company alone until he was able to garner the support of Trellix creator Dan Bricklin, who invested in it after becoming aware of Blogger's situation. As popularity of Blogger across the blogosphere increased, advertisers provided the main revenue, and in 2002 Blogger underwent a major overhaul. Google purchased Blogger in 2003.

everyday people negotiating the creative and collaborative possibilities of the web than web engineers interested in its economic possibilities.

In 2001, when Hourihan left Pyra Labs, she cofounded the Lafayette Project in New York City, which seeks to mine editorial content on blogs to improve reader news service. In February 2003, Google bought Blogger for a reputed eight figures and now hosts the website and its servers. Hourihan earned millions of dollars from the sale.

When she was thirty-one, Hourihan was named one of the Massachusetts Institute of Technology's *Technology Review* Top Innovators under 35. In 2004, she was named one of *PC Magazine*'s People of the Year, along with team members Williams and Bausch and the creators of rival software company Six Apart, the makers of Movable Type.

Hourihan has collaborated with many successful entrepreneurs, but not all projects were successful. Kinja.com, a news aggregator that Hourihan helped launched in 2003 with British journalism and Internet entrepreneur Nick Denton—founder of the blog collective Gawker Media—never managed to gain

momentum. From 2006 to 2007, Hourihan was a member of the RSS (Really Simple Syndication) Advisory Board.

Hourihan speaks frequently about online journalism and the role of women in online technology. Ironically, she often fields questions about her work with Williams (who skyrocketed to popularity after the global success of Twitter) rather than her own endeavors. Nevertheless, Hourihan remains an exemplary figure in the Internet's entrepreneurial history. A feminist, she has argued that "more proactive encouragement of women in technology needs to happen. At least now it seems like girls have more exposure to it at younger ages and the opportunity to be familiar with it from the beginning."

In a *New York Times* article, Hourihan explained how she writes for a small audience, even though everyone knows that blogging's intimacy—which is part of its allure—is accessible to a much larger audience. "My guiding principle is always to write with my grandparents in mind. It keeps me from being too personal or too technical or too complainy [*sic*]." Hourihan also notes the uniqueness of time stamps and permalinks.

Hourihan is a monthly columnist for the O'Reilly Network. In a June 2012 blog entry she wrote, "What's important [regarding blogging] is that we've embraced a medium free of the physical limitations of pages, intrusions of editors, and delays of tedious publishing systems. As with free speech itself, what we say is not as important as the system that enables us to say it."

PERSONAL LIFE

In March 2000, Hourihan met husband Jason Kottke at South by Southwest (SXSW), a popular web technology convention held annually in Austin, Texas. At the time, Hourihan was still living in San Francisco. Kottke is a web designer and pioneer blogger who created the Silkscreen typeface and won a Bloggie Lifetime Achievement Award. Hourihan and Kottke dated off and on while each maintained popular blogs; subsequently, their relationship became a cause célèbre in the blogosphere. In 2005 Hourihan and Kottke they briefly broke up, with Hourihan moving from New York City, where she had been living since 2002, to New Hampshire, where she relied on dial-up Internet access. She rekindled the relationship with Kottke, and the couple married in March 2006. They live in New York City and have two children. Hourihan is an avid runner and writes often about her children, Ollie and Minna.

Hourihan is also a foodie and publishes *Megnut*, a personal blog that boasts a self-portrait (edited with

Photoshop) taken in the mirror (a common trend among web gurus). She is the senior adviser to Serious Eats, a recipient of the James Beard Foundation's Best Food Blog award. Considered one of the first serious food bloggers, Hourihan has challenged foodie blog readers to consider not only food sustainability but also how crowd sourcing of recipe sites jeopardizes their quality and reliability.

Ellen Elder

FURTHER READING
Bausch, Paul, Matthew Haughey, and Meg Hourihan. *We Blog: Publishing Online with Weblogs.* Indianapolis: Wiley, 2002. Print. A guide to creating and maintaining weblogs written by the pioneer blogging team of Hourihan along with Blogger cocreator Paul Bausch and MetaFilter founder Matthew Haughey. The book details how to automate blogs to share ideas, voice opinions, and help businesses grow.
Greenman, Catherine. "A Blogger's Big Fish Fantasy." *New York Times* 19 June 2003. Print. Poles a number of reputed bloggers, including Hourihan, about the fundamental issues of blogging, including we-blog readership and links, how to attract desired readers, and other fundamental issues of blogging.
Mead, Rebecca. "Meg and Jason." *New Yorker* 5 June 2006: 30–31. Print. A follow-up to Mead's feature on Hourihan, this *Talk of the Town* story announces the marriage of Hourihan to fellow pioneer blogger and web designer Jason Kottke.
---. "You've Got Blog." *New Yorker* 13 Nov. 2000: 102–08. Print. A digital culture feature by journalist Rebecca Mead highlighting Hourihan's innovative career, the evolution of blogs, and how her often quirky and inspiring life parallels that of the popularity of the blogosphere.
Rosenberg, Scott, ed. "The Blogger Catapult: Evan Williams and Meg Hourihan." *Say Everything: How Blogging Began, What It's Becoming, and Why It Matters.* New York: Crown, 2009. Print. *Salon.com* cofounder Rosenberg's book is a collection of essays by technology web experts that examines blogging's technological evolution and global triumph, including a study of the team behind Blogger. Chronicles blogging's impact on media, business, politics, and people.

TONY HSIEH
CEO of Zappos

Born: December 12, 1973; Chicago, Illinois
Died: -
Primary Field: Internet
Specialty: Commerce
Primary Company/Organization: Zappos

INTRODUCTION
Internet entrepreneur Tony Hsieh sold his first company, LinkExchange, to Microsoft for $265 million in 1998. He subsequently cofounded Venture Frogs, then joined Zappos. Under his leadership, Zappos has grown to a billion-dollar online shoe retailer that is dedicated to customer service. From a young age, Hsieh has been involved in numerous flourishing companies, which he has inscribed with his own unique business and organizational culture. Hsieh's technical knowledge, creativity, leadership qualities, and entrepreneurial spirit have combined to make him a successful business innovator in today's world.

EARLY LIFE
Tony Hsieh (pronounced shay) was born the eldest of three sons to Taiwanese parents who immigrated to the United States. He spent his childhood in Marin County, California. According to several accounts, he demonstrated creativity and entrepreneurial behavior early. In 1995, Hsieh graduated from Harvard University with a bachelor's degree in computer science. His time in college provided him with the opportunity to meet diverse people and to practice his business skills in a pizza business he was operating from his dormitory. One of his best pizza customers, Alfred Lin, later became the chief financial and operating office of Zappos until he retired in 2010.

LIFE'S WORK
After graduating from college, in 1995 Hsieh started his first job with Oracle as a software engineer. However, within a year he quit and, in 1996, together with Sanjay

Mandan, his roommate at Harvard and a business partner in his pizza business, founded LinkExchange, an Internet advertising network. LinkExchange's customers were able to place advertisements on the company's website. Within months, the number of customers and banner ads they displayed had exploded. The company succeeded and during this period reached almost half of all Internet users worldwide.

Only two years after the start of LinkExchange, in 1998, Microsoft approached the then twenty-four-year-old Hsieh and offered $265 million for the company. One of the main reasons for selling the business in 1999, according to Hsieh, was that the fast growth of the company, with its increasing number of employees, had had a negative impact on the organizational culture, and he no longer enjoyed working for the company.

The sale of LinkExchange to Microsoft made Hsieh a millionaire. He next cofounded a small investment company named Venture Frogs, through which he invested in approximately twenty Internet companies, among them Ask Jeeves, MongoMusic, MyAble, and Tellme Networks. Another of the companies in which Venture Frogs invested was Zappos, which was founded by Nick Swinmurn to sell shoes online. Hsieh was initially skeptical about the quality of this business

Tony Hsieh.

proposal: Who would buy shoes unseen and unfitted? He soon realized, however, the immense size of the retail shoe market and its potential. He invested in Shoe-Site.com, which before long changed its name to Zappos, based on the Spanish word for shoes, *zapatos*. Only two months after the company was founded, Hsieh's involvement in the company changed. Having started as an adviser and investor, soon he was working together with Swinmurn to run the company.

One of the first strategic decisions they made was to develop a brand identity for Zappos. They agreed that their competitive advantage should be centred on a highly satisfying customer service experience. In order to be able to control, manage, and improve the customer relationship directly, they changed the company's supply chain and invested heavily in their own warehouse instead of continuing to have manufacturers ship directly to customers. Since then, Zappos has offered a 365-day return policy, during which customers do not have to pay for shipping or return shipping. Zappos even goes as far as recommending competitors' sites and products if it cannot immediately make a pair of shoes available. Having gone through the experience of LinkExchange, Hsieh valued the atmosphere of a small, intimate company. The company's corporate culture encourages employees to work in an informal environment, establish collegial working relationships, and have fun getting the job done.

In 2006, Swinmurn left the company. Hsieh was left to run Zappos, which had reached $265 million sales in 2005. In November 2009, the economic recession and credit crisis reduced Zappos's inventory, endangering its cash flows. As a result, the company's board of directors sold the company to Amazon.com for more than $1.2 billion. Despite the change in ownership, Hsieh, who stayed as chief executive officer (CEO), has remained loyal to the company. In a security e-mail sent to its customers following a cyberattack on the company's internal networks, the management declared that the company had in excess of 24 million customer accounts in Zappos's database (January 2012).

Hsieh plans for Zappos to expand its product line, which it has already begun to do. Zappos is headquartered in a former warehouse in Henderson, Nevada. Hsieh has continued working not only on the e-commerce success of that company but also on a $350 million project to rebuild a small downtown area of Las Vegas. Passionate about networking and social interaction, Hsieh has opted to build the city a public space that will facilitate a melding of work and personal lives.

Affiliation: Zappos

Within one decade, Zappos, which started as an online shoe retailer, became a billion-dollar company specializing in selling shoes, accessories, handbags, beauty items, and fashion. Under the leadership of CEO Tony Hsieh, Zappos has become not only a successful online store but also well known for its total dedication and commitment to customer service and to enhancing the customer experience.

When recruiting new employees, Zappos is looking primarily for people who can fit in with the company's culture and reflect the organizational philosophy of customer orientation. The company even goes as far as to offer new recruits the sum of $3,000 if they quit, on the theory that only those truly interested in the company and its vision will remain. Zappos is more than happy to pay employees to leave rather than retain unmotivated employees whose presence might affect the company's customer relationships negatively. In the final analysis, Zappos's organizational culture is central to the success of the company.

Zappos has identified the following ten core values, which summarize the company's internal culture, branding strategy, and business goals:

- Deliver WOW Through Service
- Embrace and Drive Change
- Create Fun and a Little Weirdness
- Be Adventurous, Creative, and Open Minded
- Pursue Growth and Learning
- Build Open and Honest Relationships with Communication
- Build a Positive Team and Family Spirit
- Do More with Less
- Be Passionate and Determined
- Be Humble

Zappos is now delivering more than $1 billion in gross merchandise sales annually. Its corporate success, together with its unique corporate culture, resulted in its being ranked among *Fortune* magazine's annual Best Companies to Work For in 2009.

His plan, which will involve other investors, is it to construct a creative, relaxing, and fun place in which to live and work. In the meantime, Zappos is renting the old City Hall and has started major renovation work so that the company can open its headquarters on that site and provide work for approximately two thousand employees.

PERSONAL LIFE

As of 2012, Hsieh resided in Las Vegas, Nevada, and was unmarried. His public profile is large: As of June 2012, he had more than 2.4 million Twitter followers, and he encourages employees to use social media in order to personalize the company's image.

Hsieh's involvement in social media reflects his philosophy of work and management: Among Zappos's core values, for example, is the mandate to "create fun and a little weirdness," and to secure a job with the company requires not only a professional interview focused on skills but also an interview to determine whether the applicant's personality will fit in with the company culture.

Whether Hsieh has pursued an entrepreneurial career because he did not want to be an employee or simply had a passion for following his personal dream is hard to say. Whatever his reasons, his dedication to establishing a unique corporate culture, to providing a satisfying workplace for his employees, and to customer service appear to be linked in his book *Delivering Happiness: A Path to Profits, Passion and Purpose*. Published in June 2010, it was soon listed on the *New York Times* Best-Seller List and stayed there for twenty-seven consecutive weeks. Hsieh argues that profits and customer/employee satisfaction are not dichotomous; it is possible, he claims, to achieve both simultaneously, making everybody happy.

In March 2009, during an appearance on *Celebrity Apprentice*, Hsieh asked the two competing teams to create a comic book character for Zappos to be adopted for company's marketing campaigns.

Sabine H. Hoffmann

FURTHER READING

Chafkin, Max. "How I Did It: Tony Hsieh, CEO, Zappos.com." *Inc.* 1 Sept. 2006. Web. 20 June 2012. Interview with Tony Hsieh about the beginnings of Zappos.com.

Hao, Vivien. "In His Shoes." *Asianweek* 4 Dec. 2008. Web. 20 June 2012. Gives insights into the life and work of Tony Hsieh.

Hsieh, Tony. *Delivering Happiness: A Path to Profits, Passion and Purpose.* New York: Business Plus,

2010. Print. Hsieh elaborates on his commitment to customer service and the relevance of corporate culture to the success of a company. His philosophy of creating a win-win situation for all—customers, employees, and company—is explored.

Perschel, Anne. "Work-Life Flow: How Individuals, Zappos, and Other Innovative Companies Achieve High Engagement." *Global Business and Orga-* *nizational Excellence* 29.5 (2010): 17–30. Print. Talks about leadership, employee involvement, and coaching at Zappos.

Vasanthi, Sravanthi, and Vara Vasanthi. "Designing an Organisational Culture: Tony Hsieh—Wrapping Zappo's Organisational Culture?" n.d. IBS Case Development Centre. Web. 20 June 2012. A case study about the organizational culture of Zappos.

ARIANNA HUFFINGTON

Cofounder of *The Huffington Post*

Born: July 15, 1950; Athens, Greece
Died: -
Primary Field: Internet
Specialty: News and entertainment
Primary Company/Organization: Huffington Post Media Group

INTRODUCTION

Alternately known as a "force of nature," "the patron saint of new media," and "the queen of aggregation," Arianna Huffington has helped to redefine news media on the Internet. She cofounded The Huffington Post *in 2005 as an alternative to conservative news sites. Regularly offering both original and compiled news and entertainment stories, images, and videos,* The Huffington Post *continues to draw an increasing number of visitors to its site. Even though her detractors question her transformation from staunch conservative to active liberal, they have been forced to acknowledge Huffington's flair for providing a comfortable place for "Huffsters" to vent their opinions on everything from politics to celebrity antics. When AOL bought* The Huffington Post *for $315 million in 2011, Huffington was placed at the head of the entire AOL media team. As the editor-in-chief of the Huffington Post Media Group, she was initially in charge of TechCrunch, Engadget, Moviefone, Mapquest, Pop Eater, and AOL Music. Later, her editorial role was scaled back to just* The Huffington Post.

EARLY LIFE

Ariadne Anna Stassinopoulos was born on July 15, 1950, to Constantine Stassinopoulos, a journalist and managerial consultant, and Elli Stassinopoulos, also a journalist, in Athens, Greece. Huffington has repeatedly

said in interviews that her mother has been the most significant influence on her life, because she taught her that there were no limits to what she could dream or accomplish. When young Arianna announced that she wished to be educated at the prestigious Cambridge University in England, her mother set out to help her realize her dream. The family moved to England in 1966, and within two years she was studying economics at Cambridge. Huffington's father also influence her outlook: He had served time in a Nazi concentration camp after he was

Arianna Huffinton.

arrested for running an underground newspaper during World War II. Growing up in a family with that history imbued Huffington with a respect for the printed word that she would retain throughout her life. Her desire for financial success may also be attributed to those early years, when her family was constantly short of funds. She would date high-profile men, including Conservative Member of Parliament John Selwyn and columnist Bernard Levin.

Joining the Cambridge Union debating society helped to prepare Huffington for her future as a political activist. In her final year, she was elected president of the club, becoming its first foreign-born leader and only the third female to head the club. In 1973, the year after she earned her master's in economics from Cambridge, Huffington published her first book, *The Female Woman: An Argument against Women's Liberation for Female Emancipation*, in which she argued that feminists were being unfair to women who opted for traditional roles. The book was an unexpected bestseller in England.

Over the next eight years, Huffington maintained a close relationship with Levin while experimenting with her spirituality. The latter included involvement with some socially edgy groups, such as Insight (which encouraged members to act out their fantasies) and a spiritual group headed by guru Bhagwan Shree Rajneesh, which proved to be a cult and attempted to take over a town in Oregon. During this exploratory period, Huffington read the works of Carl Jung and wrote a second book, *After Reason* (1979), which questioned the social and political failures of the postwar era, criticizing both Left and Right. By 1981, Huffington was living in New York and publishing a biography of opera singer Maria Callas. Accused of plagiarizing part of the material, she settled out of court. A similar accusation followed the publication of the biography *Picasso: Creator and Destroyer* in 1988.

As a participant in the Los Angeles social scene of the early 1980s, Arianna met oil tycoon Michael Huffington; they married in 1986. Following a lavish wedding, they moved to Washington, D.C., where he served as assistant secretary of defense for negotiations policy in the administration of President Ronald Reagan. In 1992, he won a California seat in the House of Representatives. Two years later, he challenged Democrat Dianne Feinstein for her Senate seat in what was, at the time, the most expensive Senate race in American history, spending more than $5 million of his own money. Assuming a tough anti-immigration stance,

Huffington's campaign was ultimately derailed when it was learned that his Mexican nanny was in the country illegally. During this period, Arianna wrote a syndicated column and appeared on television shows such as *Politically Incorrect*, *Crossfire*, and *Face the Music*; she also campaigned vigorously for her husband. By 1997, however, the couple were were divorced. Arianna returned to New York, where she continued to participate in political and social scenes and began to develop her public persona and her own professional life.

LIFE'S WORK

By 1996, Huffington had become disillusioned with House Speaker Newt Gingrich and the entire Republican Party, whose conflict with President Bill Clinton over the federal budget led to the 1995–96 shutdown of the federal government. Huffington announced that she had become a "progressive populist." Also in 1996, she began writing a syndicated column that appeared twice weekly in more than a hundred newspapers. In 2003, she entered the California gubernatorial race after Governor Gray Davis was recalled (her former husband backed opponent Arnold Schwarzenegger); she later withdrew amid claims that she had not paid her fair share in state taxes for the previous two years. In 2004, she endorsed Democrat John Kerry for president.

While attending a party in 2004, Huffington and Kenneth Lerer, a former AOL executive, decided to create *The Huffington Post*. They promised each other to raise $2 million apiece in start-up money. Huffington's years as a socialite, political activist, and hostess provided her with a stable of influential friends who served her well in this latest venture. She turned to them and raised her $2 million within a week. Huffington and Lerer subsequently turned to venture capitalists, particularly SoftBank Capital, for additional financial support. *The Huffington Post*, dubbed *HuffPo* by loyal followers, featured work by historian and social critic Arthur Schlesinger, Jr., politician Gary Hart, actors Julia Louis-Dreyfus and John Cusack, newsman Walter Cronkite, and comedian Larry David, among other celebrity bloggers.

The site was eventually divided into verticals on politics, business, entertainment, technology, media, life and style, culture, comedy, healthy living, women, and local news and has sections devoted to religion, black voices, world news, and the environment. *The Huffington Post* uses videos and slide shows and contains numerous links to other Internet sites. For many visitors, it is the ability to post comments on blogs that draws them to the site. Big news items or controversial story lines might generate as many as five thousand comments. When *HuffPo* ran a story discussing the possibility of former Florida governor Jeb Bush running for president in 2012, there were more than eight thousand responses. Comments are moderated in order to ensure civility.

In 2009, *The Huffington Post* partnered with the social media site Facebook to create HuffPo Social News with Facebook Connect, resulting in 3.5 million visitors connecting to *The Huffington Post* from Facebook. The partnership allowed Facebook users to create a personal site that shared the *HuffPo* content they were reading, allowing for commentary with their Facebook friends.

Huffington is credited with most of the success of *The Huffington Post*. She has never been afraid to try new technologies, and *HuffPo* works with technical experts in Ukraine, India, Chile, the Philippines, and Vietnam, as well as those in the United States. In large part because of the efforts of marketing expert Jonah Peretti, *The Huffington Post* uses search engine optimization (SEO) to ensure that articles are worded in such a way that they show up at the tops of Google searches.

The Huffington Post has been harshly criticized for taking material from other sites and using it to promote its own popularity. Huffington and her employees defend the practice by calling themselves "curators" of the news, insisting that such methods are integral to new media. Staff members also insist that including links to original content encourages visitors to visit those sites also, resulting in increased traffic to competitors' websites.

AOL (America Online) bought *The Huffington Post* in 2011 for $315 million. Huffington became the editor-in-chief of the newsroom for all AOL's media properties. Even though AOL dropped some 90 percent of its freelance journalists, Huffington began hiring journalists away from competitors. According to *Huffington Post* watchdog Jeff Bercovici of *Forbes*, with thirteen hundred full-time journalists, the newly formed Huffington Post Media Group soon had a staff larger than that of well-established newspapers such as *The Washington Post* and *The Wall Street Journal*.

The Huffington Post had acquired an archive of high-quality content in largely based on the work of unpaid bloggers. In 2011, after AOL's acquisition of the site, a group of these bloggers would file a class-action suit against Huffington, *The Huffington Post*, and AOL, arguing that their work had helped increase the financial worth of the site and demanding a share of the profits. The case was dismissed in March 2012 on the grounds

---

Affiliation: *The Huffington Post*

After going online on May 9, 2005, *The Huffington Post* quickly became one of the most frequently visited news sites on the Internet. Its unpaid bloggers have included everyone from Senator (now President) Barack Obama to author Norman Mailer to actor Warren Beatty. By 2008, the site was claiming 8.9 million unique visitors per month. Within a year, the number of bloggers had climbed to three thousand. During the summer of 2010, *HuffPo*, as followers called it, claimed 24.3 million unique visitors each month, second only to the venerable *New York Times*. For the first time, the site made a profit, garnering $30 million. By 2011, the number of bloggers had skyrocketed to nine thousand and revenue was estimated to have doubled over that of the previous year.

In February 2011, AOL, which had recently been released from its disastrous merger with Time Warner, purchased *The Huffington Post* for $315 million. *HuffPo* founder Arianna Huffington was reportedly the motivating force behind the buyout, which placed her in charge of AOL's entire newsroom and gave her a budget that allowed her to hire big name journalists, such as Tim O'Brien and Peter Goodman, away from established print media at reported annual salaries of more than $300,000. Huffington agreed to accept a quarter of the purchase price in AOL stock.

---

that the bloggers had entered into agreements to provide the paper with content with no expectation of monetary compensation, only the exposure that had been provided, and could not renegotiate those agreements ex post facto. In May, Huffington's responsibilities were scaled back to focus solely on *The Huffington Post*, which was continuing to grow.

PERSONAL LIFE

In the mid- and late 1970s, Huffington had a close relationship with London *Times* columnist Bernard Levin, whom she would later call the "love of her life" and who was her senior by more than two decades; they separated when it became clear that he did not wish to marry and have children. After her marriage to Michael Huffington in 1986, she gave birth to two daughters: Isabella in 1989 and Christina in 1991. She became a naturalized U.S. citizen in 1990.

After the couple's 1997 divorce, Huffington continued her printed commentary on political life. In 1998, she published *Greetings from the Lincoln Bedroom*, a satire on Bill Clinton's presidency. In the 2000s, her political works focused on the problems created by politicians interested in promoting their own interests over those of the American people: *How to Overthrow the Government* (2000), *Fanatics and Fools: The Game Plan for Winning Back America* (2004), *Right Is Wrong: How the Lunatic Fringe Hijacked America, Shredded the Constitution, and Made Us All Less Safe* (2008), and *Third World America: How Our Politicians Are Abandoning the Middle Class and Betraying the American Dream* (2010). Of course the accomplishment for which she is best known, founding *The Huffington Post*, was realized in 2005.

After the 1990s, Huffington also maintained a public profile as a political and social commentator. She became a cohost of the political round table *Left, Right, and Center* for public radio; the show's format incorporated viewpoints from political commentators representing different political perspectives, and Huffington represented the "independent-progressive blogosphere." With conservative political consultant and analyst Mary Matalin, Huffington hosts the syndicated radio program *Both Sides Now*. She also gives approximately one hundred speeches annually and is a frequent guest on nationally televised political and news programs.

On the lighter side, Huffington has voiced Arianna the Bear for *The Cleveland Show*, an animated television show aired over the Fox network. She is the author of more than a dozen books and works with various charities, serving on the boards for A Place Called Home, a safe house for inner-city youths in Los Angeles, and the Archer School for Girls, which provides a nourishing environment for educating girls of middle school and high school age.

Her daughters now grown, Huffington remains friendly with their father (who announced his bisexuality in 1998) and as of 2012 had not remarried. Most of her energies are devoted to ensuring the success of *The Huffington Post*. While her detractors have charged her with being manipulative and opportunistic, many others regard her as and a pioneer of new media and a strong woman whose opinions have evolved and matured over time. It is clear that her methods for creating an Internet news site that people want to visit have been highly successful.

Elizabeth Rholetter Purdy

FURTHER READING

Bankoff, Jim. "Why the *New York Times* Should Stop Complaining about *The Huffington Post*." *Page One: Inside the* New York Times *and the Future of Journalism*. Ed. David Folkenflik. New York: PublicAffairs, 2011. N. pag. Print. The former president of Netscape and vice president at AOL explores the status of the newspaper industry and journalism.

Bercovici, Jeff. "The Honeymooners." *Forbes* 187.11/12 (2011): 140–44. Print. Examines AOL's buyout of *The Huffington Post*. Includes a photograph and a graph.

Fox, Richard Logan, and Jennifer Ramos, eds. *iPolitics: Citizens, Elections, and Governing in the New Media Era*. New York: Cambridge UP, 2012. Print. Discusses the impact of social media and political websites on contemporary democracy. Includes illustrations and charts.

Huffington, Arianna. *Pigs at the Trough: How Corporate Greed and Political Corruption Are Undermining America*. New York: Three Rivers, 2009. Print. A revision of the 2003 edition, including a new preface and afterword. An anti-Bush administration examination of how big corporations have contributed to the impoverishment of Americans. Includes a list of recommended groups that promote political reform.

Lyons, Daniel. "Arianna's Answer." *Newsweek* 156.5 (2010): 44–47. Print. Detailed examination of the rise of *The Huffington Post*. Includes photographs, a chart, and a graph.

STEVE HUFFMAN

Cofounder of Reddit

Born: November 12, 1983; place unknown
Died: -
Primary Field: Internet

Specialty: Social media
Primary Company/Organization: Reddit

INTRODUCTION

Straight out of college, Steve Huffman founded the social news site Reddit with classmate Alexis Ohanian, using seed money from Y Combinator. A competitor to Digg, which began around the same time, Reddit was acquired by Condé Nast Publications while Digg turned down suitors until long after its price had fallen. Huffman left Reddit in 2009, returning to Y Combinator and forming a start-up, the travel search engine Hipmunk.

EARLY LIFE

Steve Huffman was born on November 12, 1983. His parents divorced when he was young, and each parent remarried while he was still a child. His stepfather was a successful businessman. His father sparked his interest in programming by introducing him to the BASIC programming language when he was about eight years old. Huffman graduated from the University of Virginia with a bachelor's degree in computer science in 2005.

Huffman turned down a programming job in Virginia, so he and his college roommate, Alexis Ohanian, could relocate to Medford, Massachusetts. They approached Paul Graham, founder of Y Combinator and Huffman's programming idol, about funding for an idea. Graham rejected their first idea but invited them to try again. The second idea was Reddit.

LIFE'S WORK

Reddit was a social news site, premiering in June 2005, only three weeks after Huffman and Ohanian began work on the site. Users could submit links (or text posts) and "upvote" or "downvote" other submitted links; the front page displayed the most popular stories at any given time, and the community developed around the hierarchical comment threads (also subject to up- and downvoting) attached to each story. The constantly changing display was key to Reddit's business model, because revenue was based on advertising; presenting a dynamic site rather than a static one, where every user's interaction changed the site in some way, encouraged users to stay on the site, refresh the page, and go back to another story to read more comments, all the while generating more page views (and ideally the occasional click-through).

The initial audience for Reddit came from Graham: He e-mailed friends and contacts to tell them about the site, providing the first thousand or so unique visitors. From there, the site grew organically, although Huffman

and Ohanian also created a number of fake user accounts to submit news or comments in order to keep activity going for the first few months, while waiting for the user base to reach a self-sustaining critical mass. Huffman has said that he and Ohanian used "tons of … fake users" to submit content they wanted to read. This practice helped set the bar for the site. In the early days, Huffman and Ohanian answered every feedback e-mail personally, solidifying a sense of community. Various aesthetic choices clarified Reddit's identity compared to other sites: Huffman explained that because the emphasis was on sharing links, the headline inputted by a user became a significant part of the content. Photos and videos were therefore kept off the front page in order to keep visitors' focus on those headlines—which were uncensored.

In discussing Reddit's performance compared to Digg's after the fact, Huffman noted that Digg eventually imploded, with high-level management leaving at the same time that longtime users expressed dissatisfaction with changes to the site, but that Digg had previously outperformed Reddit on the basis of several metrics. While Reddit had a strong, loyal user base, Digg was better known to outsiders, more likely to be a familiar name to people who had never used the site. Digg was more adept at public relations, and perhaps because Condé Nast bought Reddit so early in the site's history, Digg earned headlines with buyout rumors, for which Reddit had no equivalent. At the same time, Digg was the subject of fraud actions, with users accepting pay to promote stories, something Reddit largely avoided.

After leaving Reddit, Huffman founded Hipmunk in August 2010 with Adam Goldstein. Ohanian joined the start-up, shortly before launch, as marketing director. Huffman and Goldstein had spent the preceding summer in Y Combinator's summer course. Hipmunk is an online travel company offering well-organized flight search results, presented chronologically and ranked according to price, schedule, and Hipmunk's unique "agony" rating, based on travel duration and number of stops. The site also offers searches for hotels (which are ranked) and Amtrak train routes. After searching, users are redirected to purchase their tickets (usually to Orbitz, although American Airlines flights are redirected to the American Airlines website). The site is built on Python and Tornado, on Amazon EC2. Flight data are provided by QPX Solution, the same package ITA Software provides to the other major travel search engines. Revenue is accrued through commissions; the site is free to

Affiliation: Reddit

The social news website Reddit was founded by Steve Huffman and Alexis Ohanian in 2005. It was quickly acquired by publishing company Condé Nast and spun off as a subsidiary of Condé Nast's parent company.

Social news websites arguably began with Slashdot, in 1997; it is certainly the earliest site to gain significant popularity and remain in operation today. Fark, Delicious, and Digg followed soon after, all offering variations on the same mechanism: Users submit links to websites (typically news stories, although not necessarily from conventional news websites), which are posted to the site and commented on. At Slashdot, moderators selected links to post from the users' submissions. At Digg and Reddit, a voting system was used, and the articles with the most positive votes were displayed at the top of the list. The voting system democratizes the moderation process compared to sites like Slashdot.

Huffman and Ohanian founded Reddit in Medford, Massachusetts, and it was merged with Infogami a few months later, with Infogami's Aaron Swartz joining the Reddit team. The Reddit site went live after only three weeks of work. In order to encourage participation, Huffman and Ohanian submitted content under numerous false usernames in order to create the illusion of a crowd and of conversation—a gambit to which they did not admit until years after the fact. Because revenue came solely from advertising (until the introduction of Reddit Gold later), the user base needed to be large, and active users who viewed many pages would be best—especially because the click-through rate on social news sites is incredibly low. Huffman estimated it at 0.5 percent.

Magazine publishing giant Condé Nast acquired Reddit on Halloween 2006, less than a year and a half after it was founded, and the site continued to grow. Huffman and Ohanian left in 2009 to form Hipmunk with other former employees of Reddit. Shortly thereafter, in the summer of 2010, a paid service, Reddit Gold, was offered, making new features available for about $30 per year in order to fund a larger staff and greater computing resources. In 2011, Reddit was spun off from Condé Nast and became a separate subsidiary of Advance Publications, Condé Nast's parent company.

At Reddit, started in June 2005 a few months after Digg was opened to the public, both articles and comments can be voted on, which alters the order of comments in comment threads. Upvotes raise a score; downvotes lower it. Highest-scored articles appear on the front page, while articles in a given subcategory (called "subReddits") are displayed in order of score as well. One of the interesting innovations at Reddit is the "controversial" page, which lists articles in which the upvote and downvote totals are nearly equal. The controversial page and the effect of votes on comments result in an environment in which the semantic meaning of a vote is somewhat more complicated than would result from a more binary system (such as "liking" posts on Facebook).

Users of Reddit are called "Redditors," reflecting the origins of the site's name—a blend of *read* and *edit*, blurring the line between the reader and the editor, which is perhaps the essence of social news. Redditors can customize their front pages after logging in and can maintain friends lists (as on most social networks) in order to keep track of the content generated by users they want to follow. Commenting on Reddit is voracious; the community has a great many memes, traditions, tropes, and quirks that maintain a sense of community and consistency, although as with any other online community, this level of activity and involvement can render content opaque to newcomers.

SubReddits are key to the feel of Reddit, and they number in the tens of thousands. On the front page is a default list of subReddits: funny, pics, announcements, blog, askReddit, worldnews, gaming, todayilearned, politics, science, WTF, IAmA, videos, technology, music, atheism, AdviceAnimals, aww, movies, and bestof. Capitalization and grammar in subReddit naming is rather inconsistent.

The IAmA subReddit deserves special mention. It stands for "I am a ...," while also containing the abbreviation AMA, for "ask me anything." This subReddit is not a list of links to other sites but consists of posts on Reddit, in which the initial poster introduces himself or herself and invites the community to "ask me anything." The poster may have an interesting job, such as working on a movie set, or may be a member of a community about which people are curious, such as a religious community. The most famous IAmAs outside Reddit are those of celebrities, which on the whole offer franker, more candid, and more in-depth interaction than either traditional media interviews or the hosted

Affiliation: Reddit (continued)

chat rooms that once were a part of the standard public relations (PR) tour. The variable end to which celebrities put IAmA is best compared to Twitter, which some celebrities delegate to their PR or street teams, others use only for official announcements, and others use for genuine social purposes. In many ways Reddit has replaced moderated chats when it comes to interactions between the famous and the public; *Atlantic* editor Ta-Nehisi Coates answered questions on Reddit about his August 2012 editorial "Fear of a Black President," for instance, rather than hosting a chat on *The Atlantic*'s website. Awareness of Reddit among celebrities steadily rose in 2011–12, with some celebrities revealing they had read the site for a while before participating. Actress-writer Molly Ringwald's IAmA was especially successful.

The Reddit community operates the largest Secret Santa program in the world, involving nearly one hundred countries and twenty thousand participants. Reddit also operates on Amazon's Web Services, uses Pylons as its web framework, and uses RabbitMQ for offline processing. The site was rewritten in Python in December 2005, having originally been written in Common Lisp. Reddit's code is available as open source code.

The largely uncensored nature of Reddit has led to a number of controversial subReddits, the most famous of which was the "jailbait" subReddit, which included user-submitted photos of underage minors; it was removed in 2012, at which point sexual content featuring minors was explicitly banned. There are also subReddits devoted to graphic photos of violence.

use. Apps for the iPhone and the iPad were introduced in the first half of 2011.

Within a year, Hipmunk was seeing more than 1 million searches per month, and *Time* magazine included the site in the 50 Best Websites of 2011. In 2012, the staff had grown to sixteen and venture funding had grown to $20.2 million: the initial $15,000 in seed money from Y Combinator; $1 million in seed money from SV Angel, Paul Buchheit, Matt Mullenweg, Raymond Tonsing, Amitt Mahajan, Gabor Cselle, Sizhao Yang, and Ashton Kutcher; $4.2 million in Series A funding in 2011, from Ignition Partners, Erik Blachford, Jim Hornthal, Rob Glaser, Raymond Tonsing, and Richard Barton; and $15 million in Series B funding in 2012, from Institutional Venture Partners and Ignition Partners.

PERSONAL LIFE

Huffman married Katie Babiarz, whom he had met in college. She is a physician and she enjoys Suduko, so Huffman wrote a program to help solve the puzzles for her. He also teaches CS253, web application engineering, through the Udacity online classroom.

Bill Kte'pi

FURTHER READING

Bot, Sophy. *The Hipster Effect: How the Rising Tide of Individuality Is Changing Everything We Know About Life, Work, and the Pursuit of Happiness*. Suisun City: Sophy Bot, 2011. Print. Examines hipsterdom as a product of Internet culture and Reddit's role in that culture.

Gusto, M. *Rage Comics*. Scotts Valley: CreateSpace, 2011. Print. A compilation of the meme comics popularized by Reddit.

Jenkins, Henry. *Confronting the Challenges of Participatory Culture: Media Education for the 21st Century*. Cambridge: MIT, 2009. Print. Examines social media, new forms of creative expression, and their impact on media studies.

Morris, Kevin. "How Reddit Was Built with an Army of Fake Accounts." 19 June 2012. *Daily Dot*. Web. 8 Sept. 2012. *Mashable*. Web. 12 Aug. 2012. A brief account of Huffman's story of how Reddit was "founded on a lie."

Qualman, Erik. *Socialnomics: How Social Media Transforms the Way We Live and Do Business*. New York: Wiley, 2010. Print. Considers the impact of social media on the business world.

CHRIS HUGHES

Cofounder of Facebook and publisher of *The New Republic*

Born: November 26, 1983; Hickory, North Carolina
Died: -
Primary Field: Internet
Specialty: Social media
Primary Company/Organization: Facebook

INTRODUCTION

By the age of twenty-five, Chris Hughes was considered a success in the fields of both social networking and political campaigning. Never as interested in the computer side of creating Facebook as the rest of his Harvard friends, Hughes had a special knack for understanding the impact of particular features on users of the social networking site, which earned him the nickname the Empath among his fellow Facebook cofounders. After graduating from Harvard, Hughes devoted his full attention to turning Facebook into the top social networking site in the world. Much more than his friend and cofounder Mark Zuckerberg, who believed the Internet should be used for sharing information, Hughes understood the need for privacy. After leaving Facebook, Hughes expanded his interests to public policy, and he is credited with developing the online campaign, which became a primary source of funding, for Barack Obama's presidential bid in 2008. In April 2009, Fast Company *dubbed Hughes "the kid who made Obama president" in a cover story written by Ellen McGirt. In 2010, Hughes founded Jumo, a nonprofit social networking site that connects individuals with charities. In 2012, Hughes purchased* The New Republic, *becoming its publisher and editor in chief.*

EARLY LIFE

Chris Hughes was born into a typically conservative southern middle-class family in Hickory, North Carolina, on November 26, 1983. He has said that he was raised to be religious but rejected his faith after leaving North Carolina. Hughes was an only child, and his parents were older than those of most of his friends. His father, Ray, was a paper salesman, and his mother, Brenda, had taught school. Although close to his parents, he applied for a scholarship to attend the prestigious Phillips Academy in Andover, Massachusetts, without telling them. After suffering culture shock in the new environment, he settled in and began to enjoy

it. It was at Phillips that for the first time, Hughes admitted to himself that he was gay.

By the time he reached Harvard in 2002 as a scholarship student, Hughes was openly gay. While he was majoring in the literature and history of France, he also had a deep interest in public policy. Mark Zuckerberg was one of his roommates in Kirkland House dorm at Harvard, and Hughes signed on as one of the original members of what was then thefacebook.com. He soon became the spokesman for the new company. When Zuckerberg and the rest of the team headed for Palo Alto, California, in the summer of 2004, Hughes's finances were such that he could not afford to waste time, and he was much more interested than Zuckerberg in completing his degree. Zuckerberg had been much impressed by a speech in which he had heard Bill Gates suggest to students that it might benefit them to take time off from their studies before completing their degrees. When Zuckerberg headed for California, Hughes had already signed up and paid for a summer program in France, so he flew to Paris instead of Palo Alto. After

Chris Hughes.

187

a brief period in California, Hughes returned to Harvard to continue his studies.

Affiliation: Facebook

In 2004, when Chris Hughes joined his friends Mark Zuckerberg, Dustin Moskovitz, and Eduardo Saverin in creating thefacebook.com in their Harvard dorm, the site was limited to Harvard students. When students signed up, they submitted a small photograph and minimal information about themselves. Within a month of going online, the number of users had climbed to ten thousand. Over the following months, it spread to seventy universities and colleges and eventually to high schools before becoming widely available. By 2010, three years after Hughes left the company to run the online campaign for Barack Obama's presidential bid, Facebook's value had skyrocketed to $1 billion.

Generating millions of views in a single day, Facebook has entered the language as a verb; the term *facebooking* has come to be widely understood. As what came to be known as the "Facebook obsession" spread around the world; the site was used for a variety of reasons, some completely unintentional. Most people use Facebook simply to keep up with family and friends, posting information and photographs about their daily lives and sharing news and thoughts that are important to them: updates on relationships; job changes; photographs of weddings, children, or grandchildren; and so forth. Others use it as a dating site, a place to connect with others; many couples have been made or broken on Facebook. Celebrities, political figures, and writers use it to keep fans and supporters updated on their activities. Due to information unwisely shared on Facebook, some people have lost jobs, have been arrested, or even have had their homes broken into.

Today Facebook is increasingly becoming a tool of marketers. The belief is that, with the number of users approaching 1 billion as of July 2012, Facebook offers a ready-made location for potential business customers and clients. The site has also increasingly taken on social and political significance, serving as a site for information dissemination and feedback as well as a place to form movements. Although subject to concerns about privacy, Facebook and its uses continue to evolve.

Life's Work

While still at Harvard, Hughes was besieged with requests for interviews concerning the growing success of Facebook, but he was forced to balance his public relations work with his studies. In 2006, he graduated magna cum laude and left for California to serve as onsite spokesperson for Facebook. Although he was never involved in the technical side of Facebook and had never expressed interest in learning to write software, he had an instinctive understanding of how people were likely to react to new features. He later became the head of product management, taking on responsibility for overseeing the Facebook experience and making it something that users could enjoy. He also filled the essential role of serving as a sounding board for the ideas of other members of the Facebook team.

In 2006, Facebook decided to allow politicians to set up their own profiles on Facebook, and Barack Obama signed up. Thus, Hughes learned that he and Obama shared many ideas, particularly the notion that people could work together to institute change. When he told his friend Mark Zuckerberg that he was leaving the company, Zuckerberg was shocked because he could not see himself leaving Facebook for any reason. By the time Hughes left Facebook in 2007, he had amassed a fortune estimated at $700 million. When Facebook went public in May 2012, Hughes's Facebook stock became worth considerably more.

After being hired by the Obama campaign team as the director of online organizing, Hughes moved to Chicago. His experience at Facebook served him well as he worked on creating My.BarackObama.com (MyBo) to serve as the online presence for Obama's run for the presidency. The site was up and running by February 2007, following Obama's announcement that he had officially entered the race. Raising $30 million, the site was considered a major factor in Obama's successful campaign. By November 2008, the site had generated two million profiles and thirty-five thousand groups. Users had also planned two hundred thousand real-world events. Hughes had seen the site as a way for Obama supporters to find one another, promote the campaign, and raise funds. He was successful on all counts. Although they received less publicity than the MyBo site, Hughes also managed Obama sites on Facebook and MySpace, as well as those on other networks. Overall, Hughes was responsible for helping to raise $500 million for Obama, with most of that amount coming from contributions of less than $200 each.

After Obama's inauguration, Hughes accepted a position as "entrepreneur in residence" at General Catalyst Partners, a venture capital firm based in Cambridge, Massachusetts, where he helped to motivate potential entrepreneurs. The following year, he founded Jumo, a nonprofit website with a stated mission of helping people discover ways to make the world a better place. Concerned mostly with nonprofits that lacked the resources for lavish fund-raising activities, Jumo used technology to match visitors with causes that reflected their interests. By 2011, Jumo had a million users and twenty thousand followers on Facebook. Hughes sold the site to *Good* magazine that year, announcing that it would combine *Good*'s three million unique monthly visitors with Jumo's access to fifteen thousand nonprofit organizations.

In 2010, Hughes was named to the High Level Commission of the Joint United Nations Programme on HIV/AIDS (UNAIDS), a group of business leaders, activists, and scientists that focuses on promoting social and political action on issues related to HIV/AIDS. The high-profile group is cochaired by Françoise Barré-Sinoussi, a French physician who was awarded the Nobel Prize in Physiology or Medicine in 2008 in conjunction with her mentor, Luc Montagnier, for their joint discovery of the HIV virus, and Archbishop Desmond Tutu, who won the Nobel Peace Prize in 1984 for his campaign against apartheid in South Africa. Another member of the group is basketball legend Magic Johnson, who had announced in 1991 that he had tested HIV positive.

In March 2012, Hughes announced that he had purchased *The New Republic*, a liberal print magazine that has focused on politics, the arts, and social issues for more than a century. Hughes announced that he believed there was a need for "big idea journalism" in the environment of the early twenty-first century, when books, particularly e-books, are selling at an all-time high. Hughes stated that he would serve as both publisher and editor in chief. His plan was to take the magazine beyond its intellectual history to appeal to a broader audience; this included the immediate goal of bringing *The New Republic* into the computer age by making it available on devices such as tablet computers, the iPod Touch, and smart phones. On May 11, Hughes announced on Twitter that *The New Republic* was introducing the *TNR Reader*, a daily collection of "the best writing on the web" as filtered through the lens of the magazine. The *TNR Reader* is available on Facebook, Twitter, and e-mail platforms. When interviewers questioned whether Hughes's age would be a factor in his running *The New Republic*, he reminded them that the magazine had a history of young editors: Mike Kinsley, Andrew Sullivan, and Peter Beinart had all also served as editors, all starting in their late twenties.

PERSONAL LIFE

Hughes has remained friends with Zuckerberg since giving up an active role in Facebook. Like Zuckerberg and most of the others involved in founding Facebook, Hughes has insisted that the depiction of the founding of Facebook in Aaron Sorkin's screenplay for the film *The Social Network* (2010) and in Ben Mezrich's book *The Accidental Billionaires* (2009), on which the movie was based, is mostly fiction. Hughes particularly objected to the personification of Zuckerberg as a selfish egotist, insisting that his friend is kind as well as brilliant.

On a personal level, Hughes has been involved in a relationship with Sean Eldridge, the president of Hudson River Ventures, since 2005. Eldridge is an active spokesperson for gay rights and has appeared on a number of television shows to debate opponents of those rights. He also serves as a senior adviser to the gay-rights group Freedom to Marry. Hughes and Eldridge, who have announced their engagement, live in the SoHo section of Manhattan and are heavily involved in political causes, particularly in the fight to have same-sex marriages declared legal throughout the United States. They established the Telos Foundation in 2011. In 2012, Hughes and Eldridge also joined the bipartisan group New York Lead to promote campaign finance reform in the state of New York.

Elizabeth Rholetter Purdy

FURTHER READING

Bindrim, Kira. "Facebook Co-founder Has Another Network." *New York Business* 27.13 (2011): F-10. Print. Profiles Hughes's work with Jumo.

Dolan, Kerry A. "Chris Hughes on What's Next for Nonprofit Social Site Jumo." *Forbes* 21 Apr. 2011. Web. 9 Aug. 2012. Hughes reveals his plans for the next phase of Jumo: bringing in large corporations who want to publicize the nonprofits they support.

Karpel, Ari. "Forty under 40." *Advocate* 1049 (2011): n. pag. Print. Includes Hughes as one of top business people of the year. Illustrated.

Kirkpatrick, David. *The Facebook Effect: The Inside Story of the Company That Is Connecting the*

World. New York: Simon, 2010. Print. Traces the history of Facebook and its founders. Includes notes, an index, and illustrations.

McGirt, Ellen. "Boy Wonder." *Fast Company* 134 (2009): 58–97. Print. Profiles the career of Hughes

with a focus on his work with the Obama campaign. Illustrated.

Moses, Lucia. "First Mover: Chris Hughes." *Adweek* 53.20 (2012): n. pag. Print. Profile of Hughes with a focus on his acquisition of *The New Republic*. Illustrated.

CHAD HURLEY

Cofounder and former CEO of YouTube

Born: January 1, 1977; Birdsboro, Pennsylvania
Died: -
Primary Field: Business and commerce
Specialty: Management, executives, and investors
Primary Company/Organization: YouTube

INTRODUCTION

Chad Hurley cofounded the popular website YouTube, which revolutionized the way many viewed video by allowing users to share their creations online. Although YouTube does not charge users a fee to upload or view videos, it does sell advertising, making it highly profitable. After selling YouTube to Google in 2006, Hurley stayed on as chief executive officer (CEO) through 2010 and has continued to serve as an adviser to the company.

EARLY LIFE

Chad Meredith Hurley was born in 1977 and grew up near Birdsboro, Pennsylvania. Early on, Hurley demonstrated a keen interest in the fine arts, especially painting and sculpture. Hurley's entrepreneurial spirit also emerged at an early age: He set up a stand in his parents' front yard to sell his artwork to passersby. As he grew older, Hurley became interested in technology and computers. While a student at Twin Valley High School in Elverson, Pennsylvania, he was a member of the Technology Student Association and built an amplifier that won third place in a national electronics competition. He attended Indiana University of Pennsylvania and initially majored in computer science, although he later decided that this field was too technical and mechanical for his tastes. Wanting to explore a more creative field, Hurley changed his emphasis of the study to graphic design and printmaking.

As graduation neared, Hurley became aware of a new company, PayPal, which was attempting to allow individuals using personal data (or digital) assistants (PDAs) to transfer money to other PDA users. He

interviewed for a position with the company and was asked to design a logo for PayPal as part of the interview process. He did so, creating a logo that PayPal would continue to use through 2012, and was offered a job as PayPal's first designer. Within three years, PayPal was purchased by eBay for more than $1.5 billion. As an early employee of PayPal, Hurley received stock options that provided him enough money to consider starting his own Internet business. In the interim, Hurley engaged in other activities, such as designing a series of messenger bags. Hurley also worked as a designer for the 2005 film *Thank You for Smoking*, which was produced by PayPal founder Max Levchin.

Chad Hurley.

LIFE'S WORK

Perhaps the most significant developments that resulted from Hurley's employment at PayPal were his friendships with Steve Chen and Jawed Karim, two software engineers. During the winter of 2005, the three began to discuss the problems they had experienced sharing videos online.

According to company lore, the idea of YouTube originated during an after-dinner discussion between Chen and Hurley regarding the difficulty of posting video online. The YouTube website was activated on February 14, 2005, and development continued on the project over the following months. This development was funded by an $11.5 million investment by venture capital firm Sequoia Capital. Sequoia Capital has played a significant role in funding a variety of technology start-ups, including Apple, Cisco Systems, Electronic Arts, Google, and Yahoo! Pierre Lamond, a partner at Sequoia Capital from 1981 through 2009 and one of the founders of National Semiconductor, worked with Hurley and Chen to develop YouTube (Karim had returned to Stanford University to pursue graduate study). Hurley became CEO of YouTube, while Chen served as its chief technology officer (CTO). Lamond was immediately impressed by Hurley and Chen as they developed YouTube, particularly admiring their responsible approach to the financial aspects of the business. Unlike many start-up companies that moved into expensive quarters, YouTube was more frugal: Its original offices were located in San Mateo, above a pizza parlor and a Japanese restaurant.

The first video was uploaded on YouTube on April 23, 2005. Entitled "Me at the Zoo," the nineteen-second-long video featured Karim standing in front of some elephants at the San Diego Zoo. Although the site officially launched in November, a beta version was available to the public in May. In July 2006, YouTube reported that more than sixty-five thousand new videos were being uploaded to the website and more than one hundred million videos were being viewed each day. The ease of using YouTube was such that many videos became very popular, with viewers who enjoyed a video sending links to it to friends and family members. The widespread sharing of video through e-mail, websites, and social media became known as a clip "going viral," a phenomenon that coincided with the proliferation of cameras as a feature of cellular telephones.

YouTube became so popular so quickly for a variety of reasons. First, few other options for sharing video were available at the time of YouTube's launch.

Second, YouTube was relatively easy to use and accepted a variety of formats that were then displayed using the Adobe Flash player plug-in, which can be found on nearly 80 percent of all computers. Third, all YouTube content was uploaded by the public, changing the traditional model of programming in that all of the content was provided without cost by the users rather than the company. Finally, YouTube was free to users and used advertising revenue to generate income. Although investors suggested that advertisements be played before a video could be viewed, Hurley resisted this during his tenure as CEO. YouTube proved increasingly popular because of the wide variety of videos that it made available, including clips from films, television programs, and music videos as well as video blogs and other original content made by users.

The presence of commercial works on YouTube prompted the copyright owners of those works to threaten YouTube with lawsuits for enabling the public to steal their intellectual property. Hurley and YouTube's legal counsel maintained that federal copyright law required them to remove videos if and when the copyright holder informed them of the problem, not to proactively monitor new content for possible violations. Aware of the fate that befell file-sharing service Napster, however, Hurley guided YouTube to work with content providers such as NBC Universal, CBS, and the BBC to make agreements that permitted the site to host clips from their programming. Threats of potential liability perhaps in part influenced Hurley's and Chen's decision to accept a buyout offer from Google in November 2006, an agreement that allowed Hurley to maintain his position of CEO. Hurley's share of the Google buyout amounted to approximately $350 million.

Although Google purchased YouTube, it permitted a high degree of independence, valuing the separate culture and contributions of that organization. Hurley continued to work with content providers to lessen the threat of legal action for copyright violation while increasing the availability of certain content. To that end, YouTube entered into a revenue-sharing arrangement with VEVO, a consortium that includes three of the four largest music companies, Sony Music Entertainment, Universal Music Group, and EMI Group. To date, VEVO has made more than forty-five thousand music videos available and generates income by splitting advertising revenue with YouTube. Despite agreements such as these, entertainment companies such as Viacom and Mediaset have filed lawsuits against YouTube.

In November 2008, Hurley announced an agreement with several production companies, including Metro-Goldwyn-Mayer (MGM) and CBS, that would allow YouTube to stream full-length motion pictures and television programs to audiences. YouTube originally intended to compete with rival websites such as Hulu, which features programming from NBC, Fox Broadcasting Company, and the Walt Disney Company. As the streaming service evolved, however, YouTube expanded its offerings to include online film rentals. In March 2010, YouTube began to stream live sporting events with cricket matches from the Indian Premier League.

To assist in reducing abuse of the site's features, Hurley helped YouTube to establish community guidelines that govern users' behavior. YouTube's community guidelines prohibit certain types of behavior and conduct, such as posting videos that infringe on copyrights and those containing animal abuse, hate speech, sexually explicit content, spam, or extreme violence. Users are provided with a means to tag videos or comments as inappropriate, and material tagged as inappropriate is examined by a team of YouTube employees who work around the clock. Nevertheless, Hurley faced tremendous criticism from those who believed the company did not do enough to protect the public. The fact that most videos permit users to leave comments has allowed users to build a sense of community and collaboration that is different from many other web experiences. The users' comments are frequently criticized, however, for including racist, homophobic, sexist, and vulgar language. Although Hurley has acknowledged that such comments are inappropriate, he has defended the rights of those using YouTube to maintain free speech and do so without interference from the company.

Since handing over the powers of CEO in November 2010, Hurley has continued to serve as an adviser to its management. With Chen, Hurley also helped to found AVOS Systems, an Internet-based company headquartered in San Mateo, California. Among AVOS's products are the social bookmarking web service Delicious, which was purchased from Yahoo! in 2011, and Zeen.com, which provides web-based software that assists in magazine design. Hurley has described AVOS as a "sandbox" that permits a team of designers and programmers to develop new products quickly using a common set of tools. Hurley is also reported to be involved with US F1 Team, a proposed Formula One racing team that was granted permission to enter the 2010 season. Based in Charlotte, North Carolina, US F1

Affiliation: YouTube

Chad Hurley, Steve Chen, and Jawed Karim met during the late 1990s, when Hurley worked as a designer and Chen and Karim were software engineers for PayPal. After PayPal was sold to eBay, the three devised a Website that would permit anyone to post video online.

YouTube was launched in November 2005. The site grew rapidly in popularity. By July 2006, YouTube was reporting that more than sixty-five thousand new videos were being uploaded to the website daily and more than 100 million videos were being viewed each day. YouTube proved easy to use, and as a result many videos became very popular, with viewers who enjoyed the video forwarding sending links to it to friends and family members. The launch of YouTube coincided with the proliferation of cameras as a feature of cellular telephones, which meant many consumers were able to shoot video in many locations.

YouTube was purchased by Google, which has allowed the video-sharing site to operate independently while connecting many of YouTube's features with its network of services.

Team secured a base for operations, announced conditional deals with drivers, and launched its own official YouTube channel. Despite this, the team soon dismissed all employees and revealed that it would not be participating in the 2010 Formula One season.

PERSONAL LIFE

Shortly after joining PayPal, Hurley met Kathy Clark, the daughter of James H. Clark, the founder of Silicon Graphics, Netscape Communications Corporation, and Healtheon. Hurley and Clark were married in 2000 and later had two children.

Hurley has long enjoyed athletics and sports, both as a participant and as an observer. When he was enrolled at Twin Valley High School, his cross-country team was the Pennsylvania Interscholastic Athletic Association (PIAA) champion. Hurley continued to run competitively as a member of the Indiana University of Pennsylvania cross-country team. A longtime fan of Formula One racing, Hurley invested briefly in a proposed team, and rumors persist that he will soon become more involved in the sport. Hurley's love of design has him involved in numerous projects, including

Hlaska, a clothing firm that specializes in shirts, jackets, and bags. Anthony Mazzei founded Hlaska with Hurley, and the two continue to operate it via both the website and brick-and-mortar stores.

Stephen T. Schroth

FURTHER READING

Andrews, L. *I Know Who You Are and I Saw What You Did: Social Networks and the Death of Privacy*. New York: Free Press, 2011. Print. An examination of how social networks and other web tools empower the average citizen.

Chayko, M. *Portable Communities: The Social Dynamics of Online and Mobile Communications*. Albany: State U of New York P, 2008. Print. Explores how conceptions of community have become redefined in response to social networking, blogging, video sharing, and other web tools.

Christakis, N. A., and J. H. Fowler. *Connected: The Surprising Power of Our Social Networks and How They Shape Our Lives*. Boston: Little, Brown, 2009. Print. Looks at how collaboration and participation in social networking enhance an individual's effectiveness.

Kelsy, T. *Social Networking Spaces: From Facebook to Twitter and Everything in Between*. New York: Apress, 2010. Print. An introduction to some of the leading social networking websites (including Facebook, YouTube, and Twitter) and explains how to use them for social, business, or academic purposes.

Turow, J. *The Daily You: How the New Advertising Industry Is Defining Your Identity and Your Worth*. New Haven: Yale UP, 2011. Print. Investigates how today's customized media environment affects consumer power and looks at how the data are collected.

J

VAN JACOBSON

Redesigner of the transmission-control protocol

Born: Date and place unknown
Died: -
Primary Field: Internet
Specialty: Applications
Primary Company/Organization: Lawrence Berkeley National Laboratory

INTRODUCTION

Although his name lacks the public recognition of many of the giants of the late twentieth and early twenty-first century technology revolution, Van Jacobson played an important role in bringing the World Wide Web to the global public. His work on redesigning the transmission-control protocol (TCP) and expanding its scope was instrumental in providing the means of digital communication that came to be known as the Internet. Jacobson's technology, which involved the development of what is popularly known as Jacobson's algorithms, made it possible for the Internet to continue to expand without collapsing in the late 1980s. His work on networking led him to create diagnostic tools such as traceroute, tcpdump, and pathchar. Jacobson has also been responsible for creating various media technologies used on the Internet, including Mbone. He has continued to work to make computer networking and the Internet stabler with projects such as the development of content-centric networking, which improves Internet performance and stability by identifying data and cutting down on redundancy.

EARLY LIFE

Van Jacobson first began to make a name for himself while working at the Lawrence Berkeley National Laboratory as part of the lab's Network Research Group. He remained at that facility for twenty-five years. Part of his responsibilities involved leading the team that developed "multicast backbone" (Mbone) and working on Internet multimedia tools such as Vic, Vat, and wb. While at the Lawrence Berkeley National Laboratory, Jacobson worked closely with the Computer Research Group of the University of California, Berkeley.

Van Jacobson.

In the early 1990s, Jacobson transferred to the networking giant Cisco Systems, where he served as the chief scientist. Cisco had been founded in 1984 by a married couple, Len Bosack and Sandy Lerner. At Cisco, Jacobson was responsible for working on applications such as quality of service (QoS) and voice services.

LIFE'S WORK

The transmission-control protocol (TCP) was invented by Vinton Cerf and Robert Kahn, who subsequently became known as the fathers of the Internet, in 1972–73. The Internet protocol (IP) eventually became familiar to Internet users who learned the purpose of IP addresses. In 1985, what would become the Internet was actually ARPANET, and it was being operated by the U.S. Department of Defense. At the time, Jacobson was teaching at the University of California at Berkeley, one of the research institutions granted access to ARPANET. He became frustrated at the network's slow speeds when he tried to upload class material for his students. He turned that frustration into action and began working on ways to solve the problem.

In 1988, as the Internet began to be more crowded with constantly increasing traffic, it faced potential collapse. That year, Jacobson presented a paper on congestion avoidance and control, which had a major impact on the industry. His TCP/IP flow-control algorithms redesigned the original TCP, expanding the scope of the work of Cerf and Kahn and allowing the Internet to avoid collapse. By 2012, some 90 percent of Internet service providers had become dependent on Jacobson's redesigned TCP for operating their networks. Professionals employed in Internet research and development also continue to use diagnostic tools developed by Jacobson. Furthermore, his work on multimedia applications has become the standard for work done by other developers.

In 1999, an additional problem with the Internet surfaced as new technologies were developed for streaming media. Traditionally, data being sent over the Internet reacted to increased traffic by slowing its own speed, but computers streaming data continued to demand right of way, decreasing transmission speed only slightly. The result was that data transmission for other Internet users became slower as streaming demands increased. As cable modems and the Integrated Services Digital Network (ISDN), through telephone lines, replaced the dial-up modems of the past, streaming had the potential to create Internet gridlock. Jacobson responded to this problem by insisting that incentives for regulating Internet traffic needed to be put in place before streaming media became the road hog of the Internet.

In 2002, Jacobson helped found Packet Design. The company had been the brainchild of technology entrepreneurs Judy Estrin, who had been the chief technology officer at Cisco Systems, and her husband, Bill Carrico, a computer scientist. Initial backing for Packet Design, which focuses on improving the reliability, efficiency, and predictability of IP networks, came from James Barksdale, the former chief executive officer (CEO) of Netscape, and Bill Joy, chief scientist at Sun Microsystems. Packet Design ultimately raised $44 million from sources that included Advanced Technologies, Allegis Capital, Juniper Networks, Masthead Venture Partners, and the Mayfield Fund. As the chief scientist at Packet Design, Jacobson worked with a number of former Cisco colleagues on solving problems brought on by the growth of the Internet. With additional backing from a number of Menlo Park companies, including Advanced Technology Ventures, 3i, and Foundation Capital, Packet Design spun off Precision I/O in March 2003 for the purpose of improving Ethernet technologies, which provide the basis for communication among networks connecting to the Internet. In addition to cofounding Precision I/O, Jacobson served as its chief scientific officer.

Jacobson has also made contributions to computer networking by his work on improving performance through the use of network channels. In 2006, he was designated as a research fellow at PARC, formerly the Palo Alto Research Center, a division of Xerox. At PARC, Jacobson assumed responsibility for leading research in the area of content-centric networking. The same year he joined PARC, he presented "A New Way to Look at Networking," which Google Tech Talk made available throughout the Internet. It reportedly created a storm among those involved in network research and development.

In 2012, Jacobson introduced the concept of content-centric networking in the January issue of the *Communications of the ACM*. He suggests in the article that performance, salability, and security could all be improved by replacing the present practice of retrieving chunks of information with his method of retrieving information over the Internet according to content. He and his team are attempting to change the way the public understands the ways in which computer networks operate.

Affiliation: Lawrence Berkeley National Laboratory

Van Jacobson spent twenty-five years of his professional life at the Lawrence Berkeley National Laboratory, which was founded on the Berkeley campus of the University of California in 1927 when physicist Ernest O. Lawrence, the inventor of the cyclotron, was hired to head the first of the national laboratories established by the U.S. Department of Energy. By the twenty-first century, the facility was involved in advancing scientific research and development in the fields of health, technology, and the environment.

In March 1992, Allison Mankin, a member of the Internet Engineering Task Force, was in an advanced state of pregnancy and was unable to travel to an upcoming conference being held by the organization in San Diego, California. She suggested that she and others who could not attend the meeting might be able to benefit from research ideas presented via multicasting. Steve Casner of the University of Southern California Information Sciences Institute and Steve Deering of the Palo Alto Research Center (PARC) were charged with turning Mankin's concept into reality. The development of the multicasting software behind what came to be called Mbone was left to Van Jacobson, who was then employed at the Lawrence Berkeley National Laboratory, and his fellow researchers.

The use of Mbone was initially limited to universities and large computer-research laboratories because it required high-powered workstations and high-speed data connections. The use of multicasting through Mbone was soon apparent within the entertainment industry. Concerts such as one performed by the Rolling Stones in Dallas, Texas, in 1994, proved an ideal venue for the new technology. Politicians, including President Bill Clinton, Vice President Al Gore, and a prime minister of Sweden, also saw the advantage of broadcasting to a wide audience using the new technology. Other uses for Mbone's capabilities surfaced when a surgeon based in San Francisco, California, performed a complex liver surgery that was sent over Mbone to physicians as far away as London and Sweden.

Jacobson insists that one of the major problems on the Internet is redundancy. As an example, he cites an event that occurred during NBC's broadcasting of the 2006 Winter Olympics. When skier Bode Miller was disqualified from an Alpine event, some five thousand identical videos of the event were uploaded to NBC's server, which was incapable of recognizing the redundancy. With Jacobson's content-centric networking, a router is granted the capability of rooting out redundancy by allowing the data rather, than the server, to function as the point of identification in the communication process between Internet users and their data sources.

PERSONAL LIFE

In 2001, ACM's Special Interest Group on Data Communication (SIGCOMM) honored Jacobson's contributions to the industry with a Lifetime Achievement Award, recognizing his work on "protocol architecture and congestion control." Two years later, Jacobson received the Institute of Electrical and Electronics Engineers' Koji Kobayashi Computers and Communication Award in recognition of his contributions toward solving the problems with congestion on the Internet. In 2004, Jacobson was named to the National Academy of Engineering. In 2012, the Jacobson was inducted into the Internet Hall of Fame (along with Cerf), paying homage to his contributions to the development of networking performance and scaling.

Elizabeth Rholetter Purdy

FURTHER READING

"Buffer Blast: What's Wrong with the Internet?" *Communications of the ACM* 55.2 (2012): n. pag. Print. Roundtable discussion on problems faced in Internet development.

"Extreme Peer-to-Peer." *PC Magazine* 26.14 (2007): n. pag. Print. Brief explanation of Jacobson's work on Content-Centric Networking. Illustrated.

Hafner, Katie. "The M Bone: Can't You Hear It Knocking?" *Newsweek* 124.23 (1994): n. pag. Print. Overview of the development of the Mbone. Illustrated.

Jacobson, Van, et al. "Networking Named Content." *Communications of the ACM* 55.1 (2012): n. pag. Print. Discusses the field of computer networking.

King, Cecilia. "Former Executives from Top Tech Firms Launch Fourth Networking Start-Up." *San Jose Mercury News* 13 June 2000: n. pag. Print. Focuses on the creation of Packet Design.

Robinson, Sara. "Multimedia Transmissions Are Driving Internet toward Gridlock." *New York Times* 23 Aug. 1999. Print. Examination of Jacobson's role in avoiding Internet gridlock with the advent of streaming media.

JEFF JAFFE

CEO of the World Wide Web Consortium (W3C)

Born: 1954; place unknown
Died: -
Primary Field: Business and commerce
Specialty: Management, executives, and investors
Primary Company/Organization: World Wide Web
  Consortium

INTRODUCTION

*Since entering the information technology industry in
1980, Jeff Jaffe has been a committed researcher and
activist. For more than thirty years, his research-guided philosophy has centered on creating an efficient and
rapid Internet environment. His skills have caught the
attention of numerous worldwide leaders and in 2010
propelled him to a position as chief executive officer
(CEO) at the World Wide Web Consortium (W3C).*

EARLY LIFE

After graduating from high school, Jeff Jaffe was accepted into the undergraduate mathematics program at
the Massachusetts Institute of Technology (MIT), from
which he earned his bachelor's degree in 1976. He remained at MIT for graduate studies and completed a
master's in computer science in 1977. Two years later, he graduated with a Ph.D. in computer science. As
a graduate student, Jaffe received a National Science
Foundation graduate fellowship, which helped him
conduct detailed research centered on computer algorithms, languages, and the other processes associated
with computers.

LIFE'S WORK

Jaffe's first job upon the completion of his doctorate
was at IBM, where he worked in the Computer Science
Department at the Thomas J. Watson Research Center
in Yorktown Heights, New York. He was a researcher
and focused on network algorithms and combinatorial
optimization. His interests centered on computer communications and distribution. As he developed further
experience, he became the manager of the Network Architecture and Protocols Group, and in 1982 he received
an award for work in dynamic routing.

In 1984, Jaffe worked overseas for a year at the IBM
Scientific Center in Haifa, Israel. After returning to New
York, he became the manager of the IBM Communi-
cations Systems Department. He continued to progress

through IBM, and in July 1990 he was named the director of large systems and communications, which made
him responsible for developing the research plans for
future computer networks. Later with IBM, he became
the vice president of systems and software research, introducing the company to new software and advanced
technology. For example, Jaffe's division introduced
MuxMaster, a fiber-optic technology that offered a
much quicker and more efficient Internet connection for
business users.

By the late 1990s, Jaffe was leading research projects that focused on developing greater security for the
online environment. He also served as IBM's general
manager for the SecureWay business unit. Jaffe assisted
in the development of SecureWay FirstSecure, which
was a framework designed to offer businesses state-of-
the-art methods to secure entire commercial networks.
It was unique in that it centralized the security capabilities of servers on one specific network.

During this time, Jaffe had gained a reputation in
the computer industry as an individual with broad

Jeff Jaffe.

expertise and well-established connections. As a Fellow of both the Association for Computing Machinery (ACM) and the Institute of Electrical and Electronics Engineers (IEEE), he was regarded by many U.S. government officials as someone who could assist in developing a secure and efficient Internet network. In 1997, President Bill Clinton appointed Jaffe to serve on the Advisory Committee to the President's Commission on Critical Infrastructure Protection. In this capacity, Jaffe assisted in the development of methods to combat cyberterrorism along with designs to create a secure telecommunications network. Jaffe has also been involved in various government-funded research studies that have centered on telecommunications research.

In 2000, Jaffe's long career at IBM ended after he accepted a position with Bell Laboratories' Advanced Technologies Group. He immediately became the vice president of Bell Labs Research. One year later, he was named president of Bell Labs Research and Advanced Technologies. He led a team of experts who worked on innovations for the information technology industry, focusing on improved security and wireless services. Specifically, Jaffe and his team worked on methods to integrate the components of television, telephones, and the Internet.

Jaffe's arrival at Bell Labs occurred during a time of transition for the facility. By 2003, the research budget had shrunk from $350 million to $115 million and the facility's once highly complex and broad research projects had become specialized and focused on certain applications that could create revenue. Although the facility had cut the workforce in the United States, the management began to expand Bell's international operations. In 2004, Jaffe announced the opening of a Bell Labs research center in Dublin, Ireland. One year later, he opened another facility in India. His commitment to leading the development of highly effective network security attracted the attention of the International Telecommunication Union (ITU), and in 2004 the ITU announced that the Bell Labs Network Security Model would be introduced on the ITU platform.

In late 2005, Jaffe resigned from Bell Labs after accepting the position of executive vice president and chief technology officer at Novell. Working for this large multinational software company offered Jaffe new challenges, including the chance to lead new product development. In July 2006, a fresh version of the commercial desktop, Linux, was offered to business customers. The development of open source software was also at the forefront of Jaffe's work. Months after

---

Affiliation: World Wide Web Consortium

Founded in 1994 at the Massachusetts Institute of Technology (MIT), the World Wide Web Consortium (W3C) is an organization focused on realizing the full potential of the World Wide Web. The W3C develops standards and protocols for the web in order for it to be administered and transformed uniformly. The organization is administered by MIT, the European Research Consortium for Informatics and Mathematics, and Keio University. From these centers of excellence, the sixty-nine employees of the W3C work to make the Web a standardized and highly efficient information medium. W3C has relationships with dozens of organizations, including the Federal Communications Commission (FCC), the European Commission, and United Nations Educational, Scientific and Cultural Organization (UNESCO), which assist in the development of the web.

The founder and director of W3C is Tim Berners-Lee, who is also considered the inventor, along with Robert Cailliau, of the World Wide Web. In 2010, Jeff Jaffe, formerly of IBM, Bell Laboratories, and Novell, was named the new CEO of the organization. Today, the W3C is focused on updating and standardizing cascading style sheets (CSS) and hypertext markup language through HTML5, two technologies that are vital to the operations of many modern devices and applications, from computers to mobile phones. As the World Wide Web becomes even more diverse and unique in its features, the W3C is constantly forced to adapt to the changing environment.

---

beginning at Novell, Jaffe announced the release of a new Open Enterprise Server to Novell customers. He also led the development of projects that provided more efficient servers for computer users, including devices that would reduce power consumption.

In early 2010, Jaffe left Novell to become the CEO of the World Wide Web Consortium (W3C). Founded at MIT in 1994, W3C has focused on the Internet's becoming an international medium available to all. Jaffe's goal is to strengthen the World Wide Web by introducing new technology through a creative and driven philosophy. Most important, he has been committed to advancing the security features of the Internet. One of the major goals of the consortium is to create a widely available open access platform. Since 2010, W3C has focused on developing the new HTML5.

PERSONAL LIFE

Jaffe maintains a quiet life outside his business interests. Every few months, on his own personal blog at W3C, he updates interested parties about the advances of the W3C and offers observations about the World Wide Web. He is recognized by many as one of the most important people in the information technology industry.

Gavin Wilk

FURTHER READING

Berman, Dennis K. "At Bell Labs, Hard Times Take Toll on Pure Research." *Wall Street Journal* 23 May 2003. Web. 20 Aug. 2012. Reveals the financial difficulties that Bell Labs faced in the early 2000s and how the facility was forced to adopt new research measures in order to cut costs.

Galli, Peter. "Novell's vision of the Future." *eWeek* 24 Mar. 2008. Web. 20 Aug. 2012. Details Jaffe's talk at the 2008 BrainShare Conference, in which he detailed Novell's commitment to open source software and new servers.

Gehani, Nairan. *Bell Labs: Life in the Crown Jewel.* Summit: Silicon, 2003. Print. Insightful firsthand account of Bell Labs and the work environment that existed in the facility.

Grover, George A., and Jeffrey M. Jaffe. "Standoff and Standoff Resolution in Deadlock Free Networks with Virtual Circuits." *IEEE Transactions on Communications* 40.4 (1992). Print. Technical paper cowritten by Jaffe that describes how computer deadlocks occur and the steps that can be taken to prevent this phenomenon.

Larsen, Amy K. "IBM Integrates E-Business Security." *Information Week Online* 25 Jan. 1999. Web. 20 Aug. 2012. Describes the capabilities of IBM's SecureWay FirstSecure framework, a project led by Jaffe.

Lohr, Steve. "In a New Web World, No Application Is an Island." *New York Times* 27 Mar. 2011. Print. Article describes the new applications in development for the web, including HTML5.

Lyons, Tom. "Bell Labs' Arrival Creates Buzz of Activity in Irish R&D Circles." *Irish Independent* 8 July 2004. Print. Includes an interview with Jaffe that took place in Dublin, Ireland. The piece focuses on the international range of Bell Labs.

McAllister, Neil. "Open Enterprise: Can New Executives Deliver on Novell's Open Source Vision? New CTO Jeffrey Jaffe Needs to Unify the Disparate Ximian Open Source Teams." *InfoWorld* 27.48 (2005): n. pag. Print. Article that explains the role that Jaffe was expected to play in revitalizing Novell.

National Research Council Committee on Telecommunications Research and Development, R. W. Lucky, and Jon Eisenberg. *Renewing U.S. Telecommunications Research.* Washington, DC: National Academies Press, 2006. Print. Research study that included Jaffe and centers on how the United States should improve the country's telecommunications research capabilities and practices.

National Research Council Committee on the Role of Information Technology in Responding to Terrorism, John L. Hennessy, David A. Patterson, and Herbert Lin. *Information Technology for Counterterrorism: Immediate Actions and Future Possibilities.* Washington, DC: National Academies Press, 2003. Print. Research study that included Jaffe and that examines how the United States can prepare for a terrorist act through the new advancement in technology.

Shankland, Stephen. "Jeff Jaffe Lights a Fire Under Web Standardization." *CNet News* 5 Mar. 2012. Web. 20 Aug. 2012. Offers an interview with Jaffe that centers on the development of HTML.

Wessner, Charles W., and National Research Council Committee on The Telecommunications Challenge. *The Telecommunications Challenge: Changing Technologies and Evolving Policies.* Washington, DC: National Academies Press, 2006. Print. Research study that included Jaffe and examined how the United States could strengthen its telecommunications systems, especially the country's broadband capabilities.

XENI JARDIN

Coeditor of Boing Boing

Born: August 5, 1970; Richmond, Virginia
Died: -
Primary Field: Internet

Specialty: News and entertainment
Primary Company/Organization: Boing Boing

Introduction

Digital media commentator Xeni Jardin is a contributor to Wired, *a correspondent for National Public Radio (NPR), and a frequent guest commentator on television news broadcasts. She is the coeditor of the blog Boing Boing, as well as a culture journalist with publications in numerous major venues. She also hosts and executive produces Boing Boing Video.*

Early Life

Xeni Jardin was born on August 5, 1970, in Richmond, Virginia, to artist Glenn B. Hamm, Jr., and Monica Rumsey. Her father taught art education at Virginia Commonwealth University, spent much of the family's money on painting supplies and antique machines, and was often difficult to live with. He died of amyotrophic lateral sclerosis (Lou Gehrig's disease) in 1980, when Jardin was ten. As a teenager, she pierced her nose, dyed her hair, and began using drugs, leaving home at fourteen and staying with one friend or acquaintance after another, sometimes squatting in abandoned buildings. She was active in the Richmond punk scene, writing for zines and building her own art portfolio, earning a scholarship to the San Francisco Art Institute. Xeni Jardin is not her birth name; she took it in honor of her mentor and father figure, Munir Xochipillicueponi Quetzalkanbalam, during travels in Guatemala. She met him in San Francisco, and he encouraged her to get clean and sober, helping to support her in return.

Jardin studied journalism at San Diego State University after traveling with Quetzalkanbalam, taking courses in computer science. The Internet did not interest her much until she took a job as a web developer in southern California. As the tech boom of the late 1990s swept the country, she began freelance writing for various publications and left web development to take a job with Rising Tide Studios, the parent company of the *Silicon Alley Reporter*, a publication for which she had been a contributing editor. For Rising Tide, she coordinated high-profile industry events in New York and Los Angeles. In 2001, Jardin left Rising Tide to focus on journalism, which led to her joining the Boing Boing blog in 2002.

Life's Work

Boing Boing had begun as a magazine, with a website launching in 1995 and a blog following in 2000. Founder Mark Frauenfelder was one of the coeditors of the blog, along with Cory Doctorow, David Pescowitz, and Jardin.

Xeni Jardin.

Jardin's stories for Boing Boing have ranged from the Flash video uploaded by the Korean Friendship Association advertising North Korean vacations to Lars Ulrich's defense of Beatallica, Ullrich's Milwaukee band performing Beatles songs in the style of Metallica. Although Jardin is not the first to compare blogs to the fanzines of the 1980s and 1990s, for her the comparison is not off the cuff or abstracted but intimate, drawing on personal experience with both. While her writing and interests have evolved since the fanzine era, it seems fair to say that, more than most, she approaches her blog entries with much of the same attitude as a zine writer.

On September 15, 2004, Jardin was a passenger on a zero-gravity flight 32,000 feet above the earth, operated by ZERO-G, as part of the company's launch. She wrote about the experience extensively for Boing Boing, in a series of entries and photographs, as well as speaking to NPR about it. She now lists zero gravity as an interest on her home page.

In 2010, Jardin was a guest on NPR's *All Things Considered* and looked back on the major tech stories of the previous decade. Among the topics she discussed were the AOL/Time Warner merger, personal digital assistants (PDAs), and Napster. For a time, Jardin hosted "Xeni Tech," a segment on NPR's *Day to Day* covering tech-related stories. In 2011, she covered the "pepper-spraying cop" (Lieutenant John Pike), who pepper-sprayed Occupy demonstrators at the University of California at Davis, and the Photoshop meme manipulating his image in retribution.

Jardin has occasionally been the subject of criticism and controversy, as is to be expected of any prolific blogger. One of the more serious controversies occurred in June 2008, when sex blogger Violet Blue posted to her blog that Boing Boing had removed from its site all mentions of her, as well as posts she had written for them—a total of at least seventy entries, which were not deleted but "unpublished" (the data still existed but were no longer viewable on the site). Much of the controversy revolved not around the removal per se but

around Boing Boing's odd handling of it: The site announced that Violet Blue had behaved in a way that prompted Boing Boing to remove all references in order to distance the site from her, and Jardin added that she hoped the reasons would not be made public. It is worth noting that of the posts removed, few were about Violet Blue. In most cases she was simply mentioned as having e-mailed in a link to the story the entry was about, which means an unrelated story was removed from the site in order to avoid mentioning the person who had brought it to Boing Boing's attention. Other entries mention Violet Blue in passing. In a few cases, the removed posts reference comments Violet Blue made in Boing Boing's comment section, along with other reader comments. In one case, the only mention of Violet

Affiliation: Boing Boing

Boing Boing describes itself as "a directory of wonderful things," and entries range from tech news that is overlooked or misunderstood by the mainstream media to links to interesting oddities found online. Simply sifting through the links and stories e-mailed to the site by readers takes hours per day.

Boing Boing began as a zine in 1988, subtitled "The World's Greatest Neurozine." Long before *Wired* launched, *Boing Boing*, *2600*, *Phrack*, and to a lesser extent *Mondo 2000* were the periodicals most strongly associated with hacker culture and cyberculture. Over the course of fifteen irregularly released issues, it covered technology and gadgets in a way the mainstream media (even science journals) did not, as well as liberalism, science fiction, and futurism. Founder Mark Frauenfelder also coedited 1995's *Happy Mutant Handbook*, worked as an editor at *Wired* from 1993 to 1998 (all of the *Boing Boing* coeditors have been *Wired* writers), and worked with Billy Idol on his 1993 album *Cyberpunk*. More recently, he has become the editor in chief of O'Reilly Media's *MAKE Magazine*. Other editors of the magazine incarnation of Boing Boing included media critic Gareth Branwyn, who became an editor at *Mondo 2000* and collaborated with Frauenfelder on *The Happy Mutant Handbook* and Billy Idol's *Cyberpunk* (and today at *MAKE Magazine*, where he is the editorial director); activist Jon Lebkowsky, who hosted the *Factsheet Five* forum on the WELL in the 1990s; and computer scientist Paco Nathan. Nathan and Lebkowsky had also cofounded FringeWare, an early commercial website, in 1992.

The website for Boing Boing was built in 1995, and a year later it replaced the magazine. In January 2000, Boing Boing founder Frauenfelder began the Boing Boing blog, soon adding three coeditors: writer Cory Doctorow (winner of the 2000 John W. Campbell Award for Best New Writer, awarded to science-fiction writers), journalist David Pescowitz, and journalist Xeni Jardin. A year before the blog began, Frauenfelder had written an article about the web tools used in blogging; the editors to whom he submitted it at *The Industry Standard* rejected it because blogging did not seem like a significant activity.

For a lengthy period, beginning in September 2003, comments were disabled at Boing Boing because of the staff's dissatisfaction with impersonators and arguments. In August 2007, the site relaunched with Teresa Nielsen Hayden (editor and blogger at *Making Light*) moderating the comments section. By this time, it had twice won the Blog of the Year Award in the Bloggies, and it had become one of the most prominent, most widely read blogs on the Internet.

In 2004, Boing Boing incorporated as Happy Mutants LLC, with John Battelle as business manager. Advertising was added to the site, paying expenses and generating income for the staff. Boing Boing also offers several podcasts, including Boing Boing Boing (news about the blog), Get Illuminated (interviews), and Gweek (a discussion of geek culture). Boing Boing TV was added to the lineup of content in 2007, consisting of video segments produced by the editors and airing online and on Virgin America flights.

Blue in the entry is in a list of thirteen podcast interviews, one of which is with Blue.

Jardin had written most or all of the posts referring to Violet Blue. It was her decision to take the material down, and she had done so a year before Violet Blue's mention of it—presumably Blue did not realize it at the time that it was done. According to Jardin, she did not consult her coeditors before removing the posts. Serious issues were raised about media transparency, and Jardin's defense that Boing Boing felt like a personal blog—by implication, not subject to the same expectations one would place on professional journalism—did little to assuage those concerns. "This is a directory of wonderful things," Jardin wrote, referencing the blog's subtitle. "If we no longer think something is wonderful, we have every right to remove it from this directory." Eventually, the original Violet Blue–related posts were not the only ones removed; the posts about the removal, and the various defenses offered, were removed as well, silencing the dissent.

Although Jardin is sometimes criticized for her handling of comments on Boing Boing, she is also the originator of one of Boing Boing's most enduring memes, the unicorn chaser. The unicorn chaser is a picture of a unicorn posted after a post or comment containing a disturbing image, in order to cleanse the palate, as it were.

On December 1, 2011, Jardin was diagnosed with breast cancer. She announced the news via Twitter, having posted a photo of herself at the breast cancer screening clinic Pink Lotus the day before ("Instagramm[ing] my mammogram"). She continued to document the process of dealing with cancer, first taking the anticancer drug Taxol and later undergoing surgery.

Recent topics Jardin has covered on Boing Boing include the recurring nightmare Neil Armstrong had in the years leading up to the Moon landing, a LEGO film retelling the Lord of the Rings saga from the Orcs' point of view, a discussion of Lance Armstrong's Livestrong organization from her perspective as a cancer patient, and news of a cancer epidemic among Tasmanian devils.

Jardin is also a public speaker on the topics of cancer, networked culture, tech, and media.

PERSONAL LIFE
Jardin's brother Carl M. Hamm is a disc jockey in Richmond, Virginia. Jardin is interested in fine art and languages. She is an avid music fan and has guest-hosted on the Santa Monica public radio station KCRW (including the punk rock band Bad Brains in her playlist). In addition to blogging at Boing Boing, she maintains a Tumblr site, xenijardin.tumblr.com. Her favorite film is Jean-Luc Godard's *Alphaville*.

Bill Kte'pi

FURTHER READING
Jardin, Xeni. "Everything Moves to Live." *Poetry* Oct. 2011: n. pag. Print. Jardin writes about her favorite movie, *Alphaville*.

---. "NYT: 'Men Invented the Internet.'" 3 June 2012. *Boing Boing*. Web. 20 Aug. 2012. This response to a *New York Times* article is essential reading on the importance of women in the tech industry.

Rosenberg, Scott. *Say Everything: How Blogging Began, What It's Becoming, and Why It Matters*. New York: Broadway, 2010. Print. A history of blogging and of the major blogs, such as Boing Boing, by a journalist and Salon.com cofounder, without the hype, misconceptions, or fast-money tips of most other books.

SANDY JEN
Cofounder of Meebo

Born: 1981?; Silver Spring, Maryland
Died: -
Primary Field: Internet
Specialty: Social media
Primary Company/Organization: Meebo

INTRODUCTION
Sandy Jen is an entrepreneur who, together with cofounders Seth Sternberg and Elaine Wherry, launched the first web-based instant-messaging product, Meebo Messenger, in September 2005. Meebo represented a revolutionary approach to person-to-person (P2P) communication in the days before social media was a household term. As chief technology officer, Jen drove the company's back-end development and innovation as it continued to launch new products to meet the evolving communication and information needs of users. In June 2012, Jen joined Google's technology

team, working on Google+, following that company's acquisition of Meebo. She shares her experiences as a female technology leader with students and young entrepreneurs.

EARLY LIFE

Sandy Jen was born and raised in Silver Spring, Maryland. The daughter of two professional engineers, she grew up in a structured, goal-focused, achievement-oriented environment. She was a diligent student in school and from a very early age focused her attention and efforts on college. She strove not only to attain top grades but also to log extracurricular activities and prepare herself for acing college entrance exams and essays.

When she entered high school, Jen embraced the opportunity to participate in the institution's four-year computer science program. There she learned her first programming languages: BASIC, Pascal, and C++. Based on that programming foundation, Jen chose to skip the introductory courses and enrolled in the accelerated computer programming track when she began attending college at Stanford University in California. She worked as a teacher's assistant in some classes and ultimately decided to make computer science her major. Jen graduated from Stanford University with a bachelor's degree in computer science in 2003.

During her college career, Jen devoted herself to two things: academic achievement and preparing for the future. For Jen, that meant ensuring she that was well positioned to secure a solid job with a good company in her field. Once engaged in the professional workforce, however, Jen quickly became disenchanted by the realities of life as a corporate employee. She began to reevaluate her environment and her priorities. In the end, she decided that she would not be able to achieve her goals for changing the world from the confines of a cubicle.

LIFE'S WORK

After her graduation from Stanford in 2003, Jen began working as an enterprise software developer for semiconductor company Xilinx in San Jose, California. In 2012, Jen told Matthew Wise of FounderLY that the reality of sitting in a cubicle all day staring at a computer monitor made her realize that she wanted more. At about the same time, the husband of a college acquaintance, Elaine Wherry, had been contacted by his friend Seth Sternberg about recruiting some top Stanford talent to work on a start-up.

When Sternberg, Wherry, and Jen eventually got together to discuss the potential for a partnership,

they immediately recognized that their vision, talents, and personalities complemented each other. The three began to brainstorm and evaluate ideas for creating a consumer-focused technology start-up in their spare time. They purchased several servers with their personal credit cards and registered the domain name Meebo right away, even although the details of the company had not been determined. The three met weekly in their free time to discuss their options and approaches. Initially, they focused on backup software. Then they shifted their attention to peer-to-peer file sharing. By March 2005, the team had decided on instant-messaging facilitation as the core of the business.

At that time, social media was a fledgling industry. Individuals seeking to share information through real-time communication relied mainly on instant messaging (IM). However, the IM capability was desktop-specific, meaning that the application had to be installed on both the user's and the recipient's desktops in order for the information exchange to occur. The idea behind Meebo was to use the Internet to expand and facilitate access to IM by users, regardless of their physical location or individual desktop software. Jen had a strong personal need for such a service and recognized that others would as well.

Sandy Jen.

203

With that goal in mind, Jen, Wherry, and Sternberg spent the next several months developing their product while still working at their regular, full-time jobs. Jen and Wherry left their positions in August 2005 and spent a month completing the coding required to get Meebo ready for launch the following month.

Working on a shoestring budget, Jen and her Meebo cofounders used blog posts on Digg and other sites to promote the availability of Meebo Messenger, their new web-based IM service via Meebo.com. It was the first product of its kind and filled an immediate need in the marketplace. Meebo's innovative approach of asking for—and acting upon—user feedback early in its existence also spurred positive chat both in technology

---

Affiliation: Meebo

Seth Sternberg, Elaine Wherry, and Sandy Jen founded Meebo in September 2005. All three were Stanford University students who connected after graduation to partner on the creation of a consumer-focused technology start-up. Sternberg's expertise was in the area of finance and business management; Wherry's skills were centered on the front-end user experience; and Jen's contribution was concentrated in the area of back-end engineering.

As early as 2003, the threesome registered the name Meebo and purchased infrastructure in the form of two servers. After two years of development and prototypes in other areas, the team decided in early 2005 to create a web-based instant-messaging (IM) client that would enable users to communicate via IM regardless of their desktop setups. It was a revolutionary idea in an era before today's Web 2.0 mania.

Meebo Messenger was an instant success, attracting tens of thousands of users within its first few weeks. By December 2005, Sequoia Capital became Meebo's first external investor. From 2005 through 2012, Meebo continued to launch innovative products, such as MeeboBar, which is designed to coordinate relevant content for users and facilitate information exchange while engaging site publishers and advertisers.

Meebo was purchased by Google in June 2012. The new owners planned to phase out most of Meebo's product line and put their efforts behind MeeboBar. Sternberg and Jen joined Google as part of the acquisition, working on Google+.

---

circles and among consumer user groups. Within twenty-four hours of the launch, Meebo.com had attracted some five hundred users. Within weeks, tens of thousands of people were using Meebo to communicate with each other. By the end of the year, Meebo was being courted by investors and had accepted funding from Sequoia Capital.

Jen, Wherry, and Sternberg used those dollars to grow the company. As vice president of engineering for Meebo, Jen took the lead on back-end technology development. With the advent of Web 2.0 and the soaring success of social media, she quickly recognized that the way people were communicating with one another was changing and that Meebo had to expand beyond IM. She also realized that Meebo's infrastructure made it uniquely positioned to provide other innovative products designed to help users connect, navigate the Internet, and hone in on information specifically relevant to them. Jen told Christina Warren in a 2011 interview for Mashable Business that her vision for Meebo was to create an Internet that is truly driven by users and their interests rather than algorithms and assumptions. To answer that call, Jen and her team developed numerous mobile applications and sharing tools, including MeeboMiniBar, a site check-in product, and MeeboBar, a content platform that connects the user, site publisher, and site advertisers simultaneously. The products helped propel Meebo to nearly two hundred unique utilizations by 2012. As a result, the company expanded its operations to include some two hundred employees in offices across the United States.

By the time Meebo was acquired by Google in June 2012, Jen had assumed the role of chief technology officer. In that capacity, she was responsible for devising and implementing Meebo's engineering development goals and coordinating front- and back-end technology efforts across the company. She and some members of her engineering team are reportedly joining Google as part of the acquisition. She and her team worked with Google+ to transition and evolve the MeeboBar product.

PERSONAL LIFE

Jen is accustomed to the grueling schedule associated with launching and running a business, yet she remains a staunch advocate for maintaining a work-life balance. Her personal pursuits tend to fall on the physical side: yoga, running, rock climbing, and even Ultimate Frisbee. Although she resides in California, Jen has also been a lifelong fan of her hometown-area Major League Baseball team, the Baltimore Orioles.

Jen serves as a guest speaker and mentor to students and fledgling entrepreneurs, with a particular focus on female entrepreneurs in Web 2.0 and other technology-based sectors. In her messages to others, she emphasizes the importance of personal passion, strong self-confidence, excellent team support, and the ability and willingness to listen intuitively to the input of others. She was the recipient of a Founders Fund TechFellow Award in Engineering Leadership in 2009 and continues to rank on lists of important young entrepreneurs.

Shari Parsons Miller

FURTHER READING

Buckman, Rebecca, and Mylene Mangalindan. "Financing Round Values Meebo at $200 Million." *Wall Street Journal*, Eastern edition, May 2008: C3. Print. Talks about Meebo's $200 million investor valuation, $25 million in new investor funding, and the company's potential designs on international expansion into Japan and South Korea.

Cassavoy, Liane. "Meebo Tops in Web-Based IM Services." *PC World* 25.7 (2007): 66. Print. Provides a review of several web-based instant-messaging products and explains why Meebo ranked at the top: because of its viability as an alternative to a desktop instant-messaging client.

Hampton, Alison, Sarah Cooper, and Pauric McGowan. "Female Entrepreneurial Networks and Networking Activity in Technology-Based Ventures." *International Small Business Journal* 27.2 (2009): 193–214. Print. Presents the findings of an interview-based study evaluating female entrepreneurial networks and networking dynamics pertaining to science, engineering, and technology-based businesses.

Jen, Sandy. "Sandy Jen: Chill Out." *Daily Muse* 13 Sept. 2011. Web. 12 Aug. 2012. Jen talks about her personal background, perceptions, and advice to other driven individuals to relax and not put excessive pressure on themselves.

Moscaritolo, Angela. "After Google Acquisition, Meebo Shutting Down July 11." *PC Magazine* 11 June 2012. Print. Discusses the rationale for and basic details of Google's acquisition of Meebo, as well as its plans to discontinue Meebo's product line with the exception of MeeboBar.

Shields, Mike. "Meebo Finds Its Niche." *Mediaweek* 20.28 (2010): 31. Print. Provides an overview of Meebo as an Internet company and highlights the popularity of its web toolbar, which enables sharing of links among social network members.

K

Brewster Kahle

Founder of the Internet Archive and cofounder of Alexa Internet

Born: October 22, 1960; New York, New York
Died: -
Primary Field: Internet
Specialty: Content and data
Primary Company/Organization: Internet Archive

INTRODUCTION

Since the mid-1980s, Brewster Kahle has focused on developing technologies for information discovery and digital libraries. As a digital librarian, he has played a major role in making information easy to find and widely available through the Internet. Kahle is most famous for founding the Internet Archive, a nonprofit digital library with the mission of "universal access to all knowledge." An idealist with focus and discipline, Kahle would like to save a copy of every type of information resource on Earth.

EARLY LIFE

Brewster Kahle was born on October 22, 1960, in New York City and grew up in Scarsdale, New York. He graduated from Scarsdale High School in 1978 and attended the Massachusetts Institute of Technology (MIT). He also took library science courses at Simmons College. Kahle wanted to create a type of technology that would help people, and that led him to the Artificial Intelligence Laboratory, where he studied under Marvin Minsky and Danny Hills. Minsky and Hills taught Kahle two mantras: "Think big" and "What will serve the greatest good?" At the time, the two biggest concepts being discussed by those in technology and futurists were encryption and digital libraries. After graduating

from MIT in 1982 with a bachelor's degree in computer science, Kahle decided to take on both.

LIFE'S WORK

After graduation, Kahle joined Artificial Intelligence Laboratory colleague Hills and five other MIT alumni to form Thinking Machines, a parallel supercomputer

Brewster Kahle.

maker. From 1983 to 1989, Kahle was the lead engineer on the company's main product, the Connection Machine, a series of supercomputers intended for applications in artificial intelligence, symbolic processing, and text searching. The most famous invention created by Thinking Machines, however, was the Wide Area Information Server, or WAIS, system. WAIS was originally developed for supercomputers to give them fast access to very large databases. It was an electronic publishing system that allowed users to ask remote information sources questions in natural language so that the server could retrieve the best-matched documents. WAIS was a precursor to the World Wide Web and modern search engines.

In 1992, Kahle teamed with Bruce Gilliat to found WAIS, Inc., which he sold to America Online in 1995 for $15 million. Kahle used some of that money to move to San Francisco and build Alexa Internet with Gilliat In 1996. Alexa was named after the Library of Alexandria, for Kahle believed that the Internet had the potential to become a repository of knowledge as significant as the library at Alexandria had been to the ancient world. Improving on the WAIS natural language search system, Alexa Internet provided a toolbar that would make suggestions to Internet users regarding popular sites, based on the traffic patterns of its users. Alexa Internet also archived every active website on the Internet. For each website that it archived, Alexa Internet would record the person or company who registered it, how many pages it had, the number of other sites that referred to it, and how frequently it was updated. Kahle donated a copy of this archive to the Library of Congress in 1998. In 1999, Kahle sold Alexa Internet to Amazon.com for $250 million in Amazon stock.

At the same time that he started Alexa, Kahle founded the nonprofit Internet Archive, which he continues to direct. Originally, Kahle worked with Gilliat in developing software to "crawl" and download all publicly accessible Internet pages, the Gopher hierarchy, the Netnews bulletin board system, and downloadable software. These formed the first contents of the Internet Archive. In l999, Kahle decided to collect other digital materials for the archive, starting with the Prelinger Archives, a collection of films about the cultural history of the United States. Today, the Internet Archive contains e-books, text, audio, video, and software. The Internet Archive is of value not only to historians but also to web developers and computer scientists who want to solve Internet infrastructure issues.

In 2001, Kahle implemented the so-called Wayback Machine, named after the time-travel invention used by the characters Sherman and Peabody from the *Rocky and Bullwinkle* cartoons. The Wayback Machine is a service that allows public access to the archived web pages of the past, which the Internet Archive has been gathering since 1996. Kahle was inspired to create the Wayback Machine after visiting the offices of AltaVista (the search provider for Yahoo!), where he saw an enormous computer, the size of five or six Coke machines, used to store and index everything that was on the Web.

The Internet Archive hosts many other projects, including the National Aeronautics and Space Administration's Images Archive, the contract crawling service Archive-It, and the open source wiki library catalog and book information site Open Library. In 2012, the Internet Archive was working on providing information services for the print-disabled.

Kahle is a major supporter of the Open Content Alliance (OCA), a consortium of organizations contributing to a permanent, free, publicly accessible archive of digitized texts. The Internet Archive provides scanning, storage, and access services for the OCA through its website. OCA was founded in reaction to Google Book Search and Google's book digitization practices. Kahle has been a vocal critic of Google's digital practices, which he has regarded as a for-profit operation. Kahle prefers locally controlled, nonprofit information resources with access unfettered by contracts and licenses. At the same time, he realizes that the digital transition is becoming centralized, homogeneous, and for-profit because most traditional libraries do not have the money, staff, or expertise to create their own unique digital book collections.

Inspired by the Svalbard Global Seed Vault (a secure underground vault in Norway that is designed to preserve copies of plant seeds in worldwide gene banks), Kahle's dream is to collect one copy of every book ever published. He has purchased a warehouse on the West Coast, which is estimated to hold one million titles, and has converted conventional shipping containers to serve as climate-controlled storage units. One day, he would like to be able to provide a digital or print-on-demand copy to anyone in the world. In 2009, Kahle invented a technology called BookServer, which gives any author, publisher, or library the opportunity to make a scanned book available for free, for sale, or for loan. Using Bookserver, as well as a book scanner he invented called Scribe, Kahle built a print-on-demand bookmobile, which he drove around San Francisco with his son. Based on his experience, he started the nonprofit organization Anywhere Books. Anywhere Books sends

Affiliation: Internet Archive

Brewster Kahle founded the nonprofit Internet Archive in 1996. Originally Kahle worked with Bruce Gilliat in developing software to "crawl" and download all publicly accessible Internet pages, the Gopher hierarchy, the Netnews bulletin board system, and downloadable software. In 1999, Kahle decided to collect other digital materials for the archive, starting with the Prelinger Archives, a collection of films about the cultural history of the United States. The Internet Archive now contains e-books, texts, audio, video, and software. It also includes discussion forums, the most popular of which is devoted to the Grateful Dead.

print-on-demand bookmobiles to Uganda to provide books for poor and rural populations.

Kahle is a member of the Internet Hall of Fame, a Fellow of the American Academy of Arts and Sciences, and a member of the National Academy of Engineering. He serves on the boards of the Electronic Frontier Foundation, Public Knowledge, the European Archive, and the Television Archive. He is a member of the advisory board of the National Digital Information Infrastructure and Preservation Program of the Library of Congress as well as the National Science Foundation Advisory Committee for Cyberinfrastructure. He received an honorary doctorate in computer science from Simmons College in 2010 and an honorary doctorate in law from the University of Alberta. Kahle has won numerous awards, including the 2004 Paul Evan Peters Award from the Coalition for Networked Information (CNI), the 2008 Robert B. Downs Intellectual Freedom Award from the University of Illinois, the 2010 Zoia Horn Intellectual Freedom Award from the California Library Association, and the 2012 Peter Jackson Innovation Award from the Software and Information Industry of America.

Personal Life

Kahle and his wife, Mary Austin, run the Kahle/Austin Foundation. The foundation supports the Free Software Foundation for its work promoting GNU, a free, Unix-like operating system. Kahle maintains the blog Brewster.kahle.org, where he writes articles about housing, education, food, and health in the United States. Kahle has one son, Logan, who is "custom schooled."

Rachel Wexelbaum

Further Reading

Cronin, Mary J. "Brewster Kahle and WAIS, Inc." *Doing More Business on the Internet: How the Electronic Highway Is Transforming American Companies*. New York: Van Nostrand Reinhold, 1995. N. pag. Print. Detailed history of WAIS and its original uses.

Hardy, Quentin. "Lend Ho!" *Forbes* 29 Oct. 2009. Web. 20 June 2012. An article focusing on Kahle's Bookserver technology.

Kahle, Brewster. "Brewster Kahle: Founder, WAIS, Internet Archive, Alexa Internet." Interview by Jessica Livingston. *Founders at Work: Stories of Startups' Early Days*. New York: Springer, 2008. Print. Kahle discusses his development of WAIS, founding of Alexa Internet with Gilliat, and establishment and maintenance of the Internet Archive.

---. "A Conversation with Brewster Kahle: Creating a Library of Alexandria for the Digital Age." Interview by Stewart Feldman. 9 July 2004. *Association for Computing Machinery*. Web. 20 June 2012. Kahle shares with Feldman, vice president of Internet technology at IBM, the philosophy behind Alexa Internet and his opinions on the future of libraries, free access to information, electronic reading, and online privacy. This is the first article in which Kahle discusses his nonprofit start-up AnyWhere Books.

---. "Preserving the Internet." *The Future of the Web*. New York: Rosen, 2007. Print. Kahle's personal justification for creating an archive of the Internet.

Technology Quarterly. "The Internet's Librarian." 5 Mar. 2009. Web. *The Economist*. 20 June 2012. An overview of Kahle's goals for information on the Internet, with some insights into his philosophy and vision.

ROBERT KAHN

Coinventor of the transmission-control protocol and the Internet protocol

Born: December 23, 1938; New York, New York
Died: -
Primary Field: Computer science
Specialty: Internet
Primary Company/Organization: Bolt, Beranek, and Newman

INTRODUCTION

Robert Kahn's involvement with ARPANET and eventually the Internet began at the very start of the ARPANET program in 1968, when he was part of the team at Bolt, Beranek, and Newman that developed the network for the Department of Defense. Eventually joining the Advanced Research Projects Agency (ARPA) in 1973, Kahn headed what was the largest government computer research and development program to that time. Along with Vinton Cerf, Kahn developed the transmission-control protocol/Internet protocol (TCP/IP) in the early 1970s, establishing a means whereby computers on a network (such as ARPANET or the Internet) could communicate with computers on different networks. In addition, he was instrumental in creating open architecture, meaning that information could be accessed openly rather than through programs that were protected as proprietary intellectual property. Kahn's contributions have been recognized as among the most important to the creation of the Internet, earning him credit, along with Cerf, as one of the fathers of the Internet.

EARLY LIFE

Robert Kahn was born in New York City on December 23, 1938. He attended the City College of New York, where he earned a bachelor's degree in electrical engineering. Two years later, he received a master's degree from Princeton University, and two years after that he earned his doctorate from the same institution. Kahn's first job upon completing his education was at Bell Laboratories. He then became an assistant professor of electrical engineering at the Massachusetts Institute of Technology (MIT). In the late 1960s, he joined the staff at Bolt, Beranek, and Newman (BBN) in Cambridge, Massachusetts.

In late 1968, Larry Roberts, chief scientist and newly selected program manager at ARPA, released a request for proposal (RFP) in search of contractors to build a computer network for the agency, eventually to be known as ARPANET. BBN received the RFP and began to prepare a response in the form of a technical proposal. Kahn was assigned to the team that prepared this response.

In early 1969, BBN was announced as the winner and thus began to develop the network that would eventually result in computers (referred to as interface message processors, or IMPs) at four different sites: the University of California at Los Angeles, the University of California at Santa Barbara, Stanford University, and the University of Utah.

Kahn's involvement, which began with developing the proposal, would continue into 1971. He not only would help in the development but also had an influence on the approach that would be taken to design the architecture of the network. His view, which would be incorporated into the overall development, was that however the network was to be configured, it ought to be planned in such a way that its basic organization would remain the same even as the network expanded. In that way, costly changes in the future could be avoided.

Robert Kahn.

209

As time went on, Kahn's involvement in the project was accompanied by a growing conviction that the network was increasingly important, a feeling that he did not believe was being shared by BBN, which tended to develop solutions and then move on to the next problem. In 1972, Kahn was offered a position as head of ARPA's Information Processing Techniques Office (IPTO). Later that year, Kahn gave a demonstration at an international computing conference of ARPANET's capabilities, linking forty computers simultaneously.

LIFE'S WORK

While Kahn's work up to 1972 was important in defining and developing networks, his major contributions would be made in the later 1970s. First, as IPTO director, he started and managed the largest computer development program to that time, the Strategic Computing Program. Second, he and Vinton Cerf developed a solution to the problem of how networks might communicate with one another despite differences in equipment and architecture.

The computers connected to ARPANET had all been brought in as integral parts of the ARPA network. There was no problem with their ability to communicate among themselves. What would happen, however, if there was a need (and there certainly would be at some point) for ARPANET to communicate with computers on other networks? For the time being, there was no commonality in hardware or software, and consequently none in the ability of networks to contact and understand one another. That was the problem that Kahn and Cerf would solve.

Their eventual solution was to develop network protocols. A protocol is software or hardware that defines how communications are conducted so that dissimilar networks can communicate with each other. Protocols handle communications and the rules at different levels. One protocol will handle how different hardware items will interact. Another will establish how messages will be passed back and forth (the packet-switching method that Leonard Kleinrock claimed to have developed was the means of conveying messages on ARPANET and later the Internet). Another may govern how browsers will receive messages, while yet another may resolve lost packet issues or authentication.

In the spring of 1973, Cerf joined Kahn on the project. They started by conducting research on reliable data communications across packet radio networks, factored in lessons learned from the networking control protocol, and then created the next-generation transmission-control protocol (TCP), the standard protocol used on the Internet today. In the early versions of this technology, there was only one core protocol, which was named TCP. At the time, these letters did not stand for what they do today, transmission-control protocol, but instead stood for the transmission-control *program*. The first version of this predecessor of modern TCP was written in 1973, then revised and formally documented in RFC 675, "Specification of Internet Transmission Control Program" (December 1974; RFC is a standard designation in computer and Internet engineering meaning "request for comments").

What Kahn and Cerf developed, then, was to be known as the transmission-control

---

Affiliation: Bolt, Beranek, and Newman

Bolt, Beranek, and Newman (BBN) was formed in 1948 in Cambridge, Massachusetts, by two professors from the Massachusetts Institute of Technology (MIT): Richard Bolt and Leo Beranek, along with one of their students, Robert Newman. BBN's principal area of work when it started was acoustics. It was for this reason that it hired J. C. R. Licklider from MIT, a noted physioacoustics expert (and later ARPANET and Internet visionary). Acoustical research remained one of BBN's major business and research areas until that activity was spun off in the 1980s.

In the early years, BBN was staffed heavily by faculty hired from Harvard and MIT. It was widely regarded as the "third campus" in Cambridge, one that provided extensive opportunities for research without the requirement to teach. Through the 1950s, the areas of research had expanded. The company bought what were then large-scale computers in the early 1950s on the recommendation of one its vice presidents, not because the actual need had been identified but because it was realized that the company, to remain viable, would need to have advanced computing capacity to support research in any area that might materialize. For example, BBN was the proving ground for the first model PDP-1 from Digital Equipment Corporation.

As BBN's areas of research grew, one of the most important was the work done in researching the requirements for the design and implementation of networks. BBN's winning the contracting bid in 1968 to make computers for the ARPANET would lead to other networking projects for the government.

In the 1990s, BBN was purchased, spun off, and sold several times. In 2009, it became part of Raytheon.

protocol/Internet protocol (TCP/IP). These two layers form the middle of a four-layer structure that makes communication on the Internet possible. The first is known as a link layer and provides the means and the rules for communications within a specific network. The next is the Internet protocol (IP) layer, developed by Cerf and Kahn, which makes it possible for different local networks to connect and communicate. Once a connection is established, the transport layer (Kahn and Cerf's TCP) allows the host in each network to connect and communicate with the host in another network. Finally, there is an application layer, which governs how data service processes are run (for example, a web browser interacting on a machine with a web server located elsewhere).

What Kahn and Cerf did was to make it possible for individuals on different networks to communicate with one another. While this was extremely important in resolving an immediate need, its importance went beyond a technical solution. By insisting that the architecture and the protocols be open to everyone, they ensured that these protocols could be made to work anywhere by anyone and not subjected to the restrictions that would occur when using proprietary systems. The Department of Defense, even at this early stage, was making decisions regarding programs such as the Worldwide Military Command and Control System (in which proprietary solutions would hinder open communications). Kahn and Cerf's solution ensured that similar problems would not exist within ARPANET and subsequently the Internet.

Today's IP networking represents a synthesis of several developments that began to evolve in the 1960s and 1970s, namely the Internet and local area networks, or LANs (which emerged in the mid- to late-1980s), together with the advent of the World Wide Web in the early 1990s.

PERSONAL LIFE
Kahn left ARPA in 1986, thereafter serving as chief executive officer (CEO) and president of the Corporation for National Research Initiatives (CNRI), a nonprofit organization that seeks to find solutions to developing a national Information infrastructure. He has received many awards, including the Association for Computing Machinery's Alan M. Turing Award and its President's Award. In conjunction with his collaborator, Cerf, Kahn received the U.S. National Medal of Technology, the Marconi Award, and the Presidential Medal of Freedom. He shared the Charles Stark Draper Prize for 2001 with Cerf, Leonard Kleinrock, and Larry Roberts for their work on the ARPANET and Internet. In addition, Kahn has received many honorary degrees.

Kahn's cousin, Herman Kahn (1922–83), was a military analyst and theorist who made a specialty of studying the possibilities of atomic warfare and its results, publishing two books on the subject, *On Thermonuclear War* and *On Escalation*. Herman Kahn is said by some to have been one of the models for the titular character in the film *Dr. Strangelove*.

Robert N. Stacy

FURTHER READING
Beranek, Leo. "Roots of the Internet: A Personal History." *Massachusetts Historical Review* 2 (2000): 55–75. Print. One of the founders of Bolt, Beranek, and Newman discusses his and his company's role in the development of ARPANET.

Denning, Peter J.; and Robert E. Kahn. "The Long Quest for Universal Information Access." *Communications of the ACM* 53.12 (2010): 34–36. *Business Source Complete*. Web. 22 July 2012. Kahn discusses the search for a means to allow universal access while providing a short history of the development of the Internet.

Hafner, Katie. *Where Wizards Stay Up Late: The Origins of the Internet*. New York: Simon, 1996. Print. A good general history of the development of the Internet, covering the development of protocols by Kahn and Cerf.

Salus, Peter H. *Casting the Net: From ARPANET to Internet and Beyond*. Reading: Addison-Wesley, 1995. Print. A thorough history, beginning with the long-distance computing demonstrations at Bell Labs in the 1940s to the full implementation of the Internet. Kahn and the importance of his work in developing protocols is discussed in detail.

MITCHELL KAPOR

Founder of Lotus Development Corporation and cofounder of the Electronic Frontier Foundation

Born: November 1, 1950; New York, New York
Died: -
Primary Field: Computer science
Specialty: Computer programming
Primary Company/Organization: Lotus Development Corporation

INTRODUCTION

Mitchell Kapor is best known for the design, development, and marketing of the spectacularly successful spreadsheet program Lotus 1-2-3 in the 1980s. He has, however, a string of other accomplishments. He has been a significant force in making the benefits of technology available to a wide range of people, especially minorities. As an entrepreneur, investor, and founder of the Mitchell Kapor Foundation, he has sought to bring educational opportunities to minority students and to minority-owned companies trying to establish themselves in the information technology (IT) field. He has also worked in the areas of open systems development for the Internet, revising outdated copyright protection laws, and creating an effective national technology policy.

EARLY LIFE

Mitchell Kapor was born in Brooklyn, New York, on November 1, 1950. His father was the owner of a box manufacturing company, and his mother was a librarian. At a very young age, he built a primitive computer with his father, finding the instructions in a book. While in high school, he had the opportunity to attend the Summer Science program sponsored by the National Science Foundation in Ojai, California. That experience was significant in his eventual development, and later in life he supported the Summer Science program.

After high school, Kapor enrolled at Yale University, graduating with a bachelor's degree in an interdisciplinary major he had designed with a linguistics professor. His self-created major combined computer science, psychology, and linguistics. His life during the next few years was unsettled but involved some interesting experiences. He moved to Boston in 1973, worked at a public television station, and was a radio disk jockey. He returned to school and received a master's degree in

psychological counseling, eventually working in a mental hospital. Kapor enrolled at the Sloan Business School at the Massachusetts Institute of Technology (MIT) with the objective of getting a master's in business administration, but he never completed the course work.

Becoming interested in computers in the late 1970s, when the computers available were early TSR (terminate and stay resident) systems and the Apple II, Kapor inadvertently became a consultant and programmer for the Apple II. Eventually, he became seriously involved with programming for the VisiCorp, which developed a spreadsheet program known as VisiCalc. Kapor's experience programming for the VisiCalc application would exert a strong influence on his subsequent programming and development efforts.

LIFE'S WORK

In 1982, Kapor left VisiCorp and with a partner, Jonathan Sachs (with whom he had worked on VisiCalc),

Mitchell Kapor.

began the Lotus Development Corporation. The next January, Lotus released its spreadsheet, Lotus 1-2-3. The effects of this release were staggering at the time. The personal computer was new and there was even a strong belief in some circles (most famously, perhaps, on the part of Ken Olsen of Digital Equipment Corporation, who did not believe there was a market for microcomputers such as the personal computer) that it was not going to last as an innovation. Personal computers of the time were seen as the domain of hobbyists. Lotus 1-2-3 changed that, however. A personal spreadsheet program was something that many people could use in a time when slide rules and the recently marketed handheld digital calculator were among the most sophisticated consumer electronics, and now that an effective and widely applicable spreadsheet program existed there was a compelling reason to invest in a PC. The early IBM PCs came with what was referred to as a "shell" that contained and allowed access to several programs that IBM also provided. These included a word-processing program, a graphics package, and the spreadsheet program VisiCalc, on which Kapor had worked before starting Lotus Development. Lotus 1-2-3 was purchased by people who were willing to pay an additional sum for an application that worked better than the free spreadsheet they received with the computer. The success of the product took everyone, including Kapor, by surprise. He had anticipated that revenues in the first year would be $1 million. The actual revenues in the first year of Lotus 1-2-3 sales were approximately $53 million. In 1984, the revenues from Lotus 1-2-3 were three times that amount.

The success of 1-2-3 was not to be matched again, however. As the 1980s progressed, the Macintosh, with its graphical user interface, appeared with programs that could by navigated with a computer mouse; Lotus 1-2-3 was designed to be run on DOS (the "disk operating system" typical of PCs at the time), in which one navigated and performed actions using the keyboard's Tab and Enter keys and saw primarily characters on the screen. Eventually, Microsoft's Excel would overtake Lotus 1-2-3 as the spreadsheet application of choice for PC users.

Other programs and application suites developed by Lotus enjoyed limited success or were outright failures. An application suite for the PC called Lotus Symphony enjoyed some popularity. A similar suite for the Macintosh, Jazz, failed miserably, in large part because its interface was different from anything then seen on the Macintosh, having a completely look and feel

different from the interface to which Macintosh users had become accustomed. Other development projects followed, and failed: a file management application (Magellan), a word-processing program (Manuscript), and a personal information management program (Agenda). Another project was designed specifically for Steve Jobs's NeXT computer and failed as well.

There was one more success story at Lotus, however, and that was a communication and groupware application called Lotus Notes. Notes was not a PC application but one that would service an entire enterprise—an important consideration as the 1980s progressed and it was becoming ineffective for PCs to operate as stand-alones (in isolated manner) as opposed to combining in local-area networks. The effectiveness of Notes started to arouse the interest of IBM, which was attempting to create software that would successfully compete with the new array of Microsoft products that supported both individual and group-centered work projects. In July 1995, IBM would purchase Lotus for $3.5 billion.

Kapor had left Lotus by that time, however. After his departure from Lotus in the late 1980s, he became active in a number of areas, and in many of these venues he has sought to make both the development and benefits of information technology available to a wider population, with emphasis on minorities. He has also advocated the use of open systems in developing applications. He was a cofounder of the Electronic Frontier Foundation (EFF) in 1990, an organization with the stated purpose of defending free speech, privacy, innovation, and consumer rights; he was EFF's chairman until 1994. In 1997, he founded the Mitchell Kapor Foundation, which supports many social (specifically minority) initiatives by granting funds and providing technical support.

In 2001, Kapor became director of the Level Playing Field Institute, which works to expand educational and employment opportunities. Two years later, he founded and became chair of the Mozilla Foundation (developer of Firefox and a champion of open systems development). As a venture capitalist, Kapor has assisted in the successful launch of several minority-owned IT start-ups. He has been on the boards of many philanthropic organizations as well.

Kapor has not been uniformly successful, however, as seen in his involvement with the Chandler Project, a seven-year effort to create a personal information management system. Chandler was to be a rival to Microsoft's Outlook, not only as a functioning application but also as a project with open source code; its developer

Affiliation: Lotus Development Corporation

In the 1980s, Lotus Development Corporation was considered to be one of the most advanced information technology (IT) companies in the United States. It developed a revolutionary product—a spreadsheet with many new features, including graphical capabilities—available on the latest genre of computing machinery, the personal computer. In addition to its advanced product, Lotus provided its employees with one of the best, if not the best, benefits packages available at the time: not only generous but also reflective of the progressive views of its cofounder, Mitchell Kapor.

Kapor had formed Lotus Development in 1982. In early 1983, Lotus released the flagship product that would be the key to its success, Lotus 1-2-3, a spreadsheet application that brought in more than $50 million in sales in the first year. The following year, revenues for Lotus 1-2-3 were triple that amount.

Following the release 1-2-3, however, Lotus's products were not as successful, and several even failed in a dramatic fashion. A suite of applications to be used for word processing, spreadsheets, and other capabilities for the PC, using the DOS operating system (that is,

with no mouse, no graphical user interface, and navigation and command execution only by means of the keyboard) was called Symphony and was only moderately successful. A similar bundling of applications for the Macintosh, named Jazz, failed miserably. File management, word-processing, database, and personal organization applications were not well received. Complicating the picture were several copyright infringement lawsuits initiated by Lotus. The company won some of these actions but lost one. In 1989, Lotus released a collaborative and messaging application called Lotus Notes, which was successful and which still exists.

Regardless of the lackluster performance of Lotus's other products, Lotus Notes made the attractive to buyers, and one in particular, IBM, sought to compete with Microsoft's successful applications and office suites. IBM therefore purchased Lotus in 1995 for $3.5 billion. The legacy of Lotus Development is now Lotus Software, a subsidiary of IBM. The company is no longer located in the Boston area but rather several miles west, in Westford, Massachusetts.

was the Open Source Application Foundation. Development efforts began in 2001, but by 2007 it was apparent that Chandler was not ready for release, mostly because of performance issues. Kapor then announced that the following year would see him withdraw his funding. Although there was talk as late as 2009 that the project would continue, it ended without coming to fruition.

PERSONAL LIFE

Kapor has been not only a software developer, entrepreneur, and activist but also a teacher and scholar. He taught at MIT's Media Lab during the 1994–95 and 1995–96 academic years, as well as the University of California, Berkeley. Kapor also worked with President Barack Obama both during the 2008 presidential campaign and in the postelection transition, pushing for the creation of a national chief technological officer. He continued to provide advice to the Obama administration on technical issues and on how they affect society at large.

In 2011, Kapor was an adviser for a highly discussed documentary produced by CNN. Titled "The New Promised Land: Silicon Valley," the program was part of the CNN-produced series *Black in America*. The

program emphasized that, despite the belief that Silicon Valley is a complete meritocracy, it is in fact an environment in which minorities are not necessarily given an even chance to succeed or even participate. Kapor appeared in the program, articulating his beliefs and reflecting his ongoing efforts to bring greater opportunities in the technical fields to minority students.

On September 16, 2011, in Kendall Square, Cambridge, Massachusetts (just slightly more than five minutes' walk from where Lotus Development had been located), the Entrepreneur Walk of Fame was unveiled. Among its first seven inductees, whose star was embedded into the sidewalk, was Kapor, along with Steve Jobs, Thomas Edison, and Bill Gates.

Kapor is married to Freada Kapor Klein, an expert and activist on Diversity and fairness in the workplace. They live in San Francisco, California.

Robert N. Stacy

FURTHER READING

Aspray, William. *Engineers as Executives: An International Perspective*. New York: Institute of Electrical and Electronics Engineers, 1995. Print. A detailed study of the roles of executives in engineering projects by the director of the IEEE's History of Electrical Engineering project. The book includes an interview with Kapor about the development of Lotus 1-2-3, emphasizing Kapor's belief that luck had a great deal to do with his success and that organizations cannot adequately prepare for the kind of success he had with Lotus 1-2-3.

Kapor, Mitchell D., Pamela Samuelson, Randall Davis, and J. H. Reichman. "A Manifesto Concerning the Legal Protection of Computer Programs." *Columbia Law Review* 94.8 (1994): 2308–2431. Print. Kapor and his collaborators discuss aspects of software product development that are inadequately covered under current laws. Not only the source code and functionality must be covered but Kapor and his coauthors argue that the behavior and "look and feel" of applications can be can be inexpensively copied from an original. This article was written in the wake of Lotus's "look and feel" copyright infringement suits against several software companies.

Rosenberg, Scott. *Dreaming in Code: Two Dozen Programmers, Three Years, 4,732 Bugs, and One Quest for Transcendent Software.* New York: Random House, 2007. Print. An account of the Chandler project, a personal information management application that was to rival Microsoft Outlook. Led and funded by Kapor and developed at the Open Source Application Foundation over a seven-year period, the effort came to a halt when Kapor withdrew funding.

Winograd, Terry, ed. *Bringing Design to Software.* Reading: Addison-Wesley, 1996. Print. A collection of essays by leading designers of software. Kapor's "A Software Design Manifesto" emphasizes the importance of keeping the user experience in mind during software development.

JAWED KARIM

Cofounder of YouTube

Born: May 1979; Merseberg, East Germany (now Germany)
Died: -
Primary Field: Internet
Specialty: Social media
Primary Company/Organization: YouTube

INTRODUCTION

Jawed Karim was one of the three cofounders of the Internet video-sharing site YouTube, credited with the initial idea for the site; he also worked on the pioneering Internet commerce site PayPal, which facilitated the exchange of money over the Internet. Although Jawed became a multimillionaire when YouTube was sold to Google, he has largely stayed out of the limelight and later returned to his academic studies, with the goal of becoming a university professor.

EARLY LIFE

Jawed Karim was born in East Germany (the former communist nation) to a family of scientists; his father was a chemist and his mother a biochemist. The family moved to West Germany when Karim was one year old, and in 1992 they immigrated to the United States, where they settled in the St. Paul, Minnesota, suburb of Maplewood. In the United States, Karim's father worked for 3M, and his mother was a professor of biochemistry at the University of Minnesota. When he was a child, Karim's mother often brought him to her laboratory, so he was able to observe the process of scientific research from an early age. He showed an early interest in computers as well: At age ten, Karim began working with a Commodore computer, and while in high school he completed programming tasks for his school and for his mother's lab. In 1997, Karim began studying computer science at the University of Illinois at Urbana-Champaign, stating that he was attracted to the school because Marc Andreessen, one of the founders of Netscape, had been a student there. However, Karim interrupted his university studies three years later so he could go to work at PayPal, in Palo Alto, California. There he met Steve Chen and Chad Hurley, the cofounders of YouTube, and after PayPal was sold to eBay in 2002, the three were looking for a new project.

LIFE'S WORK

Karim, Hurley, and Chen created YouTube as a way for users to share videos they had shot themselves. They were also inspired by Janet Jackson's "wardrobe malfunction" during the halftime show for the 2004 Super

Jawed Karim.

Bowl (one breast was briefly uncovered during a dance routine) and an amateur video of the Asian tsunami in the same year. In both cases, there was high viewer interest in seeing video clips of the events, yet it was difficult to locate and play such clips on the Internet. Another influence was an article Karim had read that stated that a monologue delivered by Jon Stewart on *The Daily Show*, a satirical television news program, was seen by three times as many people online as the number who watched the original broadcast.

During the development of YouTube, Karim and Chen did most of the technical work, while Hurley designed the site's logo and user interface. Karim posted the first video clip to YouTube on April 23, 2005. It was unremarkable except for its historic significance; it lasted only eighteen seconds and showed Karim at the San Diego Zoo, standing in front of the elephant enclosure and saying a few words about it. The beta version of YouTube was launched in May 2005, financed by payouts that Karim, Hurley, and Chen had received when eBay had purchased PayPal. Only a few dozen videos were available on the site, and it attracted little attention; the videos were shot by the founders and their friends and thus held no interest for the public. One early attempt to popularize the website, an offer to pay

$100 to any attractive woman who would post at least ten videos to the site, received no takers at all.

Karim realized that the market for people who produced their own videos was too small to make the site popular and that the best way to attract large numbers of viewers was to provide professionally produced content. YouTube soon began began adding profesionally produced video, including clips from television, music videos, and other copyright-protected content, a process that brought a much-increased audience (several million daily views by December 2005) but that also attracted the attention of the copyright owners. One early YouTube hit was a clip from the NBC television program *Saturday Night Live* (called "Lazy Sunday"), by the comedy troupe The Lonely Island; it was viewed more than 5 million times by February 2006, when NBC demanded its removal. The widespread publicity resulting from NBC's threat to take legal action (under the Digital Millennium Copyright Act) focused attention on the ability of YouTube to reach the youth audience while raising legal questions about the boundaries of copyright and the responsibility the provider of a service has for the actions of people using it. It also highlighted YouTube's role as a content aggregator, rather than as a sight for amateurs to share their own videos. In October 2006, YouTube was sold to Google for $1.65 billion, making the three cofounders multimillionaires. However, Karim had already reduced his role to that of an adviser to the company and had resumed his academic studies in computer science.

Karim has stated that four key features enabled the rise of YouTube to dominate the market for video sharing: the ability to embed videos in websites, recommendations made to users of other videos they might like to see (the "related videos" list), allowing comments, and providing an e-mail link to facilitate sharing of videos; the latter two in particular helped create a community of people around videos they liked (or did not like) and also created wider audiences for individual videos because one person could easily tell his or her friends about videos he or she liked (or liked to make fun of).

PERSONAL LIFE

After leaving the University of Illinois to work for Pay-Pal, Karim completed his undergraduate degree in computer science by taking courses online and at Santa Clara University. He played a key role in the creation of YouTube and remained a shareholder (he gained an estimated $64 million when the company was sold to Google in 2007) but chose the role of informal adviser,

Affiliation: YouTube

Jawed Karim, Chad Hurley, and Steven Chen came up with the idea of YouTube after a dinner party in which guests had commented that it would be nice if there were an easy way for them to share the videos they had taken of one another. The original idea for the site, therefore, was to enable users to share video they had created themselves. This approach did not prove popular, and the site's growth began only when the founders started to post professionally produced content (for example, clips from television programming), marking a change in direction from a site for amateur video producers to a content supplier for people who had no interest in producing videos and viewed programming on YouTube similarly to the way they viewed programming on television or radio. At the time of its creation, YouTube was one among many sites striving to solve the technical problems involved in sharing video clips online; factors in YouTube's ascendancy include its simple interface (which allowed people without much technical knowledge to upload and play videos), the fact that it set no limits to the number of videos an individual could upload, the low demands it placed on bandwidth and browser software, the community functions (for example, the opportunity to link with other users), and the ability to embed videos into other websites.

Google bought YouTube in October 2006, paying $1.65 billion, and addressed the copyright issues through a content management program. By November 2007, it became the most popular entertainment website in the United Kingdom and globally was one of the ten most popular sites on the Internet in 2008; the same year, it hosted more than 85 million video clips. As of January 2012, YouTube was generating more than three billion views per day, and in 2012 it drew eight times as many viewers as Hulu, a rival video-streaming service. In 2007, YouTube created the YouTube Partner Program, which offers viewing "channels" supported by advertising.

rather than employee of the company from its early days, so he could focus on his studies; in fact, when Google bought YouTube, some news stories reported with surprise that the company had three rather than two founders. Karim also cofounded Youniversity Ventures with Kevin Hartz and Keith Rabois, an investment group specializing in developing projects by students from Stanford University and the University of Illinois.

Sarah Boslaugh

FURTHER READING

Burgess, Jean, and Joshua Green. *YouTube*. Digital Media and Society Series. Malden: Polity, 2009. Print. An examination of the YouTube phenomenon and the role it plays in today's society, including public debates about the site and its role in the struggles for authority in media, as well as its place in the evolving relationship among media consumers, producers, and industries. The authors are academics based in Australia and the United States.

Helft, Miguel. "With YouTube, Student Hits Jackpot Again." *New York Times* 12 Oct. 2006: C1–C4. Print. A news article about Karim, on the occasion of Google's purchase of YouTube, focusing on Karim's wish to maintain a low profile, return to academic studies, and become a professor.

Rowell, Rebecca. *YouTube: The Company and Its Founders*. Edina: ABDO, 2011. Print. A popular history of YouTube and its founders, written for schools. Provides historical and social context for their lives as well as the innovations of the company.

Seabrook, John. "Streaming Dreams." *New Yorker* 87.44 (2012): 24–30. Print. A feature article on YouTube, from its origins, as the creation of three former PayPal employees who wanted a way to share personal videos, to its current status, including the potential for YouTube to replace or supplement television as a method of delivering programming to suit narrow interest groups.

Snickars, Pelle, and Patrick Vonderau, eds. *The YouTube Reader*. Stockholm: National Library of Sweden, 2009. Print. A collection of essays about various aspects of YouTube, many written by academics; topics covered include the relationship between television and YouTube, YouTube's role in fostering participatory culture, types of materials posted on YouTube, the relationship between YouTube and other digital archives, and the business aspects of YouTube.

DAVID KARP

Founder of Tumblr

Born: July 6, 1986; New York, New York
Died: -
Primary Field: Internet
Specialty: Social media
Primary Company/Organization: Tumblr

INTRODUCTION

The founder and chief executive officer (CEO) of Tumblr, David Karp has an estimated net worth of more than $40 million. He was named one of the TR35 ("35 innovators under 35") in the Massachusetts Institute of Technology Technology Review's 2010 TR35 list when he was twenty-four years old.

EARLY LIFE

David Karp was born on July 6, 1986, in Manhattan's upper West Side, to parents Michael and Barbara (Ackerman) Karp. As a child, he attended the Calhoun School, a private school (preschool–twelfth grade), where his mother was a teacher. He also attended Bronx

David Karp.

Science, the country's premier magnet science school, for one year of high school before dropping out in favor of homeschooling. As a teenager, he interned for Fred Seibert, owner of Frederator Studios, an animation studio responsible for a number of Nickelodeon cartoon series, such as *The Fairly Oddparents*. After he finished his homeschooling, Karp worked for the online parenting forum UrbanBaby as a software consultant in 2006. In November 2007, at the age of twenty-one, he launched the site Tumblr, subletting office space from Seibert.

LIFE'S WORK

Working with Marco Arment, a web developer who simultaneously developed Instapaper and later left Tumblr to work on it full time, Karp launched Tumblr in November 2007. The funding came principally from Karp's UrbanBaby job, with later contributions from venture capital investors (including UrbanBaby founder John Maloney). A microblogging site, Tumblr streamlined the blogging experience, letting users select a category of entry to post, including photos, text posts, videos, audio, and other categories. The site is streamlined to work with popular services like YouTube and Spotify, making it easy to post links to content on other sites. Unlike blogging platforms such as Blogger or Wordpress, Tumblr focuses on link sharing as its main purpose, making it a sort of hybrid between more personal blogs and social link-sharing services such as Digg. The social feature—a dashboard on which subscribed blogs appear, with the option of broadcasting on the blog's home page which Tumblrs one subscribes to—built a greater sense of community than on sites such as Blogger, where such features are optional but rarely focal.

Perhaps because of its simplicity, the site grew in popularity quickly, especially among young people (more than half of Tumblr's audience is under twenty-five). Tumblr launched an iPhone app in 2009, and more mobile apps followed, making it—like Twitter and Facebook—a part of the increasingly relevant mobile Internet. By 2012 the site had nearly 60 million Tumblrs and nearly as many unique hits per month. Because of its strong visual focus, about 18 percent of the site's blogs are fashion-oriented.

Affiliation: Tumblr

Tumblr was launched in November 2007 as a microblogging service. The site emphasized ease of use, a simple interface, and social elements. The site grew quickly in popularity, especially among young people, for many of whom it may have been their first blog. Indeed, given the prevalence of users who interact with the web primarily through cell phones and mobile apps on tablets and other devices, for many young users the service may have been received more as an enhanced Twitter than a stripped-down Blogger.

Tumblr's interface consists of the dashboard, a scrolling page displaying entries from all of the Tumblrs the user subscribes to (or "follows"), which helps build the social focus of Tumblr—though Tumblrs can still be read by non-Tumblr users, by RSS feed subscription, or by visiting a Tumblr user's site directly. Along the top of the dashboard is a strip of icons for various types of post the user can make to his own Tumblr, including a text post, a photo, a quote, a link, an audio post, or a video post. Tumblr streamlines the posting of content from other sites by including a "reblog" button on each post, which posts a link to the post on the user's own Tumblr; reblogs, comments, and likes are tallied as "notes" and make it easy to post content from other websites and also induce a competitive element, as users hope to make popular posts. In 2011, Tumblr became the first platform to host the blog of President Barack Obama.

Many Tumblrs take on a specific focus, posting links to content related to a particular topic. Tumblr has spawned its own memes and conventions, notably the "F—— Yeah" blogs (each devoted to the celebration of its titular subject), of which there are tens of thousands, including one of the Tumblrs that won a book deal (*F—— Yeah Menswear*, published in November 2012). The first F—— Yeah Tumblr launched in April 2007, while the site was still in beta testing, although the genre was popularized by F—— Yeah Sharks, launched in October 2008. In early 2011, the number of F—— Yeah blogs created per day exceeded 150, and a year later it had diminished but was still more than 100 per day.

Because Tumblr's essential nature is to curate content, it goes virtually without saying that little of the content hosted on the average Tumblr is hosted by its copyright holder. The extent to which this actually constitutes copyright infringement is the subject of some dispute, but the adult men's magazine *Perfect 10* has sued Tumblr for copyright infringement over the amount of material from *Perfect 10* that has been reproduced by Tumblr users on Tumblr's site. The suit was filed in 2012, and it is likely that a number of such suits will be settled out of court before going to a judge. Any legal decision made in such a case could create important precedents, not only for Tumblr but for other areas of the Internet as well. (*Perfect 10* had previously attempted to sue Google because its photos appeared in Google image searches, but the judge in that case ruled that even Google's automated creation of thumbnail images—duplication of copyrighted images—constituted fair use.)

Although David Karp has expressed disdain for advertising, Tumblr has become increasingly ad friendly. For a minimum of $25,000, space may be purchased in the "Radar" section of a user's dashboard, where previously only tumblrs that the company wanted to highlight had been featured. The hope is that Tumblr will avoid conventional banner ads and will integrate advertising into its own environment and interface instead. The company has used the size of its user base and its number of hits per month to attract advertisers to this idea. The difficulty is in assigning a value to the ad. Traditional ads, as seen elsewhere on the Internet, have obvious benchmarks of comparison; at this point in the Internet's history, it is a relatively old field with rich data. The sorts of ads that Tumblr proposes do not have obvious comparisons, nor does Tumblr collect the amount of personal data of a site like Facebook or Google—an e-mail address and an idea for a post is all that is necessary to become a Tumblr user.

This also means ad buyers need to be Tumblr-literate. An ad purchased for Facebook cannot be simply ported over to Tumblr, or rather, if it is, advertisers will not be happy with the results, which in the long run is not good for Tumblr. Because ads will run only on the dashboard, they are essentially targeting Tumblr users, not readers—a major difference from ads run on blogs, for instance. On the other hand, posts featured in Radar have a much broader variety of potential content than many other ad solutions do. They can be text, links, audio, or video.

The potential versatility may be appealing to advertisers. As of 2012, Tumblr had a four-member ad sales team and planned to triple the size of the team by 2013. It was also introducing self-service tools for marketers.

In recent years, Karp has added a small number of revenue-generating features to the free service. The "Radar" space on Tumblr dashboards serves as an advertising space for sponsored posts, with a minimum buy-in of $25,000. Karp was named Best Young Tech Entrepreneur by *BusinessWeek* in 2009.

PERSONAL LIFE

Karp is an avid photographer, and took he most of the Tumblr employee photos used on the site. On weekends, he often takes road trips, renting cars from the Classic Car Club of Manhattan. As of 2012 he was unmarried and had no children. He is notable as a New Yorker in a field long dominated by denizens of California's Silicon Valley.

Bill Kte'pi

FURTHER READING

Ehrlich, Brenna, and Andrea Bartz. *Stuff Hipsters Hate*. Berkeley: Ulysses, 2010. Print. One of the many tumblrs (in this case by two professional editors) to be published as a book.

Jenkins, Henry. *Confronting the Challenges of Participatory Culture: Media Education for the 21st Century*. Cambridge: MIT, 2009. Print. Examines social media, new forms of creative expression, and their impact on media studies.

Qualman, Erik. *Socialnomics: How Social Media Transforms the Way We Live and Do Business*. New York: Wiley, 2010. Print. The impact of social media on the business world.

Welch, Liz. "The Way I Work: David Karp of Tumblr." *Inc.* June 2011. Print. A brief account of Karp's work habits.

JIM KIMSEY

Cofounder of America Online

Born: February 21, 1939; Washington, D.C.
Died: -
Primary Field: Business and commerce
Specialty: Management, executives, and investors
Primary Company/Organization: America Online

INTRODUCTION

Entrepreneur and philanthropist Jim Kimsey is best known as a cofounder of America Online, Inc. (AOL). Kimsey served as president and chief executive officer (CEO) of the company during the first decade of the Internet service provider's existence. He was the first chairman of the board of directors, a title he held after he was succeeded as CEO by Steve Case. Kimsey resigned from the board in 1997 to lead the AOL Foundation, a philanthropic organization with AOL backing, until AOL merged with Time Warner. Kimsey is chairman emeritus of AOL and served as chairman of the International Commission on Missing Persons from 2001 to 2011. He continues to be active in various cultural and charitable groups. In 2012, he recorded a privately distributed country-rock album as Verlin Jack.

EARLY LIFE

James Verlin "Jim" Kimsey was born February 21, 1939, in Washington, D.C. He grew up in nearby Arlington, Virginia, the oldest of five children born to a low-ranking civil servant and his homemaker wife. Young Jim worked to help his family from an early age, first as a

Jim Kimsey.

paperboy and later as a caddy. He was a bright student, and his mother urged him to apply for one of the scholarships awarded annually by Gonzaga, a Jesuit high school for boys in Washington, D.C. Kimsey won a scholarship and proved himself a high achiever academically. He was less successful at conforming to the rules and was expelled a few months shy of graduation. However, his mother was determined that he receive an education. She approached a priest at St. John's, another Catholic high school in the area, to plead for a second chance. Kimsey graduated from St. John's in 1957.

He enrolled at Georgetown University but left after one term when he was accepted at West Point. He graduated from West Point in 1962 and began his career with the U.S. Army as an airborne ranger. He served two tours of duty in Vietnam. During the first, he directed the building of an orphanage, which he supported for more than thirty-five years. He was in special operations for his second tour. He attained the rank of major but left the Army after eight years.

He returned to Washington, D.C., with his wife and two young sons, ready to begin life as an entrepreneur. With the help of a friend and less than $2,000, he bought a building. The plans called for a brokerage firm on the top floor and a bar downstairs. Kimsey installed a working ticker-tape machine and named the bar The Exchange. It was so successful that he was able to buy five other bars. Eventually his profits were great enough to allow him to invest in financial service companies and real estate.

Life's Work

In 1982, an old friend from West Point who had invested in Control Video, a company that offered consumers video games that could be downloaded via the telephone, wondered if Kimsey might be interested in investing as well. Since the company was in the Washington, D.C., area, he asked Kimsey to check out the company. Kimsey was soon involved as a consultant, an involvement that increased as the company's struggle to survive grew more desperate. When an attempt to interest Apple in buying the company failed, Kimsey approached Commodore, at the time the leading company in the personal computer market. Commodore was not interested in buying Control Video either, but they were interested in an online service that could be put on the Commodore 64.

Kimsey had to raise more capital and purchase software from a small company in Troy, New York, in order to provide the service. Control Video morphed into Quantum Computer Services, which, in 1985, launched Q-link, an online service for Commodore. By its second year, Quantum was in the black. The combination of Kimsey as money man, Marc Seriff as head of technology, and Steve Case in charge of marketing signaled that the company was one to watch. Quantum added new interactive services such as real-time chat and live celebrity appearances. Alliances with Apple, Tandy, and IBM followed. In 1989, instant messaging and the soon famous announcement "Welcome! You've got mail" debuted. In 1991, Quantum became America Online (AOL) and a point-and-click interface for DOS users was introduced. The next year, Kimsey turned over the position of CEO to Case and became chairman of the board.

By the time AOL went public a year later, membership exceeded 150,000, but it was in 1993 that the company's base saw its most dramatic increase, thanks in large part to a mistake by a competitor. Prodigy had more than 2.5 million subscribers to their online service when rising costs and mounting losses persuaded management to abandon the flat-fee structure and raise rates. Consumers were angry, and AOL cut their prices and, in advertisements and disk mailings, invited unhappy Prodigy users to join AOL. Soon AOL had overtaken not only Prodigy but also CompuServe. In 1994, Kimsey was named Business Leader of the Year by *Washingtonian* magazine. AOL's membership reached one million in 1995; the same year the company went international by launching AOL Germany. A year later, membership jumped to 5 million, and AOL introduced a flat-rate pricing program and the Buddy List for chatting.

Kimsey, known for his ability to spot and support talent, had been grooming Case to replace him as chairman for several years, and in 1995, he passed the position to the man who whose name would become the one most identified with the company Kimsey had helped to found. The two men were not always in agreement. Most notably, they were on opposite sides in the 1993 crisis when Case and his supporters narrowly defeated a move to sell AOL to Microsoft, a move Kimsey supported. It was common knowledge within the company that Case was eager to have more control, and much was made of the outspoken Kimsey's comment to a reporter that when Case took over as chairman of the board, AOL would need "adult supervision." However, Case has expressed his gratitude for Kimsey's belief in him. Indeed, it was Kimsey's influence with the board that saved Case's job on one occasion. In his turn, Kimsey acknowledged that Case was wise to fight selling the company to Microsoft.

In 1997, Kimsey resigned from the board of directors to serve as chairman of the AOL Foundation, a philanthropic organization he founded. Kimsey's first goal for the foundation was to improve educational opportunities for disadvantaged students in Washington, D.C., and northern Virginia. The foundation provided money to parents and educators for online learning and gave cash and computers to schools and learning centers. It also offered comp time to AOL employees who volunteer their time to the effort and encouraged employees to apply for grants for their own favorite nonprofit organizations. Kimsey continued to head the foundation until AOL's merger with Time Warner in 2000.

At the time Kimsey became chairman of the AOL Foundation, he owned more than a million shares of AOL stock worth more than $78.8 million. However, while his slice of the AOL pie may have been generous, his innovation of awarding stock options to employees, a strategy born in the years when the company lacked the funds to offer large salaries, made many of AOL's employees wealthy. One insider estimates that AOL may have created more than three thousand millionaires. Even clerical staff became rich. Kimsey's own secretary retired to spend time with her grandchildren with stock options worth $5 million.

PERSONAL LIFE

Long divorced and the father of three adult sons—Mike, Mark, and Ray—Kimsey devotes much of his time and a considerable portion of his wealth to charitable causes. In 1996, he founded the Kimsey Foundation, combining support for educational and cultural initiatives in Washington with policy research and humanitarian outreach to the international community. Kimsey has assisted numerous charitable and cultural associations, including the National Stroke Association, Big Brothers of the National Capital Area, the National Symphony Orchestra, the Washington National Opera, and the Vietnam Veterans Memorial Fund. He has served on no fewer than fifty-four nonprofit boards.

Kimsey was appointed chairman of the International Commission on Missing Persons (ICMP), the leading organization involved in the identification of remains of victims of mass atrocities around the globe, by then Secretary of State Colin Powell in May 2001. In the aftermath of the terrorist attacks on the United States in 2001, Kimsey deployed the commission's DNA experts to assist in the identification of remains found at the site of the attacks, "Ground Zero," where the World Trade Center stood. Kimsey has also traveled to Iraq to oversee ICMP efforts there. He served in that position

Affiliation: America Online

The beginnings of America Online (now AOL) can be traced to Control Video Corporation, founded by William von Meister in 1983, which Jim Kimsey restructured as Quantum Computer Services, Inc., in 1985. Kimsey, as CEO, was joined by Marc Sheriff, chief technology officer, and Steve Case, vice president of marketing to lead the new company. Q-link, the online service Quantum offered for the Commodore 64 computer, proved a success, and alliances with Apple, Tandy, and IBM followed. In 1989, the service became known as America Online. Two years later, the company was renamed America Online as well. In 1992, Kimsey yielded the position of CEO to Case, remaining as chairman of the board. The company went public the same year.

By the late 1990s, when the number of Americans first using e-mail and the Internet surged, Case's strategy of targeting the ordinary consumer had made AOL the dominant Internet service. In 2000, AOL merged with Time Warner in the largest merger in American history. Originally viewed as a coup for Case, who was

named chairman of AOL Time Warner in January 2001, the merged company soon became an albatross. By May 2002, the value of the company had fallen $50 billion, a sign of things to come. Case was held responsible for the loss, and, in February 2003, he resigned.

Neither the offer of free services nor the launching of niche content sites solved the company's problems. Finally, in 2009, Time Warner was spun off, making AOL an independent company. Tim Armstrong was named CEO and chairman of the new AOL in 2009. His most noteworthy achievement was the acquisition of *The Huffington Post*, an online site that delivers news, aggregates content, and offers blogs. In 2012, the Pulitzer Prize for national reporting was awarded to David Wood for his ten-part series on the struggles of returning wounded veterans, making *The Huffington Post* the first for-profit online news organization to win a Pulitzer Prize. Arianna Huffington, the president and editor-in-chief of Huffington Post Media Group, said the award was a direct result of the cash infusion that came with AOL's acquisition.

for a decade and continues his involvement with the organization as Chairman Emeritus. He also served as chairman of Refugees International, which advocates humane treatment of refugees around the world, from 1999 to 2005 and remains on the board as chairman emeritus.

Wylene Rholetter

FURTHER READING

Katz, Lee Michael. "Lucky Jim." *Washingtonian* May 2002: 33–43. Print. The article profiles Kimsey, identifying him as "one of the least-known corporate pioneers." It includes details of his growing up in humble circumstances in Washington, D.C., his years at West Point and in military service, and his history with AOL.

Klein, Alec. *Stealing Time: Steve Case, Jerry Levin, and the Collapse of AOL Time Warner*. New York: Simon, 2004. Print. The book focuses on the rise and fall of AOL Time Warner, looking at the role various individuals played the companies before, during, and after the merger. Kimsey is one of the individuals whose role is examined.

"The Singing Millionaire." *Washington Post* 5 Jan. 2012: CO2. Print. Describes Kimsey's decision, inspired by the role of Jeff Bridges in the movie *Crazy Heart*, to record a country-rock album and give it to two thousand of his closest friends for Christmas.

Stelter, Brian. "Huffington Gains More Control in AOL Revamping." *New York Times* 5 Apr. 2012: B1. Print. The article examines the relationship between *The Huffington Post* and AOL, with a focus on the greater independence granted to *The Huffington Post* in 2012.

Swisher, Kara. *Aol.com: How Steve Case Beat Bill Gates, Nailed the Netheads, and Made Millions in the War for the Web*. New York: Random House, 1999. Print. This biography of AOL begins with the earliest incarnation of the company as Bill von Meister's Control Video and follows it from crisis to survival until 1997. Although her focus is on the role of Steve Case, Swisher includes numerous references to Kimsey and acknowledges the importance of his role as the money man.

Vistica, Gregory, and Evan Thomas. "The New Billionaire to See." *Newsweek* 31 July 2000: 30–31. Print. Profiles Kimsey, focusing on his philanthropic activities since he retired from AOL and his ideas about the responsibilities of America's wealthiest citizens to become social activists. Three color photographs.

MICHAEL KINSLEY

Founder of *Slate*

Born: March 9, 1951; Detroit, Michigan
Died: -
Primary Field: Internet
Specialty: News and entertainment
Primary Company/Organization: *Slate*

INTRODUCTION

Michael Kinsley, an American political journalist and pundit, founded Slate*, an online magazine that was originally part of Microsoft's Internet presence. Kinsley was twice editor of* The New Republic *and he served as editor of* Harper's *and the* Washington Monthly *and American editor of* The Economist*. For six years, he was cohost of CNN's* Crossfire *and earlier was a regular with William Buckley, Jr., on PBS's* Firing Line*. A longtime contributing writer for* Time *magazine, Kinsley has also written columns for* The Wall Street Journal *and* The Times *of London. He has been a regular columnist for* Politico *and Bloomberg's* View *and is author or coauthor of half a dozen books.*

EARLY LIFE

Michael Kinsley was born in Detroit, Michigan, on March 9, 1951, the son of George Kinsley, a surgeon, and Lillian (Margolis) Kinsley. He grew up in Birmingham, a suburb of the city, with one sister, Susan. He graduated from the Cranbrook School in Bloomfield Hills, Michigan, a private, college preparatory school about ten miles outside Detroit. He attended Harvard University, where he had the reputation of being a nonconformist. An excellent student, he was editor of *The Harvard Crimson*. He received his bachelor's degree from Harvard in 1972, and then he spent two years at Magdalen College, Oxford University, as a Rhodes

Michael Kinsley.

scholar. In 1974, he returned to the United States and entered law school at Harvard.

Toward the end of his first year in law school, Kinsley went to work for the *Washington Monthly*, eventually becoming the magazine's managing editor. By the fall of 1976, he had decided that journalism rather than law was the career he should pursue. Martin Peretz, editor in chief and owner of *The New Republic*, offered the third-year law student the job of managing editor if he could begin immediately. After negotiating with Harvard Law to allow him to complete law school at George Washington University Law Center, which offered evening classes, Kinsley took the job at *The New Republic*. In 1977, he received his doctorate in jurisprudence from Harvard Law School. He was managing editor of *The New Republic* from 1976 until 1979, when he became editor.

LIFE'S WORK

In 1981, Kinsley moved to New York to become editor of *Harper's*, a job he held for twenty months. During his time there, *Harper's* received a National Magazine Award for general excellence. In 1982, he first appeared as cohost and questioner on the PBS television show *Firing Line*, hosted by William Buckley, Jr. Kinsley

returned to Washington and *The New Republic* in 1983. He wrote the TRB column for the magazine and was named editor again in 1985. He took a leave of absence in 1989 to serve for six months as American Survey editor of *The Economist*. From 1989 to 1995, Kinsley served as the representative of the political left, opposite conservative Pat Buchanan (later Robert Novak and John Sununu), on CNN's weekly political debate show *Crossfire*. Kinsley's association with *The New Republic* continued during his time at *Crossfire*. He wrote approximately one article per month for the magazine and contributed ten essays per year to *Time*.

Kinsley was ready for a change in 1995. He talked with Time Warner about a new magazine and later proposed the idea of a web magazine, but the company moved slowly. Kinsley read that Bill Gates was looking for a "big-name editor" for a new news division at Microsoft Network and contacted Microsoft. The information was wrong, but Microsoft had just decided that the network needed a new emphasis on Internet content and was interested in talking to Kinsley. In August 1995, Kinsley paid a secret visit to Microsoft.

In many ways, he was ill suited for the company. At forty-five, he was eleven years older than the average employee of the company. He was older than all but one of the executives. The Microsoft people had some concerns about the effect of Kinsley's leftist politics on the magazine. Kinsley was adamant that he have full editorial freedom and warned that trouble was a by-product of liveliness—they all agreed they wanted a "lively" magazine. Ultimately they agreed on a weekly news and current affairs magazine that would run about twenty-five thousand words (as compared to *The New Republic*'s forty thousand). In November, Kinsley announced, to general shock, that he was leaving Washington, D.C., to edit an online magazine in Seattle.

The move occurred on Christmas Day, 1995; his first day on the job was January 2, 1996. The name *Slate*, Kinsley's idea, was chosen because it was short and easy to remember and carried a connotation of toughness.

Publication of the magazine began in June 1996. In addition to Kinsley, the small staff included some respected names, such as foreign-affairs columnist Anne Applebaum, Washington bureau chief Jodie Allen, and culture editor Judith Shulevitz. Communicating via e-mail, the group were able to work together from different geographical locations.

Slate's editor came into the job with definite ideas about what the magazine should be. He thought that the

Affiliation: *Slate*

On June 24, 1996, Microsoft entered the world of online publishing with the launch of *Slate*, a news and culture magazine. The fiscal power of Microsoft and the reputation of *Slate*'s editor Michael Kinsley—former editor of *The New Republic*, and the representative of the liberal point of view on CNN's *Crossfire*—were a formidable combination. The magazine was created out of Microsoft's need for more web content at a time when the number of households with an Internet connection was growing steadily. Kinsley's original plan called for a weekly magazine that was a mix of political commentary and arts criticism in the tradition of *The New Yorker*. Experience soon taught him the necessity of modifying some of his ideas. The longer pieces he envisioned never worked as web content. The conventions of print journalism foolishly restricted the formats and tools the new medium offered, and the experiment in requiring paid subscriptions to access material was a failure that was jettisoned after one year.

Kinsley, who was named Editor of the Year in 1999 by the *Columbia Journalism Review* for his work at *Slate*, left the magazine in 2002. He was succeeded by Jacob Weisberg, who was still editor when *Slate* was purchased by the Washington Post Company in December 2004. He continued as editor under the new owners until he was named chairman and editor in chief of the Slate Group in 2008. During his tenure, *Slate* changed from a weekly magazine to a daily, continuously updated one. Podcasting and a video magazine were added, and the audience grew from 2.3 million to 6.5 million monthly visitors. David Plotz, Weisberg's deputy editor, was named *Slate*'s third editor. In 2009, *Slate* went international with the launch of a French *Slate*.

major news magazines, both print and television, were so caught up in reporting breaking events that they had abandoned the journalist's traditional role of telling the news and explaining what was going on in the world. *Slate* was particularly suited to occupy the abandoned ground because of the unique abilities the web gave the online magazine the ability to link backward to older stories for context and to add charts, graphs, photographs, and other content. Kinsley also was convinced that the magazine should be a weekly and that it should be fee-based.

Kinsley was forced to change some of his ideas. Opposed to the idea of bulletin boards, he was persuaded that they were necessary. Even though *Slate* launched as a free site, Kinsley, convinced that paid subscriptions was the only way for the magazine to be viewed as serious journalism, had not given up on requiring readers to pay for the privilege. When *Slate* did move to a subscription rate for about a year ($19.95 for one year), there were just over twenty thousand paying subscribers. The free portions of the site were attracting an audience twenty times that size. Kinsley had no choice but to admit that he was wrong and to return to free content.

Kinsley resigned as editor of *Slate* in April 2004. He was named editorial and opinion editor of the *Los Angeles Times* in June. He left with *Slate* ranked as one of the top fifteen news and information sites on the web, with 2.3 million unique visitors in a single month. He also left with the praise of colleagues and competitors for his contributions in shaping a new journalistic medium.

PERSONAL LIFE

Kinsley's tenure at the *Los Angeles Times* was brief, only fourteen months. The next year found him writing a column for *The Guardian*, but in 2007 he was at *Time* writing a regular column. He then moved to *The Atlantic* where he was hired as a columnist and charged with launching the magazine's new business site, set to go online in early 2010. In late January 2010, Kinsley and Justin Smith, president of Atlantic Media, decided that Kinsley was not right for the job. By September 2010, he had signed on with *Politico*, a newspaper and website, as a columnist representing views of the left. On April 29, 2011, Bloomberg L.P. announced that Kinsley has joined the *Bloomberg View* editorial board. Kinsley's frequent moves since leaving *Slate* may speak of his restlessness, but they also demonstrate that there is no shortage of people eager to add his name and credentials to their rosters.

In 2002, Kinsley married Patty Stonesifer, whom he had met during his secret visit to Microsoft in 1995. Stonesifer, a former Microsoft executive, was cochair and chief executive officer (CEO) of the Bill and Melinda Gates Foundation for eleven years. In 2008, she became senior adviser to the foundation. Kinsley and Stonesifer have homes in Seattle and Washington, D.C.

Kinsley announced in 2002 that he had Parkinson's disease. On February 8, 2010, the American Society of Magazine Editors announced the election of Kinsley to the Magazine Editors' Hall of Fame. He was also among thirteen journalists whose names appeared in a list of "150 Who Make a Difference in American Politics," published in the *National Journal* in the summer of 1986, and in 1999 he was named Editor of the Year by the *Columbia Journalism Review* for his work at *Slate*.

Wylene Rholetter

FURTHER READING

Auletta, Ken. "Jumping off a Bridge: Microsoft and Michael Kinsley Enter Cyberspace." *The New Yorker* 13 May 1996. Rpt. In *The Highwaymen: Warriors of the Information Superhighway*. New York: Random House, 1996. 303-332. Print. The article takes a lengthy look at Kinsley's founding of *Slate*, from his first thoughts about a web magazine through the bust period immediately before the magazine's launch. The article also includes biographical information about Kinsley's early life and the professional path that led him to *Slate*.

Kinsley, Michael. *Please Don't Remain Calm: Provocations and Commentaries*. New York: Norton, 2008. Print. A collection of Kinsley's best commentaries from *Slate*, *The New York Times*, the *Los Angeles*

Times, and other publications. The collection includes pieces on the Internet's impact on journalism and on Kinsley's coming to terms with his diagnosis of Parkinson's disease and his subsequent brain surgery.

---. Preface to *Best of Slate: A 10th Anniversary Anthology*. Ed. David Plotz. New York: Public Affairs, 2006. Print. The preface provides a retrospective view of Kinsley's years at *Slate*. He notes his proudest achievements.

Peters, Jeremy W. "Scarborough and Kinsley Will Write for Politico." *New York Times* 9 Sept. 2010: B8. Print. The article reports on Kinsley's announcement that he was leaving the Atlantic Media Company and on *Politico*'s coup in introducing opinion into its news mix with such names as Kinsley and *Joe Scarborough*.

Stein, Nicholas."*Slate* vs. *Salon*." *Columbia Journalism Review* 37.5 (1999): 56–59. Print. The article is an evaluative comparison of the online magazines *Slate* and *Salon*. The author sees both magazines as models of what electronic journalism can be, but he concludes that *Salon* focuses on reporting, whereas *Slate* opts for a heavier selection of opinion and editorials.

STEVE KIRSCH

Founder of Infoseek Corporation

Born: December 24, 1956; Los Angeles, California
Died: -
Primary Field: Business and commerce
Specialty: Management, executives, and investors
Primary Company/Organization: Infoseek

INTRODUCTION

For more than thirty years, Steve Kirsch has offered innovation to the information technology industry. As an entrepreneur who constantly strives to create cutting-edge technology, he has provided new devices and software which has assisted both individual users and companies. Furthermore, Kirsch's deep commitment to philanthropy has set an example for others inside and outside the industry.

EARLY LIFE

Steve Kirsch was born in Los Angeles, California, on December 24, 1956. He first became interested in

computers and technology after receiving a calculator in the sixth grade. He subsequently enrolled in a computer class at a museum and later registered for an advanced course at a local computer center. The instructor deemed him to be too young for the class but offered to teach Kirsch individually the intricacies of the IBM 360 computer model. Kirsch soon began to spend time around the engineering facilities at the University of California (UCLA), particularly the Defense Advanced Research Projects Agency (DARPA). There, he caught the attention of Vinton Cerf, a researcher at ARPA. Cerf was impressed with Kirsch's burgeoning knowledge and desire to learn more about the agency's computer, the Sigma 7. Kirsch was subsequently given an account with DARPA and as a teenager became responsible for creating a program that would send and receive electronic mail through the various computers in the agency. At this time, Kirsch complemented his growing knowledge of computers with a job at the local arcade that

Steve Kirsch.

involved fixing pinball machines. Making $30 an hour, Kirsch was able to hone his developing mechanical and electronic skills with this job.

Kirsch's early passion for computers and technology offered a clear indication of his future goals. Seeking a university where he could develop his skills and create a clear platform for a professional life, he applied for and was accepted into the Massachusetts Institute of Technology (MIT). As an undergraduate and graduate student at MIT, he studied electrical engineering and computer science. He subsequently developed a deep interest in optics, a major topic in his master's thesis. His enthusiasm for this dimension of physics was complemented with summer work at Bell Laboratories in New Jersey.

While enrolled at MIT, Kirsch developed the protocol for the optical mouse. At the time, all computers were equipped with an affixed mechanical mouse, a device that could occasionally cause problems for the user, especially if it became obstructed or its cord became entangled as a result of the individual's desk configuration. Kirsch attempted to market the optical mouse and even organized a meeting with Steve Jobs at Apple Computer. Although Jobs decided against incorporating the new device into Apple's hardware, Kirsch,

undeterred, secured a patent for his invention. The initial license for the optical mouse was granted to Summagraphics in Danbury, Connecticut.

LIFE'S WORK

Upon graduating from MIT with both bachelor's and master's degrees in computer science in 1980, Kirsch quickly found a job with ROLM Corporation in California. Working in the systems software department for this large Silicon Valley technology company exposed Kirsch to the intense corporate lifestyle. For Kirsch, the work was monotonous and rigid. He quickly became dissatisfied with the job and resigned after nine months.

While contemplating his future, Kirsch returned his attention to the optical mouse. Frustrated that Summagraphics had not begun manufacturing his invention, Kirsch reacquired the license and in 1982 used his nearly $40,000 in savings to start Mouse Systems Corporation. The start-up company moved steadily along, and in the first year nearly forty-eight hundred devices were sold at $300 each. One year later, sales had doubled. In 1986, Kirsch stepped away from the daily operations of the company. Two years later, it was sold to Kye System Corporation for around $12 million.

Kirsch continued to seek new entrepreneurial opportunities and in 1986 started Frame Technology Corporation with engineer Charles Corfield. The company, which focused mainly on developing desktop publishing software for businesses, became highly successful after its major product, FrameMaker, was introduced to the professional market. The company expanded rapidly before being sold to Adobe Systems in 1995 for $500 million. Kirsch's initial investment of $300,000 in the company had proven extremely fruitful, evident in the $30 million garnered by the sale.

By the late 1980s, Kirsch had become deeply interested in the rapid expansion of the Internet. As the networks associated with this new medium began to be established, Kirsch envisioned the need for an efficient search engine that could rapidly retrieve information. In 1993, he organized Infoseek Corporation. What Kirsch offered through Infoseek was a dynamic product that could provide full-texting searches that encompassed the entire spectrum of the Internet. In fact, Infoseek focused on speed and accuracy and was the first search engine to count the total number of hits on accompanying advertisements. By 1998, Infoseek had become an Internet portal and had expanded to include other features, including topical channels.

Realizing that Infoseek would have difficulty in surpassing the popularity of Yahoo! and other search engines, Kirsch began considering outside bids for the company. In 1998, Walt Disney Company, under the leadership of Michael Eisner, had begun to incorporate the Internet medium by purchasing the portal Go.com. In 1998, Disney reached out to Kirsch and bought a partial stake in Infoseek. The deal opened the door to future negotiations, and one year later, Infoseek was sold to the Disney and merged with Disney's Go Network. The sale of the company was finalized for around $1.7 billion, $100 million of which was appropriated directly to Kirsch. Kirsch remained with the new company for four weeks before departing at the end of 1999.

After the success of Infoseek, Kirsch was one of the most recognizable figures in the information technology industry. He remained committed to creating new products and enhancing the ever-evolving technology. Soon after the sale of Infoseek, he set his sights on creating software that would make the Internet easier to use. In 1999, he enticed a number of investors and started Propel Software Corporation. Propel focused initially on providing e-commerce with web acceleration by eliminating pop-up blocking and improving connection techniques with dial-up services. Today, Propel continues to evolve. It is used by more than 40 million users across the world and provides both wireless and Internet acceleration services.

Kirsch is constantly seeking methods to create efficiency for customers. During the early 2000s, he sought to contain and prevent the unwanted messages that would suddenly appear in the physical and electronic domains of offices. In 2003, he filed a lawsuit against Fax.com, a company that sent out unsolicited faxes to offices across the United States. The efforts on the part of Kirsch and others led to the Junk Fax Prevention Act of 2005. In 2007, Kirsch founded Abaca Technology Corporation, which blocks spam e-mail. Two years later, Yahoo! signed a deal with Abaca to assist in their efforts to eliminate spam from personal e-mail accounts. In 2011, Kirsch founded OneID, a company that creates a single sign-on password and ultimate security for the Internet.

PERSONAL LIFE

Kirsch lives in Los Altos Hill, California, with his wife, Michelle; they have three daughters, Julia, Alexandra, and Katherine. For more than two decades, he has been one of the leading philanthropists in the United States. Beginning in 1990, he began to donate much of his wealth to charitable organizations and programs. He has contributed money to projects that he believes will create a better world. He has also contributed significantly to his alma mater, MIT. He provided funds for a new computer science building at the university, assisted in the redevelopment of the school's *Technology Review* magazine, and has assisted in the creation of interpersonal courses for computer science students. Kirsch is committed to providing MIT students with the resources to become better business leaders.

In 1999, Kirsch and his wife established a charitable foundation to fund environmental, community, and political projects. They are committed to investing in a wide variety

---

Affiliation: Infoseek Corporation

The idea for the search engine Infoseek began in the early 1990s, when computer entrepreneur Steve Kirsch was conducting research for computer publications in a CD-ROM. Attracted to the retrieval capabilities of the CD-ROM, Kirsch began to contemplate how the functions could be applied to the burgeoning Internet. Intent on developing an accurate and efficient retrieval system, Kirsch and his team of computer engineers, with the help of investors Sun Microsystems and Eastman Kodak, created Infoseek in 1993. This search engine was the first of its kind: It offered users a full-text indexing experience. Articles from websites, Usenet newsgroups, and publications could be accessed rapidly, accurately, and efficiently. Furthermore, the engine's capabilities allowed a real-time search, so the most recent articles could be accessed.

Originally, Infoseek was a subscription service intended mainly for commercial customers. For $9.95 per month, users were allowed to conduct 100 queries. However, company management soon realized that a significant amount of money could be generated through advertisements, and the retrieval service became free. By 1998, Infoseek had become an Internet portal and expanded to include other features, including topical channels. By this time, the engine was run by new software, Ultraseek, which offered even quicker and more reliable searches.

In 1999, Infoseek was sold to the Walt Disney Company for $1.7 billion. Disney's attempts to amalgamate Infoseek and their Buena Vista Internet Group into the Go.com portal proved unsuccessful. Two years later, Disney shut down the Go.com search engine.

of programs that range from nonproliferation programs to campaign finance reforms. The foundation aspires to contribute to causes that can make a difference in local, national, and international environments, has set a precedent for philanthropists, and has been honored with various community awards.

Since 2007, the Kirsch Foundation has focused a great deal of attention and money on health-related issues. This direction began after Kirsch was diagnosed with Waldenström macroglobulinemia, a non-Hodgkin lymphoma. He dedicated his financial resources to finding a cure for this cancer.

Gavin Wilk

FURTHER READING

Green, Lelia. *The Internet: An Introduction to New Media*. New York: Berg, 2010. Print. Examines the development of the Internet and how it has changed everyday lives.

Kirsch, Steven. "Infoseek's Experiences Searching the Internet." *SIGIR Forum* 32.2 (1998): n. pag. Web. 12 Aug. 2012. Kirsch provides a firsthand look at the data that Infoseek gathered from 1994 to 1998.

Perry, Tekla S. "Steve Kirsch." *IEEE Spectrum* Aug. 2000. Web. 20 Aug. 2012. Provides insight into Kirsch's childhood through the development of Infoseek.

Price, Christopher. *Internet Entrepreneurs: Business Rules Are Good; Break Them*. Harlow: Pearson Education, 2000. Print. Includes a chapter dedicated to Kirsch and the creation of Infoseek.

Steinbock, Dan. *The Birth of Internet Marketing Communications*. Westport: Quorum, 2000. Print. In-depth study revealing how companies have adopted marketing strategies using the technology of the Internet.

PETER T. KIRSTEIN

Computer scientist and early developer of the Internet

Born: June 20, 1933; Berlin, Germany
Died: -
Primary Field: Computer science
Specialty: Internet
Primary Company/Organization: University College London

INTRODUCTION

Peter Kirstein was a pioneer in helping to establish the Internet in Europe and led the group that established the first Internet connection between the United States and the United Kingdom. He was first head of the computer science department at University College London and has been involved in many international collaborations over the course of his career.

EARLY LIFE

Peter Thomas Kirstein was born June 20, 1933, in Berlin, Germany, just a few months after Adolf Hitler and the Nazi Party had taken power. Kirstein's parents were Jewish, and by 1935, social attitudes and oppressive laws were making it increasingly difficult for Jews to live freely in Germany. The Kirsteins decided to leave for England. Peter's mother had been born in England while her parents were briefly working there, so she easily obtained a visa. She immigrated to London, England, in 1936, and Peter and his father followed in 1937. Peter attended the Highgate School in London, where he excelled at the subjects he enjoyed, such as mathematics, but did poorly in those he did not. Instead of a year of national service before starting his studies at a university, Kirstein's uncle arranged for him to study at the University of California at Los Angeles for a semester. Afterward, he took a summer job with the U.S. Army calculating statistics on rain runoff at airports.

Kirstein received a scholarship to study at Cambridge University, where he studied mathematics during his first two years and electrical engineering in his third. In 1954, he earned his bachelor's degree from Gonville and Caius College, Cambridge. He was granted a fellowship to study electrical engineering at Stanford University, earning a master's degree in 1955 and a doctorate in 1957. There had been some problems as he began his doctoral work, but once he had the right adviser, Kirstein completed his doctoral work in only six months.

Ignoring offers to join various universities, Kirstein spent the next four years at the European Organization for Nuclear Research (Conseille Européen pour la Recherche Nucléaire, or CERN) in Switzerland, where he was exposed to the latest computers. He then took a job with General Electric in Switzerland, in part so that

229

Peter T. Kirstein.

he could continue to enjoy skiing there. His job was to keep tabs on relevant research at universities throughout the world. The contacts he made while in that position shaped the course of his career. While visiting the University of London's Institute of Computer Science in 1965, he decided he would like to work there; he became a reader there in 1967 and received a D.Sc. in engineering from London University in 1970.

LIFE'S WORK

Kirstein is best known for his work in establishing the Internet in Europe and for his vision of the global possibilities for communication it offered. After receiving his doctorate from Stanford University, he worked at Stanford University, then moved to Switzerland to work at CERN in Geneva and the General Electric Research and Development Center in Zurich. However, his early scientific work was focused on electron beam design for microwave tubes and accelerators. Kirstein became a reader in the Institute of Computer Science at the University of London in 1967, and in 1970 became a professor of computer communications systems. In 1973, he joined University College London (UCL) in the Department of Statistics and Computer Science. The same year, he established one of the first two international

nodes for the Advanced Research Projects Agency Network (ARPANET), a precursor to the Internet, and led the group that established Internet links between the United States and Great Britain, maintaining them throughout the 1980s. During this period, he also managed the .int and .uk domains.

Kirstein was appointed the first head of the computer science department at UCL, serving in that capacity from 1980 until 1994. He next became director of research for the UCL computer science department; he is also the director of the United Kingdom's Virtual Centre of Excellence in Digital Broadcasting. As of 2012, he had published a book and more than 170 scientific papers. He was also involved in the technological aspects of the British Library for many years, including work in digitizing journals and establishing online access to databases; he was chair of the New Technology Group of the British Library in the 1980s, and as of 2012 he was a member of the Library Council of England.

Most of Kirstein's later work involves networked multimedia and high-speed networks. He is the leader of SILK, SPONGE, OCCASION projects, sponsored by the European Community and the North American Treaty Organization (NATO) and designed to provide Internet access to the national research and education networks (NRENs) of countries in central Asia and the Caucasus. He is involved in many projects related to Internet protocol version 6 (IPv6), a revision of the Internet protocol that will implement a new addressing system with larger address spaces (128 bits as opposed to 32 bits) and thus allow far more addresses to be created.

Kirstein has worked internationally for much of his career, involved with many international collaborations. In 1962, he spent six months working in Russia, and he has worked for extended periods in Switzerland and the United States over the course of his career. He has been involved in many collaborative efforts funded by the European Commission, including 6WINIT, a project to validate the mobile wireless Internet, using IPv6, in Europe; Convergence of Internet, Asynchronous Transfer Mode and Satellite (COIAS), a project to demonstrate the feasibility of using satellite networks and asynchronous transfer mode for the global Internet structure using IPv6; reconfigurable ubiquitous networked embedded systems (RUNES), a project to develop standardized technology for embedded network sensors and networks of them; and U-2010, a crisis management project based on IPv6.

Kirstein has also taught in Japan and Malaysia; has served as a private consultant in six countries; has chaired the International Collaboration Board (1983–2004), promoting cooperation to achieve interoperability in command and information systems among NATO defense organizations, national defense organizations, and national research organizations; and has served on the NATO Science Committee's Networking Panel.

PERSONAL LIFE

As of 2012, Kirstein was a professor of computer systems in the Department of Computer Science within the faculty of engineering science of UCL. His interests include tennis, skiing, and bridge. In 2003, he was made a Commander of the Most Excellent Order of the British Empire (CBE) for his work in developing the Internet. Also in 2003, he received the Jonathan B. Postel Service Award from the Internet Society, in honor of his work in helping establish the Internet as a global network. He has received many other awards over his lifetime, including being named a Fellow of the Institute of Physics, the Institution of Electrical Engineering, the British Computer Society, and the U.K. Royal Academy of Engineering. In 1999, he received ACM's Special Interest Group in Communications and Computer Networks (SIGCOMM) award of the Academy for Computing Machinery for his work on the Internet.

Sarah Boslaugh

FURTHER READING

Bentley, Peter J. *Digitized: The Science of Computers and How It Shapes Our World*. New York: Oxford UP, 2012. Print. A popular book about the origins of modern computers, how they affect our lives today, and what developments are expected in the future, written by a computer scientist and honorary member of the UCL Computer Science Department. Bentley's goal is to show how pervasive a role computers play in the daily lives of most people and how the different aspects of computer science relate to one another.

Gillies, James, and Robert Cailliau. *How the Web Was Born: The Story of the World Wide Web*. New York: Oxford UP, 2000. Print. A very readable account of the origins of the World Wide Web, written by two CERN employees and emphasizing the European origins of the web, including the contributions of workers at CERN.

Hafner, Katie, and Matthew Lyon. *Where Wizards Stay Up Late: The Origins of the Internet*. New York: Simon, 1996. Print. A popular history of the early days of the Internet, beginning in the 1960s with the work of Robert Taylor and others at the Advanced Research Projects Agency (ARPA). Hafner is a technology writer at *Newsweek*.

Affiliation: University College London

Peter Kirstein has played a key role in the computer science department of University College London (UCL) since being appointed its first head in 1980. He led the effort in the early 1970s to connect the U.S. ARPANET system with UCL, an idea first proposed in 1970 by Larry Roberts, head of ARPA in the U.S. Kirstein and his group at UCL were able to establish the U.S.-U.K. linkage in 1973, and provided access to the U.S. system through the UCL to other U.K. universities from as well.

The computer science department at University College London (UCL) grants several degrees, including bachelor of science, master of engineering, master of science, doctor of engineering, master of philosophy, and doctor of philosophy. The department recruits students and faculty who fit with its primary focus on experimental computer science: Work at UCL is based on forming and testing hypotheses, then conducting experiments that both based on theory and reproducible. The computer science department has ten research groups: Bioinformatics; Media Futures; Human Centred Systems; Intelligent Systems; Information Security; Networks; Programming Principles, Logic and Verification; Software Systems Engineering; Vision and Imaging Science; and Virtual Environments and Graphics. The department also has four interest groups: Complex Networks, Digital Biology, Mobile Systems (MOBISYS), and Tesla, which focuses on projects drawing on both art and science that seek to create a new amalgam of art|science. The UCL computer science department has had more than seventy collaborations with industry and governmental organizations, including the Wellcome Trust, the European Office of Aerospace Research and Development, GlaxoSmithKline, Kodak, Banque Safra, Microsoft, Phillips Electronics UK, and the Science Applications International Corporation (SAIC). The department is also home to UCL SECReT, the first center in Europe to grant a Ph.D. in security and crime science.

Malamud, Carl. *Exploring the Internet: A Technical Travelogue*. Englewood Cliffs: Prentice hall, 1992. Print. A journalistic account of the author's travels (he circled the globe three times) investigating places of importance for the history and current developments of the Internet; Kirstein's labs at University College London are among his stops.

Wu, Tim. *The Master Switch: The Rise and Fall of Information Empires*. New York: Vintage, 2011. Print. A history of a pattern the author argues information technologies (including telephone, radio, and film) in U.S. history have followed: moving from an open and entrepreneurial environment to one dominated by a few large corporations. The author, a Columbia University professor and senior adviser to the U.S. Federal Trade Commission, argues that the Internet is in danger of following the same course and losing the freedom of its early years to become dominated by one or a few companies.

LEONARD KLEINROCK

Developer of the Internet

Born: June 13, 1934; New York, New York
Died: -
Primary Field: Computer science
Specialty: Internet
Primary Company/Organization: University of California, Los Angeles

INTRODUCTION

Leonard Kleinrock's contributions to the Internet have been extensive on both the theoretical and practical levels. He has referred to himself as the father of modern data networking, a claim disputed by some. He conducted research into and enhanced the theoretical framework for packet switching, a technology that allows messages to be broken into smaller segments and then reassembled at the point where the message was to be sent. This method would allow faster transmission with the ability to share computer resources most effectively. On a practical level, Kleinrock and his staff at the University of California at Los Angeles (UCLA) supported the creation of the first major network, the Advanced Research Projects Agency Network (AR-PANET), developing and implementing its first node at UCLA. He later developed otherideas on how the resulting Internet could be improved and has been an advocate for greater mobility, or what he calls "nomadic computing."

EARLY LIFE

Leonard Kleinrock was born on June 13, 1934, in New York City. He has described how his later life was changed forever when, at the age of six, he was reading a Superman comic book. Inside the comic book was a set of instructions for making a crystal radio. After gathering the materials, he built the radio set and, as he put it, an engineer was born. He continued to make radios and other projects and, given his interests, enrolled at the Bronx High School of Science.

He graduated from high school in 1951 and later that year began attending night school at the City College of New York. He graduated in 1957 with a

Leonard Kleinrock.

bachelor's degree in electrical engineering. Kleinrock then went to the Massachusetts Institute of Technology (MIT), where he earned a master's degree in electrical engineering (1959) and a doctorate in computer science (1963). He received his Ph.D. at MIT in the same year as his later colleague and codeveloper of the ARPANET, Larry Roberts, received his.

Upon graduating from MIT, Kleinrock he joined the faculty at UCLA. In the years immediately after his arrival, Kleinrock's activities included the establishment of the Network Measurement Center (NMC), which, as a network measuring and development group, would play a large role in his own career as well as in the development of the ARPANET.

LIFE'S WORK

Kleinrock's major work can be divided into two significant areas. The first and most controversial is his claim to have developed the idea of packet switching as a means of transmitting messages. Packet switching was an important development in the effective transfer data over networks. In the 1950s and 1960s, the capability of mainframe computers was limited. The standard procedure was to send a message in its entirety, a process that required a greater share of computer resources. At this time, gaining the maximum use by a large number of users (time sharing) was becoming the subject of increasing research, as it was looked upon as the only reasonable alternative to buying larger numbers of computers. Additionally, as nearly all communications technology at that time was developed with a thought toward military applications, the vulnerability of these long message strings was a point of concern. Packet switching meant that messages would be decomposed into "packets," small portions of the message, then sent over the communication network to the destination, where the message would be reassembled.

Work on this concept had already been done from a theoretical perspective. Kleinrock produced papers in the early 1960s, based on his doctoral research in queuing, which was important to the implementation of packet switching. What he claimed was not only that his work was important for the successful development of packet switching but also that he had, in essence, invented it.

Kleinrock's role in the development of the Internet has, for some years now, been the source of controversy. That controversy began in the mid-1990s, when Kleinrock began to style himself as the "Inventor of Internet Technology" and posted his claims on his web page at UCLA. The claims were met with considerable skepticism, because it was widely known that two other individuals, Donald Davies and Paul Baran, were considered to be the inventors of packet switching. They had not only defined what packet switching was in theory but also had coined the term *packets* for the bundles of data into which messages were broken and had actually built a prototype packet-switching network in the mid-1960s.

Davies contested Kleinrock's assertions of having developed the technology in a letter released after his death (his son saying that, because Davies was ill toward the end of his life, he had not wanted to engage in a battle at that time). In his letter, Davies strongly claims that Kleinrock made no real contribution to either the practical or the theoretical aspects of packet switching. Kleinrock's claim to have written about packet switching in 1961 was disputed not only by Davies but also by several authors who analyzed Kleinrock's work from that time; their conclusions lend credence to Davies' claim. Kleinrock's work in the early 1960s was based on his investigations into queuing, which does have a connection with the operation of packet switching.

Kleinrock's reply has been that while Baran and Davies did make contributions to the concept but that the credit for developing packet switching should go to him. While some authors have noted the work done by Davies and Baran, Larry Roberts, who managed the development of ARPANET, has repeatedly come to the defense of Kleinrock and his claims.

The second part of Kleinrock's life work was in the building of ARPANET. He had already begun to establish himself as a leader in planning how networks might work and how they might be built. In 1961, he published a paper entitled "Information Flow in Large Communication Nets." Three years later, he would write a book, *Communication Nets*, that attracted wide attention. One of those who read the book was his MIT classmate, Larry Roberts, who would become the project manager for the development of ARPANET.

ARPANET, a network that would be designed and developed through the auspices of the Defense Advanced Research Projects Agency (DARPA), was the result of conversations, exchanges of ideas, and papers during the early 1960s. J. C. R. Licklider, whose idea of a "galactic" network that would allow multiple users to communicate, simultaneously found support among ARPA managers and scientists, including Roberts. The effort started under Roberts's direction in 1967, and the network of four computers, including one at UCLA that

Affiliation: Computer Science Department, University of California, Los Angeles

The University of California at Los Angeles was established in 1881, when it came into being as the State Normal School Teacher's College. In 1919, the school became the southern branch of the University of California, based in Berkeley, and it came to be known by its abbreviation, UCLA, in 1927. Enrollment at UCLA in 2012 was approximately thirty thousand undergraduates and more than ten thousand graduate students.

The school's dominance as a computer science center began in the post-World War II era. In the late 1940s, government funding, principally from the National Bureau of Standards and the Navy Department, began to be directed to UCLA. Design and building of computers and all areas of development associated with them grew dramatically in the 1950s. In 1950, UCLA faculty developed the Standards Western Automatic Computer (SWAC). Because of its increasing capabilities and its ability to attract both students and faculty, it became not only one of the prime centers of computer development but also a center where work requiring massive computing could be performed.

With all of that activity, however, computer science was conducted on a decentralized basis. It was not until 1968 that today's separate Computer Science Department was formed, taking faculty and resources from several engineering departments. The UCLA Computer Science Department's current activities include high-speed networking, artificial intelligence, and computer-aided design and manufacturing (CAD/CAM), as well as other aspects of computer science, both theoretical and practical.

PERSONAL LIFE

Kleinrock has published more than 225 papers and six books in the course of his career. He secured seventeen patents through 2011. In addition to his work at UCLA, Kleinrock has been active in private ventures. One of these is Nomadix, of which he is founder and chairman. Nomadix manufactures gateways that can more easily support the demands of what Kleinrock refers to as "nomadic computing," or *nomadicity*. This nomadicity includes the increasing number of users who depend on public and visitor-based networks or who use Wi-Fi zones.

In 2004, Kleinrock made news when he stated that, as a UCLA principal investigator for DARPA, he would no longer accept any DARPA funding because of its new policy of not granting funding to projects in which not all of the researchers were U.S. citizens.

Kleinrock is a member many professional organizations, such as the National Academy of Engineering, and he is a Fellow of the Association for Computing Machinery and the Institute of Electrical and Electronics Engineers (IEEE). Kleinrock has also participated on several committees to investigate network issues. He has received many awards, including the Marconi Award, the IEEE Internet Millennium Award, the UCLA Outstanding Teacher Award, and the National Academy of Engineering's Charles Stark Draper Prize. It was this last award, received with Larry Roberts, Robert Kahn, and Vinton Cerf, combined with his statements beginning in the mid-1990s about his role in developing the Internet, that has created the controversy surrounding Kleinrock.

Robert N. Stacy

FURTHER READING

Hafner, Katie. "A Paternity Suit Divides Net Pioneers." *New York Times*. 8 Nov. 2001: n. pag. Print. An account of the controversy over the importance of Kleinrock's role in developing the Internet and that of earlier developers in the area of packet switching.

Kleinrock, Leonard. "Busting Loose." *Communications of the ACM* Sept. 2001: 41–45. Print. Kleinrock's account of his career in development as well as a discussion of decreasing constraints that existed in the Internet circa 2001. This article begins to define what he refers to as nomadicity as well as the increasing need for mobile, or nomadic, computing.

---. "Creating a Mathematical Theory of Computer Networks." *Operations Research* 50.1 (2002): 125–31. Print. Discusses Kleinrock's theories of computer networks.

Kleinrock's NMC staff had assisted in developing, went into operation in October 1969.

Kleinrock and his group did not cease their affiliation with ARPANET after the successful implementation. A large part of the NMC's charter had been to test and suggest improvements to ARPANET. Through the 1970s, Kleinrock and his team worked on expanding the capabilities of the network, especially in terms of performance through stress testing and increasing robustness of the network.

---. "Nomadic Computing and Smart Spaces." *IEEE Internet Computing* 4.1 (2000): 52–53. Print. A somewhat shorter description of Kleinrock's idea of nomadicity and increased requirements for mobility.

Kurose, James F., and Keith W. Ross. *Computer Networking: A Top-down Approach Featuring the Internet.* Boston: Pearson/Addison Wesley, 2005. Print. Includes an interview with Kleinrock.

Salus, Peter H. *Casting the Net: From ARPANET to Internet and Beyond.* Reading: Addison-Wesley, 1995. Print. Now a standard history of the evolution of ARPANET into the Internet as it existed in the mid-1990s.

TIMOTHY KOOGLE

Former President and CEO of Yahoo!

Born: July 5, 1951; Alexandria, Virginia
Died: -
Primary Field: Internet
Specialty: Content and data
Primary Company/Organization: Yahoo!

INTRODUCTION

Timothy Koogle was the first president and chief executive officer (CEO) of Yahoo, Inc. He was recruited by investor Mike Moritz of Sequoia Capital to be Yahoo!'s sixth employee. In the company of Stanford Ph.D. dropouts, he was comparatively a wise old sage at forty-five. His folksy and reasoned style guided the company through the first six years of explosive growth on the world stage. In 2001, Koogle was replaced at the helm of Yahoo! by entertainment executive Terry Semel. A mechanic at heart, Koogle then retired to a couple of board seats and the occasional race car seat.

EARLY LIFE

Timothy Andrew Koogle (who goes by TK) was born in Alexandria, Virginia, on July 5, 1951. His mechanical interests were fostered by his father, who was a machinist. In high school and college, he cofounded and performed in two rock bands, the Tides and Paraphernalia. He attended the University of Virginia, graduating as valedictorian with a bachelor's degree in mechanical engineering in 1973. This was followed with two more engineering degrees, a master of science in 1975 and a Ph.D. in 1977, both from Stanford University. Learning how to rebuild engines at an early age paid off later in life, as Koogle augmented his graduate student scholarship with income that he earned repairing other students' broken cars in and around Palo Alto. He made so much money doing this between classes that he bought his own machine shop.

LIFE'S WORK

Prior to Yahoo, Koogle had two corporate experiences of note. At Motorola for most of the 1980s and the first few years of the 1990s, he played an operational role that evolved into corporate venturing. This gave him a solid background in risk-based decision making. For two years afterward, he greatly increased sales as the president of Seattle's Intermec, a manufacturer of barcode-related equipment. This was also good training for the wild ride he was about to take. In his forty-fifth year, Koogle was chosen to be the first CEO of Yahoo, Inc. which was just a few months old in the summer of 1995.

Timothy Koogle.

Affiliation: Yahoo!

Sergey Brin and Larry Page, cofounders of Google, were not the first two Internet billionaires whose business was born out of the electrical engineering Ph.D. students' office trailer on the Stanford University campus. At the dawn of consumer awareness of the World Wide Web, in early 1994, Stanford Ph.D. students David Filo and Jerry Yang cofounded the index of websites that later became known as Yahoo!

Something like a virtual telephone book, Yahoo! organized all known websites into categories and subcategories. Yahoo! was a portal, a place where regular people started their Internet session. Quickly this unique and very useful index attracted a cultlike following. Through word of mouth, that growing usage snowballed into a great deal of Internet traffic. At this time, Stanford asked that the site, which was hogging space, be moved off its servers. Befriending Marc Andreessen of Netscape yielded a temporary hosting solution that kept the site alive and growing.

In 1995, engineer cofounders Filo and Yang met another key businessperson. Randy Adams, who ran the Internet Shopping Network, saw the promise in their product and brought them to meet Mike Moritz of the powerful Sequoia Capital venture firm. "Jerry and Dave's Guide to the World Wide Web" was renamed Yahoo, an acronym that stands for "yet another hierarchical officious oracle." Sequoia led an investment that culminated in a very lucrative 1996 initial public offering (IPO). As the dot-com boom came peaked at the end of the 1990s, the Yahoo! brand name, website, and associated yodel were familiar to hundreds of millions worldwide. Popular products included Yahoo! Mail and Yahoo! Finance.

The tide turned in 2001, when, for the first but certainly not the last time, Yahoo! laid off hundreds of employees. Yang was seen crying at the related analyst's call. Timothy Koogle, Yahoo!'s first CEO, was replaced by Terry Semel, who had a Hollywood entertainment background.

Strong competition in the most lucrative vertical markets—search, e-mail, auctions, shopping, and classifieds—demonstrated emphatically that in the new millennium Yahoo! would no longer be all things to all users. Leadership turnover, myriad priorities, and problematic decisions regarding mergers and acquisitions have all been blamed for exacerbating this fall from grace. Following a scandalous ousting of its fourth CEO within one calendar year, in 2012 Yahoo! hired a new CEO: thirty-seven-year-old engineer Marissa Mayer, who brought fifteen years of experience from Google's search business.

Koogle was affable and cool but not zany or off-the-wall. This distinguished him as a grown-up among the Yahooligans. Together, they made a worldwide brand and an incredible amount money in a very short period of time. As CEO, Koogle is credited with convincing founders David Filo and Jerry Yang to adopt the advertising model. Carefully, the company rolled out a 468-by-60-pixel banner ad that adorned the top of each page in the directory that used to be "Jerry and Dave's Guide to the World Wide Web." Koogle assured them of the need to make money for their investors and explained that the ad model enabled that, while continuing to provide a service to their users free of charge.

Unlike contemporary search engine competitors, such as Excite or AltaVista, Yahoo!'s mechanism for sorting web content into a usable taxonomy was different; it was human. Under Koogle's leadership, hundreds of Yahoo! employees were paid to look at websites and make informed decisions and judgment calls about where and how they ought to be categorized. These people, appropriately called surfers, continued to differentiate the incumbent Yahoo! from upstart Google at the beginning of the twenty-first centry.

For many years, Koogle could do no wrong. Advertising sales were so fast and easy that Yahoo! was scrambling to handle the phones. Without much evidence of an eventual sales payoff, major advertisers like Ford Motor Company and Pepsi spent seven or eight figures on integrated campaigns across the site, which had branched out to provide content-themed home pages on more than forty topics, such as games and pets. In part, the motivation for these expenditures seems to have included the cachet of the Yahoo! brand.

In the late 1990s, during the period now known as the dot-com boom, the atmosphere in Silicon Valley was feverish, a purple and yellow contagion initiated by Koogle's Yahoo! Stock that might have beeen bought for $13 in 1996 was trading for more than ten times that amount by the end of the decade. Despite the fact that Yahoo!'s price-to-earnings ratio exceeded 1,500:1, investors and would-be employees flocked to YHOO and Santa Clara in droves.

Perhaps the greatest compliment to Koogle's leadership style and ability was paid in an academic journal article. In David Thomson's *Leader-to-Leader* piece entitled "Inside Outside Leadership for Exponential Growth," the Yahoo! pair of chief operating officer Jeff Mallet and CEO Koogle are held up as exemplars. According to the author, working together on these distinct internal and external leadership elements is what makes such a pairing so effective.

Under Koogle's leadership, Yahoo! made several acquisitions. Rebranded, this intellectual property extended the company's product and service lines to include Yahoo! Mail and Yahoo! Messenger, among others. When acquired, the shares that employees had held in these smaller companies typically converted into YHOO stock and vested immediately. In this fast-moving melee, many people made more money in a few months than their parents had earned in an entire lifetime. Legend has it that at least one customer service representative made more than $10 million "answering phones" and that many a foosball game was played to win or lose a $10,000 bet. Koogle himself was outed for splurging on late-night eBay purchases that included a new $130,000 Aston Martin, a Versace wallet, and an Armani jacket.

What Koogle did not buy might have been more important, ultimately to his future and to YHOO shareholders. In the spring of 2000, news emerged that Yahoo! was holding meetings with eBay. Nothing ever came of this promising Internet commerce conversation. Instead, the story goes that a merger of equals was blockaded by egos.

Had he made or publicly championed any such bold or strategic moves, Koogle might have held onto the reins longer or been remembered differently. Unfortunately, after the overheated NASDAQ crashed in April of 2000, neither the company nor his reputation as a charming and reasonable leader would ever be the same. The equity that was once part of the plot of the Hollywood film *Frequency* (in which the main character travels back in time and implores a friend to buy stock at the IPO price) fell. Almost a year later, after an unpopular one-day trading embargo, Koogle resigned as CEO. Soon after, YHOO was trading below its IPO price of five years earlier.

PERSONAL LIFE

Previously divorced, Koogle was remarried to Pam Scott, an advertising and marketing professional who cofounded The Curious Company. Together they share a passion for beautiful mechanical things and have attended prestigious car shows and racing schools. They are now developing luxury estates near Puerto Vallarta, Mexico, called El Banco.

Koogle remained on the board until 2003, when he stepped down as chairman of the board. He is a director of the social networking firm Friendster, having served as interim CEO there in 2003–04. He then became chairman of ecofriendly cleaning supply purveyor Method Products and the cochairman of Room-to-Read, which establishes libraries in developing countries.

Geoffrey R. Archer

FURTHER READING

Ackman, Dan. "Top of the News: Koogle Quits." *Forbes* 8 Mar. 2001. Web. 19 Aug. 2012. Sarcastic explanation of why YHOO stock trading was halted on the day before Koogle resigned.

Himelstein, Linda. "Tim Koogle: The Grown-Up Voice of Reason at Yahoo!" *Business Week* 7 Sept. 1998: n. pag. Print. Profiles Koogle as a racy car-guy and provides a brief history of Yahoo!

---, Heather Green, Richard Siklos, and Catherine Yang. "Yahoo! The Company. The Strategy. The Stock." *Business Week* 7 Sept. 1998: n. pag. Print. Profiles Yahoo! in its heyday.

Koogle, Tim. "Public Profile." *LinkedIn.com*. Web. 19 Aug. 2012. Koogles own profile, listing professional history and accomplishments, on this popular professional networking site.

Lardner, James. "Search No Further." *U.S. News and World Report* 18 May 1998: 49–53. Print. Describes the Internet start-up with the crazy stock price as run by sane people, nevertheless.

Sherman, Josepha. *Jerry Yang and David Filo (Techies)*. Brookfield: 21st Century, 2001. Print. Written for a younger audience, this eighty-page softcover gives an account of the early years of Yahoo!

Taylor, Chris. "Yahoo! Lowers the Net." *Time* 19 Mar. 2001: 54–55. Print. An account of the dot-com bubble and how it burst all over Yahoo! shareholders.

Thomson, David G. "Inside-Outside Leadership for Exponential Growth." *Leader-to-Leader* 40 (2006): 22–29. Print. Academic management article that describes Koogle as part of a high-functioning leadership team.

Weston, Michael R. *Jerry Yang and David Filo: The Founders of Yahoo!* New York: Rosen, 2006. Print. These 112 pages are meant to inspire youth to accomplish great things.

GARY KREMEN

Founder of match.com

Born: 1963; Skokie, Illinois
Died: -
Primary Field: Internet
Specialty: Social media
Primary Company/Organization: match.com

INTRODUCTION

Gary Kremen is an Internet and software engineer known for capitalizing on the value of Internet domain names; among the names he has registered are jobs.com, autos.com, and sex.com. His eleven-year battle to reclaim sex.com was highly publicized and established the legal principle that a domain name is property and thus can be stolen, even if the original owner did not pay for it. Kremen also cofounded one of the world's first open source software companies and created a pioneering green power company to encourage the use of solar energy.

EARLY LIFE

Gary Kremen grew up in Skokie, Illinois, a Chicago suburb; both his parents were teachers. As a teenager, he was a computer hacker and was involved in minor juvenile delinquency. After graduating from Niles West High School in Skokie, he enrolled in Northwestern University in Evanston, Illinois (also a Chicago suburb) in 1981, studying business and electrical engineering. After graduation in 1985, he went to work with an aerospace contractor and was introduced to the ARPANET, a forerunner of the Internet. Kremen also earned a master's degree in business administration from Stanford University in 1989.

LIFE'S WORK

Kremen's distinguished himself with an ability to be among the first to recognize trends and meet emerging needs in the software industry. In 1991, he and Ben Dubin created one of the world's first open source software companies, Full Source Software; their business model was built by capitalizing on the number of software programs available on the Internet, at a time when many individuals had computers but not Internet access. The company operated by downloading and testing open source programs, putting them together into packages, and selling them to people who did not have access to the Internet and to corporations. Setting a price point of

$99 per package, Full Source Software was soon selling several thousand dollars' worth of software per day.

Kremen made his biggest fortune by spotting another trend: the value of domain names. In the early days of the Internet, domain names were free, but they had to be registered so that each would be used only once, Kremen reasoned that the Internet would one day carry classified advertising similar to that carried in newspapers, and so he registered domain names based on the traditional headings in a newspaper's classified listings: autos.com, jobs.com, housing.com, and most famously sex.com. In 1993, he founded Electric Classifieds, Inc., the first Internet classified ads company, and with backing by private investors launched the dating site match.com in 1995. Match.com allowed users eighteen years old and older to post information about themselves, to browse other listings, and to search for matches based on criteria of their choosing. Kremen obtained financing from a group of investors led by Canaan Partners, and as Internet dating became more popular, the company prospered, even while some of the

Gary Kremen.

Affiliation: match.com

Gary Kremen created match.com in 1995 to test his idea of using the Internet as a medium for classified ads, fulfilling a function then still largely the domain of newspapers. One key feature of the operation was a database allowing people to store their personal information and search for potential dates based on specified criteria; this feature remains with match.com today, which specifies on its website that its search algorithm helps people find good matches.

Although Internet dating was a new concept in the mid-1990s, it proved extremely popular and also profitable for its investors. Match.com sold to Cendant for $7 million in 1998 and to Ticket Master in 2000 for $50 million. As of 2012, match.com operated in twenty-five countries on five contents and in eight languages. According to Alexa, a company that tracks web traffic, match.com is the most often visited dating site on the Internet.

---

investors were reluctant to be associated with a dating service, considering it tacky. In 1997, match.com was sold to Cendant for $8 million; it was sold again in 1999 to Ticket Master for $50 million.

Kremen may be most famous for his battle with Stephen Michael Cohen over ownership of the domain name sex.com. Kremen registered the name in 1994 but learned in 1995 that ownership of sex.com had been transferred to Cohen, who presented forged documents to Network Solutions, LLC, the company in charge of registering Internet domain names. Cohen had already served prison time for fraud and had a string of convictions for other crimes, including car theft, forgery, and passing bad checks. Network Solutions had no interest in helping Kremen regain the website, in part because Kremen paid nothing to register it in the first place, and Kremen spent an estimated $5 million in legal fees on the case. He ultimately won it, however, and in 2000 a judge ordered Cohen to return the domain name to Kremen and to pay $65 million in damages. Kremen was unable to collect the settlement, however, because Cohen fled the country and had already transferred most of his wealth outside the United States as well. One material benefit Kremen did enjoy as part of the settlement was ownership of Cohen's mansion in Rancho Santa Fe, California, a wealthy suburb near San Diego, after Cohen fled the United States. Cohen was extradited from Mexico on October 27, 2005, and Kremen has since been awarded more of Cohen's properties, including land in Tijuana, Mexico, a shrimp farm in Mexico, and a partial interest in a Mexican strip club.

The value of sex.com fell rapidly after the domain was returned to Kremen, although not entirely because of any fault of his. Under Cohen's management, sex.com had been making $500,000 to $750,000 per month, primary through advertising, and kept earning at this pace for a few months after the site was returned to Kremen.

However, demand for Internet pornography fell rapidly within a few months, as what had once been a scarce property had become commonplace and was available free through sharing services such as Kazaa. Kremen was also not an efficient manager, and revenue from the site dropped to one-third of what it had been a year earlier. Given this competition, Kremen shifted the focus of sex.com toward selling sponsored links to appear on the sex.com site and on search engines. In 2006, Kremen sold sex.com for $14 million, the largest sum ever paid for a domain name, although much less than what Cohen appears to have made on the site when he was operating it.

Also in 2006, Kremen began a new venture by founding Clean Power Finance, a company whose stated goal is to get more Americans to use solar power by simplifying the processes of designing, installing, and financing it. Clean Power Finance (CPF) uses two complementary approaches to encourage the adoption of solar technologies. First, it created CPF Tools, a software program used by solar installers to help them design, quote, and sell solar power systems for residential customers; about 40 percent of all residential solar sales use CPF Tools. Second, it provides access to financing to residential consumers. Kremen holds three patents, the most significant of which is for dynamic web pages, meaning web pages that change as an individual uses them; dynamic web pages have become a standard feature of most websites. He sold this patent for more than $1.25 million.

PERSONAL LIFE

Kremen lives in San Diego, in Stephen Michael Cohen's former house (awarded to Kremen as part of the settlement of the sex.com case), and maintains a residence and business office in San Francisco as well. In 2007, he estimated his net worth at $10 million. He is married and has a child.

Sarah Boslaugh

FURTHER READING

Carreon, Charles. *The Sex.Com Chronicles: A White-Hat Lawyer's Journey to the Dark Side of the Internet*. Tucson: Prime, 2008. Print. An insider's account of the lawsuit Kremen filed against Stephen Michael Cohen, charging him with stealing Sex. Com; this book is written by Kremen's lawyer in the case.

McCarthy, Kieren. *Sex.com: One Domain, Two Men, Twelve Years, and the Brutal Battle for the Jewel in the Internet's Crown*. London: Quercus, 2007. Print. A straightforward account of the theft of the domain name sex.com, Kremen's legal battle to get it back, and the legal precedents established in the process. The author is a journalist and expert on Internet issues.

Mooallem, Jon. "Sol Man: The Founder of Match.com Is Making the Case for Solar Energy, One Roof at a Time." *Mother Jones* 33.3 (2008): 46–48. Print. A feature article on Kremen, focusing on his start-up company, Clean Power Finance, with which he intends to convince average Americans that it is in their interests to make some use of solar power—for example, by installing solar panels on their roofs.

O'Brien, Chris. "Kremen: Life after Match.com, Sex. com; Entrepreneur Is Now a Family Man, Angel Investor in Cleantech." *San Jose Mercury News*, Business Valley final, 16 Mar. 2010: n. pag. Print. News article about Kremen, focusing on the changes in his life (Kremen was forty-six years old at the time) after settlement of the Sex.com case and after his marriage and the birth of his child.

---. "The Prisoner of Sex.com." *Wired* 11.8 (2003): n. pag. Print. A news article about Kremen's lawsuit against Stephen Cohen, which ended in a decision that Cohen had stolen the domain through forgery, and the current state of the website, which was in disarray after being managed by Cohen.

L

MAX LEVCHIN

Cofounder of PayPal

Born: July 11, 1975; Kiev, Ukraine
Died: -
Primary Field: Internet
Specialty: Commerce
Primary Company/Organization: PayPal

INTRODUCTION

Max Levchin is a Ukrainian-born, but primarily American-raised, computer scientist who has used his technology skills and business savvy to become a successful Silicon Valley entrepreneur. As a founder and key driving force behind the online payment-processing company PayPal, in 2002 he helped lead the first successful initial public offering (IPO) of a technology company after the terrorist attacks of September 11, 2001. After selling the post-IPO PayPal to eBay later in 2002, he then founded, invested in, and became chief executive officer (CEO) of Slide, an online service designed to give people an easy way to improve their blogs and personal pages with photo slide shows, videos, and other visual content. After selling Slide to Google in 2010, Levchin founded a company named HVF, which is reported to be an incubator employing tactics similar to those that Levchin used to launch Slide and other companies in which his role was more limited (such as Yelp, whose board includes Levchin).

EARLY LIFE

Maximilian Rafael Levchin is one of four children of a theoretical physicist mother and a poet-playwright father, born on July 11, 1975, in Kiev, Ukraine. His family emigrated from Ukraine to Chicago in 1991 under political asylum for reasons having to do with religious persecution (he is Jewish). Once in Illinois, his family settled in the West Ridge neighborhood on the border of Chicago and its adjacent suburb to the north, Evanston. After graduating from Mather High School in 1993, Levchin went to the University of Illinois at Urbana-Champaign, graduating in 1997 with a bachelor's degree in computer science. While an undergraduate, he became infamous for his all-night coding sessions. That

Max Levchin.

241

notoriety led him to meet others with similar interests in technology and coding, with whom he cofounded companies named NetMeridian Software (which developed early palm-top security applications) and SponsorNet New Media (which provided advertising services on the Internet); each ultimately failed.

LIFE'S WORK

Shortly after his graduation from the University of Illinois in 1997, Levchin relocated to Silicon Valley and cofounded a company named Fieldlink, which eventually became known as Confinity and then Pay-Pal. Fieldlink was a payments and cryptography company limited to the Palm Pilot platform. In 2000, after having changed its name to Confinity, the company merged with a company named X.com, an Internet financial services company that focused on e-mail payments and was founded by Elon Musk. The combined entity was then renamed PayPal, and Levchin became its chief technical officer.

While Confinity was forming, merging with X.com, and ultimately becoming PayPal, the online payments space began to burgeon with competitors, including Citibank's c2it, Yahoo!'s PayDirect, and Western Union's BidPay. At the same time, eBay was becoming increasingly interested in the space, and this interest led eBay ultimately to acquire an online payments company named Billpoint. It renamed Billpoint as eBay Payments and reduced its functionality so that it worked only with eBay auctions. Despite the leverage of eBay behind it, the limited functionality of the eBay Payments product made it unpopular with consumers, and by early 2000 PayPal was being used as the payment mechanism for far more eBay auctions than not only Billpoint but also all other mechanisms combined.

In February 2002, PayPal sold an initial public offering (IPO) of just less than 10 percent of its then-outstanding stock, raising more than $70 million, with its stock price rising more than 50 percent on the first day of trading. In the process, PayPal became the first

---

Affiliation: PayPal

PayPal is worldwide online payment-processing company that had its origins in a company named Confinity, which ultimately merged with a company called X.com to form a combined firm that was renamed Pay-Pal.

While Confinity was forming, merging with X.com, and becoming PayPal, the online payments space began to burgeon with competitors, including Citibank's c2it, Yahoo!'s PayDirect, and Western Union's BidPay. At the same time, eBay was becoming increasingly interested in the space, and this interest led eBay to acquire an online payments company named Billpoint. It renamed Billpoint as eBay Payments and reduced its functionality so that it worked only with eBay auctions. Despite the leverage of eBay behind it, the limited functionality of the eBay Payments product made it unpopular with consumers. By early 2000, PayPal was being used as the payment mechanism for far more eBay auctions than not only Billpoint but also all other mechanisms combined.

In February 2002, PayPal sold an initial public offering (IPO) of just under 10 percent of its then-outstanding stock, raising more than $70 million, with its stock price rising more than 50 percent on the first day of trading. In the process, PayPal became the first successful Internet IPO following the terrorist attacks of September 11, 2001. In October 2002, PayPal was acquired by eBay for $1.5 billion worth of eBay stock, and it remains wholly owned by eBay.

Today, PayPal operates under three primary brands: PayPal, Payflow Gateway, and Bill Me Later. It has more than 100 million active registered accounts and is available in nearly two hundred markets. It supports payments in more than twenty currencies, including the U.S. dollar, the Hong Kong dollar, the Euro, the Chinese yuan, the British pound sterling, and the Japanese yen. It has localized websites in more than twenty markets, including China, Germany, Hong Kong, Japan, and the United Kingdom.

PayPal's 2011 annual revenue was $4.4 billion, half of which was generated internationally. This revenue represented 38 percent of eBay's total revenues for the year. The total value of transactions processed through PayPal in 2011 was $118 billion, up 29 percent from the prior year.

PayPal is headquartered in San Jose, California, with its European headquarters in Luxembourg and its international headquarters in Singapore. It has multiple operations centers, located in such places as Berlin, Dublin, Omaha, São Paulo, and Shanghai, and multiple development centers, located in such places as Austin, Singapore, and Tel Aviv.

---

successful Internet IPO following the terrorist attacks of September 11, 2001. Levchin's 2.3 percent share of the company had a value of roughly $17 million.

In October of 2002, PayPal was acquired by eBay for $1.5 billion worth of eBay stock. Levchin was then twenty-six years old and had a net worth of roughly $34 million. He remained a PayPal executive after the eBay acquisition until December 2002. Although he left only two months after acquisition, that was longer than any other PayPal executive had remained.

After leaving PayPal, Levchin spent a year traveling, putting his newfound wealth and financial affairs in order, and contemplating returning to school to earn a doctorate. During this time, he decided that his true passion was starting and running companies, and he decided to return to entrepreneurship. He also began dabbling in angel investing, which has led over time to a portfolio that includes Yelp (a local-area shopping and social networking company for which he was chairman of the board, of which he remains a member), IronPort (sold to Cisco), LiveOps, Mixpanel, WePay, Quid, Emerald Therapeutics, and others.

In August 2005, Levchin founded a company named Slide, with an initial funding of $78 million, $7 million of which was his. Slide was launched as a service designed to give people an easy way to improve their blogs and other personal web pages with photo slide shows, videos, and other visual content. By 2005, the Internet already had multiple popular photo-sharing sites, but Levchin envisioned a new way to share visual content with products such as the multimedia FunWall and SuperPoke, which let users virtually "hug," "punch," or "throw" animal images at other users.

In August 2010, Google announced that it was acquiring Slide for $182 million. That acquisition added another $34 million to Levchin's net worth and, when he agreed to work for Google after the acquisition, the title of Google vice president of engineering to his résumé. While the purchase price of $182 million was significant, it was far less than the valuation of up to $500 million that Slide had sometimes garnered during its fund-raising rounds. Neither Slide's products nor its personnel successfully integrated into Google, and only a year after the acquisition, in August 2011, Google announced both that it was shuttering the Slide service and that Levchin was leaving Google to pursue other opportunities.

In early 2012, Levchin launched a new venture, named HVF, which is reported to be an incubator employing tactics similar to those that Levchin used to launch Slide and other companies in which his role was more limited (such as Yelp). He continues to participate in the governance of the companies included in his investment portfolio and sits as an outside director on numerous boards, as well as on the San Francisco Symphony Orchestra's board of governors. As of mid-2012, estimates of Levchin's net worth ranged from $100 to $300 million.

PERSONAL LIFE

In September 2008, Levchin wed longtime girlfriend Nellie Minkova. They settled in the South Park neighborhood north of San Francisco with their wheaten terrier, Uma, and maintained a vegetarian lifestyle. The only reported visible extravagance of Levchin's wealth is the house in which he and his wife live, which they purchased for approximately $5 million.

In his leisure time, Levchin enjoys endurance road cycling, fermented foods, music (particularly electronic), art, general science, mathematics (particularly discrete math), literature, theology, and geometry.

Joe Bogdan

FURTHER READING

Jackson, Eric M. *The PayPal Wars: Battles with eBay, the Media, the Mafia, and the Rest of Planet Earth.* Torrance: World Ahead, 2008. Print and digital. Tells the story of PayPal's history from the view of a former insider, author Eric Jackson.

Kasparov, Garry, Max Levchin, and Peter Thiel. *The Blueprint: Reviving Innovation, Rediscovering Risk, and Rescuing the Free Market.* New York: Norton, 2012. E-book. Levchin, along with Kasparov (the globe's youngest World Chess Champion) and Thiel (former CEO of PayPal and initial investor in Facebook)—billed as "three of the world's most original thinkers"—deliver a manifesto addressing their thoughts on research and development, disruptive technologies, job creation, education, and financial discipline.

Livingston, Jessica. *Founders at Work: Stories of Startups' Early Days.* Berkeley: Apress, 2008. Print. A collection of interviews with founders of well-known technology companies, including Levchin and PayPal, about what happened in the very earliest days.

ROBIN LI

Cofounder of Baidu

Born: November 17, 1968; Yangquan, China
Died: -
Primary Field: Computer science
Specialty: Internet
Primary Company/Organization: Baidu

INTRODUCTION

Robin Li is a Chinese Internet entrepreneur and co-founder, chairman and chief executive officer (CEO) of Baidu, Inc., the Chinese web services company that runs China's most popular search engine and the world's third-largest independent search engine. In 2011, Forbes *named him the richest man in China and the ninety-fifth richest in the world, with an estimated worth of $10.2 billion. Li excels at improving algorithms for search engines; for example, he developed the RankDex site-scoring algorithm for ranking search engine pages, which was awarded a U.S. patent. This technology is used in the Chinese-language search engine Baidu, which Li cofounded in 1999 and which now holds 85 percent of the Chinese market share.*

Robin Li.

EARLY LIFE

Robin Li was born Li Yanhong in the city of Yangquan in Shanxi Province in northern China on November 17, 1968. His parents worked in factories. Li was the fourth of five children (and the only boy). He grew up during China's Cultural Revolution. A smart student, Li gained admission to Yangquan First High School by earning the second-highest grade on the entrance exam. In high school he studied computer programming and participated in various citywide programming competitions. In 1987, Li scored among the highest in China's National Higher Education Entrance Examination. In 1991, he received a bachelor's degree from the prestigious Beijing University (formerly known as Peking University), where he had studied information management. Li was a college sophomore when, in 1989, the pro-democracy demonstrations in Tiananmen Square caused the university campus to be shut down.

LIFE'S WORK

Li, who speaks fluent English, was interested in studying abroad after high school. In the fall of 1991, he went to the State University of New York at Buffalo (SUNY-Buffalo), where he earned a master's degree in computer science. He initially planned to continue with his studies and earn a Ph.D. In 1994, however, Li joined IDD Information Services, a New Jersey division of Dow Jones and Company, where he helped create a software program for the online edition of *The Wall Street Journal*. He worked at IDD from May 1994 to June 1997.

Li always had a passion for Internet searches and was interested in solving one of the Internet industry's biggest dilemmas in its early years: how to sort information. Li knew that the importance of search results could be automatically ranked by citations, or by how many websites linked to that information, so he focused his research on developing better algorithms for search engines to rank sites.

Li's breakthrough came in 1996, when he developed a "link analysis" search mechanism for IDD that he named RankDex. RankDex ranked websites based on how many other sites had linked to it. RankDex received a U.S. patent in 1996. (Around this time, two Stanford students, Larry Page and Sergey Brin, devised a similar algorithm they called BackRub, which later became Google.)

In 1997, Li attended a computer conference in Silicon Valley where he demonstrated his algorithms. William Chang, then chief technology officer at the early search firm Infoseek (partly owned by Disney), hired Li as a staff engineer. Li also published widely circulated papers at this time. Although shy, Li retained his passion for developing Internet search tools in an entrepreneurial setting and became disappointed with Infoseek's lackluster interest in pursuing innovative search techniques.

In 1998, Li's friend Eric Xu, then a thirty-four-year-old biochemist and sales representative for a U.S. biotech firm, introduced the thirty-year-old Li to Jerry Yang, the Taiwanese-born cofounder of Yahoo! Xu, who was making a documentary about American innovation at the time, was working with Chinese American documentary filmmaker Ruby Yang. Together they had interviewed Jerry Yang. Xu and other Yahoo! employees were invited to a playback of the interview. Li's wife, who worked at Yahoo! as a sales representative, brought her husband to the event. Li and Xu were inspired by the success of the Yahoo! cofounder, with whom they could identify.

In 1999, the Chinese communist government, aware of Li's computer science expertise, invited Li to return to China for the regime's fiftieth anniversary celebrations. Dedicated to their vision of building a major media company and inspired by Jerry Yang, Li and Xu started Baidu in a hotel room in Beijing that year. They left their wives in the United States and worked tirelessly, armed with $1.2 million from U.S. venture firms Integrity Partners and Peninsula Capital. In 2000, Draper Fisher Jurvetson and IDG Technology Ventures invested another $10 million.

Baidu, Inc.'s search engine, Baidu, was launched on October 11, 1999. The name Baidu comes from an eight-hundred-year-old Song Dynasty poem. Its literal translation means "hundreds of times" and stands for finding retreating beauty in chaos or searching for an ideal. Li's inventions, which are considered the gold standard in web search relevance, are still under the control of the Chinese government. Baidu is heavily censored by China's government, and priority is often granted to advertising companies rather than relevant search results. Baidu has been accused of penalizing the search rankings of websites that decrease their advertising spending. With its near monopoly of search engines in China, Baidu has also been accused of Internet piracy. Li disputes all these allegations. Nonetheless, Baidu complies with the Chinese government's search restrictions, including blocking pornography sites and

pages that reference politically sensitive topics, such as Taiwanese independence, the Dalai Lama, and the 1989 Tiananmen Square uprising.

By 2004, Baidu, with its Internet traffic skyrocketing, allowed advertisers to pay to appear at the tops of searches. Although known as the "Chinese Google," Google never became a big threat to Baidu, perhaps because of Baidu's software's better ability to parse sentences into Chinese, as well as Google's unwillingness—perhaps because of its ties to the entertainment industry—to allow copyright infringement with music, where Baidu is popular for its free music downloads. In 2004, Google invested $5 million in Baidu, laying the groundwork for acquisition. However, several problems at Google's headquarters in China the next year, including e-mail hacking, may have given rise to Baidu's ability to oust Google and gain control of the market. Google accused Baidu of poisoning the Domain Name System, among other discriminatory practices.

In 2005, Baidu filed to go public; on August 5, it was listed on NASDAQ. Shares jumped from its initial public offering (IPO) price of $27 to $122 that day, the biggest one-day gain since the final days of the dot-com boom, when IPOs regularly soared. Baidu's dazzling debut was due both to its connections to Google and to its own potential.

In 2005, Google made a failed $1.6 billion bid for Baidu, which many think was a missed opportunity. That year, Li was listed in CNN Money's 50 People Who Matter Now. The next year, he was named *American Business Weekly*'s Best Business Leader for 2006. Around the same time, Baidu introduced an online encyclopedia, Baidupedia, modeled on Wikipedia but without the ability for users to create or edit entries. Baidupedia is filtered by Baidu, Inc., to comply with Chinese government restrictions. It was meant to replace Li's first attempt at offering a Chinese-language version of Wikipedia in 2005. In 2007 Baidu became the first Chinese company to be included in the NASDAQ-100 Index.

There have been some controversies with regard to Baidu's control. In 2008, the government-owned China Central Television (CCTV) aired several in-depth programs investigating Baidu, alleging that the web company earned millions of dollars by advertising unlicensed medical practitioners. The headlines ran on Li's fortieth birthday. When Baidu later increased its ad spending, with most of the money going to CCTV, the negative coverage stopped.

Li is dedicated to making Baidu a global company and exporting the Baidu brand abroad with such services

Affiliation: Baidu

Baidu, Inc., is the Chinese Internet services company known for the popular search engine Baidu, considered the Chinese equivalent of Google. Baidu, Inc., was founded by Chinese Internet entrepreneurs Robin Li and Eric Xu in 1999. With an index of more than 740 million web pages, Baidu's Chinese-language search engine offers millions of Chinese-languages users services to locate information, products, and services.

With an estimated worth of $15 billion, Baidu is the first Chinese company to be included in the NASDAQ-100 index. It is ranked sixth overall in the Alexa Internet rankings.

Baidu's search engine follows censorship regulations set by the Chinese government, which blocks pornography sites and references to topics such as Taiwanese Independence, the Dalai Lama, and the 1989 Tiananmen Square uprising.

Baidu generates revenues from online marketing services with a pay-for-placement (P4P) platform and keyword bidding/pay-per-click (PPC) advertising model. Baidu TV, its advertising service, allows advertisers to access the websites of its Baidu Union members so that they can strategically choose websites for marketing. Other components include Baidu Map, Baidu Legal Search, Baidu Entertainment, and social networking sites.

Although accused of censorship, Baidu remains the most trusted Chinese search engine and dominates the Chinese market. Headquartered in the bustling Shangdi district of Beijing, China, Baidu is symbolized by a bear's paw. Its name comes from an eight-hundred-year-old Song Dynasty poem representing the persistent search for ideal beauty.

as games, e-commerce, online payments, a Hulu-like video site, and maps. Engineers have been translating the site into a dozen languages, and Li holds an annual Baidu World conference at the Baidu headquarters in Beijing. In November 2010, Li participated in his first Silicon Valley public forum at the Web 2.0 Summit in San Francisco, California. He has never sold a share of his Baidu stock, according to public financial records.

PERSONAL LIFE

Li is married to Dongmin (Melissa) Ma and lives in Beijing. The couple met in 1995 at a ballroom dancing event for Chinese students in the Greater New York area. They married on October 10 that year in New Jersey, after dating for only six months.

In 1998, when Li and Xu met Jerry Yang, Melissa was instrumental in getting Li to pursue his passion as it was awakened by Yang's success. She urged him to found an Internet company, something Li says he would not have done without her encouragement and motivation. The couple had a daughter in 2000.

Li is an avid fan of the English Premier League Everton Football Club.

Ellen Elder

FURTHER READING

Greenberg, Andy. "The Man Who's Beating Google." *Forbes* 184.6 (2009): 82–87. Print. The article discusses Li and his success with Baidu, the most popular search engine in China and a rival to Google. At the time of the article's publication, Li was the seventh richest person in China and Baidu's stock was worth around $2.1 billion.

---, and Jie Li. "Internet Intermezzo." *Forbes Asia* 5.14 (2009): 30–33. Print. This article presents information, pictures, and a graph related to Li and Baidu, China's most popular search engine, which racks up approximately 8 billion monthly searches. It discusses Baidu's relevance along with China's growth in digital population.

Li, Yanhong (Robin). "Toward a Qualitative Search Engine." *IEEE Internet Computing* 2.4 (1998): 24–29. Print. One of Li's published papers that explains site-scoring algorithms for search engines that result in page rankings, as in his development of the patented RankDex.

Margolis, Jonathan. "Great Wall of Silence." *New Statesman* 15 Aug. 2011: 36–39. Print. This article focuses on Baidu's dominant role in Internet searching in China as compared to the role of Google in Western countries, focusing on censorship. It notes Baidu's attempts to present information as freely as possible without conflicting with the Chinese government.

Stone, Brad, and Bruce Einhorn. "How Baidu Won China." *Bloomberg Businessweek* 11 Nov. 2010: 60–67. Print. The article discusses how Baidu, which had captured a 73 percent market share in China at the time of publication, alters search results to conform with Chinese law. It also discusses Li's future plans for Baidu, including games, electronic commerce, and online payments.

J. C. R. LICKLIDER

Developer of the Internet

Born: May 11, 1925; St. Louis, Missouri
Died: June 26, 1990; Arlington, Massachusetts
Primary Field: Computer science
Specialty: Internet
Primary Company/Organization: Massachusetts
    Institute of Technology

INTRODUCTION

Sometimes known as the Johnny Appleseed of twentieth-century computing, J. C. R. Licklider has been credited by various sources as the creator of the Internet, cloud computing, libraries as repositories for information accessed electronically, and e-commerce. Licklider's accomplishments were not based on design and development of system architectures, hardware, or software. Instead, his great contribution was as a visionary, an "idea man," who conceives concepts and then brings them to the attention of those who eventually design and implement his vision. On a more practical level, Licklider's positions in key organizations (particularly the Defense Advanced Research Projects Agency and Bolt, Beranek, and Newman), as a leader of efforts backed by funds that he freely and judiciously applied, went far toward making his visions, including his concept of what is now the Internet, reality.

EARLY LIFE

Born on March 11, 1915, in St. Louis, Missouri, Joseph Carl Robnett Licklider was the only child of Joseph and Margaret Licklider. He earned his bachelor's degree in 1937 with three majors: physics, mathematics, and psychology. That combination of physical science, study of the mind, and mathematics would inform his thinking in coming years as he conceived of general problems and then how existing technologies might be used to solve them. Remaining at Washington University, he earned a master's degree in psychology the following year.

Five years later (in 1942), he received a doctorate in psychoacoustics from The Johns Hopkins University. He went immediately into research to support the war effort, working at Swarthmore before going to Harvard the following year. From 1943 until 1950, he worked in the Psychoacoustics Laboratory at Harvard. One of his colleagues was Leo Beranek, who would be instrumental in bringing him to Bolt, Beranek, and Newman in the late 1950s.

Licklider's specialty at this time was the study of the effects of sound as people perceive it and its effects on physiology. He remained very active in this field for several years. Even as late as 1960, the year he published his major work on the man-machine interface, he coauthored a significant article, "Suppression of Pain by Sound." The article reported on the results of a study of the effectiveness of sound in alleviating pain of those undergoing dental procedures.

In 1950, Licklider moved to the Massachusetts Institute of Technology (MIT). In addition to teaching and research, one of his earliest activities there was helping to establish the Lincoln Laboratory. Developed originally as an organization to investigate how air defense technologies could be designed and implemented, it still exists today as a major research and development organization supporting government initiatives.

During his association with the Lincoln Laboratory, Licklider became involved the Semi-Automatic Ground Environment (SAGE), which was to support the command and control function of a large-scale integrated

J.C.R. Licklider.

air defense system. The heart of that system was the Whirlwind computer. Unlike earlier computers, which operated in batch mode in response to a particular problem, this computer delivered information to the user at a computer station, who would then respond interactively. There were several of these computers working together, which raised the possibilities of not only what computers could do for users but also how they could be used to work together on a large scale.

LIFE'S WORK

By 1957, Licklider had enjoyed a career of some significance. His main life's work can be said to have begun

---

Affiliation: Defense Advanced Research Projects Agency

The Defense Advanced Research Projects Agency (DARPA) is a true child of the Cold War. It was initiated by President Dwight D. Eisenhower in February 1958, when it was named simply the Advanced Research Projects Agency (ARPA). Licklider had said that the belief by a great many people in the early 1950s that fifty thousand Russian bombers might appear over American soil was an encouragement for the kind of research and development that led to the development and implementation of the Semi-Automatic Ground Environment (SAGE) defense system. The urgency was increased substantially as a result of successful Soviet space exploration at the end of 1957. ARPA was meant to be a funding and management agency that would identify technological areas that ought to be explored to gain military advantage. As befitted an era in which quick success was essential, there were few restrictions on funding, on imagination, or on ideas. In 1962, when the agency's Information Processing Techniques Office (IPTO) was created, J. C. R. Licklider was selected as its first head. He served to disburse funds and encourage development.

DARPA's name has changed over the years, and it has variously been known with and without the "Defense" in its title: The name was changed to DARPA in 1972, changed back to ARPA in 1993, and returned to DARPA in 1996. Likewise, the focus of its projects has varied, but it remains an important agency in selecting technologies to solve the tactical and strategic problems of the day and to developing and implement solutions.

---

when he accepted the position of vice president at Bolt, Beranek, and Newman (BB&N). In discussing the origins of the Internet for the *Massachusetts Historical Review*, Beranek described how he had convinced Licklider to give up his tenured position at MIT by offering him stock as part of his compensation, a rather unusual offer at the time. One of Licklider's earliest accomplishments was to convince BB&N to buy a computer for $30,000, an enormous investment at the time. Beranek recalls asking Licklider what he would use it for and receiving the reply that Licklider himself did not know but that the future success of the company would depend on having and using that capability. Within a short time, BB&N would receive an offer from Ken Olsen of Digital Equipment Company (DEC) to try the new model PDP-1. Eventually there would be several of those machines at BB&N.

Licklider was now working in computers, a departure from his background, in which psychology had predominated. He never abandoned that experience and academic training, however; it informed nearly everything that he was to do in the future. In 1960, he published a major paper on what he referred to as "man-computer symbiosis." In that paper, he identified many of the characteristics that now define the experience of personal computing. This symbiosis was a close partnership between human and machine that would allow the human to ask questions and make decisions and to do so in a flexible manner (one can see the influence of working on SAGE/Whirlwind here). A promising aspect of this symbiosis was that the machines could take care of the routine tasks, leaving the human free to perform more intellectual functions. Although Licklider's ideas and work touched on the discipline now known as artificial intelligence (AI), it is important to note that he never entertained the notion that computing machines could replace human beings.

In 1962, Licklider left BB&N and joined the four-year-old Defense Advanced Research Projects Agency (DARPA). Within this organization, which sought to encourage and manage new technologies that might be used to enhance the defense of the United States, a new department had been created, the Information Processing Techniques Office (IPTO). There Licklider had a budget of approximately $10 million, a huge sum in the early 1960s, and used it to fund projects that included systems and application development and time-shared processing. One of the organizations that he funded was the Palo Alto Research Center (PARC), where Douglas Engelbart would invent and demonstrate the computer mouse a few years later.

Also in 1962, Licklider wrote a series of memoranda that culminated in a paper in which he described what he called an intergalactic network: a network of computers with multiple users having access to each computer (time sharing computer resources was a major goal at that time; the idea of multiple users, each with a personal computer, was not at that time widely foreseen). The paper was important in two ways. First, Licklider predicted the way that networks would develop into the Internet as we now know it. Second, and most important, he managed to convince his colleagues that it was an achievable goal and not only could be done but would offer significant advantages. One of the colleagues he managed to convince was Larry Roberts, who would later take the first steps toward that vision by managing the development of ARPANET, the forerunner of the Internet.

In 1963, Licklider left IPTO to become director of DARPA's Behavioral Sciences and Command and Control Research. The following year, he left government service to work for IBM as manager of information sciences, systems, and applications, a position he would hold until 1968, when he returned to MIT. There, he was director of the Project on Mathematics and Computation (Project MAC), an effort to implement time-shared computing, with up to thirty individuals using a mainframe computer at the same time. He remained at MIT until 1985, when he retired.

PERSONAL LIFE

During his life, Licklider received two major awards: the Franklin V. Taylor Award for Outstanding Contributions in the Field of Applied Experimental and Engineering Psychology (1966) and, along with five others, the Commonwealth Award for Distinguished Service (1990). The Commonwealth Awards are designed to award human achievement on a worldwide basis in virtually any discipline. Others who received the award that year included Jerome Robbins and Aharon Appelfeld.

Licklider was married to Louise Carpenter Licklider; the couple had three children and two grandchildren. Despite his religious upbringing (his father was a minister), Licklider did not practice any religion. After retiring from MIT in 1985, he died five years later of complications from asthma. He was sixty-five years old.

Robert N. Stacy

FURTHER READING

Arif, Mohammed. "Where Did Cloud Computing Come from and Where Is it heading" *Computer Weekly* 7 Apr. 2009. Print. A discussion of the cloud and its origins, giving credit to Licklider for his ideas, eventually developed by others.

Belfiore, Michael P. *The Department of Mad Scientists: How DARPA Is Remaking Our World, from the Internet to Artificial Limbs.* New York: Harper, 2009. Print. An overview of the history, projects, and applications of DARPA.

Beranek, Leo. "Roots of the Internet: A Personal History." *Massachusetts Historical Review* 2 (2000): 55–75. Print. A very personal view of the early projects and activities that gave rise to the Internet. Beranek provides a great deal of detail about the role of BB&N at the time, with particular emphasis on the role of Licklider.

Licklider, J. C. R. *Libraries of the Future.* Reprint. Cambridge: MIT, 1971. Print. An important study by Licklider, performed at BB&N from 1961 to 1963 as part of a project commissioned to BB&N by the Council of Library Resources. He discusses how computers can be used in libraries in the year 2000, predicting that libraries will no longer be based on books but instead on accessing knowledge by using computers.

---. "Man-Computer Symbiosis." *IRE Transactions on Human Factors in Electronics* HFE-1 (1960): 4–11. Print. An important paper by Licklider in which he works out how humans and machines can operate together. Although this paper has some implications for artificial intelligence, Licklider saw computing as a tool and not a replacement for human thought.

Stefik, Mark, ed. *Internet Dreams: Archetypes, Myths, and Metaphors.* Cambridge: MIT, 1996. Print. A discussion of the functions and roles performed by the Internet, nearly all of which Licklider foresaw and wrote about.

Waldrop, M. Mitchell. *The Dream Machine: J. C. R. Licklider and the Revolution That Made Computing Personal.* New York: Viking, 2001. Print. A view of Licklider and his role in the development of advanced computing. While Licklider was probably the least flamboyant of the group that eventually laid the foundation for the Internet, Waldrop makes a good case for Licklider's being perhaps the most essential.

M

ANDREW MASON

Founder of Groupon

Born: October 22, 1980; Pittsburgh, Pennsylvania
Died: -
Primary Field: Internet
Specialty: Commerce
Primary Company/Organization: Groupon

INTRODUCTION

Andrew Mason is the founder of Groupon, a Chicago-based Internet company that offers discounted gift certificates that are localized to major markets. The name is a composite of the words group *and* coupon.

EARLY LIFE

Andrew Mason was born October 22, 1980, in Pittsburgh, Pennsylvania, and grew up in Mt. Lebanon, Pennsylvania, a suburb of Pittsburgh. Both his parents were entrepreneurs: His father sold diamonds, and his mother had a photography business. Mason's entrepreneurial spirit emerged at age fifteen, when he started a Saturday-morning bagel delivery service called Bagel Express. He graduated from Mt. Lebanon High School in 1999 and enrolled in Northwestern University, where he earned a bachelor's degree in music in 2003.

After college, he worked in web design and at Electrical Audio, the studio of recording engineer Steve Albini (producer of hundreds of albums and member of the band Big Black), whom Mason credits as an influence. He briefly attended the University of Chicago's Harris School of Public Policy in the master's program but dropped out after a semester.

LIFE'S WORK

Mason's first online entrepreneurial effort was The Point, funded with $1 million in seed money from Eric Lefkofsky, for whom Mason had worked after college, an Internet entrepreneur with a mixed reputation. The Point was named for Malcolm Gladwell's 2000 book

Andrew Mason.

Affiliation: Groupon

Groupon was started by Andrew Mason in 2008 and quickly became the most successful collective online buying site. The Groupon model is based on Mason's previous start-up, The Point, in which people pledged money to social initiatives but would be charged only if a collective minimum was met (similar to Kickstarter's model). Groupon negotiates deals with local businesses and offers them to customers, who are signed up for the Groupon service and live in the covered area. If enough customers sign up for the deal, it becomes available and customers are charged; if not, the deal is not made. The coupons work for the businesses like quantity discounts, similar to the discounts sold to travel agencies and other companies. Groupon takes a 50 percent cut plus the fees for processing credit cards. Businesses pay nothing to participate, and thus there is no risk as long as they make sure to offer only those discounts they can afford to honor. Health, beauty, spa, fitness, and restaurant deals are popular, in part because businesses offering these services (as opposed to a car dealerships and pet stores, for instance) depend on repeat customers and stand a good chance of seeing the discounted customers return, and in part because the site's user base skews decidedly female and young.

Collective online buying did not begin with Groupon. Companies like MobShop and Mercata were offering a similar model in the 1990s. However, they were not generally localized. Instead they would offer deals on goods and services such as consumer electronics and travel packages. Moreover, they were rarely able to bring the price down as much as Groupon typically does. An advantage to Groupon's operating locally is that a local restaurant benefits more from a guaranteed sale of, say, two hundred customers than a television wholesaler does, because, proportional to the size of its enterprise, that number of customers offers a local business a better deal.

There are a number of criticisms of Groupon. Some have noted that the experience can be addictive: The copy is so persuasive, and the deals so good, that people buy things they would not usually buy and do not need, compelled by the great bargain. Of course, that is largely the point: No business needs a middleman to sell discount coupons to its existing customer base. Some businesses despair that Groupon erodes cus-

tomer loyalty, too; while the so-called groupons can introduce new customers to a business, who might be retained as repeat customers, those customers are just as likely to return to their usual place of business (whether a hairdresser or a restaurant) or to migrate with the herd, following the next Groupon offer to the next business. If that were to happen on a large scale, it would arguably be disproportionately in the best interest of Groupon, and perhaps the customer, rather than the business, to participate in the system.

Restaurants often view Groupon as a necessary evil. It is a truism in the restaurant world that coupon-using customers tend to be the cheapest; they often do not tip well, and they often order only what their coupon covers. Restaurants make their profits on appetizers, desserts, beverages—the upsells that, in effect, subsidize the cost of other elements of the meal and make it possible to offer coupons in the first place. A well-run business charges the price it does because that is the price it needs to charge, after all, in order to pay its expenses and overhead and make enough profit to stay afloat. Although it may seem to the customer that a coupon benefits the restaurant—or other business—just by getting the customer in the door, in actuality coupon use, especially of the magnitude of Groupon's offerings, can cost a restaurant money, a loss it takes on the gamble that it is generating repeat customers in the process. An ideal situation might be a party of four in which two people have Groupon discounts, for instance; they fill a table, they leave enough of a tip to keep the wait staff earning a living wage, and their ticket will not be discounted down to cost. The Restaurant Intelligence Agency, an industry website, has worked to correct the misconception, which restaurant owners sometimes have, that Groupon users will all or mostly become regular customers—an outcome that motivates them to offer discounts they really cannot afford to offer.

Groupon has also had to remind customers that tips are supposed to be based on the menu price, not the coupon price, a practice that sometimes meets with disgruntled customers if they are using Groupon. However, in some cases the business simply needs to learn how to use Groupon to its best advantage. Many cities have a "restaurant week during which restaurants offer

Affiliation: Groupon (continued)

special menus or prix fixe meals, intended to get people who do not go out often to do so and experience their city's restaurants; Groupon can be approached the same way. By creating a prix fixe meal or limiting Groupon usage to a specific part of the menu, costs can be controlled somewhat; similarly, the number of coupons sold can be capped. Seasonal businesses especially find that Groupon is helpful in creating business during a slow period—again, a strategic use of Groupon, one that requires some consideration.

In 2011, Groupon went public, trading as GRPN on NASDAQ. Although it closed at a price higher than the initial offering price, the stock subsequently fell when a series of accounting errors and bad practices were revealed. Today, Groupon's management team includes chief executive officer Andrew Mason, chief financial officer Jason Child, senior vice president of global sales and operations Kal Raman, senior vice president of cor

porate development Jason Harinstein, general counsel David Schellhase, senior vice president of human resources Brian Schipper, and senior vice president of engineering and operations Brian Totty. The company employs more than ten thousand people.

According to surveys, the average Groupon user is a single female between the ages of eighteen and thirty-four, usually with a college degree, usually earning between $50,000 and $100,000 per year. More than five hundred markets are served. Groupon competitors include LivingSocial, BuyWithMe, Scoop Street, and YouSwoop.

A sitcom scheduled to premiere on CBS in spring 2013, *Friend Me*, stars Christopher Mintz-Plasse (who portrayed McLovin in the film *Superbad*) and Nicholas Braun as two midwesterners who move to Los Angeles to work for Groupon. The series will be directed by Pamela Fryman of *How I Met Your Mother*.

The Tipping Point, which examines processes of sociological change. The Point was a social initiatives site, but Mason had difficulty marketing it and in 2008 dismantled most of its features in order to turn it into Groupon. Mason has credited the idea for The Point with an origin story that may be apocryphal: Having trouble canceling his cell phone contract, he found himself wishing he could take collective action with other people having the same problem in order to leverage their power. The way The Point was supposed to work was that users would commit to participation in some social initiative as long as the total number of participants exceeded a certain threshold. This could involve monetary donations: For example, Mason proposed a $10 billion project to build a dome over Chicago to protect it from snow, which yielded $234,395 worth of pledges. Monetizing The Point was a challenge, however, and although it still exists (with a staff of few than ten employees), Mason no longer works on it day to day, having replicated one of its core features for Groupon.

Groupon preserves the "this will happen if enough people participate" element: the idea of using a crowd to leverage collective power, and little else. Groupon, which has since inspired numerous similar sites, acts a middleman between businesses and local customers and then offers a deal to customers who have signed up for e-mail notifications. If the number of customers who accept the deal exceeds a certain number, the deal

is made official (and credit cards charged accordingly). Typically, the deals are for about half off of some local product or service, such as a spa service, car wash, or restaurant meal. Groupon takes 50 percent and the fee for processing credit cards, giving the balance to the local business. Instead of leveraging the power of a crowd to enact social change, Groupon leverages the crowd in order to get a discount.

One of the keys to Groupon's success is Mason's insistence on copywriting that is compelling: Brandon Copple, the former managing editor of Crain's Chicago Business, was hired as Groupon's managing editor and oversees a staff of copywriters who are given a manual the size of a midsized city's phone book. Groupon deals are meant to be interesting to read. This is a solid sales technique—the longer customers spend reading the pitch, especially if they are entertained by it, the more positively disposed they will be toward accepting the sale—and it helps define Groupon's brand identity.

A former Yahoo president, Rob Solomon, was hired to help shape Groupon's infrastructure in 2010. One of the experiments launched was the "hyperlocal" deal—a deal offered to specific neighborhoods of large metropolitan areas such as Chicago, New York, and London.

In 2010, Groupon received $135 million in venture capital from Digital Sky Technologies, Battery Ventures, and other groups, at which point it had sold more than 6 million deals. That May, it acquired CityDeal, a

European copycat site, in order to add Groupon coverage to eighty more cities in sixteen countries. Later in the year, Groupon turned down a $5.3 billion acquisition bid from Google. Much of Groupon's appeal for investors and potential buyers is how effectively it has monetized the Internet, whereas many dot-coms (Twitter, for instance) do not appear to have monetization models that are equal to their popularity, particularly since the Internet generally eschews paying for online services.

In 2011, Groupon issued an initial public offering (IPO), trading as GRPN on the NASDAQ, and Mason's 45.9 million shares, at a stock price of $27.90, made him a billionaire—and made billionaires of Lefkofsky (Groupon's biggest shareholder) and Brad Keywell, Lefkofsky's longtime business partner. However, after going public in November, Groupon reported a loss of revenues in February, at a time when investors expected profits to be reported.

As a result, 2012 saw challenges for Groupon. It was forced to revise its first-quarter financial results as a public company when it was discovered by auditor Ernst and Young that those results did not include refunds paid back to customers. The stock had already fallen below its IPO price of $20, and with this news the share value fell to $17.20. Numerous questions were raised about accounting procedures and accountability at Groupon. The following quarter, revenues were again lower than expected or projected, and the day after reporting, Groupon's shares dropped 27 percent—for a total drop of 70 percent since the IPO.

PERSONAL LIFE
Mason lives in the Ukrainian Village neighborhood of Chicago with his girlfriend. He plays the piano. Mason has imposed only one rule concerning dress at Groupon: no sunglasses indoors. The impetus for this rule was his dislike for rock star Bono's tendency to wear sunglasses indoors.

Bill Kte'pi

FURTHER READING
Qualman, Erik. *Socialnomics: How Social Media Transforms the Way We Live and Do Business.* New York: Wiley, 2010. Print. Examines the impact of social media and e-commerce on twenty-first-century business.

Sennett, Frank. *Groupon's Biggest Deal Ever: The Inside Story of How One Insane Gamble, Tons of Unbelievable Hype, and Millions of Wild Deals Made Billions for One Ballsy Joker.* New York: St. Martin's, 2012. Print. Sensationalist but entertaining, the only book-length treatment of Mason and Groupon, focusing on Mason's idiosyncrasies and Groupon's rapid rise.

MICHAEL MAULDIN
Founder of Lycos

Born: March 23, 1959; Dallas, Texas
Died: -
Primary Field: Internet
Specialty: Content and data
Primary Company/Organization: Lycos

INTRODUCTION
In 1994, Michael Mauldin created the Internet search engine Lycos with three pages of code. A year later, the venture capital company CMGI purchased program and built it into a publicly traded company. Mauldin went on to cofound Conversive (formerly Virtual Personalities, Inc.) in 1997, which creates computer-generated human characters. In 2000, his obsession with robots was initiated by an episode of the television show Battle Bots, *and robotics have fascinated him since.*

EARLY LIFE
Michael Loren "Fuzzy" Mauldin was born on March 23, 1959, in Dallas, Texas. He attended Rice University, with a double major in computer science and mathematics and a minor in linguistics. While at Rice, he was introduced to ELIZA, an early chatterbot developed in 1966, and became fascinated by it, leading to his interest in linguistics as he sought a better understanding of language and natural language processing. Mauldin went to graduate school at Carnegie Mellon, where he was earned a master's degree in 1983 and a Ph.D. in 1989, both in computer science. Jaime Carbonell, whose work has encompassed artificial intelligence, information retrieval, and machine learning, was the chair of his dissertation committee and adviser.

After graduation, Mauldin worked as a research associate at Carnegie Mellon from 1989 to 1991 and as a research computer scientist in the university's Center for Machine Translation from 1991 to 1995, after which he founded Lycos, Inc., spinning off a Carnegie Mellon research project.

LIFE'S WORK

Mauldin's work in the computing industry has covered a variety of areas and has left a lasting influence. In 1984, he was one of three programmers who developed Rog-O-Matic, which they described as "a belligerent expert system [in the artificial intelligence sense]." It was a bot programmed to play the dungeon crawling computer game *Rogue*, an exceptionally popular Unix game in the 1980s. Because *Rogue* was a text adventure (like the better-known *Zork*, for instance), its output could be piped to Rog-O-Matic, which could therefore easily be given the same information a human player would have. The bot was designed to respond to a dynamic environment in a way that artificial intelligence theorists continue to study and cite.

After Rog-O-Matic, Mauldin created Gloria, a bot built to play *TinyMUD*, an online text adventure environment launched in 1989. Gloria was succeeded by Julia, which gradually developed greater conversational skills as a result of interacting in the game, as well as the ability to play the card game Hearts.

Mauldin coined the term *chatterbot* to describe other bots that, instead of playing games, were programmed to simulate conversation with human users. The first such was ELIZA, introduced in 1966 in response to Alan Turing's 1950 article "Computing Machinery and Intelligence," which proposed a conversation-based test of artificial intelligence. More recent chatterbots have been used online for commercial purposes—sometimes as spam, sometimes to automate customer assistance (a fictional chatterbot named JARVIS was even featured in the *Iron Man* movies). The design and implementation of chatterbots has been an important area of artificial intelligence and specifically of developing the subfield of natural language processing. The annual Loebner Prize is awarded to chatterbots considered the most convincing; in 1991, Julia came in third. Mauldin continued to work on her regularly, deploying her into chat environments as well as various multiuser dungeons (MUDs) and other online games.

Eventually the Julia work led to collaboration with clinical psychologist and animator Peter Plantec, and Mauldin and Plantec founded Virtual Personalities, Inc., which became Conversive. Conversive develops verbally enhanced software robots, or verbots—chatterbots with animation and speech that convey more information and personality than text alone can do. The first verbot was Sylvie, which took Mauldin's Julia work and went further, offering more flexible interfacing, a voice, and an animated face.

Mauldin's chatterbot work led directly to his best-known accomplishment, the Lycos search engine, named for the wolf spider, *Lycosidae lycosa*. Julia explored virtual game worlds defined by text descriptions and, in order to navigate the dungeons and other areas of these games, needed to be able to map the paths through them. Lycos, in turn, explored the World Wide Web, with its hyperlinks and pages of text, learning information about its contents just as Julia learned about the dungeons.

Mauldin was working at Carnegie Mellon's Informedia Digital Library when he developed Lycos. Mauldin was the principal investigator in charge of natural language, indexing, and retrieval. Informedia is a research program developed by the university to carry out research in information visualization, information retrieval, face recognition, search engines, and other issues related to intelligently sifting through large

Michael Mauldin.

Affiliation: Lycos

As the World Wide Web became increasingly accessible, the "web" needed a "spider" that could navigate it. Computer science research professor Michael "Fuzzy" Mauldin, working at Carnegie Mellon University's Informedia Digital Library—an ongoing research project addressing the challenges of digitization and information retrieval—took the concepts of the science of information retrieval, translated them into three pages of code, and applied them to the then-new World Wide Web in 1994. The result was the Lycos search engine was named for the wolf spider, *Lycosidae lycosa*. Mauldin had previously worked on (and would return to work on) chatterbots, automated programs that emulated conversation, as well as bots programmed to interact with game environments. The search engine was an extension of that work, a spider that navigated the hyperlinked sites of the Internet instead of the rooms of a computer game's dungeon.

In 1995, Lycos, Inc., was spun off from Carnegie Mellon, with Mauldin and the university splitting the intellectual property equally, each retaining a 10 percent ownership of the company after taking it public in 1996—the briefest period of time between founding and initial public offering (IPO) in NASDAQ history.

Bob Davis became the CEO and at first tried to turn Lycos into a software company before focusing on advertising as the source of revenue and purchasing Tripod in order to transition into the web portal market. Lycos's IPO preceded the wave of dot-com IPOs that would lead to the dot-com bubble. Also in 1996, Lycos was one of the five search engines that paid $5 million per year to be one of the featured search engines on the Netscape browser's search page—which showed how much had changed in the previous two years.

Lycos had indexed 54,000 documents when it was first made available to the public. By August 1994, that number had increased to nearly 400,000. In 1996, the year of Lycos, Inc.'s IPO, it had indexed more than 60 million documents, the most of any search engine at that time.

Lycos was acquired by Terra Networks in 2000, which then sold it to the Korean company Daum Communications Corporation in 2004. Since then, the company has restructured to focus less on search. It introduced media services, social media applications, and location-based services. The company was purchased in 2010 by the Indian Internet marketing firm Ybrant Digital.

bodies of data. It was begun in preparation for the large amounts of information expected to become available as a result of the Internet, the popularity of personal computers, and the growing digitization of data previously available only in hard copy.

The amount of information available on the Internet even in its early days made search engines increasingly necessary. Archie, the first Internet search tool, had been introduced in 1990 for searching the directory listings of public anonymous file transfer protocol (FTP) sites. Unlike later search tools, it did not create indices of contents, so every time a search was performed, it had to go through the whole process again. Veronica and Jughead were created a year later to search gopher servers, and in 1993 a primitive search of the web was available in the form of W3Catalog, which was indexed by compiling numerous catalogs that had been assembled by hand. The first web robots followed. Web robots, web crawlers, or spiders are programs that automatically browse the web, beginning with specified sites called seeds, followed by the sites linked from those sites, then the sites linked from those sites, and so on. While crawling

the web, a web crawler maps what it finds and in some cases downloads some of the web pages it accesses for faster later retrieval. The first search engine to resemble modern web search engines was WebCrawler, which allowed users to search the full text of web pages for any string.

Lycos was developed the same year as WebCrawler, released in 1994, and became the first search engine to be commercialized. Lycos, Inc., was spun off from Informedia, with Mauldin as its founder and chief scientist. Mauldin later downplayed the accomplishment—the search engine was written in three pages of code, using principles of information retrieval that had already been developed, and simply applied those principles to the web. He was savvy in commercializing the product, delegating the proper tasks to lawyers and accountants. Mauldin owned half of the intellectual property and Carnegie Mellon the other half (which translated into each owning 10 percent of the company after it went public). Mark Coticchia, the director of the CMU Technology Transfer office, functioned as the business manager. The company's initial public offering

255

followed in 1996, opening at $16 per share with 3 million shares. Lycos was one of the first Internet companies to go public, preceding the flurry of initial public offerings (IPOs) that led to the Internet bubble at the end of the decade.

Mauldin left Lycos in 1997, when Virtual Personalities (Conversive) was formed. He has pointed out that his knowledge of search engines quickly became dated and that he never learned Java, as his interests went in different directions.

Mauldin has been granted five patents, two related to the Informedia Digital Library, two related to Lycos, and one in his virtual personalities work. A tattoo on his arm displays the Lycos spider, along with its patent number. He retired in 2006 and settled in Texas, although he remained on the board at Conversive.

PERSONAL LIFE

Mauldin is a fan of the Robot Fighting League (established in 2002), which promotes robotic sports and competitions, and he is an active competitor in it. He is a former vice president of Robot Club and Grille, a robot-themed restaurant that hosted robot fighting events. He competed on the Comedy Central program Battle-Bots from 2000 to 20002, and his robot Icecube won the middleweight division of the Robot Fighting League national championship in 2006.

Mauldin and his wife, Debbie, have two sons, Gregory Bernard and Daniel Baird. He is also a licensed pilot.

Bill Kte'pi

FURTHER READING

Abbate, Janet. *Inventing the Internet*. Cambridge: MIT, 2000. Print. An Internet history with a focus on the early days.

Berners-Lee, T. "Long Live the Web: A Call for Continued Open Standards and Neutrality." *Scientific American* Nov. 2010: n. pag. Print. A recent look at issues of search engines and neutrality.

Carr, N. *The Shallows: What the Internet Is Doing to Our Brain*. New York: Norton, 2011. Print. A critical look at psychological and neurological effects of Internet usage, including the impact of search engines.

Hafner, Katie. *Where Wizards Stay Up Late: The Origins of the Internet*. New York: Simon, 1998. Print. A history of the Internet, though old enough to be noticeably incomplete now, nevertheless thorough in its coverage of the Internet's origins and early days.

Introna, L., and H. Nissenbaum. "Shaping the Web: Why the Politics of Search Engines Matters." *The Information Society* 16.3 (2000): n. pag. Print. Another discussion of the importance of neutrality in search engines and the problems of search engine bias.

Mauldin, Michael, G. Jacobson, A. Appel, and L. Hamey. "ROG-O-MATIC: A Belligerent Expert System." 16 May 1984. Carnegie Mellon University Department of Computer Science. Web. 12 Aug. 2012. Mauldin's paper on the *Rogue*-playing bot, which influenced later bots, his own and others, as well as the field of artificial intelligence.

Plantec, Peter. *Virtual Humans: A Build-It-Yourself Kit, Complete with Software and Step by Step Instructions; Creating the Illusion of Personality*. New York: AMACOM, 2004. Print. Plantec is Mauldin's partner at Conversive and here presents some of the company's work in chatterbots.

Wu, Tim. *The Master Switch: The Rise and Fall of Information Empires*. New York: Vintage, 2011. Print. An analytical look at the Internet and its role in history.

MARISSA MAYER

CEO of Yahoo!

Born: May 30, 1975; Wausau, Wisconsin
Died: -
Primary Field: Computer science
Specialty: Computer programming
Primary Company/Organization: Yahoo!

INTRODUCTION

Marissa Mayer is one of the Internet world's most prominent female executives and has attracted considerable attention as the youngest CEO of a Fortune 500 company (Yahoo!) who did not found the company. By June

2012, when she began her tenure at Yahoo, she was best known for her thirteen years with Google, during which she worked as a product manager, engineer, and designer for a range of services, including Gmail, Google Books, and Google Maps. Her competence and vision enabled her to rise through the ranks to an executive position at Google, and she demonstrated her potential for further growth when, at the age of thirty-seven and pregnant, she struck a blow for women in technology (and in the corporate world generally) by taking the top spot as chief executive officer (CEO) at Yahoo!

EARLY LIFE

Marissa Mayer was born in Wausau, Wisconsin, on May 30, 1975, to a mother who was an art teacher and an engineer father. She has cultivated both aspects of her personality and, at school, was captain of the debate club and the pom-pom team. She also had a job as a grocery clerk. Her intellectual prowess was recognized and celebrated as well.

Mayer enrolled at Stanford University in California at a time when the Silicon Valley cluster of intellectuals, investors, and engineers was beginning to form. She received degrees in symbolic systems and then computer science, specializing in artificial intelligence. She had

Marisa Mayer.

the opportunity to work as a consultant before taking the chance to join Google, where she was employee number 20, the first female engineer at the company.

LIFE'S WORK

Mayer's work with Google provided the foundation for her career, and what she has learned during more than a decade with the Internet behemoth would be instrumental in determining her success at Yahoo! The latter is a technology company that was a dominant Internet presence in its early years but, by 2012, seemed to have lost its identity and purpose. Mayer had filled a range of roles for Google, moving from engineer to headhunter, product designer, project manager, and often the human face of the company. In an industry in which many of the enormously successful and rich founders and entrepreneurs struggle to make a favorable impression in mass media, Mayer stood out as the attractive, human, youthful, and successful face of the company. Both she and Google used her presence—she has been named among the private sector's most glamorous as well as most influential people—to their benefit.

However, Mayer is also a formidable computer scientist in her own right. Although she has patent applications in the area of artificial intelligence, it seems that her greatest achievement in career terms is to be able to relate to Google users and their use of the services provided. The term *google* has become a household word around the globe, in no small part thanks to her design of the uncluttered search page and the user experience that it provides. Mayer has likened the Google experience to the elegance of a Swiss army knife, which combines many tools for specific tasks but which manages to tuck them all away, inconspicuously, until the user chooses to pull them out and make use of them. In her influential slide show "The Nine Notions on Innovation," Mayer identifies the secret to this success as the desire to think of users and usage, not money. She also mentions an effective if small and often overlooked concept: Google regularly releases incremental changes in service in the form of beta releases, which facilitate development of the most up-to-date technological approaches to using the Internet by allowing the public to test these enhancements and suggest improvements.

Mayer also continued to oversee the human resources of the company until her departure in mid-2012 and was said to scrutinize every hiring decision made at Google, a company of some six thousand employees. Her expressed preference is for "brilliance" and, indeed, the more brilliance the better. Clearly, considerable

Affiliation: Google

Google was started by Larry Page and Sergey Brin in 1996, when both were doctoral students at Stanford University. Their initial concept was that a better Internet search engine than was then available could be possible if it were based on the PageRank approach, which took into account the relationships between different web pages and sites. The Google search, partly because of its technical approach and partly because of its image and sense of style, has become the market leader, and the neologism *to google* has entered many languages. Google's workplace and management style reflect Silicon Valley's reputation for casual dress and a sense of play combined with an intense work ethic. The unofficial motto "Don't Be Evil' has inspired generations of young people to wish to join the company and to use its products.

It has been estimated that Google has more than one million computer servers located in a variety of "server farms" dispersed geographically, which are needed to provide the various Google services. In addition to the basic search engine, Google provides blogging services (having bought Blogger) and video sharing (having bought YouTube). It also announced plans to digitize the world's stock of books—an initiative that ran into some trouble with copyright and intellectual property rights issues.

Despite a strategy of diversification, Google continues to derive the great majority of its income from online advertising. However, the success of its initial public offering (IPO) and the subsequent performance of its shares seem to have persuaded people generally that the company has been successful in monetizing services ostensibly offered free.

thought must be put into the company's corporate culture and workplace conditions to ensure that so many brilliant people are able to work together smoothly. The level of work this would require helps to explain the punishing work schedule to which Mayer has subjected herself. She is believed to be worth some $300 million, reflecting the value she gave to the company.

In addition to the basic search engine, Google has diversified its processes and services through acquisition and invention. Mayer was involved with the invention side of this development. She has been associated with Google Maps, Books, Images, and Gmail, both from the programming standpoint and (as her job title, Vice President of Search and User Experience, suggested) from the human perspective. Google's philosophy of not doing evil and of "being cool" has been reinforced by the ability to provide unfussy and sleekly functional service interfaces. These services have not all been without controversy, however. Google's attempt to digitize all the books in the world, for example, and make them available free of charge to anyone with Internet access led to a significant legal struggle concerning the ownership (and revenue streams) of the intellectual property involved. Google Maps and Google Earth, meanwhile, which seek to create and update an accurate interactive image of every part of the world at a variety of scales, have also been controversial in terms of privacy and secrecy issues.

Another stream of complaint has turned on what Google actually intends to do with all the information it has gathered on its millions of users and whether the company is guilty of the further commodification of knowledge and of space—that is, turning information such as knowledge about neighborhoods into products that can be marketed and sold even though they may are derived from private property rather than being part of the public domain or commons. Commodification of Google customers (that is, as consumption units for advertising) has also been discussed.

On July 17, 2012, Mayer started work as the CEO of Yahoo! after a surprising and secretive switch from Google. The move was particularly unexpected because she was six months pregnant at the time—she promised to work through a brief maternity leave—and because of the turmoil at Yahoo, which had thereby appointed its fifth CEO in as many years and appeared to have left its best days some time in the past. It remains to be seen to what extent she will be able to transfer her skills and competencies to a new workplace and whether it will be possible to turn around a company of such scope. Nevertheless, as the youngest CEO of a Fortune 500 company who had not founded the company, a high-profile life will surely continue as long as she is active in the field.

PERSONAL LIFE

In 2009, Mayer married Zachary "Zack" Bogue, an entrepreneur, investor, and cofounder of Founders Den, which is a shared club space for entrepreneurs. The couple was expecting their first child in the fall of 2012. Mayer's move to Yahoo! was accompanied by claims that she would work through the end of her pregnancy and her child's early days insofar as possible. This approach is considered controversial because, as a prominent woman in executive, all of her acts are considered representative of state of women and feminism, irrespective of her own desires, and most feminists seek parity in the workplace regardless of their biological roles, which above all includes accommodations for their roles as mothers. After the birth of her son on September 30, 2012, Mayer turned to social media to crowdsource baby name suggestions; eventually, however, she settled on a name she had previously considered, Macallister.

It is certainly true that Mayer has become known for her intense diligence: for example, by treating her weekends as the opportunity for fourteen-hour-long e-mail sessions. Her workdays have lasted until 9:00 P.M. (at times, midnight), and in the past she allowed herself only five hours' sleep per night. She makes efforts to maintain her femininity despite this intense lifestyle, and debate surrounds the kind of role model she might offer for girls interested in joining the industry.

Regardless of how various members of the public perceive her, to have achieved such success as a woman in a field dominated by men indicates Mayer's sense of determination and ambition. This is complemented by an interest in artistic expression (she is a member of the San Francisco and New York ballet companies' boards as well as that of the San Francisco Museum of Modern Art) and designer clothes. She was once a dancer herself and has climbed Mount Kilimanjaro, Africa's highest peak, and has snorkeled around the world. She lives in Palo Alto, California, in a house capable of holding large fund-raising parties.

John Walsh

FURTHER READING

Battelle, John. *The Search: How Google and Its Rivals Rewrote the Rules of Business and Transformed Our Culture*. Rev. ed. London: Nicolas Brealey, 2006. Print. Detailed discussion of rise of Google and its transformative impact on business thinking.

Chang, Andrea. "Marissa Mayer Biography." *Los Angeles Times* 18 July 2012. Web. 12 July 2012. Newspaper story consisting of a list of facts on Mayer's life.

Fuchs, Christian. "Google Capitalism." *Triple C: Cognition, Communication, Cooperation* 10.1 (2012): 42–48. Web. 12 July 2012. Academic paper considering some aspects of Google's capital accumulation model.

"Marissa Mayer: The Talent Scout." *Businessweek* 18 June 2006: n. pag. Web. 12 July 2012. Magazine story describing Mayer's character and daily schedule.

Mayer, Marissa. "Nine Notions of Innovation." *Businessweek* June 2006. Web. 12 July 2012. Simple slideshow of Mayer's philosophy with respect to innovation and its application at Google.

Perlroth, Nicole. "Mayer Hopes to Brighten User Experience at Yahoo!" *New York Times* 16 July 2012. Web. 20 July 2012. Newspaper coverage of Mayer's move to Yahoo! with some career details and analysis.

Rushe, Dominic, and Charles Arthur. "Google Executive Marissa Mayer to Become Yahoo! CEO in Surprise Move." *The Guardian* 16 July 2012. Web. 20 July 2012. Newspaper story covering Mayer's move to Yahoo! Includes some analysis and a career retrospective.

KEVIN MITNICK

Founder of Mitnick Security

Born: August 6, 1963; Van Nuys, California
Died: -
Primary Field: Computer science
Specialty: Security
Primary Company/Organization: Mitnick Security

INTRODUCTION

Kevin Mitnick is one of the most famous computer hackers in history. He became fascinated with breaking into mechanical and computer systems at an early age and progressed into hacking the computer networks of large companies, copying their software and reading their records, e-mails, and other private information.

Like many other hackers, he was allegedly motivated by intellectual curiosity and the desire to demonstrate to corporate interests that their property was not as safe as they believed and did not wish to benefit materially from his crimes. After having been a convicted criminal and a fugitive, Mitnick has reinvented himself as a computer security specialist particularly well positioned to advise companies on how to repel hackers like him.

EARLY LIFE

Kevin David Mitnick was born on August 6, 1963, in Van Nuys, California, and grew up in Los Angeles. He attended Monroe High School and then enrolled at the

University of Southern California (USC). He has been described as a disempowered youngster from a lower middle-class background who viewed social engineering as a means of making friends and gaining acceptance and access to data and resources more exciting than his normal life.

The first indication of Mitnick's future career was his collusion with a bus driver to obtain a punch card machine that enabled him to use the bus system without paying. Over the next few years, he became associated with a series of so-called phone phreakers, who used interpersonal skills to telephone networks with a view to carrying out a series of stunts and practical jokes on individuals and organizations. When he was sixteen, Mitnick was given a telephone number that enabled him to access, through phreaking techniques, the RSTE/S network of Digital Equipment Corporation (DEC) and copy the proprietary software found there. This was an act of theft. As is common with young hackers, Mitnick's subsequent career was marked by a combination of pranks and criminality, aligned with the risk-taking behavior often associated with young men. By the time he was nineteen, Mitnick had graduated to physical entry of the premises whose systems he and his colleagues had compromised, and such a venture in the Los Angeles COSMOS phone center of Pacific Bell resulted in extraction of passwords and meddling with records to permit subsequent future access. The social engineering aspect of this crime was more professionally managed than the physical infiltration, and the police were able to follow up several leads.

By this time, Mitnick seems to have begun to confuse his virtual world exploits with genuine achievement and began using the handle Condor and to take ever greater risks. At USC, where he had already been in trouble for attempting to hack the university's part of the ARPANET system, he was caught trying to hack into the Pentagon from university premises and was sentenced to six months' imprisonment at a juvenile facility.

LIFE'S WORK

Mitnick's criminal career was comparatively short, and for most of that time he was under suspicion by various representatives of the authorities as a result of having been caught for previous crimes. The DEC escapade resulted in a twelve-month prison sentence for Mitnick, followed by three years of supervision; this latter measure is taken to try to prevent people with suspected addiction to computers and their illegal use from being

Kevin Mitnick.

able to commit further crimes. The measure has become more complex with the profusion of devices such as cellular telephones (which have more computing power than supposedly high-capacity research computers of a couple of decades ago); their ubiquitous use has made it increasingly difficult for people to lead fully functional lives without them. In Mitnick's case, the supervision was also shown to be ineffective.

Mitnick hacked the Pacific Bell database toward the end of his period of supervision, and a warrant was issued for his arrest. Emboldened by his ability to confuse people regarding his location and who he really was, Mitnick embarked on a two-and-a-half-year period as a fugitive. Cloned cellular phones and surreptitiously arranged free telephone calls enabled him to maintain a low profile while on the run and, at the same time, continue his various activities. His desire to obtain access to proprietary software and copy it for no particular material benefit at the risk of a lengthy period of imprisonment appears irrational and lends weight to the plea of computer addiction.

Eventually, in 1995, Mitnick was arrested as a part of a well-publicized police operation: The police were part of an attempt to convince the public that Mitnick and people like him were willing and able to undertake actions causing major damage to the country and its people. He served more than four years in detention before admitting to a small number of sentences and then being transferred to solitary confinement, apparently for symbolic purposes. He also received a three-year supervisory period after his release in 2000. His activities undoubtedly caused considerable expense and inconvenience to the organizations he targeted, leading to additional transaction costs for them and, hence, higher costs for everyone. Furthermore, in a world in which intellectual property rights have become resources to be fiercely defended in the United States, Mitnick's reading of personal e-mails and copying of software are considered serious offenses against not just individuals but corporations as well. All computer users face threats and additional costs and inconvenience as a result.

In addition to the technical damage from Mitnick's exploits, it is probable that the most important result of his activity was to make clear the importance of social engineering techniques to obtain access to sensitive or expensive proprietary data. Mitnick began his career as a phone phreaker: a person capable of calling people by telephone and using social skills to persuade the person called to yield access to a network. This may be accomplished, quite legally in fact, by persuading people to direct their web browsers to specific sites that then capture data from the user, which can subsequently be used to penetrate the system. The human element has always represented the potentially weakest spot in any security system, and many hackers find it convenient to exploit this fact, relying on the minor laziness and venality of individuals who will (for example) chase down apparent bargains using systems whose default settings they have not changed, thereby making their systems vulnerable. With the spread of Internet technology and the great expansion of social networking, many millions of people are being introduced to computer networks with little experience of the threats that might be involved. The security implications for the providers of these services are of considerable moment, and Mitnick often appears on media shows to talk about the issues involved and, whether intentionally or not, increase the overall awareness of the use of companies such as his.

After being released, Mitnick sought to support himself by making appearances in the media as owner of a computer security firm that aims to advise companies on how to resist the ill-intentioned efforts of people like him. It is not clear whether or to what extent he is able to maintain cutting-edge knowledge of hacking and

---

Affiliation: Mitnick Security

Mitnick Security Consulting LLC is a firm providing a full range of services relating to computer security. It offers physical testing of virtual and physical network environments, in addition to assessment of the human element, on the basis that the easiest way to break into any valuable place is always likely to be in cahoots with or by exploiting the vulnerability of people who are part of the system. In addition to these assessments, the company provides training programs for relevant individuals and forensic examination of previous attempts at hacking to try to determine the level of success and perpetrators. Kevin Mitnick himself also seems to have time and desire to diversify income-generating activities by writing books trading on his notoriety and making media appearances to promote these. These efforts include personal speaking engagements.

---

phishing techniques without practicing them himself; as a result, his perspective is increasingly that of one taking a retrospective look at how he behaved in the past and the lessons we can draw from that period that remain vital in the present.

PERSONAL LIFE

Mitnick is generally considered to be a computer addict with a desire to continue illegal activities for excitement. His evidently insurmountable desires have effectively ruined his life: He pleaded guilty to crimes while using such a plea of mitigation, which was accepted. He is said to have entered into serious relationships with girlfriends whose influence has enabled him to fend off the addiction for periods of time, but has returned to his addictive behaviors eventually.

There are also some indications of the reality of struggling to survive in urban California when unable to create and sustain a stable position and situation. The lengthy periods during which Mitnick and his colleagues were maintaining campaigns against various corporate targets might have had a veneer of glamour but were in reality enacted in small offices, rented apartments, and hastily arranged low-salaried jobs offering a place to continue computer activities. Mitnick's personal life after his release from prison has been otherwise unexceptional.

John Walsh

261

FURTHER READING

Gold, Steve. "Social Engineering Today: Psychology, Strategies and Tricks." *Network Security* 11 (2010): 11–14. Print. Combination of journalism and academic analysis of the relative importance of social engineering techniques in hacking and how this has changed over the years.

Mitnick, Kevin, and William L. Simon. *Ghost in the Wires: My Adventures as the World's Most Wanted Hacker.* New York: Back Bay, 2012. Print. Mitnick returns to his hacking days to provide an account of his adventures and lessons that may be drawn from them.

---, and William L. Simon. *The Art of Intrusion: The Real Stories behind the Exploits of Hackers, In-*
truders and Deceivers. Indianapolis: Wiley, 2005. Print. Mitnick lends his name to an exposé of hacking incidents.

"Prominent Hacker Mitnick Hacked." *BBC News Online* 11 Feb. 2003. Web. 20 July 2012. News report of hacking attempts on the hacker Mitnick's own computer security company.

Shimomura, Tsutomu, and John Markoff. *Takedown: The Pursuit and Capture of Kevin Mitnick, America's Most Wanted Computer Outlaw, by the Man Who Did It.* New York: Hyperion, 1996. Print. Uneven account of Mitnick's pursuit and capture that was subsequently made into a film.

PAUL MOCKAPETRIS

Inventor of the Domain Name System

Born: November 18, 1948; Boston, Massachusetts
Died: -
Primary Field: Computer science
Specialty: Internet
Primary Company/Organization: Nominum

INTRODUCTION

Paul Mockapetris is best known for creating the Domain Name System (DNS), which for twenty years has helped structure the distribution of e-mail messages and Internet communications on multiuser networks. He is also responsible for a number of other Internet-related achievements that have led to his induction into the Internet Hall of Fame and having received numerous awards and distinctions. After a lengthy career in academia, in 1995 he entered the commercial sector to work as chair and chief scientist at Nomunim, Inc., which creates software to assist in DNS applications and is based in Redwood City, California.

EARLY LIFE

Paul V. Mockapetris was born and grew up in Boston, Massachusetts, and attended high school there. At that time, the Massachusetts Institute of Technology (MIT) offered free summer classes to anyone interested. The classes were often taught by MIT students, and Mockapetris took two, both taught by students who went on to become MIT professors. One class was on programming, and through it he gained his first experience with

a computer, an IBM 1620. The computer the class used was part of the Department of Aeronautics and Astronautics. One day, a department secretary asked him if he was a student and whether he would like a key to

Paul Mockapetris.

the computer room. Mockapetris said yes, accepted the key, and began using the computer late at night, when it was free; later he realized that the secretary had been asking whether if he was a MIT student, not a student in the summer program. In any case, Mockapetris quickly developed an aptitude for computers that inspired him into studying the subject at the tertiary level. He earned undergraduate degrees in physics and engineering from MIT in 1971 and a Ph.D. in information and computer science from the Bren School of Information and Computer Sciences at the University of California at Irvine in 1982.

LIFE'S WORK

In his early career, Mockapetris found himself working on research projects that were poorly funded and reliant on small computers that had been donated rather than the larger machines then available on a permanent or time-share basis. This inspired a career-long interest in the issues of dealing with distributed information systems and how to organize networks to improve productivity from using them. As a member of USC's Information Science Institute, where he was later to become director of the High Performance Computing and Communications Division, he was at first involved with the development of simple mail transfer protocol (SMTP). SMTP was introduced in 1983 as part of the introduction of the e-mail system internationally. Mockapetris then began to work on the creation of the Domain Name System (DNS). DNS is important in that, since the 1990s, it has enabled the conversion of the names entered by users (URLs or e-mail addresses) into the unique numerical string that identifies the actual location of the required machine and destination on the network concerned. This system has worked successfully to date, and Mockapetris believes it has the scope to continue to work and grow in the future. Nevertheless, it is true that the system evolved in a setting determined first by university researchers in Western, developed countries and then spread to industrial settings and the general population around the world. The use of different alphabets, which has become increasingly practicable, may nevertheless pose problems for the DNS that might require a transition to a newer system, such as electronic numbering (ENUM).

While Mockapetris was instrumental in the technical aspects of DNS and later developments, he has always tried to steer clear of the political aspects: for example, controversies over whether consistency of usage over international borders is required or new

Affiliation: Nominum

Having previously designed the Domain Name System (DNS), Paul Mockapetris subsequently sought to take commercial benefit from it and its iterations in his capacity as chief scientist and chair of the board at Nominum, Inc., a company that was formed in 1999 in part as a collaboration with Mockapetris and Ted Lemon, responsible for the first widely used dynamic host configuration protocol (DHCP) system. The company provides products that leverage these two principal technologies and aims to provide thought leadership (and hence consultancy services) with respect to new developments in the systems. It has also incorporated enhanced security features into its product offerings after the revelation in 2008 that a significant and DNS harbored a dangerous backdoor fault.

Nomium's corporate headquarters are located at Redwood City, California, and the company prides itself on a working environment in which the most vibrant and brilliant minds are can easily interact. It is the intellectual capacity and property of the company that constitutes its principal offering to stakeholders and which it leverages into new products and projects.

designations should be introduced. In some sources, Jon Postel is described as a cocreator of the DNS.

The DNS was one of the original Internet standards that was designated by the Internet Engineering Task Force (IETF), with which Mockapetris has been associated subsequently and which he chaired from 1994 to 1996. In the first half of the 1990s, he was a member of the U.S. Department of Defense's Advanced Research Projects Agency (ARPA) and was involved in developing more sophisticated networking technologies, including optical networking. In 1995, he moved into the corporate sector and became involved with a number of start-up operations. In doing so, he has developed his own entrepreneurial philosophy, which revolves around the needs for simplicity, clear communication of objectives and methods to stakeholders, and early planning for extensions and sophistication of the original base system.

As of 2012, Mockapetris was chair and chief scientist at Nominum, Inc., a company based in Redwood City, California, that provides software solutions related to DNS and the dynamic host configuration protocol (DHCP). He is also associated with a number of other software companies, including Acord Technologies, UrbanMedia Communication Corporation, and Sandlot Capital.

Personal Life

Mockapetris and his wife, Elizabeth, have three sons: Alexander and fraternal twins Eric and William. He lists wine tasting and tennis as his favorite pastimes. He is the recipients of several honors, including induction into the Internet Hall of Fame and the Association for Computing Machinery's Special Interest Group on Data Communication (SIGCOMM) lifetime award.

John Walsh

Further Reading

Levy, Steven. *The Perfect Thing: How the iPod Shuffles Commerce, Culture, and Coolness*. New York: Simon, 2006. Print. A discussion of the iPod in the context of both Apple's innovative history and twenty-first century world culture.

Ludwig, Sean. "DNS Inventor Paul Mockapetris to Startups: 'Complexity Is Your Enemy,'" 13 July 2012. *Venture Beat*. Web. 12 July 2012. A brief description of an address given by Mockapetris on his start-up philosophy.

Mockapetris, P., and K. J. Dunlop. "Development of the Domain Name System." *ACM SIGCOMM Computer Communication Review* 18.4 (1988): 123–33. Web. 12 July 2012. Academic description of the process of development of DNS from the technical perspective.

Naughton, John. *Brief History of the Future: The Origins of the Internet*. Woodstock: Overlook, 2000. Print. Well-written history of the development of the Internet from various perspectives.

"Paul V. Mockapetris: Ph.D. Chief Scientist and Chairman Nominum." 2006. *WIWIW (Who Is Who in the Internet World?)*. Web. 12 July 2012. Interview in which Mockapetris discusses his career and opinions about the future of the Internet.

"Peter Mockapetris: Chairman and Chief Scientist." 2012. *Nominum*. Web. 12 July 2012. Brief profile that appears on the website of Mockapetris's employer, Nomium.

Dustin Moskovitz

Cofounder of Facebook

Born: May 22, 1984; Gainesville, Florida
Died: -
Primary Field: Internet
Specialty: Social media
Primary Company/Organization: Facebook

Introduction

Dustin Moskovitz is one of the cofounders of Facebook, one of the world's most prominent social media networks and the focus of considerable attention. He left Harvard University after two years majoring in economics in order to move to Palo Alto with Mark Zuckerberg. There they founded the company in 2004, with Moskovitz acting as chief technologist and development strategist. In 2008, he left Facebook to start a new company, Asana, which aimed to provide applications that mirrored in working life what Facebook does for social life. He retains his holding in Facebook and, after the flotation of the company in 2012, was estimated to have a net worth in excess of $5 billion.

Early Life

Dustin Moskovitz was born in Gainesville, Florida, on May 22, 1984, and attended Vanguard High School in Ocala, Florida, where he undertook the international baccalaureate program. He had no particular interest in computers or the Internet and enrolled in Harvard University to study economics. His roommate, Mark Zuckerberg, and he were soon working together to create the prototype of Facebook, which was then designed to be a means of making contact with other Harvard University colleagues. Moskovitz began to teach himself the computer programming skills necessary for this work as he continued. Within two years, the two, with some other collaborators, decided to leave Harvard and move to Palo Alto as a means of working on Facebook on a full-time basis. Their initial plan was to return to Harvard in a year, but they did not return.

Life's Work

Moskovitz's prowess as a strategist and programmer has developed in line with the scope and sophistication of

Facebook as a whole. Initially, the concept of Facemash was used by Zuckerberg alone as a means of getting to know other Harvard University colleagues. Security and privacy have been recurrent issues in the history of social networking ever since.

Facebook opened for operations in February 2004 and reached 100 million users by 2008, when Moskovitz left to start his own venture. It has subsequently risen to more than 900 million users, with growth coming largely in the mobile sector, which accounts for more than half of all users. Facebook's services in the early years were rudimentary compared to the present version. Additions have been made both through internal developments and by acquiring technology from external companies or buying those companies outright. As leading technologist and strategist for the mobile service, Moskovitz was involved in both means of improving the service. The results have been hugely popular, with people quickly taking to the opportunities to make contact with friends and family members, as well as others, by exchanging information and photographs with each other digitally.

Contacts can be divided according to categories such as friends, close friends, and family members, and privacy settings can be adjusted to limit the information exchanged with people not in those categories. In its early years, it was observed that many users were casual about their use of the service and did not always appreciate or modulate the amount of information about themselves that they made available; some shared information indiscreetly, which had both social and career consequences. Facebook management has also admitted that some of the changes in policy made with respect to privacy settings could have been made more carefully. There have been other controversies relating to ownership of intellectual property and the order with which certain applications and processes were developed. These issues bedevil software development in the private sector, since there are so many sets of people aiming to achieve approximately the same effects using slightly different means and with so many stages of development that it is not easy to determine exactly when a project is sufficiently advanced to be considered completed.

At first, Facebook was limited to Harvard University users. Then it spread to other universities and then to high schools across the Northeast and then the rest of the world by 2006. Users must be thirteen years old to be permitted to join and must possess a genuine e-mail address. However, it is widely established that these

Dustin Moskovitz.

requirements are not difficult to meet (or appear to meet); Facebook employees are constantly at work closing accounts and deleting content deemed to contravene corporate policies. These interventions are estimated to number in the thousands daily. Inevitably, some mistakes have occurred—a message outlining abuse by security forces in Syria was apparently deleted accidentally, for example. Other interventions have attracted less attention but may still be just as problematic.

In 2007, Microsoft purchased a 1.6 percent share in Facebook, both as an investment and as a means of shaping the placing of advertisements on the system. It is through advertisements that the company has sought to monetize the user base of Facebook and the content uploaded to it. The willingness of users to share so much time and information with the system has encouraged valuations of each one to range as high as an average of $200. However, obtaining the value of each customer has been problematic for all online businesses and was a significant contributory factor in the dot-com crash at the beginning of the century. That Facebook was able to float on the stock exchange with a valuation of billions of dollars suggests that investors have confidence that this problem can be overcome.

In 2008, Moskovitz announced that he was leaving Facebook to start his own venture, Asana, along with Justin Rosenstein, who had joined Facebook the year before after some years working as a software engineer at Google. Moskovitz explained his decision in lifestyle terms: He wanted the experience of establishing a start-up company and the opportunity to reinvent himself as a person independent from Facebook who could operate as a philanthropic investor and entrepreneur as well as a company executive—all the while continuing the low-key lifestyle and personal freedoms to which he aspired.

The new venture, Asana, is named after a term associated with yoga. The company is designed to operate along nontraditional lines that will enhance productivity and creativity. The principal product is a form of collaborative software aimed at improving the productivity of people working together that will inevitably be compared to Facebook, fairly or otherwise. The company appears to be prospering at a comparatively early stage of product release and is benefiting from investment support and advice from a cluster of entrepreneurs, venture capitalists, and Internet thinkers who have become associated with the West Coast of the United States. This fuzzily defined group of people share a philosophy involving the power of technology to liberate people (at least those people able who take advantage of it), the ability of science to conquer nature and the responsibility of gifted individuals to return benefits to society by supporting new ventures and entrepreneurial individuals.

Affiliation: Facebook

Facebook was originally envisioned by its founders to be a means of providing an online database of Harvard University members and neighbors. It has subsequently grown in scope and sophistication to link many millions of members across numerous countries and has become the means of communication of choice for large numbers of people, particularly young people. Integrating various online technologies—and not without some controversy over intellectual property rights—the Facebook experience enables people to post their photos online, comment on one another's lives as represented by personal documentation, and connect with celebrities and organizational contacts. Braving unchartered territory in terms of breadth of coverage, Facebook has encountered problems with privacy issues and accidental deletions, not to mention cooperation with heavily financed political activism (super PAC) groups and the way in which flotation of the company was handled.

The degree of fascination that Facebook and its creators engendered is clear from the publication of numerous books about it and the successful feature film *The Social Network*, which (somewhat controversially) portrays its founding. Facebook continues to offer new features to users and has vanquished one-time competitors such as Myspace. For many users, Facebook has *become* the Internet, and this means that the monetization of customer members (the service is free and, it is promised, always will be) is more feasible.

PERSONAL LIFE

Like Facebook originator Zuckerberg and other Internet entrepreneurs, Moskovitz places great importance on the personal freedom of software creators in the workplace and embodies the dressed-down informality this implies. At Asana, employees can enjoy regular yoga sessions and, famously, up to $10,000 to improve their workplace equipment. Moskovitz's wealth has enabled him to follow Bill and Melinda Gates in pledging himself to philanthropic giving, and this aspect of his activities is handled by his fiancée, Cari Tuna, who is a graduate of Yale and a technology journalist for *The Wall Street Journal*. The couple are said to have met on a blind date. She will run the philanthropic organization under the title Good Ventures and has already made donations to charities dealing with malaria and poverty, among others. Moskovitz and Tuna live together in San Francisco.

One of Asana's corporate values is "chillness," and this seems to reflect Moskovitz's personality, which has been described as sedate and almost taciturn. When he started Facebook, he had only a rudimentary knowledge of computer science and he taught himself what he needed to know as he needed to know it. He has maintained a comparatively low public profile, with few if any of the excesses associated with other billionaires.

John Walsh

FURTHER READING

"Dustin Moskovitz, Facebook Billionaire, Shuns Luxury for Startup Life." 30 Apr. 2012. *CNBC*. Web. 1 May 2012. Journalistic profile of Moskovitz during the Asana start-up period.

Fuchs, Christian. "An Alternative View of Privacy on Facebook," *Information* 2.1 (2011): 140–65. Print.

Academic analysis of the privacy issues involved with Facebook, linking these with capitalism and the commodification of users.

Kirkpatrick, David. "The Facebook Effect." *The Inside Story of the Company That Is Connecting the World*. New York: Simon, 2010. Print. Discusses the history and impact of Facebook. Includes notes, an index, and illustrations.

Mezrich, Ben. *The Accidental Billionaires: The Founding of Facebook; A Tale of Sex, Money, Genius, and Betrayal*. New York: Doubleday, 2009. Print. The lurid and not entirely factual account of Facebook's founding that inspired the film *The Social Network*.

Vance, Ashlee, and Douglas MacMillan. "Asana: Dustin and Justin's Quest for Flow," 2 Nov. 2011. *Bloomberg Businessweek*. Web. 1 July 2012. Covers Moskovitz's character as it is expressed in the corporate philosophy of Asana.

Westlake, T. J. "Friend Me If You Facebook: Generation Y and Performative Surveillance." *TDR: The Drama Review* 52.4 (2008): 21–40. Print. Academic discussion of the panopticon effect of Facebook and the modified behavior of its users in response.

MARKOS MOULITSAS

Founder of *The Daily Kos*

Born: September 11, 1971; Chicago, Illinois
Died: -
Primary Field: Internet
Specialty: News and entertainment
Primary Company/Organization: *The Daily Kos*

INTRODUCTION

Markos Moulitsas is one of the most influential voices on the Internet, with a community blog, The Daily Kos, *that reaches 2 million readers and is a leading site for left-central readers as well as regular columns for traditional media.* The Daily Kos *has become such an important part of progressive politics that Moulitsas has become incorporated, informally, into the Democratic Party's intelligentsia, and his opinion on potential candidates a valued one. As a proponent of grassroots activism and bottom-up self-organization as a means of effecting political change, Moulitsas aims to promote* The Daily Kos *as a seamless link between mainstream journalism and citizen journalism. He balances his activities there with work for the mainstream media and his other commercial interests, which include a network of sports blogs.*

EARLY LIFE

Markos "Kos" Moulitsas Zúniga was born on September 11, 1971, in Chicago, Illinois, to a mother who was Salvadoran and a father who was Greek. Moulitsas subsequently spent several years (1976–80) in El Salvador during the time when the civil war between a U.S.-backed military junta and communist insurgents was under way. The family returned to the United States as a result of the fighting and fear of violence.

As a young man, Moulitsas exhibited a right-wing sensibility. On finishing high school, he joined the U.S. Army. He spent a period at a U.S. base and the bulk of his three years in Germany as part of a missile launch

Markos Moulitsas.

team. His experiences in the military persuaded him that he had been pursuing the wrong course: The use of paid and unaccountable mercenaries (for example, the private security contractor Blackwater in Iraq), the general management of the wars in Iraq and Afghanistan, and the role of corporate interests in dictating foreign policy all seemed to have been influential in effecting this transition.

When he left the military, therefore, Moulitsas resolved to get more education and then chart a new course for his career. He read for undergraduate degrees in philosophy, journalism, and politics at Northern Illinois University and then a postgraduate law degree at Boston University. In 1999, he decided to move to California to embark on a new career in proximity to the emerging Internet industry, although it was not immediately apparent what the course of that career would be.

LIFE'S WORK

To a certain extent, Moulitsas has followed the same route into Internet success as many of the other members of the network of investors, entrepreneurs, and engineers in that field. That is, he has found a successful business model after being at first discouraged by attempts at political consultancy and other ventures relying principally on his own efforts.

His success came when he adopted a network model of entrepreneurism, which means identifying a technological platform that important other stakeholders wish to share. In contrast to some other ventures (for example, Facebook and Google), the important stakeholders in this case were members of the public—or at least people and organizations motivated to get their message across on a larger connected network than they could achieve based on their own efforts. Both *The Daily Kos* and the SN Nation of sports blogs rely on positive externalities: that is, the willingness of other people to contribute their physical and mental labor to a venture without being initially compensated for it. Contributors provide content and assistance in the hope that their opinions will become better known, perhaps because they have a personal ideology they would like to see advanced at a broader social level or because their partiality to a sports team or sporting league also represents something of an evangelical aspiration that requires them to tell other people their opinions. This approach minimizes, within reason, capital asset investment and maximizes external input from network connections in a set of self-extending networks. That is, people who become part of the network by reading and

---

Affiliation: *The Daily Kos*

The Daily Kos was started May 26, 2002 as a community blog that would be home to individuals and organizations wishing to contribute to the progressive cause by holding elected and unelected officials of both parties and of the establishment to account for their actions. Markos Moulitsas was inspired by the fierce grip held on the mainstream media by corporate interests and the huge amount of attention given to extreme right wing radio-based shock jocks to create a counterblast that would go some way toward balancing the stridency of debate.

That this was an important and popular cause is attested by the 2 million unique visitors to the site per month and the 300,000 registered users. It is also attested by the range of prominent individuals who have contributed comment to the site, including then-Senator Barack Obama, President Jimmy Carter, and Speaker of the House Nancy Pelosi.

The Daily Kos consists of areas given to individual bloggers (who are rated for performance) and forum posts on a range of progressive topics, including self-organization for Occupy Wall Street–type protests and similar campaigns. There is space for headlining writers and also for the very popular comics section. It is both a source of information and a place where people can spend time in the company of being of generally like-minded opinions. In common with all crowded parts of the Internet, Daily Kos communities are occasionally prone to hysterical outbreaks by individuals or groups and the gap between citizen journalism and mainstream journalism is not yet fully abridged.

---

contributing to the community blogs have a powerful incentive to increase the number of people also reading and contributing to them. This is both a positive externality (that is, it provides additional benefits to the community and stakeholders at large above and beyond what is intended by the creator) and a network externality (that is, the more people that log onto, read, and then comment on *Daily Kos* posts, then the more that contributors and everyone else will obtain value from the process).

There have of course been controversies along the way. These have arisen from two principal causes. First, since *The Daily Kos* is read (depending on estimates) by editors at more than the top ten political magazines in the United States combined, it has aroused the interest of its ideological opponents and, given the nature of political discourse in contemporary America, any questionable statement or misstatement by a member of the public or regular contributor can be seized upon as a means of obtaining political leverage. Second, the contributors themselves are indeed occasionally prone to overstatement, hysteria, or paranoia. These phenomena seem endemic to online contributions, which can be effected at great speed and without the period of reflection and checking that traditional journalistic principles require to be incorporated into the process (although these have also eroded in the face of today's cost reductions).

The extent to which *Daily Kos* content has become recognized as an important part of the media landscape in the United States is demonstrated by the fact that content analysis is now being performed on it for publication in academic journals. For example, the occasion on which Virginia senator George Allen made racist comments during a floundering campaign (although disputed, they were caught clearly on tape) and the subsequent exchange of comments became an important case study measuring the nature and extent of public political discourse. One research question in this case is the extent to which comments received are genuine representations of grassroots mobilization or are responses from large-scale organizations masquerading as the genuine voice of the people.

It remains to be seen whether online communities such as those surrounding *The Daily Kos* will be able to provide the kind of citizen journalism that has been forecast and whether such communities will genuinely function as partnerships with mainstream journalism.

PERSONAL LIFE

Moulitsas was married in 2000 and lives in California with wife and two children, son Artistotle and younger daughter Elisandra. They are described as living a healthy and happy Californian lifestlye featuring sports and music. Moulitsas is said to be an enthusiastic composer.

He has been included in a variety of "most important" lists in the media, including lists of important Hispanics, important Internet personalities, and so forth.

These are subjective judgments, but their accumulation suggests that a level of significance in the industry does exist. The Zúniga portion of Moulitsas's name only occasionally appears in print, presumably in part because it interferes with the Kos brand name.

John Walsh

FURTHER READING

"About Daily Kos." n.d. *Daily Kos.* Web. 20 July 2012. Informative biography of Moulitsas and colleagues, which seems to have formed the basis of most other profiles and description on the Internet.

Armstrong, Jerome, and Markos Moulitsas. *Netroots, Grassroots, and the Rise of People-Powered Politics.* White River Junction: Chelsea Green, 2006. Print. Energetic polemic excoriating both the Democratic and Republican parties for their failures and calling on grassroots groups and individuals to hold the establishment accountable when using contemporary political techniques.

Karpf, David. "Macaca Moments Reconsidered: Electoral Panopticon or Netroots Mobilization?" *Journal of Information Technology and Politics* 17.2–3 (2010): 143–62. Print. Considers misconceptions about so-called macaca moments, or high-profile gaffes, that have been captured on YouTube and have instigated discussion and debate, including the case of Virginia senator George Allen.

Moulitsas, Markos. *American Taliban: How War, Sex, Sin, and Power Bind Jihadists and the Radical Right.* San Francisco: Polipoint, 2010. Print. Entertaining polemic in which Moulitsas compares the Islamic jihadists of Al Qaeda with the right wing of the Republican Party, to the credit of neither.

---. *Taking on the System: Rules for Change in a Digital Era.* New York: Celebra, 2009. Print. Handbook for self-organization for the progressive movement, with detailed instructions on how to use social media to mobilize people and increase the impact of campaigns.

Wallace-Wells, Benjamin. "Kos Call." *Washington Monthly* Jan./Feb. 2006. Web. 20 July 2012. Extensive magazine profile of Moulitsas and the evolution of his career.

ELON MUSK

Cofounder of PayPal

Born: June 28, 1971; Pretoria, South Africa
Died: -
Primary Field: Internet
Specialty: Commerce
Primary Company/Organization: PayPal

INTRODUCTION

Elon Musk is a used his technology skills and business savvy to become a successful, serial, U.S.-based entrepreneur. Musk's first company, which he cofounded with his brother shortly after leaving the graduate physics program at Stanford University, was called Zip2; it provided online content publishing software for local news organizations and was acquired by Compaq. As a founder and early driving force behind online payment-processing company PayPal, Musk in early 2002 reaped significant financial rewards from PayPal's initial public offering (IPO)—the first successful IPO of a technology company after the U.S. terrorist attacks of September 11, 2001. After eBay acquired the post-IPO PayPal later in 2002, Musk then used the significant wealth he had accumulated from Zip2 and PayPal to cofound, invest in, and become chief executive officer (CEO) of both Space Exploration Technologies (SpaceX) and Tesla Motors. In these roles, Musk is largely credited with having developed the Falcon 9/Dragon, a commercial successor to the Space Shuttle, and the Tesla Roadster, the first viable electric car of the modern era. He also became chairman of SolarCity, which designs, audits, finances, and installs solar energy systems.

EARLY LIFE

Elon Musk is one of three children born to an engineer father and a nutritionist/dietitian mother (now divorced), on June 28, 1971, in Pretoria, South Africa. He left high school and emigrated from South Africa to Canada in 1988 at the age of seventeen, primarily because he objected philosophically to mandatory conscription into the South African military, which at the time was the primary enforcement vehicle for apartheid, the country's former system of racial segregation, which had been shrined in law and enforced for nearly fifty years until it was ended in the mid-1990s.

After studying for two years at Queen's University in Kingston, Ontario, Canada, Musk relocated to the United States to pursue business and physics at the University of Pennsylvania, from which he received a separate bachelor's degree in each subject. Following his graduation from that institution, Musk relocated to Silicon Valley, California. Originally, the reason for the relocation was to earn a doctorate degree in applied physics and materials science from Stanford University, but Musk participated in that program for only a few days before leaving it to cofound Zip2, an online content publishing software company.

LIFE'S WORK

After leaving Stanford's graduate physics program, Musk and his brother cofounded a company named Zip2, which provided online content publishing software for local news organizations, such as *The New York Times* and the *Chicago Tribune*. Ultimately, business pressures forced the Musk brothers to sell a controlling interest in Zip2 to venture capitalists; in 1999, Compaq acquired Zip2 in the hope of using it to buttress its AltaVista search engine division. The reported cash

Elon Musk.

and stock purchase price for Zip2 was nearly $350 million, out of which Musk's reported share was $22 million.

Following the successful sale of Zip2, Musk cofounded a new company, named X.com, which was an Internet financial services company focused on e-mail payments. In early 2000, X.com merged with a company named Confinity, which initially was a payments and cryptography company limited to the Palm Pilot platform and cofounded by Max Levchin and Peter Thiel, among others. Musk became CEO of the combined entity for a time, then chief product officer; ultimately he was credited with having been the primary architect of a viral campaign that quickly fueled the company's growth. Because of personality conflicts and political struggles on the management team, however, Musk left the company in late 2000, keeping his significant equity stake in the company, by then renamed PayPal.

In February 2002, PayPal sold an IPO of just less than 10 percent of its then-outstanding stock, raising more than $70 million, with its stock price rising more than 50 percent on the first day of trading. In the process, PayPal became the first successful Internet IPO following the terrorist attacks of September 11, 2001, and Musk's 11.7 percent share of the company had a value of roughly $86 million.

In October 2002, PayPal was acquired by eBay for $1.5 billion worth of eBay stock. Musk, then thirty-one years of age, made roughly $172 million from his ownership stake in PayPal. Shortly after the eBay acquisition of PayPal, Musk reportedly used $100 million of his own money to found Space Exploration Technologies (SpaceX), which develops rockets and spacecraft and has developed to launch several products, including Falcon 1, a launch vehicle that in 2008 was the first privately developed liquid fuel rocket to put a satellite into Earth orbit; Falcon 9, also a launch vehicle, which in 2012 was the first privately developed rocket of any type to deliver to the International Space Station; and Dragon, a free-flying, reusable spacecraft used to transport cargo and crew members into low Earth orbit, which in 2012 was launched to the International Space Station using SpaceX's Falcon 9. SpaceX has another product deep in the development stage: Falcon Heavy, which, if successful, will be the world's most powerful rocket, possessing the ability to carry payload weighing more than twice the payload of the U.S. Space Shuttle (the next closest vehicle). In December of 2008, SpaceX was awarded a National Aeronautics and Space Administration contract having a value of up to $3.1 billion for

---

Affiliation: PayPal

PayPal is worldwide online payment-processing company that had its origins in a company named X.com, which ultimately merged with a company called Confinity to form a combined firm that ultimately was renamed PayPal.

In February of 2002, PayPal sold an initial public offering (IPO) of just under 10 percent of its then-outstanding stock, raising more than $70 million and seeing its stock price rise more than 50 percent on the first day of trading. In the process, PayPal became the first successful Internet IPO following the terrorist attacks of September 11, 2001. In October 2002, PayPal was acquired by eBay for $1.5 billion worth of eBay stock, and it remains wholly owned by eBay.

Today, PayPal operates under the three primary brands: PayPal, Payflow Gateway, and Bill Me Later. It has more than 100 million active registered accounts and is available in nearly two hundred markets. It supports payments in more than twenty currencies, including the U.S. dollar, the Hong Kong dollar, the Euro, the Chinese yuan, the British pound sterling, and the Japanese yen. It has localized websites in more than twenty markets, including China, Germany, Hong Kong, Japan, and the United Kingdom. PayPal's 2011 annual revenue was $4.4 billion, half of which was generated internationally. This $4.4 billion represented 38 percent of eBay's revenues for the year. The total value of transactions processed through PayPal in 2011 was $118 billion, up 29 percent from the prior year.

PayPal is headquartered in San Jose, California, with a European headquarters in Luxembourg and an international headquarters in Singapore. It has multiple operations centers, located in such places as Berlin, Dublin, Omaha, São Paulo, and Shanghai, and multiple development centers, located in such places as Austin, Singapore, and Tel Aviv.

---

not less than twelve flights of its Falcon 9/Dragon to the International Space Station, replacing the Space Shuttle after it retired in 2011. In addition to having been the primary founder and funder of SpaceX, Musk has been its CEO and chief technology officer.

In 2003, Musk was one of five cofounders of Tesla Motors, an electric car company. It is reported that Musk has used nearly $50 million of his own money to participate in the various funding rounds of Tesla, where he became its first chairman and product architect, helping design the groundbreaking Tesla Roadster. At Tesla, Musk also has become the CEO and is credited with many of the company's achievements, including the design, engineering, and manufacturing of the company's products (with sales of around two thousand vehicles as of mid-2012); launching the company's regional sales and service centers across two continents; securing a $50 million investment and strategic partnership from Germany's Daimler; spearheading a successful cost-down program that enabled the company to achieve profitability in mid-2009; and guiding development of a new, all-electric family sedan that is scheduled for production in late 2012. Musk is reported to have a 32 percent stake in Tesla, which is has been valued at more than$1 billion.

In 2006, Musk reportedly again used his own money to launch (and provided an initial concept for) SolarCity, the largest provider of solar power systems in the United States. Unlike SpaceX and Tesla, SolarCity has seen Musk take a limited operational role; two of his cousins are the cofounders and run the company on a day-to-day basis. Musk remains, however, the largest shareholder and chairman of the board.

Musk has received numerous awards and accolades for his work, including appointment to *Time* magazine's list of 100 People Who Most Affect the World in 2010, the Fédération Aéronautique Internationale (FAI) Gold Space Medal (the highest award in air and space) in 2010, appointment to *Forbes* magazine's list of America's 20 Most Powerful CEOs 40 And Under in 2011; the National Wildlife Federation's National Conservation Achievement Award in 2008; and *IncMagazine*'s Entrepreneur of the Year award for 2007.

PERSONAL LIFE

In 2000, Musk married Canadian-born author Justine Wilson, whom he met while attending Queen's University and with whom he has five children, a set of twins and a set of triplets, all boys. A sixth child, also a boy, died of SIDS at the age of ten days. Musk and Wilson announced their separation in September of 2008, have since divorced, remain estranged, and share joint custody of their children. By some estimates, Musk's net worth exceeds $2 billion. By contrast, in papers he filed in 2010 in his divorce proceedings, he claimed to have personal financial problems and to have been subsisting on loans from wealthy friends. In September 2010, Musk married British actor Talulah Riley-Milburn. They announced the end of their relationship in January 2012.

Musk, who lives in Bel Air, California, is a self-described workaholic who claims to work more than a hundred hours per week, leaving scarce time for leisure activities. He is, however, an active philanthropist, counting among his philanthropic endeavors the Musk Foundation, which focuses its philanthropic efforts on science education, pediatric health, and clean energy; the X Prize Foundation, which promotes renewable energy technologies; and the boards of the Space Foundation, the National Academies' Aeronautics and Space Engineering Board, and the Planetary Society.

In April 2012, Musk joined the Giving Pledge, first popularized by Warren Buffett and Bill Gates, joining them in offering his moral commitment ultimately to donate the majority of his fortune to philanthropy.

Joe Bogdan

FURTHER READING

Belfiore, Michael. *Rocketeers: How a Visionary Band of Business Leaders, Engineers, and Pilots Is Boldly Privatizing Space*. New York: HarperCollins, 2007. Print. A candid look behind the curtain in the nascent industry of privatized space travel and exploration, and the people whose dreams are helping to make that a reality.

Dubbs, Chris, and Emeline Paat-Dahlstrom. *Realizing Tomorrow: The Path to Private Spaceflight*. Lincoln: U of Nebraska P. Print. A perspective on the lives of those who have shared the conviction that private individuals and private enterprise belong in space.

Jackson, Eric M. *The PayPal Wars: Battles with eBay, the Media, the Mafia, and the Rest of Planet Earth*. Torrance: World Ahead, 2008. Print and digital. Tells the story of PayPal's history from the view of a former insider, author Jackson.

N

ASHWIN NAVIN

Cofounder of BitTorrent

Born: 1977; Sacramento, California
Died: -
Primary Field: Internet
Specialty: Applications
Primary Company/Organization: BitTorrent

INTRODUCTION

Ashwin Navin cofounded BitTorrent, Inc., in 2004 with brothers Bram and Ross Cohen to maintain and promote the peer-to-peer file-sharing protocol developed by Bram. Navin served as the company's first president, handling business matters, while the Cohens dealt with product development. In 2008, Navin resigned from BitTorrent to focus on other businesses, Flingo and i/o Ventures.

EARLY LIFE

Ashwin Navin was born in 1977 in Sacramento, California, and graduated from Claremont McKenna College in 1999 with a double major in economics and government. He worked on Wall Street as an analyst and investment banker for Goldman Sachs and Merrill Lynch and was instrumental in founding the financial services company Epoch Partners. Epoch provided investment banking services for online investment brokerages such as TD Waterhouse, Ameritrade, and Charles Schwab. It was founded in 2000 and acquired by Goldman Sachs in 2001. Navin went to work for Yahoo!'s Corporate Development group in 2002, handling corporate strategy. It was in that capacity that he first came in contact with BitTorrent, presenting an evaluation on the recently released software.

LIFE'S WORK

Bram Cohen developed the BitTorrent application in 2001, in nine months of coding, after he left his job working on the software for Mojo Nation, peer-to-peer (P2P), open source system for sharing everything from resources to digital cash. It was a leap forward in P2P file sharing, allowing files to be downloaded from

Ashwin Navin.

273

Affiliation: BitTorrent

Less than a decade after its introduction, the BitTorrent protocol accounts for almost half of all Internet traffic. Even in 2005—four years after its introduction—the Internet-analysis firm CacheLogic reported that BitTorrent accounted for a third of the Internet's traffic. Perhaps only streaming video has so quickly claimed such a large a portion of traffic—and for that matter, arguably only the popularity of streaming video services such as Hulu and Netflix, offering movies and television programs, can account for BitTorrent's consuming only half the Internet's traffic. The protocol was developed by Bram Cohen in 2001 and is maintained by BitTorrent, Inc. BitTorrent addressed one of the fundamental challenges that has faced the Internet since its early days: the task of transfering large files (where "large" has scaled over time, in accordance to technological advances) efficiently and without the inconvenience of continually restarting failed transfers. The fundamentals of peer-to-peer file sharing had already been pioneered and popularized by Napster, which made the act of sharing files a passive one; unlike many previous forms of file transfers, with BitTorrent the user from whom the file was downloaded did not need to be present to initiate or agree to the transfer but could passively host files and open a program that would allow others to initiate downloads. This alone was a considerable advance over the software available to most users who were not operating servers.

The BitTorrent protocol was inspired in part by Cohen's work on Mojo Nation, a digital cash economy and file-sharing platform that stored pieces of files on users' computers, as in cloud computing, with the storage burden shifted to the client side. BitTorrent similarly shifts some of the burden to the client side. Rather than creating file transfers between two peers, as Napster did, with BitTorrent the file may be downloaded from any of the connected users who have a copy and have agreed to share it—and critically, the BitTorrent client programs download from multiple source copies simultaneously. The fact that BitTorrent allows users who are still downloading to be downloaded from in turn—that incomplete copies of a file are still used as sources for other downloaders—is key to BitTorrent's efficiency, because this eases the load from the server

(or from seeds). The moment a user begins downloading, every bit of data downloaded reduces the demand on the seed, and thus the more users are downloading, the faster the file can be downloaded—which is the reverse of the situation experienced in traditional downloading-from-server scenarios.

Mojo Nation encouraged sharing by compensating users for their computing resources with mojo, a digital cash that was then spent on downloaded files. BitTorrent sites (although this is not formally encoded by the protocol) have developed a different incentive: Users are incentivized through various means to maintain a reasonable ratio of bytes uploaded to bytes downloaded, which encourages them to continue seeding files they have successfully downloaded, since this is a passive, resource-light method of increasing their bytes-uploaded count.

BitTorrent arrived at just the right time, as MP3 files were becoming, if not passé, no longer the amazing novelty they had been; with streaming video becoming more common, video, not audio, was the medium of the moment. BitTorrent was much better suited for transferring video files (which are much larger than audio files); even a half-hour video was several times larger than a high-quality MP3 of an entire music album. Of course, BitTorrent's adroitness at handling large files made it well suited to the copyright-infringing transfer of movies, television shows, software, and other files—and it became common, surprisingly quickly, to find television shows available by torrent within hours of their airing and full DVD downloads available the week of release if not sooner—but BitTorrent, Inc., which Cohen founded with his brother Ross and business partner Ashwin Navin in 2004, made an alliance with the MPAA, a move predecessors such as Napster had been unable or unwilling to do. While BitTorrent, Inc., could do nothing to stop the use of its software for illegal purposes, the official BitTorrent site complies with the requirements of the Digital Millennium Copyright Act. BitTorrent is often used as the official means of distribution for legitimate files, from movies to software, and allows files to be released from individuals or companies that cannot afford the resources to offer it for direct download from a server. One well-known example early in BitTorrent's history,

Affiliation: BitTorrent (continued)

in 2003, was the open source Red Hat Linux 9 operating system; Red Hat's servers crashed under the demand of downloaders when the operating system was released, but once a copy was made available via BitTorrent, 21.15 terabytes of data were exchanged over three days, an amount of traffic that would have cost as much as $50,000 in bandwidth through conventional means but, with BitTorrent, never exceeded the amount of traffic allowed by the host's $99 server rental fee. The Red Hat release demonstrated that BitTorrent had arrived at exactly the right time, when the Internet was on the verge of suffering from its own growth. It prevented the stifling that could have occurred, and enabled sharing that simply could not have happened otherwise, such as when graduate student Gary Lerhaupt convinced the filmmakers behind the Fox News exposé *Outfoxed* to let him release it as a torrent file; fifteen hundred people downloaded it, at a cost to Lerhaupt of $4.

The BitTorrent protocol is always being developed. Recent changes have included a shift to delay-based congestion control in 2012, in order to be friendlier to the limitations of the transmission-control protocol (TCP) and those of the routers that provide the Internet with its infrastructure—and in order to consume less bandwidth to address the common problem of users who are unable to use BitTorrent (or use it effectively) at the same time as resource-intensive applications such as *World of Warcraft* and other massively multiplayer online role-playing games.

BitTorrent, Inc., supports BitTorrent, Codeville (a distributed revision control system developed by the Cohen brothers), BitTorrent DNA (a "disruptively effective" content delivery technology to reduce bandwidth costs to websites), and the BitTorrent Device Partners program for hardware and software companies manufacturing Internet-enabled consumer electronics. Bram Cohen remains cofounder and chief scientist of BitTorrent (as well as cofounder of related projects CodeCon and Codeville) and serves on the board of directors. The remaining board members are CEO Eric Klinker, previously of Internap and Excite@ Home; David Chao, cofounder and general partner of DCM; Ping Li, general partner of Accel; and John J. Cadeddu, managing director of DAG Ventures. The rest of the management team is chief strategist and executive vice president of marketing Shahi Ghanem, previously of STL and DivX; vice president of data science Simon Morris, previously of Openwave; vice president of engineering Ilan Shamir, previously of Check Point Software Technologies and SideTalk, Inc.; vice president of finance and operations Claude Tolbert, previously of Covad Communications; and vice president of marketing and business development Ro Choy, formerly of Formspring.

multiple sources at once—with those sources being fellow users, rather than a centralized server that might crash under the demand. The protocol was ideally suited to the problem of transferring large very large files—from gigabyte-big movies and exact copies of DVDs. Prior P2P clients had scaled poorly, doing a considerably worse job if files were larger than a hundred megabytes or so (roughly the size of an album's worth of MP3 music files). BitTorrent handled more, handled them more quickly, and handled them using less bandwidth on the part of the uploader, which made the service ideal for sharing large amounts of data without incurring significant bandwidth usage fees.

Navin's role in cofounding the company in 2004 was to help at the business end to commercialize and mainstream it, while the brothers worked to maintain the BitTorrent protocol (and related works). BitTorrent's capacity to transfer large files had alarmed the film industry, which now faced the dilemma the music industry had faced with Napster. Learning from Napster's example, Navin continued Cohen's work in clearly delineating the difference between the software's possible uses and its intended uses. In 2005, an agreement was reached with the Motion Picture Association of America (MPAA) whereby the official BitTorrent site would abide by the procedures of the Digital Millennium Copyright Act and no copyright-infringing files would be listed on the site. Because BitTorrent provided only software, not servers, it could not monitor how that software was used.

Furthermore, Navin dealt with movie executives carefully, pointing out that BitTorrent is simply a means of distributing data—one that could be used commercially, particularly as digital distribution of commercial media became more common. Just as iTunes became the legal, commercial successor to early MP3-sharing programs, a legitimate movie distribution system could follow the illegal pirate sites. Through Navin's work,

BitTorrent cultivated relationships with most of the major studios, notably Warner Bros., 20th Century Fox, and Paramount.

Navin was also behind BitTorrent's acquisition of uTorrent, the most popular BitTorrent client, and the launch of the BitTorrent software developer's kit for consumer electronics, the BitTorrent DNA package for websites, and the BitTorrent Entertainment Network. He negotiated BitTorrent's critical deal with Comcast over net neutrality issues and traffic management policy.

In late 2008, Navin resigned from BitTorrent, having given several months' notice, in order to help the company make a transition while hiring a new management team. He continued to support and advocate the software, and the departure seems to have been amicable. He moved on to two new ventures: Flingo and i/o Ventures. Flingo, of which he became chief executive officer (CEO), was founded in 2008 to develop apps for smart televisions, working with the major TV studios and networks—contacts Navin had made at BitTorrent—to develop apps for their content. Flingo investors include billionaire entrepeneur Mark Cuban.

Navin founded i/o Ventures in 2009 with Aber Whitcomb (cofounder of Myspace), Paul Bragiel (cofounder of Lefora), and Jim Young (cofounder of Hot or Not). Based in San Francisco, i/o Ventures provides venture capital and a six-month business incubation program to start-ups. Mentors involved with the program include founders of Digg, Mint.com, Myspace, YouTube, Yelp, and TechCrunch.

PERSONAL LIFE

Navin is an avid skiier, a fan of board games, and a vegetarian. His childhood dream was to work at Apple.

Bill Kte'pi

FURTHER READING

Aigrain, Philippe. *Sharing: Culture and Economy in the Internet Age*. Amsterdam: Amsterdam UP, 2012. Print. Considers BitTorrent as one of several technologies enabling the sharing of information and media, and the effects thereof on culture.

Botsman, Rachel, and Roo Rogers. *What's Mine Is Yours: The Rose of Collaborative Consumption*. New York: HarperCollins, 2012. Print. Botsman and Rogers do not address BitTorrent by name—nor do they mention many other file-sharing technologies, perhaps fearing sounding dated—but discuss generally the role of the Internet in sharing and collaboration.

Gold, Lorna. *The Sharing Economy: Solidarity Networks Transforming Globalization*. Burlington: Ashgate, 2004. Print. Covers BitTorrent and sharing applications in the context of globalization.

Roth, Daniel. "Torrential Reign." *Fortune* 31 Oct. 2005: n. pag. Print. Examines the alliance between the MPAA and BitTorrent, which in retrospect was likely instrumental in the company's long-term success.

Thompson, Clive. "The BitTorrent Effect." *Wired* 13.1 (2005): n. pag. Print. An in-depth, technically informed profile of BitTorrent and the spike in movie piracy.

COL NEEDHAM

Founder and CEO of the Internet Movie Database

Born: January 26, 1967; Manchester, England
Died: -
Primary Field: Internet
Specialty: News and entertainment
Primary Company/Organization: Internet Movie Database

INTRODUCTION

Hewlett-Packard technological engineer Col Needham founded the Internet Movie Database, commonly known by its web address acronym IMDb, in 1990. The searchable entertainment industry database grew from the movie credit lists of Needham and other online film enthusiasts. IMDb had emerged as one of the most popular entertainment websites by the late 1990s, in part driven by its frequent appearance at the top of results returned for movie-related Internet searches. Needham remained with the Internet Movie Database after its 1998 acquisition by online entertainment e-commerce leader Amazon. The Internet Movie Database's growth placed him within the ranks of the leading Internet entrepreneurs. He is among the pioneers of telecommuting to maintain a role as the site's managing director and is also known for his business philosophy, which is centered on the vital importance of the site's visitors' contributions to its success.

Col Needham.

EARLY LIFE

Colin "Col" Needham was born on January 26, 1967, in the Denton, Tameside, neighborhood of Manchester, England. He received his early education at Audenshaw School and Hyde sixth form (currently Hyde Clarendon). His childhood interests centered on technology and entertainment. Needham became a technology entrepreneur at fourteen years of age, when he founded a computer games software business. He attended the University of Leeds, graduating with a bachelor's degree with honors in computer science in 1988.

Shortly after graduation, Needham began his adult career in technology at the computer company Hewlett-Packard in Bristol, England, where he was an engineer in the field of technology research. Outside work, he continued to pursue his childhood interests in technology and in the movies. These twin passions were combined in his creation of a computerized informational database on the movie industry that would shape his future career. He also began sharing his passion on Internet discussion boards such as the Usenet group rec.arts.movies.

LIFE'S WORK

Needham continued to pursue his interest in movies while working at Hewlett-Packard, building the personal film diary and film credits database he had begun as a teenager. Beginning in the late 1980s, he and other film enthusiasts collated his personal database with other film information lists on the online Usenet bulletin board site rec.arts.movies. The earliest data points included actor and director credits and biographies of deceased filmmakers. The database soon expanded to include television programs.

Another breakthrough came when Needham made the collated database searchable through his authorship of Unix shell scripts. The first searchable version appeared in 1990 and is considered the origin of today's IMDb. The database was the first dedicated movie website and the first to be available for searching free of charge. The site was also housed mostly on volunteer server space in its formative years. Early servers included that of Cardiff University in Wales, where site volunteer Rob Hartill was a graduate student. Interested users initially had to install the database locally on their home computers. The site became known as the Internet Movie Database and adopted the www.IMDb.com web address in 1993. Needham is credited as IMDb's founder and chief executive officer (CEO).

Volunteer site participants continued to build the credit lists that form the site's core, adding such categories as writers and composers. The uploading of digital content has increased exponentially since IMDb's founding, in terms of both content and number of participating users. The IMDb had been among the first sites to encourage users to upload such information, much of which had been locally stored on personal computers, as had the original movie lists at IMDb's core. This was a departure from the early days of the Internet, when users had mostly downloaded available content.

Hartill, Jake Dias, Murray Chapman, and Ron Higgins joined Needham as early volunteer workers, most of whom held salaried jobs at other companies. Hartill was responsible for the technological changes needed to create the first IMDb website. Needham left Hewlett-Packard in 1995 to devote himself to the IMDb full time, reflecting its rapid growth and success. The core group of volunteers also decided to transform the site into a commercial operation after a lengthy debate. The IMDb incorporated in the United Kingdom in January 1996. Its volunteer workers were also its first shareholders. and Needham charged the cost of its server space to his personal credit card. Improved technological capacity resulted in improved speed and service quality.

The IMDb quickly became a leading entertainment site and frequently topped Internet search engine results for queries based on movie and television titles, greatly increasing the site's traffic. Data submissions from the site's visitors also continued to increase, expanding the site's database but overwhelming its server space and volunteer workers. Needham had developed no master business plan when launching what became IMDb; it was created before the development of e-commerce. The site made its first advertising revenue in 1996. Its first movie advertising revenue, also in 1996, came from its promotion of the Fox blockbuster *Independence Day*. Needham soon began receiving buyout offers from numerous companies. Amazon.com founder Jeff Bezos was one of the Internet entrepreneurs offering to purchase the IMDb, realizing its potential to aid in the sales of his site's entertainment products.

Amazon acquired the IMDb in April 1998, making it a wholly owned subsidiary of the site. The acquisition provided technological improvements and upgrades, but Needham remained to run the site as managing director, telecommuting from his Bristol, England, home office. He is one of the pioneering business leaders in the use of instant messaging and other electronic communication avenues to telecommute. The site collaborates with Amazon's staff and advisers, but it is known for successfully maintaining its original business practices with little interference from the parent company.

The formerly volunteer IMDb staff became salaried employees. Employee Murray Chapman relocated from Australia to Seattle, Washington, to serve as liaison to Amazon. The IMDb began raising revenue through advertising sales, content licensing, business partnerships in movie ticket sales, and sales of advanced site features and subscription services. Needham often credited the participation of site visitors as one of the key forces behind the site's depth, growth, and popularity, noting (in his words) that the customer is the celebrity. Others have credited his ongoing leadership as crucial to IMDb's continuity and success.

Users also study and debate content, and both users and site editors check for factual accuracy. The site has added features such as the popularity rankings Starmeter and Moviemeter, as well as features designed for film and television industry workers. The Publicity Photos Service was added in 2001, and the paid subscription service IMDbPro.com was added in 2002. The subscription service provides more detailed information on a variety of industry data. IMDb was also enhanced with features addressing current events, entertainment industry news, and information on upcoming films.

Affiliation: Internet Movie Database

The Internet Movie Database (IMDb) had its origin in the personal film database built from the movie credits data set of founder Col Needham. Needham and others with similar interests collated their information online into one large bulletin-board database. Needham programmed the database to be searchable, publishing the earliest version to the Usenet newsgroup rec.arts.movies in 1990. The site adopted the Internet Movie Database name and the www.IMDb.com web address in 1993 and is commonly known by its abbreviation, IMDb.

IMDb was incorporated in 1996. The volunteers who had developed the site were also its first shareholders. Needham soon received numerous offers to purchase the site; Amazon closed the deal in 1998, and IMDb has remained a wholly owned subsidiary of the e-commerce giant ever since. The acquisition provided technological improvements, but Needham still runs the site independently. IMDb had emerged as one of the most popular entertainment websites by the late 1990s. Site visitor participation continues to play a vital role, helping the database expand its movie data and add other entertainment media such as information on television programs and series.

IMDb was not developed as an e-commerce site. Amazon's founder, Jeff Bezos, however, saw the potential for IMDb to help sell Amazon's entertainment products. IMDb raises revenue through advertising sales, content licensing, premium IMDb Pro service sales, and sales of products such as movie tickets and publicity photos. The site's twentieth anniversary was in 2010, marking the longevity of the site, and today IMDb has more than fifty employees and locations in Great Britain, the United States, Germany, and Switzerland. IMDb has acquired two subsidiaries, Withoutabox and BoxOfficeMojo.

The IMDb celebrated its twentieth anniversary in 2010, with Needham still at the helm. The site remains among the world's most popular online sites dedicated to the entertainment industry and has grown to include more than 1.5 million titles. The site also remains profitable, maintaining a staff of more than fifty employees as well as locations in Great Britain, the United States, Switzerland, and Germany. It has acquired two subsidiaries, Withoutabox and Box Office Mojo. Future development plans center on downloadable DVD services and further integration with Amazon's retail enterprises.

PERSONAL LIFE

Needham married his wife Karen in 1989. The couple have twin daughters and lives in a house in Bristol, England. Needham amassed a personal fortune as a result of his acquisition of Amazon shares through that company's 1998 purchase of the IMDb. Needham telecommutes, working alone from an office in his former residence in the Stoke Gifford suburb of Bristol, which the couple maintained after purchasing a larger house nearby.

Needham has retained a lifelong passion for the twin hobbies that launched the IMDb: movies and technology. He has a vast collection of films, largely consisting of DVDs and approaching eight thousand titles. He has stated that he was watching the 1981 motion picture *Body Heat* on the date the IMDb was founded. He has cited *Vertigo* as his favorite film. In 1999, he received Webby Award from the International Academy of Digital Arts and Sciences for his role in the founding of the IMDb.

Marcella Bush Trevino

FURTHER READING

Aspray, William, and Paul E. Ceruzzi. *The Internet and American Business*. Cambridge: MIT, 2008. Print. A series of essays that examine the commercialization of the Internet, including social networking, information searching, and entertainment. Covers business models, e-commerce, and the successes and failures of dot-com companies.

Johnson, Brian David. *Screen Future: The Future of Entertainment, Computing, and the Devices We Love*. Santa Clara: Intel Press, 2010. Print. Exploration of the potential future impacts of computers on the television and entertainment industries. Covers televisions, phones, cars, and computers as personal entertainment delivery systems.

Rose, Frank. *The Art of Immersion: How the Digital Generation Is Remaking Hollywood, Madison Avenue, and the Way We Tell Stories*. New York: Norton, 2011. Print. The contributing editor for *Wired* magazine discusses the impact of the Internet and the impact of digital technology on the social, production, business, and marketing aspects of the entertainment industry.

Tapscott, Don. *Grown Up Digital: How the Net Generation Is Changing Your World*. New York: McGraw-Hill, 2009. Print. A description of the Net Generation, young adults who have grown up in a digital world, based on extensive surveys. Provides insight into their revolutionary use of technology, including the active participation vital to sites such as the Internet Movie Database, and its impact on society.

Ulin, Jeff. *The Business of Media Distribution: Monetizing Film, TV and Video Content in an Online World*. Burlington: Focal, 2009. Print. An insider's look at the media distribution field from a longtime Lucasfilm employee. Traces the process of creating profits in the industry from a project's concept through its distribution across multiple markets, including online aspects.

CRAIG NEWMARK

Founder of Craigslist

Born: December 6, 1952; Morristown, New Jersey
Died: -
Primary Field: Internet
Specialty: Social media
Primary Company/Organization: Craigslist

INTRODUCTION

Craig Newmark founded Craigslist to build a community that could use the Internet as a tool to help others: a simple site that connects people around the world, where they can satisfy basic human needs in finding work, shelter, and relationships in one place. Despite Craigslist's success, Newmark stuck to his core values and remained a "customer service representative" for his own site, using undisclosed profits to fund citizen journalism projects and other causes involving civic participation.

EARLY LIFE

Craig Alexander Newmark was born to Jewish parents on December 6, 1952, in Morristown, New Jersey. His father, Lee, was a salesman who dealt in food, insurance, and promotional items. His mother, Joyce, was a book-keeper. The pair met at a synagogue dance. Tragically, Newmark's father died of cancer just six months after the young boy's bar mitzvah. Newmark was rarely invited to other children's parties; one teacher sent him to a school counselor, who gave up on therapy and taught him chess. Newmark embraced his social awkwardness as part of "being a nerd," and to complete the image he wore thick glasses with a piece of tape holding them together. As a boy, he also loved science fiction and comic books.

Newmark graduated from Morristown High in 1971. He was active on the debate team and the forensics club, and he had also started a go club. Newmark attended college at Case Western Reserve in Cleveland, Ohio, originally planning to study physics. Instead, he earned bachelor's and master's degrees in computer science in 1975 and 1977, respectively. His social problems continued; a book called *Language in Thought and Action* made him realize that he—not other people—had a communication problem.

LIFE'S WORK

After college, Newmark worked for IBM from 1976 to 1993, first spending six years in Boca Raton, Florida, then ten years in Detroit, Michigan, attempting to work his way up the corporate ladder. Craig moved to San Francisco in 1993 to work for Charles Schwab and Company as a systems security architect and general consultant. In 1995, Newmark became an independent contractor and developed software for companies such as Bank of America, Xircon (now Intel), and Sun Microsystems.

While working as an independent contractor, Newmark observed people on the Internet, the WELL, and Usenet helping one another. He started socializing with computer and technology experts, who saw their emerging field as revolutionary, blending art, social media, and science. In early 1995, Newmark decided to join this community of helpers and technologists, using e-mail to inform people about art and technology events in San Francisco.

News of the list spread through word of mouth, and people asked to be added to the e-mail list, which led to their friends requesting to be added. Soon people were asking Newmark to include job listings and items for sale. Newmark realized that he could add apartments for rent to this list as well. By the middle of 1995, Newmark's e-mail list included 240 addresses, exceeding the limit of e-mail addresses he could include in a cc box.

Craig Newmark.

At that point, Newmark posted the list for public consumption using a list server that required a name. Craig wanted to call it "sf-events" (for San Francisco events), but his friends told him to call it Craigslist because that is what everyone was already calling it, and the name reinforced the list's personal and down-to-earth nature.

For a few years, Newmark ran Craigslist as a hobby site. In the beginning, it ran on a single PC with a 128-megabyte hard drive in his living room. In 1998, Craigslist's popularity had increased to the point where Newmark had recruited some volunteers to help him run the site, with little success. The site had thousands of readers, and communication with this number of people became overwhelming for Newmark. During that year, tech recruiter Christina Murphy, a frequent poster to the early list, teamed with Internet consultant Nancy Melone to get Newmark to join them in starting a nonprofit called the List Foundation. Melone intended for the List Foundation to serve as a host for Craigslist; job recruiters would pay $30 per ad, and any money left after paying the cost of upkeep and administration would be given away.

Newmark made Melone chief executive officer (CEO) of Craigslist, but he had no interest in making money or becoming a dot-com company; he wanted to maintain the integrity of Craigslist as a community service. Newmark and Melone split as a result of their philosophical differences. In late 1999, Craigslist users who entered the site through listfoundation.org were bounced to a new, for-profit website called Metro Vox, run by Melone, offering community listings similar to those of Craigslist but for a profit. Craigslist fans rejected Metro Vox, and the site went bankrupt in 2001.

In 2000, Newmark devoted his energy full time to Craigslist. That year, he hired Jim Buckmaster, a self-taught computer programmer who lived in a communal housing development, making sandals out of car tires. Buckmaster transferred Craigslist to a multiserver environment and a number of other cities. He redesigned Craigslist so that users could search, review, post, send and receive messages, and flag problems, which greatly reduced the amount of staff support needed for the site, as well as the need for Newmark to answer as many e-mails and phone calls. Buckmaster launched Craigslist in Boston in June 2000, then two months later in New York, Chicago, Los Angeles, Seattle, and Washington, D.C. He expanded the categories to include child care, political and legal discussion forums, the Missed Connections list, and, in the interest of plainness, a category headed "Men Seeking Sex." After a week, Newmark, a devotee of the television series *Sex and the City*, came up with the title "Casual Encounters." In December 2000, Newmark appointed Buckmaster as CEO, and Buckmaster would continue to hold that position.

Both Newmark and Buckmaster see Craigslist in social, rather than financial, terms. Newmark is not interested in taking Craigslist public or selling it for billions of dollars. "Make a comfortable living and then make a difference" is Newmark's philosophy.

As of 2012, Craigslist was active in more than one hundred cities in seventy-five countries, one of the top ten most frequently visited websites in the world. In San Francisco, city authorities declared October 10 Craigslist Day. The site attracts millions of users but also much criticism. The newspaper industry blames its demise in part on Craigslist and its free online classified ads. Others have found fault in Craigslist security measures, particularly after an episode in 2009, when the so-called Craigslist Killer posted an ad to the adult services section in order to entice and kill prostitutes. CEO Buckmaster claimed that Craigslist manually reviewed every adult service ad posted and required phone verification by the person placing it, but this was not sufficient. The fact that Craigslist even allowed an adult services section where pimps or prostitutes could advertise

Affiliation: Craigslist

In early 1995, Newmark decided to join a community of helpers and technologists using e-mail to inform people about art and technology events in San Francisco. News of the list spread through word of mouth, and people asked to be added to the e-mail list, which led to their friends requesting to be added. Soon people were asking Newmark to include job listings and items for sale. Newmark realized that he could add apartments for rent to this list as well. Midyear, Newmark's e-mail list included 240 addresses, exceeding the limit that could be distributed via a cc line. At that point, Newmark posted the list for public consumption using a list server that required a name. Craig wanted to call it sf-events, but his friends told him to call it Craigslist; everyone was already calling it Craigslist already, and the name reinforced the list's personal and straightforward style.

By 2012, Craigslist was active in more than 100 cities and in 75 countries and had become one of the top ten most visited websites in the world. In San Francisco, city authorities declared October 10 to be Craigslist day.

their services was declared tantamount to a promotion of prostitution by the state of South Carolina and therefore an illegal activity. The Craigslist Killer case forced Craigslist to shut down its adult services category in the United States and its erotic services category elsewhere. The episode also focused international attention on the dangers of the Internet and debate about the responsibility of website owners in monitoring and regulating potentially criminal activity facilitated by the service.

PERSONAL LIFE

In 2001, Newmark founded the Craigslist Foundation, a 501(c)3 nonprofit organization that helps emerging nonprofit organizations. His first two contributions through this foundation were for eye examinations and glasses for Israeli and Palestinian children. He has also given thousands of dollars to other Israeli and Palestinian organizations devoted to peace in the Middle East, as well as women's shelters and a free clinic for sex workers.

In 2005, *Time* magazine ranked Newmark as twenty-eighth on its list of the world's 100 Most Influential People. Newmark expressed his goal of using the revenues from Craigslist to replace newspapers and reporters with "citizen journalists" who would cover the news online without the influence of political parties or corporate advertisers. His zeal for citizen journalism derives from his disgust for how the mainstream media covered the Iraq War. Politically, Newmark has described himself as both moderate and libertarian; he has donated money to the campaigns of both Democrats and Republicans.

In spite of the enormous influence that Newmark has had in global communications, his widely acknowledged social awkwardness has led writers to theorize that he might have Asperger's syndrome. Interviewers have often cited his canned conversation topics, difficulty in remembering names as well as associating faces with names, and struggles to read facial expressions, but Newmark vehemently denies any Asperger's diagnosis. He simply maintains that he is a product of nerd culture.

True to his core beliefs, Newmark lives a modest lifestyle in spite of his Craigslist earnings. He lives in a San Francisco apartment and regularly frequents a neighborhood coffee shop. He owns a Toyota Prius but usually takes public transport. Although he claims that he does not believe in having fun, he admits that he enjoys socializing with friends at the coffee shop. His hobbies include listening to music, reading, and watching television. He also maintains a website and blog, where he encourages people to show support for military families and veterans, "back to basics journalism," the Israeli-Palestinian peace process, open government, consumer protection, voter protection, and technology for the common good. Newmark has never married or had children, but he does have a girlfriend. His younger brother, Jeff, is a finance director for an Acura dealership in Springfield, New Jersey.

Rachel Wexelbaum

FURTHER READING

Freese, Susan M. *Craigslist: The Company and Its Founder*. North Mankato: ABDO, 2011. Print. Designed for the young adult audience, this biography provides a good overview of Newmark and the genesis of his famous website.

Newmark, Craig. "Craig Newmark: Founder of Craigslist." Interview by Jessica Livingston. *Founders at Work: Stories of Startups' Early Days*. New York: Springer, 2008. Print. Newmark responds to questions about the development of Craigslist and its corporate values.

---. *Craigconnects: Connecting the World for the Common Good*. 28 June 2012. Web. 12 Aug. 2012. Newmark's personal website and blog, where he shares news, opinions, and links to provide support for his many causes.

LUKE NOSEK

Cofounder of PayPal

Born: 1975; Tarnów, Poland
Died: -
Primary Field: Internet
Specialty: Applications
Primary Company/Organization: PayPal

INTRODUCTION

Polish-born American Internet entrepreneur Luke Nosek is known for his leading roles in the fields of e-commerce and venture capitalism. He was a cofounder of the payment and cryptography services company Confinity, which merged with Internet financial services company X.com to form the online financial transactions broker PayPal in 1998. Nosek remained with PayPal until its acquisition by online auction site eBay in 2002. PayPal emerged as one of the lead-ing online payment options both within and outside eBay. Meanwhile, Nosek gained renown as a member of the so-called PayPal Mafia, the group of company leaders who had been together since their early days at the Stanford Review *newspaper. The PayPal Mafia are known for their innovative approach to business philosophy and methods. After making millions through the sale of PayPal, Nosek turned his attention to his other passion of venture capitalism, utilizing his personal funds through angel investing as well as establishing the Founders Fund in 2005. The Founders Fund pursued a revolutionary approach to venture capitalism through its development of Series FF stocks, which allow start-up entrepreneurs and chief executive officers (CEOs) to recoup some of their investments before an initial public offering (IPO) or company sale.*

EARLY LIFE

Luke Nosek was born in Tarnów, Poland, in 1975. Little information is publicly available regarding his birth and childhood. He attended the University of Illinois at Urbana-Champaign in the early to mid-1990s, graduating with a bachelor of science degree in computer science. His studies included work on supercomputers. He began his entrepreneurial career while in college, teaming with fellow students Max Levchin and Scott Banister to develop SponsorNet New Media, Inc., in 1995. Upon graduation, Nosek moved from Illinois to the Silicon Valley region of California to pursue a career.

He began his career working in business development at the computer services company Netscape Communications Corporation after spending almost a year getting his footing in the Silicon Valley business world. Nosek served as an evangelist for Netscape, seeking to promote the company's proprietary technology as the industry standard. Nosek also served as an editor of the *Stanford Review* in his early career. Stanford University Law School graduate Peter Thiel had founded the *Stanford Review* in 1987 as a student.

Nosek next cofounded Confinity, Inc., with fellow Internet entrepreneurs Thiel, Levchin, and Ken Howery in 1998. Confinity made its name through the provision

Luke Nosek.

of online payment and cryptography services for the Palm Pilot (a "personal digital assistant," now largely superseded by other consumer electronics such as smart phones), in the early days of e-commerce development. Nosek served as Confinity's vice president of marketing.

LIFE'S WORK

In 2000, Nosek and the other Confinity founders merged their company with the Internet financial services company X.com, which had been founded by Elon Musk in 1999. The new incarnation was renamed PayPal and was headquartered in rented office space in Palo Alto, California. Many of the business and technological staff of both former companies continued to be employed at PayPal, helping develop the new company into a success. Many *Stanford Review* alumni also worked at PayPal, where Thiel served as CEO. These alumni, including Nosek, became known as the PayPal Mafia. Nosek served as the company's vice president of marketing and strategy, helping expand the site's customer base to approximately one million after six months of operations. He also developed the company's profitable Instant Transfer product.

PayPal is an e-commerce business that serves as an online financial transactions broker through the processing of online payments and money transfers. PayPal is licensed as a money transmitter rather than a bank in the United States. PayPal Europe became a licensed bank within the European Union in 2007. PayPal users require a PayPal account, a valid e-mail address, and a valid credit card or bank account. Convenience of service and user trust helped PayPal become one of the leading online financial services companies. PayPal protects the confidential information of users and offers fraud protection for buyers and sellers who use the service. Common commercial users include online auction sites and vendors. Buyers are not charged to transfer money to sellers or vendors; rather, sellers or vendors pay a surcharge to receive money.

PayPal's initial business model relied on the interest earned through funds in user accounts rather than its low fees to generate revenue and the payment of new account bonuses to attract users, a model that quickly proved financially ineffective, because most users did not let funds accumulate in their accounts. The company was losing millions each month and was close to going out of business by 2000 before it gained new life through the infusion of $100 million in venture capital. The company's successful 2002 initial public offering (IPO) saw a 55 percent rise in share price and raised

$1.2 billion. PayPal also survived a number of legal challenges from banks and local governments.

One of PayPal's largest early customer bases comprised users of the popular online auction site eBay. The growing success of eBay had driven the site to explore online payment options. PayPal had emerged as the first choice of eBay customers for online payment services—topping rivals Billpoint, c2it, PayDirect, BidPay, Google Checkout, Wirecard, and Moneybookers. In October 2002, eBay acquired PayPal as a wholly owned subsidiary for a purchase price of $1.5 billion. PayPal had grown to approximately two hundred employees; its corporate headquarters was relocated to San Jose, California.

When eBay purchased PayPal, Nosek left the company to pursue other business and personal interests. The sale to eBay divided the original leadership team, but they maintained connections with one another. The PayPal Mafia are known for their business innovations, such as the early belief that PayPal could emerge as a type of universal currency. Other successful businesses connected to the PayPal Mafia include YouTube, Facebook, and LinkedIn. PayPal continued its phenomenal growth after Nosek's departure, managing more than 200 million international accounts representing twenty-five different currencies and expanding to include local operations in twenty-one countries by 2011. The company now relies on fees that are determined based on currency, country, amount, payment option, and account type.

Nosek's enjoyed another success when he reteamed with PayPal cofounders Thiel and Howery to launch the Founders Fund in 2005. Nosek is a managing partner of the Founders Fund, along with Thiel, Howery, and Sean Parker. The Founders Fund is a venture capital company based in San Francisco, California, and seeks to bridge the often contentious relationship between entrepreneurs and the venture capitalists that fund their start-up businesses. Its founders believe their experiences as both entrepreneurs and venture capitalists give them a unique perspective.

The Founders Fund is known for its innovative approach, challenging the traditional practices of the venture fund investment field. Most notable among these innovations is the introduction of Series FF stock. FF shares are offered to the owners and CEOs of the companies in which the company is investing, allowing them to convert and sell these shares to investors during later preferred stock offerings. The Founders Fund's partners believe that this system gives them an advantage in seeking investment opportunities among cash-strapped and heavily indebted entrepreneurs, who often have sunk their personal wealth into their businesses and would otherwise have to wait for an initial public offering or company sale to recoup their investments. Other venture capitalists feel that less risk will weaken an owner's drive to maximize the business's success.

The Founders Fund bases its investment priorities on companies whose revenue streams are driven by user subscriptions or product sales as opposed to advertising sales. The company currently holds stakes in numerous

---

Affiliation: PayPal

PayPal is an international e-commerce business based in the United States. Internet entrepreneurs Luke Nosek, Max Levchin, Peter Thiel, Ken Howery, and Elon Musk launched PayPal in 2000 by merging Confinity and X.com. Its corporate headquarters are located in San Jose, California, while its main operations center is in Omaha, Nebraska. PayPal has developed a significant international presence as well, with offices in Luxembourg and Singapore. By 2011, PayPal managed more than 200 million accounts utilizing twenty-five different currencies.

As an online system for financial transactions, PayPal allows Internet users with active PayPal accounts to transfer money over the Internet with a valid e-mail address and credit card or bank account. PayPal profits are derived from charging sellers a percentage of the amount of money transferred to cover the costs of processing the payments it facilitates as a financial broker. Fees are determined based on currency, country, amount, payment option, and account type. Ease of use, the security of confidential user information, and the development of user trust have been integral to PayPal's success.

By the early twenty-first century, the popular online auction site eBay had begun to pursue online payment methods for its buyers and sellers. PayPal quickly emerged as the favorite among eBay customers. In 2002, eBay acquired PayPal for $1.5 billion. After building its national and international eBay business, PayPal expanded to other Internet applications. PayPal Labs searches for additional innovative methods of expansion, such as storefront locations and payment methods adapted to mobile phones and social networking sites.

and diverse companies, including social networking giant Facebook, rocket designer Space Exploration Technologies (SpaceX), Internet advertising facilitator Clickable, and robotics manufacturer RoboteX. The company has enjoyed success but has also had to adjust to the impact of the tighter market conditions that accompanied the economic downturn that began in 2008.

PERSONAL LIFE

Nosek moved to the Silicon Valley area of California in the early 1990s, shortly after his graduation from the University of Illinois at Urbana-Champaign. His main interest outside venture capitalism is travel, which is one of the reasons he left PayPal after its acquisition by eBay made him a millionaire. He also enjoys reading, citing Ayn Rand's novel *Atlas Shrugged* as having influenced the development of his business philosophy to use the industry to create good. He is also an active financial contributor to political campaigns, such as Libertarian Ron Paul's bid for the Republican presidential nomination in 2012.

Nosek has dedicated his post-PayPal career to the identification, promotion, and mentoring of young entrepreneurs through angel investing, defined as the provision of personal funds to back such businesses or individuals. Nosek has maintained his own entrepreneurial career through the start-up of several Internet-based businesses, founding and serving as president and director of Halcyon Molecular, Inc., in 2009. He has also served on the boards of directors for various companies, including Yammer, Space Exploration Technologies (SpaceX), SSE Labs, Pathway Genomics, Powerset, Zivity, and ResearchGate.

Marcella Bush Trevino

FURTHER READING

Aspray, William, and Paul E. Ceruzzi. *The Internet and American Business*. History of Computing series. Cambridge: MIT, 2008. Print. A series of essays, which examine the commercialization of the Internet, including social networking, information searching, and entertainment. Covers business models, e-commerce, and the successes and failures of dot-com companies.

Bhide, Amar. *The Venturesome Economy: How Innovation Sustains Prosperity in a More Connected World*. Princeton, NJ: Princeton UP, 2008. Print. Examines the link between U.S. venture capital–backed businesses and the global development of technology in the modern economy as well as the roles of scientists, engineers, entrepreneurs, financiers, consumers, and other key players.

Jackson, Eric M. *The PayPal Wars: Battles with eBay, the Media, the Mafia, and the Rest of the Planet*. Los Angeles: World Ahead, 2010. Print. A history of the company from a former insider, including a description of the site's business strategy and its successes and challenges within and outside eBay.

Schneider, Gary P. *Electronic Commerce*. 9th ed. Boston: Course Technology Cengage Learning, 2011. Print. Introduces the dynamics of the electronic commerce industry from both the technological and business perspectives, including the development and future of online technologies and the e-commerce marketplace.

Shah, Tarang, and Sheetal Shah. *Venture Capitalists at Work: How Venture Capitalists Identify and Build Billion-Dollar Successes*. New York: Apress, 2011. Print. An overview of venture capitalism through the personalities and business approaches of leading venture capitalists. Discusses how venture capitalists identify and develop entrepreneurs, markets, and products.

O

KEVIN O'CONNOR

Cofounder of DoubleClick

Born: April 4, 1961; Livonia, Michigan
Died: -
Primary Field: Internet
Specialty: Commerce
Primary Company/Organization: DoubleClick

INTRODUCTION

Best known for his founding of DoubleClick, which at its prime was the most successful Internet advertising company in existence, Kevin O'Connor is also an author, a college professor, and an astute investor. He became successful in business immediately after graduating from college and continued to hone his computer and financial skills. O'Connor has said that one of the most influential jobs he ever had in his life was working as an assistant wrestling coach, a job that taught him what he needed to understand human nature. O'Connor has spent his life trying to make things happen rather than waiting for events to unfold. He has been called a "serial entrepreneur" because of his tendency to leave a company once it has become successful and move on to the next venture. When people complain about ubiquitous advertising on the Internet, O'Connor reminds them that it is the presence of advertising that keeps the Internet free for the public.

EARLY LIFE

Kevin O'Connor was born on April 4, 1961, in Livonia, Michigan, near Detroit. As a child, he loved to experiment. He discovered computers at the age of twelve, and by the age of thirteen he was already demonstrating a flair for electronics and inventions. Both parents were supportive of his efforts, and he found a ready partner for his adventures in his father, an electrical engineer. When O'Connor set the garage on fire when he attempted to launch a hot-air balloon he had built, losing the balloon, his father helped him build another one. Young Kevin and a friend spent hours building go-carts. O'Connor attended Detroit Catholic Central High School, graduating in 1979. In 1983, he completed his bachelor's degree in electrical engineering at the University of Michigan.

After completing his undergraduate degree, O'Connor began graduate school, intending to obtain a doctorate, but he soon dropped out. Instead, he and his friends Bill Miller and Michael Schier founded the Intercomputer Communications Corporation in Cincinnati in 1983. O'Connor had become friendly with Miller while serving an internship at Texas Instruments in Houston, where O'Connor had worked on an IBM computer. The year following the internship, O'Connor worked on another IBM project in Austin. Miller and Schier had become friends in high school. Financing for the new company came from Miller and Schier's consulting business and from a $25,000 investment from Miller's parents.

During this period when company mainframes controlled all computers, the idea of personal computers that operated on their own was alien to most employers. Thus, the Intercomputer Communications Corporation (ICC) was involved in the process of linking microcomputers to mainframe computers through local networks. O'Connor chiefly concentrated his efforts on what he calls "hard-core coding" and developing ICC's product line. In 1992, ICC was sold to DCA.

Between 1988 and 1992, which was the same time that O'Connor was making a name for himself in computer programming, he also worked as an assistant to Cincinnati Moeller High School wrestling coach Jeff Gaier. O'Connor said that working with young, sometimes reluctant, athletes taught him all he needed to know about life in order to succeed.

After ICC was purchased by DCA, O'Connor became chief technical officer and vice president of research and development. However, he chose to leave DCA in 1995, only a week after the company had been acquired by Attachmate, a San Francisco–based software company.

LIFE'S WORK

Toward the end of 1995, O'Connor and Dwight Merriman founded the Internet Advertising Network, the company that was to become DoubleClick. The company was founded in the basement of O'Connor's home in Alpharetta, a suburb of Atlanta, Georgia. Double-Click's sole purpose was to make money by promoting the Internet. Discarding the notion of basing the service on subscriptions, O'Connor and Merriman opted to sell advertising. Internet advertising was still in its infancy at the time, and it was up to O'Connor and Merriman to devise the best possible strategy for accomplishing their goals. They divided responsibilities, with O'Connor serving as manager and product designer and Merriman writing code. The entire workforce of DoubleClick consisted of the two founders, a computer programmer, and a salesperson.

Learning that a group of academics had created a company called DoubleClick that sold advertising over the Internet but lacked the technology to make the company profitable, O'Connor and Merriman worked out a deal to combine forces with them, raising their total workforce to eight individuals. When it became evident that DoubleClick needed to be where media companies and publishers were located, O'Connor and Merriman chose to relocate DoubleClick to New York City rather than following the technology trend to Silicon Valley on the West Coast. That move was profitable for New York, which subsequently developed as Silicon Alley. Doubleclick brought in Wenda Harris Millard, a marketing expert with twenty years of experience to her credit, and for his business acumen Kevin P. Ryan, who became chief executive officer (CEO) when O'Connor chose to step down in 2006 (he felt the company had grown to such an extent that it no longer suited his needs).

When O'Connor and Merriman joined forces with the existing DoubleClick, BJK&E owned a large share of DoubleClick, but company executives were anxious to divest themselves of DoubleClick as the Internet exploded on the public consciousness. O'Connor entered into negotiations with Yahoo! to buy DoubleClick for $95 million, but financial backing amounting to $40 million was generated from West Coast technology investors and Boston's venture capitalists. That funding allowed DoubleClick to spend $25 million to buy out BJK&E's interest in DoubleClick.

DoubleClick continued to place a strong emphasis on the needs of its customers, and the company went public in 1998, eight months after that first round of financing. By that time, the company had generated $80 million in revenue over a two-year period. In 1999, $1.6 billion shares were offered for stock purchasing. By 2000, DoubleClick was employing twenty-five hundred workers in twenty separate companies. At the same time, the company was faced with a number of lawsuits filed by privacy advocates over the decision to tie data derived from new credit card purchases to information gathered on web users. O'Connor quickly backtracked and created new positions to protect privacy rights. He hired Jules Polonetsky, a former consumer affairs commissioner, as chief policy officer and recruited Robert

Kevin O'Connor.

Abrams, a former New York State attorney general, as the chairman of DoubleClick's Privacy Board.

Amid the privacy lawsuits and the dot-com collapse in 2000, DoubleClick saw its fortunes begin to decline. Stock prices fell by 50 percent, and the company began laying off workers. Within three years, it had begun to recover. In July 2005, DoubleClick was sold to Hellman and Friedman, a company that specializes in private equity, for $1.1 billion. Two years later, Google acquired DoubleClick from Hellman and Friedman for $3.1 billion. Google continues to make use of the technology created by O'Connor and Merriman, such as the DoubleClick Ad Planner, which allows advertisers to research and identify websites that are visited by their target audience.

During DoubleClick's glory years, O'Connor, along with coauthor Paul Brown, wrote *The Map of Innovation: Creating Something Out of Nothing*. The book explains how to take an idea or service and turn it into a successful business enterprise. O'Connor's business philosophy focuses on the notion that it is necessary to make lightning strike rather than wait on the off chance that it might strike on its own. He has summarized his ideas in a method that he calls the "brainstorming prioritization technique" (BPT), admitting that it is poor name. The technique involves brainstorming ideas before settling on a single one to pursue. Success is derived, according to O'Connor, from choosing the correct strategy for marketing the product so that it reaches the proper client base.

PERSONAL LIFE

O'Connor has repeatedly said that he enjoys building up a company and then moving on, leaving the running of the companies he started to individuals who are better at maintaining ongoing operations. He founded O'Connor Ventures in 2001 to manage his investments. Because of his interest in innovation, he specializes in investing in start-up technology companies such as 9 Star, Surfline, Travidia, ProCore, and Campus Explorer. O'Connor serves on the board of Flexplay Technology, a start-up that manufactures recyclable DVDS that allow customers to bypass trips to video stores and forgo late fees for failing to return items on time.

At the urging of Internet Security Systems founder Chris Claus, O'Connor invested in the Atlanta-based company. It proved to be a wise investment: The company issued its initial public offering four years later. In 2006, IBM purchased Internet Security Systems for $1.3 billion.

Affiliation: DoubleClick

When Kevin O'Connor and Dwight Merriman decided to move DoubleClick's emerging operations from Atlanta to New York City rather than to California's Silicon Valley, the move had strong implications for its new home. It paved the way for New York's technology sector, which came to be known as Silicon Alley.

DoubleClick was the first new media company to set up headquarters in New York, and it ultimately became the most successful. Following the trend, other new media companies created by young techies just out of college, along with those who left more settled jobs to risk it all on the chance of getting rich quick in the new industry, relocated to the advertising capital of the world, with the result that the overall economy of New York benefited. The 250,000 workers employed in the new industry needed housing, resulting in a score of neighborhood renewal projects.

When O'Connor and Merriman arrived in New York along with their two employees, a computer programmer and a salesperson, they could afford only a one-room office that was located on West 23rd Street. The time was ripe for DoubleClick's success, and O'Connor guided the company into becoming an industry giant, eventually amassing a worth of $8 billion by the start of the twenty-first century. By that time, the company had hundreds of employees working in twenty different countries. The company survived the dot-com collapse and was eventually sold to Google.

In 2009, O'Connor cofounded the Santa Barbara, California–based FindTheBest.com, a search engine that operates on the principle of locating the best matches for search terms by comparing possible matches. Promoting itself as a service offering "easy-to-use tables with smart filters," the site insists that its data are free of marketing involvement. Categories include business, education, electronics, health, home and family, motors, software, sports and recreation, and travel and lifestyles. Visitors to the site are encouraged to log in with Facebook to facilitate linking their personal interests with information available through FindtheBest.com.

O'Connor lives in Santa Barbara, California, with his wife; they have three children. He spends part of his time lecturing at local universities. O'Connor has announced on his O'Connor Ventures website that he continues to pursue his hobbies of surfing, skiing, he-liskiing, weightlifting, and basketball. He strengthens bonds with his children by coaching their soccer, basketball, and wrestling teams.

Elizabeth Rholetter Purdy

FURTHER READING
Budman, Matthew. "Kevin O'Connor Says That Hunkering Down Is Never a Good Idea." *Across the Board* 40.4 (2003): 11–12. Print. Profile of O'Connor that focuses on his business philosophy.
Messina, Judith. "Kevin O'Connor and the Mouse That Roared: The Founder of Online Advertising Network DoubleClick Paved Way for City's Fastest Growing Sector." *Crain's New York Business* 16.20 (2000): 30–32. Print. Focus on role of DoubleClick in creating the new media sector in New York City. Illustrated.
O'Connor, Kevin. "Interview with Kevin O'Connor." *Kaizen: Ethics and Entrepreneurship* 20 Apr. 2009: n. pag. Print. Interview with O'Connor that focuses on O'Connor Ventures.
---, and Paul B. Brown. *The Map of Innovation: Creating Something Out of Nothing.* New York: Crown, 2003. Print. How-to book on successfully marketing an idea. Illustrated.
Rankin, Rose. "Insights for Online Targeting with DoubleClick Ad Planner." *Marketing Week* 33.16 (2010): n. pag. Print. Explanation of DoubleClick's Ad Planner that shows advertisers how to target Audiences.

ALEXIS OHANIAN

Cofounder of Reddit

Born: April 24, 1983; New York, New York
Died: -
Primary Field: Internet
Specialty: Social media
Primary Company/Organization: Reddit

INTRODUCTION
Alexis Ohanian founded the social news site Reddit with Steve Huffman immediately after the two graduated the University of Virginia. He later joined Huffman's travel search engine start-up, Hipmunk, as well as working as Y Combinator's "Ambassador to the East," mentoring East Coast start-ups.

EARLY LIFE
Alexis Ohanian was born on April 24, 1983, in New York City. He attended the University of Virginia, where he met fellow student Steve Huffman. Upon graduating in 2005 with a bachelor's degree in history, Ohanian, along with Huffman, approached the seed accelerator Y Combinator with an idea for a start-up. Paul Graham, Y Combinator's founder, rejected the first proposal but told the two to brainstorm another idea and try again. Ohanian and Huffman proposed an idea for a social news site and secured $15,000 in seed money to move to Medford, Massachusetts, living on a shoestring budget and coding for three weeks in order to create Reddit.

LIFE'S WORK
The social news site Reddit (styled with a lowercase *r*) premiered in June 2005, three weeks after Ohanian and

Alexis Ohanian.

Huffman began work on it. Social news sites like Reddit, Slashdot, and Digg are websites where registered users submit links to external sites (or the occasional text-only post, of which there are several specific traditional forms on Reddit) and other users can vote on their level of interest. A vote is meant to indicate not enjoyment or approval, like Facebook's "like" button, but the appropriateness and relevance of the link, particularly if it is submitted in a given category. By 2012, Reddit had tens of thousands of "subReddits" to which links could be submitted.

While Huffman was principally responsible for Reddit's code and engineering and the two worked jointly on establishing its feel and philosophy—in the early days, for instance, both partners contributed content to the site under false names in order to establish the illusion of activity and community in the six months it took to attract a real user base—Ohanian is the more social and gregarious of the two, and his primary responsibility was what Huffman called "strategic hanging out." The first summer, for instance, when they were the only two people running Reddit, Huffman focused on the code and structure of the site. Ohanian took care of their expenses, paying the rent and bills, while dealing with the lawyers, paperwork, and other practical aspects of starting a business. When those functions were subsumed in 2006 by Condé Nast after it bought Reddit, Ohanian transitioned into a role combining marketing, defining the company vision, and acting as a liaison between Huffman and external contacts, whether Condé Nast or other employees.

Ohanian was also important as the public face and persona of Reddit. Although both Huffman and Ohanian responded to feedback e-mails, especially in the first year, Ohanian made a point of sending something personal to people who took the time to point out a bug, who helped with the site in some way, or who were especially enthusiastic in their participation: He would send a T-shirt, a handwritten letter, or another response that was clearly not automated.

In 2009, Ohanian gave a TED talk on Mister Splashy Pants, a humpback whale being tracked by Greenpeace in the South Pacific Ocean. Mister Splashy Pants was an interesting example of the convergence of social awareness, memes, and the Internet's sense of humor. Greenpeace had held an online poll to name the whale in order to personalize him as part of a campaign to raise awareness of the Japanese Fisheries Agency's plan to hunt fifty humpbacks. The name Mister Splashy Pants received a sudden spike in votes from someone who had disabled cookies in order to get around the one-person-one-vote limit. When this was brought to the attention of sites like Reddit, users flocked to the poll to continue voting for the name, and the Reddit logo was even temporarily changed to feature the whale with a doodle drawn by Ohanian. Mister Splashy Pants won the poll with 78 percent of the vote, and although Greenpeace leaders were wary— the name did not seem serious enough and they were afraid that it might trivialize their cause—they honored the results. In fact, the poll may have been even more effective than Greenpeace had initially hoped; "Save Mister Splashy Pants" clothes have been sold, and shortly after the poll the Japanese government, under the weight of publicity, announced that it was canceling the humpback hunt. Movements to support Mister Splashy Pants continue to be tracked on Greenpeace's website.

Ohanian used the incident as an example of how social media can both effective and unpredictable—and, most important, that the unpredictability should be embraced, not feared. Social media are at their most effective when not overly controlled, allowing emergent phenomena.

Huffman and Ohanian left the day-to-day business of Reddit in 2009, because of a combination of factors; Ohanian was having some family problems at the time, and both cofounders were unhappy after having had to let go of an employee who had not worked out. Ohanian remains on Reddit's board of directors. He spent his first three months after leaving Reddit in Yerevan, Armenia, working with the microfinance nonprofit organization Kiva. When he returned, he joined Hipmunk—the travel search engine site started by Huffman—days before its 2010 launch. He plays a role at Hipmunk similar to his role at Reddit, advising and marketing. Hipmunk received its seed money from Y Combinator, the same firm that provided Reddit with its seed money. Ohanian continues to work closely with the company as its "Ambassador to the East." He meets with and evaluates applicants on the East Coast and acts as a mentor to successful applicants in the New York City area. He also runs Das Kapital Capital, a start-up investment and consulting company launched in June 2010.

Since 2007, Ohanian has run Breadpig, a geek-centric vendor that donates its proceeds to charity. Breadpig is best known as the publisher of the *xkcd* book,

Affiliation: Reddit

The social news website Reddit was founded by Steve Huffman and Alexis Ohanian in 2005. It was quickly acquired by publishing company Condé Nast and spun off as a subsidiary of Condé Nast's parent company.

Social news websites arguably began with Slashdot, in 1997; it is certainly the earliest site to gain significant popularity and remain in operation today. Fark, Delicious, and Digg followed soon after, all offering variations on the same mechanism: Users submit links to websites (typically news stories, although not necessarily from conventional news websites), which are posted to the site and commented on. At Slashdot, moderators selected links to post from the users' submissions. At Digg and Reddit, a voting system was used, and the articles with the most positive votes were displayed at the top of the list. The voting system democratizes the moderation process compared to sites like Slashdot.

Huffman and Ohanian founded Reddit in Medford, Massachusetts, and it was merged with Infogami a few months later, with Infogami's Aaron Swartz joining the Reddit team. The Reddit site went live after only three weeks of work. In order to encourage participation, Huffman and Ohanian submitted content under numerous false usernames in order to create the illusion of a crowd and of conversation—a gambit to which they did not admit until years after the fact. Because revenue came solely from advertising (until the introduction of Reddit Gold later), the user base needed to be large, and active users who viewed many pages would be best—especially because the click-through rate on social news sites is incredibly low. Huffman estimated it at 0.5 percent.

Magazine publishing giant Condé Nast acquired Reddit on Halloween 2006, less than a year and a half after it was founded, and the site continued to grow. Huffman and Ohanian left in 2009 to form Hipmunk with other former employees of Reddit. Shortly thereafter, in the summer of 2010, a paid service, Reddit Gold, was offered, making new features available for about $30 per year in order to fund a larger staff and greater computing resources. In 2011, Reddit was spun off from Condé Nast and became a separate subsidiary of Advance Publications, Condé Nast's parent company.

At Reddit, started in June 2005 a few months after Digg was opened to the public, both articles and comments can be voted on, which alters the order of comments in comment threads. Upvotes raise a score; downvotes lower it. Highest-scored articles appear on the front page, while articles in a given subcategory (called "subReddits") are displayed in order of score as well. One of the interesting innovations at Reddit is the "controversial" page, which lists articles in which the upvote and downvote totals are nearly equal. The controversial page and the effect of votes on comments result in an environment in which the semantic meaning of a vote is somewhat more complicated than would result from a more binary system (such as "liking" posts on Facebook).

Users of Reddit are called "Redditors," reflecting the origins of the site's name—a blend of *read* and *edit*, blurring the line between the reader and the editor, which is perhaps the essence of social news. Redditors can customize their front pages after logging in and can maintain friends lists (as on most social networks) in order to keep track of the content generated by users they want to follow. Commenting on Reddit is voracious; the community has a great many memes, traditions, tropes, and quirks that maintain a sense of community and consistency, although as with any other online community, this level of activity and involvement can render content opaque to newcomers.

SubReddits are key to the feel of Reddit, and they number in the tens of thousands. On the front page is a default list of subReddits: funny, pics, announcements, blog, askReddit, worldnews, gaming, todayilearned, politics, science, WTF, IAmA, videos, technology, music, atheism, AdviceAnimals, aww, movies, and bestof. Capitalization and grammar in subReddit naming is rather inconsistent.

Affiliation: Reddit (continued)

The IAmA subReddit deserves special mention. It stands for "I am a ...," while also containing the abbreviation AMA, for "ask me anything." This subReddit is not a list of links to other sites but consists of posts on Reddit, in which the initial poster introduces himself or herself and invites the community to "ask me anything." The poster may have an interesting job, such as working on a movie set, or may be a member of a community about which people are curious, such as a religious community. The most famous IAmAs outside Reddit are those of celebrities, which on the whole offer franker, more candid, and more in-depth interaction than either traditional media interviews or the hosted chat rooms that once were a part of the standard public relations (PR) tour. The variable end to which celebrities put IAmA is best compared to Twitter, which some celebrities delegate to their PR or street teams, others use only for official announcements, and others use for genuine social purposes. In many ways Reddit has replaced moderated chats when it comes to interactions between the famous and the public; *Atlantic* editor Ta-Nehisi Coates answered questions on Reddit about his August 2012 editorial "Fear of a Black President," for instance, rather than hosting a chat on *The Atlantic*'s website. Awareness of Reddit among celebrities steadily rose in 2011–12, with some celebrities revealing they had read the site for a while before participating. Actresswriter Molly Ringwald's IAmA was especially successful.

The Reddit community operates the largest Secret Santa program in the world, involving nearly one hundred countries and twenty thousand participants. Reddit also operates on Amazon's Web Services, uses Pylons as its web framework, and uses RabbitMQ for offline processing. The site was rewritten in Python in December 2005, having originally been written in Common Lisp. Reddit's code is available as open source code.

The largely uncensored nature of Reddit has led to a number of controversial subReddits, the most famous of which was the "jailbait" subReddit, which included user-submitted photos of underage minors; it was removed in 2012, at which point sexual content featuring minors was explicitly banned. There are also subReddits devoted to graphic photos of violence.

collecting strips from the webcomic; sales of *xkcd: volume 0* raised more than $50,000 to construct a school in Laos.

PERSONAL LIFE

Ohanian is active in Internet free speech causes and was involved in the nationwide protests against the Stop Online Piracy Act (SOPA) and Protect Intellectual Property Act (PIPA) in 2012, as well as speaking to members of Congress to explain problems with the bills.

Ohanian has revealed that at the time of Reddit's founding, he was going through the hardest part of his life and that work on the site helped keep him afloat. A month into work on the site, his then-girlfriend had fallen out of a five-story window and had slipped into a coma. She eventually recovered, after the better part of a year. During the period when his girlfriend was recovering, Ohanian's family dog, Max, was put to sleep after a long struggle with illness; that same day, his mother had a seizure, likely induced by the stress of the loss, and her hospitalization revealed a class IV glioblastoma multiforme: terminal brain cancer. She died two and a half years later, on March 15, 2008.

Working at Reddit allowed Ohanian to travel, to visit both his girlfriend and his mother in the hospital, and to engage in deeply consuming and distracting work that allowed some respite from the stresses of his personal life.

Bill Kte'pi

FURTHER READING

Bot, Sophy. *The Hipster Effect: How the Rising Tide of Individuality Is Changing Everything We Know About Life, Work, and the Pursuit of Happiness.* Suisun City: Sophy Bot, 2011. Print. Examines hipsterdom as a product of Internet culture, and Reddit's role in that culture.

Gusto, M. *Rage Comics*. Scotts Valley: CreateSpace, 2011. Print. A compilation of the meme comics popularized by Reddit.

Jenkins, Henry. *Confronting the Challenges of Participatory Culture: Media Education for the 21st Century*. Cambridge: MIT, 2009. Print. Examines social media, new forms of creative expression, and their impact on media studies.

Qualman, Erik. *Socialnomics: How Social Media Transforms the Way We Live and Do Business*. New York: Wiley, 2010. Print. The impact of social media on the business world.

PIERRE OMIDYAR

Founder of eBay

Born: June 21, 1967; Paris, France
Died: -
Primary Field: Internet
Specialty: Commerce
Primary Company/Organization: eBay

INTRODUCTION

Throughout his career as a software engineer at Claris and a developer services engineer for General Magic, Pierre Omidyar's major interest was in online commerce and online auctions. With the establishment of the auction site eBay.com, he brought together buyers and sellers of huge numbers of different products and services. EBay is now the most widely recognized site where buyers and sellers meet, and Omidyar is widely recognized as one of the most innovative and creative Internet entrepreneurs. He and his wife are passionate philanthropists who have donated millions of dollars to social causes.

EARLY LIFE

Pierre Morad Omidyar was born on June 21, 1967, in Paris, France, to Iranian parents. Both of his parents went to school in France and have academic backgrounds. His mother graduated with a doctoral degree in linguistics from the Sorbonne in Paris, and his father pursued a medical degree. The family moved to the United States so Pierre's father could perform his residency at the Johns Hopkins University Medical Center in Baltimore. At the time, Omidyar was six years old. Even as a child, he was interested in computers. After completing high school, he enrolled at Tufts University, where he graduated with a computer science degree in 1988. Working as an intern at innovative data design during a summer break gave him his first experience in the computer industry. His first job was in software development at Claris, a subsidiary of Apple Computer.

LIFE'S WORK

In 1991, while still working full time at Claris, Omidyar cofounded a company called Ink Development Corporation with three of his friends. The company developed software for pen-based computers and also a program to enable Internet shopping. Omidyar was a software engineer for this company, which later focused on e-retailing and was duly renamed eShop, Inc. When later, in 1996, eShop was sold to Microsoft, Omidyar, who still owned shares in the company, became a millionaire.

In 1994, Omidyar left eShop and joined General Magic as a developer services engineer. In September

Pierre Omidyar.

1995, working in his home in San Jose, Omidyar created the code for AuctionWeb, an online service to enable person-to-person auctions and provide a marketplace for individual buyers and sellers. The first product he sold was a broken laser pointer: He was surprised by the sale and, after questioning the buyer about why he would want to buy damaged goods, was told that the buyer collected broken laser pointers. The epiphany that followed—that a market existed for practically anything, given the ability to link the right seller with the right buyer—led Omidyar to recognize the untapped potential of his service. The business grew quickly, but the increasing number of users visiting his sites led Omidyar's Internet service provider to increase his fees. In order to be able to pay for his Internet access, he started to charge a relatively small fee to his clients based on the final price of the product sold. From the first month, his business became profitable: Soon AuctionWeb dominated Omidyar's entire domain, www.ebay.com. (The name eBay came from an abbreviation for Echo Bay, the name of Omidyar's consulting company.)

Recognizing the importance of a good customer experience to the success of the site and realizing that he alone could no longer deal with all the incoming questions from users of the site, in February 1996 Omidyar added a feedback forum through which buyers and sellers could evaluate one another. He also added a bulletin board to enable and encourage all eBay users to discuss their issues, problems, and questions openly. Now users could help themselves and one another. The business grew quickly. In March 1996, Omidyar's revenues totaled $1,000, in April $2,500, in May $5,000, and in June $10,000. Concomitant with these growing revenues, however, Omidyar faced another problem. All payments were being sent directly to his house, and he was now unable to cope with the huge volume of mail. He hired his first part-time employee, Chris Agarpao, to open his mail and deposit all the money in a bank. This significantly relieved Omidyar from having to respond to a barrage of inquiries and allowed him to focus on business operations and expanding the site to allow the sale and purchase not only of the small collectibles with which he had started but also larger items, such as furniture, electronics, and cars. Ultimately, he quit his day job at General Magic to focus his energy solely on the development of AuctionWeb.

In August 1996, Omidyar hired Jeffrey Skoll, a graduate of Stanford University with a master's in business administration, as the company's first official employee and first president. In November, the company

---

Affiliation: eBay

Pierre Omidyar founded his auction website, eBay, Inc., in 1995 as AuctionWeb. The early e-commerce platform would become one of the largest online marketplaces in the world, connecting buyers and sellers across the globe. Although the company started as an online auction site for collectibles, today it is a shopping website for all kinds of products and services bought and sold by individual buyers and sellers as well as small businesses using an auction and bidding format. The company is headquartered in San Jose, California.

Soon after eBay's inauguration, Omidyar added a feedback forum to the site to enable users to solve their disputes among themselves and to decide on the value of a product or service. Over time, various improvements were made to the site and the user experience. These included an improved search engine, daily deals, and mobile applications. Moreover, with the addition of the payment-processing service PayPal, through which individuals and businesses can make payments worldwide, domestic and international transactions have increased. Omidyar and eBay have together changed the world of e-commerce.

---

was licensed to offer airline tickets online. In the same year, 250,000 auctions were hosted; by January 1997, that number had grown to 2 million. By mid-1997, the site was hosting as many as 800,000 auctions per day. In September, Omidyar officially renamed the company eBay; he would remain eBay's chairman as well as developing other ventures.

In order to market and expand the company, in March 1998 eBay recruited Meg Whitman, a Harvard Business School graduate with a deep record of experienced in corporate branding strategies, as chief executive officer (CEO). Whitman strengthened the company by hiring senior staff with technical experience who were well versed in the establishment of a strong corporate brand. They helped her communicate that eBay was not only about buying and selling things but also about connecting people. EBay now started to expand business to include more expensive products and services. The products had a higher average sale price (ASP), which determined eBay's transaction fee. By facilitating the sale of more expensive items, eBay, in return, could increase revenues. This prompted eBay to enter into partnerships with numerous brands, including GM, Disney, and Sun, which started to sell their products on eBay's online marketplace. On September 21, 1998, eBay went public and made both Omidyar and Skoll billionaires.

In 1999, eBay's site was down for twenty-two hours: the company had to apologize to its customers for this significant interruption in service—a mark of how big it had become. The business continued to grow: In 2002, eBay acquired two companies, iBazar, an auction website in Europe, and PayPal, an online payment-processing service. In 2005, another acquisition was made, Skype, for $2.5 billion plus $500 million later paid out to Skype's founders. This decision, led by Whitman in an effort to develop the online community aspect of the site, received harsh criticism, and the expected usage by eBay users did not materialize. By early 2008, however, eBay's revenues had increased to almost $7.7 billion. In January 2008, Whitman stepped down as president and CEO and was succeeded by John Donahoe.

In 2009, eBay announced that it had sold 65 percent of its share in Skype for $1.9 billion. In May 2011, after Skype was bought by Microsoft for $8.5 billion, eBay, still holding 35 percent in Skype, made a profit, defying those who had previously criticized the purchase of Skype. In the same year, eBay purchased GSI, a company specializing in e-commerce marketing.

As of the end of 2011, ebay was connecting more than 100 million people around the world. Through PayPal, ebay's online payment service, buyers and sellers can buy and sell in 190 markets and twenty-four currencies. Clearly, PayPal has driven the growth of eBay significantly. In the first three months of 2011, eBay's net income totaled $476 million, which was 20 percent higher than that of the previous year. In 2011, eBay sold goods estimated at $68.6 billion, more than $2,100 every second. In the first quarter of 2012, eBay's revenues increased by 29 percent to $3.3 billion and the company's profits rose from $476 million to $570 million.

While Omidyar remained as chairman of the board at eBay, he also developed other enterprises, including an online news service in Honolulu, *Civil Beat* (2010), and the Omidyar Network, a philanthropic investment firm (2004). As of 2012, *Forbes* listed Omidyar as the 141st richest person in the world, worth $6.7 billion.

PERSONAL LIFE

Omidyar met his future wife, Pamela Wesley, a biologist turned management consultant, while he was working in the San Francisco Bay Area. Connecting people is not only his business motto but also a matter close to the couple's heart. The two are recognized as important philanthropists, having been engaged in bringing individuals and whole communities together, supporting personal growth and encouraging empowerment for social change. The Omidyar Network helps people to better themselves and supports innovative nonprofit organizations. It has invested more than $383 million in the promotion of positive social change.

Omidyar is active in Tuft University's alumni organization, having, with Pam, been one of the cochairs of the Beyond Boundaries Campaign. In 2005, the Omidyars made a donation of $100 million to Tufts, enabling the creation of the Omidyar-Tufts Microfinance Fund, designed to support people in developing countries. On May 22, 2011, Tufts awarded Omidyar an honorary doctorate of public service for his contribution to the business world and his social engagement.

Sabine H. Hoffmann

FURTHER READING

Cohen, Adam. *The Perfect Store*. New York: Little, Brown, 2002. Print. A history of eBay that describes the corporate philosophy and the life of Omidyar.

Houser, Daniel, and John Wooders. "Reputation in Auctions: Theory and Evidence from eBay." *Journal of Economics and Management Strategy* 15.2 (2006): 353–69. Print. Examines the effect of reputation on price in eBay auctions.

Prince, Dennis L. *How to Sell Anything on eBay ... and Make a Fortune*. New York: McGraw-Hill, 2004. Print. A guide to help eBay users to sell more successfully.

P

LARRY PAGE

Cofounder and CEO of Google

Born: March 26, 1973; Lansing, Michigan
Died: -
Primary Field: Business and commerce
Specialty: Management, executives, and investors
Primary Company/Organization: Google

INTRODUCTION

As a codeveloper of the PageRank algorithm, Larry Page provided the tools that led to the creation of Google, Inc., a multinational corporation that provides a variety of Internet-related products and services. Based on the success of its Internet search engine, Google has extended its products to include e-mail, an office productivity suite, social networking tools, and other online productivity software. Page, who serves as chief executive officer (CEO) of Google, is responsible for the operation of the company responsible for the most often visited website on the Internet.

EARLY LIFE

Lawrence "Larry" Page was born on March 26, 1973, in Lansing, Michigan. Both of Page's parents were professors of computer science at Michigan State University (MSU), located in nearby East Lansing. Page's father, Carl, earned a Ph.D. in computer science from the University of Michigan in 1965 and taught at the University of North Carolina before joining MSU in 1967. One of the first members of MSU's Department of Computer Science and Engineering, Carl was a pioneer in the field and was a specialist in artificial intelligence. Page's mother, Gloria, taught computer programming classes. Although Page's mother was Jewish, he was raised in a

home without religion, favoring his father's view that his religion was technology.

Page began his schooling at the Okemos Montessori School and graduated from East Lansing High School in 1991. As a child, Page became interested in computers, whetted by the availability of computers and computer science journals. Page's older brother, Carl, Jr., encouraged his propensity to disassemble common

Larry Page.

household appliances. Even before he reached his teens, Page states that he realized he wanted to be an inventor as an adult, and he tried to learn what he could about business and technology. While in high school, Page demonstrated a high degree of proficiency in mathematics and the sciences, and he was accepted into the University of Michigan as a student. While a student at Michigan, Page participated in a variety of competitions, including making a solar car and an inkjet printer from Legos. Page graduated from Michigan with honors with a bachelor of science degree in computer engineering. He was accepted at Stanford University to do graduate work in computer science.

Page quickly earned a master's degree in computer science from Stanford, and he applied to and was accepted by its doctoral program in that subject in early 1995. At a new student orientation in March of that year, Page first met Sergey Brin, who had been a computer science doctoral student at Stanford since 1993. Brin was assigned to give a group of the new students, including Page, a campus tour, and the two quickly became friends.

LIFE'S WORK

While completing course work at Stanford, Page began thinking about possible dissertation topics. Page thought it might be interesting to determine the number of website links to a given page, including the number and nature of such connections, known as backlinks. Page's adviser, Terry Winograd, encouraged him to pursue this line of research, and he was soon joined in this work by Brin. Together, Page and Brin devised a web crawler, BackRub, that would measure the number of links a given website had. To then access the data, Page and Brin created an algorithm known as PageRank that would sort websites based on the number of links that site had. Page and Brin soon recognized that this could help establish a web browser that provided better results than those then available. Until this point, most web browsers had sorted websites on the vague concept of "relevance," as based on the number of times a term appeared on that website. Using BackRub and PageRank, Page and Brin were quickly able to create a web browser that returned a results list in which those websites that were most frequently referenced by others appear at the top of the screen. By August 1996, an early version of the web browser that was to become Google appeared on Stanford's website, as google.stanford.edu.

The Google search engine quickly became very popular with web users. As more users flocked to the website, Stanford requested that Page and Brin find a different host, as the rush of users was causing the Stanford website to respond very slowly. On September 15, 1997, Page and Brin registered Google's domain name, and they incorporated it as a business the following year. Originally working from a borrowed garage in Menlo Park, California, Google was able to move its offices to nearby Palo Alto in 1999. Google was granted a patent for PageRank, and although the patent was assigned to Stanford, the company received an exclusive license to use the algorithm in exchange for stock in Google.

In mid-1998, Google received its first funding, $100,000, from Sun Microsystems' cofounder, Andy Bechtolsheim. In early 1999, Page and Brin decided that Google was taking up too much of their time and entered into negotiations to sell it to Excite, a popular web portal, for $1 million. After this offer was turned down, Page and Brin dropped out of Stanford to devote their efforts to building Google, and by June they had received funding of $25 million from a group of venture capitalists. While Page and Brin had initially wanted to keep Google free of advertising, by 2000 they had begun selling advertisements that were linked to certain search words. As Google's revenues began to grow rapidly, Page and Brin determined that they needed someone with management experience to help run the company. To that end, they hired Eric Schmidt, the former president of Sun Technology Enterprises and president and chairman of Novell, Inc., as Google's chairman March 2001, and he became Google's CEO in August. While Schmidt "ran" Google, he shared responsibility for many of the company's daily operations with Page and Brin. At this point, Google began a series of mergers and acquisitions that greatly expanded its appeal and scope.

Google's most popular service continues to be its search engine, the web page for which is the most often visited page on the Internet and used for two-thirds of searches conducted in the United States. Because Google generates 99 percent of its revenues from advertising, it has continued to search for other services to provide that will attract users to its website. To augment its search services, Google hosts Google Books, which makes scanned copies of book previews, and in some cases full books, available to users at no cost. Google has also invested in a series of online productivity tools, beginning with Gmail, a free online e-mail service. A beta version of Gmail was made available to the public in 2007 and upgraded two years later to provide its nearly 150 million users with one gigabyte of storage, with additional storage available for a fee.

Affiliation: Google

Google became a wildly popular search engine during the late 1990s, largely because of its reputation for providing users with more hits than its rivals did. Known for its minimalistic design and bright primary colors, the Google website is the most popular in the world and has maintained its status as the most widely used search engine even in the face of strong competition.

As Google has grown, it has made a variety of free services available to the public, including Gmail, Google Maps, Google Earth, Google Docs, Google Calendar, and the social networking service Google+. While Google charges a fee to certain heavy users of these services who elect to upgrade, more than 99 percent of the company's revenues come from advertising, making it essential that the site draw users to it.

Google maintains more than 1 million servers in global data centers and processes more than 1 billion searches per day. As the owner of other websites, such as YouTube and Blogger, Google has managed to stay on the cutting edge of Web 2.0 developments, permitting users to create, share, and interact with information in a variety of ways. As Google's position in many markets has grown more dominant, criticism of its policies regarding privacy, copyright protection, and censorship have also grown.

Google Docs provides users with word-processing, spreadsheet, drawing, and presentation software, along with cloud-based storage and web-based access. Google Calendar supplies users a way to share schedules with families and friends. Google also offers geospatial software services through Google Earth and Google Maps, and Google Translate is a free translation service. In response to the popularity of social networking sites, such as Facebook, Google introduced Google+, which permits users to stream information, form and join affiliation circles, "hang out" with friends, or coordinate information with smart phones. As rival Microsoft Corporation has increased its efforts to divert users from Google's search functions with its own search engine, Bing, Google has even developed a free web browser, Google Chrome, although to date it ships only on equipment made by Google's partners. Google has also been a driving force behind the development of the Android smart phone.

Page was deeply involved with Google's move to its new headquarters in Mountain View, California, a complex known as Googleplex. The corridors at Googleplex are filled with bicycles and other exercise equipment, and all employees are encouraged to make use of the Google recreation center. Weight rooms, locker rooms, laundry facilities, game rooms, and snack rooms are available to employees for no cost. Page believes that such progressive amenities make for a happier and more productive workforce for Google, also serving as an example for other employers. Google has also worked, under Page's guidance, to assure that its operations are as environmentally neutral as possible. To this end, Google makes use of solar energy, uses goats to trim the grass around Googleplex, and uses servers that are as energy-efficient as possible.

PERSONAL LIFE

In 2007, Page married Lucinda Southworth, whom he had been dating for a year. Southworth earned a master's degree from Oxford University and was a doctoral student studying biomedical informatics at Stanford when she and Page met. Page and Southworth had a son in 2009 and live in Palo Alto.

Long interested in environmental issues, Page has a keen attraction to alternative energy vehicles. He owns a Zero X motorbike, a Tesla electric roadster, and a Toyota Prius. Indeed, Page has been an active investor in alternative energy companies, including Tesla Motors, and works with Google.org, Google's philanthropic organization, to encourage the development of renewable energy sources. Long a participant in outdoor adventure sports, Page enjoys kite boarding and hiking. The owner of the 193-foot yacht *Senses*, Page also shares a 767-200 jet airplane with Brin.

Page has been honored by a number of organizations, including the University of Michigan, which granted him an honorary doctorate in 2009; the American Academy of Arts and Sciences, which named him a Fellow in 2005; and the Marconi Foundation at Columbia University, which gave him the Marconi Foundation Prize and elected him a Fellow in 2004. With a net worth of nearly $19 billion in 2012, Page is one of the richest individuals in the world.

Stephen T. Schroth and Shayna Hargraves

FURTHER READING

Auletta, Ken. *Googled: The End of the World as We Know It*. New York: Penguin, 2009. Print. Explores some of the consequences resulting from the fast pace at which Google permits information to be found, analyzed, and acted upon by a variety of individuals.

Brandt, R. L. *The Google Guys: Inside the Brilliant Minds of Google Founders Larry Page and Sergey Brin*. New York: Penguin, 2009. Print. Recounts the history of Page's and Brin's meeting and their decision to form what became Google.

Jarvis, J. *What Would Google do?* New York: HarperCollins, 2009. Print. Investigates how Google's business

dealings combine the visionary with the ruthless, in an effort to both save the planet and decimate the competition.

Stross, R. *Planet Google: One Company's Audacious Plan to Organize Everything We Know*. New York: Free Press, 2009. Print. A look at Google's plans to become a one-stop location for information needs, including its potential to serve as a gatekeeper for data and the potential consequences arising from this dominance.

SEAN PARKER

Cofounder of Napster and founding president of Facebook

Born: December 3, 1979; place unknown
Died: -
Primary Field: Internet
Specialty: Social media
Primary Company/Organization: Napster

INTRODUCTION

Sean Parker was the cocreator of the pioneering music file-sharing site Napster, which demonstrated the viability of distributing individual songs over the Internet as MP3 files. The success of Napster helped both artists and users bypass traditional record companies, tapping years of frustration at the music industry, and led to the creation of the Apple iTunes store, a profitable commercial operation selling individual songs over the Internet. Parker also played a crucial role in the creation of the social networking site Facebook, helping founder Mark Zuckerberg obtain funding; Parker also served as president of Facebook and has been involved with several other web products, including Plaxo and Spotify.

EARLY LIFE

Sean Parker was raised in Herndon, Virginia, in the Washington, D.C., metropolitan area. He began writing computer programs in the second grade, using an Atari 800 computer given to him by his father, an oceanographer at the National Oceanic and Atmospheric Administration (NOAA). His mother was an infomercial media buyer and thus employed in an arm of the technology business. Sean became known as a computer hacker by age fifteen, having broken into numerous companies' and universities' networks; he was

sentenced to community service for these activities. At age sixteen, he designed a web crawler that won first prize at a Virginia state computer science fair, and interned with several companies, including FreeLoader and UUNet, during his senior year of high school. Parker did not attend college after graduating from high school; instead, he went to work with Shawn Fanning, creating the site that would become Napster. Parker has referred

Sean Parker.

to this project as Napster University because he learned about law, finance, and entrepreneurship, as well as programming, while working on Napster.

LIFE'S WORK

Parker first met Fanning on Internet relay chat (IRC), where they discovered they had common interests, including hacking. Fanning enrolled at Northeastern University in Boston, while Parker skipped college and went to work for UUNet, an Internet service provider (ISP) for businesses. The first investor Parker signed up for Napster was Ben Lilienthal, who also referred the company to an angel investor with whom he was familiar.

When Yosi Amran decided to invest $250,000 in the company, Fanning and Parker moved to California to devote their full time to the business. Napster's business plan, such as it was at this time, amounted to building a large user base of people interested in trading copyrighted music; ideas for generating revenue included charging a subscription fee, charging for each song, and selling merchandise to subscribers.

By July 2000, Napster had more than 20 million users and had become so popular on college campuses that some banned it because it used so much bandwith that it interfered with other uses of the computer system. However, such measures were met with student protests, often couched in terms of free speech and against the record labels, which were accused of overcharging for inferior music. In other words, Napster fit into the rebellious spirit that is characteristic of many college students. Napster also inspired some bands to bypass the record industry or expose their financial dealings. For instance, Courtney Love gave a speech at a Digital Hollywood conference in 2002, publicized through the website Salon.com, in which she pointed out how little money a band might make on even a highly successful album compared to how much the record company might make. In 2000, Radiohead promoted an album by releasing tracks on Napster, and the reggae-rock band Dispatch used Napster as a sort of radio service to publicize its work and build its audience for its live concerts.

Much of the music shared on Napster was copyrighted, and this drew the attention of the music industry. On December 6, 1999, the Recording Industry Association of America (RIAA) filed suit against Napster, charging copyright infringement. The lawsuit generated publicity for Napster, with front-page stories in *The New York Times* and *Los Angeles Times* and interviews on MTV. This publicity was reflected in a tripling of

Napster users, from 50,000 to 150,000, over the course of the month, and trading music over Napster became for some users an act of self-righteousness and an expression of freedom rather than an act of theft. Napster argued that they could not be held responsible for any copyright infringement on the part of Napster users, because the service was acting merely as an innocent middleman, like the phone company or the manufacturers of videocassette recorders (VCRs).

The success of Napster pointed out to the major music companies that there was demand for a different way of obtaining music, and the fact that music could be obtained for free on Napster was not the only reason the service was popular. Some record company executives realized that their business was changing and looked into ways to capitalize on consumers' desire to obtain individual songs in MP3 format. For instance, after Mark Ghuneim of Sony Music observed that downloads on Napster increased sharply during and after the 2001 Superbowl half-time show (of songs performed by the bands featured in that show), he investigated the possibility of having his company release singles on vinyl. However, this proved impossible: Not only did Sony no longer produce singles, but the company could not efficiently meet demand, because it took fourteen days to get a product ready for sale.

In March 2001, Napster received an injunction to stop allowing users to trade copyrighted music on its service, and in July 2001 the company shut down its network. Napster paid substantial settlements ($36 million in total) to the music industry and attempted to convert to a subscription service model. However, this was unsuccessful and the company filed for bankruptcy on May 14, 2002. Although Napster ceased to exist in its original form, its existence left the music business unalterably changed. Not only did other services, such as Gnutella and Freenet, emerge, but in 2003 Apple Computer demonstrated that users would pay to download music from its iTunes music stores.

Parker became a managing parter in the venture capital firm the Founders Fund after leaving Facebook; this company, created by Peter Thiel, focuses on investing in technology companies at their early stages. Parker also founded Project Agape, a social network for political activists, as well as Plaxo, a free system to store and update contact information, similar to an online Rolodex. However, Plaxo had a dark side: When an individual signed up for Plaxo, the program would send an e-mail message to everyone in that individual's address book inviting them to sign up. The number of e-mails thus increased geometrically, because some of the contacts of the first user would sign up for the service, triggering a new set of e-mails, and so on. The details surrounding Parker's departure from Plaxo are not completely clear; he claims he was forced out by Ram Shriram, while others involved in the company said that Parker was no longer doing his job and was a disruptive influence.

Parker met Facebook cofounders Mark Zuckerberg and Eduardo Saverin in the spring of 2004 and then ran into Zuckerberg again a few weeks later in Palo Alto, where Zuckerberg and several others were living in a rented house and working on the new social networking site. Parker helped Facebook connect with potential investors in Silicon Valley and, according to Zuckerberg, played a crucial role in transforming Facebook from a college project into a real company. Parker is also credited with helping design the look of Facebook (he emphasized the importance of design as well as engineering) and for promoting the photo-sharing capabilities of Facebook. Parker's greatest influence on Facebook, however, may have come from the corporate structure he developed to give Zuckerberg complete control of the company; the structure gave Zuckerberg multiple board seats and "supervoting shares" (B shares, worth ten times as many votes as the A shares held by, for instance, Saverin). Parker based this structure on his experience with Plaxo, where he felt he was unfairly cut out of the business.

In 2009, Parker became involved with the Swedish music site Spotify, which is supported by advertising and offers users unlimited legal access to music. He is also an investor in Airtime, a project created by Shawn Fanning to allow real-time communication and file sharing over the Internet. Parker and Joe Green created the Facebook application Causes.com, designed to use the power of social networking to support charitable causes. When a user posts a cause to a web page, the action is communicated to all that person's Facebook friends, creating social pressure for the friends to support the cause as well. According to Green, as of November 2009, $17 million had been raised for charities through Cause, and 90 million people were taking part in the system.

PERSONAL LIFE

In 2005, Parker was questioned by police in North Carolina after cocaine was discovered in a rented beach house registered under his name, but he was never charged or arrested. However, this incident, along with some internal disputes, persuaded him that it was time

---

Affiliation: Napster

Sean Parker was a cocreator of Napster and is well known for his involvement in Facebook, particularly after the popularity of the 2010 feature film *The Social Network* in 2010 (in which Justin Timberlake portrayed Parker). Napster was a service that allowed individuals to share music files in MP3 format and thus was known as a peer-to-peer file-sharing service. It was one of the first companies to capitalize in a big way on the possibilities inherent in MP3 files, which could easily be copied and exchanged and thus encouraged users to consume music as individual songs rather than entire albums. Although Napster ceased operation in 2001, following charges of copyright infringement, it made a lasting impression on the music business because it demonstrated that people wanted to acquire music encoded in MP3 files rather than on physical media such as tapes or compact discs, and they wanted to be able to purchase individual songs rather than complete albums.

---

to leave Facebook. In 2012, he was engaged to Alexandra Lenas, a musician and a copywriter.

Sarah Boslaugh

FURTHER READING

Alderman, John. *Sonic Boom: Napster, MP3, and the New Pioneers of Music.* New York: Basic, 2003. Print. A journalistic history of the changes in the record industry brought about by the ubiquity of MP3 recordings and the influence of Napster, as well as key websites such as the Internet Underground Music Archive, which enabled musicians to bypass the conventional recording industry.

Bertoni, Stephen S. "Sean Parker: Agent of Disruption." *Forbes* 188.6 (2011): 58–73. Print. A profile of Parker, focusing on his personality and abilities as an "idea catalyst" who has helped create some of the most influential technology companies of recent history while amassing a personal fortune of more than $2 billion.

Kirkpatrick, David. *The Facebook Effect: The Inside Story of the Company That Is Connecting the World.* New York: Simon, 2011. Print. A clearly written and straightforward history of *Facebook*, from its origins as Facemash to its worldwide success, written by a *Fortune* journalist with the cooperation of Facebook executives.

Knopper, Steve. *Appetite for Self-Destruction: The Spectacular Crash of the Record Industry in the Digital Age.* New York: Simon, 2009. Print. A book-length analysis, written by a contributing editor from *Rolling Stone*, of the record industry's response to the threat to their business model posed by digital recordings. Knopper argues that the record companies should have made a deal with Napster rather than shutting it down and driving people to other sites.

Mezrich, Ben. *The Accidental Billionaires: The Founding of Facebook; A Tale of Sex, Money, Genius, and Betrayal.* New York: Doubleday, 2009. Print. An account, written in a dramatic and colloquial style but based on interviews and other research, of the events surrounding the creation of Facebook. This book served as a major source for the 2010 movie *The Social Network.*

BOB PARSONS

Founder of GoDaddy

Born: November 27, 1950; Baltimore, Maryland
Died: -
Primary Field: Computer science
Specialty: Internet
Primary Company/Organization: GoDaddy

INTRODUCTION
Vietnam War veteran Bob Parsons founded the highly successful domain registry website GoDaddy.com. A

Bob Parsons.

determined spirit and charitable heart have helped Parsons's endeavor flourish into the multimillion-dollar industry it is today. GoDaddy came into being during the early years of the Web 2.0 evolution and soon became the dominant website registry and hosting service. It has experienced some controversy, however, most of it surrounding its founder, Parsons. His determined nature and ability to capitalize on bad press have made him a major player in the virtual world and an example for those who did not perform well during school and succeeded despite growing up with more disadvantages than advantages. Hard work and persistence despite failure are the hallmarks of Parsons's professional career.

EARLY LIFE
Robert "Bob" Parsons was born in Baltimore, Maryland, on November 27, 1950. Raised in the blue-collar inner-city world of Baltimore, he learned early that hard work was essential to a successful life. His early education was no success story, however: He nearly did not graduate from high school. Fortunately, his teachers took pity on him after he decided to sign up for the U.S. Army; he received his diploma at the height of the Vietnam War.

Parsons served in the Army from 1968 to 1970. He was wounded during his short tour in Vietnam and became eligible for assistance under the G.I. Bill. After leaving the Army, Parsons had started working at a steel mill. After watching several coworkers get seriously hurt on the job, he decided that it was not the career choice for him. He began studying at the University of Baltimore, randomly choosing accounting as his major (the unconfirmed story is that he simply picked the first major in the booklet).

During his college years, Parsons studied computers as a hobby, reading a computer programming book that he had found at a campus bookstore. After graduating in 1975, he worked for several years in the accounting field for several different companies. Every time he needed a program for his computer, he wrote it himself. Parsons then decided to start his own software company.

LIFE'S WORK

Working from his basement in Cedar Rapids, Iowa, Parsons taught himself how to write computer code and used this newfound skill to design some computer software. His first programs were related to accounting, and Parsons used them in his day job. It was not long before he went into business for himself.

Parsons named his first company, begun in 1984, Parsons Technology. He used direct-mail marketing to sell his products, reducing advertising costs and eliminating the need for a storefront. The company did not succeed immediately; in fact, Parsons admits to nearly losing the business several times because of cash-flow problems. Credit cards kept it afloat long enough to establish a solid customer base, and thereafter the company began to thrive. At its height, Parsons Technology had one thousand employees and showed returns in the $100 million range.

Intuit, Inc., a major accounting and tax software company, purchased Parsons Technology in 1994 for $64 million. Part of the deal with Intuit was that Parsons would not design new programs or software for at least a year. He agreed and went off to Florida to play golf. During that year, he got divorced and his golf game did not improve. He then returned to the world of business; he had not enjoyed resting on his laurels and was eager to get back to work. Parsons took some of the money from the Intuit sale to start a new company, which he named Jomax Technologies, in 1997 (the name was derived from a road Parsons traveled regularly). The employees of the new company were handpicked from former colleagues and who had responded well to Parsons's laid-back management style.

Jomax Technologies experimented with several types of software, website development, and online content building before settling down into the world of domain registry. The only other major company offering domain registry services at the time was Network Solutions, and it charged a high price for its services. Parsons believed he could offer the same kind of services for a much lower price. He also wanted to provide what he believed was missing from the world of online businesses: high-quality customer service. After a brainstorming session during which a staff member shouted out "Go, daddy!" Parsons changed the name of the company and relaunched his business as GoDaddy in 1999. Founded at the height of the dot-com bubble, GoDaddy did not really register in the world of registry services. It was not until a Super Bowl commercial in 2005 that the company began to get noticed.

Using a part-time pornography star as the main player in a risqué commercial, Parsons managed to put the GoDaddy name on the virtual map. By creating hype, he increased traffic, and it was not long before the quality of product and pricing far outweighed the issue of lowbrow advertising. Between 2005 and 2006, cash flow increased 80 percent. GoDaddy has become the market leader in the world of domain registry. By 2012, Parsons's company consisted of three different branches: the original GoDaddy.com domain service, Wild West Domains, and Starfield Technologies, LLC. By offering services such as web hosting and online privacy, Parsons has managed to extend his brand in several directions.

In 2006, Parsons considered making GoDaddy a public company. He did not care for the rules surrounding the move from a private to a public concern. Parsons found the process so restricting, however (it included not being able to post his blogs or execute his online video and radio shows), that he pulled his application. GoDaddy remains a private company.

In 2011, Parsons decided to sell 65 percent of the company to an entrepreneurial group called Kohlberg Kravis Roberts, Silver Lake, and Technology Crossover Ventures for a reported $2.25 billion and stepped down as chief executive officer. In 2012, GoDaddy had 53 million domain names on its registry, 5 million web hosting customers, and thirty-five hundred employees.

PERSONAL LIFE

Parsons enjoys writing his personal blog and hosting an online radio show. His blog is one of the most widely consulted personal blogs on the Internet. The radio show airs weekly and often comprises Parsons interviewing GoDaddy customers and interviewing them about their personal and professional websites. Since stepping down as CEO of GoDaddy, Parsons has focused his energy on marketing, spending his time casting commercials and enjoying his substantial success. Occasionally Parsons travels to Africa to cull elephants

Affiliation: GoDaddy

Bob Parsons began Jomax Technologies in 1997, changing its name to GoDaddy in 1999. Originally, Parsons intended to offer software development and website building, but he soon discovered a gap in the growing world of domain registration. Parsons established GoDaddy with the philosophy of selling a quality product cheaply to a large number of people. Unlike its competitors, GoDaddy offered round-the-clock customer support, including a follow-up telephone call the day after the purchase of a domain name, no matter how low the price tag. This personal touch attracted businesses large and small to the GoDaddy brand, and it was not long before the company outsold its biggest competitor, Network Solutions.

GoDaddy did not really make its mark in the world until 2005. A commercial for GoDaddy, aired during the Super Bowl, that caused a lot of controversy. Parsons had chosen a part-time pornography actress to speak for the GoDaddy brand, presenting women in skimpy outfits during the commercial. There was an immediate outcry from women's groups, calling the commercial exploitive and sexist. Parsons used the negative press to build hype for his product.

GoDaddy has received numerous awards for its customer service and its working environment. The company now comprises three main branches: GoDaddy.com, WildWest Domains, and Starfield Technologies, LLC. GoDaddy has branched out into the world of domain hosting and Internet privacy. GoDaddy Cares is the charitable branch of the company that donates millions of dollars annually to charities large and small.

In 2011, Parsons stepped down as CEO of the company and sold 65 percent of the business to the entrepreneurial firm Kohlberg Kravis Roberts, Silver Lake, and Technology Crossover Ventures for $2.25 billion. GoDaddy quickly became the market leader in domain registration. As of 2012, the company had 53 million domains in its registry. GoDaddy is based in Scottsdale, Arizona, and has some thirty-five hundred employees.

---

as part of a herd-thinning village feeding program. He has received much negative press for this activity, including a boycott of the GoDaddy brand. Although the boycott did not stop the company's growth, People for the Ethical Treatment of Animals (PETA) and the Humane Society of the United States have publicly denounced Parsons's choices, despite his attempts to explain them.

Parsons is an active lobbyist for the Internet and has supported unpopular online legislation, including an antipiracy law vehemently opposed by giants such as Google and Yahoo! He has been a vocal critic of the way China accesses personal information online and actually stopped registering .cn domains (the country domain for China) to make his point.

Despite a mountain of negative press from animal rights activists and several larger online companies who disagree with his politics, Parsons is well known in some circles for his charitable giving. GoDaddy donated $3 million to charity in 2011, and there seems to be little focus to the giving. Parsons and his company donate money to numerous charities in numerous fields, although they have raised a large amount for children's charities.

Parsons received the Muhammad Ali Entrepreneurial Award in 2011 and was named Arizona Business Leader in 2007. The University of Baltimore gave him an honorary doctorate in 2008 and the University of Baltimore Distinguished Entrepreneur award in 2010.

Trish Popovitch

FURTHER READING

Parsons, Bob. "Bob Parsons Doesn't Do Subtle." Interview by Andrew Goldman. *New York Times* 1 Jan. 2012. Print. 24 Aug. 2012. Interview with Bob Parsons discussing the purchase of 65 percent of the GoDaddy website by Kohlberg Kravis Roberts, Silver Lake and Technology Crossover Ventures. Parsons explains his marketing philosophy.

---. "GoDaddy's Bob Parsons: We're Only Seeing the Tip of the Iceberg." Interview by Michael A. Cox. *Practical Ecommerce* 5 Oct. 2005. Web. 24 Aug. 2012. This early interview with Parsons offers details regarding the sale of Parsons Technology and the beginning of Jomax Technologies. Includes an overview of the GoDaddy company.

---. "My Bio." 17 Dec 2004. Web. 24 Aug 2012. Parsons's explains his upbringing, his work ethic, his military service, and his college education choices.

Sloan, Paul. "Who's Your Go Daddy?" *Business 2.0* 19 Dec. 2006. Web. 24 Aug. 2012. Provides biographical details on Parsons as well as some background on the GoDaddy brand. Includes a chart comparing GoDaddy with its closest competitors as well as Parsons's four keys to entrepreneurial success.

Vance, Ashlee. "The Challenge of Classing Up GoDaddy." *Bloomberg Businessweek*. 24 May 2012. Web. 24 Aug. 2012. Provides facts and figures regarding the success of the GoDaddy brand as well as the

sale of a portion of the company and Parsons's life after heading the company.

Welch, Liz. "The Way I Work: Michael Arrington of TechCrunch." *Inc.* 1 Oct. 2010. Web. 24 Aug. 2012. Arrington describes his workday and approach to work. Includes details about his personal life as well as his attitude toward his staff and business.

RADIA PERLMAN

Inventor of the spanning tree protocol

Born: 1951; Portsmouth, Virginia
Died: -
Primary Field: Internet
Specialty: Applications
Primary Company/Organization: Sun Microsystems

INTRODUCTION

Although she dislikes the title, software engineer and inventor Radia Perlman is known as the mother of the Internet for her design of the spanning tree protocol (STP), which has kept the Internet accessible through networking even as it has continued to expand. She also developed TRILL (for Transparent Interconnection of Lots of Links), a more sophisticated protocol that fixed problems with STP. She is also a pioneer in tangible computing and is responsible for the development of link-state routing. In the field of Internet security, Perlman has developed sabotage-proof networks, certificate revocation, and password protection. She holds more than one hundred patents, approximately half of in conjunction with Sun Microsystems, her longtime employer, and has other patents pending. Her textbooks have become required reading for both students and professionals.

EARLY LIFE

Radia Perlman was born in Portsmouth, Virginia, in 1951, but she spent most of her childhood in New Jersey. Her father, Julius Perlman, was a radar technician for the U.S. Navy, and her mother, Hope Sonne Perlman, worked as a civilian computer programmer. Thus, both parents were interested in engineering, even though they discouraged their daughter from engaging in hands-on experimentation. Perlman grew up with a strong interest in both mathematics and science. She continues to insist that she hates technology, despite

spending her entire professional life in the field of computer technology.

In 1969, Perlman enrolled at the Massachusetts Institute of Technology (MIT) in Cambridge and discovered computer programming. As part of her undergraduate program, she worked in the MIT Artificial Intelligence Laboratory, which later became the LOGO Lab. Her mentor was Seymour Papert, the South African–born educator and computer scientist who developed the Toddler's Own Recursive Turtle Interpreter System (TORTIS), which was designed to track cognitive development in small children.

Radia Perlman.

Perlman earned her bachelor's degree in mathematics in 1973. She spent the years between 1974 and 1976 working on her master's degree and redesigning

Affiliation: Sun Microsystems

While Radia Perlman has worked for a number of companies and designed the spanning tree protocol (STM), for which she is best known, while working at Digital Equipment Corporation (DEC), she is most closely associated with Sun Microsystems, where she was involved in the company's work on Internet security for more than a decade.

In early 1982, while involved in graduate studies at Stanford University, Vinod Khosla, Andy Bechtolsheim, and Scott McNealy founded Sun Microsystems. They were soon joined by Bill Joy, a Berkeley developer. Sun sold computers, computer components, software applications, and computer services. The business was headquartered in Silicon Valley in Santa Clara, California, and had manufacturing facilities in both the United States and Scotland. In 1987, Sun began a series of acquisitions with the purchase of Trancept Systems, Sitka Corporation, and Centram Systems West; such acquisitions would continue throughout Sun's history as an independent company.

Over time, Sun became best known for its processors, storage systems, and workstations and for technologies such as Java, a now ubiquitous programming language; MySQL, an open-source database; and the Solaris operating system. Always a strong proponent of open source software, Sun was also involved with the development of the Unix operating system.

Sun prospered throughout the 1980s and 1990s. In 1995, Sun came "within hours" of purchasing Apple when it was in decline; the deal fell through, however. At the dawn of the twenty-first century, as the dot-com bubble burst, Sun also began to falter. Despite continuing to acquire other companies, Sun consolidated its American manufacturing facilities in Hillsboro, Oregon, to help deal with declining revenues. However, the Hillsboro facilities were also closed in 2006.

Both IBM and Oracle entered into talks to buy Sun Microsystems. In April 2009, Oracle won and purchased Sun Microsystems for $7.4 billion. Shortly after merging Sun into its existing operations, Oracle became Oracle America.

TORTIS. She worked with children, some as young as three and one-half years, teaching them to program the Turtle robot by plugging items together. As a result of that work, Perlman came to be considered the inventor of the field of tangible computing, which uses physical objects plugged together to program computers. She completed her master's degree in 1976 and received her doctorate from MIT in 1988. Her dissertation, "Routing with Byzantine Robustness," dealt with failures that occur on networks in response to malicious activities.

LIFE'S WORK
Perlman's first job after completing her master's work at MIT was as a software designer with Bolt, Beranek, and Newman, a company that developed networking equipment for use by the U.S. government. In 1980, while giving a speech on network routing, she was recruited by the Digital Equipment Corporation (DEC). After starting her work there, she was asked if she could solve the problem the company was having in getting its computers to communicate with one another. In response, Perlman, in less than a week, invented the spanning tree protocol (STP), which is made up of algorithms that work behind the scenes to connect the bridges and switches that support Ethernet, the technology that controls local networking.

Before Perlman invented the spanning tree, Ethernet technology was confined to use by small networks within a limited area. With STP, legitimate connections on the network were recognized and anything beyond the tree itself was disabled. Although few members of the public are even aware of STM, it has been identified as the "heart" of the Ethernet, allowing computers to connect to the Internet, which had begun to be taken for granted by much of the world by the end of the twentieth century. Greg Papadopoulos, who later worked with Perlman at Sun, explained STM by describing it as a road map for moving traffic in the virtual world of the Internet.

Perlman's quirky sense of humor is evident in her work. She penned the poem "Algorhyme," patterned on Joyce Kilmer's "Trees," to explain the spanning tree protocol, and her son later set it to music. The poem reads in part: "I think that I shall never see/ a graph more lovely than a tree./ A tree whose crucial property/ is loop-free connectivity. …/ A mesh is made by folks like me,/ then bridges find a spanning tree." Perlman's STM has been embraced by the International Organization for Standardization, which renamed the protocol IS-IS.

In 1993, Perlman accepted a job with Novell, working on information exchange and security. Four years later, she moved to Sun Microsystems, where she spent thirteen years. As a Sun Distinguished Engineer, she specialized in network security. Of the more than one hundred patents Perlman holds, some fifty of them arose from her work at Sun. In order to solve problems encountered with the spanning tree as Internet technology became more sophisticated, Perlman invented Transparent Interconnection of Lots of Links (TRILL). Unlike STM, TRILL is designed to optimize available bandwidth by taking the shortest path available and making use of multipathing. In 2004, Perlman invented link-state routing, which is one of two major protocols used in connecting computers to networks and the Internet. Her link-state routing is credited with helping to keep the Internet stable, scalable, and robust.

Although she has become widely identified as the "mother of the Internet," Perlman rejects the title, insisting that, in fact, there are a number of individuals responsible for creating and maintaining the Internet. She is also adamant that gender should not be an issue when discussing someone's life work.

Sun Microsystems was acquired by Oracle in 2009. After spending thirteen years at the company, Perlman decided to leave. In 2011, she became the director of network security technology at Intel, and she has been awarded the distinguished honor of being named an Intel Fellow.

PERSONAL LIFE

Perlman, who maintains her base in Redmond, Washington, is married to fellow software engineer and author Michael Speciner and is the mother of two children. Her son, Ray, is a musician, and her daughter, Dawn, is an amateur opera singer. While Perlman and Michael were on a cruise to Russia, he persuaded her to try her hand at stand-up comedy. She was a huge success, according to fellow passengers.

Perlman has extended her knowledge to students through classroom teaching, and she has taught at MIT, Harvard University, and the University of Washington. In 1997, Prentice-Hall began publishing the Perlman Series in Computer Networking and Security, beginning with James Solomon's *Mobile IP: The Internet Unplugged*. By 2012, the series included thirteen books.

In the January 15, 1992, issue of *Data Communications* magazine, Perlman was recognized as one of the twenty most influential people in the industry. She was again recognized by the same publication in the January 15, 1997, issue, becoming the only figure in the industry to be so named in two issues. In 2004, the Silicon Valley Intellectual Property Law Association (SVIPLA) designated Perlman as its Silicon Valley Inventor of the Year.

Perlman is considered to be one of the most significant contributors to the field of women in technology. In recognition of those contributions, the Anita Borg Institute awarded Perlman its Women of Vision Award for Innovation in 2005, the first year the awards were given. In 2006, the Advanced Computing Systems Association (USENIX) honored Perlman with a lifetime achievement award. In 2012, she was recognized by the Association for Computing Machinery's Special Interest Group on Data Communication (SIGCOMM) for her work on Internet routing and bridging protocols. In 2000, Perlman's work was also recognized by the prestigious Royal Institute of Technology in Sweden, which awarded her an honorary doctorate in recognition of her contributions to data networking, communications, and security technology.

Elizabeth Rholetter Purdy

FURTHER READING

Barlas, Pete. "Puzzle Solver: Radia Perlman's Determination Helped Make Web Surfing a Reality." *Investor's Business Daily*, February 9, 2006. Print. Profile of Perlman, covering both her educational and her professional history. Illustrated.

Boudreau, John. "Technology's Women of Vision." *San Jose Mercury News* 19 Oct. 2005. Print. Salute to the inaugural winners of the Anita Borg Institute's Women of Vision Award winners, which included Perlman.

Diffie, Whitfield. "Information Security: 50 Years Behind, 50 Years Ahead." *Communications of the ACM* 51.1 (2008): n. pag. Print. Detailed look at the field of Internet security.

Kaugman, Charlie, Radia Perlman, and Michael Speciner. *Network Security: Private Communication in a Public World*. New York: Prentice-Hall, 2002. Print. Updated from the 1999 edition, this is considered the standard textbook for anyone interested in the fields of networking and Internet security. Illustrated.

"The Many Sides of Radia Perlman." 20 Apr. 2011. *Intel Free Press*. Web. 12 Aug. 2012. Excellent profile of Perlman's life and work. Includes a head shot of Perlman.

"McNeely, Zander Dish on Sun's Glory Days." *eWeek* 28.5 (2011): n. pag. Print. Profile of Sun Microsystems.

Perlman, Radia. *Interconnections: Bridges, Routers, Switches, and Internetworking Protocols*. Boston: Addison-Wesley, 1999. Print. Considered a must-have for both students and professionals in the field. Illustrated.

Southwick, Karen. *High Noon: The Inside Story of Sun Microsystems*. New York: John Wiley, 1999. Print. Traces the history of Sun and its role in the development of the Internet.

CHRISTOPHER POOLE

Founder of 4chan

Born: c. 1988; New York State
Died: -
Primary Field: Internet
Specialty: Social media
Primary Company/Organization: 4chan

INTRODUCTION

Christopher "moot" Poole is the founder of the popular Internet image-sharing board, 4chan.org, and the online image remix site Canvas (URL canv.as). Poole was declared Time *magazine's Most Influential Person of 2008 in an online poll. A strong proponent of online anonymity and privacy rights, he speaks at conferences and on panels as an advocate of free online culture.*

EARLY LIFE

Christopher Poole, also known as moot (always with a lower-case *m*), was born in 1988 in New York. Little else is known about him, since he intentionally keeps his private life and his public "moot" persona separate—there has even been speculation as to whether or not Christopher Poole is his real name.

He is the child of divorced parents and spent most of his youth in suburban Westchester County, New York. Poole briefly attended Virginia Commonwealth University to major in anthropology and sociology in 2009 but dropped out after only a few semesters. His father, Tom Poole, described him as a "bit obsessive" in a 2008 *Wall Street Journal* article, explaining that as a young boy Chris once built a water-cooled computer in his spare time.

LIFE'S WORK

Inspired by the Japanese image-sharing board 2chan, Poole founded 4chan in October 2003, when he was fifteen years old, and funded the site's storage with his mother's credit card. Originally focusing on Japanese anime and manga—and Otaku culture generally—the site has expanded over the years to include forums for physical fitness, automobiles, literature, and many other subjects.

4chan's anonymous user community has become a significant cultural force in the twenty-first century. Users post with complete anonymity, and there is no archive of site activity. This gives users tremendous freedom to collaborate, conspire, and communicate. This

freedom is noteworthy for two reasons in particular: the proliferation of Internet memes—phrases, images, and ideas that pervade online culture, such as "lolcats" and "Rickrolling"—and anonymous "hacktivism"—a collaboration of technologically savvy Internet users working together to coordinate denial-of-service attacks on offending websites as well as real-life protests, usually against supporters of Internet censorship. While both phenomena existed before the inception of 4chan, it is on 4chan that the phenomena matured into a more legitimate form of culture.

Despite being one of the most popular sites on the Internet, 4chan has not proved to be commercially viable. In the early months of its existence, hosting and bandwidth costs were partly covered by donations, but in 2005 Poole began running advertisements on the site both to raise money for its operation and to reify his commitment to keeping the site free for everyone to use. Because of the often controversial content posted to the website, advertisers have remained wary of 4chan and have tended to stay away.

Christopher Poole.

Affiliation: 4chan

In 2003, while living in his mother's house in Long Island, Christopher "moot" Poole created 4chan, which quickly became one of the most notorious and influential sites on the internet. A simple and anonymous image-sharing board, 4chan began as a resource for fans of Japanese anime and manga to share images and enthusiasm for their favorite art form, but the site quickly grew beyond this narrow focus, incorporating subsections for topics as diverse as cooking, weapons, and fashion. The design of the site has changed little since its inception, in part to keep development and hosting costs low (4chan is a free-to-use forum) and as in homage to the original image-sharing forums of the past.

4chan has been described as a "meme factory" and is the original source for such prevalent cultural tropes as "lolcats" (creatively labeled pictures of cats in humorous situations) and "Rickrolling" (a bait-and-switch prank in which a target is promised interesting or relevant content and then is redirected to a video of Rick Astley's 1987 single "Never Gonna Give You Up").

4chan and its community of anonymous users are frequently subjects of controversy. Because posting is anonymous and is not archived, users often feel free to post questionable or even illegal content such as instructions on drug use and making explosives or outlawed pornography.

Additionally, 4chan users and other hacktivists have conspired to act as an amorphous whole, collectively calling itself Anonymous (or anon) to perform various feats of mayhem and Internet vandalism. In 2008, anon launched Operation: Chanology, a series of vigorous denial-of-service attacks and real-life protests against the Church of Scientology, when they perceived some the church's actions as acts of Internet censorship and intimidation. This is widely reputed to be Anonymous's most famous and successful operation. A similar operation in 2010, codenamed Operation Payback, targeted the popular Internet payment site PayPal after that organization deleted an account collecting donations for controversial WikiLeaks founder Julian Assange. Targets in this ongoing operation have included former vice presidential candidate Sarah Palin, Senator Joe Lieberman, and MasterCard.

Although Anonymous exists independently of 4chan, the site is a frequent communication forum for hacktivists, and the two entities are often (though incorrectly) referenced interchangeably. While Anonymous appears to have initially formed on 4chan (posters who do not enter a handle are tagged Anonymous and thus the name), the loose affiliation has extended well beyond the confines of the website's popular /b/ Random board.

In a 2009 Internet poll, "moot" was named *Time* magazine's World's Most Influential Person of 2008. It was in the process of this nomination that Poole, who had previously only gone by his online alias moot, revealed his real name. Additionally, the competition was suspected of being rigged by enthusiastic 4chan users who apparently managed, through careful manipulation of votes, to spell out two popular memes (MARBLE-CAKE ALSO THE GAME) as an acrostic using the first letter of each of the nominees' names.

The *Time* magazine nomination introduced a new stage in Poole's career: that of Internet privacy activist and cultural analyst. This led to a number of speaking engagements beginning in 2009, when he spoke at the Paraflows Symposium in Vienna, Austria, to discuss the relationship between 4chan's crowd mentality and meme generation.

In 2010, Poole spoke at the annual TED conference in order to stress the importance of anonymity and online privacy as cultural forces and as conduits of innovation. At that talk, he portrayed 4chan as a sort of antithesis to more personally invasive sites such as Facebook and Twitter, which require full user profiles.

Also in 2010, Poole gave testimony in the trial of David Kernell, who had hacked the e-mail accounts of former vice presidential nominee Sarah Palin and her daughter, Bristol. Poole defined and explained much of the activity and terminology used on the 4chan boards and was instrumental in helping the court to explain the coded language of the evidence in the trial.

Using $625,000 in funds collected through venture capitalist and angel investors in 2010, Poole launched a new website, Canvas (or, per its URL, Canv.as) in 2011. Like 4chan, this site encourages anonymity, but as a "media remix" site, it maintains a tone and intent that are markedly different. In 2012, Canv.as was in open beta testing.

PERSONAL LIFE

Little is known about Poole's private life. He is an online privacy and anonymity advocate who very much exemplifies his own ideals. He announced his real name only when, in 2008, he was nominated as *Time* magazine's World's Most Influential Person. He continues to speak out in favor of online privacy and anonymity at college campuses such as New York University, Yale University, and the Massachusetts Institute of Technology, as well as conferences such as the annual TED talks. One of his friends is Christina Xu, from the Awesome Foundation and the Institute of Higher Awesome. In 2012, he was living in Cambridge, Massachusetts.

Vytautas Malesh

FURTHER READING

Brophy-Warren, Jamin. "Modest Web Site Is Behind a Bevy of Memes." *Wall Street Journal* 9 July 2009: n. pag. Web. 27 July 2012. In this article, the author describes the mimetic cultural impact of 4chan, describing successful popular memes, such as "Lolcats" and "I heard U like Mudkips," and explains the concept of an Internet meme to the uninitiated.

Chen, Adrian. "4chan Attack Brings down MPAA Website." *Gawker.com*. 18 Sept. 2010. Web. 25 July 2012. This short article announces attacks by Anonymous on the Motion Picture Association of America in response to that group's targeting of the popular Pirate Bay torrent download site. The article also describes Anonymous's weapon of choice, the Low Orbit Ion Cannon (LOIC) botnet.

Dibbell, Julian. "Radical Opacity." *Technology Review*. Massachusetts Institute of Technology, Sept. 2010. Web. 25 July 2012. This article covers the history of 4chan and some biographical information on Poole, including fan responses to his appearances and the celebrity culture that has developed around this otherwise extremely private individual. This article also analyzes 4chan's revenue potential, announces capital procurement for the Canv.as site, and digresses into Poole's inability to monetize 4chan.

Ewalt, David. "4chan's Christopher Poole: Why Anonymity Rules." *Forbes* 13 Mar. 2011. Web. 27 July 2012. This extremely short article highlights Poole's position and talking points on anonymity as with regard to innovation, as described at 2011's South by Southwest (SXSW) tech conference. Emphasis is on the removal of cultural barriers and the freedom provided by anonymity.

"FAQ." *4chan.org*. n.d. Web. 26 July 2012. The official frequently-asked-questions page of 4chan.org, authored by Christopher "moot" Poole and his team

of administrators. This web page details the procedures and practices of posting to the 4chan image boards, including protocol for off-list activity such as panel hosting and donations.

Fisher, Ken. "4chan's Moot Takes Pro-Anonymity to TED 2010." *arstechnica*. 11 Feb 2010. Web. 25 July 2012. This article describes the significant points of Poole's 2010 TED talk and aptly paraphrases the 4chan creator's pro-anonymity argument: that users who are uninhibited by name-associated social pressure and protected by total privacy will produce innovative and exciting content organically.

Hesse, Monica. "A Virtual Unknown: Meet 'moot,' the Secretive Internet Celeb Who Still Lives with Mom." *Washington Post Online*. 17 Feb. 2009. Web. 25 July 2012. Primarily a lengthy biography of Poole, this article features observations of Poole interacting with his fan base and a commentary on the cultural significance of 4chan. The article also discusses the financing and commercialization of both 4chan and Canv.as.

Jeffries, Adrianne. "From the Creator of 4chan Comes the More Mature Canvas." *Observer.com*. 31 Jan. 2011. Web. 28 July 2012. This look-out-report article summarizes the announcement of, and venture capital financing for, Poole's commercial venture Canvas and makes light mention of Poole's inability to monetize 4chan while comparing and contrasting the purpose and intent of both sites.

Landers, Chris. "Serious Business: Anonymous Takes on Scientology (and Doesn't Afraid of Anything)." *Citypaper.com*. 2 Apr. 2008. Web. 25 July 2012. Citypaper presents an exhaustive look at Operation: Chanology, one of the most significant Anonymous raids to date. The article features interviews with Anonymous activists, an exploration of the motives and methods of the operation, and some history on 4chan, Anonymous, and the /b/ random board in particular.

Singel, Ryan. "War Breaks Out between Hackers and Scientology: There Can Be Only One." *Wired.com*. 23 Jan. 2008. Web. 29 July 2012. Operation: Chanology thrust the loose affiliation of hacker activists, or hacktivists, into the national spotlight. This piece from 2008 gives a cursory overview of the network's actions against the Church of Scientology and some context for those actions.

"The World's Most Influential Person Is...." *Time.com*. 26 Apr. 2009. Web. 26 July 2012. This article is the formal announcement of and response to criticism of the awarding of *Time*'s 2008 World's Most Influential Person award to moot. The piece briefly touches on the evident vote tampering perpetuated by Anonymous but continues to support Poole's win while partially dismissing the significance of the win by noting that this is an Internet-based poll and not a formal journalistic survey.

R

John Rezner

Cofounder of GeoCities

Born: 1964; California
Died: -
Primary Field: Internet
Specialty: Content and data
Primary Company/Organization: GeoCities

INTRODUCTION

John Rezner was in the right place at the right time in November 1994, when he and his partner, David Bohnett, cofounded GeoCities, which has been called the Internet's "first cybercommunity." Rezner helped guide the company in its revolutionary efforts to give the public a voice in creating the Internet as it was becoming a part of the everyday lives of people around the world. He developed technology that made GeoCities so user-friendly that even those uninitiated in computer technology or web publishing could create their own sites. Despite a few missteps, such as mandating a floating GeoCities watermark for all member pages and attempting to target user interests for advertisers, Rezner demonstrated great foresight in understanding that many individuals wish to share information about themselves with others. He played a major role in cultivating the strong sense of community among GeoCities' neighborhoods that led the web-hosting service to become the third most often visited site on the Internet. Even though GeoCities was acquired by Yahoo! in 1999 and the company eventually closed, the site continues to hold a place in the history of the development of the Internet, having paved the way for the success of social networking sites of the early twenty-first century.

EARLY LIFE

John C. Rezner was born in California in 1964. Little is known about his personal life. He received a bachelor's degree in computer science from California State Polytechnic University in Pomona, California. He received his master's degree in computer science from the University of Southern California in 1992.

Rezner spent the early years of his professional life at the aerospace giant McDonnell Douglas, where he worked for nine years and held technology and development positions with various aerospace and defense programs, including the C-17, Mast Mounted Sight, ASW, and SDI. In 1986, he accepted a position as the head of information systems at AISF Group. He left AISF in 1995, after he and David Bohnett decided to create the web-hosting service that became GeoCities.

At GeoCities, Rezner and working for Bohnett eventually brought in Thomas R. working for Evans, the publisher of both the *Atlantic Monthly* and *U.S. News and World Report*, to serve as chief executive officer (CEO) of GeoCities. Evans had serious misgivings about the possibility of the Internet becoming successful; he thought web users would give up on the slow transmission speeds they were forced to endure at a time when access was mainly via dial-up connections. Regardless of his lack of enthusiasm, Evans applied his financial expertise to help the founders make the company a success.

LIFE'S WORK

In November 1994, entrepreneurs Rezner and Bohnett bought a computer for $5,000 that was capable of acting

Affiliation: GeoCities

The popularity of GeoCities was based in large part on the popularity of individual member sites. The websites that made up each city came to be known as GeoCities neighborhoods. Site owners were called homesteaders. Partly because John Rezner's cofounder, David Bohnett, is openly gay, GeoCities touted itself as offering a wide range of opportunities for members to express themselves freely.

The most popular cities were the technology-related site Silicon Valley and the entertainment-related site Hollywood. Other popular cities included Area 51, which concentrated on science fiction and fantasy, and Bourbon Street, which served as an umbrella site for jazz, Cajun food, New Orleans, and the American South in general. Many cities were issue-specific to certain topics or locales, with names such as Broadway, Capitol Hill, Sunset Strip, Wall Street, Rodeo Drive, Madison Avenue, Napa Valley (wine), Augusta (golf), and Rain Forest.

One of the most popular communities on GeoCities was Rick Brown's tribute to Monty Python, the British comedy troupe that taken on cult status. In June 1998, more than one hundred thousand visitors stopped by Brown's site to examine his collection of photographs, sound clips, scripts, and other memorabilia.

After GeoCities was purchased by Yahoo! in 1999, many homesteaders insisted that the new owner destroyed the sense of community that had been so integral to GeoCities' popularity. A number of financial analysts insisted that Yahoo! lost a major opportunity for expanding its own fortunes by failing to accommodate GeoCities' devoted members, who moved to rival sites.

To Internet historians, the early history of GeoCities is reflective of the early history of the World Wide Web. To maintain access to that history, sites such as OoCities.org, geocities.ws, and archive.org have created archives of former GeoCities websites.

as a web server. They then became partners in creating Beverly Hills Internet, a web-hosting service that took full advantage of the burgeoning interest in the World Wide Web. The site allowed members to create their own websites, providing them with the opportunity to share whatever information they wished with the rest of the world. Some people simply shared their family photographs, recipes, poetry, or opinion pieces; others shared their love of collecting or information on their interests or hobbies. Other sites were devoted to specific celebrities, figures from history, or events. Each site was loosely categorized into "cities."

Because dial-up modems were the main technology providing access to the Internet at this time, many users depended on Internet service providers (ISPs) that charged a set rate that increased if users went over their allotted plans. Uploading photographs and various other media could be a lengthy process, requiring dedication for any user interested in participating in the virtual neighborhoods of GeoCities. The quality of the pages varied greatly according to individual users' dedication and technological expertise.

Rezner and Bohnett designed GeoCities to serve as virtual cities named after their real-life counterparts, such as Silicon Valley (a gathering place for computer technology buffs) and Hollywood (a collection of sites devoted to the entertainment industry). Whenever a site

began attracting a lot of visitors, site owners responded by making their sites more elaborate, a move that generated more traffic for GeoCities.

By the beginning of 1995, with Bohnett serving as CEO and Rezner taking on responsibilities as vice president of operations and chief technology officer, GeoCities was well on its way. Rezner oversaw design and development of new products. Rezner and Bohnett added the new virtual cities of Capital Hill, Paris, and Tokyo. By that time, the GeoCities was attracting more than 6 million visitors per month. As the service grew, GeoCities added new features: bulletin boards, mailing lists, and chat rooms. The sense of community deepened, and volunteers within each community helped to keep it going by serving as block captains, heading up welcome wagons, and monitoring chat rooms. Approximately fifteen hundred volunteers donated their time to keeping communities free of pornography.

On December 6, 1995, Rezner and Bohnett officially changed the name of the new company from Beverly Hills Internet to GeoCities. Within a year, the company had moved into well-appointed offices in Santa Monica, California, and established a second office on Park Avenue in New York City. GeoCities also began attracting new investors, including Yahoo! Within three years of its founding, the web-hosting service was one of the most frequently visited sites on the Internet.

Because the basic site was free, revenue was generated not from users but from items sold through the GeoStore, where customers spent GeoCities cash to purchase a range of products related to GeoCities. More revenue was derived from creating a subscription service that offered additional features and selling advertising spots on GeoCities. The company also negotiated deals with companies such as Amazon, earning commissions from sales that originated with GeoCities. By the fall of 1997, GeoCities was reporting that it had 1 million members, and revenue had climbed to $4.6 million. The following year, revenues exploded to between $20 and $25 million.

In June 1998, GeoCities prompted an uproar when it began requiring the so-called homesteaders on its site to display a translucent watermark identifying the site as located on GeoCities. Members objected on the basis that the watermark detracted from the design of their pages and argued that it was distracting to viewers. Some GeoCities homesteaders created new sites that were devoted solely to forcing GeoCities to remove the watermark. Rick Brown, whose Monty Python tribute site was one of the most popular on GeoCities, replaced his front page with one that was all black.

In the summer of 1998, Rezner and Bohnett took GeoCities public, with stocks rising from an initial public offering (IPO) of $17 per share to $100 per share at the height of GeoCities' popularity. Since Rezner owned 826,000 shares, the IPO swelled his worth to $103 million. With 3 million shares in the company, Bohnett earned greater profits from going public, netting some $367 million.

In 1999, new headquarters were established in Los Angeles when GeoCities was at its peak. By that time, it had become the third most visited site on the Internet, outranked only by America Online and Yahoo! GeoCities recorded 3.5 million unique visitors for the year. In January, Yahoo! purchased GeoCities for $4.6 billion. Rezner left the company at that time. According to most fans and many critics, the new owner set about destroying all that had been good about GeoCities communities. One of the first moves was to change addresses of individual websites to so-called vanity addresses, with members being forced to include their Yahoo! member names in their URLs.

With Yahoo! continuing to establish new guidelines for GeoCities websites, the homesteaders that had felt a sense of community under GeoCities complained that the camaraderie had gone. As a result, they abandoned GeoCities. Yahoo! launched a layoff of GeoCities employees, with the result that decisions dealing with site operations were made by Yahoo! employees who were not always familiar with the ways in which GeoCities had operated. Those GeoCities employees who remained insisted that both entrepreneurship and innovation were being sacrificed. Over time, however, dissatisfaction with the way Yahoo! was operating GeoCities was reflected in falling numbers, with 18.9 million visitors recorded in 2006. Visitors fell to only 11.5 million recorded in 2008.

Despite GeoCities' ongoing popularity, ten years after acquiring the web-hosting service from its founders, on October 26, 2009, Yahoo! closed the site down, shutting out more than thirty-eight thousand site owners in the United States. Canadian sites were also shut down. The initial enthusiasm expressed by Yahoo!'s president, Jeff Marlett, had long since declined, and outsiders insisted that GeoCities and Yahoo! simply had distinct cultures that had never successfully merged.

By 2012, GeoCities was operational only within Japan, where it continued to thrive from its Tokyo base. Other web-hosting websites continued to offer users a way of expressing themselves, including Tripod, Angelfire, Hotmail, Switchboard, and Xoom. Many users opted for social media sites instead, drifting to Friendster, Facebook, Twitter, and Myspace.

PERSONAL LIFE

Rezner serves on the boards of companies that include the Dorado Corporation and Space4Rent.com. He lives in Manhattan Beach, California, with his wife; they have three children.

Elizabeth Rholetter Purdy

FURTHER READING

Borzykowski, Bryan. "The Ode." *Canadian Business* 82.21 (2009): n. pag. Print. Traces the history of GeoCities as Yahoo! closed it down in the United States and Canada.

Hansell, Saul. "GeoCities' Cyberworld Is Vibrant, but Can It Make Money?" *New York Times* 13 July 1998: n. pag. Print. Examination of the development of the GeoCities as it rose to popularity. Illustrated.

Mandiberg, Michael, ed. *The Social Media Reader*. New York: New York UP, 2012. Print. Provides a context for the development of social media on the Internet.

Swisher, Kara. "Tired of Tales about Quick Internet Riches? Try Sleeping on This: Those Who Tied Their Fortunes to GeoCities Yell Yahoo! All the Way to the Bank." *Wall Street Journal* 29 Jan. 1999: n. pag. Print. Examines the sale of GeoCities to Yahoo!

LARRY ROBERTS

Former chief scientist at the Advanced Research Projects Agency

Born: 1937; Westport, Connecticut
Died: -
Primary Field: Computer science
Specialty: Internet
Primary Company/Organization: Advanced Research Projects Agency

INTRODUCTION

Of all of the individuals credited as having contributed to the development of the Internet, Larry Roberts was not only present at the creation but also one of the most critical involved. His participation began with the first small-scale and primitive networks at the Massachusetts Institute of Technology's Lincoln Labs in the early to mid-1960s. His interest in and comprehension of J. C. R. Licklider's concept of an "intergalactic network" informed his eventual role as program manager responsible for all aspects of the management and design of the ARPANET. Like many early developers of ARPANET and its successor, the Internet, Roberts has remained deeply involved in making

Larry Roberts.

improvements to its capabilities in both infrastructure and the means to communicate on a daily basis. Expressing dissatisfaction with the Internet's current capabilities in regard to the demands placed on it, he has launched several companies with the intention of making improvements and has articulated a vision of how the Internet should develop in the future.

EARLY LIFE

Larry Roberts was born in Westport, Connecticut, in 1937 to Elliot and Elizabeth Roberts. Both of his parents were chemists and both had Ph.D.s. Like many innovators, to include George Stibitz and Leonard Kleinrock, Roberts from an early age loved to tinker with electronic and electrical equipment. Among his projects was a small telephone network and a working television set. These interests persisted as he began college. He entered the Massachusetts Institute of Technology (MIT) in 1955, earning his bachelor's degree in 1959, his master's in 1960, and his doctorate in 1963 with concentrations in electrical engineering. One of his classmates in the doctoral program was Kleinrock, with whom he would be involved in later years during the development of ARPANET.

In the early 1960s, Roberts read the series of memoranda written by J. C. R. Licklider that described what Licklider called an "intergalactic network." Licklider was able to envision what would eventually become ARPANET and ultimately the Internet, but his areas of technical expertise were not in fields that would allow him to design and implement it. Roberts, however, was in such a position, and after reading the memos and discussing them in depth with Licklider in November 1964, he was convinced that creating such a network could be done.

In October 1965, Roberts helped take a step toward the intergalactic network at Lincoln Labs in Massachusetts when he created the first network in which computers communicated with one another. With this working network, Roberts had begun to develop the solution to the problem of finding a way for computers to communicate. In 1966, he published a paper, "Toward a Cooperative Network of Time-Shared Computers," which not only discussed networking but also addressed another major problem. Computers were becoming more powerful but were expensive, both to acquire and to use, and since George Stibitz's computing machine had gone into operation at Bell Laboratories in 1940, they could be operated by only one person at a time. Roberts saw that this limitation could be removed by the same technology that made networking possible.

In the same year that Roberts published his paper, he began work at the Advanced Research Projects Agency (ARPA, later the Defense Advanced Research Projects Agency, or DARPA), where he would make the network a reality.

LIFE'S WORK

Roberts's first job at ARPA was as chief scientist. He was initially unwilling to work on ARPANET, being quite happy with his current position. He eventually accepted the responsibility for heading the program, however, and would not only manage all aspects of contracting and development but also design the system. In June 1967, he published the initial design paper for ARPANET: "Multiple Computer Networks and Intercomputer Communication." In August 1968, he and his staff prepared the request for proposals (RFP) that would detail the planned project and specified the technical and programmatic (including financial) requirements the winning contractor would have to meet.

Two months after the release of the RFP, Roberts contacted Leonard Kleinrock of the University of California at Los Angeles (UCLA), who headed the Network Measurement Center, there to support measurement and quality functions. In December of that year, Bolt, Beranek, and Newman of Cambridge, Massachusetts, won the contract to build the ARPANET, based on a proposal written, in large part, by Robert Kahn, whose association with ARPANET and similar ARPA projects would be of long standing.

In April 1969, Kahn submitted ARPANET's architecture specification, describing how the host computers would interface with the machines that would pass communications (interface message processors, or IMPs), to Roberts. The specification was approved by ARPA, and in September the first of what would be four nodes was installed at the UCLA Measurement Lab. In May, a second node was installed at Stanford University (which had been chosen because Douglas Engelbart, inventor of the computer mouse and hypertext, worked there). The first message to be carried on ARPANET was transmitted between these two nodes in the same month. The third and fourth nodes of ARPANET were installed in November and December. In the meantime, in addition to remaining involved with the ARPANET project, Roberts was named head of the Information Processing Techniques Office (IPTO), whose first head, Licklider, had convinced Roberts some years before about the possibilities in creating wide-ranging computer communications networks. Upon Roberts's departure, Licklider returned as head of IPTO.

Affiliation: Defense Advanced Research Projects Agency

The Defense Advanced Research Projects Agency (DARPA), originally simply the Advanced Research Projects Agency (ARPA), began in February 1958, when President Dwight Eisenhower directed its foundation. Only a few months previously, the Soviet Union had launched Sputnik, the first artificial satellite to orbit Earth. The dire possibilities envisioned by the Soviets' capability, along with the political and military tensions of the Cold War, brought an extreme sense of urgency to establish a centralized agency that would manage and fund projects capable of delivering technical solutions for the defense of the United States. The agency was extremely well funded and enjoyed few bureaucratic restrictions in the early years, when the computer research and technical programs that would culminate in ARPANET were initiated. Other projects and funding included the beginning of the Augmentation Research Center (ARC), where Douglas Engelbart would work.

DARPA's name has changed over the years: It became the Defense Advanced Research Projects Agency (DARPA) in 1972, returned to the Advanced Research Projects Agency (ARPA) in 1993, and again became DARPA in 1996. Similarly, the focus of its projects has also evolved, but DARPA remains an important agency in selecting technologies to solve the tactical and strategic problems of the day and to develop and implement solutions. In the 1970s and 1980s, command, control, and communications programs, along with tactical armor projects, lasers, and stealth technology, were very high priorities. Today, priorities focus on computers and communications and—particularly in the post-9/11 world with its concern over decentralized terrorist threats—have shifted from long-range programs to technologies that can deliver short-term results.

Roberts remained at ARPA for another four years, leaving in 1973 at a time when ARPANET had grown to twenty-three machines (although demonstrations of temporary arrangements of up to forty machines had been given). However, he continued to be actively involved in developing operational hardware and software, improving the infrastructure and shaping the way the Internet would evolve.

Roberts's first post-ARPA position was as chief executive officer (CEO) of Telenet. This carrier, which employed the packet-switching technology used by ARPANET, pioneered methods whereby computers on a network without standard hardware could communicate. That contribution was the X.25 set of protocols, which are still used today. Seven years after taking this position, Roberts left. The year before, Telenet had been purchased by GTE, and it would later become part of Sprint.

Roberts continued to be a major presence in commercial venues, developing and improving communications and networking mostly by concentrating on routers (their design and manufacture), protocols, and packet and Ethernet switches. The companies for which he worked after leaving Telenet included DHL, NetExpress, ATM Systems, Packetcom, Caspian Networks, and Anagran.

Roberts has been extremely critical of the current state of the Internet; his main concern is that it was never designed for either the volume or type of traffic that it now supports. One of his projects has been to invent a technology that would "create" the bandwidth required for specific types of communication on an as-needed basis. E-mails, for example, require substantially less than the films and videos one downloads from YouTube or other entertainment venues. Roberts has noted that the Internet was not designed for watching television and that such activity, with the amount of bandwidth it requires, is putting a strain on the Internet's infrastructure.

PERSONAL LIFE

Since the mid-1990s, as the Internet has established itself as a major and permanent presence in our lives, and widespread recognition has been conferred on Roberts. Along with his colleagues in the development of ARPANET (including Kleinrock, Kahn, and Vinton Cerf), Roberts has received many awards for his work, including the Association for Computing Machinery (ACM) Special Interest Group on Data Communication (SIG-COMM) Communications Award, the Charles Stark Draper Prize (along with his colleagues) for his contributions to the development of both ARPANET and the Internet, a Meritorious Service Medal from the U.S. Secretary of Defense, and awards from the Institute of Electrical and Electronic Engineers (IEEE). He was inducted into the Internet Hall of Fame in 2012.

Starting in 1999, Roberts became involved in the controversy surrounding the claims of Kleinrock in developing the Internet. Kleinrock, who was brought on board the ARPANET project to support measurement and quality aspects, has claimed that he essentially invented the packet-switching technology that was adopted for ARPANET. This claim has been disputed rather strongly by individuals who not only developed the theory but also actually built prototypes years before ARPANET was developed. Roberts has insisted on the validity of Kleinrock's claims, although some commentators have noted that Roberts did not assign such great importance to Kleinrock's work during the development of ARPANET.

In addition to his continuing work in developing communications, Roberts has also become involved in research to extend the typical human life span.

Robert N. Stacy

FURTHER READING

Hafner, Katie. *Where Wizards Stay Up Late: The Origins of the Internet*. New York: Simon, 1996. Print. A good general history of the development of the Internet, covering the development of protocols by Kahn and Cerf.

Mathison, Stuart, Lawrence Roberts, and Philip Walker. "The History of Telenet and the Commercialization of Packet Switching in the U.S." *IEEE Transactions on Communications* 50.5 (2012): 28–45. Print. In collaboration with others, Roberts describes how technologies developed for ARPANET were adopted for commercial venues.

Roberts, Larry. "Its Creators Call Internet Outdated, Offer Remedies." Interview by Bobby White. *Wall Street Journal* 2 Oct. 2007: n. pag. Print. An interview with Roberts in which he describes shortcomings in the current Internet and how these might be remedied.

---. "Multiple Computer Networks and Intercomputer Communication." *From Gutenberg to the Internet*. Ed. Jeremy M. Norman. Novato: Historyofscience.com, 2005. Print. Roberts's 1967 paper is included in this collection of sixty-three seminal readings in the history of computing.

Salus, Peter H. *Casting the Net: From ARPANET to Internet and Beyond*. Reading: Addison-Wesley, 1995. Print. A thorough history, beginning with the long-distance computing demonstrations at Bell Labs in the 1940s to the full implementation of the

Internet. Kahn and the importance of his work in developing protocols is discussed in detail.

MICHAEL ROBERTSON

Founder of MP3.com

Born: April 4, 1966; Orange County, California
Died: -
Primary Field: Business and commerce
Specialty: Management, executives, and investors
Primary Company/Organization: MP3.com

INTRODUCTION

Long recognized as a groundbreaking entrepreneur and a businessman with a defiant streak, Michael Robertson has pushed the boundaries of the information technology industry. Best known for his creation of MP3.com, Robertson has exhibited a willingness to test the limits of technology, business, and copyright laws, which has placed him at odds with stakeholders both inside and outside the computer industry.

EARLY LIFE

Born in Orange County, California, in 1966, Michael Robertson experienced a difficult childhood that included much financial insecurity. He nevertheless was able to graduate from the University of California at San Diego (UCSD) in 1990 with a bachelor's degree in cognitive science. As a student at UCSD, he interned at the San Diego Supercomputer Center and was involved in a research project using Apple computers.

LIFE'S WORK

After graduating from UCSD, Robertson was employed as a Macintosh technical supporter at the San Diego Super Computer Center and wrote weekly columns for *ComputerEdge* magazine. These weekly articles were for a column called "Mr. Mac" and centered on the various developments associated with the Apple Macintosh. In 1994, Robertson founded MR Mac Software, a business that focused mainly on developing computer networking. Two years later, he started Media Minds, Inc., which created software for digital photo albums. In 1996, Robertson also started a search engine called Filez, also known as Z Company. Unlike other search engines, Filez indexed file transfer protocol (FTP) servers. Users of Filez could search for nearly five thousand

files (a large number at the time) associated with movies, games, and graphics.

As Filez gained popularity, Robertson noticed that users preferred to locate audio files in the Moving Pictures Expert Group 1, Layer 3 (MP3) format. After listening to an MP3 music file, Robertson was deeply impressed with its clear sounds and quickly moved forward with a friend, Greg Flores, in securing the rights to the domain name MP3.com. Upon gaining ownership of the site in November 1997, Robertson was startled to see that nearly ten thousand people visited the site on its first day of operations.

Initially, Robertson offered information in the form of articles about MP3s. However, after receiving numerous requests about incorporating actual music files into the site, Robertson developed a format that allowed

Michael Robertson.

MP3 files to be accessed and downloaded. He began contacting emerging artists and bands that were seeking to publicize their work and offered to place their songs on the website. Within months, nearly eighteen thousand artists and one hundred thousand songs were on MP3.com, and the site had an astounding three hundred thousand visitors per day. By July 1999, the company offered the first public sale of its stock. The initial public offering (IPO) was the largest at the time.

Determined to expand his company, Robertson developed a plan whereby users could store their own music in individual music "lockers" at my.mp3.com. In order to access this service, each user had to place a personal CD in his or her computer, which would then automatically lead to a download of a digital version of the song from the MP3.com library, where eighty thousand songs were stored. The service immediately raised the ire of those in the music industry, who complained that Robertson was violating copyright laws. The five major record labels—Universal, BMG Entertainment, Sony Music Group, EMI Recorded Music, and Warner Music Group—all filed a lawsuit claiming copyright violations.

After major deliberations, on April 28, 2000, a New York State judge declared that the service offered by MP3.com was indeed in violation of copyright law. MP3.com ultimately lost $170 million in settlements with the record companies and music publishers. Robertson was forced to form licenses with the major record companies, and under these licenses royalties were properly administered. At the end of 2000, a resurrected MP3.com was launched as a subscription service for $49.95 per year. However, the company could not fully regroup from the financial losses it had suffered. In 2001, Robertson sold MP3.com to Vivendi Universal for $372 million.

Robertson soon turned toward the computer industry and started a company called Lindows. The central feature of this business was the creation of a desktop operating system that could function on both Linux and Windows platforms. Robertson hoped that this new operating system would rival Microsoft's dominant Windows. However, he once again faced scrutiny after Microsoft sued Robertson for trademark infringement. Microsoft officials believed that the name, Lindows, was too similar to the name of their established operating system, Windows. Judges in the United States supported Robertson. However, in Europe, Lindows software was banned as a result of these copyright issues. In April 2004, Robertson changed the name of Lindows to

---

Affiliation: MP3.com

Michael Robertson first became aware of a Moving Pictures Expert Group 1, Layer 3 (MP3) file while conducting data research for his search engine Filez during the mid-1990s. Upon examining the relevant statistics, he noticed that users of his search engine had a great interest in music files. After listening to an MP3 file for the first time, Robertson became fascinated with the special quality of sound. Soon afterward, he bought the domain MP3.com for $1,000 and he and business partner Greg Flores, started the company MP3.com.

This rudimentary website, which initially offered only articles on MP3 technology, quickly evolved into a domain where independent artists could offer their music to the public for free. Within months, nearly eighteen thousand artists had placed nearly one hundred thousand songs on the website. In July 1999, MP3.com mounted an initial public offering (IPO) of $28 per share, which was the largest IPO at that time. Robertson continued to consider new ways to expand his site. In early 1999, my.mp3.com was launched, allowing users with certain records to access the MP3 versions of their albums from the MP3.com audio library. This service created immediate controversy, however: Leaders in the music industry believed that copyright laws had been broken and their rights infringed with each song that was downloaded from MP3.com's library.

After a lawsuit by the five major record labels—Universal, BMG Entertainment, Sony Music Group, EMI Recorded Music, and Warner Music Group—Robertson was forced to defend his actions. In April 2000, a judge declared Robertson's actions illegal. For the remainder of the year, Robertson was forced to settle lawsuits, which cost the company nearly $170 million. Eventually, he devised a new subscription service for MP3.com that was properly licensed. However, the company would never again regain its popularity. In 2001, Robertson sold MP3.com to Vivendi Universal for $372 million.

Linspire. Although this operating system offered greater specialization and affordability, it could not firmly establish itself among the competition. In 2008, Robertson sold Linspire to Xandros, a company that specialized in Linux desktop operating systems.

Robertson has been a major player in the Internet phone service industry, also known as Voice over Internet Protocol (VoIP). In 2003, he started SIPphone, a company that sold telephones that could be used on the Internet. After receiving further funding in 2006, Robertson launched the Gizmo Project through SIPphone. The features included VoIP service and allowed users to connect with noncomputer phones. The company progressed and launched software, including Gizmo Project and Gizmo5, both of which used open standards, that is, the ability to connect with multiple networks. In 2009, Robertson sold Gizmo5 to Google for around $30 million.

In 2007, Robertson once again turned to the medium of online music. He started MP3tunes.com, which provided remote storage for songs. Subscribers could download music and then, through cloud technology, play their selections from any location. In November 2007, EMI filed a copyright suit against Robertson, claiming that MP3tunes.com was legally required to obtain licenses from record labels before allowing the storage and subsequent playback of songs. For more than four years, Robertson was forced to deal with litigation arising from this case. Faced with no clear conclusion to the case, in May 2012 MP3tunes.com filed for bankruptcy.

Robertson's other music start-up, DAR.fm, which began in 2010, has thus far escaped any lawsuits or confrontations with those in the music industry. The service is unique, allowing users to record streamlined radio shows, which can then be placed on an iPod, tablet, or smart phone.

PERSONAL LIFE

Robertson resides in San Diego and is the head of Robertson Education Empowerment Foundation, a nonprofit organization that offers students information about financial options pertaining to higher education. Since 2001, he has written a weekly electronic newsletter called "Michael's Minute," which is available on his personal website. He provides weekly commentary about the technology industry and related topics.

Gavin Wilk

FURTHER READING

Bigelow, Bruce V. "Michael Robertson on Gizmo5, and How the World Has Changed for Internet Start-ups." *Xconomy* 1 Dec. 2009. Web. 20 Aug. 2012. Describes why Robertson's start-up, Gizmo5, was sold to Google.

Borland, John. "Lindows Chief Hears Net Phones Calling." *CNet News* 6 Aug. 2003. Web. 20 Aug. 2012. A description of Robertson's move into the Internet phone service industry.

Haring, Bruce. *Beyond the Charts: MP3 and the Digital Music Revolution*. Los Angeles: JM Northern Media, 2000. Print. An in-depth look at the rise of the MP3 and the role that Robertson and MP3.com played in its evolution.

Levy, Steven. *The Perfect Thing: How the iPod Shuffles Commerce, Culture, and Coolness Millennia Makeover*. New York: Simon, 2006. Print. Examines the formation of the Apple iPod and provides a broad overview of the development of music on the Internet.

Reno, Jamie. "Michael Robertson Rolls the Dice." *San Diego Magazine* June 2000. Web. 20 Aug. 2012. Examines the controversy surrounding MP3.com, providing solid background on Robertson's early career.

Richtel, Matt. "Market Place: Will Mp3.com Soar to No. 1 with a Bullet, or Languish in the Wall St. Cut-out Bins?" *New York Times* 20 July 1999: n. pag. Print. Overview of the IPO of MP3.com.

Robertson, Michael. "Michael Robertson: Digital Music's Bad Boy Was Right." Interview by Greg Sandoval. *CNet News* 25 Aug. 2009. Web. 20 Aug. 2012. Interview with Robertson that delves into his various confrontations with the leaders of the music industry.

---. "Michael Robertson: Internationally Renowned Visionary, Technology Authority, and Entrepreneur Shares His Views." Interview by Stephen Ibaraki. n.d. *Canada's Association of I.T. Professionals*. Web. 20 Aug. 2012. Robertson covers his college studies and the creation and development of his various start-up companies.

Sandoval, Greg. "MP3tunes.com Locker Service Files for Bankruptcy (Exclusive)." *CNet News* 10 May 2012. Web. 20 Aug. 2012. Reveals the troubles that MP3tunes faced since its inception in 2007.

Stone, Brad. "Michael Robertson Bucks the Music Industry Again." *Businessweek* 23 Feb. 2011. Web. 20 Aug. 2012. Describes Robertson's development of MP3Tunes.com and DAR.FM. Provides background information on Robertson's business history.

KEVIN ROSE

Cofounder of Digg

Born: February 21, 1977; Redding, California
Died: -
Primary Field: Internet
Specialty: Social media
Primary Company/Organization: Digg

INTRODUCTION

Kevin Rose left a career in broadcasting at TechTV to cofound Digg and Revision3, a social news site and web TV developer, respectively. He oversaw Digg's most successful period, founded the short-lived but financially successful Pownce social network, and was eventually hired by Google Ventures.

EARLY LIFE

Robert Kevin Rose was born on February 21, 1977, in Redding, California, but spent most of his childhood in Las Vegas, Nevada. As a teenager, he was a computer aficionado, running a Wildcat bulletin board system (BBS) with two nodes, door games, and shareware available for downloads. He was a member of the Boy

Kevin Rose.

Scouts of America, achieving the Eagle Scout rank (an experience he later talked about on his television show *Diggnation*), and he attended a Montessori school and then a vocational-technical high school in Las Vegas. He majored in computer science at the University of Nevada Las Vegas (UNLV) but dropped out in 1988 to take a job with the Department of Energy at the Nevada Test Site. He then moved to San Francisco to work as a production assistant on the computer-centric news program *The Screen Savers* at ZDTV (later TechTV) .

LIFE'S WORK

The Screen Savers launched on May 11, 1998, the first broadcast day for ZDTV, the twenty-four-hour cable network founded by the publishing company Ziff Davis, which had begun as a publisher of magazines for hobbyists (and the fiction magazine *Amazing Stories*) but since the personal computing revolution of the late 1970s had focused mainly on computer and technology magazines. The original incarnation of *The Screen Savers* was hosted by creator Leo Laporte, who had previously hosted a show about the Internet on PBS, and television personality Kate Botello. ZDTV was acquired by CNET and renamed TechTV in 2000, and for the next few years TechTV struggled as cable provider Comcast dropped it from some of its regions to keep it from competing with the Comcast-owned G4, a cable news and entertainment network with a similar niche.

When Laporte left *The Screen Savers* in 2004 to host the new show *Call for Help*, Rose replaced him as main host. TechTV was bought out by Comcast and merged with G4, resulting in widespread layoffs and a relocation of the studios to Los Angeles. Alex Albrecht became Rose's cohost. In late 2004, an informal announcement was made that *The Screen Savers* would change its focus to pop culture for the technology community, as opposed to technology alone. The show continued under the name *The Screen Savers* until March 2005, at which point it was renamed *Attack of the Show*. Rose continued to host briefly, but on May 22, 2005, he reached an agreement with G4 to release him from his contract.

In the months before leaving G4, Rose had founded two start-ups: Digg in February and Revision3 in March. Both were collaborations with Jay Adelson, chief executive officer (CEO) of data center and Internet services company Equinix, whom Rose had met while interviewing

Affiliation: Digg

The social news site Digg was founded after Kevin Rose, host of Tech TV's *The Screen Savers* (the predecessor to G4's *Attack of the Show*) met Equinix founder Jay Adelson while interviewing him. Digg began in February 2005, with the collaboration of Adelson (the first CEO), Rose, Owen Byrne, and Ron Gorodetzky. The site's initial design was developed by Dan Ries.

Digg allows users to share and recommend content on the web, with a focus on news. Members vote on shared content, using a system familiar from Slashdot, Reddit, and other sites: A given page shared with the site may be voted up (a "digg") or voted down (a "bury"). The front page displays currently popular and trending content, which is constantly in flux as users read and respond to content and share new links. Changes to the website in the first year included adding categories for stories (technology, science, world and business, videos, entertainment, gaming), the capacity for users to build a friends list and keep track of their friends' stories, and improvements to the interface. Popularity grew steadily, and, like Slashdot, Reddit, and other sites, Digg experienced spikes in traffic resulting from a story becoming popular. One of Digg's primary merits was its ability to focus a spotlight on something on the Internet that might otherwise go unnoticed by most, so that audiences no longer had to rely as heavily on the news "curation" of traditional media.

The impact of user votes on the site inevitably led to attempts to game the system. There were several known attempts, uncovered by sting operations, to upvote stories for cash (with the implied threat of a downvote if no payment were made—a sort of protection racket). There was also the explicit, openly conducted Bury Brigade, which responded to the popularity of Ron Paul among Digg users—social news users in the United States long having included a vocal libertarian contingent—by downvoting every Paul story submitted in an attempt to bury any mention of him. Digg's popularity led to a high ranking on Google's PageRank, meaning that "digged" stories would feature prominently in Google search results—providing a clear financial motivation for abuses of the system.

Around the height of the site's fame, Google attempted to purchase Digg for $200 million but eventually walked away from the table without completing the deal. Digg was considered one of the ripest websites for purchase, and other deals were entertained, but by the end of the year, then-CEO Adelson announced that the company was not for sale. Fox News, Microsoft, and Yahoo! had been among the suitors. Over time, the shine may have left the apple, although hits remained high, with about 20 million visitors per month; Digg never developed the level of mainstream awareness that Facebook or Twitter did, and its niche competitor, Reddit, began to attract mainstream media attention because of several high-profile news stories and the celebrity involvement in AMA/IAMA threads. In 2010, the site had to lay off more than a third of its staff, and Adelson left after disagreements with Rose and others.

Google's AdSense was originally used to provide ads, the source of Digg's revenue, but in 2007 the company switched to Microsoft's ad service.

In 2012, Digg went through significant changes. Although it was widely reported that the site was sold for a paltry $500,000—an extremely low amount relative to both the market for popular websites and the previous offers that had been made—this price, paid by Betaworks, was only for the website, technology, and Digg brand. Patents developed under Adelson were sold to LinkedIn for an additional $4 million, and staff were transferred to *The Washington Post* for $12 million. The total was still a far cry from the $200 million once bandied about, but that reflected the financial realities of the intervening years as much as anything else.

On July 31, 2012, a new version of Digg launched, based in part on user surveys collected through Betaworks' RethinkDigg.com. The new site integrated better with social media (the site had been integrated with Facebook Connect since 2009 and offered an iPhone app, although a previously offered Android app was no longer available with the relaunch), featured a more image-heavy design, and was built around an editorially centered front page.

him for *The Screen Savers*. Adelson became the CEO of both Digg and Revision3, as well as chairman of Revision3's board, and acted as business mentor to the other founders while raising venture capital. Rose contributed $6,000 of start-up funds for Digg. Digg was founded as a

social news website, beginning as an experiment in late 2004 by Rose, Adelson, Owen Byrne, and Ron Gorodetzky, before the company was officially formed. The site allows registered users to submit interesting links from the web—with an intended focus on recent news—at which point other users may vote for ("digg") or against ("bury") the link, resulting in constantly changing lists of links to content, with the most popular stories becoming the most visible. Digg became popular quickly, and an early version was featured on *The Screen Savers* before Rose left the show to pursue his start-ups full time. The site was changed several times in the first two years, including a revamped interface, categories for stories, and the ability for users to maintain lists of friends. Later innovations included iPhone and Android apps and integration with Facebook through Facebook Connect.

Revision3's name referred to the first two "revisions" of the television content delivery model: broadcast and cable. Revision3, founded by Rose, Adelson, and *Screen Savers* segment producer David Prager, was established as a developer of television shows for the web, including *Diggnation*, a show much like *Screen Savers* that used stories found on Digg as discussion topics. Revision3 makes shows for a niche audience of tech and gaming fans, reflecting the general tendency of television to produce shows for smaller and smaller shares of the overall audience. Rose's *Screen Savers* cohost Albrecht soon joined Revision3 as well. Most of Revision3's shows are talk or news shows.

Jim Louderback succeeded Rose as CEO of Revision3, bringing media expertise from his stint as editor in chief of *PC Magazine*. Website redesigns followed, as well as the first shows not produced by Revision3 itself. Revision3 has begun producing shows for the sites affiliated with Gawker Media, including io9's *Screen Savers*-like show *We Come from the Future*.

Revision3 also produced *Systm*, beginning in May 2005, the day after Rose left G4. He hosted the show with Dan Huard for several episodes before it went on a temporary hiatus, returning with new hosts. Each episode of *Systm*, which varies in length, focuses on a single how-to topic, including building homemade DVRs and making homemade audio-video cable. After the 109th episode in 2009, *Systm* was folded into the tech news show *Tekzilla* (another show similar to *The Screen Savers*) and became a segment of that show.

In 2007, Rose cofounded Pownce, a social networking site, with Leah Culver and Daniel Burka, Digg's creative director. Launched invitation-only at first, Pownce received disproportionate media coverage due to Rose, the rumors that Digg was the subject of high-priced buyout offers (and the speculation that Pownce would be a similar success), and the site's similarity to Twitter, then the major social networking success story. Unlike most social networks, Pownce provided an option to purchase a "pro" account with extra features, which was a major part of its business model; in this it had more in common with LiveJournal and Flickr than Facebook or Twitter. Pownce was bought out by Six Apart, owners of Movable Type and Typepad, at the end of 2008, after less than a year of going public. It was promptly shuttered.

Although several offers were made to buy Digg, Rose and his partners accepted none of them, and a decline in revenue led to the need to lay off 37 percent of the staff in 2010. Adelson left after a disagreement. Rose ascribed Digg's relative failure—it still attracted millions of hits per month—to the popularity of Facebook and Twitter and to problems with its database system at a critical time. The company was eventually sold in several pieces—the brand and site were sold to Betaworks, much of the staff departed for *The Washington Post*, and $4 million in patents were sold to LinkedIn. Rose had resigned from Digg a year earlier, in March 2011, several months after Amazon's Matt Williams succeeded him as CEO, as he had succeeded Adelson.

Rose's first post-Digg project was Milk, a mobile app developer. In 2012, the Milk team joined Google to work on Google+, and that summer Rose left the Google+ team to work at Google Ventures.

PERSONAL LIFE

A self-described serial entrepreneur, rock climber, product builder, and tea drinker, Rose lives in San Francisco and sits on the board of the Tony Hawk Foundation. A partner at Google Ventures, he is also a fan of the Star Wars and Indiana Jones films. In 2012 he became engaged to Darya Pino, who earned a doctorate in neuroscience from the University of California at San Francisco in 2010 and blogs about food at Summer Tomato.

Bill Kte'pi

FURTHER READING

Jenkins, Henry. *Confronting the Challenges of Participatory Culture: Media Education for the 21st Century*. Cambridge: MIT, 2009. Print. Examines social media, new forms of creative expression, and their impact on media studies.

Qualman, Erik. *Socialnomics: How Social Media Transforms the Way We Live and Do Business*. New York: Wiley, 2010. Print. Discusses the impact of social media on the business world.

Sarno, David. "Digg Gets $28.7M Boost, Plans to Double Size, Go Global." *Los Angeles Times* 23 Sept. 2008. Print. Covers Digg's rise from the company's peak period.

S

SHERYL SANDBERG

Chief operating officer of Facebook

Born: August 28, 1969; Washington, D.C.
Died: -
Primary Field: Internet
Specialty: Social media
Primary Company/Organization: Facebook

INTRODUCTION

Sheryl Sandberg is credited with helping to build Google into the powerhouse it became before moving to Facebook, where she became a major force in expanding both the fortune and the user base of the social networking site. She has risen to the height of her career while raising a family and maintaining a strong base of friendships and promoting women's issues. When she left Google in 2008, her loss was considered a major setback for Google but a major victory for Mark Zuckerberg and Facebook. In 2007, Sandberg was the youngest woman to be included among Fortune*'s 50 Most Powerful Women. That year, she was ranked fifth on* Forbes*' list of 100 Most Powerful Women. She has also been named to* The Wall Street Journal*'s list of 50 Women to Watch and to* Business-week*'s 25 Most Influential People on the Web. In 2012,* Time *magazine named Sandberg to its list of 100 Most Influential People. She has served on the boards of companies and institutions that include Starbucks, the Brookings Institution, Women for Women International, V-Day, and the Ad Council.*

EARLY LIFE

Sheryl Kara Sandberg was born August 28, 1969, in Washington, D.C., while her father Joel, an ophthalmologist, was working for the National Institutes of Health.

Her mother, Adele, taught English as a second language. Sandberg has two younger siblings, David, a pediatric neurologist, and Michelle, a pediatrician. When she was two years old, the family moved to North Miami Beach.

Sandberg entered Harvard in 1987 as an economics major. Harvard helped to hone her activist inclinations, and she was particularly concerned with women's issues. One of her pet causes was encouraging other

Sheryl Sandberg.

women to major in economics and government. She wrote her undergraduate honors thesis on the correlation between domestic violence and socioeconomic status.

She graduated summa cum laude in 1991 with a bachelor of arts degree and was awarded the John H. Williams Prize for top economic student in her class. Her mentor, Lawrence Summers, became extremely important in her career, and she spent two years working with him as a research assistant while he served as a chief economist and vice president for developing economies at the World Bank. Her job responsibilities focused on issues such as leprosy, HIV/AIDS, and blindness in India. In 1993, Sandberg began graduate work at Harvard, receiving a master's of business administration with highest distinction in 1995. She then went to work as a management consultant at McKinsey and Company, a blue chip consulting firm.

LIFE'S WORK

Sandberg moved to Washington, D.C., in 1999 to serve as chief of staff for her former mentor, Summers, when he was appointed secretary of the Treasury under President Bill Clinton. She remained in that position until January 2001, when Clinton left office. At Treasury, her focus was on debt forgiveness during the economic crisis in Asia. As chief of staff, she made a particular point of visiting each undersecretary to discover what she could do to facilitate the goals of their jobs and make their professional lives easier. Sandberg gained a reputation for genuinely liking people and is considered a gracious hostess. She became well known for the parties she gave in Washington.

In 2001, Sandberg moved to California to begin working for Google, concentrating on the advertising side of the business. At the time, Google, which had been founded by Larry Page and Sergey Brin in 1998, was still a small company, with only three hundred employees. As the vice president of Global Online Sales and Operations, Sandberg was a major player in Google's rise to the top. She was responsible for advertising, publishing, and consumer sales and for sales related to Google Books Search. She was also closely involved in establishing Google's philanthropic arm, which was created by earmarking 1 percent of equity and 1 percent of profits for Google.org, which focuses on issues such as global warming, poverty, pandemic disease, and drought. In 2005, Sandberg helped to set up a system for awarding grants to individuals and groups working on these issues. By the time she left the company, she was a millionaire.

By 2007, Sandberg was looking for a job change, either within Google or with another company. She met Facebook's Mark Zuckerberg at a Christmas party given by Silicon Valley executive Dan Rosensweig. At the time, Zuckerberg was only twenty-four years old, and he recognized the need to bring in someone with more experience than he had. However, he was being careful about the kind of person he brought in. Zuckerberg had pledged to keep Facebook free for users, and the company was spending more money than it was bringing in. He wanted someone who shared his goals for the company but who could also make the company profitable. Zuckerberg and Sandberg began a series of lengthy meetings in restaurants and in her home. When she announced that she had decided to leave Google for Facebook, which had only 130 employees at the time, there was widespread surprise.

Sandberg came to Facebook as the chief operating officer, outranked only by Zuckerberg as cofounder and chief executive officer (CEO). With the goal of raising Facebook profits, Sandberg was put in charge of advertising and sales. Under her leadership, advertising became Facebook's chief source of revenue. Her responsibilities also included business development, human resources, communication, and public policy. Facebook began placing ads that run alongside user pages, encouraging users to click on particular products. Whenever a user "likes" a company or a product, that action is posted on the user's newsfeed, serving as an advertisement to friends and family or to anyone who has access to the user's profile page. The site also began selling virtual birthday cards.

As Facebook advertising skyrocketed, companies flocked to the site, with the number of advertisers tripling between 2008 and 2009. A study conducted by National Advertisers revealed that 66 percent of advertisers were marketing their products on social media sites, with the majority of them choosing to do so on Facebook. In 2009, Sandberg led Facebook into selling Facebook credits that could be used to purchase virtual items in games such as Zynga's ever-popular FarmVille.

Once Sandberg was on board, Zuckerberg left for a monthlong vacation, allowing her free rein. She won over most employees by demonstrating that her advertising model works. As a boss, she is generous with praise, and she saves criticisms for one-on-one meetings with employees. By 2010, with one-third of all Internet display advertising appearing on Facebook, sales had climbed to $2 billion and were expected to double in 2011.

Affiliation: Facebook

When Sheryl Sandberg joined Facebook in 2008, the company had 66 million users around the globe. Half of those users fell into the target advertising age range of eighteen to twenty-five. Sandberg was charged with growing profits while maintaining the atmosphere of Facebook's early days. That atmosphere had been maintained in large part by keeping the total number of employees small. By 2011, Sandberg had helped to grow Facebook's user base to 640 million and its employee base to 2,500.

Privacy is an ongoing issue on Facebook, and Sandberg has been at the forefront of protecting the rights of users. While users do have to check their privacy settings frequently, Facebook gives them much more control of their information than do most Internet sites. The site allows users to create groups of selected "friends," with information posted to those groups restricted to members approved by group administrators.

In 2009, Facebook faced a hailstorm of criticism when new privacy settings were instituted, setting the default at "everyone" having the ability to access information. As users learned about the new setting, they posted information about protecting privacy on their newsfeeds, urging their friends to change their settings. A number of organizations concerned about the threat to privacy filed a suit with the Federal Trade Commission (FTC).

In 2010, Facebook received new criticism when the site introduced "instant personalization," which allowed other websites to tailor their sites to information publicly available about Facebook users. Again, users were given the choice of opting out of the feature. The FTC launched a new investigation, leading Facebook to announce that any future changes concerning access to information would require user permission.

Sandberg and Zuckerberg have continued to work well together. While he allows her a great deal of autonomy, he does not intend to lose control of his company. Sandberg is much more conscious than Zuckerberg of the right of Facebook users to control access to their own information. When Facebook went public in 2012, she became a billionaire.

PERSONAL LIFE

Sandberg's first marriage, to businessman Brian Kraff, ended in divorce. In 2004, Sandberg married Dave Goldberg, a former executive of Yahoo! and a cofounder of Launch Music. The wedding took place at Boulders Resort in Carefree, Arizona, with Rabbi Jay Moses officiating. Goldberg became the CEO of SurveyMonkey. The couple has two children, a son born in 2005 and a daughter born in 2007.

Sandberg continues to host parties similar to those she gave in Washington. She has also managed to combine her love of entertaining with her passion for women's issues. She regularly entertains the Women of Silicon Valley, a group of women that includes doctors and teachers as well as technology wizards. Actor Geena Davis, tennis legend Billie Jean King, media mogul Rupert Murdock, business executive Meg Whitman, Senator Kirsten Gillibrand, former secretary of the Treasury Robert Rubin, and Cambodian activist Somaly Mam have all been guest speakers. A benefit that Sandberg sponsored for Mam's work raised more than $1 million. When Sandberg attends the 2012 World Economic Forum in Davos, Switzerland, she was the only woman on the board. Women in the audience, however, included heads of state and chiefs of international organizations.

2012, Sandberg unwittingly became the center of a debate on women executives when Eric Johnson of Forbes.com published the article "Sheryl Sandberg Is the Valley's It Girl—Just Like Kim Polese Once Was" (May 24, 2012). Polese, a Silicon Valley entrepreneur who cofounded the software company Marimba, fired back via an article by Caroline Howard ("Kim Polese: Stop Comparing Female Executives and Just Let Sheryl Sandberg Do Her Job," Forbes.com, May 25, 2012). Polese accused Johnson of expressing outmoded views on the roles of women. Amid protests, the article was pulled. The reason that Sandberg has been so successful at Facebook, in Polese's view, is simply that she does her job well.

Elizabeth Rholetter Purdy

FURTHER READING

Andrews, Lori B. *I Know Who You Are and I Saw What You Did*. New York: Free Press, 2011. Print. Detailed examination of the privacy issue on Facebook and other social network sites. Includes illustrations and Index.

Auletta, Ken. "A Woman's Place." *New Yorker* 11 July 2011. Print. Profile of Sandberg and her impact on Facebook. Illustrated.

"Facebook Growing Up Fast." *San Jose Mercury News* 25 Oct. 2007. Print. A brief look at the history of Facebook.

Kirkpatrick, David. *The Facebook Effect: The Inside Story of the Company that Is Connecting the World.* New York: Simon, 2010. Print. Traces the history of Facebook and its founders. Includes notes, index, and illustrations.

Rushe, Dominic. "Sheryl Sandberg: The First Lady of Facebook Takes the World Stage." *The Guardian* 24 Jan. 2012. Print. An excellent profile of Sandberg with a brief biography and a focus on her professional accomplishments. Illustrated.

Stone, Brad. "Everybody Needs a Sheryl Sandberg." *Businessweek* 44.29 (2011): 50–58. Print. Profile of Sandberg and her roles at Google and Facebook. Illustrated.

LARRY SANGER

Cofounder of Wikipedia

Born: July 16, 1968; Bellevue, Washington
Died: -
Primary Field: Internet
Specialty: Content and data
Primary Company/Organization: Wikipedia

INTRODUCTION

Larry Sanger is an American philosophy professor best known as the cofounder of Wikipedia. It was Sanger who gave the online, collaboratively written encyclopedia its name, combining the term wiki, *which denoted the server software that allowed users to create and edit web page content on any browser, with* pedia, *a root of* encyclopedia, *meaning "education." He was responsible for the day-to-day oversight of Wikipedia until he left the project in 2002 and became a vocal critic of the open source encyclopedia in the years after he severed his connection with the group. Later, he founded Citizendium, another wiki encyclopedia project more strictly regulated and edited than Wikipedia. Sanger also served as executive director of WatchKnowLearn.org, a directory of free educational videos for students in grades 1 through 12.*

EARLY LIFE

Lawrence Mark Sanger was born July 16, 1968, in Bellevue, Washington, a suburb of Seattle. His parents, a marine biologist and a homemaker, moved the family to Anchorage, Alaska, when Sanger was seven. A bookish teen and an excellent student, he was also a debate champion. Other early interests included the piano, cross-country running, and skiing. He was also a Dungeons and Dragons player and enjoyed tinkering with computers. He coded a text-based adventure game in BASIC, the first popular programming language. A mild hearing loss from the age of eight heightened a tendency toward introspection. Growing up in the Lutheran Church, he wandered about the distinctions among body, soul, and spirit but found the orthodoxy of his parents' responses to his questions unsatisfactory. Pondering existence led him to the work of René Descartes, in which he found a model.

After graduating from high school in 1986, he enrolled in Reed College, a liberal arts college in Portland, Oregon, known for its rigorous academic program and its independent study. He graduated from Reed in 1991 with a bachelor's degree in philosophy. A fascination

Larry Sanger.

with epistemology led him to enroll in graduate school at Ohio State University, where he received his master's degree in philosophy in 1995 and a Ph.D. in the same field in 2000. In the late 1990s, Sanger developed an interest in the year 2000 (or Y2K) "millennium bug" and the pervasive fears concerning computer crashes (which some foresaw resulting from programming codes that stored dates using two digits for the year) as the twentieth century changed to the twenty-first. He created a digest of news reports relating to the issue, "Sanger's Review of Y2K News Reports," that garnered attention among Y2K experts. His success with this project led him to consider careers beyond academia.

LIFE'S WORK

In January 2000, Sanger sent a business proposal for a cultural news blog to Jimmy Wales, the creator of Bomis, a dot-com company that created and hosted web rings designed to appeal to male users. Wales had for several months been considering an online encyclopedia created by volunteers. He even had a name for the project, Nupedia, and he was looking for someone who had both academic credentials and computer expertise to run it. Sanger's proposal was timely. With funding from Bomis, Wales started Nupedia and hired Sanger as editor in chief. In February, Sanger moved to San Diego, where Bomis was based. Sanger made clear that Nupedia was to be an open encyclopedia, welcoming all contributors and available to anyone, but he left the details to Sanger. Sanger drew from his academic experience to plan an encyclopedia shaped by experts, a few who would make up a guiding board and many others who would use their expertise to write articles that they submitted for peer review.

On March 9, Nupedia went online. Although there was no shortage of experts volunteering to write articles, the process made haste impossible. Nupedia had been operating for seven months by the time the first article, an entry on atonality by German music scholar Christoph Hust, was approved. Fortuitously, a couple of months before the encyclopedia's first anniversary, Sanger had dinner with an old friend, Ben Kovitz, who told him about a program called WikiWikiWeb, which simplified collaboration because it allowed anyone to edit any page at any time. Sanger saw the possibilities, especially the ability for many people to work on a page without the delays that were making it difficult to grow Nupedia. A few days later, Sanger invited Nupedia's volunteers to make a wiki. The group's first wiki went online on January 10, 2001. The intention was that the

wiki be a means of collaborating on peer reviews for Nupedia, but some of the experts were skeptical about the value of the wiki. On January 15, the wiki was named Wikipedia and began operating under a separate domain. Within a few days, the number of articles on Wikipedia exceeded those on Nupedia, in quantity at least.

By October 2001, Wikipedia had thirteen thousand articles. Some were written by Nupedia's expert volunteers, but many were not. Vandalism and dogmatism were increasing. Sanger as Nupedia's editor in chief had the authority to settle disputes and enforce standards, but, by his own choice, he was head organizer for Wikipedia with none of chief's status. The vandalism could be dealt with, but Sanger was ill-equipped to manage contributors who posted erroneous information, who used the site to argue a point of view, or who delighted in acrimonious exchanges with other contributors or even Sanger himself. The larger the site grew, the larger the problems loomed from Sanger's perspective. The growth was undeniable. In its first year, Wikipedia included twenty thousand articles and eighteen languages. Nupedia had lost momentum, and Wales's attempt to calm troubled waters, by addressing the Wikipedia community via his role as moderator of the discussion list, indicated that he and Sanger were not in agreement regarding openness and authority. In December 2001, Wales, whose company had suffered when the dot-com bubble burst, used financial reverses as the reason for cutting staff and dismissed Sanger. Although Sanger continued as a Wikipedia volunteer for a few months longer, he soon despaired of finding support for his belief that articles should be approved by experts. In January 2003, he cut all ties with Wikipedia and returned to teaching philosophy.

His conviction that Wikipedia needed experts was undiminished, however. In December 2004, Sanger wrote an essay, "Why Wikipedia Must Jettison Its Anti-Elitism," explaining why experts were necessary for Wikipedia to be perceived as a credible source by "librarians, teachers, and academics." Sanger's argument gained force in September 2005 when seventy-eight-year-old John Seigenthaler, a retired journalist who founded the Freedom Forum First Amendment Center at Vanderbilt University, discovered that a false biography that identified him as a suspect in the assassinations of John and Robert Kennedy had been on Wikipedia since late May. A correct version of Seigenthaler's biography was posted on September 23, but the malicious biography was not deleted until October 7. Seigenthaler's account of the incident appeared November 29 in an editorial he wrote for USA Today. Sanger, who was contacted by Seigenthaler, wrote and spoke about his hope that the incident would pressure Wikipedia to address its problems. In September 2006, he chose a more active response and founded Citizendium, an alternative to Wikipedia that rejects anonymous contributions and develops "expert-approved" articles by those who have credentials to perform as editors. Citizendium's charter (on its website) defines the latter as "citizens whose expertise in some field of knowledge is recognized and formally acknowledged by the community. Official recognition of expertise—obtained through education or experience—and its scope shall be based on guidelines established by the Editorial Council."

PERSONAL LIFE

Sanger left his job at the Digital Universe Foundation, where he had been working on other open content projects, and started Citizendium as a pilot project October 17, 2006. Citizendium began as a fork of Wikipedia, but in 2007 it deleted imported Wikipedia articles that had not yet been modified. By late January 2007, the project more than five hundred individually screened people had volunteered to work as authors and editors, and the site opened to public participation. The project had 16,270 articles by August 2012, but only 164 had passed the peer review process to earn the "approved" designation. Sanger discovered that academics were no less prone to disagreements than the larger, less credentialed population. Arguments over the charter resulted in a board half the size of the original, and clashes over esoteric points of diction and grammar can delay approval of articles indefinitely. The rate of new articles per day declined from a high of thirty in 2009 to two in 2011.

In 2009, Sanger began devoting most of his attention to a new job. He was hired by the Community Foundation of Northwest Mississippi and its president, Tom Pittman, to plan a new, nonprofit educational video service, WatchKnowLearn, funded by a Tennessee philanthropist. Sanger served as executive director of the project, originally called WatchKnow. The website, which both aggregated and organized videos on the web and invited users to upload original content, launched in a beta version the fall of 2008. It was decided to defer the official launch for additional testing. In November 2009, after Sanger teamed with a web development firm and a graphic design company, the website launched with a new name, WatchKnowLearn, with more than

---

Affiliation: Wikipedia

Wikipedia is, as its tagline famously boasts, "the free encyclopedia that anyone can edit." Founded in 2001 by Jimmy Wales and Larry Sanger, the project began as Nupedia, an open source, online version of the traditional encyclopedia written by experts and vetted by other experts. However, when Sanger, whom owner Wales had hired as editor in chief, was introduced to Ward Cunningham's new wiki software, technology that allowed collaborative, real-time editing, the site quickly grew beyond all expectations.

Within less than a week of adding the wiki software, Wikipedia was operating under its own domain name, and by the end of 2001, it consisted of more than twenty thousand articles in eighteen languages. As of February 2012, Wikipedia's had become the sixth most popular site on the web, and in August its own article page on its statistics boasted 10.6 million articles, 400,000 editors, contributions in 250 languages, and 2,500 views per second. The average volunteer was in the mid-twenties, and less than fifteen percent were women.

Since 2003, the various national Wikipedias, along with such projects as Wiktionary, a free collaborative dictionary (one for each Wikipedia), and the Wikimedia Commons, a database of more than 13 million freely usable media files, have been controlled and operated by the Wikimedia Foundation, a nonprofit based in San Francisco. Wales is one of the directors and the public face of Wikipedia. Sanger, who was dismissed by Wales in 2002, is a vocal critic of the site.

Sanger is not alone in his criticism. Charges of inaccuracy and irresponsibility have been leveled frequently at the site. Wikipedia has responded by barring anonymous users from creating new articles and by requiring attribution for facts. More recently, the site has implemented a flagged revision system that requires articles about living persons to be cleared by a trusted editor before they are released to the public.

---

ten thousand videos and more than two thousand categories. A year later, the directory included more than twenty thousand videos and added four part-time editors to its staff. Sanger left the project in the summer of 2010 to work on special projects.

Wylene Rholetter

FURTHER READING

Lapp, Alison. "Wikipedia's Opponent." *PC Magazine* 22 May 2007: 19. Print. The article reports on Sanger's launch of Citizendium as a rival to Wikipedia. It notes that while Sanger's new site follows the Wikipedia model, it has implemented an expert review process and requires contributors to provide real names and sign an agreement that they will abide by certain rules.

Lih, Andrew. *The Wikipedia Revolution: How a Bunch of Nobodies Created the World's Greatest Encyclopedia.* New York: Hyperion, 2009. Print. The author, a veteran Wikipedian, journalist, and academic, covers the history of Wikipedia from early influences on its original owner to the site's origin in the peer-reviewed Nupedia championed by Larry Sanger to the in-fighting and external critics. He sees Wikipedia's importance as more cultural than technical.

Poe, Marshall. "The Hive." *Atlantic Monthly* Sept. 2006: 86–94. Print. The article takes a comprehensive look at Wikipedia, including its history, its development, and its growth. It also profiles cofounders Jimmy Wales and Larry Sanger and reports on the criticism the encyclopedia has faced. Includes one color photograph and six charts.

Reagle, Joseph Michael. *Good Faith Collaboration: The Culture of Wikipedia.* Cambridge: MIT, 2010. Print. The book places Wikipedia in the context of other efforts, also fired by new technology, to create a freely shared, universal encyclopedia and analyzes the "good faith collaboration" the author views as Wikipedia's defining characteristic.

Roush, Wade. "Larry Sanger's Knowledge Free-for-All: Can One Balance Anarchy and Accuracy?" *Technology Review* Jan. 2005: 21. Print. The article includes biographical information on Sanger and reports on the interests and experiences that led to his role as cofounder of Wikipedia. It also relates Sanger's ideas on the neutral point of view. Includes one color photograph.

EDUARDO SAVERIN

Cofounder of Facebook

Born: March 13, 1982; São Paulo, Brazil
Died: -
Primary Field: Internet
Specialty: Social media
Primary Company/Organization: Facebook

INTRODUCTION

Eduardo Saverin, born to a wealthy Jewish family in Brazil and raised in the United States from age thirteen, is best known as the cocreator, with Mark Zuckerberg, of Facebook (dramatized in the 2010 feature film The Social Network *with Andrew Garfield as Saverin). Saverin was friends with Zuckerberg when they were both students at Harvard University, and he was the first investor in Facebook; he later sued Zuckerberg. Saverin has more recently invested in other technology start-ups, including Qwiki and Jumio. His decision to renounce his U.S. citizenship (he remains a citizen of Brazil) and take up residence in Singapore before Facebook's initial public offering (IPO) attracted public scrutiny, many charging that the move was designed to avoid paying U.S. taxes (Singapore has no capital gains tax), but Saverin insists the move was motivated only by his desire to live and work in Singapore.*

EARLY LIFE

Eduardo Saverin was born in São Paulo, Brazil, the third child of Roberto and Sandra Saverin; later his family moved to Rio de Janeiro. His father was an industrialist whose business endeavors included clothing, shipping, export, and real estate; his mother was a psychologist. In the early 1990s, Roberto decided to fulfill a dream and move his family to Miami, Florida, a popular destination for Brazilians. Contrary to rumor, the impetus for the move was Brazil's economic situation and its president's move to freeze savings accounts; it was a year after the family had left Brazil that Roberto learned that his father, Eugênio, was on a list of individuals to be kidnapped for ransom. Today Roberto heads a Miami business that exports pharmaceuticals.

Eduardo had to learn English and how to fit into a new society just as he was starting adolescence. Although he was not a computer nerd, this experience of being an outsider has been hypothesized to have helped him understand the motivations of computer geeks such as Zuckerberg. He attended Gulliver Preparatory School in Miami and became an American citizen at age eighteen. Saverin graduated magna cum laude from Harvard University with a bachelor's degree in economics in 2006. While at Harvard, he was a member of the Phoenix S.K. Club, a finals club founded in 1902, and was president of the Harvard Investment Association. Saverin was also known as an expert chess player and was a member of the Jewish fraternity Alpha Epsilon Pi, as was Zuckerberg.

LIFE'S WORK

Zuckerberg and Saverin met during their freshman year at Harvard. They created thefacebook. the forerunner to Facebook, working from their dormitory. Zuckerman was the technical expert and programmer, while Saverin managed the service as well as providing the initial financial investment, handling the incorporation process, and managing the advertising and business end of the operation. Saverin and Zuckerberg registered thefacebook in Florida on April 13, 2003, as a limited liability corporation; the company partners were Zuckerberg, Saverin, and Dustin Moskovitz. On the online "about" page for thefacebook they gave themselves humorous titles: Zuckerman was "Founder, Master and

Eduardo Saverin.

Commander, Enemy of the State," Saverin was in charge of "Business Stuff, Corporate Stuff, Brazilian Affairs" and Moskovitz was "No Longer Expendable Programmer, Paid Assassin."

Although thefacebook was producing almost no revenue, the rapidly increasing popularity of the service (by June 2004, it had almost 100,000 users at thirty-four schools) attracted the attention of investors; despite the fact that the company was producing no significant revenue at this point, in June 2004 Zuckerberg was offered $10 million for it. One of the first advertisers on thefacebook was the credit card company MasterCard, and the ads proved immediately successful: The company received twice as many applicants in one day as had been expected for four months, demonstrating thefacebook's ability to get ads in front of well-off undergraduates at prestigious schools.

In the summer of 2004, Saverin took a summer internship at an investment bank in New York City, while Zuckerberg went to California to work on thefacebook and a new project, Wirehog. Saverin also intended to solicit more advertising for thefacebook, reasoning that many of the logical companies to approach were located in New York. At this point, both Saverin and Zuckerberg also agreed to invest $20,000 in Facebook, although Saverin would later charge that Zuckerberg did not live up to his end of the bargain. The money was needed to buy servers and other equipment and to support the programming team; while in California, Zuckerberg rented a house in Palo Alto and worked on Facebook, assisted by Moskovitz and several interns. Those involved recall it as an intensive, work-focused experience, with most time spent writing code, punctuated by music, beer, and horseplay. During this summer, Sean Parker (cofounder of Napster) became interested in Facebook and introduced Zuckerberg to potential venture capitalist investors.

In July 2004, Zuckerberg and Saverin had a dispute, the details of which are not entirely clear. Saverin felt he was being muscled out of the company, despite his dedication to producing revenues for it, while Zuckerberg and the other programmers felt Saverin was not working nearly as hard as they were. Parker led the effort to reincorporate the company in Delaware, and, according to legal filings, Zuckerberg informed Saverin that he (Saverin) was no longer an employee of the company and that his stock was subject to dilution (meaning that Saverin's share of the company would decline when more stock was issued through employee stock options and when new investors bought into the company). In the newly reincorporated company, Zuckerberg owned 51 percent, Saverin 34.4 percent, Moskovitz 6.81 percent, Parker 6.47 percent, and the law firm handling the deal the remaining shares. In response, Saverin froze the company's Florida bank account; Zuckerberg drew on his savings and contributions from his parents to buy needed equipment and keep the Palo Alto house running.

By December 2004, Facebook had 1 million users—a remarkable achievement for a company that had been in business less than a year. In January 2005, Parker was appointed president of Facebook; he resigned in October. Also in 2005, Facebook started allowing high school students to join, and soon it had 5.5 million users.

In September 2011, Saverin filed papers to renounce his U.S. citizenship, but the information did not become widely known until the U.S. Internal Revenue Service released it on April 30, 2012. This choice was highly criticized in the media, which charged that he had made this choice in order to avoid paying taxes in the country (the United States) that had allowed him to become prosperous. However, Saverin stated that he had already been living in Singapore for some time and that the location was also convenient because he would be investing in Asian companies. Saverin's stake in Facebook was first revealed publicly on May 18, 2012, in a filing by the U.S. Securities and Exchange Commission (SEC). The filing revealed that Saverin owned just under 2 percent of Facebook shares, worth about $2.2 billion; Saverin had previously sold off more than half his shares from the settlement of his lawsuit against Facebook. All Saverin's shares are Class A stock, giving him virtually no actual control over the company (Class A shares have one-tenth the voting rights of Class B shares).

PERSONAL LIFE

Saverin has been described as shy but strong willed. When he was thirteen, he beat a chess master during a match in Orlando, Florida—a feat so unusual that it earned him his first mention in international news. Before making his final move, he turned to his mother and asked, "Do you think it's all right if I win?" Since 2009, Saverin's home and work base has been a multimillion-dollar condo in

---

Affiliation: Facebook

Eduardo Saverin was a cocreator of thefacebook as well as its initial investor and manager; this social media tool was the precursor to Facebook. As of 2010, an estimated 70 million people logged onto Facebook on any given day, and about 150,000 new members join every day. People use Facebook to share information about themselves with their friends, and the company makes money by mining that information and selling it to advertisers.

The germ of the idea that became Facebook was called "Harvard Face Mash" and was based on the dormitory facebooks already available at Harvard. At about the same time, another Harvard student, Divya Narendra, had the idea for a Harvard social network and shared his idea with Tyler and Cameron Winklevoss. The three contacted Mark Zuckerberg about doing the programming for a site, which they called "Harvard Connection," that would allow students to post pictures and social information and would be searchable.

Thefacebook was launched on February 4, 2003, and more than four thousand people joined it in the first two weeks. Dustin Moskovitz was brought on to help with programming, and the company expanded to a few more elite colleges, including Yale, Columbia, and Stanford. Although rival social networks already existed on some of these campuses (such as Club Nexus at Stanford and CUCommunity at Columbia), thefacebook proved quite popular. The founders filed letters of incorporation for Facebook; Zuckerberg owned 65 percent of it, Saverin 30 percent, and Moskovitz 5 percent. By the end of the Harvard spring term, Facebook had more than 200,000 users nationwide; notably, an e-mail address from one of a select list of elite colleges was required to join, setting Facebook apart from rivals such as Friendster and Myspace.

Facebook was not the first social networking site launched at Harvard. Aaron Greenspan had created a networking portal allowing Harvard students to post personal information, but it was criticized as an invasion of privacy and Greenspan shut it down. In September 2003, he launched a revised version of this portal, with a section called TheFaceBook; however, the site was not popular. He and Zuckerberg had multiple communications over the next few months, and eventually Greenspan asked for a job on Zuckerberg's site, only to be refused because he lacked technical experience.

Singapore. He relies on his iPhone, iPad, and three Macs to stay connected with the rest of the world. One of the Macs continually displays weather information on hurricanes and tsunamis. Since witnessing the devastation wrought by Hurricane Andrew in Florida, Saverin has been fascinated by the big storms.

When asked in 2012 about his current investments, Saverin said he was investing "like a crazy person, mostly in Internet start-ups." He believes that a Facebook-like enterprise involving health care will emerge sometime in the future. As of July 2012, Saverin's net worth was estimated at $2.2 billion (U.S. dollars), making him the eighth-richest person in Singapore.

Sarah Boslaugh

FURTHER READING

Hoffman, Claire. "The Battle for Facebook." *Rolling Stone* 1055 (2008): 64–71. Print. Describes the creation of Facebook, with emphasis on disputes over the origins of the idea of a social networking site and the lawsuits filed against Zuckerberg by those who believe they deserve a larger share in Facebook.

Kirkpatrick, David. *The Facebook Effect: The Inside Story of the Company That Is Connecting the World*. New York: Simon, 2011. Print. A clearly written and straightforward history of Facebook, from its origins as Facemash to its worldwide success; the author is a journalist who has written for *Fortune* magazine, and the book was written with the cooperation of Facebook executives.

Mezrich, Ben. *The Accidental Billionaires: The Founding of Facebook; A Tale of Sex, Money, Genius, and Betrayal*. New York: Doubleday, 2009. Print. A popular account of the events leading up to the creation of Facebook, concentrating on the years 2003n}05 and the central "characters": Mark Zuckerberg, Saverin, Parker, and Tyler and Cameron Winklevoss. Mezrich's account of these events is notable for its dramatic retelling of incidents, based on interviews and other sources of information. However, some have called into question the accuracy of the account (which formed the basis for the film *The Social Network*).

Saverin, Eduardo."Eduardo Saverin Finally Opens Up: 'No Hard Feeling Between Me and Mark Zuckerberg.'" Interview by Anderson Antunes. *Forbes* 27 May 2012. Web. 6 Aug. 2012. A candid interview with Saverin in which he looks back on his Facebook involvement and discusses current projects.

Schermerhorn, John R. *Organizational Behavior*. 12th ed. Hoboken: Wiley, 2011. Print. A well-regarded textbook used in business schools. Includes an analysis of the story of Saverin, Zuckerberg, and Facebook as an example of philosophical and stylistic differences that can lead to conflict and eventually the dissolution of a business relationship.

MARC SERIFF

Cofounder of America Online

Born: May 5, 1948; Austin, Texas
Died: -
Primary Field: Internet
Specialty: Content and data
Primary Company/Organization: America Online

INTRODUCTION

American Internet executive Marc Seriff is known for his technical, entrepreneurial, and investment knowledge and experience with Internet-based start-up companies (commonly known as dot-coms). He was an early employee of the data communications company Telenet Communications, Inc., joining the company in 1974 and helping to develop the first commercially available e-mail. He then worked at several start-up companies, including Digital Music, where in 1981 he helped develop the first downloading service for music. Seriff's most notable achievement was the 1985 cofounding of the Internet service provider Quantum Computer Services with Jim Kimsey and Steve Case. The company was renamed America Online, Inc. (AOL) in 1991. Seriff served as the company's first chief technical officer. After retiring from America Online in 1996, Seriff and his wife returned to his home state of Texas, where they became active in the local Austin nonprofit community. He has also remained active in the entrepreneurial and investment communities both within and outside the greater Austin area and sits on several boards of directors. He joined Austin-based G-51 Capital Management as an adviser in 2011.

EARLY LIFE

Marc S. Seriff was born May 5, 1948, in Austin, Texas. He graduated from the University of Texas at Austin with a bachelor of science degree in mathematics and computer science in 1971. He then earned his master's in electrical engineering and computer science from the Massachusetts Institute of Technology (MIT) in 1974. Seriff's education provided him with the business and technological skills that would define his career path.

Seriff was among the first to be employed at the start-up Internet service provider (ISP) Telenet Communications, Inc., which had been established by the firm Bolt, Beranek, and Newman (BBN). He joined the new company after graduating from MIT. The company offered the first commercially available packet-switched network. While at Telenet, Seriff was a member of the team that developed the first commercially available e-mail. Telenet would later be acquired by and Sprint.

Seriff acquired his interest in the Internet-based business world while at graduate school and during his time at Telenet. He has cited both J. C. R. Licklider (one of his graduate professors at MIT) and Larry Roberts (a former boss at Telenet) as key influences on his business career. His role with Telenet, at the time one of the trend-setting online data communications companies, also played a vital role in establishing his career path as an Internet executive in the exploding dot-com industry centered in Silicon Valley.

LIFE'S WORK

Seriff used his experience with Telenet to launch his executive career. He found executive opportunities at several dot-com companies, including Venture Technology, Control Video Corp., GTE Corp., and Digital Music, Inc. While employed with Digital Music, he was among the developers of the first online service allowing the downloading of music from the Internet, which debuted in 1981. He has also served as director of InteliHome from 1997 to 1998, director of U.S. Online Communications, and chief executive officer (CEO) of Eos Management, LLC.

Seriff is best known as a cofounder of America Online and an executive with the company for almost a dozen years. America Online (AOL) began its corporate existence in 1985 as Quantum Computer Services, founded by Internet entrepreneurs Steve Case and Jim Kimsey as an Internet service provider (ISP) for Commodore computer users and headquartered in Dulles, Virginia. The new company's customer base soon expanded to include users of the computers produced by

Marc Seriff.

Apple Computer, Tandy Corporation, and International Business Machines (IBM). Quantum began to develop the software required to use its Internet services. Seriff's technical knowledge contributed to America Online's improvement of these products and hence the company's expansion.

Quantum Computer Services changed its name to America Online in 1991, quickly becoming known by its initials, AOL. The company also underwent a leadership change that year. Founding CEO Kimsey became chairman, while Case began his long-standing term as CEO. Seriff was the start-up company's founding chief technical officer. He later served as senior vice president, a position he held until his 1996 retirement from the company. Seriff's responsibilities involved both the technological and business aspects of the company, which would emerge as one of the dot-com era's most successful providers of Internet services and technologies.

During Seriff's tenure at America Online, the company's subscriber base grew to approximately 6 million members, eclipsing competitors such as Prodigy and CompuServe. America Online would later acquire CompuServe. New CEO Case built the company's membership through a marketing strategy centered on low prices and the mass mailing of software (on a CD-ROM) that lured customers with a free trial membership and immediate access. America Online also overcame early financial difficulties and went public in 1992, raising $66 million during its initial public offering (IPO). The start-up company had originally been funded with venture capital.

America Online had started as a closed network, meaning that subscribers received access only to the online content provided through AOL's business partnerships rather than open access to the larger World Wide Web. Successful product introductions and offering expansions during Seriff's tenure included new content providers and content access, greater World Wide Web

access, a flat-rate monthly subscription service, and improved customer support services. "You've got mail," an audible recording that alerted users to new e-mail messages, became a catchphrase commonly associated with AOL.

Seriff helped foster and sustain the company's business partnerships, a key part CEO Case's growth strategy. Company acquisitions during this period included Advanced Network Services, BookLink Technologies, and the Global Network Navigator. In 1996, agreements with Netscape and Microsoft provided America Online subscribers with access to those companies' popular Internet browsers. America Online continued its growth and profitability after Seriff's 1996 retirement, acquiring new companies and market capital infusions and expanding into new online markets such as e-commerce, instant messaging, and mobile communications. In one of the most celebrated mergers of the era, the company joined with Time Warner to form AOL Time Warner in 2001. America Online became a wholly owned subsidiary of the new parent company. Seriff has received recognition for the vital role he played in setting the foundation for the company's ongoing success.

Since his 1996 retirement from America Online, Seriff has maintained his commitment to the Internet-based business community, serving during both his later career and his retirement on the boards of directors of several Internet-based companies, including iExchange.com, InteractiveFunds, Isochron (Isochron Data Corp.), Hire.com, and Unwired Nation (UnWired Buyer). He has also served as a member of the advisory board for Activerse.

Seriff brought his extensive business experience, technical knowledge, and investment advisory skills to the greater Austin, Texas, business community, renewing his commitment to the development of his Texas hometown. He has been active in both an advisory and investment capacity since returning to Austin. He has invested in the company Techxas Ventures and its principal subsidiary companies since 1998. He began his role as an adviser with G-51 Capital Management, headquartered in Austin, in 2011.

PERSONAL LIFE
Seriff is married and settled with his wife, Carolyn, in his hometown of Austin, Texas,

---

Affiliation: America Online

America Online, Inc. (now AOL) is an Internet service provider headquartered in Dulles, Virginia. It began as Quantum Computer Services, founded by Steve Case and Jim Kimsey in 1985. Marc Seriff was a founding member and the company's first chief technical officer. Kimsey was the company's first CEO, followed by Case in 1991. The name was changed to America Online that year and is now widely known as AOL. Case built the service's customer base through low membership prices, widespread publicity, and mass-mailed free trial offers.

The company began its career offering online services that were limited to Commodore computer users. After several years, America Online expanded its reach to include Apple Computers, Tandy Corp., and IBM. Later expansions included the offering of additional content and Internet access for members, e-commerce services, and support for new digital platforms and devices. The audible "You've got mail" message alerting users to new e-mail messages entered the lexicon as a popular catchphrase widely associated with the company.

America Online's initial public offering (IPO) came in 1992, netting $66 million. The company's success attracted investor attention and helped it to weather two takeover attempts in 1993, the first from Microsoft founders Paul Allen and CEO Bill Gates. Notable acquisitions included rival online service provider CompuServe and Netscape Communications Corp.

America Online announced its intention to acquire Time Warner, Inc., in 2000, and the two companies merged in 2001 to create AOL Time Warner, Inc. Case was named chairman and Time Warner chairman Gerald Levin was named CEO. America Online became a wholly owned subsidiary of the newly formed company. AOL Time Warner is headquartered in New York City, while America Online retains its headquarters in Dulles, Virginia.

after his 1996 retirement from America Online. During his employment, the couple had lived near the America Online corporate headquarters in Dulles, Virginia. Seriff and his wife began to work closely with the greater Austin area nonprofit community soon after their move to Texas. They founded The Seriff Foundation (TSF), an organization dedicated to a new approach to nonprofit support not based solely on the awarding of grant funding. TSF instead provided management assistance and training for area nonprofit organizations. TSF served the local community from 2001 through 2008, when it became defunct.

Seriff served on the boards of the Highland Lakes Legacy Fund and the Austin Community Foundation and was an establishing member of the Dell Jewish Community Center and the Boys and Girls Club of the Highland Lakes. He is dedicated to the performing arts, serving on the boards of the Long Center for the Performing Arts and the Austin Musical Theatre.

Seriff's Austin, Texas home base has also allowed him to maintain close ties with his alma mater, the University of Texas at Austin, where he serves as a member of the university's Commission of 125 and as a member of the Longhorn Fund's Advisory Council. He sits on the advisory councils for the College of Natural Sciences, the Department of Computer Science, and the Department of Theatre and Dance.

Marcella Bush Trevino

FURTHER READING

Aspray, William, and Paul E. Ceruzzi. *The Internet and American Business*. Cambridge: MIT, 2008. Print. A series of essays that examine the commercialization of the Internet through such developments as information searching, e-mail, and social networking. Covers business models, e-commerce, and the successes and failures of dot-com companies such as AOL.

Munk, Nina. *Fools Rush In: Steve Case, Jerry Levin, and the Unmaking of AOL Time Warner*. New York: HarperBusiness, 2004. Print. Inside story of the blockbuster merger that examines the history of both companies, the two chief executive officers in question, and the long-term implications of the deal.

Stauffer, David. *Big Shots: It's a Wired, Wired World: Business the AOL Way*. North Mankato: Capstone, 2001. Print. Details the company's rise in the dot-com era under chief executive officer Steve Case and the business plans and deals that made its success possible.

Swisher, Kara. *AOL.com: How Steve Case Beat Bill Gates, Nailed the Netheads, and Made Millions in the War for the Web*. New York: Times, 1998. Print. Details the corporate history of AOL during Seriff's tenure, focusing on the company's success and ability to fight off acquisition by Microsoft.

---. *There Must Be a Pony in Here Somewhere: The AOL Time Warner Debacle and the Quest for a Digital Future*. New York: Crown, 2003. Print. Discusses the blockbuster merger and its aftermath, including the financial implications and its impact on Internet-based business strategy and the digital revolution.

DAVE SIFRY

Founder of Technorati

Born: 1968; Long Island, New York
Died: -
Primary Field: Internet
Specialty: News and entertainment
Primary Company/Organization: Technorati

INTRODUCTION

A vocal member of the open source movement, entrepreneur Dave Sifry moved from Linuxcare—his start-up offering Linux consulting and tech support in order to encourage the adoption of Linux by business-es—to Technorati, which began as a blog search tool and added numerous blogs' worth of content and an innovative advertising platform. Technorati has since become the third-largest social media property, after Facebook and Twitter.

EARLY LIFE

David L. Sifry was born in 1968 and grew up on Long Island. An early computer aficionado, he learned to program on the Commodore PET, the first full-featured Commodore computer (1977n}82). He graduated from

Dave Sifry.

Oceanside Senior High School in 1986. Determined from a young age to start a computer business, he studied computer science at Johns Hopkins University and received a bachelor of science degree in 1991. In 1996, he set up Secure Remote to sell private networks to large companies. Sifry described the venture as "a horrendous failure." His early experience in the computer industry, after working for Mitsubishi Electric in Kobe, Japan, included cofounding the Wi-Fi company Sputnik, and in 1998 he founded Linuxcare with Arthur Tyde and Dave LaDuke. Linuxcare offered twenty-four-hour phone support for Linux, a Unix-variant operating system that had grown in popularity in the late 1990s but had faced resistance in being adopted as the operating system for businesses because of the lack of professional technical support—something offered by Apple and Microsoft, for instance.

LIFE'S WORK

The Linuxcare concept was to hire and professionalize a class of Linux experts to offer paid on-demand technical support. Dell was enticed to bundle coupons for Linuxcare support with its Red Hat Linux-running desktops. Linuxcare hired a number of high-profile experts, including Rasmus Lerdorf, the developer of PHP, and Martin Pool, one of the developers of Apache.

The company evolved considerably over time, adding four divisions: a research and development division to develop open source software; the professional services division, offering Linux consulting; Linuxcare University, for Linux training; and Linuxcare Labs, which certified hardware systems as Linux-compatible. In addition to offering its own Linux technical support, Linuxcare trained other companies' staffs in Linux issues related to technical support, customer support, and sales matters.

After canceling plans for an initial public offering (IPO), Linuxcare shifted again, shedding most of its staff and focusing on Linux software, which led to the company's renaming in 2004 as Levanta (after its bestselling software package). In 2005, Levanta changed focus again to hardware and gradually declined, going out of business in 2008. The Linuxcare name was purchased by original founder Arthur Tyde, who would later provide cloud computing information technology services under that name.

In the meantime, Sifry had moved on from Linuxcare, founding Technorati in 2002. Technorati began as a search engine for blogs. While blogs and online journals had been around for most of the history of the web—personal blogging began in 1994 with bloggers such as Swarthmore student Justin Hall—the late 1990s saw a spike in the popularity of blogging, which would continue to the present day: Open Diary introduced comment threads to blogs in 1998, and LiveJournal, Diaryland, and Blogger.com all opened the following year. Even in 2002, when Technorati was founded, blogs were by then sufficiently developed and varied that a significant number of political blogs (the political blogosphere) had begun covering political news overlooked by the mainstream media. Talking Points Memo, for example, began shortly after the 2000 U.S. presidential election and was later awarded a George Polk Award in Journalism.

A vast and growing number of blogs made it increasingly difficult to sift through them. The first Internet search engines had been introduced in order to allow users to engage efficiently with the mountains of content on the web, and Technorati saw a niche to fill in offering a tool to allow users better discovery of the breadth of blogs. The name, playing on *literati*, reflects the belief that blog-reading Internet users were likely among the better-read and better-educated portion of the demographic, although since the time of Technorati's founding, blogs have become mainstream and most Internet users read them. In addition to searching

Affiliation: Technorati

Technorati, Inc., is an Internet social media services company consisting of Technorati.com, the world's largest search engine for blogs; Technorati Media, an advertising network for blogs and social media; the self-service advertising platform AdEngage; and the Blogcritics webzine, which the company calls a "journalism 3.0 site."

The popularity and prevalence of blogs rose steadily over the first decade of the twenty-first century, with most magazines, many large newspapers, and other media outlets adding blogs to their other content, in addition to the "unaffiliated" professional or hobbyist blogger. By 2010, the overwhelming majority, more than three-quarters, of American Internet users read at least one blog on a regular basis: Blogs had become mainstream reading material. Many argued that bloggers wielded more influence on the reading public than the major newspapers, particularly given the decline of print journalism and the contraction of newspaper staffs across the country. What is commonly called "social media" now, encompassing both blogging and social networks like Facebook and Twitter, was then often referred to as "conversational media," which underscored the importance of the comments sections in blogs and of the tendency of blogs to write responses to one another; indeed, it is not trivializing them to point out that some blogs do little else other than write commentary on other blogs, such is the information-richness of the modern blogosphere.

In response, Technorati was formed, beginning with a search engine to help users find blogs in areas in which they are interested. Dave Sifry, an entrepreneur and open source advocate who had previously cofounded the twenty-four-hour Linux tech support service Linuxcare, founded Technorati, freely admitting that it was an "ego project"—he was building something that he himself wanted to use, a search engine he wished existed. Software engineer Tantek Celik (of Microsoft, formerly of Sun Microsystems, Oracle, and Apple) served as chief technologist. Celik wrote the Election 2004 section of the Technorati site, featuring blog coverage of the U.S. presidential election (and gubernatorial and congressional elections). Technorati's focus on Election 2004 coverage reflected this core tenet of the site, that blogs included not only disposable fluff or personal journals but also up-to-the-minute, in-the-moment journalism that conventional news media could not provide.

By 2006, Technorati was tracking 27.7 million blogs and noted that there were approximately 75,000 new blogs added daily. Numerous mechanisms had had to be put in place in order to prevent blogs from gaming the system in order to spam search results or manipulate rankings through link farming. Sifry also promoted the practice of bloggers pinging Technorati when updating their blogs; while this helped make Technorati's results better, he appealed to bloggers' egos by pointing out that it was the best way to guarantee that a blogger got credit for being the first to say something.

Much of the focus on the site at the time was on political blogging, corporate news blogging, and tech blogging, but that changed as Technorati acquired content for the first time. Blogcritics was its first acquisition, in 2008. Founded in 2002, the site published blog entries from anyone who contributed—having been founded with an initial roster of fifty bloggers—although all content was approved by editors first. The editorial control had given it a reputation for quality reflected by several awards and its use by Google News and Yahoo! News. At the time of its acquisition, it was visited by approximately 1 million unique visitors per month. Blogcritics' founder, Eric Olsen, and lead developer, Phillip Winn, were made Technorati employees. Key to the acquisition was the assurance that blogs controlled by Technorati would not be given favorable treatment in search results.

The Silicon Valley Moms Group, SV Moms, a network of female bloggers in the Silicon Valley, was acquired in 2010, and its cofounder Jill Asher became Technorati's editorial director. The SV Moms blogs were folded into the newly created Technorati Women Channel, along with a number of other blogs by women.

Since 2004, Technorati has published an annual "State of the Blogosphere" address, which in 2007 was streamed live by Sifry. The 2011 address, delivered by chief executive officer Shani Higgins, identified the predominant new trend as the entrepreneur-blogger—a (usually) small business owner using a blog to promote that business. Internal surveys revealed that the biggest influence on bloggers' content was other bloggers and that they were increasingly concerned with remaining transparent in their relationships with any products they promoted. Facebook and Twitter were the primary sources of blog traffic, with Digg in a serious decline.

blogs, Technorati rates each blog based on the number of other blogs that have linked to it over the previous six months. Its categorizes search results—and its blog directory—according to the tags bloggers use on their sites. Tag descriptions in recent years have been written by Blogcritics bloggers.

Sifry is an advocate of open source software, as he had been at Linuxcare, and Technorati both uses and contributes to open source software, including a publicly accessible wiki for developers. Since the founding of Technorati.com, Technorati, Inc.—the company behind the search engine—has grown to include Technorati Media, the company's advertising network, and the Blogcritics webzine. Blogcritics was acquired in 2008, its founders made full-time Technorati staffers, and the site was completely redesigned in 2009. More content acquisition followed in 2010, when Technorati acquired SV Moms, the Silicon Valley Moms Group, a network of blogs by women and mothers, which was folded into the new women's channel at Technorati. Again, some of the SV Moms staff were given positions at Technorati.

Every year since 2004, Technorati has issued a "State of the Blogosphere" address, based in large part on an internal survey of bloggers. The "State of the Blogosphere" address has repeatedly drawn criticism; virtually without fail, Technorati's statements about the Blogosphere are challenged by some. The validity of the criticism varies; some merely offer counterexamples in response to Technorati's descriptions of patterns, which can lead to interesting and valuable conversations but does not ultimately disprove the pattern. On other occasions Technorati's facts, or the conclusions drawn from those facts, have been challenged. In particular, Technorati and Sifry are sometimes criticized for being too uncritical about the concept of paid blogging (blogging paid for by brands promoted in those blogs, not ad- or donation-supported blogging). This issue came up after the 2006 address, which heavily promoted Edelman, a widely criticized public relations (PR) agency with which Technorati was working at the time, which had been using fake blogs as a PR tool. There has been a mixed reaction to the 2009 decision to index only English-language blogs, in order to focus on a more or less self-contained segment of the blogosphere. (In 2011, Shani Higgins issued a statement that paid blogging was not stigmatized if it remained transparent.)

Sifry served as CEO of Technorati from its inception until 2007, when he was succeeded by Richard Jalichandra (who was succeeded by Shani Higgins). Sifry became chairman of the board of directors. He is also a board member with Linux International.

Sifry also created Projectdocs, an online collaboration and document management service. In 2008, he launched Hoosgot, a reimagining of Matt Jones and Ben Hammersley's Lazyweb service. Lazyweb had launched in 2002 and was an early web 2.0 initiative, relying on crowd sourcing to answer questions to which users were "too lazy" to find themselves. Spam shut the site down in 2006. Hoosgot took the same concept and integrated it with Twitter, blogging, and RSS/Atom feeds. The name is a play on "who's got [an answer to my burning question]?" Sifry installed spam-fighting tools in the hope of avoiding the problems that had sunk Lazyweb.

Sifry is also the founder and CEO of Offbeat Guides, which launched at the end of 2008. Offbeat Guides sells customized travel guides with up-to-date information, based on customers' answers to questions about when they plan to travel, from where they are leaving, and where they will be staying. The guides cover the same categories of information as conventional travel guides—with maps, key phrases, and recommendations for attractions and restaurants—but also incorporate time-dependent information such as events, holidays, a weather forecast, and the most recent information about currency exchange.

PERSONAL LIFE

Sifry is a vocal advocate of open source software. He lives in San Francisco and enjoys traveling, especially to Yosemite National Park, London, and Paris.

Bill Kte'pi

FURTHER READING

Benedictus, Leo. "Technorati, David L. Sifry." *Guardian.* 3 Nov. 2006. Web. 10 Sept. 2012. A profile of Sifry.

Jenkins, Henry. *Confronting the Challenges of Participatory Culture: Media Education for the 21st Century.* Cambridge: MIT, 2009. Print. Examines social media, new forms of creative expression, and their impact on media studies.

Qualman, Erik. *Socialnomics: How Social Media Transforms the Way We Live and Do Business.* New York: Wiley, 2010. Print. The impact of social media on the business world.

Rosenberg, Scott. *Say Everything: How Blogging Began, What It's Becoming, and Why It Matters.* New York: Broadway, 2010. Print. A history of blogging by a journalist and Salon.com cofounder, without the hype, misconceptions, or fast-money tips of other books.

BEN SILBERMANN

Cofounder and CEO of Pinterest

Born: 1982; Des Moines, Iowa
Died: -
Primary Field: Internet
Specialty: Social media
Primary Company/Organization: Pinterest

INTRODUCTION

Ben Silbermann is cofounder and chief executive officer (CEO) of Pinterest, one of the world's most popular social networks. In 2009, Silbermann, along with Paul Sciarra and Evan Sharp, began working on a site on which people could share collections of things that interested them by electronically pinning images of those things to an interactive virtual bulletin board. Less than three years later, Pinterest had nearly 20 million unique visitors each month and $138 million in funding. The network has been valued as high as $1.5 billion, and by 2012 it was recognized as the fastest-growing social media site, outdistancing both Facebook and Twitter.

EARLY LIFE

Ben Silbermann was born in 1982 in Des Moines, Iowa, His parents, Jane Wang and Neil Silbermann, are ophthalmologists with a family practice in Urbandale, Iowa. Silbermann grew up in West Des Moines, the wealthiest suburb of Des Moines. He was a collector as a child, avidly accumulating stamps and leaves. His greatest enthusiasm was reserved for insects, which he remembers collecting "maniacally."

He attended Roosevelt High School, where he competed on the debate team and played cello for the Des Moines Youth Symphony. He graduated from Roosevelt High School and from Central Academy, an educational program specifically designed for highly gifted and talented students, where qualified students from every Des Moines Public middle and high school spend part of their day. In 1998, he attended the Research Science Institute at the Massachusetts Institute of Technology (MIT), a summer science and engineering program. Attendance at the institute is an honor reserved for eighty of the nation's most accomplished high school students.

Silbermann entered Yale University in 1999. With grandparents, both parents, and his sisters (doctors), becoming a premedical student was a logical choice for Silbermann, but in his junior year he changed his mind

and decided that medicine was not for him. He graduated from Yale in 2003 and moved to Washington, D.C., where he worked for an information technology consulting firm, making charts and giving presentations. A history buff and a fan of sites like Digg, Reddit, and TechCrunch, he decided that the Internet defined his generation and he wanted to be a part of it. He and his then girlfriend, Divya Bhaskaran, packed up and moved across the country to California in 2006. Silbermann cajoled his way into a job with Google, where he spent two years as a product designer. While he enjoyed the Google culture, he knew that without an engineering degree, his future with the company was limited. He thought about a start-up, but it was his girlfriend's encouragement to stop talking and act that pushed him into leaving Google in August 2008.

LIFE'S WORK

At the same time Silbermann was leaving Google, a friend from Yale, Paul Sciarra, was cutting ties with the New York venture capital firm that had employed him.

Ben Silbermann.

Affiliation: Pinterest

In 2008, Ben Silbermann and Paul Sciarra, former classmates at Yale, neither of whom had a background in engineering or information technology, founded Cold Brew Labs, a mobile shopping start-up. When their first venture failed, they turned their focus to what they called "social cataloging." Pinterest, named by Silbermann's then girlfriend and later wife, Divya Bhaskaran, launched in March 2010. Evan Sharp joined the group as designer and cofounder in 2011. The site, which allows users to collect and share images, attracted little attention at first. However, traffic began to build, and *Time* magazine named Pinterest one of the Best Websites of 2011. That recognition, combined with the release of a Pinterest iPhone app, helped to drive visitors to the site in substantial numbers.

In May 2012, the company raised $100 million from a group of investors led by Japanese online retailer Rakuten, Inc. Pinterest was valued at around $1.5 billion. Headlines proclaimed it the fastest-growing social network ever when as many as 12 million visited the site in January 2012—well in excess of the number of Facebook users during a similar period in that company's history. By March 2012, Pinterest had registered 17.8 million users. On August 9, 2012, the site, which had offered membership on an invitation-only basis since its founding, became open to all.

By mid-2012, experts were expecting Pinterest to announce monetization plans. Tim Kendall, formerly director of monetization at Facebook, became director of monetization at Pinterest. Barry Schnitt, once director of policy at Facebook, joined Pinterest as head of policy. Several other significant employees at Facebook followed suit. Advertisers are well aware of Pinterest's potential. Recent data suggest the site drove more traffic per month in mid-2012 than Google+, Reddit, YouTube, and Myspace combined. One study found that Pinterest surpassed Facebook in terms of retail outlets or brands that users "follow" or "like." A survey by a price comparison site found that 21 percent of Pinterest users polled had purchased items they had seen on the site. Pinterest users are heavily female, ranging from 68 to 97 percent by some counts. Any figure in that range makes Pinterest a natural tool for extending the features of the meta catalog from look to buy.

The two started a company called Cold Brew Labs. Because Sciarra brought some venture capital experience to the start-up, they agreed that he would be CEO and Silbermann would be the idea man. His first idea was Tote, an application for the iPhone that took data from online catalogs to create a meta catalog. By early 2009, the app was ready to launch. Sciarra found an investor, and the app was visually appealing. However, it did not work. No one was using mobile apps for shopping. Nonetheless, some people were using it to send images of products to themselves.

Silbermann considered the use of the Tote app, remembered his childhood fascination with collections, and thought about the different things people collected and their desire to display them. From this rumination came an idea for a website that would allow users to collect and display images online. Silbermann worked with a small group to create the site. The group spent two and a half months working on the basic screen, trying fifty coded versions before arriving at the one that seemed the best fit for their purpose. Silbermann's fiancée suggested the name Pinterest (combining the words *pin* and *interest*). The site launched in March 2010.

Although Silbermann and his cofounders contacted friends and family several months before the launch to tell them about the site and invite them to try it, the early months were slow. Cash was limited, and investors showed little interest in a start-up founded by three men without a technical degree among them. Investors who were willing to review Pinterest saw no purpose in people collecting and posting a bunch of images. By the end of their first quarter year, Pinterest had only a few hundred users.

Then the site began to attract an audience. Silbermann's friends in Iowa began using it. When he traveled to a Utah design conference, the interior designers attending the conference found it useful. As numbers increased, it was clear that the growing base was made up not of the usual early adapters located primarily on the two coasts but rather from Middle America, where people were using Pinterest for sharing things that were important to them. A bride-to-be used it to plan her wedding, a homeschooling parent kept and shared boards of lesson-plan ideas, and cooks found that it was a great way to collect recipes. Silbermann personally contacted the first five thousand users, even meeting with some of them.

The growth of Pinterest proved consistent, growing on average 40 to 50 percent each month. The company's future looked bright when 2010 ended, but no one was prepared for the rate of change that came in 2011. Silbermann started the year by making Evan Sharp, a designer who had interrupted his graduate studies in architecture at Columbia to design products for Facebook, officially a part of Pinterest, listing him as a cofounder. In March, the company added an iPhone app that brought new users on board. In May, Pinterest raised $27 million from venture capital. Marc Andreessen, whose firm Andreessen Horowitz led the investors, credited a woman at his firm, a researcher, with fostering his interest in Silbermann's company.

On August 16, 2011, *Time* magazine included Pinterest in its list of the fifty best websites of the year, driving traffic numbers still higher. Between May and November 2011, traffic at the site increased from 500,000 to 5 million active monthly users. Another 2 million had joined by the end of the year. A substantial majority of those users, like Andreessen's researcher, were women. The site lent itself to beautiful displays of fashion and food that appealed to women accustomed to leafing through glossy magazines. This growth took place while Pinterest was operating with an invitation-only policy.

During this period of phenomenal growth, Sciarra was nominally at least president and CEO of the company, but in 2012, as everyone from the U.S. Army to *The New York Times*, from Silbermann's fiancée to Michele Obama and Ann Romney established a presence on Pinterest, Silbermann became the public face of the company. It was Silbermann who described his vision for the company in interviews, and it was he who was a featured speaker at conferences such as South by Southwest (SXSW), the annual music, film, and interactive conference and festival in Austin, Texas. Sciarra resigned as CEO in April 2012, although he remained on the board. Silbermann became CEO in title as well as role.

PERSONAL LIFE

Pinterest was named Best New Startup of 2011 by TechCrunch, one of the online technology publications that inspired Silbermann to move to California to realize his dream of a start-up. In 2012, *Inc.* magazine named him one of America's Coolest Young Entrepreneurs. The modest Silbermann carefully restricts his public comments to information on his company and remains silent on the subject of awards.

Silbermann married longtime girlfriend Divya Bhaskaran on July 22, 2011, in a ceremony at Nestldown, a private retreat in Los Gatos, California. The festivities combined Western food and music with Hindi wedding traditions, honoring the cultures of both the Indian bride and her groom. Like thousands of other brides, Bhaskaran pinned her wedding plans and photographs on a board on Pinterest, the site she named; the title read, "So it turns out we're getting married." A board she posted in 2012 read, "Preparations for baby b&d."

Wylene Rholetter

FURTHER READING

Habash, Gabe, Calvin Reid, and Diane Roback. "The Pinterest Experiment." *Publishers Weekly* 30 Apr. 2012: 4–5. Print. Considers Pinterest and its demographics and looks at publishers' use of Pinterest for brand marketing, devoting particular attention to their use of the online site to promote books for children, teens, and parents. Three charts.

Hempel, Jessi, and Alex Konrad. "Is Pinterest the Next Facebook?" *Fortune* 9 Apr. 2012: 108–14. Print. Focuses on the purpose of Pinterest and the company's dramatic growth in funding and traffic. Covers Pinterest's hiring of Tim Kendall, former director of monetization at the social network Facebook, and Silbermann's response to the concerns of lawyer, photographer, and blogger Kristin Kowalski about possible copyright violations on Pinterest. Four photographs, two charts.

Li, Shan. "Pinterest Rises Fast in Social Networking, but Can It Stick It Out?" *Los Angeles Times* 13 Apr. 2012: A1. Print. The article examines the phenomenal rate of growth at Pinterest and raises the question of whether the company's achievement in its first two years can be sustained.

MacMillan, Douglas. "A Startup Builds the Bulletin Board 2.0." *Bloomberg Businessweek* 21 November 2011: 48–49. Print. The article describes the way Pinterest functions as a site that allows users to curate images. It also names some of the retailers who have set up boards on the site. One color photograph.

Wortham, Jenna. "A Site That Aims to Unleash the Scrapbook Maker in All of Us." *New York Times* 12 Mar. 2012: B1. Print. Provides an overview of Pinterest and compares users of the site to scrapbookers. Quotes the opinions of several professionals in technology and related fields.

CRAIG SILVERSTEIN

First director of technology at Google

Born: 1972; Guam
Died: -
Primary Field: Internet
Specialty: Content and data
Primary Company/Organization: Google

INTRODUCTION

As the first employee hired by Google founders Larry Page and Sergey Brin, Craig Silverstein will always have a special place in the history of the organization. Google's rapid rise was greatly assisted by Silverstein's deep computer programming skills and his commitment to providing users of the Google search engine with efficiency, accuracy, and speed.

EARLY LIFE

Craig Silverstein was born in Guam. At the age of four, he, along with his parents, Burton and Janet, who were both practicing physicians, moved to Chapel Hill, North Carolina. The family then settled in Gainesville, Florida, two years later. In Gainesville, he attended Brentwood

Craig Silverstein.

School, Westwood Middle School, and Gainesville High School. After receiving a perfect 1,600 on his Scholastic Aptitude Test (SAT), he was accepted into Harvard University in 1990, where he studied computer science. He was a highly decorated student at Harvard and received the Microsoft Technical Scholarship in 1993, along with the Derek Bok Award for Teaching Excellence in 1992 and 1993. In 1994, he graduated from Harvard with an A.B. degree in computer science.

In the summers of 1992 and 1993, Silverstein worked as a software design engineer at Microsoft Corporation in Seattle, Washington. With this job, he was offered a unique and deep glimpse into the computer software development process. With his deep academic and work experience, Silverstein was accepted in the computer science doctoral program at Stanford University. As a doctoral student, he was supervised by Rajeev Motwani. Silverstein's research focused on data mining, algorithms, and information retrieval. He became extremely proficient at organizing large data sets and, in particular, was an accomplished user of Scatter/Gather, a document-browsing tool. He complemented his research with summer work at the nearby Palo Alto Research Center (Xerox PARC).

LIFE'S WORK

In 1996, Silverstein was shown a search engine that had been developed as a research project by friends and fellow Stanford doctoral students Larry Page and Sergey Brin. Referred to as BackRub, this search engine could direct searches to the backlinks of websites. Silverstein was immediately impressed and began creating certain compression algorithms for the development of the search engine. Slowly, the search engine evolved into a tool that could navigate quickly and efficiently through the Internet. Most important, the search engine used a system called PageRank, which determined the significance of certain websites based primarily on the number of links each website possessed.

The search engine caught the eye of several Stanford professors, including Silverstein's supervisor, Motwani, and further guidance was given. After the founders received $100,000 from Andy Bechtolsheim, a Stanford alumnus and a founder of Sun Microsystems, Google, Inc. was founded. Initially, Google was run from Sergey Brin's dormitory room, but after a few weeks the small-scale operations were moved to a garage in Menlo Park. Susan Wojcicki, the owner of the garage, rented the space to Page and Brin for $1,700 per month.

After Google was created, Silverstein became the company's first employee and was named the director of technology. Upon accepting the position, Silverstein decided to take a leave of absence from his doctoral studies. His new responsibilities centered on refining and updating Google's capabilities through new programming projects. He was also a central figure in the company's product development.

By 1999, Google had become recognized in information technology circles as a dynamic search engine. By August, the company had moved out of its garage offices and settled into a Mountain View, California, location. In 2000, Google partnered with Yahoo! and became the main search engine for Yahoo!'s directory. Soon afterward, the company, with the assistance of Silverstein, released a new index that had more than 1 billion uniform resource locators (URLs). This retrieval capability made Google the largest search engine on the World Wide Web.

The rapid success of Google did not diminish the unique company culture, which, from the outset, centered on providing a comfortable atmosphere for all of its employees. What separates Google from other major companies is an open and relaxed, if intense, environment that connects senior management with every employee in the company. The ethos of Google is centered on the belief that each employee can offer a special skill, no matter how trivial or humorous. For example, Silverstein complemented his deep programming and technology skills with baking. Once a week, Silverstein would bake a loaf of bread and share the bread with his coworkers.

Throughout the 2000s, Google rapidly progressed and became the premier online search engine. In 2002, the company's revenue was near $300 million. By 2003, nearly 150 million searches per day were being processed. The search engine remained geared toward the user and ultimately never used any banner ads. As the decade progressed and under Silverstein's quiet guidance, dynamic products were introduced. In 2003, the company started using a news service. Later in the decade, Gmail was introduced, along with Google Maps, Google Books, and the Android. These products and many other accessories assisted in Google's evolution and helped to maintain its popularity.

In 2004, the company had an initial public offering (IPO); initial valuation of the company was around $27 billion. Five years later, the value of Google was near $140 billion. Although Silverstein has never revealed

---

Affiliation: Google

In 1996, Larry Page and Sergey Brin, two Stanford doctoral students, developed a search engine called BackRub. The search engine was unique, for it could delve into the backlinks of websites and produce extremely accurate results. They demonstrated the search engine's capabilities to friend and fellow doctoral student Craig Silverstein, who then proceeded to revise many of the algorithms and ultimately provided enhancements. The revised search engine used PageRank, an algorithm that based the significance of searchable websites on the number of links each website possessed.

After receiving an investment of $100,000, Page and Brin founded Google, Inc., in 1998. Silverstein was the company's first employee. Success came extremely rapidly for Google. Within two years, the small company, which had begun in a garage, had moved into a complex in Mountain View, California. By 2000, the search engine had become the largest in the world, with more than 1 billion uniform resource locators (URLs). Throughout the 2000s, Google would continue to grow rapidly. The company opened offices throughout the world and by 2012 had around thirty-two thousand employees.

Google has long been recognized as an employee-friendly company. Free meals are the norm, massage therapists are available, and office outings are common. Google offices throughout the world are largely casual and conducive to free and open thinking.

The products devised by Google since its founding, including Google Maps and Google Earth, take advantage of cutting-edge technology. Furthermore, the company remains committed to its users—as demonstrated in 2007, when Gmail, with its 4 megabytes of free storage, was introduced. Today, Google is estimated to be worth close to $200 billion.

---

his net worth to the public, financial experts in 2010 believed that his assets exceeded $800 million.

By the late 2000s, Silverstein could often be spotted giving lectures about Google at universities and other public forums. His humble and laid-back personality appealed to many, and he was known as an excellent company representative. By 2010, Silverstein was working in Google's New York office, where he was involved in a project that focused on offering to the public some of Google's internal programming codes.

By early 2012, Silverstein was at a crossroads in his Google career. After fourteeen years, he was searching for greater challenges. After being offered a programmer position with Khan Academy, a small online education company, he decided to resign from Google. Upon announcing his resignation, Silverstein emphasized in an e-mail to his fellow Google employees that his fourteen years in the company were extremely special and memorable. At Khan, Silverstein assists in the development of free online education tools for children across the world. He believes that online education offers students and educators a transparent environment for learning and is convinced that technology in the academic environment has tremendous room for advancement. Silverstein is once again faced with tackling the challenges that exist in a small start-up company.

PERSONAL LIFE

Silverstein maintains a quiet life outside his business interests. In a 2010 interview, he revealed that he was a Muppets fan and that he was a strict vegetarian. At that time he was driving a ten-year-old Nissan.

Gavin Wilk

FURTHER READING

Clark, Anthony. "Gainesville's Silverstein Excited about Life after Google." *Gainesville Sun* 29 Feb. 2012. Web. 20 Aug. 2012. Details the departure of Silverstein from Google for Khan Academy. Provides some personal details about Silverstein.

Edmonston, Peter. "Google's I.P.O., Five Years Later." *New York Times* 19 Aug. 2009. Web. 20 Aug. 2012. Analysis of the company's IPO in historical context. Examines how the company evolved after the milestone day of the offering.

Edwards, Douglas. *I'm Feeling Lucky: The Confessions of Google Employee Number 59.* Boston: Houghton, 2011. Print. A unique perspective on Google offered by the company's first director of marketing and brand management.

Levy, Steven. *In the Plex: How Google Thinks, Works, and Shapes Our Lives.* New York: Simon, 2011. Print. An inside look at the company culture of Google. The author was given direct access to the major figures in Google; the book is thus based on numerous discussions and interviews with the leading personalities in the company.

Silverstein, Craig. "In Conversation with Craig Silverstein, Khan Academy." Interview by Arun Saigal. *Lokvani* 16 Aug. 2012. Web. 20 Aug. 2012. One of the first interviews with Silverstein, published after his departure from Google. Topics covered include Silverstein's childhood, his experiences at Google, and his new role at Khan Academy.

---. "Mercury News Interview: Craig Silverstein, Google's First Employee." Interview by Mike Swift. *Mercury News* 8 Oct. 2010. Web. 20 Aug. 2012. Silverstein details everything from his first car to his SAT scores.

---, Hannes Marais, Monika Henzinger, and Michael Moricz. "Analysis of a Very Large Web Search Engine Query Log." *SIGIR Forum* 33.1 (1999). Web. 20 Aug. 2012. A technical analysis of the query methods of the AltaVista search engine. Provides an interesting look into the query methods prevalent during the mid- to late 1990s.

Tate, Ryan. "How a Tech Non-profit Became the Hottest Ticket in Silicon Valley." *Wired* 25 June 2012. Web. 20 Aug. 2012. Covers the evolution of the start-up Khan Academy and provides insight into why Silverstein decided to join the company.

Vise, David A., and Mark Malseed. *The Google Story: Inside the Hottest Business, Media and Technology Success of Our Time.* New York: Delacorte, 2008. Print. An in-depth description of Google's rise. Emphasis is on Larry Page and Sergey Brin.

RUSSEL SIMMONS

Cofounder of Yelp

Born: 1979; place unknown
Died: -
Primary Field: Internet
Specialty: Commerce
Primary Company/Organization: Yelp

INTRODUCTION

Russel Simmons (not to be confused with hip-hop mogul Russell Simmons) is best known as the cofounder, along with Jeremy Stoppelman, of the social media and review site Yelp. Simmons worked as lead software architect at PayPal during its early days; he also worked at an incubator started by the company's cofounder, Max Levchin. Simmons is interested not only in computer entrepreneurship but also in exploiting the flexibility of the computer and the Internet for educational applications.

EARLY LIFE

Russel Simmons was always interested in mathematics and science, and from the moment he had his Apple II computer, he had some project in the works, whether creating a computer game or working on an algorithm. He attended the Illinois Mathematics and Science Academy from 1992 to 1995, then entered the University of Illinois at Urbana-Champaign, from which he graduated with honors and a bachelor of science degree in computer science in 1998. The Urbana campus was the alma mater of many of Web 2.0 top engineers and designers. While at school there, Simmons befriended Jeremy Stoppelman, with whom he would found the review and social media website Yelp.

LIFE'S WORK

Most Internet followers associate Simmons with Yelp, but he has been instrumental in several other websites

Russel Simmons.

and projects as well. After graduating from the University of Illinois, Simmons went to work with PayPal, the online payment-processing service. He was PayPal's first computer engineer and its lead software architect, ultimately becoming its chief technical officer (CTO). Simmons says in his own online biography that he "helped design and develop [the] PayPal system from scratch." Between 1999 and 2003, he headed a team of senior engineers in developing "software aspects of site scalability, security, availability, internationalization, management of codebase, mentoring engineers, technology decisions."

Stoppelman was working at PayPal at the same time that Simmons was there. PayPal had revolutionized the ease and security with which people could do business over the Internet, and it grew increasingly linked to eBay. When eBay bought PayPal, both Simmons and Stoppelman took advantage of cash-out offers, and they left PayPal. Stoppelman entered Harvard Business School, studying there for a brief time, and Simmons traveled.

Simmons also worked for five months in 2004 at Max Levchin's MRL Ventures in California. MRL was known among computer engineers and designers as an "incubator" for new Internet and software ideas. Levchin often contributed seed money to help develop ideas.

In 2004, Simmons and Stoppelman teamed again to create Yelp. Internet lore holds that Yelp—a combination customer-review and social media site—began when Stoppelman was looking for recommendations for a doctor in San Francisco. However, both men are aficionados of San Francisco food and entertainment, and both wanted an easily referenced, Internet-based index of reviews for personal use. They envisioned using reviews e-mailed to a common account, then linked to review categories. The men admittedly spent only a little time developing the idea, and Levchin spotted them $1 million to develop the idea.

Within three months, Simmons and Stoppelman had the nexus of Yelp online. Although the results were not initially to their liking, Stoppelman noted that people seemed to love writing reviews about consumer experiences. It remained for Simmons and Stoppelman to channel that energy into readable, reliable, searchable reviews. In 2005, Simmons and Stoppelman relaunched Yelp. This time it included a "review filter"—an algorithm that weeds out suspicious reviews, such as those created by business owners themselves or favorable reviews that business owners have purchased. The filter also targets critical reviews written by one competitor against another. Yelp quickly gained popularity around San Francisco, becoming the "go-to" site for information not only about food and entertainment but also all types of other businesses, including doctors, veterinarians, and plumbers. Yelp now canvasses the entire United States, all the major countries of Europe, and Australia. Chief executive officer (CEO) Stoppelman took the company through several rounds of venture capitalization, and in early 2012 he took the company public.

By then, Simmons had left Yelp. His departure was preceded by little fanfare and no hint of acrimony. Stoppelman said Simmons was transitioning to an advisory role with Yelp and that he would remain a significant shareholder in the company.

Simmons did not sit idle. In 2011, he rolled out the educational web company Learnirvana. Also based in San Francisco, Learnirvana is Simmons's attempt to match the flexibility of the Internet with the educational needs of users. The impetus for the site may have come from its founder's opinions about traditional American educational systems, of which he has been a staunch critic. A donor to the Bay Area's nontraditional Brightworks school, Simmons told *San Francisco* magazine writer Diana Kapp, "Education is one of the most talked-about things in the Valley right now.... The first wave of Internet entrepreneurs have kids who are school

age. They're like [referring to standardized education], 'Screw this.'"

Simmons used that attitude to create Learnirvana. On Learnirvana's landing page, site designers say, "Learnirvana is reimagining the experience of learning. Breaking from traditional models of education, we build streamlined products for students to explore the subjects of their curiosity." The site links to various "sources of inspiration" that are also critical of standardized education, especially curricula that stifle creativity. Learnirvana rolled out its first product hub, Lentil, in 2012. Lentil endeavors to teach users Japanese, Korean, and geography through online, repetitive lessons.

PERSONAL LIFE

Little is known of Simmons's private life. He has indicated that he hopes to do for younger entrepreneurs the same service Levchin performed for him and Stoppelman. Simmons is one of the lead financial backers of Upstart.com, which collects donations for venture capital to help people develop their own business ideas.

Steve Jones

Affiliation: Yelp and Learnirvana

In 2004, Russel Simmons teamed with his friend Jeremy Stoppelman to create Yelp, a website that mixes nonprofessional business reviews with social media. Simmons and Stoppelman were both graduates of the University of Illinois at Urbana-Champaign and veteran start-up employees of PayPal, the online payment site. After taking a cash out at PayPal, they created Yelp as a local San Francisco site to review eating establishments. After a poor rollout, they integrated social media recognition and rewards for reviewers into Yelp. The site has since grown into a nationwide and semiglobal entity. Simmons departed Yelp in 2010 with little fanfare; Stoppelman took Yelp public in 2012 with a successful IPO.

Simmons has gone on to found Learnirvana, a site dedicated to Web-based education. In 2012, it rolled out its first product, Lentil, to teach languages. Simmons also lent his support to modern educational techniques in the San Francisco Bay Area and to the entrepreneurial start-up site Upstart.

FURTHER READING

Alburger, Carolyn. "Yelp Co-founder Russel Simmons: Over It and Out." *Eater SF.* 15 June 2010. Web. 12 Aug. 2012. A brief article about the departure of Russel Simmons from Yelp, the Internet company he helped found. Includes a link to an article about the departure of Yelp brand director Nish Nadaraja.

Balcita, Angela. "The Start-up Boys: A Conversation with Yelp.com Founders Jeremy Stoppelman and Russel Simmons." *imagine.* Jan./Feb. 2008. Web. 12 Aug. 2012. An online magazine interview with the founders of Yelp. Includes insights into their business vision and model and how they used their previous experiences to launch Yelp.

Hansell, Saul. "Why Yelp Works." *Bits.* 12 May 2008. *New York Times.com*. Web. 12 Aug. 2012. Says that Yelp has succeeded because of its use of nonprofessional, social-media-motivated user reviews to stimulate readership, rather than relying on professional reviews.

Kamenetz, Anya. "The Perils and Promise of the Reputation Economy." *Fast Company*. 131 (2008/2009). Web. 12 Aug. 2012. An examination of the websites and Internet companies that deal in product and business reviews, which in turn create a "reputation economy." (Also available online as "Next on the Internet, Everyone Knows You're a Dog.")

Kapp, Diana. "The New and Hopefully Improved Totally DIY School." *Modern Luxury.com*. Apr. 2012. Web. 12 Aug. 2012. An article discussing new ideas of education in Silicon Valley, especially popular with the Web 2.0 generation. Mentions Simmons's support of the Brightworks.

Kucera, Danielle. "Yelp's Stoppelman Leads IPO by Snubbing Google, Yahoo Offers." *Bloomberg.com*. 2 Mar. 2012. Web. 12 Aug. 2012. Details Stoppelman's desire for control and how it led to a successful Yelp IPO.

Lacy, Sarah. *Once You're Lucky, Twice You're Good: The Rebirth of Silicon Valley and the Rise of Web 2.0*. New York: Gotham, 2008. Print. An overview of the renaissance of computer and web entrepreneurs in California's Silicon Valley.

O'Brien, Jeffrey M. "The Next Wave: Yelp Effecting Business Paradigm Shifts (Through Free Food and Tequila Shots)." *Fortune* 156.2 (2007). Web. 12 Aug. 2012. Details the way Stoppelman and Simmons created Yelp and gives insight into their casual approach to organizing their office.

Rusli, Evelyn M. "Yelp Hires Goldman and Citigroup to Lead I.P.O." *Dealb%k*. 8 Nov. 2011. *NewYork-Times.com*. Web. 12 Aug. 2012. Brief article about Stoppelman's hiring of Goldman and Citigroup to underwrite Yelp's IPO.

Smalera, Paul. "Yelp Grows Up." *Cnn.com*. 9 Apr. 2010. Web. 12 Aug. 2012. An article about the success of Yelp, plus the responsibility it has created, including facing three lawsuits.

Stoppelman, Jeremy."Q&A with Yelp CEO Jeremy Stoppelman." Interview by James Temple. *SFGate*. 12 Oct. 2011. Web. 12 Aug. 2012. Stoppelman reveals facts about the start of Yelp, as well as personal, sometimes trivial, information about the founders.

Tuttle, Brad. "The Yelp Conspiracy: How a Group of Businesses Conspired to Get Better Yelp Ratings." *Time*. 6 July 2012. Web. 12 Aug. 2012. Discusses how Yelp owners Stoppelman and Simmons cracked a group of business owners who were conspiring to get superior ratings on Yelp.

Wauters, Robin. "Yelp Co-founder and CTP Russel Simmons Is Out." *Techcrunch*. 14 June 2010. Web. 12 Aug. 2012. Brief article detailing Simmons's departure from Yelp, the online business review site he cofounded.

BIZ STONE

Cofounder of Twitter

Born: March 10, 1974; Boston, Massachusetts
Died: -
Primary Field: Internet
Specialty: Social media
Primary Company/Organization: Twitter

INTRODUCTION

Biz Stone has been called a serial entrepreneur because of his involvement with several enterprises: blogging sites Xanga and Blogger, podcasting company Odeo, and start-up incubator Obvious Corporation. He was a cofounder of the latter two. He is best known as a cofounder of Twitter, the free microblogging service that enables subscribers to send and receive text-based messages of 140 or fewer characters. He served as the company's creative director until 2010. He is also the author of Blogging: Genius Strategies for Instant Web Content *(2002) and* Who Let the Blogs Out? A Hyperconnected Peek at the World of Weblogs *(2004).*

EARLY LIFE

Christopher Isaac Stone was born in Boston, Massachusetts, on March 10, 1974. He acquired the name "Biz" as a toddler when his struggle to pronounce his first name yielded something that sounded like "Biz-ah-bah," which was soon shortened to Biz. His parents, Christopher Stone, a Boston mechanic, and Marjory Pugh, divorced when Biz was young, and he dropped the name "Christopher" at that time. Biz grew up in Wellesley, Massachusetts. He has three sisters. He graduated from Wellesley High School, where he founded a lacrosse team and coordinated the senior play. He entered Northeastern University in Boston on a scholarship with plans to major in English, but he dropped out after one year when he realized his only reason for going to college was that it was what one did after high school. He gave college another try when he enrolled at the University of Massachusetts on a theater arts scholarship, but he again dropped out after a year.

Biz Stone.

A summer job moving boxes at the Little, Brown publishing company led to work as a designer Stone helped the art director, who was having problems with a new Mac computer. While the art director was at lunch one day, Stone designed a book cover and left it in a stack of jacket designs with no comment. The director approved the design and offered the box mover a job as a designer. When Little, Brown moved its design division to New York, Stone, who by this time had met Livia McRee, whom he would later marry, chose not to leave Boston. Instead, he became a freelance graphic designer and taught himself web design. When friends decided in 1999 to start Xanga, an early blogging community, they invited Stone to join them. Xanga launched in 2000, and Stone served as the company's creative director until 2001, when he moved to Los Angeles and wrote his first book on blogging. He left California to move back to Massachusetts, where he wrote software for the alumni association of Wellesley College.

In 2003, Stone received an invitation from Evan Williams, whose company Blogger had just been acquired by Google, to join him and help revamp Blogger. Stone helped create the newly designed Blogger with additional features and remained as creative director

until 2005, when he went to work for Odeo, a new company founded by Williams and Noah Glass.

LIFE'S WORK

Odeo had been founded by Williams and Glass as a podcasting company. When Apple's iTunes added a podcasting directory, Odeo needed a new plan. Williams set the staff to brainstorming, and Jack Dorsey, a young programmer, tossed out an idea that he had been mulling for years, a service that combined instant messaging with qualities of dispatching. Dorsey, Stone, Glass, and engineer Florian Weber were charged with producing version 0.1.

Glass, with the help of a dictionary, came up with the name "Twitter," meaning "a short burst of inconsequential information" and "chirps from birds." Within two weeks, they had the prototype. On March 21, 2006, at 12:50 P.M. Pacific time, Dorsey sent the first message: "just setting up my twttr." The prototype was tested internally for several months before the public launch on July 15, 2006. Williams bought out the Odeo shareholders, and in October 2006, Stone joined Williams, Dorsey, and a few others from Odeo in forming a new company, The Obvious Corporation, which now owned all Odeo's assets, including Twitter.

Hopes were high, but growth was slow at first. It was not until March 2007 at the South by Southwest (SXSW) Interactive conference in Austin, Texas, that the service really began to attract attention. The annual conference is part of a larger festival that runs for a week or more and includes music and film as well as technology. Twitter negotiated with the festival to place flat panel screens in the hallways and created a Twitter visualizer that showcased tweets on the screens to demonstrate how the service worked. The tech-savvy crowd was hooked by the opportunity to tweet conference news and locations of the best parties, Twitter usage went from twenty thousand tweets per day to sixty thousand. In April 2007, Twitter became a separate company, with Dorsey as chief executive officer (CEO) and Stone as creative director.

Two years later, on June 8, 2009, in New York City, Stone accepted the Webby Award for Breakout of the Year, an award presented annually by the International Academy of Digital Arts and Sciences. The award was presented to Twitter, which had grown by 900 percent in that year alone. Stone, more outgoing than the Dorsey or Williams, became the public face of Twitter. He appeared on television shows such as *The Colbert Report* and Conan O'Brien's show to explain how people use the service and to relate human interest stories of people using Twitter for purposes weightier than "short bursts of inconsequential information." He has done interviews with *The New York Times*, *The Wall Street Journal*, *The Guardian*, *Vanity Fair*, *Mother Jones*, and dozens of other publications, some provocative and thoughtful, some witty and tongue-in-cheek.

The affable Stone is annoyed that Twitter is still dismissed as lightweight by some. One of his favorite stories concerns James Buck, a photojournalism student at the University of California in Berkeley, who went to Egypt to take photos of the protests of 2006–08 and was arrested by police. Buck tweeted "Arrested" on his cell phone, and friends at home who saw the message contacted the dean, who contacted the consulate, and so on until Buck could tweet "Freed." Stone also insists that Twitter is more information service than social medium. Despite the fact that Lady Gaga is the most followed person on Twitter, evidence suggests that Stone is right about its informative role. In addition to the famous tweets about the 2009 Iranian election protests, Janis Krum's message and photograph of the emergency landing of US Airways flight 1549 on the Hudson River, the National Aeronautics and Space Administration astronaut Timothy Creamer's first live tweet from space, and the tweet by Keith Urbahn, chief of staff for former defense secretary Donald Rumsfeld, that al-Qaeda leader Osama bin Laden had been killed by U.S. forces in Pakistan are just samples of important news that has been tweeted. As a result, much breaking news is now being announced via Twitter. Some celebrities are prolific tweeters, but ill-conceived tweets can have consequences, as icon Oprah Winfrey, NASCAR driver Kasey Kahne, and actors Ashton Kutcher and Alec Baldwin have discovered. Artists, authors, and actors use Twitter to promote their work, regional emergency preparedness organizations use Twitter to reach people during a disaster, and political dissidents use Twitter to promote their causes. Stone has an abundance of ammunition to respond to the charges of shallowness.

Stone remained in his position as Twitter's creative director through the company's first five years and saw the total tweets per day reach 200 million in 2010. He also worked through tense times with three CEOs: his two partners, Jack Dorsey (2006-2008) and Evan Williams (2008-2010), and Dick Costolo, who joined Twitter as chief operating officer in 2009 and became CEO in October 2010. Stone remained friends with both Dorsey and Williams when the two were not speaking to each other. However, on June 28, 2011, a few weeks

---

Affiliation: Twitter

Twitter is a communications network that allows people to send and receive text messages of 140 characters or less and link to photographs and videos using the Internet or appropriate mobile devices. The company was founded by Jack Dorsey, Biz Stone, and Evan Williams, and the service was publicly launched on July 15, 2006. It takes its name from the characteristic short bursts of conversation that generate behavior analogous to the flocking of twittering birds. The service, which is free but requires users to subscribe, celebrated its sixth anniversary in 2012 with 250 million users and a monetary valuation estimated by some to be as high as $13 billion.

The network is famous for its celebrity tweeters, such as U.S. president Barack Obama, popular singer/songwriter Lady Gaga, and Portuguese footballer Cristiano Ronaldo, but Twitter was also used during the 2008 Mumbai attacks to send emergency information and report on the injured and the dead, to send astronaut Mike Massimino's updates during the Hubble Space Telescope repair mission in 2009, and to celebrate Japan's 1–0 victory over Cameroon in the 2010 World Cup. The Library of Congress, the venerable U.S. repository of historical records, acknowledged Twitter's effect on culture and history and announced in 2010 that it would collect all tweets for scholarly and research purposes. The Twitter archive is part of the library's "Web Capture" project.

---

before Twitter entered its sixth year, Stone announced that he was leaving Twitter in his official role but would continue to be available in an unofficial advisory capacity. At the same time, he explained that he was joining Williams and Jason Goldman, who resigned in December 2010 as Twitter's vice president of product, in relaunching the Obvious Corporation. Less than a week later, he announced that he would also serve as strategic adviser to Spark Capital, a venture capital firm that is invested in Twitter.

Personal Life

Stone married his longtime girlfriend, Livia McRee, an artist and author turned wildlife rehabilitator, in June 2007. She was on the staff of WildCare, an urban wildlife rehabilitation center in Marin County, California. Stone was an honorary member of the center's board of directors. The Stones live in Marin County with their son Jacob, born in November 2011. They are vegans.

In 2010, the Stones established the Biz and Livia Stone Foundation, a private nonprofit that supports education and conservation in the Bay Area, with priority given to programs that benefit underserved children. Livia runs the foundation with one employee. The foundation held its first fund-raiser, cosponsored by AOL and *The Huffington Post*, in September 2011. The event raised more than $50,000. Stone holds the title Strategic Advisor for Social Impact for AOL's Huffington Post Media Group, where he offers counsel on cause-based initiatives and best corporate practices for philanthropy and corporate responsibility. Stone also donated to the foundation his fee for a Stolichnaya vodka advertisement in which he appeared.

Stone is an adviser to several other companies and organizations and is a visiting scholar at several universities. In 2009, he was named one of 100 Most Influential People in the world by *Time* and Nerd of the Year by *GQ*. In 2012, Stone signed a contract with Grand Central Publishing, a division of Hachette Book Group, for his third book, *Things a Little Bird Told Me*.

Wylene Rholetter

FURTHER READING

Korn, Melissa, and Amir Efrati. "Business Education: Biz Stone Goes Back to College, This Time as Adviser to M.B.A.s." *Wall Street Journal* 1 Sept. 2011, Eastern edition: B6. Print. The article shares what Stone thinks about the advantages of an advanced degree in business and considers what he has learned through on-the-job experience.

Smith, Chris, and Marcie McGrata. *Twitter: Jack Dorsey, Biz Stone, and Evan Williams*. Greensboro: Morgan Reynolds, 2011. Print. Looks at the early lives of the three founders of Twitter. Discusses Dorsey's early fascination with city maps and computer programming and the interest Williams and Stone had in blogging that led to careers. Traces the development of Twitter and the roles each founder played. The book is written for young adults, but it contains a wealth of information anyone interested in Twitter or its founders will find useful.

Stone, Biz. "Biz Stone." Interview by Sharon Gaudin. Computerworld 43.13 (2009):16–20. Print. Stone talks about expanding Twitter's real-time network internationally and his vision of how the service can help people. A sidebar with biographical data is included.

Switzer, Cody. "A Twitter Co-founder Starts Small with Family Charity." *Chronicle of Philanthropy* 24:4 (2011): 2. Print. The article discusses the private charity founded by Biz Stone and his wife Livia to support education and conservation in the Bay Area. It gives examples of their personal involvement in fund-raising and in selecting causes.

Williams, Evan, and Biz Stone. "The Weekend Interview with Evan Williams and Biz Stone: The Twitter Revolution." Interview by Michael S. Malone. *Wall Street Journal* 18 Apr. 2009, Eastern edition: A11. Print. Stone and Williams, two of the cofounders of Twitter, consider Twitter's success. Stone shares stories about how Twitter has helped people in a variety of ways.

LISA STONE

Cofounder and CEO of BlogHer

Born: 1967?; Atlanta, Georgia?
Died: -
Primary Field: Internet
Specialty: Social media
Primary Company/Organization: BlogHer

INTRODUCTION

Lisa Stone, along with Internet entrepreneurs Elisa Camahort Page and Jory Des Jardins, cofounded BlogHer in 2005 to create opportunities for women bloggers around the world to access and engage in a community dedicated specifically to the interests and information relevant to today's women. Stone serves as the company's chief executive officer (CEO) and was the chief architect behind BlogHer's distributed, diversified media business. She helped grow the company from a grassroots conference into a top-ranked women's community through the development of innovative models to deliver profitable, high-quality online media and to attract and compensate a massive base of new content contributors. The BlogHer Conference has emerged as the world's largest in-person event for the blogging

351

community, and BlogHer.com has secured its place as an award-winning, high-traffic social hub. Prior to BlogHer, social media-saavy women barely had a grip in the male-dominated blogosphere.

EARLY LIFE

Stone spent most of her childhood in Montana. Her parents, John and Janet Stone, moved Lisa and her siblings—sisters Nancy and Anna and brother John—to Missoula, Montana, in 1976. Her parents had become enamored of the small college town in the state's far west after visiting friends from their medical school days who resided in the area. Stone was instantly attracted to the mountain landscape and snow. The family settled in an part of town close to the University of Montanta, Missoula.

Stone attended the city's historic Hellgate High School. At the time, she was more interested in cheerleading and dating than academics. College was not on her personal agenda until after she received some prodding and encouragement from several of the school's teachers, who saw potential in her intellect and ideas. She then became more focused on the future: Once high school graduation was behind her, she left Montana and moved across the country to attend Wellesley College, a prestigious women's institution in Wellesley, Massachusetts.

During her college years, Stone took a trip to California to visit her sister. who was studying at Stanford University. She decided the West Coast fit her style and moved to the San Francisco Bay Area after graduating from Wellesley, taking a job working in fuel futures with a local management consulting company. While learning about the industry and the markets and cultures of Europe, Stone decided on a different career path: She wanted to become a journalist. The realization prompted her to leave her consulting position and take a job as a writer with the local newspaper, *The Oakland Tribune*.

LIFE'S WORK

The Oakland Tribune was a daily newspaper in Oakland, California. During her tenure there, Stone gained valuable experience as a writer and investigative journalist. After originating a series of hard-hitting articles revealing the Federal Aviation Administration's lack of emergency preparedness, she was offered and accepted a job as a journalist with the powerhouse Cable News Network, or CNN.

Stone was a successful print journalist for CNN, but life changes instigated another career transition in

Lisa Stone.

1997. Stone's eight-year marriage had recently ended and she found herself in the role of a single working mother with an infant son. Her job with CNN required extensive travel and she did not want to be an absentee mother, so she decided to leave traditional journalism and begin a career in the then-novel field of online journalism. She looked for opportunities that would give her scheduling flexibility or the option to work from home so she could be there for her son.

Stone's first online journalism job was with WebTV, where she learned and honed her skills with hypertext markup language (HTML). Then she moved on to a position with Women.com as the company's executive producer, editor in chief, and vice president of programming. In that capacity, she was responsible for launching and developing online content communities for Bloomberg, E! Television/Online, the Gallup and Knight Ridder news organizations, HBO's *Sex and the City*, and Hearst and Rodale magazines. Under Stone's leadership, Women.com became a top-tier site.

When Women.com was acquired by iVillage in 2001, Stone took the opportunity to try something new. She left the company and applied for a Nieman fellowship at Harvard University. The fellowship recognizes the evolving face of journalism by awarding a small and select group of journalists from around the globe with an opportunity to engage in a year of study at the esteemed Harvard University with their peers and time to pursue their own individual areas of interest and expertise. Stone was the first Internet journalist to be accepted as a Nieman Fellow. She and her son moved to Massachusetts, where she spent the first six months of the program at the Massachusetts Institute of Technology (MIT) observing gaming technology. The next six months she spent at Harvard assessing business models that could be leveraged to fit the new technology she had just discovered.

As soon as the Nieman fellowship ended, Stone and her son moved back to the San Francisco Bay Area. She took a job with Law.com, where she built the first sponsored social media blogging network. During that time, Stone was also writing blogs covering the 2004 presidential election for the *Los Angeles Times*. She knew by then that there was a lack of resources for, and representation of, women in the blogosphere. However, it was not until connecting with two like-minded Internet entrepreneurs, Elisa Camahort Page and Jory Des Jardins, at a blog conference that the BlogHer took root. The three women discussed a project that would enable women bloggers to connect and share with one another. They decided on hosting their own blog conference specifically targeted at women bloggers. They agreed on the name BlogHer and held their first conference in 2005. Some three hundred women attended.

As a way to help conference attendees and other interested women stay connected outside the conference, Stone and her partners launched a blog hosted by Typepad. Within just one year, the blog became so popular that the three founders committed themselves full time to their new venture. Camahort Page, Des Jardins, and Stone quit their regular jobs and launched BlogHer as a limited liability company in 2006. With expectations high, the team realized that they needed to upgrade their platform from Typepad and moved the blog onto Drupal, which offered improved functionality and design options. Also in 2006, the three partners created an advertising and publishing network under the BlogHer umbrella to promote blogging among women and to make it easier for any woman to participate. With BlogHer's rapid success and expansion, Stone rallied to secure venture capital and big-name conference sponsorships to support the continued growth of the company.

By 2011, BlogHer had emerged as the fifth-largest online women's network. In addition, the company

---

Affiliation: BlogHer

BlogHer was launched in 2005 by Internet entrepreneurs Elisa Camahort Page, Jory Des Jardins, and Lisa Stone. The media company was formed to meet the needs of women bloggers, who were having difficulty finding a voice in the male-dominated blogosphere. BlogHer.com enables women to share with one another information and advice relevant to their roles as professionals, wives, mothers, friends, and the many other positions they fill. BlogHer.com attracts roughly 40 million unique users per month, according to April 2012 site statistics.

Along with providing women with an online environment for open communication, BlogHer hosts the world's largest social media conference for women each year. The event attracts thousands of participants from across the globe and hosts an array of influential guest speakers. U.S. president Barrack Obama gave an address at the 2012 BlogHer Conference in New York.

BlogHer also operates an expansive publishing network that boasts approximately three thousand high-quality blogs written by women. Operated by more than fifty staff members at the company's offices in New York and Silicon Valley, BlogHer receives funding support from Azure Capital Partners, Comcast Interactive Capital, and Venrock.

---

experienced huge revenue growth, saw its conference participation soar into the thousands, achieved top-tier distribution status for its advertising enterprise, and recorded utilization rates of nearly half a billion hits per month for the BlogHer.com community. BlogHer has been honored as one of AlwaysOn's OnMedia Top 100 for 2011 and among the Global 250 for 2010 and 2011. Separately, BlogHer.com was ranked among the Top 100 Websites for Women by *Forbes* in 2010, 2011, and 2012.

For her contributions, Stone has been recognized in the Ernst and Young Winning Women Class of 2011, as a recipient of the 2011 PepsiCo Women's Inspiration Award, and as one of the Most Powerful Moms in Media by *Working Mother* magazine in 2011. She was listed as one of the most influential women in Web 2.0 and technology by *Fast Company* in 2008, 2009, and 2010 and as one of the 100 Most Creative People in Business by *Fast Company* in 2010. In 2009, Stone was identified as one of the seven most powerful people in new media as ranked by *Forbes* magazine, as one of

AlwaysOn's Top 25 Women in Tech, and among the Influencers of Silicon Valley by the *San Jose Mercury News*. She frequently speaks at industry events and is an active member of the board of directors for the International Women's Media Foundation.

PERSONAL LIFE

Stone was married in the late 1980s, but the marriage ended by 1997, shortly after the birth of the couple's son, Jake. In 2003, she met Christopher Carfi, a senior strategist with Ant's Eye View, who helps clients such as Google and Visa develop their own social business strategies. Stone met Carfi, a blogger and single father, via Twitter. The two decided to live together in the San Francisco Bay Area of California with Jake, Carfi's son Gordon, and two Australian cattle dogs named Ike and Max. Gordon has a daughter, Meghan, who lives on the East Coast.

To try to balance her demanding career and family life at home, Stone has had to relinquish some of her favorite down-time activities, such as sewing, painting, reading, and—most coveted of all—skiing. Stone makes sure she has a chance to get on the slopes at least once a year when she returns to Missoula to visit family for the Christmas and New Year holidays.

Shari Parsons Miller

FURTHER READING

"Experiences with Internet Journalism." *Nieman Reports* 56.2 (2002): 35. Print. Provides excerpts from remarks made by journalists such as Teresa Hanafin, Stone, and Ken Doctor about their experiences with Internet-based journalism sites.

Stone, Lisa. "Lisa Stone Interview, Founder of BlogHer, Talks to Us About Her Success." Interview by Michael Dunlop. *Income Diary* June 2009. Web. 20 Aug. 2012. An interview in which Stone discusses the inspiration for BlogHer, the site's success, and her advice for other female Internet entrepreneurs.

"Study: 3 in 4 Online Women Are Active Social Media Users." *Public Relations Tactics* 17.5 (2010): 10. Print. Presents the results of the *BlogHer-iVillage 2010 Social Media Matters Study*, which found that 73 percent of female Internet users are active in social media and participate on leading social media platforms such as Facebook, Twitter, and blogs.

Swartz, Jon. "The New Faces of Tech." *USA Today* 5 June 2012: n. pag. Print. Discusses the ways in which female technology entrepreneurs and their start-up companies are changing Silicon Valley and driving the new web economy.

Tobias, Vicki. "Blog This! An Introduction to Blogs, Blogging, and the Feminist Blogosphere." *Feminist Collections: A Quarterly of Women's Studies Resources* 26.2–3 (2005): n. pag. Print. Provides an overview of blogs and their evolution into an effective communication mechanism for sharing ideas and opinions in general, and regarding women's issues in particular.

Viveiros, Beth Negus. "Picking Up Chicks." *Chief Marketer* 2.5 (2010): 41–42. Print. Explains that BlogHer views female users of social media as a unique marketing segment and talks about the ways in which some companies are using the site's targeted community to market and sell their products.

JEREMY STOPPELMAN

Cofounder of Yelp

Born: October 1977; Arlington, Virginia
Died: -
Primary Field: Internet
Specialty: Commerce
Primary Company/Organization: Yelp

INTRODUCTION

Jeremy R. Stoppelman is one of a new generation of Internet entrepreneurs revolutionizing Internet commerce and opinion sites. Stoppelman learned about Internet commerce while working as a vice president of engineering at the online payment company PayPal. Online auction site eBay bought PayPal while Stoppelman was employed there. With the introduction of Yelp in 2005, Stoppelman and partner Russel Simmons made it possible for customers in the San Francisco area to rate local businesses. Yelp has since gone nationwide, and ventured into public stock trading.

EARLY LIFE

Jeremy Stoppelman was born in Arlington, Virginia, in October 1977. His family moved to McLean, Virginia,

Jeremy Stoppelman.

during his early childhood. His father, John, was a securities lawyer, and his mother, Lynn, a schoolteacher before she began a marketing business. After graduating from Langley High School in McLean, he entered the University of Illinois at Urbana-Champaign in 1995, graduating with honors in 1999 with a bachelor's degree in computer engineering.

Stoppelman went to work for Excite@Home, where, according to his LinkedIn profile, he "designed and implemented various website features using Netscape Livewire for @Home's proprietary billing and provisioning system." After six months with the company, Stoppelman moved to PayPal. PayPal was the premier online payment site, allowing customers to pay safely for items purchased online by linking PayPal accounts either to credit cards or to bank accounts. The ease of PayPal usage also facilitated easy usage of the auction site Ebay. At PayPal, Stoppelman managed a forty-three-person team in charge of software development.

In 2003, Stoppelman entered the Harvard Business School. Stoppelman says his enrollment there was "deferred" after "successful completion of one year." In reality, he had begun work on the project that would become Yelp. The success of that start-up would preclude his return to graduate school.

LIFE'S WORK

As of 2012, the preeminent element of Stoppelman's career was Yelp. Stoppelman and Russel Simmons were both at PayPal when eBay bought the company. They both took cash-out offers, then started looking for new opportunities. Both men were fans of San Francisco food (burritos are a favorite of Stoppelman), and Yelp sprang from an idea to help people find good food and services. Their original idea was to take reviews in the form of e-mails from friends, load them into an algorithmic database, then make the reviews available online. Stoppelman and Simmons approached an old friend from PayPal (and another University of Illiniois almnus), Max Levchin, who advanced them $1 million to try the idea. They did three months of preparation, then rolled out the site.

It failed. "It didn't work perfectly right off the bat," Stoppelman told writer Angela Balcita. "We had to do quite a bit of tuning." Stoppelman noted, however, that they discovered that their friends loved writing reviews, so he and Simmons set about changing their vehicle to include witty reviews from local people writing about businesses they knew.

With this new idea in mind, Stoppelman and Simmons got another $5 million in venture capital from Bessemer Venture Partners and another $10 million from Benchmark Capital. The new idea was to marry the popularity of reviewing with the viral capability of the Internet. If enough reviews on a business began appearing on Yelp, then Yelp ad reps would contact the business's owners and try to sell them advertising space.

Yelp functions like an interactive Yellow Pages, or perhaps a cross between the Zagat review site and Facebook. Yelp encourages users to write witty reviews, then marries them to the popular aspects of social media. Yelpers can see which reviewers are becoming popular, their style of reviewing, and the businesses they patronize. That type of social popularity encourages more people to review, which, in theory, encourages more people to patronize featured businesses. In turn, that should equate with more paid ads on Yelp sites. Reviewers can become "elite" Yelpers over time, earning badges and online notoriety, as well as invitations to Yelp parties. Stoppelman, however, has not elaborated on what it takes to become a member of the elite.

Stoppelman explained the name Yelp on the question-and-answer site Quora:

> David Galbraith (a guy in Max's incubator MRL Ventures who was helping us with Yelp in the early days)

found it on his own. It was available for purchase from a squatter for 5k. Russ and I didn't immediately like the name since it was "the sound of a dog being kicked" and I was strangely enamored with "yocal," a terrible name. Fortunately Scott Bannister (another guy hanging out in the incubator, who was also involved in the naming of PayPal) immediately loved it. He told us he'd buy it and sell it to us the next day when we came to our senses. In the ensuing discussion Jared Kopf (yet another incubator employee) put down his credit card and actually bought the domain. The next day it was transferred to the company (we paid back Jared) and the rest is history.

Stoppelman and Simmons realized early that their site would not work if it became deluged with fake reviews—either bogus good reviews written by business owners themselves or bad reviews that business owners targeted at their competition. Stoppelman says that Yelp has encountered both types, along with attempts by business owners to pay friends to write reviews for them. They therefore created a "review filter," an algorithm (maintained in secret), that looks at patterns and weeds out fake reviews. Stoppelman said Yelp probably would not have lasted five years without the filter. Stoppelman explains on Yelp's "about us" site that the algorithm is not perfect, and Yelp staffers are constantly tweaking it for the best results. The filter is "conservative" in its approach, and Stoppelman admits that some legitimate reviews may be rejected and some shills may get through. The site also encourages "self-policing," which dedicated reviewers seem to embrace. In early 2012, the Yelp review filter busted a "business association" for posting bogus reviews. Members of the association allegedly competed with each other for prizes to see who drive up Yelp ratings the most.

After Simmons's departure from Yelp in 2010, Stoppelman expanded Yelp from a one that covered only the San Francisco area to one with nationwide coverage. Yelp has also entered all the major European countries and Australia. As of mid-2012, Yelp had 78 million unique monthly viewers, and reviewers had written more than 30 million local reviews.

Stoppelman long remained opposed to any outside control of Yelp or buyouts. In 2009, after low-key talks with Google, Stoppelman abruptly walked away from a $500 million buyout offer. Soon after, he reportedly did the same thing to a $700 million purchase offer from Microsoft. He opted instead for another round of venture capital, this time $100 million, to either compensate employees better (most of whom sold advertising the old-fashioned way, by phone) or allow them to cash out shares. As of 2012, Yelp had yet to make a profit. In 2011, it made $83 million but lost $16.9 million.

By 2012, however, Stoppelman was ready to take Yelp public. With Citigroup and Goldman underwriting its initial public offering (IPO), Yelp placed 7.15 million shares on sale on March 2, 2012, for $15 each. Trading was strong, reaching a high of $26 per share and closing at $24.58.

Yelp's popularity was not without some controversy. Some business owners have feared that they would not get good reviews if they did not buy ads on Yelp. Stoppelman has assured customers, however, that 85 percent of all reviews are three stars or more on a five star scale, regardless of advertising status. In 2009, a California dentist who was the target of a bad Yelp review sued to have the review removed. While the Yelp reviewers argued it violated their right to free speech, a California court upheld the dentist's request.

Stoppelman has also tangled with Internet giant Google. In testimony before a U.S. Senate antitrust

---

Affiliation: Yelp

In 2004, Jeremy Stoppelman teamed with his friend Russel Simmons to create Yelp, an online site that mixes nonprofessional business reviews with social media. Stoppelman and Simmons were both graduates of the University of Illinois at Urbana-Champaign and veteran start-up employees of PayPal, the pioneering online payment site. After taking a cash-out deal at PayPal, Stoppelman and Simmons created Yelp as a local San Francisco site to review eating establishments. After a dismal rollout, they integrated into Yelp social media recognition and rewards for reviewers. The site has since grown into a nationwide and semiglobal entity. With the creation of a "review filter," Stoppelman has successfully protected the credibility of Yelp's reviews, fending off attempts by businesses to manipulate their own reviews. Stoppelman has guided Yelp's survival of several lawsuits originated by recipients of poor Yelp reviews.

Since Simmons's departure from Yelp in 2010, Stoppelman has run the site on his own. He has steadfastly held on to control by refusing buyout attempts, notably from Google and Microsoft. In early 2012, he took Yelp public with a successful IPO.

subcommittee on September 21, 2011, Stoppelman alleged that, rather than maintaining a search engine that drives users to "the best sources of information" on the Internet, Google hopes to be "a destination site itself for one vertical market after another." He also charged that Google Local was favoring its own content in site searches and forcing Yelp content out of merged search results.

PERSONAL LIFE

Stoppelman is a private individual in a very public business. He eschews the manic, long-hour, day-into-night work schedule that so many computer geniuses embrace, preferring an orderly schedule of work and relaxation. He is devoted to his vizsla, Darwin, and is an avid reader of nonfiction.

Steve Jones

FURTHER READING

Alburger, Carolyn. "Yelp Co-founder Russel Simmons: Over It and Out." *Eater SF.* 15 June 2010. Web. 12 Aug. 2012. A brief article about the departure of Russel Simmons from Yelp, the Internet company he helped found. Includes a link to an article about the departure of Yelp brand director Nish Nadaraja.

Balcita, Angela. "The Start-up Boys: A Conversation with Yelp.com Founders Jeremy Stoppelman and Russel Simmons." *imagine.* Jan./Feb. 2008. Web. 12 Aug. 2012. An online magazine interview with the founders of Yelp. Includes insights into their business vision and model and how they used their previous experiences to launch Yelp.

Hansell, Saul. "Why Yelp Works." *Bits.* 12 May 2008. *New York Times.com.* Web. 12 Aug. 2012. Says that Yelp has succeeded because of its use of nonprofessional, social-media-motivated user reviews to stimulate readership, rather than relying on professional reviews.

Kamenetz, Anya. "The Perils and Promise of the Reputation Economy." *Fast Company.* 131 (2008/2009). Web. 12 Aug. 2012. An examination of the websites and Internet companies that deal in product and business reviews, which in turn create a "reputation economy." (Also available online as "Next on the Internet, Everyone Knows You're a Dog.")

Kapp, Diana. "The New and Hopefully Improved Totally DIY School." *Modern Luxury.com.* Apr. 2012. Web. 12 Aug. 2012. An article discussing new ideas of education in Silicon Valley, especially popular with the Web 2.0 generation. Mentions Simmons's support of the Brightworks.

Kucera, Danielle. "Yelp's Stoppelman Leads IPO by Snubbing Google, Yahoo Offers." *Bloomberg.com.* 2 Mar. 2012. Web. 12 Aug. 2012. Details Stoppelman's desire for control and how it led to a successful Yelp IPO.

Lacy, Sarah. *Once You're Lucky, Twice You're Good: The Rebirth of Silicon Valley and the Rise of Web 2.0.* New York: Gotham, 2008. Print. An overview of the renaissance of computer and web entrepreneurs in California's Silicon Valley.

O'Brien, Jeffrey M. "The Next Wave: Yelp Effecting Business Paradigm Shifts (Through Free Food and Tequila Shots)." *Fortune* 156.2 (2007). Web. 12 Aug. 2012. Details the way Stoppelman and Simmons created Yelp and gives insight into their casual approach to organizing their office.

Rusli, Evelyn M. "Yelp Hires Goldman and Citigroup to Lead I.P.O." *Dealb%k.* 8 Nov. 2011. *NewYorkTimes.com.* Web. 12 Aug. 2012. Brief article about Stoppelman's hiring of Goldman and Citigroup to underwrite Yelp's IPO.

Smalera, Paul. "Yelp Grows Up." *Cnn.com.* 9 Apr. 2010. Web. 12 Aug. 2012. An article about the success of Yelp, plus the responsibility it has created, including facing three lawsuits.

Stoppelman, Jeremy."Q&A with Yelp CEO Jeremy Stoppelman." Interview by James Temple. *SFGate.* 12 Oct. 2011. Web. 12 Aug. 2012. Stoppelman reveals facts about the start of Yelp, as well as personal, sometimes trivial, information about the founders.

Tuttle, Brad. "The Yelp Conspiracy: How a Group of Businesses Conspired to Get Better Yelp Ratings." *Time.* 6 July 2012. Web. 12 Aug. 2012. Discusses how Yelp owners Stoppelman and Simmons cracked a group of business owners who were conspiring to get superior ratings on Yelp.

Wauters, Robin. "Yelp Co-founder and CTP Russel Simmons Is Out." *Techcrunch.* 14 June 2010. Web. 12 Aug. 2012. Brief article detailing Simmons's departure from Yelp, the online business review site he cofounded.

T

JEFF TAYLOR

Founder of Monster

Born: October 4, 1962; place unknown
Died: -
Primary Field: Internet
Specialty: Social media
Primary Company/Organization: Monster.com

INTRODUCTION

Jeff Taylor has been an Internet entrepreneur for most of his life. He invented the job search site Monster.com, the social networking site Eons.com, and the online obituary site Tributes.com. Despite selling Monster early on, he stayed with the company after the sale to develop, implement, and communicate its corporate strategy. He has extensive marketing experience with baby boomers and their changing needs as they grow older. By transforming newspaper sections into online marketplaces, he has changed the landscapes of traditional media and careers; in addition, by aligning online commerce and social networking, Taylor has become one of the most innovative entrepreneurs in today's consumer industry.

EARLY LIFE

Jeffrey C. Taylor grew up in Peoria, Illinois. Later, he moved to Boston, where he started his first business while still a student at the University of Massachusetts, Amherst, selling "freshman survival kits." However, before long he dropped out of school and started working as a disc jockey in several nightclubs in Boston. Later, he returned to school and graduated with a degree. He would credit his later business success to the numerous extracurricular activities he became involved in during his college years, work opportunities that afforded him

both practical knowledge and experience. In his first professional business job, he worked as a contingency recruiter—a headhunter. In 1989, he founded his first company, a recruitment advertising agency called Adion, Inc., which specialized in human resource communication.

LIFE'S WORK

In December 1993, Taylor conceived the idea for Monster.com after realizing that for centuries people had been looking for jobs in newspapers, an activity that he thought outdated but adaptable and well suited to the technologies available on line. His popular Monster.com job search site, which was officially launched in April 1994, was registered as the 454th dot-com company on the Internet. In the process of attracting his first customers, Taylor approached two hundred potential clients, hoping to convince them to advertise on his new job search site. However, only forty of them acquiesced. He subsequently found, to his surprise, that the visitors to his site were not coming from the Boston area, where most of the jobs were located; they were coming from overseas. This proved frustrating for many of his clients. The ensuing struggle to attract clients and investors finally convinced him to put the company up for sale. In 1995, he sold Monster.com to TMP Worldwide for $900,000. The company then went public and was renamed Monster Worldwide. Taylor stayed with the company until August 2005, holding numerous management positions and eventually becoming chief executive officer (CEO). As a result of its famous Super Bowl ad in 1999, Monster became the indisputable market leader; by 2005, Monster was in thirty-four countries and had become a well-known brand around the world.

Jeff Taylor.

The name signified something huge; a huge idea, a monstrous, gigantic job database, an employment site with thousands of résumés. The business model was designed to attract job seekers: employers and recruiting agencies are required to pay for the service to search and contact posted online résumés. This project has revolutionized the ways in which résumés are being written and stored. Now, applicants' job histories and their availability are made evident over a long period, rendering a job search, a résumé, and an application easily reusable. Monster also used a localization strategy of linking the job site to local environments and needs. While many companies struggle in times of economic crisis and unemployment, Monster actually benefits from economic downturns; the numbers of job seekers inevitably grow during recessions.

When Taylor sold Monster to TMP Worldwide two years after it started, many voices claimed that he had sold too early and that by selling later he could have made much more money. Taylor, when asked about the sale in recent times, stated that he never regretted selling at that time and for that price. Without the resources and infrastructure of TMP, Monster would never have become as successful as it is today. Moreover, the mentoring he received from TMP's chairman, Andy McElvey, proved of immense value to him.

Taylor then focused his energy on his next start-up, Eons.com, a social network site for baby boomers (people over the age of fifty). The idea for this enterprise was based on his thoughts about what the average baby boomer would be doing around retirement age. Eons offered various interest groups and facilities for baby boomers, including a message board. It raised $32 million in funding, but around 2008 Eons laid off approximately one-third of its workforce. Taylor explained this move as the transition of Eons from a portal site to a social networking site with which baby boomers could become more engaged. At the beginning of 2011, Eons was sold for an undisclosed sum. Eons.com was the umbrella for four companies that emerged out of it: Eons.com, Eons BOOM Media, Meetcha, and Tributes.com.

Subsequently, Taylor founded Tributes.com, a website that published online obituaries. Taylor's focus was mainly on baby boomers, an age group rapidly reaching retirement age, and it seemed clear as deaths in this age group would increase over the coming years and decades. Therefore, according to Taylor, "Death is a growing business." He reasoned that, with social networks becoming more popular and people being able to communicate with one mouse-click with huge numbers of people, there would be many who would want to communicate regarding not only their lives but also their legacies, as well as their contemporaries' lives. Tributes was designed to give families and friends the opportunity to review a departed loved one's life in the public sphere: to memorialize them, grieve for them, and keep them alive in their memories and in their social network profiles.

Another spin-off from Eons.com was Meetcha, a social dating site for forty-plus individuals interested in meeting others. Taylor founded the company in 2009 not only to bring people together but also to enable people who share the same interests to meet in group settings. Recognizing that dating can become more challenging as people grow older, he thought that it might be easier for people in the older age group to make new contacts when out with others. Moreover, as members of this age group tend to have more established interests, the Meetcha search engine includes specific categories of interest that can match people more effectively.

In 2011, Taylor started another new venture, Buffalo.dj. The business idea behind this company is to record, represent, and promote disc jockeys who write their own songs and are interested in participating in music festivals. Taylor takes a much more active and hands-on role in the career building of people, which has emerged as a lifelong passion.

Affiliation: Monster.com

Jeffrey Taylor, a human resources specialist and founder of Monster.com, came up with the idea for a digital recruiting and job search site in 1994. Monster Board, as the company was called then, was acquired by TMP in 1995. Taylor was appointed head of TMP Interactive. At the time, job seekers from forty-eight countries uploaded their digital curricula vitae to the site, which saw as many as fifteen thousand visitors per day. In 1998, Monster became the world's leading online job search site, with more than 2 million visitors per month. In 1999, Monster Board and Online Career Center merged into Monster.com. In 2003, TMP changed its name to Monster Worldwide, showcasing the company's successful expansion. In 2004, Monster.com added the Monster Employment Index to the site to track employment market developments. In 2005, Taylor left the company and started Eons.com.

Today, with an online presence in approximately fifty countries, Monster has become a global company, highly specialized in local and international recruitment. Later, Monster entered into numerous strategic alliances with local newspapers in its home market in such cities as New York, Boston, Philadelphia, and Chicago. Since 2008, the company has increased its engagement in Asia, especially in the huge labor market in mainland China, where it increased its investment in ChinaHR to 100 percent and in the Asia-Pacific region by cooperating with News Limited in an Australian online website called CareerOne. Through its huge web presence, Monster can offer attractive advertising space for companies. Since 2009, Monster has enhanced its website services and functionality by offering new features, such as Monster Career Mapping, Monster Career Snapshots, and Monster Career Benchmarking. In 2010, Monster bought Yahoo! Hot Jobs for $225 million. In the following year, the company launched BeKnown, a Facebook application that connects employers and job seekers, and SeeMore, a search platform for employers.

In 2007, Salvatore Iannuzzi became Monster's chairman, president, and CEO. In 2011, Monster had six thousand employees.

PERSONAL LIFE

Taylor, whose disc jockey name is Jefr Tale, has been a passionate disc jockey for many decades. He loves dance music, electro, and house and has performed on Sirius satellite radio, at the Ultra Music Festival, and in clubs in Massachusetts, among venues. He is one of the organizers of the Root Society "party dome," the annual Burning Man festival in Nevada. Taylor sits on the board of Sonicbids, a start-up company in Boston that connects musicians with employers. He also serves on the board of directors of Boston's Citi Center for the Performing Arts and the board of advisors for the Berklee College of Music. He has owner/president management (OPM) and executive education certificates from Harvard Business School and was awarded an honorary doctorate from Bentley College.

Taylor has been married twice: He had three children—Ryan, Brooke, and Cole—with his first wife. In 2009, he married for a second time, and they have had a child together.

Sabine H. Hoffmann

FURTHER READING

Buss, Dale. *How to Think Like the World's Greatest New Media Moguls: Business Lessons from Geraldine Laybourne (Oxygen.com), Jeff Taylor (Monster.com), Steve Case (AOL.com), and Other New Media Sensations*. New York: McGraw-Hill, 2001. Print. Overview of several Internet entrepreneurs and their businesses, including Taylor and Monster.com.

Kronstadt, Sylvia. "Monster.com Founder Has a Monstrous New Scheme." 9 Aug. 2012. *The Motley Fool*. Web. 14 Aug. 2012. A review of Tributes.com.

Taylor, Jeffrey. "The Making of Monster.com (by a DJ Entrepreneur)." Interview by Andrew Warner. 15 Dec. 2010. *Mixergy.com*. Web. 14 Aug. 2012. Rehearses the history of Taylor's most successful start-up and his current activities.

---, and Doug Hardy. *Monster Careers: How to Land the Job of Your Life*. London: Penguin, 2004. Print. Provides insights into effective job-search strategies from multiple perspectives: recruiters, career counselors, human resources professionals, and other job seekers. Explains how to write effective and successful resumes and cover letters and how to succeed in negotiations.

---. *Monster Careers: Interviewing; Master the Moment That Gets You the Job*. London: Penguin, 2005. Print. Taylor provides job seekers with tips and suggestions on how to survive the interviewing process, including techniques for conducting Internet searches and how to build confidence.

---. *Monster Careers: Networking*. New York: Penguin, 2006. Print. Taylor explains the importance of social networking for job hunting and career development. He gives recommendations on how to build good relationships and helpful connections.

PETER THIEL

Cofounder of PayPal

Born: October 11, 1967; Frankfurt, Germany
Died: -
Primary Field: Business and commerce
Specialty: Management, executives, and investors
Primary Company/Organization: PayPal

INTRODUCTION

Peter Thiel is an investor, hedge fund manager, and entrepreneur who cofounded PayPal with Max Levchin. He was the first outside investor in Facebook and has a lengthy record of supporting successful Internet innovators. He has used his substantial personal wealth to fund a range of projects, through the Thiel Foundation and other vehicles, in line with his scientific and libertarian interests. In doing so, he has established a reputation as a leading philanthropist in venture capitalism. These efforts are in part an attempt to prevent what he believes to be a coming catastrophe by developing necessary preventive technology.

EARLY LIFE

Peter Andreas Thiel was born in Frankfurt, Germany, on October 11, 1967, but moved as a small child with his younger brother and parents to California, after several other stops due to his father's career as a chemical engineer. Peter became an excellent chess player and achieved the rank of master. He attended Stanford University and received a bachelor's degree in philosophy. He helped found the *Stanford Review*, which has become a well-known forum for right-wing views on society and politics.

Thiel now offers substantial fellowships of $100,000 each to college students to drop out of college for two years to become full-time entrepreneurs. The award reflects his skepticism about the value of formal education. Like-minded friends whom he met at Stanford went on to form the so-called PayPal Mafia. After graduation, Thiel worked in the legal profession and then joined Credit Suisse and traded derivatives for three years before starting his own firm, Thiel Capital Management, in 1997.

LIFE'S WORK

Thiel started PayPal with Levchin in 1998 as a means of transmitting cash payments via the Internet safely. The company subsequently merged with Elon Musk's X.com and, for four years, struggled to survive in an unfriendly business environment, which included attempts by organized crime to hack and overtake the PayPal network and the traumatic events of the collapse of the dot-com bubble. However, the company's biggest struggle was with the online trading giant eBay, which resisted the presence of PayPal at a time when a number of payment options were competing for market share. The rapid formulation of business strategy by company leaders at this time has become a staple of business school case studies.

Peter Thiel.

PayPal was bought by eBay in 2002, and Thiel's share made him rich; reportedly, he made $55 million from the total $1.5 billion sale. Freed from corporate responsibilities, Thiel founded Clarium Capital as a vehicle for investments in a wide range of activities that suited his development interests. The company prospered in its early years and, although profits declined in the years since the ongoing economic crisis of 2008, Thiel's fortune had already become self-sustaining.

Thiel's investments were inspired by the dot-com bubble and by the philosophy of René Girard, whom he had met at Stanford, in addition to interests in innovative scientific research. Some of the investments have been angel investments and venture capitalism. The most significant example of this was the 2004 investment of half a million dollars in Facebook, after Thiel was introduced to founder Mark Zuckerberg. Thiel's investment provided him with more than 10 percent of the company and was particularly important in signaling to other potential investors that Facebook was a promising investment opportunity. His relationship with Facebook has been restricted to the financial side, and he has shown little personal aptitude for technological innovation other than the desire to help fund and inspire it.

With a personal fortune estimated to be in excess of $2 billion, despite the dramatic decline in the profitability of Clarium Capital, Thiel has been able to establish numerous investment projects supporting long-term scientific research that may not meet the normal criteria of venture capitalism and that are better described, therefore, as philanthropic in nature. These have included funds for the Singularity Institute and Thiel's seasteading interests. Support for antiaging technology stems from his belief that death is a phenomenon that appropriate technology could postpone indefinitely. More conventional early-stage investment has helped in the success of such Internet ventures as LinkedIn, Yammer, Friendster, and Vator.

In 2004, Thiel was one of the leading investors in a new firm, Palantir Technologies, which also received funding from the Central Intelligence Agency's investment arm. The concept of Palantir derives from experience at PayPal in the conflict with organized criminal attempts to hack or cheat the system. This gave rise to the insight that augmented human intelligence, given an appropriate data-mining environment, would outperform purely machine intelligence. The company aimed to provide such an environment and has been credited with success in fighting potential fraud associated with the Recovery Accountability and Transparency Board.

Affiliation: PayPal

Peter Thiel met Max Levchin and other future PayPal colleagues at Stanford University. Many of them contributed to the right-wing journal *The Stanford Review*, which Thiel helped to found. Thiel and Levchin established Confinity in 1998 to research and market cryptography software applications and two years later merged it with Elon Musk's X.com to form the current incarnation of PayPal. The company aimed to provide a secure online payment receipt system and worked in competition with systems from Yahoo, Citibank, and others, including credit card companies. Competition was fierce and it was far from certain that PayPal would prevail. However, victory was signaled when eBay decided to acquire PayPal for $1.5 billion in 2002.

The founders of PayPal are among a group of Silicon Valley investors and entrepreneurs informally known as the PayPal Mafia, who are credited with reinvigorating Internet development and the Web 2.0 concept. The company has subsequently developed its range of services while fighting off cyberattacks, not least from Anonymous in 2011 after actions against WikiLeaks. The corporate culture established by Thiel and Levchin has also been diluted, and the work experience there is now little different from that at any other publicly owned corporation.

It is not clear how the data-mining and civil liberties issues arising from the system square with libertarianism.

In addition to investments, Thiel is active in promoting libertarian ideas and their proponents, including presidential candidate Ron Paul. He also writes occasional articles for the *Wall Street Journal*, *Forbes*, and other publications; has funded films such as *Thank You for Smoking*; and has taught at Stanford University. He once claimed that freedom and democracy are incompatible and indicated that the former was preferable to the latter. When he has been challenged on his political views in the public sphere, he has tended to modify his earlier claims or indicate that his thinking has continued to evolve over the course of time. His philosophy mixes promotion of financial capitalism with the fear that various disasters threaten humanity or at least human society, which can best be tackled through technological innovation. However, he fears that the pace of technological change remains at an unsustainably low rate and is characterized more by extensive change (spread to all parts of the world by processes of globalization) than by intensive change, which involves the creation of disruptive new technologies. This requires unconventional thinking, which is compromised by social norms, the contemporary educational system, and modern life. This philosophy led Thiel to establish the Thiel fellowships, which offer up to twenty young people a total of $100,000 each to spend two years away from college and pursue entreprenurial goals.

PERSONAL LIFE

Thiel lives in California and enjoys a seemingly healthy lifestyle alone, but he has been reluctant to discuss his private life. He has never married and has been described as one of the world's leading bachelor billionaires. Unsurprisingly, these circumstances have provoked gossip that Thiel is gay, and he is indeed a supporter of gay rights, among many other issues. Personal profiles of him do suggest that he is relentlessly engaged on an intellectual basis with the world and its future and that his personal lack of charisma incline him to keeping a position in the background, funding projects rather than leading them personally. His portrayal in the film *The Social Network* is of a person who is brooding, secretive, and calculating rather than compassionate. Although the film's portrayals have been roundly criticized by many, other descriptions of his personality relating to this period follow a similar line.

Thiel's right-wing politics have become increasingly extreme and important in his life, and he has made some plans for creating a "microstate" through "seasteading"—that is, building some a large ship or floating platform that can declare independence as a corporatestate ruled by its shareholders; in this entity he foresees

the ability to experiment with new governmental forms. He has also enthusiastically pursued technological ideas that may derive from his love of science fiction: antiaging technology, for example, as well as space exploration and nanotechnology. Despite an occasionally apocalyptic vision of the future, Thiel remains optimistic that technological advancement can be intensified, primarily through market means, to the extent necessary to fend off potential disaster.

John Walsh

FURTHER READING

Fitzpatrick, David. *The Facebook Effect: The Inside Story of the Company That Is Connecting the World*. New York: Simon, 2010. Print. Corporate history of Facebook from its origins until 2010.

González, Andrés Guadamuz. "PayPal: The Legal Status of C2C Payment Systems." *Computer Law and Security Review* 20.4 (2004): 203–9. Print. Detailed treatment of PayPal's operations and legal implications.

Jackson, Eric M. *The PayPal Wars: Battles with eBay, the Media, the Mafia, and the Rest of Planet Earth*. Washington, DC: World Ahead, 2010. Print. Corporate history of PayPal from its formation until it was purchases by eBay.

Rahnesar, Romesh, and Peter Thiel. "21st Century Free Radical." *Bloomsberg Businessweek* 2 Feb. 2011. Web. 15 May 2012. Magazine profile of and interview with Thiel.

Sacks, David O., and Peter A. Thiel. *The Diversity Myth: Multiculturalism and Political Intolerance on Campus*. Oakland: Independent Institute, 1998. Print. Rightwing consideration of multiculturalism and its impact on educational standards at Stanford University.

DANIELLE TIEDT

Vice president of marketing at YouTube

Born: c. 1975; Iowa
Died: -
Primary Field: Business and commerce
Specialty: Marketing
Primary Company/Organization: YouTube

INTRODUCTION

Danielle Tiedt is recognized in the technology industry as a marketing innovator who helped Microsoft

Corporation launch and promote many of its successful computer networking and web-related products and services during her fifteen-year tenure with the industry behemoth. She is most closely associated with the roles she played in showcasing MSN and in launching the Bing search engine in 2009. Tiedt was recruited by Bing's main rival, Google, in February 2012 to lead the search engine leader's marketing efforts for the popular online video-sharing service YouTube. She was brought in specifically to devise new and creative ways not only to position YouTube as the primary destination for original video content but also to make it extremely attractive to advertisers so that it will ultimately generate advertising revenue rivaling that traditionally seen in television.

EARLY LIFE

Danielle Tiedt is the daughter of two educators, Lowell and Ann Tiedt. She was raised in Anamosa, Iowa, a small city in the Cedar Rapids metropolitan area surrounded by rolling green hills, sprawling farms, and picturesque communities along the Wapsipinicon River. As a child, Tiedt excelled at hay-stacking and pig-wrestling competitions. She attended Anamosa High School and graduated in 1993. After receiving her diploma, she moved to Madison, Wisconsin, to attend the University of Wisconsin. She majored in business administration and received a bachelor's degree with honors in that field in 1997. She was hired by Microsoft Corporation right out of college and moved to the Seattle area of Washington to begin what would be a fifteen-year career with the computer and new-technology industry giant.

LIFE'S WORK

When Tiedt joined Microsoft in 1997, it was just beginning to redefine its offerings and expand its product line into computer networking and the Internet. Tiedt's main area of focus was to develop the company's cutting-edge products and market them to consumers. In connecting consumers to Microsoft's products, Tiedt consistently employed a straightforward data-driven approach derived from her formal business education and combined it with her personal passion for devising innovative new approaches to launching and promoting technology products. During her tenure at Microsoft, Tiedt was responsible for a U.S. media budget in excess of $118 million and was a key player involved in approximately fifteen major product launches for various sectors of the company's business.

One of the product launches with which Tiedt was involved was the 2004 rollout of MSN's services, targeted at high-speed broadband users. The expanded offering included optimized content services, sophisticated communication tools, digital photo sharing, and comprehensive online security solutions. The successful launch of the revitalized MSN.com was critical to Microsoft Corporation's strategic shift from an Internet service provider (ISP) to a purveyor of broadband

Danielle Tiedt.

services. Tiedt led the marketing charge, which included a yearlong U.S. advertising and marketing campaign incorporating print, television, and online media as well as a rebirth of the brand's butterfly logo.

Two years later, in 2006, Tiedt led the marketing effort behind Microsoft's launch of Windows Live Academic Search, a specialized Internet search service targeting researchers and other academics. The service searches the content of academic journals to find associated journal abstracts and enable easy extraction of information for citations. Although it was designed to compete with Google Scholar, it was expected to be less of a moneymaker and more of a component in Tiedt's broader effort to foster brand loyalty for Microsoft's burgeoning Internet search services. At the same time, Tiedt recognized the importance of building a brand relationship with users of academic search engines. She identified a select group of librarians, academic researchers, and others from among the heavy users of Google Scholar and invited them to the Microsoft campus in Washington to preview the company's product and provide input on its development. The company also connected with top businesses in the reference arena, including industry association CrossRef and various academic publishers, during the development phases of

Windows Live Academic Search. That type of relationship building is a signature strategy for Tiedt, who recognizes that connections are just as critical as cash in establishing the success of a product or service.

In 2009, Tiedt was responsible for launching another Google rival product, the search engine Bing. Backed by $100 million in advertising funds, Tiedt faced the uphill battle of creating a market need among users who seemed to be content with the leading search engines, Google and Yahoo! Essentially, she had to convince satisfied customers to switch their loyalties. The campaign was largely successful, and by 2012, Microsoft had secured some 15 percent of the U.S. search market, slightly ahead of Yahoo! but still significantly behind Google, which held nearly 66 percent of the U.S. search engine market. Microsoft Corporation put Tiedt in charge of a Bing rebranding effort. Tiedt helped take the brand's tagline in a more consumer-friendly direction, from "Decision Engine" to "Bing Is for Doing."

Shortly after the Bing rebranding effort, Tiedt was recruited by Google to join the YouTube team as vice president of marketing. She switched to Microsoft's chief rival in February 2012. At that time, YouTube was in the midst of launching ninety-six entertainment channels designed to attract television-level advertising dollars. Tiedt is responsible for guiding those channel launches and building consumer loyalty for them, which in turn was expected to lure the support and funding of big-ticket advertisers.

Tiedt's hire signals Google's larger focus on the consumer as a significant part in the overall success and growth of YouTube. Until early 2012, the YouTube brand was known primarily as a source of comical amateur videos that had gone viral. While YouTube was the top-ranked video-sharing site in the United States—with more than 150 million unique viewers—its parent company, Google, planned a major transformation. With Tiedt's help, Google expected to transform YouTube into a genuine entertainment brand and leading destination for original content, capable of serving as a desirable alternative to television and other forms of mainstream entertainment. In the past, the company's advertising and marketing efforts have centered on utilization of its service or platform. Google recognized that such an approach would not drive the change it is seeking for YouTube. Therefore, after months of searching for a marketing executive, the company decided that Tiedt's extensive experience with consumer-focused campaigns and heavy emphasis on building loyalty was the right mix to lead the rebranding effort for YouTube.

Affiliation: YouTube

YouTube is a video-sharing website founded in February 2005 in San Bruno, California. The site enables the public to view and share original digital videos. Although it is essentially a distribution platform for amateur video producers, the site also attracts advertisers and media corporations, including CBS, the BBC, and Hulu, which post some of their content offerings online for added exposure and cost-effective promotion.

When YouTube originally debuted, users could upload unlimited content, but in 2006 analysis revealed that users were posting unlicensed copies of movies and television shows to the site. YouTube instituted a ten-minute length restriction (increased to fifteen minutes in July 2010) to correct the problem, although trusted users may be invited to upload videos up to twelve hours in length upon account confirmation.

Although highly successful, the site has not been without its controversies: notably, ongoing disputes concerning intellectual property and copyright infringement and controversial or prohibited material.

In September 2012, for example, a denigratory film about the Prophet Muhammad, produced in the United States by an extremist, appeared on YouTube and incited anti-American demonstrations and violence in major cities across the Middle East. YouTube is blocked or censored, or has been blocked or censored, in a number of countries, including Morocco, Thailand, Iran, Pakistan, and most infamously China (which has issued an outright ban of the site for all Chinese users). In the case of the 2012 demonstrations, Google blocked access to the offensive film on YouTube in several countries where it was illegal and extremely politically sensitive, including Singapore, Malaysia, Indonesia, and Saudi Arabia.

In 2006, the founders of YouTube sold it to the search engine company Google for $1.65 billion in stock. Under Google, YouTube continues to be the most popular video site on the Internet and the third most popular website of all time. According to a 2008 *New York Times* report, YouTube consumes more bandwidth in one year than the entire Internet did in 2000.

Instead of persuading consumers to try a new product, as she had done with the Bing launch, Tiedt would put her efforts into getting consumers to view an established and successful brand, YouTube, in an entirely new light.

PERSONAL LIFE

Tiedt lives in the greater Seattle, Washington, area. While at Microsoft Corporation, she was a recipient of the company's Outstanding Contributor Award in recognition of her stellar work on multiple key projects.

In April 2012, it was reported that Tiedt was listed as an owner of the high-end handbag manufacturer Tradesrogue. Tiedt's boyfriend, leather artisan and designer Nathaniel Smith, serves a manager for the company. Allegations of impropriety were made when the company's handbags were featured at New York Fashion Week in 2011 as part of a Bing marketing event. While it was determined that Tiedt properly disclosed her relationship with Smith in compliance with Microsoft's conflict-of-interest policies, the question about disclosure of her individual affiliation with Tradesrogue was posed.

Shari Parsons Miller

FURTHER READING

Artero, Juan P. "Online Video Business Models: YouTube vs. Hulu." *Palabra Clave* 13.1 (2010): 111–23. Web. 20 Aug. 2012. Discusses the beginnings and evolution of the leading U.S. online video services, YouTube and Hulu. Examines the different business models implemented by the two companies, their respective success in terms of site traffic and revenue, and their strategic outlook for the future.

Green, Lelia. *The Internet: An Introduction to New Media*. New York: Berg, 2010. Print. Examines the history of the Internet, its roles in new media, and its emerging future. Explores case studies and new research from around the world to present various aspects of Internet use as a reflection of social, political, and economic circumstances.

Nasr, Dara. "With So Much Content on YouTube, How Do I Ensure My Marketing Stands Out?" 25 July 2012. *Marketing*. Web. 20 Aug. 2012. An opinion piece on the use of YouTube's video website for online marketing. Concludes that the key element of success using this marketing channel lies in creating content that users want to share with others.

Wasserman, Todd. "Why Microsoft Chose the Name 'Bing.'" *Brandweek* 50.22 (2009): 33. Web. 20 Aug. 2012. Examines why Microsoft Corporation decided to name its Internet search engine Bing. Includes commentary from Tiedt, a former executive at Interbrand, which assisted Microsoft in the naming process.

---. "You Tube." *Brandweek* 47.37 (2006): M14–M17. Web. 20 Aug. 2012. Highlights the rapid and significant success of the online video-posting website YouTube. Explains that the site capitalized on the dual new-media trends of video sharing and social media as they hit their peak.

RAY TOMLINSON

Inventor of e-mail

Born: October 2, 1941; Amsterdam, New York
Died: -
Primary Field: Computer science
Specialty: Computer programming
Primary Company/Organization: ARPANET

INTRODUCTION

Ray Tomlinson achieved what became his principal career success in 1971, when he was working on the ARPANET system and devised the means for the world's first network e-mail system. His innovations led to the development of systems that would one day become the Internet.

EARLY LIFE

Raymond "Ray" Samuel Tomlinson was born October 2, 1941, in Amsterdam, New York; he was one of four boys. He spent his first four years in Worcestershire, and then the family moved to the small, unincorporated village of Vail Mills, New York. He attended Broadalbin Central School in nearby Broadalbin, New York. In 1965, he received a bachelor of science degree in electrical engineering from Rensselaer Polytechnic Institute in Troy, New York; while at Rensselaer, he participated in a program jointly coordinated by Rensselaer and IBM. He entered the Massachusetts Institute of Technology (MIT) to continue his study of electrical engineering.

He earned a master's degree in electrical engineering in 1965; Tomlinson developed an analog-digital hybrid speech synthesizer as part of his master's work. In 1967, he took a job with Bolt, Beranek, and Newman, which was involved in work related to ARPANET. There he helped develop the operating system TENEX and a file transfer protocol (FTP) called CPYNET.

LIFE'S WORK

In 1971, Tomlinson was a young engineer at Bolt, Beranek, and Newman (BBN, now Raytheon BBN Technologies) in Cambridge, Massachusetts. He had been working on network control protocol for TENEX and on file transfer protocols such as CPYNET and SNDMSG. The group with which he was working was given responsibility for finding applications for ARPANET, which was a network of four U.S. computers linked together as part of the Department of Defense's Advanced Research Projects Agency (ARPA). The network featured data packet switching, thereby enabling (at least hypothetically) communications between one and many other computer systems. The concept of single-user-to-single-user communications had already been established, and Tomlinson could move from one machine to another to check whether a message he had sent had arrived correctly.

Ray Tomlinson.

Since the 1960s, it had been possible to leave messages for other researchers using the same time-sharing computer. Unlike today's e-mail, the messages did not travel over a network but sat waiting for pickup on the computer. CPYNET allowed files to be transferred over the ARPANET. Tomlinson came across a request for comments (RFC) about a protocol for a messaging system using the network that struck him as far too complicated. He thought he could devise a better and simpler system.

Tomlinson had the idea of combining two existing programs, one for the single-user communication and one for distribution of files among ARPANET computers, to form an application that could send a message from one user to as many recipients as desired. A file on the recipient's machine was designated as the mailbox and was configured such that, although others could attach their material to the end of the existing file (as individual e-mail messages), they could neither access the file themselves nor change any of its contents apart from appending messages at the end. Tomlinson also had the idea of providing a unique identifier for multiple users on the same machine, but he needed something to separate the user's identification from the designation of the computer or network being used. Tomlinson studied the keyboard, wondering what character he could use to set off the username that would not be assumed to be part of the username. He chose the @ symbol because it is the only character on the keyboard that typically would not be part of an individual's name. The symbol has subsequently been accepted by the New York Museum of Modern Art's permanent design collection.

The first e-mails were tests of the system that Tomlinson sent to himself; Tomlinson does not recall the specific text he used for those first e-mails. He assumes that it was the QWERTYUIOP keyboard string. After a few successful e-mails, Tomlinson showed them to a colleague with the caveat that he not tell anyone else because the project was not part of their assignment. In later years, Tomlinson was also involved in the formulation of e-mail standards and formats that continue to be used today through his coauthorship of RFC 561 in 1973, which defines name of sender, subject, and date fields. He was also involved with the enhancement of the file transfer protocol (FTP) system, which was used extensively until being replaced by simple mail transfer protocol (SMTP) in 1982.

In 2000, Tomlinson received the George R. Stibitz Computer and Communications Pioneer Award from the American Computer Museum in recognition of his

Affiliation: ARPANET

The Advanced Research Projects Agency (ARPA) was created by the U.S. Department of Defense as a means of fostering and developing innovative new systems and concepts at a time when the Cold War represented an apparently existential threat to the country. The ARPA Network, or ARPANET, was one aspect of this process.

ARPANET scientists had developed the conceptual understanding of what is today known as the Internet by the 1960s, but they were constrained from delivering their vision because of technological and engineering imitations. ARPANET scientists solved one of the more important of these limitations through the development of data packet switching. The network thereby created consisted of four computers in the United States, linked with one another, but it was not clear exactly how they would communicate.

Working at Bolt, Beranek, and Newman, Ray Tomlinson was a young engineer among a group of programmers whose job it was to identify tasks that ARPANET could usefully perform. He was the first to send the networked communication (others had already sent computer-to-computer messages) that has come to be known as e-mail. He also devised the use of the @ symbol to denote a particular user at a particular computer (or communication node). ARPANET continued for several years thereafter and was associated with various computer hardware developments before being superseded by more sophisticated networks.

role in creating what became the Internet's most popular application. He has also been inducted into the Internet Hall of Fame. The question of whether Tomlinson or, indeed, anyone else, can be genuinely credited the inventor of e-mail has been much contested over the years, partly because a number of different projects were developed more or less contemporaneously to make e-mail possible; thus there is no single invention that defines e-mail so much as a collection of different protocols and systems that need to be combined in order to provide a recognizable experience and because the people involved were mostly known to one another and, as scientists rather than members of commercial operations, were willing to share ideas and knowledge. The subsequent cluster of activities located in California's computer and Internet cluster has at some stages followed a similar principle of mutual knowledge and

competency sharing, but this has been significantly constrained as ideas and technologies have become embedded in specific companies that have aimed to protect what they believe is their intellectual property. It may be telling, however, that on *The Boston Globe*'s 2011 "MIT 150," a list of what it described as 150 ideas that "have had a profound impact, in one way or another, on society, culture, politics, economics, transportation, health, science, and, oh yes, technology," Ray Tomlinson was ranked in fourth position.

PERSONAL LIFE

Tomlinson enjoys playing the piano and skiing. He is known to reminisce fondly about his collegial working life, when he made his greatest contributions, and to compare it unfavorably with current conditions, in which, although e-mail has become embedded in everyday life, the problems caused by spam, viruses, and other ill-intentioned innovations occasioned by good technological advancements have made many people's experience of technology problematic and unenjoyable.

Tomlinson is not a fan of abbreviations or acronyms—such as LOL (for "laugh out loud") or AFAIK (for "as far as I know") in e-mails or the dropping of opening salutations. In the early days of e-mail, after mistakenly copying an e-mail to a number of people who were unrelated to the project that was the subject of his e-mail message, Tomlinson sent the world's first spam message.

John Walsh

FURTHER READING

Gillies, James, and Robert Cailliau. *How the Web Was Born: The Story of the World Wide Web*. New York: Oxford UP, 2000. Print. A detailed history of the development of the early Internet covering ARPANET.

Metz, Cade. "Meet the Man Who Put the '@' in Your Email." *Wired* 30 July 2012. Web. 30 July 2012. A profile of Tomlinson focusing on his years with ARPANET.

Pasternack, Alex. "Q+A: Ray Tomlinson Sent the First Email But His Inbox Is Still a Mess." *Motherboard* 20 Apr. 2010. Web. 30 July 2012. Magazine-style interview in question-and-answer format primarily covering developments arising from Tomlinson's work on ARPANET.

Rawsthorn, Alice. "Why @ Is Held in Such High Esteem" *New York Times* 21 Mar. 2010. Web. 30 July 2012. Newspaper story covering the acceptance of the @ symbol into the Museum of Modern Art and its significance in popular culture.

Tomlinson, Ray. "The First Network Email: A History from Ray Tomlinson, the Inventor of Email." BBN Technologies. 13 Apr. 2010. Web. 30 July 2012.

Notes by Tomlinson about the creation of the first networked e-mail communications.

GINA TRAPANI

Founder of Lifehacker

Born: September 19, 1975; New York, New York
Died: -
Primary Field: Internet
Specialty: News and entertainment
Primary Company/Organization: Lifehacker

INTRODUCTION

The founder of the Lifehacker blog in 2005, Gina Trapani continued to oversee the blog until 2009. She continues to work as a blogger and tech commentator, cohosting the This Week in Google *netcast, and developing Expert Labs' crowdsourcing platform.*

EARLY LIFE

Gina Marie Trapani was born on September 19, 1975, in Brooklyn, New York. As a high school student, she wrote for New Youth Connections, a teen-written magazine published by Youth Communication. In 2005, she founded the Lifehacker blog.

LIFE'S WORK

Lifehacker is part of the Gawker Media blog network run by British journalist Nick Denton, which includes an assortment of other blogs on subjects from cars to gossip to science fiction. Lifehacker was written solely by Trapani for the first nine months after it launched, and associate editors were added toward the end of the year, with more contributors joining soon after. Few of the early Lifehacker contributors remain with the site today.

Lifehacker offered posts on "life hacks"—tricks and tips for one's life, especially in increasing productivity, or finding more efficient or easier ways of doing things. Many of the posts on Lifehacker concern "Getting Things Done" (GTD), a management system introduced in the book by the same name by David Allen in 2002, although as a management philosophy it has grown far beyond Allen. The core idea of GTD is to write necessary tasks down and rely on an external to-do list or task management system, rather than try to keep track mentally of everything one needs to do—even when those tasks are short-term (such as making a grocery list). Trapani has compared the Lifehacker site to Merlin Mann's 43 Folders, a similar productivity blog.

In 2009, Trapani left Lifehacker to join Expert Labs as a product director and began ThinkUp, a web-based application that archives the user's social media information—friends, followers, tweets, and so on—and generates data about friends and followers. Among the kinds of data it generates are visualizations of where conversations are occurring in the world; analyses of how many retweets and replies a tweet receives; and easy tools for publishing, exporting, or searching social media data. ThinkUp can be run from the cloud or

Gina Trapani.

installed on a web server. It began as a project within Expert Labs and then became a separate company. Expert Labs ended after ThinkUp essentially superseded it; it was a nonprofit tech company incubator that was formed after discussions between blogger Anil Dash and the White House Office of Science and Technology Policy in 2009. It was originally intended to enable access to expertise by the public and was funded with a MacArthur Foundation grant. In March 2012, Anil Dash announced the end of Expert Labs in a blog post in which he noted that a company was no longer needed to

demonstrate the use of social networks to influence public policy; the people had done that on their own.

Also after leaving Lifehacker, Trapani was tapped to write the guide to Google Wave, a highly anticipated collaborative editing platform announced by Google in 2009 and launched at the end of the year. However, within two months of its public release, Google Wave development was suspended, and existing Waves were deleted in 2012. The application simply never appealed to most people beyond workers in certain areas of business, science, and education who enjoyed a particular

---

Affiliation: Lifehacker

Lifehacker is a group blog about "life hacks," an extension of the hacking concept into daily life, especially when dealing with productivity, common distractions, decision making, and information overload. In general usage, a life hack must be a trick or procedure of some kind, a technique that is not an immediately obvious or already common procedure: Heating a can of SpaghettiOs on the stove is not a hack, but cooking a fish filet wrapped in Saran wrap in the dishwasher is. Usefulness, novelty, cleverness, efficiency, and expediency are the hallmarks of a life hack.

Lifehacker is part of the Gawker Media blog network which includes Gawker.com, Deadspin (sports), Gizmodo (gadgets and tech), io9 (science fiction), Kotaku (video games), Jalopnik (cars), and Jezebel (women's interests, defined on the site as "celebrity, sex, fashion"). Gawker Media was founded by controversial British entrepreneur Nick Denton, a former *Financial Times* journalist. The controversy around Denton frequently centers on what he chooses to cover and how often he is willing—even eager—to cross the line into exploitative tabloid-style stories. He publicly downplays the profitability of Gawker Media and blogs in general, although the company is estimated to be worth several hundred million dollars, with advertising revenues in excess of $50 million.

Gawker launched in 2003 and has gone through a number of expansions and contractions, as sites were added, acquired, or folded into other sites, while sites that were less commercially successful or did not fit the Gawker Media vibe were sold off. Former Gawker blogs include the travel site Gridskipper, the music site Idolator, the D.C. gossip site Wonkette, the consumer advocacy blog The Consumerist, the gambling blog Oddjack, the online video blog Screenhead, the news blog Sploid, the Silicon Valley gossip blog Valleywag, the

Hollywood gossip blog Defamer, and the pornography news blog Fleshbot. Defamer and Valleywag have been folded into Gawker.

In 2010, commenter accounts across Gawker Media were compromised by a hacker group—a total f 1.3 million accounts, as well as the site's source code—one of the more prominent major breaches of the period. That and an early 2011 site redesign led to a loss of traffic—more than an 80 percent decrease at first (representing the loss of frequent visitors more likely than an 80 percent decrease in the participating userbase) before the decrease slowed down. As of 2012, commenting on Gawker Media sites required signing in with a Google, Facebook, or Twitter account, an increasingly common practice in the blogosphere.

Lifehacker, which was founded by Gina Trapani in January 2005 and added associate editors Erica Sudan and Keith Robinson in September, has two international editions, Lifehacker Australia and Lifehacker Japan, replicating American posts that are not country-specific while adding posts related to local content. The site was originally sponsored exclusively by Sony but has since shifted to advertising from numerous tech-oriented companies. It was named one of the 50 Coolest Websites by *Time* magazine in its year of launch, as well as in CNET's Blog 100. It won the Best Group Weblog award in the 2007 Webbies.

In 2009, Trapani resigned as editor and was succeeded by Adam Pash, who remains editor in chief. The rest of the staff included senior editor Whitson Gordon, senior writer and art director Adam Dachis, contributions editor Tessa Miller, community editor Walter Glenn, contributing designer Brett Yoncak, and writers Melanie Pinola, Thorin Klosowski, David Gallaway, and Alan Henry.

working style; Google had mistakenly expected it would be "the next big thing."

Trapani writes a weekly column for *Harvard Business Online* and cohosts *This Week in Google*, a netcast with Leo Laporte, as well as *In Beta*, a podcast about open source web and mobile apps. *In Beta* launched in 2012, and episodes have focused on Twitter's relationship with developers, the appointment of Marissa Mayer as chief executive officer (CEO) of Yahoo, the Olympics coverage in the United States, Google Wallet, changes to Twitter's API, and the question of when to hire a professional designer. Trapani's articles have been published in *Macworld*, *PC World*, *Popular Science*, *Wired*, and *Women's Health*. Her *Harvard Business* columns have focused on productivity, especially for freelancers, covering topics like creative sabbaticals, free texting, and securing laptops in public places.

Trapani also operates the website NarrowTheGapp.com, which presents data about the still real, still alarming pay gap between men and women in the United States. The site presents and organizes data from the U.S. Bureau of Labor Statistics and other open data sources. Clicking on any job field or subfield on the page—divided into Management, Professional, and Related Occupations; Service Occupations; Sales and Office Occupations; and Natural Resources, Construction, and Maintenance Occupations—presents data on pay discrepancies in that field, in terms of cents out of every dollar, pay out of every weekly paycheck, and differences in annual income. The site's data may be easily shared with Twitter, Facebook, Pinterest, and Google+.

Trapani is a Sun-certified Java programmer, primarily building websites and programming extensions for Firefox (she wrote the Better Gmail extension). She also wrote the text-based task manager Todo.txt, which takes a user-created file called todo.txt and converts it into a manageable, manipulable task list on a mobile device. The app is simple to use, consisting of basic fields like priority and deadline, in order to be equally useful whether read by a human or a machine. The shell script allows command-line access in a Unix-like environment. Recent updates have included swipe-to-complete. Todo.txt is available for both Apple and Android products.

PERSONAL LIFE

Trapani maintains a presence on Twitter and Google+, as well as a personal blog, smarterware.org. She lives in San Diego, California.

According to interviews, Trapani uses a 15-inch MacBrook Pro with an iCurve laptop stand and a desktop PC she assembled from parts, as well as a widescreen monitor (for both), an ergonomic keyboard and optical mouse, external backup hard drives, a modular Ikea Jerker desk, and an HTC G1 phone running Android. The need for both a Mac and a PC is a result of her software development, and her PC triple-boots with three versions of Windows: XP, Vista, and Windows 7. Most of her work is done in Firefox using web apps, and she keeps Gmail, Google Reader, Google Calendar, Google Docs, Twitter, and WordPress open most of the time in Firefox. She also uses Google Chrome as a secondary browser and organizes her photos with Picasa. SyncBack Free backs up her files to the external drives.

On the Mac, Trapani uses TextMate for coding, Smultron for writing, and Time Machine for backups. In addition to backing up to the external hard drives, she uses Mozy for online backups. She also uses KeePass for password management.

Bill Kte'pi

FURTHER READING

Jenkins, Henry. *Confronting the Challenges of Participatory Culture: Media Education for the 21st Century*. Cambridge: MIT, 2009. Print. Examines social media, new forms of creative expression, and their impact on media studies.

Pash, Adam, and Gina Trapani. *Lifehacker: The Guide to Working Smarter, Faster, and Better*. New York: Wiley, 2011. Print. Compiles and organizes many of the tips from the Lifehacker site.

Trapani, Gina. *Upgrade Your Life: The Lifehacker Guide to Working Smarter, Faster, Better*. New York: Wiley, 2008. Print. A Lifehacker book that offers more tips from the site.

Qualman, Erik. *Socialnomics: How Social Media Transforms the Way We Live and Do Business*. New York: Wiley, 2010. Print. The impact of social media on the business world.

Rosenberg, Scott. *Say Everything: How Blogging Began, What It's Becoming, and Why It Matters*. New York: Broadway, 2010. Print. A history of blogging by a journalist and Salon.com cofounder, without the hype, misconceptions, or fast-money tips of most other books.

MENA TROTT

Cofounder of Six Apart and creator of Movable Type

Born: September 16, 1977; Woodland Hills, California
Died: -
Primary Field: Internet
Specialty: Social media
Primary Company/Organization: Six Apart

INTRODUCTION

Mena Trott was the president of Six Apart, a company she cofounded with her husband, Ben Trott. Mena was an early blogger, and the Trotts developed Movable Type, one of the tools within Six Apart, because she was dissatisfied with the blogging software available to her. Mena Trott is sometimes called the "founding mother" of the blog revolution because of the popularity of Six Apart and its tools, including not only the easy-to-use blogging tool Movable Type but also the blog-hosting service Typepad; these tools made it possible for people with limited technical skills to become involved in blogging.

EARLY LIFE

Mena Grabowski Trott grew up in California and was the teenage sweetheart of her husband, Ben Trott. She was not a particularly good student in high school, except in English and history, but she became interested in her studies when she began dating Ben, who was the class valedictorian. The couple also attended Santa Clara University together, and Mena has recalled that they were competitive with each other in their studies. Both graduated in 1999, Mena with a bachelor's degree in English and Ben with a bachelor's degree in mathematics.

LIFE'S WORK

After graduating from college, Trott entered the workforce in Silicon Valley just as the dot-com bust of 2000 was about to occur. In this volatile atmosphere, many companies that had been founded on an idea or product that seemed promising went bankrupt rapidly. Trott's first job was at a start-up company that was building a portal to help parents monitor their children's school performance. When that company went broke, she joined a design firm, which also went broke. She began keeping an online diary, dollarshort.org, in 2001, and the attention and response granted her fairly ordinary personal thoughts persuaded her that blogging had a

commercial future, as people's interests seemed to be shifting away from being passive recipients of media and toward creating their own.

Part of the reason Trott became interested in blogging was that she wanted to connect with people online; she felt isolated because of her heavy work schedule and the fact that most of her nonwork time was spent with her husband. During a period in 2001 when both Mena and Ben were out of work, they collaborated in creating Movable Type, a program to facilitate blogging; Mena did the design for the program and Ben did the coding. The impetus for creating Movable Type was Mena's dissatisfaction with the tools available to post her own blogs, and initially they distributed Movable Type for free, asking only for donations (as was the custom with much shareware at the time). Neither Mena nor Ben was familiar with the process for starting a business, but the entrepreneur Joi Ito was a Movable Type user and arranged for a meeting with Barak Berkowitz, who would later become Movable Type's chief executive officer (CEO). Initially the Trotts' venture received less than 1 million dollars in start-up

Mena Trott.

Affiliation: Six Apart

Mena Trott was one of the first individuals to build a successful business model around blogging. She and then-husband Ben Trott founded Six Apart in 2002, but the roots of the company go back to 2001, when Mena and Ben developed Movable Type, a dynamic publishing platform, for their own use. Their timing was fortunate, because there was a huge explosion of interest in blogs in the early 2000s, and software developed by the Trotts enabled people with limited technical ability to join in online blogging conversations. In 2004, the company grew to employ fifty employees. By 2006, more than half of people using the Internet were reading blogs, and blogs had become an important commercial tool as well as a means of self-expression.

Typepad is a customizable blogging platform intended for nonexpert users; it shares some features with Movable Type, but it is less complex and includes some features popular with individual bloggers, such as photo albums. It is also available at three price levels—Plus, Unlimited, and Premium—with the higher levels allowing greater customization, the opportunity to create multiple blogs, and higher levels of support.

By 2012, Movable Type was in its fifth version (Movable Type 5), which allows users to easily build websites and blogs. It employs a content management system (CMS) that provides a dashboard to help manage blogs and websites, and a revision history feature to track changes. The program allows users to build a website, then add blogs to it, and to build multiple blogs and websites from a single installation. The 2012 iteration comes in three versions: Movable Type 5 (for developers), Movable Type 5 Pro (for individual power bloggers, small to medium businesses, primary and secondary schools, and media and publishers), and Movable Type 5 Advanced (for universities, media companies, and other institutions that need a product integrated with the Oracle and SQL server databases).

As of 2008, an estimated 20 million bloggers used Six Apart programs, and 100 million people were reading blogs fueled by Six Apart. In the 2000s, Six Apart acquired and then sold or closed two other blogging platforms. One was LiveJournal, another blogging company, in 2005 (sold in 2007 to Sup, a Russian media company). LiveJournal's tenure at Six Apart was not without incident. Six Apart angered many LiveJournal users in 2007 by closing down five hundred discussion groups it considered too sexual, although some turned out to be harmless sites devoted to fan fiction or literary criticism, while others were devoted to aiding victims of sexual abuse; in response, LiveJournal users took several acts of revenge, including publishing the social security numbers of company executives, and CEO Barak Berkowitz's profile was defaced. Six Apart acquired another blogging service in 2006, Vox, which focused on social networking with privacy controls so the user could control the content other users could see. Six Apart closed Vox in September 2010. As of 2012, Movable Type was the most popular busines content management system in Japan.

funding, and the company expanded slowly; Trott recalls that she and her husband were reluctant to spend the investor's money, and in retrospect she regrets that they did not hire more programmers and get a marketable product ready more quickly.

Movable Type was immediately popular with bloggers: soon after Trott announced it on her blog, about two thousand people signed up to be notified when Movable Type became available. However, the Trotts were slow to adopt a commercial attitude toward Movable Type: Until 2004, it was offered under a number of different license options, and all licenses but the commercial one were free. Even the commercial license was underpriced: It cost $150 for any number of installations within a company. Trott eventually realized that if other companies were using her product to make money, she should be able to make money off them. In 2004, Movable Type changed the licensing structure and began charging all users, a decision that generated some backlash from personal users and highlighted a philosophical issue that is still germane to software creators: Is their software just another commercial product that they are entitled to sell at a price the market will bear, or is it more like information to which everyone should have access? Trott takes a middle ground on this question, stating that while she is in business to make money, she also has the goal of facilitating blogging for millions of people.

As of 2004, the Trotts' Six Apart (a name chosen because its two founders were born six days apart) had more than 1 million registered users. In 2004, Trott was named one of *PC Magazine*'s people of the year and was also named one of the top innovators under age thirty-five by *Technology Review*, a journal published by the Massachusetts Institute of Technology (MIT). Trott gave an invited talk at a TED conference in 2006. Six Apart went through several name and ownership changes in 2010 and 2011; as of 2011, Six Apart was owned by the Japanese IT company Infocom, and Typepad and Movable Type are developed, marketed, and supported by SAY Media.

PERSONAL LIFE

Trott was married to Ben Trott, with whom she founded Six Apart; they have a daughter together. In May 2012, Trott announced their divorce. After they sold the company, she remained an active blogger, posting on sixapart.com, dollarshort.org, and sewweekly.com, the latter a blog devoted to sewing projects.

Sarah Boslaugh

FURTHER READING

Lacy, Sarah. *Once You're Lucky, Twice You're Good: The Rebirth of Silicon Valley and the Rise of Web 2.0*. New York: Gotham, 2008. Print. A popular history of Silicon Valley companies from the Internet Bust of 2000 to the rebirth of the industry with companies such as Facebook, PayPal, and Six Apart; the author is a journalist specializing in technology and entrepreneurship stories.

Livingston, Jessica. *Founders at Work: Stories of Startups' Early Days*. New York: Springer, 2007. Print. A collection of interviews with successful technology entrepreneurs, focusing in particular on the original idea that led to their product and company, and the process of moving from an idea to a successful company.

McNulty, Scott. *Building a Typepad Blog People Want to Read*. Berkeley: Peachpit, 2010. Print. A guide to using Typepad to create a blog, beginning with a discussion of blogging and the different purposes it may fulfill, a brief history and overview of Typepad, and discussion of specific features and capabilities. This book is targeted at TypePad users and explains how to accomplish basic tasks with the program, including choosing a theme, designing one's own, customizing a blog, using the dashboard to manage the blog, dealing with comments and spam, and monitoring and analyzing the blog's traffic.

Myers, Greg. *The Discourse of Blogs and Wikis*. London: Continuum, 2010. Print. A study of how blogs and wikis have changed methods of communications, and have changed social relations through means such as enabling the creation of virtual communities and challenging hierarchical approaches to information. Myers is a university professor of linguistics and cites examples from a wide range of wikis and blogs to support his argument that these forms of communication are distinctive genres that are changing the way we use language.

"The Universal Diarist." *The Economist* 25 Nov. 2006: 68. Print. Feature story on the originals of Six Apart, the changes in expectations (from mass media to personal or intimate media) that fueled the rapid growth of blogs, and Six Apart's acquisition of Vox.

W

Jimmy Wales

Cocreator of Wikipedia

Born: August 7, 1966; Huntsville, Alabama
Died: -
Primary Field: Internet
Specialty: Social media
Primary Company/Organization: Wikipedia

Introduction

Jimmy Wales, cofounder of Wikipedia, has believed that everyone should have the freedom to access information and the ability to add to our human knowledge base. While Wikipedia operates as a nonprofit organization, Wales has used his background in finance to provide sustainable capital for the free online encyclopedia. Charismatic but controversial, labeled as "benevolent dictator" and "spiritual leader" by his colleagues, Wales is the public face of Wikipedia, spreading the gospel of free access to information while the net worth of Wikipedia grows into hundreds of billions of dollars.

Early Life

Jimmy Donal Wales was born to a middle-class southern family on August 7, 1966, in Huntsville, Alabama. His father, also Jimmy, worked as a grocery store manager, while his mother, Doris, and grandmother, Erma, ran the House of Learning, a small private school founded on the principles of the one-room schoolhouse and the Montessori method. Wales and his three siblings received their early education from the House of Learning; the number of students was so small that the environment was almost like a home school. An early, inquisitive reader, Wales spent many hours at the House of Learning reading the *Encyclopedia Britannica* and *World Book Encyclopedia*.

Although Wales did not come from a wealthy family, they considered education extremely important for success and were willing to pay the price for further private education. After eighth grade, Wales attended a university preparatory school, the Randolph School, in Huntsville, graduating at sixteen. He attended Auburn University, where he earned his bachelor's degree in finance. He then entered the doctoral program in

Jimmy Wales.

finance at the University of Alabama, but he left with a master's degree to transfer to the Ph.D. finance program at Indiana University. While enrolled in doctoral studies, Wales taught courses at Indiana University and the University of Alabama but did not write his doctoral dissertation.

LIFE'S WORK

During his college years, Wales developed a fascination with the developing Internet and wrote computer code in his spare time. While studying at the University of Alabama, he became addicted to multiuser dungeons (MUDs), an early type of online role-playing game. From this experience, as well as his undergraduate exposure to Austrian school economist Friedrich Hayek's essay "The Use of Knowledge in Society," Wales grasped Hayek's concept of decentralized information and the potential of computer networks to foster large-scale collaborative projects to collect, organize, and disseminate this information. Wales recognized this theme again when reading about the open source movement, particularly through an essay by a founder of that movement, Eric S. Raymond, "The Cathedral and the Bazaar," which emphasized mass collaboration.

In 1994, Wales took a job with Chicago Options Associates, a futures and options trading firm in Chicago, Illinois. Through the information he gained in this position, Wales amassed his own capital bby speculating on interest rates and foreign currencies. This work, in turn, led to an interest in game theory and the effect of incentives on human collaborative activity, information that he combined with the philosophy of open source for the Wikipedia concept. In 1995, after Netscape went public, Wales decided to abandon financial trading to become an Internet entrepreneur.

In 1996, Wales and two partners founded Bomis, a male-oriented search engine and web portal featuring entertainment, user-generated web rings, and erotic photographs. While the Bomis venture landed Wales in trouble later for its pornographic content, it would provide the initial funding for the peer-reviewed free encyclopedia Nupedia and its successor, Wikipedia.

In the early 1990s, while moderating an online philosophy discussion group, Wales met Larry Sanger. Wales and Sanger had engaged in a lengthy online debate on Objectivism, which resulted in a meeting offline to continue the debate in person, giving birth to their friendship. When Wales was ready to pursue his online encyclopedia project, he knew that he needed a credentialed academic to lead it. Wales remembered

Sanger—a doctoral student in philosophy at Ohio State University at the time—and hired him to be the editor in chief.

In March 2000, Wales and Sanger launched the first free, peer-reviewed, open-content encyclopedia, Nupedia. Wales's vision was for Nupedia to have peer-reviewed, expert written entries on all subjects in all languages and to sell advertising on the site to generate profit. Unfortunately, the initial process to receive, review, edit, and publish entries on Nupedia was extremely time-intensive and led to very few entries actually getting published. Wales himself felt too intimidated to submit a first draft of an entry to Nupedia, because he knew the committee of highly esteemed finance professors who would review it. Wales wanted to change the Nupedia model to streamline the publishing process and make the site more user-friendly for volunteer writers.

In 2001, Sanger met with computer programmer Ben Kovitz to discuss the challenges of Nupedia. Kovitz introduced the concept of a *wiki* to Sanger, suggesting that a wiki would allow editors and writers to contribute and edit simultaneously, thus eliminating the bottleneck of backlogged entries. Sanger proposed the idea to Wales, and on January 10, 2001, they integrated the wiki into Nupedia. This first wiki was intended for the public to collaborate on articles that would then be reviewed by Nupedia's experts for publication. The majority of Nupedia's editors rejected the wiki, however, believing that blending content written by nonacademics with professionally researched and edited articles would compromise the academic integrity of Nupedia and destroy its credibility. On January 15, 2001, Wales and Sanger placed the wiki project, named "Wikipedia" by Sanger, on a separate domain and made it live.

Wales and Sanger had differences in opinion regarding the role of Wikipedia. While Sanger saw Wikipedia as the medium to hasten Nupedia's development, Wales saw Wikipedia as the one true collaborative open encyclopedia that would provide infinite, evolving information to the world. A few days after the launch of Wikipedia, the number of articles published there had exceeded that of Nupedia, and a collective of Wikipedia editors had formed. These first Wikipedia contributors and editors sympathized with the open source movement and promoted the free culture movement through their activities on Wikipedia.

In 2002, Bomis discontinued funding for Sanger's position. Sanger resigned as editor in chief of Nupedia and as "chief organizer" of Wikipedia. This significantly reduced maintenance costs for Wikipedia. Wales

Affiliation: Wikipedia

In March 2000, Wales and Sanger launched the first free, peer-reviewed, open-content encyclopedia, Nupedia. Wales's vision was for Nupedia to have peer-reviewed, expert-written entries on all subjects in all languages, and to sell advertising on the site to generate profit. Unfortunately, the initial process to receive, review, edit, and publish entries on Nupedia was extremely time-intensive, and led to very few entries actually getting published.

In 2001, Sanger met with computer programmer Ben Kovitz to discuss the challenges of Nupedia. Kovitz introduced the concept of a wiki to Sanger, suggesting that a wiki would allow editors and writers to contribute and edit simultaneously, thus eliminating the bottleneck of backlogged entries. Sanger proposed the idea to Wales, and on January 10, 2001, they integrated the wiki into Nupedia. This first wiki was intended for the public to collaborate on articles that would then be reviewed by Nupedia's "experts" for publication. The majority of Nupedia's editors rejected the wiki, believing that blending content written by nonacademics with professionally researched and edited articles would compromise the academic integrity of Nupedia and destroy its credibility.

On January 15, 2001, Wales and Sanger placed the wiki project, named "Wikipedia" by Sanger, on a separate domain and made it live. In a few days, the number of articles published on Wikipedia far exceeded that of Nupedia, and the original Nupedia was eventually abandoned.

While Wikipedia is still criticized by K–12 teachers and university faculty for publishing anyone's content, it does have peer reviewers and quality rating scales for every subject area. Students and researchers can use the quality rating scales to help them decide whether or not a Wikipedia entry would serve as an authoritative, credible, valid source of information. As of 2012, the English-language Wikipedia contained nearly four million entries. Wikipedia is also available in 260 languages, and that number will continue to grow as developing countries and small indigenous populations wish to preserve their languages in a free, open source environment. The Wikimedia Foundation, which provides support to Wikipedia, has also invested in open source textbooks (Wikibooks) and open education opportunities (WikiUniversity and WikiClassroom).

abandoned the idea of placing advertisements on Wikipedia and decided to turn it into a nonprofit foundation. Wales has been accused of editing Sanger out of the history of Wikipedia; in 2005 Wales edited his own biographical Wikipedia entry, deleting all references to Sanger as cofounder. Wales also tried to modify references to Bomis as a site that provided pornographic photos. As each individual Wikipedia entry displays a log of its edits, Wales could not hide his actions, and he apologized for editing his own biography. At the same time, he continued to refute Sanger's claims of cofounding Wikipedia in other forums.

In 2003, Wales set up the nonprofit Wikimedia Foundation (WMF) to establish policy for Wikipedia and related projects. It is a charitable organization that also generates funding for Wikipedia. Wales serves as board member and chairman emeritus on WMF's board of trustees. While Wales does not get paid by WMF, in 2008 he was accused of using WMF funds for recreational purposes and was forced to relinquish his WMF credit card. In 2004, Wales cofounded Wikia, a for-profit wiki-hosting service, with former WMF board of

trustees member Angela Beesley. Wikia allows people to host individual wikis on different subjects on the same website. Originally chief executive officer (CEO) of Wikia, Wales stepped down in 2006, when former vice president and general manager of eBay Gil Penchina stepped in and made Wikia profitable by 2009. Wales is also a public speaker, represented by the Harry Walker Agency. He has given talks around the world on the future of the Internet, open access to information, and related topics.

As Wikipedia became one of the most prominent websites around the world, Wales became an Internet celebrity and the public face of Wikipedia. At the same time, opinions of Wales range from "benevolent dictator" to "spiritual leader." Because of the Sanger controversy, Wales has developed a reputation for rewriting his personal history, editing out any perceived wrongdoings on his part.

Wales's role in creating Wikipedia, which has become the world's largest online open access encyclopedia, prompted *Time* magazine to name him in its 2006 list of the 100 Most Influential People in the world. He is also twelfth in *Forbes* Web Celebs 25. In 2007, Wales was identified by the World Economic Forum as one of its Young Global Leaders. His awards have included a Pioneer Award, the 2008 Global Brand Icon of the Year Award, the 2009 Nokia Foundation Annual Award, the Business Process Award at the Seventh Annual Innovation Awards and Summit by *The Economist*. He has received honorary degrees from Knox College, Amherst College, Stevenson University, Argentina's Universidad Empresarial Siglo 21, and Russia's MIREA University.

Wales identifies as an Objectivist, following twentieth-century writer Ayn Rand's philosophy, which promotes reason, individualism, and capitalism. He has identified his political views as "center-right" but also claims that he is an atheist. While he refused to comply with a request from the People's Republic of China to censor "politically sensitive" Wikipedia articles, Wales criticized WikiLeaks editor in chief Julian Assange for publishing Afghan war documents and identifying their website as a wiki, since it does not allow for collaborative editing.

PERSONAL LIFE
At twenty years old, Wales married his first wife, Pam, a coworker at a grocery store in Alabama. After moving to Chicago for his first job, Wales met his second wife,

Mitsubishi steel trader Christine Rohan. Their marriage lasted one year, and they had a daughter before separating. In 2008, Wales had a brief relationship with Canadian conservative columnist Rachel Marsden. In 2012, he and Kate Garvey, former British prime minister Tony Blair's former diary secretary, were planning to marry.

Wales identifies Wikipedia as his sole hobby, but he also enjoys reading and philosophy and maintains a blog on his personal website, www.jimmywales.com.

Rachel Wexelbaum

FURTHER READING
Anderson, Jennifer Joline. *Wikipedia: The Company and Its Founders*. Edina: ABDO, 2011. Print. Traces the history of Wikipedia and provides biographical information for Wales, Sanger, and Kovitz.

Bruns, Axel. *Blogs, Wikipedia, Second Life, and Beyond: From Production to Produsage*. New York: Peter Lang, 2008. Print. An examination of collaborative content creation in a variety of environments, including Wikipedia.

Lih, Andrew. *The Wikipedia Revolution: How a Bunch of Nobodies Created the World's Greatest Encyclopedia*. New York: Hyperion, 2009. Print. The philosophy of Wikipedia and its development.

JAY S. WALKER
Founder of Priceline

Born: November 5, 1955; Yonkers, New York
Died: -
Primary Field: Internet
Specialty: Commerce
Primary Company/Organization: Priceline

INTRODUCTION
Jay S. Walker is the founder, chairman, and chief executive officer (CEO) of Walker Digital LLC, a developer of new and patentable digital business models. He is the founder of numerous Internet-based start-up companies. Walker's most recognized accomplishment was the founding of the e-commerce site Priceline.com, for which he served as vice chairman until 2001. The site revolutionized both the travel industry and digital commerce in general through its introduction and popularization of buyer-driven commerce, a market-

ing tool that allows consumers to set their own price for goods and services and be matched with suitable companies. Walker Digital received a patent for the business model in 1998. Walker was the driving force behind Priceline, a pioneer of buyer-driven commerce on the Internet and one of the most successful companies to emerge from the so-called dot-com boom of the late twentieth century.

EARLY LIFE
Jay Scott Walker was born to Arthur and Jeanette Walker on November 5, 1955, in Yonkers, New York, where he was also raised. His father was a real estate developer. Walker cited his mother, who had escaped from Nazi-occupied Europe as a child, as the role model for his entrepreneurial drive. He also cited inventor Thomas Edison as an early hero. Walker began developing his

Jay S. Walker.

business skills as a teenager, working as a door-to-door salesman and newspaper deliveryman. In high school, he participated in student government, learning leadership skills as a representative during meetings between the city and local teacher's union. He graduated from high school in 1973 and began attending Cornell University.

During his course of study, Walker briefly left Cornell to begin his first entrepreneurial enterprise, launching a weekly Ithaca, New York, newspaper known as the *Midweek Observer*. The Gannett Company, which owned the local daily paper, soon put Walker out of business. This first failed enterprise left him with a debt reported to be between $150,000 and $250,000. He returned to Cornell, receiving a bachelor's degree in industrial relations in 1977. He and Jeffrey Lehman coauthored a book about winning strategies for the Parker Brothers board game Monopoly in 1975, bringing about a lawsuit from Parker Brothers that the company later dropped. Walker's first job after graduation was as research director of the Connecticut-based Folio Publishing Corporation, which produced the publishing industry trade journal *Folio*. He settled in Connecticut and held the job until 1984. After leaving *Folio*, Walker decided to reenter the entrepreneurial ranks.

LIFE'S WORK

Walker founded a series of companies in the 1980s and 1990s. The first, Visual Technologies Corporation, based in Glenbrook, Connecticut, lost more than $5 million and went bankrupt selling mail-order interactive glass sculptures through the Sharper Image company. Walker served as its president in 1984 and 1985. The Catalog Media Corporation, founded in Ridgefield, Connecticut, in 1985, sold advertising space in catalogs and promoted bookstore sales of catalogs. These ultimately unsuccessful ideas, coupled with a breach-of-contract lawsuit, brought by Trans World Airlines led to the company's end in 1988. Walker cofounded NewSub Services with Michael Loeb in 1991. The company, which later changed its name to Synapse Group, successfully pioneered the use of credit card companies as a base through which to sell magazine subscriptions. Walker also cofounded the publishing company Target Communications. Media conglomerate Time Warner purchased Synapse, and another media company, Primedia, purchased Target Communications.

Walker next founded Walker Digital LLC, his longest-running company, in 1994. Walker Digital is a business research and development company headquartered in Stamford, Connecticut. The company specializes in the development of new business models and systems that utilize digital technology, such as the Internet. Walker has served as the company's chairman and CEO since 2000, establishing its corporate vision as well as taking a lead role in business systems development. The company states that under Walker's leadership it has created and patented hundreds of business systems spanning a wide range of industries.

Walker Digital has patented many of its innovative business models, ensuring its profitability from the granting of exclusive licenses to other companies. Walker Digital has launched numerous affiliated operating companies, including Walker Digital Management, Walker Digital Gaming, Walker Digital Table Systems, Walker Digital Lottery, and Walker Digital Vending. The company also licenses its models to other, nonaffiliated companies of all sizes in order to maintain its core commitment to research and development as opposed to operations. The company maintains close relationships with many of its licensees.

Walker and his company achieved their biggest success with the 1997 founding of Priceline.com in Norwalk, Connecticut. Priceline was one of the most successful of the hundreds of e-commerce companies that were founded during the so-called dot-com boom of the 1990s. Its business model was representative of Walker's concern with the development of innovative selling methods rather than innovative products. The site applied the public use of buyer-driven Internet commerce (e-commerce), which allowed customers to name the price they were willing to pay for certain goods and services, to the travel industry. Those customers were then matched to companies willing to accept the offered price. Bill Perell of the San Francisco-based company Marketel had introduced the model but had quickly gone out of business. Walker was able to acquire the model and apply it to Internet commerce. The company received a U.S. patent for its buyer-driven commerce model in 1998, making it the first U.S.-patented business model.

Priceline opened for business in 1998 and its stock went public in 1999. Walker partnered with airlines to offer the site's first product, unsold airline tickets. The idea was successful for both parties, as airlines were able to sell open seats while customers received discounted fares. The site soon branched out to include hotel rooms and car rentals. Walker also proved his marketing talent as the creative force behind the hiring of popular former *Star Trek* actor William Shatner as the site's spokesman. The company's stock was soon trading at a high of more than $160 per share, while the company was valued at close to $12 billion. It was also one of the fastest-growing start-up businesses in U.S. history in terms of annual sales. Walker himself also made billions, helping to finance a lavish lifestyle and winning him national recognition as one of the world's leading Internet entrepreneurs.

Priceline's initial profitability did not last, as most customers found their offered prices rejected and the company was forced to subsidize losses on those discounted products, such as airline tickets, that were sold. Customers also had to be willing to accept company terms, such as flights at inconvenient times. Walker had also launched the affiliate Priceline WebHouse Club, Inc., selling his stock in Priceline to raise the necessary capital. Priceline WebHouse Club sought to apply the buyer-driven commerce business model to the gasoline and grocery industries, but ultimately it failed because it was unable to meet technological challenges and overwhelming public demand. The affiliate lost billions of dollars. Both companies were also victims of the dot-com bust of the early 2000s. Priceline's stock price dropped from a high of more than $160 per share to just a few dollars per share. Walker and the company lost billions.

Affiliation: Priceline

Priceline.com was one of the leading e-commerce companies of the late 1990s. The explosion of Internet-based companies during the 1990s had given the period the moniker of the dot-com boom. Priceline.com was founded in 1997 in Norwalk, Connecticut. It was based on the most successful business model developed by Walker Digital LLC, a research and development company, founded by Priceline.com founder and Internet entrepreneur Jay S. Walker.

Priceline.com's successful model centered on buyer-driven commerce within the travel industry, starting with airlines and expanding to include accommodations and car rental agencies. The site allowed customers to name their acceptable prices for an airline ticket or hotel room and the matched them to companies willing to accept their offer. The model allowed customers to receive discounted prices, but at the sacrifice of convenience, as they had to accept tickets or rooms on the company's terms.

Priceline.com began business in 1998, going public the following year. At first stock prices soared, but the company encountered financial difficulties through its subsidization of the losses incurred through the discounted prices of sold airline tickets. These losses were coupled with the failure of the affiliated Priceline WebHouse Club, launched soon after Priceline.com with the idea of extending buyer-driven Internet commerce to the gasoline and grocery industries. Founder Walker resigned as the company's vice chairman. Priceline.com later rebounded under chairman and CEO Richard Braddock and remains a successful public company.

Former Citicorp president Richard Braddock was hired as Priceline chairman and CEO, and the company later regained its profitability. Walker resigned his vice chairmanship of Priceline and sold his stocks in 2001, returning to Walker Digital. This company continues to develop new business models and oversee its various affiliated operating companies, listing more than 100 million customers and billions in revenue. Walker also continued to have business setbacks. In 2003, he unsuccessfully sought federal funding for US Home Guard, a proposed national security system based on paying citizens an hourly wage to conduct Internet surveillance.

PERSONAL LIFE

Walker married Eileen McManus on April 18, 1982. The couple had two children, Evan and Lindsey, and settled in Ridgefield, Connecticut. His hobbies include collecting books, artifacts, space memorabilia, and fine wines, as well as photography. Walker's extensive personal collection of rare books and historical artifacts formed the basis for the Walker Library of the History of Human Imagination, built in Ridgefield in 2002. The library hosts global leaders and scholars from a variety of fields, as well as children and librarians. Walker is also a licensed pilot, a skill he acquired in college.

Walker is a popular public speaker in the fields of business, technology, and motivational speaking. Awards and recognition have included Ernst & Young's Entrepreneur of the Year (1998), *Target Marketing* magazine's Direct Marketer of the Year (1998), and the Yonkers Legend Award (2002). He has been cited as a leading Internet pioneer by *Time*, *Businessweek*, and *Newsweek* magazines. He was a member of the Sigma Phi fraternity and served as the chairman of its board of directors from 1988 to 1990. Walker serves as a member of numerous organizations, including the World Information Transfer, an organization associated with the United Nations. He is a member of the TED (Technology, Entertainment, and Design) conference series and the chairman of TEDMED, which facilitates discussions on health and medicine.

Marcella Bush Trevino

FURTHER READING

Elkind, Peter. "The Hype Is Really, Really Big at Priceline." *Fortune* 6 Sept. 1999: 193. Print. A behind-the-scenes examination of Walker and his company's operations.

Ericksen, Gregory K. *Net Entrepreneurs Only: Ten Entrepreneurs Tell the Stories of Their Success*. New York: Wiley, 2000. Print. Walker shares his own account of his success as an Internet entrepreneur.

Price, Christopher. *The Internet Entrepreneurs: Business Rules Are Good; Break Them*. London: FT.com, 2000. Print. Walker is among the Internet entrepreneurs who exemplify the value of challenging conventional business practices.

Raju, Jagmohan Singh, and Z. John Zhang. *Smart Pricing: How Google, Priceline, and Leading Businesses Use Pricing Innovation for Profitability*. Upper Saddle River: Pearson, 2010. Print. Shows how Priceline developed its innovative pricing strategies and their benefits to the company.

Rust, Roland T., Valarie A. Zeithaml, and Katherine N. Lemon. *Driving Customer Equity: How Customer Lifetime Value Is Reshaping Corporate Strategy*. New York: Free Press, 2000. Print. Uses Priceline as an example of a company that has employed competitive metrics to build the value of its customer base.

NEIL CLARK WARREN

Founder of eHarmony

Born: September 18, 1934; Urbandale, Iowa
Died: -
Primary Field: Internet
Specialty: Social media
Primary Company/Organization: eHarmony

INTRODUCTION

Neil Clark Warren is best known as the founder of eHarmony, an online matchmaking service, and as an author of popular articles and books giving relationship and marriage advice. A professional psychologist, Warren has said that he founded eHarmony as an outgrowth of his counseling practice and that his motivation was to help people identify partners with whom they could form a lasting and happy marriage. Warren is the public face of eHarmony: His image appears in many advertisements for the site, and he makes many media appearances (on more than three thousand radio and television programs, according to the eHarmony website). Warren has also published nine books and hundreds of articles promoting his views on relationships and marriage. Although eHarmony began as a primarily Christian dating site, in 2005 Warren moved away from focus on that particular market and toward appealing to a much broader market; today. eHarmony presents itself (on its website and through advertising) to potential users as similar to many other online dating services.

EARLY LIFE

Neil Clark Warren was born in Urbandale, Iowa, a suburb of Des Moines, and grew up on a farm. During his childhood, Warren's father pursued many business endeavors: He owned a Chevrolet dealership, a John Deere store, and a grocery. Warren describes his father as very bright man and his mother as a very sweet woman who was not in her husband's intellectual league. Consequently, his parents rarely spoke to each other, and Warren found home life boring. He left for Long Beach, California, to study at Pepperdine University. It was there that he met his wife. He earned his bachelor's degree in social sciences from Pepperdine University in 1956, his master's degree in divinity in 1959 from Princeton Theological Seminary, and his doctorate in psychology from the University of Chicago in 1967.

LIFE'S WORK

In 1967, Warren accepted a position as assistant professor in the Graduate School of Psychology of Fuller Theological Seminary, a Christian, multidenominational institution headquartered in Pasadena, California, with branch campuses in Washington, Arizona, Colorado, Texas, and California. He also maintained a private practice in psychology in the years 1967–2000. Warren

Neil Clark Warren.

founded eHarmony, an Internet matchmaking site designed to be compatible with his Christian beliefs; the site began operation on August 22, 2000.

From the beginning, eHarmony has emphasized some characteristics that make it distinct from many other online dating services. One difference is eHarmony's explicit restrictions on who may use the service: The goal of eHarmony is to make matches resulting in successful marriages, and individuals are barred from using the service if they are younger than twenty-one, have been divorced more than twice, or do not state that their goal is marriage. Another key difference is the method whereby clients are matched with prospective partners. When clients join eHarmony, they fill out an extensive questionnaire (containing 436 questions) intended to determine aspects of their personality and to facilitate matching them with members of the opposite sex with whom they would be compatible. This information, along with preferences stated by the user (such as age and location), are used by eHarmony to provide lists of potential matches; unlike most online dating services, eHarmony does not allow users to browse the profiles of other users in order to select people in whom they might be interested in dating. Some individuals who take the test are rejected by the site because they are considered poor matches: for instance, those assumed to be lying, depressed, or emotionally unstable, based on their answers to the questionnaire. The matching algorithm is proprietary and thus not available for public scrutiny; it is registered with the U.S. patent office (under U.S. patent no. 6,735,568).

In 2005, Warren decided to downplay the Christian origins of eHarmony and to seek a wider clientele. The site's advertising (the company spent an estimated $80 million on advertising in 2005) made no mention of Warren's seminary background, and Warren explicitly distanced himself from Focus on the Family, a conservative Christian organization founded by James Dobson. (Prior to 2005, Warren had been a regular guest on Dobson's radio program, and Focus on the Family had published several of Warren's books. In fact, Warren bought back the rights to three of them—*Learning to Live with the Love of Your Life, Make Anger Your Ally*, and *Finding the Love of Your Life*—so he could remove the name of Focus on the Family from their covers. Because of this change in the company's image, Warren's public image, and the site's emphasis on marriage, many users are aware of the service's religious background and orientation toward moral issues, and for some this background offers a

Affiliation: eHarmony

Neil Clark Warren founded eHarmony in 2000 as an outgrowth of his work as a professional psychologist. He believed that there should be a scientific way to evaluate which individuals would be compatible and able to make a good marriage together. In pursuit of this goal, he developed the Compatibility Matching System, based on responses to a 436-item questionnaire. Prospective matches are compared on twenty-nine "areas of compatibility" including family values (such as background and spirituality) and emotional makeup (such as anger and mood issues); only individuals with matches on at least twenty-five of the twenty-nine categories are deemed compatible. The site began operation in the United Kingdom in 2007, after about one year during which the compatibility characteristics of British couples were studied in order to adjust the matching system for cultural differences between the United States and the United Kingdom. However, when the company expanded to Canada and Australia, no extra research was done, and the same matching system used in the United States was applied in both countries.

One of the leading matchmaking sites on the Internet, eHarmony as of 2012 claimed 20 million subscribers and $250 million in revenues, making it second only to match.com, which claims 29 million subscribers and $350 million in revenues. eHarmony is also second to match.com in terms of the number of marriages it claims to have facilitated: eHarmony claims that it is responsible for an average of 236 marriages per day, while match.com claims responsibility for 472 per day. eHarmony is the most expensive of the leading Internet matchmaking websites; as of 2010, eHarmony charged $59.95 for a one-month subscription, $39.95 per month for a three-month subscription, $29.95 per month for a six-month subscription, and $19.95 per month for a twelve-month subscription. In contrast, match.com charged $34.99 per month for one month, $19.99 per month for three months, and $16.99 per month for six months (the service does not have a different rate for a twelve-month subscription), and Yahoo! Personals charged $29.99 for one month, $19.99 per month for three months, and $15.99 per month for six months.

One notable characteristic of the eHarmony is the amount of money it spends on advertising, which far outstrips most of its rivals' spending. For instance, in 2008 eHarmony spent more than $100 million on advertising, primarily for ads on cable and network television; in comparison, match.com spent about $50 million on advertising in that time frame, and the only other online matchmaking service to spend more than $1 million on advertising in that period was chemistry.com, with advertising expenditures of about $30 million.

---

particular appeal, bringing eHarmony a niche market of users who may perceive that rival dating sites do not serve their needs as well because they are not founded on conservative moral values.

The eHarmony website allows anyone to sign up for free, take the personality test, and review information about people with whom they have been matched; however, to use the service requires payment of a subscription fee ranging from $59.95 per month for one month to $19.95 per month for twelve months. The website also includes a number of free articles on different aspects of dating and relationships, including advice for specific population groups (African Americans, Latinos, Indians, senior citizens, Jews, and Asians), people in particular geographic locations, and people involved in or contemplating an interracial relationship.

When it first began operation, eHarmony recognized only opposite-sex relationships. The company was sued, in both California and New Jersey, for discrimination against individuals seeking same-sex matches. In his defense, Warren said that his matching system was based on heterosexual couples, and he did not know that it would work for same-sex couples. As part of the settlement in the New Jersey case, eHarmony in 2010 began directing those seeking same-sex matches to Compatiblepartners.net, an affiliated website. Settlement for the California suit included making the option of same-sex matches more visible on the eHarmony website and creating a $2 million settlement fund to compensate Californians who can demonstrate that they were wronged by the company's policies. As of August 2012, however, the eHarmony website allowed users to specify their gender and the gender of the person they were seeking, so it was possible to sign up as a man seeking a man or a woman seeking a woman, as well as a man seeking a woman or a woman seeking a man. In 2010, eHarmony was also sued by Lynda Kelly and Miranda Soegi, who claim that eHarmony does not deliver on its promise to match people using a scientific process and that many of the people in the eHarmony database are scam artists; Kelly and Soegi filed their case in the U.S. District Court of Los Angeles with class action status.

The core concept most identified with Warren's work is the "twenty-nine dimensions of compatibility," a series of dimensions that can be determined through a simple questionnaire and are based on his years of experience as a psychologist; Warren claims that he has demonstrated empirically that these dimensions can predict which couples will be compatible and have a successful marriage and which will not. However, high-quality scientific research supporting this assertion is difficult to find, as is noted in a review article by James Houran and colleagues that appeared in the *North American Journal of Psychology* in 2004.

PERSONAL LIFE

Warren is married to Marilyn Mann Warren, who is a senior vice president at eHarmony but spent eleven years as vice president and head of development for the Huntington Library. The couple have three daughters and nine grandchildren, and one of their sons-in-law, Gregory Fogatch, is eHarmony's chief executive officer.

Sarah Boslaugh

FURTHER READING

"eHarmony Settles Lawsuit, Will Offer Same Sex Matches." *Quest: Wisconsin's Gay News Leader* 15.19 (2008): 8. Print. A news article detailing the settlement of a lawsuit in New Jersey against eHarmony, in which eHarmony was charged with discrimination for not allowing people to seek same-sex matches on the website.

Gupta, Atul, Rebecca Murtha, and Niharika Patel. "EHarmony: More than Traditional Internet Dating." *Journal of the International Academy for Case Studies* 18.1 (2012): 43–52. Print. An analysis of the business strategy of eHarmony, comparing it to those of other dating sites and noting the company's shift of identity from a specifically conservative Christian site to one attempting to reach a much larger audience. The article includes many tables and charts comparing the business aspects of eHarmony to those of its rivals in the online matchmaking services market.

Houran, James, Rense Lange, P. Jason Rentfrow, and Karin H. Bruckner. "Do Online Matchmaking Tests Work? An Assessment of Preliminary Evidence for a Publicized 'Predictive Model of Marital Success.'" *North American Journal of Psychology* 6.3 (2004): 507-526. Print. A review of Warren's claims about the scientific bases for eHarmony's matching program and an examination of the empirical evidence supporting it; they find the latter wanting.

Paumgarten, Nick. "Looking for Someone." *New Yorker* 87.19 (2011): 36–49. Print. Feature article on the history and current practice of computer matchmaking and a review of how contemporary computer dating services claim to match compatible couples: from DNA samples (ScientificMatch) to Warren's "twenty-nine dimensions of compatibility."

JEFF WEINER

CEO of LinkedIn

Born: 1971; place unknown
Died: -
Primary Field: Business and commerce
Specialty: Management, executives, and investors
Primary Company/Organization: LinkedIn

INTRODUCTION

Internet executive Jeff Weiner began his career at Warner Bros., where he was employed in a variety of roles from 1994 through 2000, helping expand the company's Internet presence. He oversaw the develop-ment of Warner Bros. Online in 1996 and served as the new division's vice president. He next cofounded Windsor Digital and was an executive in residence at Accel Partners and Greylock Partners before joining Yahoo! in 2001. His executive experience at Yahoo! included senior vice president of corporate development, senior vice president of search and marketplace, and executive vice president of its Network Division. Weiner left Yahoo! in 2008 to become acting president of the leading global online professional networking company LinkedIn. He took the role of LinkedIn's chief executive officer (CEO) in 2009, helping the company expand its global presence. He is recognized for his skills in management, corporate and product development, and business operations as well as his creativity, marking him as one of the prototypical of Silicon Valley start-up executives.

EARLY LIFE

Jeff Weiner was born in the United States in 1971. He is reluctant to provide details of his personal life, and there is little information regarding his childhood. He does note a lifelong interest in technology. He graduated from the prestigious Wharton School of Business at the University of Pennsylvania with a bachelor's degree in economics in 1992. He then began his professional career as a strategic planning analyst for Braxton Associates, a division of Deloitte and Touche dedicated to strategic management consulting. His duties included scenario planning and shareholder value analysis.

Weiner was employed in several capacities with the entertainment conglomerate Warner Bros. from 1994 through 2000, starting in the role of senior analyst. His accomplishments centered on the growth of the company's Internet presence, building his experience in what would become his career field. From 1994 to 1996, he worked on interactive services for the Corporate Strategic Planning and Development Division.

Beginning in 1996, Weiner helped develop the initial business plan and oversaw the implementation of Warner Bros. Online, where he was promoted from manager to director to vice president of the Planning, Development, and Administration Division. He also helped launch both ACMEcity and the website Entertaindom.com in his capacity at Warner Bros. Online, serving as the latter's senior vice president and chief operating officer.

Weiner resigned from Warner Bros. in 2000 after its parent company, Time Warner, entered into a renowned merger with Internet service provider America Online (AOL) to form AOL Time Warner. He became a founding partner of Windsor Digital that year and was the new company's managing director until 2001. The company, cofounded by Yahoo! Chairman Terry Semel, is a private equity digital and media investment firm. Weiner left Windsor Digital in 2001 to join one of the leading Internet service providers, Yahoo, Inc.

LIFE'S WORK

Weiner served in a variety of capacities at Yahoo! from 2001 through 2008, putting into practice the leadership

Jeff Weiner.

skills and Internet business experience he had gained at Warner Bros. His most significant positions were senior vice president of corporate development, senior vice president of search and marketplace, and executive vice president of its Network Division. His chief goal was the improvement of the company's Internet search capabilities and options.

Weiner's responsibilities at Yahoo! included management, strategic business development, and the oversight of mergers and acquisitions, such as Yahoo!'s purchase of software manufacturer Inktomi. Areas for which he was responsible included the company's commerce and listings business and its consumer web products, such as the Yahoo! search engine and Yahoo! Mail. One of the company's leading problems during Weiner's tenure and since has been competition from other Internet service providers, notably Google.

Weiner resigned from Yahoo! in 2008, taking a break of several months from the corporate world to help raise his newborn child before resuming his career. He then joined Accel Partners and Greylock Partners as an executive in residence from 2008 through 2009. His advisory duties with both firms involved the evaluation of and recommendations for both companies' current and potential investments in consumer technology firms.

Weiner took the next key step in his career when he joined leading online professional networking company LinkedIn as interim president in 2008. After a trial period in the interim role, he rose to the position of CEO the following year. He also sits on the company's board of directors. Former PayPal executive Reid Hoffman had founded LinkedIn in December of 2002 alongside a team of former PayPal and SocialNet.com employees. The company was funded through a combination of venture capital investments and Hoffman's portion of the proceeds from the sale of PayPal.

The LinkedIn site was launched on May 5, 2003, with founder Hoffman as its first CEO. The company is headquartered in Mountain View, California. It also maintains corporate offices in more than twenty worldwide locations, including a European headquarters in Dublin, Ireland, opened in 2010. LinkedIn's initial public offering came in 2011. The company has also grown through acquisitions, purchasing Internet start-up companies Rapportive and SlideShare in 2012. The site has become the main Internet option for professional networking.

The company has shown a profit since 2006 and has emerged as one of the most profitable of the Internet start-ups from the Silicon Valley region during Weiner's tenure, reporting earnings of more than $500 million the year it went public. Revenues are raised through advertising and premium membership sales. By 2012, the site had more than 175 million registered members from around the world and was available in a variety of languages. The United States represented approximately half of the membership base, with Europe comprising the next largest group. Although LinkedIn maintains fewer registered users than Facebook or Twitter, its members fit the demographic groups most sought by advertisers, helping drive advertising-based revenues. Competing professional networking companies, including Viadeo and XING, have much smaller membership bases.

Users design a profile that may include a photograph and can upload their résumés. The site is open, but users must establish connections to interact with others through the maintenance and expansion of contact lists. Those seeking contact with a person not among their direct (first-degree) connections may seek the desired connection by soliciting a mutual connection for a introduction, which can be done by examining the profile of the member the user is interested in contacting. LinkedIn's cybersecurity measures and threat responses were questioned in 2012 after hackers intercepted and published more than 6 million user passwords.

The site's professional use drives both its core philosophy and its success. Users seeking employment can post profiles or resumes detailing their skills and experience, search for or be alerted to job openings, research and follow companies, and network with professionals in their field. Employers can list job openings and search for potential candidates. Employers may also receive applications through use of the Apply button with LinkedIn, a plugin introduced in 2011, which allows candidates to apply with their LinkedIn profile.

Those with similar professional interests or fields, career issues, or common schools or companies may form interest groups. Other features include LinkedIn Answers, which allows users

---

Affiliation: LinkedIn

LinkedIn is the largest and most successful of the Internet sites dedicated to professional networking. Reid Hoffman founded it in 2002 and served as the company's first CEO. Other members of the founding team consisted of a group of professionals with previous experience at Internet start-ups PayPal and SocialNet.com. The site was launched on May 5, 2003. Corporate headquarters are in Mountain View, California, with European headquarters in Dublin, Ireland.

Jeff Weiner joined LinkedIn as interim president in 2008, becoming CEO in 2009. He also serves on the company's board of directors, where LinkedIn founder Hoffman serves as chairman of the board. LinkedIn's initial public offering came in 2011. The company acquired SlideShare and Rapportive in 2012.

LinkedIn is popular among both business professionals and job seekers. Site features allow users to create profiles, maintain contact lists, upload resumes, search for jobs or job candidates, research companies, form interest groups, and ask or answer questions. Users benefit from either a previous relationship or an introduction from an existing contact to communicate directly with other business professionals.

The site has grown to a global membership base of approximately 175 million, about half of whom are from the United States, and supports more than a dozen languages. The company's main source of revenue is advertising sales. Other revenue sources include premium membership subscription sales. The site's success has made it one of the most profitable of the Internet start-up companies.

to post questions and receive advice from other members, and LinkedIn Polls. After logging in, members can also access recent job listings, elect to follow particular organizations, and post comments in ongoing discussions within the groups they have joined. Weiner has emphasized in interviews that one vital feature of a social networking site dedicated to professional networking is the avoidance of the nonprofessional and sometimes embarrassing personal photographs or information that often appear on the profiles of general social networking sites such as Facebook.

PERSONAL LIFE

Weiner is reluctant to discuss details of his personal life, instead preferring to discuss his professional career and the importance of LinkedIn. He is married to European wife Lisette Weiner. In 2012, the couple had one child. Weiner briefly left the professional world between his stints at Yahoo! and LinkedIn to help raise his new infant. He lists his interests and hobbies as spending time with his family, golfing, and volunteer and charity work. His voluntary pursuits center on the fields of economic empowerment, education, and health, and he is a supporter of the Boys and Girls Clubs.

Weiner maintains the professional and personal passion for digital technology that has largely shaped his career. He has cited the 1995 book *Being Digital*, by Nicholas Negroponte, as providing him with a demystifying overview of the field of digital technology and forming a key influence on his professional views. He is known for an executive style that blends business sense and creativity, common among Silicon Valley start-ups. He serves on the boards of directors of numerous companies, including LinkedIn (starting in 2009), Intuit (2012), DonorsChoose (2007), and Malaria No More (2009). He is also a member of the Compensation and Organizational Development Committee at Intuit.

Marcella Bush Trevino

FURTHER READING

Aspray, William, and Paul E. Ceruzzi. *The Internet and American Business*. Cambridge: MIT, 2008. Print. A series of essays that examine the commercialization of the Internet, including social networking, information searching, and entertainment. Covers business models, e-commerce, and the successes and failures of dot-com companies.

Butow, Eric, and Kathleen Taylor. *How to Succeed in Business Using LinkedIn: Making Connections and Capturing Opportunities on the Web's #1 Business Networking Site*. New York: American Management Association, 2009. Print. User guide to the site, providing a detailed overview of its features and how they work, along with an understanding of the company's business strategy and the site's success. Includes a chapter on other business networking sites by way of comparison.

Hoffman, Reid, and Ben Casnocha. *The Start-up of You*. New York: Crown, 2012. Print. A guide to building a career or industry using the methods of the Silicon Valley entrepreneurs from a cofounder and former chief executive officer of LinkedIn. Offers insights into the business philosophy behind LinkedIn.

Negroponte, Nicholas. *Being Digital*. New York: Knopf, 1995. Print. Explains digital technology, including bandwidth, multimedia, virtual reality, and the Internet, and debunks common myths surrounding these topics. Cited by Weiner as a key influence on his career.

Tapscott, Don. *Grown Up Digital: How the Net Generation Is Changing Your World*. New York: McGraw-Hill, 2009. Print. A description of the Net Generation, young adults who have grown up in a digital world, based on extensive surveys. Provides insight into their revolutionary use of technology, including their use of professional networking sites such as LinkedIn.

TIM WESTERGREN

Cofounder of Pandora

Born: December 21, 1965; Minneapolis, Minnesota
Died: -
Primary Field: Internet
Specialty: News and entertainment
Primary Company/Organization: Pandora

INTRODUCTION

Tim Westergren is a former rock and jazz musician who is best known as the cofounder and chief strategy officer of Pandora, a service that assists users in creating their own radio stations. A record producer with two decades of experience, Westergren is also an award-winning composer and an accomplished pianist and plays the bassoon, drums, and clarinet as well. He has managed artists and scored feature films. In 1999, Westergren and Will Glaser devised the Music Genome Project, a typology for categorizing a piece of music according to almost two thousand traits. The Music Genome Project, which is updated continually, is the base upon which Westergren built Pandora.

EARLY LIFE

Timothy Brooks Westergren was born December 21, 1965, in Minneapolis, Minnesota. He lived abroad as a child but returned to the United States as he entered his teens. His family moved to Michigan and California, but Westergren has always considered Minneapolis, where he has extended family, home. He was seven when he was introduced to the piano. It was the beginning of a lifelong passion for music. In 1984, he graduated from Cranbrook Schools, a private, college preparatory boarding school in Bloomfield Hills, Michigan. He studied music theory and composition at Stanford University, but Westergren admits that he spent most of his time at the Center for Research in Musical Acoustics, a campus think tank focused on the integration of

computers and music. After receiving his bachelor's degree from Stanford in 1988, he played piano with a series of acoustic rock bands—Late Coffee and Oranges, Barefoot, and Yellowwood Junction—but by 1995 he was weary of living in a van or in friends' basements and frustrated with the bands' failure to win significant attention.

Westergren found work composing scores for low-budget, independent films. To help him compose, he asked directors to describe the sounds they were looking for, and he would take their often vague descriptions (such as "scary" or "happy") and translate them into rhythm and melody. He was doing film work when he read an article about Aimee Mann, a singer-songwriter whose record company would not release her current album despite respectable sales and critical acclaim for two earlier albums. Mann's story awakened Westergren's resentment about the history of Yellowwood Junction. The ideas he had been mulling over—about a musical database organized by musical characteristic that would enable listeners to find the music they wanted and his conviction that there had to be a way for good musicians to find their audiences—synthesized.

LIFE'S WORK

Westergren thought music could be analyzed by trained musicians who would examine melody, harmony, instrumentation, rhythm, vocals, lyrics, and so on. Once a song was analyzed, the results could be used to find other songs with characteristics from the same "family." He gave the idea a name, the Music Genome Project, playing off the name for the concurrent project that was then mapping the human genome, and developed a list of about six hundred musical qualities. Westergren also had the right friends. Jon Kraft had already started and sold a technology company, and Will Glaser had the necessary technological knowledge. Kraft drew up a business plan, Glaser worked on the software, and Westergren worked on the music. They hired a musicologist to polish the idea. In 1999, the three raised $1.5 million from angel investors and started Savage Beast Technologies. At first, they sold music recommendation services to companies like electronics retailer Best Buy. However, by 2001 the company was broke. Its fifty employees were not getting paid regularly, and investors, scarred by the bursting of the dot-com bubble, were not interested. In late 2003, four former employees sued Pandora for deferring salaries. Westergren argued his case before the California Division of Labor Standards. It took most of his money to settle with the

Tim Westergren.

former employees. He dismissed his current employees, although some loyalists remained without pay. Westergren was desperate enough to consider taking his last $25,000 to Las Vegas in an attempt to increase his funds.

In March 2004, Westergren made one more pitch to a prospective backer, his 348th. However, this time the pitch was, if not perfect, at least good enough to keep the backer, venture capitalist Larry Marcus, listening. Marcus, a musician himself, led a $9 million investment. Westergren took $2 million to pay the back salaries of his loyal staff. Next, he made changes. The company would focus on consumers rather than businesses, and it would be called Pandora. He also yielded his position as chief executive officer (CEO) to Joe Kennedy, who brought experience at building consumer products to the job. Pandora launched in September 2005 and sold its first ad in December.

In the beginning, Pandora offered listeners ten free hours with higher use requiring a paid subscription. When some users avoided the fee by logging in with different e-mail addresses, Westergren decided to move to a free service and depend on advertisers for revenue. Because Pandora could offer segmented audiences, advertisers were pleased. The number of listeners was doubling monthly. Investors liked the changes and gave the company another $12 million. However, Westergren and his partners had only a brief span to enjoy success before a new problem arose that could mean the end of Pandora.

On May 1, 2007, the Copyright Royalty Board changed the amounts that Internet radio stations had to pay, switching from a fee charged per listener per hour to one charged per listener per song. The change would almost triple Pandora's costs. To this increase would be added a new charge of $500 a year per individual station. For Pandora, with each of its millions of listeners having a personalized "station," the costs would be devastating. Westergren and Kennedy considered shutting down immediately. Instead, Pandora hired a lobbyist in Washington and appealed to listeners to contact their congressional representatives. Because of Westergren's habit of meeting with listeners in groups ranging from fewer than ten to several hundred during his travels to look for new music, Pandora's connection to its listeners was closer to star-fan bond than to radio station-listener connection. Westergren sent an e-mail to all Pandora listeners, identifying their congressional representatives and senators and asking that they write to them. The result, according to Westergren's estimate, was about one million e-mails, phone calls, or faxes.

California Democratic senator Dianne Feinstein alone received twenty-five thousand e-mails. The Copyright Royalty Board agreed to negotiations, and although it took two years, the board eventually settled on a lower rate of increase. Even with the adjustment, Pandora's costs doubled, but the company stayed in business.

At the same time that Westergren was rallying the troops politically, the company was prospering. In 2008, Pandora added thirty-five thousand new users in a single day when it offered an iPhone application that made it possible to stream music. By 2010, 15 million people had the Pandora app on their iPhones. Pandora was also finding ways to work more directly with artists and provide listeners with original content. In 2010, the Dave Matthews Band hosted a listening party on Pandora, sponsored by Brita. Soon other artists were viewing Pandora as a way to boost sales and sell concert tickets. In 2011, Ford announced that Pandora would be included in its voice-activated Sync system, and there were also deals to make Pandora-capable after-market car

---

Affiliation: Pandora

Pandora is a free Internet radio service that allows users to create their own radio stations. Users enter the title of a favorite song and the name of the artist, and almost instantly a station is created that streams musically similar songs. The service is based on the Music Genome Project with a taxonomy that consists of four hundred musical attributes that cover melody, harmony, rhythm, form, composition, and lyrics. Each song is analyzed by analysts trained in music theory, composition, or performance. Typically, each analysis takes from twenty to thirty minutes. As of 2012, the service included more than nine hundred thousand, by more than ninety thousand artists.

The company was founded by Tim Westergren, who conceived the idea and served as the musical expert; Will Glaser, who developed the software; and Jon Kraft, who drew up the business plan. Savage Beast Technologies began in 1999, but it was not until 2004, when an $8 million cash infusion revived the near-death company, that the company in its current form evolved with a new name, Pandora, and a new focus on consumers. A year later, it launched on the web. With 80 million listeners in June 2011, Pandora went public. By 2012, with service available on mobile devices—notably Apple's iPhone—Pandora reached 150 million registered users.

stereos from Pioneer and Alpine. Consumer electronics companies began integrating Pandora into Blu-ray players, televisions, and music systems.

Pandora's biggest news in 2011 came on June 15, when the company officially began trading on the New York Stock Exchange at a price of $16 per share, giving Pandora a valuation of nearly $2.6 billion. In 2012, the company announced that it had more than 150 million registered users, making Pandora one of the most heavily used Internet sites in the United States. The hours listeners spend on Pandora have increased 87 percent from one year ago, and Pandora is the second most downloaded iPhone application of all time. Pandora has a 68 percent market share of Internet radio listening, according to Triton Media. Westergren still dreams of seeing Pandora become an international company. In the meantime, with Pandora's audience growing and the majority of the artists in the database independents who have never before had significant radio promotion, Westergren may be on his way to fulfilling another dream: to provide digital touring for emerging musicians that will find the audience who wants the music they are making.

PERSONAL LIFE

Westergren, who was one of *Time* magazine's 100 Most Influential People in the World in 2010, spends about one hundred days a year on the road in the United States, researching new music and talking to Pandora's listeners. He depends on those listeners to tell him the best places to stay, to recommend the best restaurants, and to steer him to the right places to hear live music. The music is the most important, personally and professionally. He has been a music lover since childhood. He trained as a jazz musician. Tenor saxophonist Stan Getz was one of his professors at Stanford. Except for Prince and his album *Purple Rain*, Westergren paid little attention to rock music until his college years. However, those years provided an education in rock along with more formal learning, and he spent the decade after college on the road playing in a rock band.

Two of Westergren's favorite spots to add to his store of music knowledge are Grimey's in Nashville, an independent record store named as one of the best in the

United States by *Rolling Stone* magazine in 2011, and the music scene in Denton, Texas, where the University of North Texas, which graduates the most professional musicians of any college in the United States, is located. His personal Pandora stations are based on songs by Muddy Waters, Ben Folds, Josh Fix, Oscar Peterson, Art Farmer, Elvis Costello, and James Taylor.

Wylene Rholetter

FURTHER READING

Copeland, Michael V. "Pandora's Founder Rocks the Music Biz." *Fortune* 5 July 2010: 27–28. Print. The article describes Pandora's founding and the services it offers. It also explains the Music Genome Project and Pandora's software applications that are in Apple's iPhones. Five color photographs.

Glitford, Stephanie. "Pandora's Long Strange Trip." *Inc.* Oct. 2007: 100–8. Print. The article recounts Pandora's long struggle to survive, including its early money problems. It also describes the company's foray into mobile devices that will allow consumers to access their personalized radio station away from the computer.

Levenson, Eugenia. "Road Warrior." *Fortune* 26 May 2008: 59. Print. The brief article provides information about Westergren's life on the road. It includes such details as his fondness for puzzles and a particular eye mask he uses when he is on an airplane. Five color photographs.

Miller, Claire Cain. "How Pandora Slipped Past the Junkyard." *New York Times* 8 Mar. 2010: B1. Print. The article provides a comprehensive look at Pandora's journey from a start-up company with a doubtful future to its success following deals with Apple and Ford.

Westergren, Tim. "Tim Westergren, Interviewed February 24, 2009." Interview by Bill Moggridge. *Designing Media*. Cambridge: MIT, 2010. 131–46. Print. The chapter, by the inventor of the laptop, includes a detailed explanation of what inspired Westergren's idea for the Music Genome Project, how the project developed, and how it works for Pandora. The author describes it as human choice within algorithmic structure.

ELAINE WHERRY

Cofounder of Meebo

Born: 1978; Willard, Missouri
Died: -
Primary Field: Internet
Specialty: Social media
Primary Company/Organization: Meebo

INTRODUCTION

Elaine Wherry is one of the cofounders of the social media platform Meebo, created in 2005. She started the company with two other college friends in a California apartment. Meebo was a Web 2.0 company, part of a group of start-ups founded on the concept that the Internet is a platform of information sharing, interoperability, user-centered design, and collaboration on the web. Web 2.0 companies center on user-generated content and include blogs, wikis, and social networking sites. Meebo was a major web-based instant-messaging (IM) system in that, while it was not the first chat service, it quickly became the most popular because it was the most accessible and most convenient, allowing users to bypass software hurdles. Wherry developed Meebo's initial JavaScript framework in 2004. She was integral in creating products such as Meebo Messenger, Meebo Mobile, and the Meebo Bar. She oversees the look and feel of all Meebo products.

EARLY LIFE

Elaine Wherry was born in the small town of Willard in southwest Missouri in 1978. She grew up on a farm, where her family raised and showed dairy goats. She described her childhood as humble, saying that it taught her the value of hard work. Farm work was full of ups and downs, creating situations to which Wherry later found parallels in the business world.

Wherry was also a dedicated member of the 4-H Youth Development Organization, a national youth-oriented group that develops citizenship, leadership, and responsibility. She began playing the violin at five and was classically trained as a violinist. However, she declined a full scholarship in music at a local college because she was not sure what she wanted to study. She credits hard work and talks with her parents in helping her make her decision to pursue a career in computer science. Wherry spent a year after high school working as a volunteer before deciding to attend Stanford University in Palo Alto, California.

LIFE'S WORK

Wherry first became interested in computers in a freshman calculus class, where she had to buy a graphing calculator. One day she was on a plane and tried to program the calculator to play a simple tic-tac-toe game. Although she could not get it to work, she was fascinated with the concept. Friends then suggested that she enroll in a computer programming class. Wherry earned a bachelor's degree in symbolic systems with a concentration in human/computer interaction at Stanford University in Palo Alto, California, in 2001.

While in college, Wherry worked for the web development company Synactics, Inc., where she was a human factors researcher and later the manager of usability and design. She also quantified performance for devices such as touch sticks. She worked there for four years.

Wherry cofounded Meebo with college friends Seth Sternberg and Sandy Jen in 2005. All were in their twenties. They used Wherry's Palo Alto apartment as their programming hub. The origin of the name Meebo

Elaine Wherry.

came from ideas the three scribled on napkins in a pizza restaurant. Wherry and her cofounders wanted a two-syllable name that began with M. They plugged different names into browsers to see what was available. Meebo struck them as catchy and humorous.

Wherry developed Meebo's initial JavaScript framework in 2004, before cofounding Meebo. She was integral in creating products such as Meebo Messenger, Meebo Mobile, and the Meebo Bar, and she would lead Meebo's web, product management, and user experience teams; she has designed the look and feel of all Meebo's products.

Although Meebo was not the first instant-messaging (IM) service, it was the first one to combine online chat services effectively to allow users to access any IM platform without needing to download and run multiple software products. This allowed users around the world to connect easily and quickly, because they could access their screen name and communicate via IM from anywhere and from any computer just by going to a single web page. Users could instant-message via Meebo regardless of whether they had AOL Instant Messenger, Yahoo! Messenger, Google Talk, Jabber, MSN Messenger, and/or an ICQ account.

Meebo was also innovative in web design in that it allowed users to send and receive messages without its interfering with the page display and behavior. Meebo also became quickly popular because it bypassed college campus and workplace IM restrictions on their servers, providing the platform to continue chatting. Thus, some people viewed it as a nuisance. Meebo is enabled by the messenger-engineering software Ajax, which provides users with a software-like experience within a web browser.

Wherry describes Meebo as a baroque balancing act between two very different worlds: an application displayed in a web document viewing medium and a metaphor of a software dialogue. Wherry draws a parallel between the way classical music developed and the way web applications have evolved today. She uses the example of classical Baroque harpischord music, arguing that the progression of classical music can guide webmasters to a subtler web design, without overwhelming audiences with lots of notes and ornamentation. Like classical music, Wherry argues that web design should utilize concrete and specific devices via subtle, simple experimentation. By way of comparison, Wherry points out that mashups inundate users with a mess of often disharmonious data culled from different websites, making navigation and comprehension difficult.

Affiliation: Meebo

Meebo was a leading web-enabled social media platform and messaging service that allowed users to communicate across all public instant-messaging (IM) services.

Three twenty-something start-up technicians, Sandy Jen, Seth Sternberg, and Elaine Wherry, founded Meebo in Wherry's apartment in Palo Alto, California, in September 2005. It was the first of the IM services to let users communicate without having to download and run IM software. Meebo's popular toolbar was ideal for users all over the world to communicate from anywhere, whether from a personal or a multiuser computer, regardless of college or workplace barriers. Meebo features included an invisible sign-on and the ability to connect to multiple IM services.

Meebo received up to $200 million in funding from angel investors and venture capitalist groups such as Sequoia Capital, which invested $3.5 million in an "A" round of funding in December 2005. In 2008, Meebo secured $25 million in venture capital funding, and Sternberg announced that Meebo would expand its market into East Asia, such as with the Japanese firm JAFCO and South Korea's Treasury Bond (KTB) Ventures.

Meebo's initial tag line was "Together Is Better" (2007–11); it later was changed to "More of What You Love." In 2008, Meebo was featured by technology magazine *Red Herring*, and in 2010 Meebo was named one of the Hottest Silicon Valley Companies by Lead411. In 2011, Meebo announced that it had reached 250 million monthly global visitors. In June 2012, Meebo was acquired by Google, Inc., as a companion to Google+. In July, all Meebo products except the Meebo Bar were discontinued.

Meebo received $3.5 million from venture capitalist firms such as Sequoia Capital and Draper Fisher Jurvetson in 2005 and $25 million in financing from Jafco Ventures, KTB Ventures, and Time Warner Investments in 2008 (the latter an investment arm of Time Warner, Inc.). By 2008, Meebo had 29 million users sending more than 150 million messages daily. Meebo was named one of the Hottest Silicon Valley Companies by Lead411 in 2010. In 2011, Meebo announced that it had reached 250 million monthly global visitors. In 2012, Google bought Meebo for an undisclosed sum speculated to be $100 million.

PERSONAL LIFE

Wherry met her husband, Todd, at Stanford. They live in San Jose, California, and enjoy biking and traveling. Wherry also enjoys reading. When she's not coding, she blogs about the art of design. Wherry has said that a background in computer sciences may have made her more comfortable in male-dominated and technical environments, but she looks forward to the day when women technological entrepreneurs will come as no surprise.

Wherry is a classically trained violinist and draws parallels between the refined austerity of classical music and the evolution of web design. She says that web pages succeed in attracting users when their use of design is subtle.

In 2009, Wherry was a recipient of the Founders Fund Tech Fellows Award in Engineering Leadership.

Ellen Elder

FURTHER READING

Bedwell, Linda. "Making Chat Widgets Work for On-line Reference." *Online* 33.3 (2009): 20–23. Print. This article discusses the advantages of using chat widgets for online reference, making an online service, such as Meebo, more accessible to patrons.

Buckman, Rebecca, and Mylene Mangalindan. "Financing Round Values Meebo at $300 Million." *Wall Street Journal* 1 May 2008: C3. Print. Focuses on Meebo's finances, valued by investors at $200 million. The article also announced that Time Warner Investments would invest $25 million and with such new revenue the company would expand its market into Japan and South Korea.

Geron, Tomio. "Google Buying Social Toolbar Company Meebo, Team Joins Google+." *Forbes* June 2012: 31. Print. Reports on Google's agreement to acquire Meebo and its plan to use it for the Google+ social networking service.

Risdahl, Aliza Pilar Sherman. *Entrepreneur* 35.8 (2006): 32. Print. Profiles female entrepreneurs, including Wherry, who are engaged in Web 2.0 business enterprises. Wherry believes that being a woman is not a problem in male-dominated and technical environments.

Wherry, Elaine. *What Web Application Design Can Learn from the Harpsichord.* 2 Feb. 2010. *BayCHI Conversation Network.* Association for Computing Machinery Special Interest Group of Computer Human Interaction. Web. 12 Aug. 2012. In this podcast, Wherry, a classically trained violinist, provides a brief lesson on the history of classical music from the Baroque to the Romantic periods and then draws a parallel with web applications today to illustrate ways that websites can achieve subtler designs.

MEG WHITMAN

CEO of eBay and Hewlett-Packard

Born: August 4, 1957; Cold Spring Harbor, New York
Died: -
Primary Field: Business and commerce
Specialty: Management, executives, and investors
Primary Company/Organization: eBay

INTRODUCTION

Meg Whitman is a business leader who has served in executive positions in a variety of companies, from Disney to Hasbro to eBay. Her bid for governor of California in 2010 did not succeed but was quickly followed by invitations to apply her talents 1and experience to new ventures, notably as Hewlett-Packard's chief executive officer (CEO) in 2011. Well connected with other corporate leaders, she continues to contribute to American business development, serving on the boards of several major corporations.

EARLY LIFE

Margaret "Meg" Cushing Whitman was born the daughter of Hendricks Hallett Whitman, Jr. (businessman) and Margaret Cushing (née Goodhue) a homemaker, on August 4, 1957, in Cold Spring Harbor, Long Island, New York. On her father's side, Whitman is a descendant of Elnathan Whitman (1785–1868), a member of the Nova Scotia House of Assembly, and U.S. senator Charles Benjamin Farwell (1823–1903) of Illinois. Her mother was from Boston. On her mother's side she is related to several distinguished Americans, including General Henry Shippen Huidekoper (1839–1918).

Cold Spring Harbor is a small hamlet on the north shore of Long Island in Suffolk County. Whitman was educated in the Cold Spring Harbor school system, graduating from Cold Spring Harbor High School in 1974. She then entered Princeton University, where she

Meg Whitman.

studied mathematics and science in anticipation of becoming a physician. She changed her major to economics after she spent a summer selling advertisements for a student magazine. Her bachelor's degree in economics was granted with honors in 1977. She received a master's of business administration in 1979 from Harvard Business School.

Between graduation and 1981 Whitman worked for Procter & Gamble in Cincinnati, Ohio, and met Griffith Rutherford Harsh IV, a Harvard medical student, whom she married. Harsh was born in St. Louis in 1953, the son of a neurosurgeon. He became a Rhodes scholar after graduating summa cum laude from Harvard University. He earned a master's degree in neurological sciences at Oxford University and then studied at Harvard Medical School, graduating in 1980.

LIFE'S WORK

Whitman's work at Procter & Gamble was with the Noxzema skin care products team. Her work was an education in marketing of brands of a company and its products that was to serve her well in the future. In 1980, she left Procter & Gamble in order to follow her husband to San Francisco, where he had been accepted as a resident in neurosurgery at the Department of

Neurosurgery and the Brain Tumor Research Center of the University of California. In 1981, Bain and Company, a leading business consulting firm, hired her as a consultant. She worked for Bain until 1989, by which time she had become a vice president. Her work was with Mitt Romney, the future Republican Party presidential nominee.

In 1989, Whitman accepted a job with Walt Disney Company as a senior vice president of marketing consumer products and strategic planning. She helped to launch Disney-themed stores abroad (the first in Japan), using the knowledge of marketing she had learned at Procter & Gamble. She also led the acquisition of *Discover* magazine as a publishing venture for Disney.

In 1992, Whitman again followed her husband, this time to Boston, where Harsh had been hired as the co-director of the brain tumor program at Massachusetts General Hospital in Boston. She took a job as president of Stride Rite Shoes in Lexington, Massachusetts. Stride Rite was a maker of children's shoes, including Sperry topsiders and Keds sneakers.

In 1995, Whitman moved to Florists' Transworld Delivery (FTD) as CEO. The job was a challenge, because she had to transform FTD into a privately held company. Higher-ups resisted some of her moves, and she also had to contend with the growth of Internet floral delivery services.

In 1997, Whitman moved to Hasbro, Inc., as general manager of the Playskool division. The division was responsible for a number of toys, including Mr. Potato Head and Teletubbies. Soon afterward, a corporate headhunter approached her about an Internet start-up in Silicon Valley. She was reluctant at first because it would mean uprooting the family; however, she visited the offices of eBay in San Jose in February 1998 and soon afterward moved to California to take the helm of eBay.

EBay had begun in 1995, when Pierre M. Omidyar had set up an auction website. A message board allowed visitors to the website to develop a sense of community. Soon a small listing fee was charged. By 1998, eBay was growing rapidly and needed a brand builder who could take the company public. Whitman quickly improved the appearance of the website and began making eBay a household name. She oversaw its initial public offering in September 1998.

In 1999, Whitman got Lloyd's of London to issue free insurance for eBay purchases of $200 or less. She also had eBay purchase the 134-year-old auction house of Butterfield and Butterfield. The move cost $260

Affiliation: eBay

The online auction company eBay was founded on September 3, 1995, by Pierre M. Omidyar in San Jose, California. It is one of the great success stories among many Internet failures during the ensuing years. The original name of the company was AuctionWeb. Its initial public offering in September 1998 was an enormous success.

From the beginning, eBay was an Internet company connecting people rather than simply selling things: It created an Internet community. People who list an item for auction on eBay are charged a small fee and then pay a small percentage fee when the item is sold. To facilitate its business, eBay acquired several auction companies, e-classified advertising companies, and e-commerce payment systems. In 1998, Met Whitman joined eBay as the company's CEO.

When Whitman began, the company had thirty employees and $4.7 billion in revenues. The company went public in September 1998 and its stock soared to nearly three times the target price of $18 per share. Whitman oversaw the expansion of eBay's services and acquisitions. On October 3, 2002, eBay acquired PayPal, giving it control of the company's e-payment system. By March 2005, eBay had pieced together several companies to form Kijiji, which is a network of online urban communities. These operate like a village where online classified advertisements can be posted. In October 2005, eBay completed its acquisition of Skype for $2.5 billion. Whitman was ridiculed for this move; she thought that the online texting, calling, and video communications service would facilitate and grow the eBay community, but that vision did not materialize. She was vindicated, however, when Microsoft purchased Skype in 2011 for $8.5 billion.

Whitman left eBay to enter politics in 2008. Her successor, John Donahoe, was chosen from within the company; he had headed eBay Marketplaces, the core of the business, and had achieved some major acquisitions. Since then, eBay has continued to develop its foreign operations and specialty sites. In 2012, the company was estimated to be worth approximately $40 billion.

---

million, but it helped eBay to move into higher-end transactions. Other acquisitions soon followed, including Kruse International (collectable automobiles), alando.de AG (the largest online European auction company), and Billpoint (which facilitated person-to-person credit card transactions).

The dot-com bubble was at its peak in 1999, with a thousand other entities competing with eBay, including Amazon.com. Whitman was able to meet the competition. She joined forces with AOL, which opened eBay to an increase in Internet traffic. She was also able to keep the company moving when the price of its stock was halved in 2004–06.

Skype was purchased by eBay in 2005 for $4 billion, despite criticism from some quarters. It was sold to Microsoft for $8 billion several years later. Whitman also had eBay purchase Rent.com and Shopping.com to gain access to the real estate and commercial markets.

In 2008, Whitman left eBay, also leaving its board of directors in 2009 and the boards of Procter & Gamble and DreamWorks SKG. She then prepared to campaign in the 2010 California gubernatorial race. She defeated Steve Poizner in the Republican primary but lost to former governor Jerry Brown in the general election.

After the November election defeat, Whitman continued her activities in the private sector. In January 2011, she was appointed to the board of directors of Hewlett-Packard (HP). In February, she took a seat on the board of directors of Zipcar, a car-sharing venture whose members can use a land or mobile phone to reserve a car for transport and avoid having to keep and maintain their own vehicles; the idea is to facilitate urban mobility, lessen traffic, and lower pollution, thus creating more livable cities. Between March and September 2011, Whitman was a part-time strategic adviser to the private equity firm Kleiner, Perkins, Caulfield and Byers. She also joined the board of Teach for America.

In September 2011, Whitman was apppointed president and CEO of HP. Former CEO Leo Apotheker had led HP in the purchase of British software maker Autonomy Corporation. However, HP was facing difficult challenges. Soon after it announced that it would probably spin off its personal computer business, there were moves to remove Apotheker. He was replaced as CEO by Whitman. The move was not viewed as an improvement by many. Some analysts looked upon HP as a victim of bad decisions and upon Whitman as the wrong "fixer." The price of HP's stock dropped dramatically the day Whitman became CEO.

In the year after Whitman began leading HP, she made a number of significant decisions. These include putting webOS operation system into open source status, reducing staff by 8 percent, and engaging in a lawsuit with Oracle over Internet servers. In May 2012, she announced a plan for revitalizing HP. Included in the plan was the merger of the personal computer and printer divisions in order to increase sales of HP's PCs. Other plans included trimming jobs, restructuring, and product improvements. Whitman publicly stated that it would probably take four or five years to turn the company around.

PERSONAL LIFE

Ownership of eBay stock has made Whitman a billionaire and Internet mogul. She has shared her talents and wealth with Princeton University as a member of its board of trustees and as a donor. Harsh and she donated $30 million to Princeton in 2002 to build a new residential college. Other donations have been made to preservation work in Telluride, Colorado; to the Environmental Defense Fund for its Center for Rivers and Deltas; to the Neurosurgery Research and Education Foundation in Rolling Meadows, Illinois; and to Menlo Park Presbyterian Church, where the family worships. Other substantial sums have been given to Whitman's family foundation.

Whitman and Harsh have two sons. Griffith "Grif" Rutherford Harsh V is a Princeton University graduate and younger brother William W. "Will" Harsh also attended Princeton. The family lives in Atherton, California, with their pet dog. Winter vacations are usually spent skiing and summer vacations fly fishing. Whitman usually travels for business on commercial airlines. She is often recognized and enjoys hearing eBay stories from fellow travelers.

During the California gubernatorial campaign, the family's residence was the target of demonstrators protesting Whitman's positions. Whitman spent more than $160 million of her own fortune to finance the campaign. She has stated that she has no regrets, seeing such expenditures for public office as a sacrifice for the public good.

Andrew J. Waskey

FURTHER READING

Cohen, Adam. *The Perfect Store: Inside eBay*. Boston: Little, Brown, 2002. Print. Offers insight into early history of eBay and its operations, including stories such as the fact that the story that eBay was created to please Pierre Omidyar's girlfriend was a public relations fabrication.

Horvitz, Leslie Alan. *Meg Whitman: President and CEO of eBay*. New York: Ferguson, 2005. Print. Part of the publisher's Career Biographies series, this concise biography focuses on Whitman's work at eBay as an instructive and inspirational guide for young career seekers.

Whitman, Meg. "Meg Whitman." Interview by Lois Romano. *Newsweek* 157.21/22 (2011): 26. Print. Whitman gave this interview shortly before her appointment as CEO of Hewlett-Packard. It covers her failed campaign for California governor, her work with eBay and other companies, and her then current work with the venture capital company Kleiner, Perkins, Caulfield and Byers.

---, and Joan O'C Hamilton. *The Power of Many: Values for Success in Business and in Life*. New York: Crown, 2010. Print. Addresses issues of core corporate values, seeking to answer the question of whether it is possible to run a corporation on the power of trust. Also addresses issues of technology.

EVAN WILLIAMS

Cofounder of Twitter

Born: March 31, 1972; Clarks, Nebraska
Died: -
Primary Field: Internet
Specialty: Social media
Primary Company/Organization: Twitter

INTRODUCTION

Evan Williams is a computer programmer and entrepreneur from Nebraska who has been involved with two of the Internet's most visited sites: Blogger and Twitter. He has worked at a number of prominent Internet companies on both full-time and contract bases but has become best known as one of the three founders of Twitter, where he continues to work in an executive position, developing strategy. Twitter has hundreds of millions of users and has revolutionized online communications for many of those people. Twitter and tweet have entered the lexicon as verbs familiar to nearly *everyone with a mobile phone or computer, and few news, entertainment, and other major corporations do not offer interactive communications with viewers and listeners via their websites and social media pages.*

EARLY LIFE

Evan Clark "Ev" Williams was born in Clarks, Nebraska, on March 31, 1972, and lived and worked on a farm during his childhood and teenage years. Although he attended the University of Nebraska for a year and a half, the isolated agricultural lifestyle did not appeal to him, and he longed to invent and create in a more technologically sophisticated environment. This led him to a variety of positions across the country, where he sought to make a mark for himself. Initially he was involved on the marketing and publishing but, at O'Reilly Media in Sebastopol, California, he was given the opportunity to switch to programming, which yielded further opportunities on contract bases with various well-known computer and Internet companies. Contacts he made during this process and the confidence and skills he acquired from the various jobs he performed facilitated the major stage of his career, which was to take a role in start-up companies providing new products for the Internet world.

Evan Wiliams.

LIFE'S WORK

In 1999, Williams and Meg Hourihan founded Pyra Labs as a company that would produce project management software. Almost serendipitously, the concept of blogging was introduced from a note-taking application that was intended to be part of a larger suite of programs. Williams rapidly became involved with making this application, Blogger, popular and is credited with inventing the term; today, many millions of people use blogging software to record their opinions on a wide range of subjects, and the term and concept have been embraced in commercial and organizational circles as important means of communication with stakeholders as well as marketing and public relations.

The Pyra Labs version of blogging was comparatively limited in scope, but it was successful in grasping the imagination and thereby enlisting the energy of users in developing the initial premise. Google recognized the further potential of the application and in 2003 purchased the company in its entirety. This was just as well for Williams, because investment money had already run out and most employees had either left or were on the verge of doing so, some of them with harsh words to say about Williams's management style and his seeming unwillingness to put human above business interests, as is common in situations when staff are expected to work without pay.

Within a year, Williams had left Google to start new ventures. These included Odeo, a company involved with producing podcasts. Again, this was a venture that provided a new medium that sparked the enthusiasm of people interested in both producing and consuming content. However, as in the case of Blogger, it was not clear to users why they should pay for such services when elsewhere user-produced content (albeit often not of the highest quality) was being made available for free in such profusion.

From 2003 to 2007, Williams was involved not just with Odeo but with a variety of other start-up companies as well. He became part of the cluster of talented entrepreneurs and engineers living in California and forming networks with one another to find complementary resources and competencies in the hope of discovering the next big Internet idea. Williams was at different times an investor, innovator, and manager.

Twitter emerged as an independent company in 2007 founded by Jack Dorsey, Biz Stone, and Williams, who supplanted Dorsey as chief executive officer (CEO) shortly thereafter. The single product that Twitter offered, the eponymous microblogging service,

Affiliation: Twitter

Twitter is an Internet service that permits users to post online and read from other users messages of up to 140 characters. Messages can be accessed from any web-enabled device, and it has become particularly popular with people who use mobile devices. In March 2012, Twitter announced that it had 140 million users making around 340 million tweets daily, and the numbers continue to grow.

Most tweets are of direct interest only to personal friends and family members, although when users are celebrities, politicians, journalists, or otherwise famous or expert persons, every tweet may be treated with great interest by thousands or even millions of users. In July 2012, for example, singer and entertainer Lady Gaga was ranked first, with more than 27 million followers. President Barack Obama was ranked sixth, with more than 17 million followers.

Twitter has become of great interest to corporations and politicians interest because of the opportunities it provides for data mining and following trends. Various applications are available for aggregating tweets to determine which subjects are "trending" or are most popular at any moment of the day. This information is used by media organizations and the marketing depart-

ments of corporations to shape the immediate media discourse, attitudes, and opinions. Companies, political groups, and other organizations can sift through tweets relevant to themselves to understand what people are thinking and saying about them through data mining techniques; they can also participate in that conversation in an attempt to influence or alter these trends. Such benefits should help in the monetization of the service, in addition to the provision of "promoted" or sponsored tweets.

Twitter has also become strongly associated with rapid self-organization of crowds, enabling political protesters during Middle Eastern uprisings that began in 2011, collectively known as the Arab Spring, to plan events; according to reports, rioters in London used Twitter do the same thing. The poorly considered or even deliberate use of Twitter has also influenced certain high-profile trials in the United Kingdom, where secrecy laws make it comparatively easy for well-known people to obtain injunctions against publishing information on their private lives, by naming the individuals involved. The implications of Twitter and its capacity to be used and manipulated by a variety of forces are likely to produce other unintended consequences in the future.

became enormously popular. Subscribers could send messages, called tweets, through the service, which were limited to 140 characters to meet the requirements of mobile device short-message services; many, already accustomed to texting short messages, found the format and character limit compatible. Twitter took off among users interested in rapid communication without any particular intellectual content and thereby overcame the initial skepticism about the professional communication industries, in the same way that blogging had done. Twitter subsequently fine-tuned the product, but the essential service remained the same and continued to be provided for free to all registered users. Third-party applications relying on Twitter began to proliferate.

In 2010, Williams stepped down as Twitter's CEO, remaining to work on strategy. The new CEO, Dick Costolo, had been chief operating officer and had joined the board the previous year. This move seemed to make sense from a personal point of view: Williams was considered to be more of a technical expert than a manager. Williams has described Twitter as a maturing high

school student, which has achieved physical size but lacks organizational sophistication. He planned to focus on strategy issues such as the realization of income from users (in such a way that people do not feel alienated by, for example, intrusive advertisements or blatantly inauthentic tweets), as well as privacy issues and the ownership of tweets, which can have commercial value. The importance of Twitter had already become apparent. In 2009, the U.S. State Department requested that the company postpone some scheduled maintenance work on the system because it would have coincided with important moments in the Iranian elections and it was thought that many people, not relying on official sources of information, were using Twitter as a means of social and political organization while avoiding official scrutiny and censorship. Subsequently, any large-scale social gathering has routinely had the extensive use of Twitter ascribed to it, whether it is the protestors of the Arab Spring in 2011 or the rioters in parts of London later that year. It is certainly true that Twitter has become a leading application for citizen journalists and for those caught up in natural disasters, terrorist attacks, and other events of great and immediate public importance.

One of Twitter's principal benefits in this context is the use of the hash key (#), which users append to messages with a short "tag" or text string that indicates the subject of the message. Tweet aggregators can easily identify these tags and thereby provide summary reports that reveal both the most popular subjects people are discussing at any moment and important user or customer feedback for companies and marketers. The ubiquity of tweets on radio and television programs inviting interactivity has brought the terminology into general use, and numerous academic studies have sought to consider what impact the process has had on people and society. Although it is not clear to what extent Williams was fully aware of all the implications of the new technology, from a commercial point of view it really does not matter. What he has achieved is to provide communication tools—blogging and tweeting—that any millions have felt inspired to develop for a wide variety of purposes.

PERSONAL LIFE

Williams has been described as an independent thinker, creative and innovative with respect to technology, if he is less interested in the fine but necessary details of organizational management. He is considered good company in a small crowd, although public speaking seems to be something of an ordeal for him.

Williams lives in San Francisco with his wife, Sarah Morishige Williams, and their two children. Notwithstanding his background in enabling people to make their thoughts and opinions known, Williams has evidently made a decision to reveal very little of his personal life to the public domain.

John Walsh

FURTHER READING

Arthur, Charles. "Twitter CEO Evan Williams Steps Down." *The Guardian* 4 Oct. 2010. Web. July 2012. Media story of Williams's departure from Twitter's CEO position and some analysis.

Diaz-Ortiz, Claire, and Biz Stone. *Twitter for Good: Change the World One Tweet at a Time*. San Francisco: Jossey Bass, 2011. Print. Twitter executives reveal the official corporate thinking on how tweeting can be used in the service of worthwhile social change.

Grossman, Lev. "Iran's Protest: Why Twitter Is the Medium of the Movement." *Time* 17 June 2009. Web. July 2012. Media analysis of the expansion of use of Twitter and its role in providing self-organizing support for protesters during the 2009 elections in Iran.

Jansen, Bernard J., Mimi Zhang, Kate Sobel, and Abdur Chowdury. "Twitter Power: Tweets as Electronic Word of Mouth." *Journal of the American Society for Information Science and Technology* 60.11 (2009): 2169–88. Print. One of many academic studies of the power of Twitter. Examines 150,000 tweets related to branding and marketing issues.

Miller, Claire Cain. "Putting Twitter's World to Use." *New York Times* 14 Apr. 2009. Web. July 2012. Newspaper story with some personal details and discussion of the increasing use of Twitter.

Thomases, Hollis. *Twitter Marketing: An Hour a Day*. Indianapolis: Wiley, 2010. Print. A self-help business book professing to educate readers in how to use Twitter in their own businesses and careers, by a professional in the trade.

Williams, Evan. "Evan Williams on Twitter." 5 Oct. 2010. *The Economist*. Web. 15 Aug. 2012. Interview with Williams after he stepped down as Twitter's CEO, focusing on how the site will attract revenue while maintaining the free service.

STEVE WOLFF

Early developer of the Internet

Born: c. 1936?; place unknown
Died: -
Primary Field: Computer science
Specialty: Internet
Primary Company/Organization: ARPANET

INTRODUCTION

Steve Wolff was a seminal figure in the early development of the Internet, particularly through popularizing the network with leading decision makers and helping to make its potential clear. This has led to his classification as one of a small group of people regarded as fathers of the Internet. He was involved with the creation of ARPANET and numerous other important developments in a career lasting more than fifty years.

EARLY LIFE

Stephen S. "Steve" Wolff received a bachelor's degree with highest honors in electrical engineering from Swarthmore College in Pennsylvania in 1957. He earned a doctoral degree in electrical engineering from Princeton University in 1961. He followed this with postdoctoral work in 1962 at Imperial College, London, under Colin Cherry and Dennis Gabor. Then he returned to the United States and taught electrical engineering at Johns Hopkins University for a decade, specializing in statistical communication theory.

LIFE'S WORK

Wolff began his close involvement with the development of the Internet when he became a communications technology researcher for the U.S. Army in 1981; he worked for the Army for fourteen years. He led a team that introduced Unix to the Army and was part of the team working on the Advanced Research Projects Agency network, ARPANET. This was the principal forerunner of the Internet and, through the use of data packet switching, represented something of a paradigm

Steve Wolff.

switch in network communication through changing from a one-to-one to a many-to-many model of communication. The development of the networks moved in parallel with technological and engineering capabilities, and each stimulated progress in the other.

In 1986, Wolff joined the National Science Foundation (NSF) as divisional director for network and communications research and was responsible for establishing NSFNET, which was intended to link academic institutions as a means of promoting research and scholarship. When asked to create the NSF network, Wolff said that it would be easy; the Army's ARPANET could simply be reproduced. When everything was up and running, Ron Natalie, a member of the team, telephoned the NSF network operations center to give them the good news. Wolff's team was disheartened when the people at the center were in complete disbelief. Wolff told his team that it did not matter what they had said or who had done what to get the network running; all that mattered was that it worked.

NSFNET was also a part of ARPANET. Wolff's role not only was technological in nature but also somewhat evangelical, in that he persuaded potential stakeholders of the importance of networked communications and the benefits it could bring. It is in this aspect and the visionary imagination that fueled it that Wolff's principal contribution lies. From the moment he joined NSF, Wolff realized that the group needed to get research collaborators who were overseas linked to the network. He struck a deal with IBM whereby NSF would pay half the cost of all international lines if IBM would run the transmission-control protocol/Internet protocol (TCP/IP) on the lines and connect with the NSF network.

Under Wolff's direction, the system was transformed and expanded from an ad hoc 56 kilobits per second (kbps) backbone to a T1 and later T3 backbone. Much of the credit for the rapid expansion of the Internet goes to Wolff for tirelessly enlisting regional and campus links and seeking funding for international network links. When he received the prestigious Jonathan B. Postel Service Award from the Internet Society (ISOC) in 2002, his leadership in fostering cooperation in the growth of the Internet was specifically mentioned.

While at NSF, Wolff was part of the gigabit testbed project that was jointly funded by the Defense Advanced Research Projects Agency (DARPA).

In 1995, Wolff joined Cisco Systems and took responsibility for the University Research Project (URP),

Affiliation: ARPANET

ARPANET was an application of the Advanced Research Projects Agency (ARPA), which in 1972 was renamed the Defense Advanced Research Projects Agency (DARPA). It was the world's first network to employ a data-packet-switching technique, which greatly increased the flexibility and power of network communications. The network was established at four universities in 1969 (three in universities in California and the fourth at the University of Utah) and then spread across the country in subsequent years and, by 1973, had some international nodes. By 1983, the military network (MILNET) was calved into a separate domain and, although this reduced the size of ARPANET, it made it possible for future civilian use and growth by eliminating access to sensitive military information.

The network was formally decommissioned in 1990, but part of its infrastructure formed an input into the subsequent Internet. This was then built with the assistance of Senator Al Gore and its popularity recognized in part by the persuasive efforts of Steve Wolff.

which had an annual budget of some $1.5 million for academic researchers looking for new ways to develop and use network communications. He was also involved with Internet2 (which he later joined full time) and the Abilene project: Abilene was a new-generation, optical fiber network (with optical fiber networks provided by Qwest Communications and in cooperation with Cisco, Nortel, and Indiana University) which offered a major advance in network connectivity and later became the Internet2 network (which is separate from the organization).

As of 2012, Wolff was the interim vice president and chief technology officer of Internet2, an advanced networking consortium that links government agencies, universities, and research centers and private sector corporations to promote the development and use of Internet-based technologies so that partners can achieve their objectives.

PERSONAL LIFE

Wolff is a member of the Association for Computing Machinery (ACM), a member of the American Association for the Advancement of Science (AAAS), a life member of the Institute for Electrical and Electronics Engineers (IEEE), and a pioneer member of the ISOC. He and Jonathan Postel raced to complete the membership form and submit their payments, each trying to be the first member of the ISOC. Postel won.

John Walsh

FURTHER READING

"Abilene Network Establishes Coast-to-Coast Connectivity." 20 Jan. 1999. University Information Technology Service, Indiana University. Web. 12 July 2012. This press release describes the Abilene network and its stakeholders.

Bass, Ryan. "Steve Wolff Named New Internet2 Interim Vice President and Chief Technology Officer." *Internet2 News.* 31 Mar. 2011. Web. 12 July 2012. Corporate press release describing Wolff's new position, his qualifications for the job, and some personal history.

Malamud, Carl. *Exploring the Internet: A Technical Travelogue.* Upper Saddle River: Prentice Hall, 1992. Print. Provides coverage of the development of the early Internet.

Leiner, Barry M., et al. "Brief History of the Internet." n.d. Internet Society. Web. 12 July 2012. History of the development of the Internet by many of the individuals responsible for that development, including contributions from Vinton G. Cerf, David D. Clark, Robert E. Kahn, Leonard Kleinrock, Daniel C. Lynch, Jon Postel, Larry G. Roberts, and Steve Wolff, as well as Leiner.

Salus, Peter H. *Casting the Net: From ARPANET to Internet and Beyond.* Reading: Addison-Wesley, 1995. Print. Detailed history of the development of computer communications networks, covering ARPANET and the role of Wolff.

Waltner, Charles. "Steve Wolff—Hustling for Innovation." *Cisco Newsroom.* 30 July 2002. Web. 12 July 2012. Corporate press release celebrating Wolff's ISOC award and describing his work at Cisco.

Y

JERRY YANG

Cofounder of Yahoo!

Born: November 6, 1968; Taipei, Taiwan
Died: -
Primary Field: Business and commerce
Specialty: Management, executives, and investors
Primary Company/Organization: Yahoo!

INTRODUCTION

With Stanford University colleague David Filo in 1994, Jerry Yang created a directory of websites located on the Internet that eventually became known as Yahoo! Quickly evolving into one of the leading Internet websites, Yahoo! enjoys some of the highest rates of traffic of any website, second only to Google as of 2012. Although Yahoo! continues to be highly successful, the failure of its stock price to keep up with that of Google led to a series of new chief executive officer (CEO) s after Yang stepped down in 2009.

EARLY LIFE

Jerry Yang was born Yáng Zhìyu n in Taipei, Taiwan, on November 6, 1968. His father died when he was two years old. In 1978, his mother, an English teacher in Taiwan, moved to San Jose, California, with Yang and his younger brother. Although he knew only a few words of English when he began as a student San Jose's Sierramont Middle School, by the time Yang graduated three years later he was considered fluent. A resident of San Jose's Berryessa district, Yang attended Piedmont Hills High School, where he did well academically, taking a variety of advanced placement (AP) classes, including AP English. Upon graduation from Piedmont Hills, Yang entered Stanford University, where he studied electrical engineering.

Yang excelled while at Stanford. While an undergraduate, he was a member of the Phi Kappa Psi social fraternity. Upon graduation, Yang was accepted into a doctoral program in electrical engineering at Stanford, and he worked as a research assistant while doing his graduate work. In 1989, Yang met David Filo, who became his fast friend and future business partner. In April 1994, Filo expressed frustration to Yang regarding

Jerry Yang.

difficulty he was experiencing keeping track of favorite websites that he found while browsing the Internet with the then-new Mosaic browser software. Yang and Filo created what they termed "Jerry and Dave's Guide to the World Wide Web." This site, which evolved into Yahoo, was a directory of other websites arranged in a hierarchy based on relevance rather than as a searchable list or index. The website soon began to consume so much of their time that Yang and Filo requested, and received, an academic leave of absence from Stanford to work on their website. Although Yang has a master's degree in electrical engineering, he never returned to Stanford to complete his doctorate.

LIFE'S WORK

In short order, news of the new web portal swept the Internet, causing Stanford to request that Yang and Filo find a commercial host for their website, as increased traffic was causing problems for the university's Internet service. By this time, other popular web portals, such as Netscape Communications and America Online (AOL) had taken notice of Yang and Filo's work and made offered to buy them out. The two decided to establish their own company instead, and they adopted the name Yahoo! for their website. Although various stories regarding reasons for the change exist, the change was made essentially to establish a brand for the service and the yahoo.com domain was created in January 1995. Because of trademark issues related to the name, Yang and Filo included an exclamation mark in the official name of the site (although it is often omitted in media references). Yang and Filo chose the term *yahoo* because they felt it encapsulated the Internet's wild and untamed image. Yahoo! has sometimes been purported to stand for "Yet Another Hierarchical Officious Oracle," although this acronym was developed after the adoption of the name.

When Yahoo! had more than a million hits before the end of 1994, Yang and Filo recognized the potential for their search engine. The business was incorporated in March 1995 and immediately generated interest from venture capitalists. Sequoia Capital invested approximately $3 million in April, paving the way for the company's initial public offering (IPO) the following year. The IPO was a success, with 2.6 million shares sold at $13 apiece, allowing the company to raise almost $34 million.

By the late 1990s, Yahoo! faced competition from a variety of other web portals, including Lycos, excite, and Ask Jeeves. In an effort to attract as many users

as possible, Yang determined that Yahoo! must compete by offering other services in an attempt to gain as many users as possible. To further this goal, Yang led Yahoo! to acquire Four11 Corporation in 1997. Four11 had developed the popular RocketMail, a free e-mail service that rivaled Microsoft Corporation's Hotmail as the most popular messaging service during the late 1990s. Yahoo! rebranded RocketMail as Yahoo! Mail, which continued to be popular and as of 2012 had more than 300 million accounts, making it the most popular e-mail service In the United States. Yahoo! also purchased ClassicGames.com, which evolved into Yahoo! Games. Yahoo! Games permits users to play electronic games, either with themselves or by interacting with other users. Offering both free games and those that can be downloaded for a fee, Yahoo! Games has proven especially popular with the otherwise hard-to-reach young male demographic. During this period, Yahoo! also acquired GeoCities, a website that allowed for the hosting of user-created websites, and eGroups, an e-mail list management system. These services were rebranded as Yahoo! GeoCities and Yahoo! Groups. Although these acquisitions were sometimes controversial with investors, they drew many users to the parent site and helped Yahoo! achieve the status as one of the top two Internet sites by 2000 (trailing only AOL.com).

The dot-com boom, sometimes referred to as the dot-com bubble, was a period stretching from 1995 until 2000 that saw the value of stocks associated with the Internet and other related technology fields increase exponentially. The dot-com boom was advantageous to Yahoo, which saw its stock price double during December 1999 alone. By January 3, 2000, Yahoo!'s stock hit an all-time high value of more than $118 per share. By September 2001, this would drop to an all-time low of $8.11. Although this drop was dramatic, and devastating to many shareholders, unlike many other dot-com rivals, Yahoo! survived the dot-com downturn. In an effort to survive the dot-com downturn, Yang instituted a series of partnerships that allowed Yahoo! to join with other Internet companies to provide content, access, and other services. Companies with which Yahoo! entered such partnerships included AOL, Southwestern Bell Corporation (SBC), and Verizon Communications, Inc. These partnerships helped to stabilize Yahoo! and allowed its stock price gradually to rebound.

While Yahoo! had been founded on its ability to provide users with access to a variety of other websites, the search engines used on Yahoo!'s website have at times been outsourced to others. In 1996, for example,

AltaVista, a division of Digital Equipment Corporation (DEC), became the exclusive provider of search functions for Yahoo! By 2000, Yahoo! had entered into a similar agreement with Google, Inc., whereby Yahoo! used Google's search engines for searches conducted on the Yahoo! site. As Google became increasingly dominant as a search engine, Yahoo! sought to bolster its search capabilities by providing these services on its own. As a result, Yahoo! Search set out to develop its own search technology, acquiring Inktomi Corporation in 2002 and a year later purchasing Overture Services, Inc., which by then owned AltaVista. By 2003, Yahoo! was able to abandon its agreement with Google and provide its own search results, using a reinvented web crawler termed Yahoo! Slurp. By 2009, Yahoo! was the search engine of choice of approximately 6.5 percent of web users, trailing market leader Google, which claimed 85 percent of users. At that point, Yahoo! decided once again to abandon its own search capacity and entered into an agreement with Microsoft Corporation whereby that entity's Bing web search engine would be used by Yahoo!'s site.

Dealings with Microsoft led to one of Yang's most controversial and unpopular decisions as CEO. In 2005, Microsoft was alarmed by Google's increasing dominance as an Internet search engine. In an effort to combat this, Microsoft entered discussions to acquire Yahoo, talks that took place from 2005 through 2007. When the two companies were unable to come to an agreement regarding Microsoft's acquisition of Yahoo, Microsoft made an unsolicited takeover bid for Yahoo! in 2008. Microsoft's offer valued Yahoo! at $44.8 billion, significantly more than what many analysts believed Yahoo! to be worth. After Yang demanded that Microsoft increase its bid by $3 per share, Microsoft withdrew its bid and the share value of Yahoo! plunged, leaving the company with a value of $20 billion by November 2008.

Yang also displeased many in 2005 when Yahoo! cooperated with the Chinese government and provided government officials the IP addresses of Chinese dissidents who used Yahoo! Mail to circulate statements critical of the Chinese government. Yahoo!'s disclosure led to the arrest of activist journalist Shi Tao, who was ultimately sentenced to ten years in prison for his release of a document relating to the fifteenth anniversary of the Tiananmen Square uprising. Yahoo! was criticized by a variety of groups, and Yang was called to Washington, D.C., to answer questions from members of the U.S. House Committee on Foreign Affairs regarding Yahoo!'s role in the arrest of Shi Tao and other

---

Affiliation: Yahoo!

Yahoo! evolved from the work of Jerry Yang and his friend and fellow Stanford University student Dave Filo to devise a way to organize the many offerings on the Internet and make these more accessible and useful. While originally a search engine, Yahoo! quickly evolved into an Internet service provider that offered users an online community, games, music, videos, e-mail accounts, and other services.

Throughout its history, Yahoo! has demonstrated an interest in and ability to acquire rival concerns that have created the content or services it desires to provide its users. Yahoo! has acquired Broadcast.com, eGroups, GeoCities, Four11, and a variety of other companies as a means of enhancing user experiences at the Yahoo! site.

Although Yahoo! remains one of the most visited Internet websites, second only to Google as a search engine, its failure to define itself has caused many business analysts to question its long-term viability. While Yang led Yahoo! through a variety of acquisitions, many of these purchases did not generate profit, and several were shut down or sold at a loss. Starting in 2011, the company had a succession of half a dozen CEOs. On June 16, 2012, former Google executive Marissa Mayer took the helm, announcing on the same day that she was pregnant. At thirty-seven, she was with the youngest CEO of a Fortune 500 company.

Chinese journalists. Yang later asked then Secretary of State Condoleezza Rice for assistance in freeing the imprisoned dissidents. Yahoo! also settled a series of lawsuits filed by dissidents who were arrested by the Chinese government as the result of documents released to them by Yahoo! relating to Yahoo! Mail accounts.

Although always a member of Yahoo!'s management team, Yang officially became CEO of the company for the first time in June 2007. In early 2009, Yang resigned as CEO to be replaced by Carol A. Bartz, although he maintained his membership on Yahoo!'s board of directors. Bartz was removed from her job in September 2011, and Yang, who had remained on the board announced his resignation as a director on January 17, 2012. A succession of CEOs followed Bartz, culminating in the appointment of former Google executive Marissa Mayer on June 16, 2012.

PERSONAL LIFE

In 1992, while part of a Stanford exchange program in Kyoto, Yang met fellow Stanford student Akiko Yamazaki, whom he later married. Yamazaki is of Japanese ancestry and was born and grew up in Costa Rica. Yang and Yamazaki are both involved in the Wildlife Conservation Network, indicating their support for environmental sustainability. In 2007, Yang and Yamazaki donated $75 million to Stanford University for the construction of a building devoted to environmental education.

Yahoo! developed out of Yang's hobby for programming code that would improve his Internet experience. While a part of Yahoo!'s management team, Yang continued to advocate for those experiences that made use of the web portal fun and engaging. Yang serves as a member of the boards of directors of Cisco Systems and the Asian Pacific Fund, as well as the Stanford University Board of Trustees.

Stephen T. Schroth and Jason A. Helfer

FURTHER READING

Cassidy, John. *Dot.con: How America Lost Its Mind and Money on the Internet.* New York: HarperCollins, 2002. Print. Financial analyst and *New Yorker* contributor Cassidy relates the histories of such Internet successes as Yahoo! and examines the practices that let the dot-com bubble to burst.

Perlroth, Nicole, and Evelyn M. Rusli. "Jerry Yang, 'Chief Yahoo,' Steps Down from Board." *New York Times* 18 Jan. 2012: 6. Print. Reports on Yang's decision and its context.

Smith, Bob, and Anthony Vlamis. *Do You? Business the Yahoo! Way: Secrets of the World's Most Popular Internet Company.* North Mankato: Capstone, 2000. Print. Written at Yahoo!'s height, this book examines the ten principles that led to the company's success.

Weston, Michael R. *Jerry Yang and David Filo: The Founders of Yahoo!* New York: Rosen, 2007. Print. Written for a young adult audience, a basic history of the company.

"Yahoo! Why Yang Is Holding Out." Business Week 4088 (2008): 30–31. Print. Surveys the company's current state, focusing on Yang's thoughts about letting the Microsoft deal slip through his fingers.

Z

NIKLAS ZENNSTRÖM

Cofounder of Skype and Kazaa

Born: February 16, 1966; Järfälla, Sweden
Died: -
Primary Field: Internet
Specialty: Applications
Primary Company/Organization: Skype

INTRODUCTION

Niklas Zennström has been termed one of the leading technology "disrupters." He has leveraged licensing, corporate start-up logistics, ownership, and litigation to disrupt, delay, and disguise information in many technology businesses. With his vision to allow consumers and businesses to interact freely over the Internet, Zennström exploited peer-to-peer (P2P) networks with his Danish collaborator and business partner Janus Friis. Early on, Zennström used these file-sharing code systems so consumers could download files with Kazaa and later stream music with Rdio. Subsequently, Zennström and Friis were responsible for the development of the Internet video service Skype, which bypassed conventional telecommunications companies to facilitate global Internet communication. A billionaire entrepreneur and visionary, Zennström serves as a role model for many technology start-ups and, along with Friis, invests in the ideas of others through his venture capital company Atomico.

EARLY LIFE

Born in Järfälla, Sweden, on February 16, 1966, to parents who were teachers, Niklas Mårten Zennström knew at an early age that he wanted to own his own company. He says this desire was more about making it big and earning money than about entrepreneurship. Summer holidays spent in the family's house south of Stockholm in Sodermanland overlooking the Baltic Sea fueled his passions. Here young Zennström enjoyed sailing, swimming, and fishing. Although the family's summer house still stands, the surroundings have changed dramatically. Algae now thrive in the waters and make swimming unappealing, and fish are scarce. These probably account for Zennström's concerns for the environment.

Niklas Zennström.

Earning degrees in business as well as engineering physics and computer science from Sweden's Uppsala University (with a final year at the University of Michigan in the United States), Zennström's first jobs exposed him to low-cost Internet technologies and shaped his philosophy of free access for users. His career began in the 1990s at Swedish Tele2's Copenhagen office. There Zennström met Dane Janus Friis, who had dropped out of high school but was gifted in software scripting. Tele2, a pioneering telephony company, was a fast-growing telecommunications provider in Nordic and Baltic countries and an alternative provider elsewhere. At Tele2, the duo launched Get2Net.com, a satellite-based broadband connection providing high-speed Internet, telephone, and television services through a dish and modem. They also tackled Tele2's European portal of Everyday.com to provide e-mail packages at no charge.

Impressed with peer-to-peer (P2P) technology's capacity to move data through the Internet efficiently and cheaply, the collaborators left Tele2 for Amsterdam in 1999 to work on their own ideas. Heading up FastTrack, a powerful file-sharing utility not requiring a centralized server, Zennström refined its indexing protocol with Friis for a network backbone. They patented an indexing software version through Joltid, a company they formed in 2001. Called Global Index, their distributed computing system was popularized as Kazaa, a website for music sharing founded in 2001.

LIFE'S WORK

Ten years older than Friis, Zennström was the visionary technologist, while Friis was the hacker extraordinaire. Their P2P endeavors with Kazaa benefited from the shutdown of Napster servers by the Recording Industry Association of America (RIAA) in mid-2001, while U.S. courts determined copyright infringement merits. Millions of Napster users switched to Kazaa: It was free and easy to use. However, in October 2001, the two software rogues were sued and they disappeared.

About this time, Zennström also founded Altnet, Inc., in Australia to promote commercial content integrating payment on a secure P2P network. Their real dealings surfaced in a January 2002 announcement that Kazaa had been sold to Sharman Networks. Formed just before Kazaa's sale, Sharman listed an office in Sidney but had been established on Vanuatu, a South Pacific island-nation known as a tax haven. Essentially Sharman's investor and board member information was hidden from scrutiny and subpoenas. Unlike Napster, Kazaa distributed to millions of individual users who traded and shared billions of music, video, and movie files. The longer it took for a court decision, the harder it would be to track software downloads, particularly since Kazaa had become the world's most downloaded software by 2003.

In January 2003, the two music disrupters were again in the spotlight when the courts ruled against them. The decision meant that RIAA could identify and sue any file-sharing individual for infringement. Legal wrangling lasted until July 2006, when Australian courts declared that Kazaa's file-sharing service encouraged infringement of MP3 and movie downloads. Codefendants Zennström and Friis contributed more than $100 million to settle the case, although by then Sharman had converted Kazaa to a subscription service.

Right after the 2001 Kazaa sale, Zennström and Friis concentrated on modifying their music P2P technology for phone applications. Capital was scarce, but Timothy Cook Draper of Draper Fisher Jurvetson rescued their efforts. Draper helped launch this new Voice over Internet Protocol (VoIP) business, Skype (organized in Luxembourg in 2003), with an infusion of $8.5 million in 2004. A more sophisticated VoIP, Skype used another variant of the Global Index as its backbone.

By 2005, Skype had become the fastest-growing start-up in history, even faster than the online auction service eBay. That is when eBay's chief executive officer (CEO) Meg Whitman came calling. Whitman thought a Skype acquisition would close more eBay online transactions, especially of big-ticket items such as cars. In September 2005, eBay purchased Skype for $3.1 billion. The newly minted billionaire Zennström stayed on as Skype's CEO until the third quarter of 2007, when he became nonexecutive chairman of Skype's board to devote more time to other pursuits.

When Skype's initial public offering was announced in early 2009, Zennström sued eBay in British courts for copyright infringement. Apparently eBay had not acquired Skype's root certificates (its intellectual property) when it bought Skype. Its underlying source code also was encrypted remotely. This meant that Skype's platform could be disabled by Zennström and Friis, who licensed Skype their software from Joltid. When eBay inked a $1.9 billion deal in September for a 65 percent stake, Joltid sued eBay and the new investors, claiming Skype had breached its licensing agreement. Zennström also threatened to pull Joltid's backbone technology and render Skype useless for millions of registered users. Litigation frightened some investors away; then eBay countersued.

Affiliations: Kazaa, Skype, and Atomico

Swede Niklas Zennström met Dane Janus Friis in the mid-1990s at the Copenhagen office of Swedish firm Tele2. They worked together on Get2Net.com and Everyday.com. In 1999, the pair left Tele2 for Amsterdam to explore peer-to-peer (P2P) technology. Zennström ended up creating companies to exploit disruptive technologies using P2P and became notorious for litigation to protect the Zennström-Friis interests.

Ten years older than Friis, Zennström was the technology visionary, but high school dropout Friis was the software genius. Using file-sharing P2P, the duo developed Internet access to free music, telephone calls, and television. This P2P platform drew scrutiny when Kazaa's music site was targeted for copyright infringement and sued in January 2002, along with developers Zennström and Friis. Ultimately, the courts ruled in favor of the industry in 2006.

However, Zennström and Friis were at work on a modified P2P backbone to facilitate Internet phone calls and founded Skype in 2003. The fastest-growing start-up by 2005, Skpye was purchased by eBay in 2006, turning the collaborators into billionaires. Zennström and Friis sued eBay in 2009 over source code licensing, when eBay announced a initial public offering for Skype. Their settlement and purchase of a 14 percent stake realized even more money for them when Microsoft bought Skype outright in May 2011 for $8.5 billion.

Also in 2006, Zennström cofounded Atomico. This venture capital company identifies, funds and develops disruptive technologies. Rovio, Fon, Technorati, and Fab are just some of its start-up beneficiaries.

Not until November 2009 were the Skype lawsuits settled. Zennström and Friis transferred software ownership to Skype and received a 10 percent stake in the new Skype and two seats on its board. They also purchased another 4 percent stake for $83 million. This was good a deal for Zennström and Friis, especially when Draper solicited another suitor, and Skype was sold to Microsoft in May 2011 for $8.58 billion cash.

Even after eBay's initial purchase of Skype, Zennström continued to extend his own interests. He and Friis formed Joost N.V. in 2006 to push Internet television further. Their Venice Project was beta-tested at one point as a secure, rights-protected site supported by advertising. Joost, however, was sold in 2009 to the United Kingdom's Adconion Media Group. Also in 2006, Zennström cofounded an investment firm to fund disruptive technologies with Friis, who is no longer involved. Headquartered in London, Atomico scouted entrepreneurs with the potential to transform technology on a global scale. The remarkable start-ups have included Angry Birds developer Rovio, Technorati, Fab, Jawbone, and Quid; some of these ventures have included Zennström on their boards.

In 2008, the Zennström-Friis team went back to their roots by providing on-demand music from Rdio.com. An ad-free web subscription service, Rdio was beta-tested in 2010 to share licensed music across multiple platforms, including computers, in-home devices, and mobile applications. Based in San Francisco, California, the company competes with the likes of iTunes, Pandora, and Spotify.

Perhaps Zennström's greatest achievement is the work funded through his foundation. Started in 2007 with his wife, Catherine, Zennström Philanthropies supports the projects of nonprofit organizations consistent with its mission to advocate and intervene for human rights, encourage social entrepreneurship, and mitigate climate change and its effects.

PERSONAL LIFE

Zennström has granted few media interviews but has been recognized with numerous awards, including the OII Lifetime Achievement Award in July 2011 from the Oxford Internet Institute for his founding roles and transformative techonologies and the KTH Great Prize in 2009 from Sweden's oldest technical university. In 2006, he was included in *Time* magazine's 100 Most Influential People List, and he was named Business Leader of the Year by *European Voice*, Entrepreneur of the Year by the European Business Leaders Awards, and Innovator in Computing and Communications by the *Economist* Innovation Awards.

Zennström met his French wife, Catherine Loing, when they both worked at Tele2. They settled in London and spend time working with their UK-based Zennström Philanthropies. He is active in combating global warming and travels to see firsthand the devastating effects of global warming on places such as his childhood Baltic Sea region and the polar locations of dwindling icebergs.

An avid sailor, Zennström also competes in major races on his yacht *Ràn 2*. His team won back-to-back races in the Rolex Fastnet competition out of Sidney in 2009 and 2011, a victory only a few have achieved.

Abby Dress

FURTHER READING

Giblin, Rebecca. *Code Wars: 10 Years of P2P Software Litigation*. Northampton: Edward Elgar, 2011. Print and e-book. Recounts the legal and technological history of the first decade of the P2P file-sharing era companies.

Miller, Michael. *Discovering P2P: Everything You Need to Know about P2P, to Understand It, to Use It, and to Benefit from It*. Alameda: Sybex, 2001.

Print. Describes the P2P technology, including how it was adapted by early companies and is used today.

Strowel, Alain. *Peer-to-Peer File Sharing and Secondary Liability in Copyright Law*. Northampton: Edward Elgar, 2009. Print. Examines ramifications, now and for the future, of court decisions about third-party P2P developer liability that involve issues of international law and data protection.

MARK ZUCKERBERG

Cofounder, chairman, and CEO of Facebook

Born: May 14, 1984; Dobbs Ferry, New York
Died: -
Primary Field: Internet
Specialty: Social media
Primary Company/Organization: Facebook

INTRODUCTION

Computer programmer and social media visionary Mark Zuckerberg was the motivating force behind the

Mark Zuckerberg.

creation of Facebook, which became the top-ranked social networking site in the world. Facebook users sign up with the site to share their lives with selected friends or with the public if they so choose. While still a student at Harvard, Zuckerberg and a group of friends launched the site as a way of connecting students to one another. Continuing to serve as chief executive officer (CEO) while retaining 56.9 percent of Facebook's voting power, Zuckerberg has remained firmly in control of the company, refusing buyout offers, including those from Google, Viacom, and Yahoo! He did allow Microsoft to buy a 1.6 percent interest in the company in 2007. Time magazine named Zuckerberg as its Person of the Year in 2010. That year, a chance meeting resulted in his donating $100 million to keep the public school system in Newark, New Jersey, from going under. Zuckerberg, whose net worth has been estimated at more than $10 billion even after Facebook's stock price fell following its initial public offering in 2012, has signed the Giving Pledge, initiated by Bill Gates and Warren Buffet, in which American billionaires promise to give away at least half of their vast fortunes during their lifetimes.

EARLY LIFE

Mark Elliot Zuckerberg was born on May 14, 1984, in White Plains, New York, and grew up in Dobbs Ferry. His father, Edward, is a dentist and his mother, Karen, a psychologist. Zuckerberg has three sisters, Randi, Donna, and Arielle. Randi is a senior marketer at Facebook. Zuckerberg got his first computer, a Quantex 486 DX that ran on Windows 3.0, at the age of ten and began customizing it to fit his own needs. At the age of twelve, he created a messaging program, Zucknet, that his father used in the office and the family used at home. Zuckerberg also designed computer games, using graphics drawn by his artistic friends. His parents hired a tutor to teach him even more about computers.

While still in high school, Zuckerberg began taking classes at Mercury College. His parents felt that he was not getting everything he needed from his local high school, so after two years they sent him to the prestigious Phillips Exeter Academy in New Hampshire in 2000. At that preparatory school, he took honors in math, astronomy, and physics, also serving as captain of the fencing team. He had a special talent for languages and could read and write in French, Hebrew, Latin, and ancient Greek.

At Phillips Exeter, Zuckerberg and Adam D'Angelo, his roommate, created Synapse, an MP3 software program with the capability of creating playlists from users' music libraries. The program aroused the interest of Microsoft and AOL, and both companies offered to buy the program and wanted to hire Zuckerberg straight out of high school. Instead, Zuckerberg chose to attend Harvard University, where he began majoring in computer science and psychology in 2002.

During his sophomore year, Zuckerberg archived *The Harvard Crimson* as a way of identifying connections among students. He also created Facemash, a program that displayed images of students, which Zuckerberg had loaded after hacking into Harvard students' online House identity photos, and encouraged other students to compare two photographs and rank them according to who was "hottest." The ensuing outrage led school authorities shut down the site; Zuckerberg escaped expulsion.

LIFE'S WORK

Zuckerberg was only twenty years old in January 2004, when he cofounded thefacebook.com with Harvard roommates Chris Hughes, Dustin Moskovitz, and Eduardo Saverin. The initial program, which was created over a two-week period, was online by February. As the site became more popular, it spread to other universities. Zuckerberg and his pals realized that they could make a fortune off the site and moved to Palo Alta, California, in June 2004, leaving Hughes to finish his degree while managing public relations for Facebook. Almost immediately, controversy arose over the rights to thefacebook.com. Classmates Divya Narendra and twins Cameron and Tyler Winklevoss filed a lawsuit, claiming that Zuckerberg had stolen the idea for the program after being asked to work with them on a dating site,

the Harvard Connection. While insisting that he had not stolen their idea, Zuckerberg was advised by his lawyers to settle the suit with a package that included Facebook shares as well as cash. A subsequent suit by cofounder Eduardo Saverin was also settled.

After meeting Zuckerberg, Sean Parker, the founder of the controversial music-sharing site Napster, became part of the early Facebook team. He negotiated the deal with PayPal cofounder Peter Thiel, who invested $500,000 in the new company. In 2005, Accel Partners invested $12.7 million in the growing company, and Zuckerberg and company raised another $27.5 million from other investors, including Greylock Partners and Meritech Capital Partners.

When Viacom attempted to buy Facebook in 2006, Zuckerberg upped the asking price to $2 billion and Viacom backed down. He subsequently turned down a $1 billion offer from Yahoo, leading *Fast Company* to dub him "The Kid Who Turned Down $1 Billion." By 2007, Facebook had climbed to 20 million users, introduced a new design, added network portals, and allowed outside developers to run applications on the site. That year, Facebook was valued at $15 billion.

By the end of 2009, Facebook had more than a thousand employees and was claiming more than 350 million users. That year, Ben Mezrich published *The Accidental Billionaires*, containing information largely based on interviews with cofounder Eduardo Saverin, who was in the process of suing Zuckerberg. The book formed the basis for the movie *The Social Network* (2010), starring Jesse Eisenberg as Zuckerberg. The Facebook camp insisted that the book was fiction rather than true to life, and the general feeling was that filmmakers had added fictive material to the history to make the founding of Facebook more dramatic than it had been in real life. One fact that supported Facebook's claim was Zuckerberg's ongoing relationship with Priscilla Chan, whom he had met at Harvard. Another is the fact that he is considered kind rather than selfish and is well liked by his coworkers. After viewing the film, Zuckerberg commented that the only thing filmmakers had rendered accurately was his wardrobe. Other Zuckerberg biographers, including David Kirkpatrick, have also insisted that the film is more fiction than fact.

While Zuckerberg remained at the helm, other cofounders left the company. Chris Hughes departed in 2007 to run Barack Obama's online campaign. Dustin Moskovitz retained the position of vice president of engineering until 2008.

Affiliation: Facebook

Mark Zuckerberg left Harvard University and moved to Palo Alto, California, in 2004 at the end of his sophomore year. He had developed Facebook (originally Facemash and then thefacebook.com) with a few fellow students at the university, and in California he and his cofounders raised $40 million in venture capital for their new endeavor. By the end of the summer, Facebook had spread to other Ivy League colleges and universities and had 200,000 active users. By November, the user base had reached one million. By September 2005, the service had been rebranded as Facebook, and by December, 1 million students were registered with the site.

In 2006, Facebook was opened to the public; within a year, it was ranked second among social networking sites. By 2010, it was ranked number one, and *Time* magazine noted that one out of every twelve people on the planet was a registered Facebook user. It was widely reported that if Facebook were a country, it would be the third largest country in the world in terms of population.

The Facebook color scheme of blue and white was chosen because Zuckerberg suffers from red-green color blindness. The site has remained popular because it is much more than a network of friends. In 2007, Facebook started partnering with other companies to offer applications on Facebook. By 2010, some ten thousand sites had become affiliated with Facebook. Affiliates include such sites as Pinterest, Goodreads, Zynga, and even the venerable *Washington Post.*

In September 2009, a survey identified Facebook as the tenth most trusted company in the United States, outranking Apple, Google, and Microsoft. Even as Americans suffered through a major economic downturn, Facebook's revenues continued to soar, rising from $300 million in 2008 to $550 in 2009 and to $1 billion in 2010. That year, Facebook reported that 500 million users throughout the world were spending an estimated 10 billion hours on the site each month. In Europe, physicians identified Facebook addiction as an actual medical condition.

Facebook's initial public offering (IPO) created a stir in May 2012. Stock opened at $38 per share and climbed to $42.05, raising $16 billion by the end of the day. Although the stock price would fall over the next weeks and months, this opening was the third largest IPO in American history, bringing Facebook's total worth to approximately $107 billion. Even after selling personal shares worth $1.2 billion, Zuckerberg still owned a significant number of shares. Subsequently, some shareholders filed suit against Zuckerberg, claiming that he had concealed information, and the Securities and Exchange Commission considered launching an investigation.

By 2011, Facebook was facing a steady stream of high-tech employees moving to other companies. That year, a new lawsuit surfaced with Paul Ceglia, an ex-convict, claiming that he had e-mails to prove that Zuckerberg had promised him half of Facebook in 2003, when he was hired to work on the application then in progress. Facebook officials insisted that the case was without merit. Despite problems, Facebook's users continued to grow. By 2011, 47 percent of Americans were registered. Facebook also claimed large memberships in countries around the world, including 31.8 million users in Germany, 31.6 million users in India, 19.9 million users in Canada, 18.6 million users in Brazil, 9.5 million users in Russia, and 7.1 million users in Egypt.

Part of the reason that Facebook was able to maintain the feel of a small company for as long as it did was that all desks, even those of Zuckerberg and chief operating officer Sheryl Sandberg, were in a general area. When moving to a much larger campus in Menlo Park, California, in 2012, Facebook maintained some of its former atmosphere by creating a cozy downtown area, complete with cafeterias and shops. Training sessions are regularly held at Facebook to emphasize the need for new employees to learn to adopt Zuckerberg's mode of thinking, and periodic all-night sessions are mandatory for Facebook developers. *Hack*, a word that has positive connotations for most techies because of its connotation of innovative exploration, is widely displayed in Facebook's offices.

PERSONAL LIFE

Given his enormous success, it is easy to forget that Zuckerberg is still a young man with a strong sense of fun. In 2010, he took his entire family to Orlando, Florida, to visit the Wizarding World of Harry Potter, where he bought a wand at Ollivander's Wand Shop. In December, the Zuckerberg family headed for Vietnam. That sense of fun is also evident on the Facebook campus, where conference rooms bear names that lampoon characters from popular culture, such as Darth Vader from George Lucas's *Star Wars* films.

The day after taking Facebook public on May 18, 2012, in a surprise wedding, Zuckerberg finally married his girlfriend of nine years, Priscilla Chan. The timing was due more to her completing medical school the previous week than to the IPO. Giving up his casual wear, Zuckerberg turned out in a suit, while Chan wore a $4,700 dress designed by Claire Pettibone. Chan was escorted down the aisle by the couple's Hungarian sheepdog, Beast. Music was provided by Billie Joe Armstrong of Green Day, who sang "Last Night on Earth." Two months earlier, the couple had moved from a rental home into a $7 million five-bedroom home in Palo Alto.

Elizabeth Rholetter Purdy

FURTHER READING

"Facebook Growing Up Fast." *San Jose Mercury News* 25 Oct. 2007. Print. Traces the history of Facebook.

Grossman, Lev. "2010 Person of the Year: Mark Zuckerberg." *Time* 176.26 (2010): 44–75. Print. Cover story highlighting the life and career of Zuckerberg. Illustrated.

Hasday, Judy L. *Facebook and Mark Zuckerberg*. Greensboro: Morgan Reynolds, 2012. Print. Part of the Outstanding Business Leaders series for young adults, the book presents a biography of Zuckerberg and details the founding of Facebook. Illustrated.

Helft, Miguel, et al. "Inside Facebook." *Fortune* 165.4 (2012): 112–22. Print. Focuses on the current status of Facebook. Includes illustrations and charts.

Kirkpatrick, David. *The Facebook Effect: The Inside Story of the Company That Is Connecting the World*. New York: Simon, 2010. Print. Chronicles the history of Facebook and its founders. Includes notes, index, and illustrations.

Mezrich, Ben. *The Accidental Billionaires: The Founding of Facebook; A Tale of Sex, Money, Genius, and Betrayal*. New York: Doubleday, 2009. Print. The lurid and not entirely factual account of Facebook's founding that inspired the film *The Social Network*. Illustrated.

Moggridge, Bill. *Designing Media*. Cambridge: MIT, 2010. Print. An examination (by the designer of the original laptop) of both digital and traditional media through interviews with individuals, such as Zuckerberg, who made significant contributions to particular fields. Includes illustration, index, and a CD-ROM.

Stone, Brad. "Everybody Needs a Sheryl Sandberg." *Businessweek* 44.29 (2011): 50–58. Print. Discusses the role played by the number-two person at Facebook, its chief operating officer, Sandberg.

Appendixes

TIMELINE

These milestone events below represent a concise history of the Internet, both theoretical and commercial in scope.

DATE	MILESTONE
1957	After the Soviet Union launches Sputnik 1, the United States forms the Advanced Research Projects Agency (ARPA) to create a communications network that links the country in the event that a military strike renders conventional communication useless.
1961	"Information Flow in Large Communications Nets," a paper by computer science professor Len Kleinrock, is published; it outlines packet switching, which groups together transmitted data into suitably-sized blocks.
1965	At the federally-funded MIT Lincoln Laboratory, a research center dedicated to the application of advanced technology, the first network experiment for ARPA is conducted. During the experiment, two computers interacted with each other using packet switching technology.
1969	The Advanced Research Projects Agency Network (ARPANET), considered the predecessor of the Internet, is commissioned by the Department of Defense for research into networking. To many, this marks the official "birth of the Internet."
1969	The first APRANET message—"Lo"—is sent in an attempt to spell log-in, but the system crashed.
1972	Electronic mail is introduced by Ray Tomlinson, a computer engineer from Cambridge, Massachusetts. He used the @ sign to distinguish between the sender's name and the name of the network.
1973	The term "Internet" first came into modern usage.
1973	The first international connections to the APRANET are established to the University College of London and the Norwegian Seismic Array, or NORSAR (Norway).
1974	The first Internet Service Provider (ISP) is created with the introduction of a commercial version of APRENET called Telenet.
1975	The first all-inclusive email program is introduced, providing replying, forwarding, and filing functionalities and options.
1975	Often attributed as the first personal computer (PC), the Altair 8800 is introduced and is surprisingly sold in high quantities. Because of the computer's surprising sales and because it used Microsoft's first product (Altair BASIC), the introduction of the microcomputer becomes an important milestone in the personal computer revolution.

DATE	MILESTONE
1975	The Microsoft Corporation is founded on April 4 by Bill Gates and Paul Allen to develop BASIC (Beginner's All-purpose Symbolic Instruction Code) interpreters for use in the Altair 8800 microcomputer. It marks the first of numerous high-level programming languages developed and sold by Microsoft, which came to dominate the PC market for decades.
1976	Apple Computer, Inc., which became known for their signature Macintosh personal computers in the 1980s, is founded by Steve Jobs and Steve Wozniak. In terms of market capitalization, Apple would overtake the once behemoth Microsoft Corporation in August of 2012,
1976	Approximately five years after the first email is sent, Queen Elizabeth II sends out an e-mail on ARPANET. It marks the first usage of networking technologies by an acting head of state.
1976	For $40,000, the Computer Corporation of America offers Comet, recognized as the first commercial email product or service.
1978	The first possible unsolicited email message, known as "spam," is sent by a marketing representative advertising an upcoming presentation of new computers. By 2012, the amount of spam recorded is estimated to be in the trillions.
1980	Renowned computer scientist Tim Berners-Lee writes the program "Enquire Within," the predecessor to the World Wide Web (abbreviated simply as the Web or WWW).
1981	Though the history of personal computers arguably spans back to the 1950s, IBM announces its first personal computer in August. At the time of its introduction, the IBM Personal Computer (model number 5150) is marketed as the "smallest, lowest-priced computer system" and offers read-only memory (ROM) of 40K. The success of the IBM PC establishes it as the standard in the personal computer market.
1981	Microsoft begins distributing and licensing its operating system, Microsoft DOS, or MS-DOS (with DOS an acronym for Disk Operating System).MS-DOS and similar operating systems were standard in the PC marketplace for the next fifteen years or so.
1982	Although widely criticized at first, emoticons are introduced to integrate emotion and feeling into messages.
1983	Domain Name System (DNS) is designed by Jon Postel, Paul Mockapetris, and Craig Partridge; .edu, .gov, .com, .mil, .org, .net, and .int are all created.
1984	William Gibson writes the science-fiction novel Neuromancer, coining the term cyberspace.
1984	Apple introduces the first Macintosh personal computer, successfully ushering a graphical user interface and the ubiquitous mouse into the personal computer marketplace.
1984	The number of hosts on the ARPANET surpasses 1,000.
1985	Symbolics.com becomes the first registered .com domain on the Internet. It is registered by a computer manufacturer.

DATE	MILESTONE
1986	The ARPANET/Internet exceeds an estimated 5,000 hosts, a number which would double within one year.
1987	Cisco Systems ships its first product, a multiprotocol router.
1987	An estimated 25 million PCs are sold in the United States.
1989	World.std.com becomes the first commercial provider of Internet dial-up access to the Internet.
1989	The Internet reaches an estimated 100,000 hosts.
1989	Security software company McAfee Associates is founded; Symantec Corp. releases Norton AntiVirus for the Macintosh; antivirus expert Eugene Kaspersky begins his career as an expert in computer viruses.
1991	ARPANET ends; that same year, Tim Berners-Lee creates the World Wide Web, making access to information from around the world easier and revolutionizing modern communication.
1991	The Stanford Linear Accelerator (SLAC) becomes the first web server on the Internet.
1992	The number of hosts on the Internet surpasses 1 million. The World Bank goes online.
1992	Librarian Jean Armour Polly is credited with coining the term "surfing the Internet."
1993	Jim Clark and Marc Andreessen establish Netscape Communications Corp., the company responsible for the commercially successful and once dominant web browser Netscape Navigator.
1993	The World Wide Web is developed within CERN, or the European Organization for Nuclear Research, which houses and maintains the largest particle physics laboratory in the world.
1994	The business plan for commerce company Amazon.com is written by Jeff Bezos. Amazon.com would go on to become the largest online retailer in the world.
1994	Online pizza ordering is available through the Hut online, the web portal for the Pizza Hut restaurant chain.
1995	Yahoo! Inc. is founded in Santa Clara, California, and offers Internet users a bevy of services and products, including a web search engine, email services, mapping, and more.
1996	The WWW browser war, with Netscape and Microsoft being the two main contenders, ushers in a new age of software development in which new products are released quarterly.
1997	The term "web log" is coined; it is later shortened to "blog."
1998	Internet behemoth Google Inc., which set out to collate all the information in the world in its founding mission statement, begins operations in Menlo Park, California.

Date	Milestone
1999	Programmer Shawn Fanning creates Napster, opening the realm of peer-to-peer file sharing and sparking a copyright war in the music industry.
1999	It is reported that Internet traffic doubles every 100 days.
2000	Approximately 20 million websites exist on the Internet, a number which doubled in under a year
2001	Supported by a nonprofit foundation, Wikipedia is launched.
2004	The dominant social media service Facebook is launched; by 2009, the service boasts over an estimated 200 million active users.
2005	The video-sharing site YouTube.com launches; one year later, the site is purchased by Google for an estimated $1.65 billion.
2006	There are an estimated 92 million web sites online.
2006	The microblogging platform Twitter is founded in San Francisco, California; as of 2012, the social networking service has a reported 500 million active users.
2007	Developed as a program to service Apple's numerous personal devices, iTunes surpasses 1 billion downloads.
2009	According to world stats, an estimated 1.114 billion people are using the Internet.
2010	iPad announced by Steve Jobs in San Francisco at the Yerba Buena Center for the Arts
2010	MetroPCS becomes the first to offer 4G LTE service.
2011	Apple launches the iCloud storage and computing service, which allows users to store data on remote computer servers. The iCloud currently has over 150 million users.
2011	The Amazon Kindle Fire is introduced.
2012	Siri voice control for the iPod 4S is introduced.
2012	Facebook goes public with an IPO of $104 billion ($38 per share), closing at $38.23 on the first day of trading.

BIBLIOGRAPHY

Abbate, Janet. *Inventing the Internet.* Cambridge: MIT, 2000. Print. A history of the Internet with a focus on ARPA, including a discussion of Baran's packet-switching technology.

Aigrain, Philippe. *Sharing: Culture and Economy in the Internet Age.* Amsterdam: Amsterdam UP, 2012. Print. Considers BitTorrent as one of several technologies enabling the sharing of information and media, and the effects thereof on culture.

Alderman, John. *Sonic Boom: Napster, MP3, and the New Pioneers of Music.* Cambridge: Perseus, 2001. Print. The dazzling success of Napster put into perspective, with an enthusiastic vision of the future evolution of the music market.

Anderson, Chris. *The Long Tail: Why the Future of Business Is Selling Less of More.* New York: Hyperion, 2006. Print. The editor of Wired examines trends in the technology business.

Anderson, Jennifer Joline. *Wikipedia: The Company and Its Founders.* Edina: ABDO, 2011. Print. Traces the history of Wikipedia and provides biographical information for Wales, Sanger, and Kovitz.

Andrews, L. *I Know Who You Are and I Saw What You Did: Social Networks and the Death of Privacy.* New York: Free Press, 2011. Print. An examination of how social networks and other web tools empower the average citizen.

Angwin, Julia. *Stealing MySpace: The Battle to Control the Most Popular Website in America.* New York: Random House, 2009. Print. An account of Myspace's peak, examining both the online culture and the impact of the company in the business world.

Armstrong, Jerome, and Markos Moulitsas. *Netroots, Grassroots, and the Rise of People-Powered Politics.* White River Junction: Chelsea Green, 2006. Print. Energetic polemic excoriating both the Democratic and Republican parties for their failures and calling on grassroots groups and individuals to hold the establishment accountable when using contemporary political techniques.

Aspray, William, and Paul E. Ceruzzi. *The Internet and American Business.* Cambridge: MIT, 2008. Print. A series of essays that examine the commercialization of the Internet through such developments as information searching, e-mail, and social networking. Covers business models, e-commerce, and the successes and failures of dot-com companies such as AOL.

Assange, Julian, and Suelette Dreyfus. *Underground: Tales of Hacking, Madness and Obsession on the Electronic Frontier.* Edinburgh: Canongate, 2011. Print. Detailed account of the work of the computer hacking collective known as the International Subversives, of which Assange was a member known as Mendax.

Auletta, Ken. *Googled: The End of the World as We Know It.* New York: Penguin, 2009. Print. Explores some of the consequences resulting from the fast pace at which Google permits information to be found, analyzed, and acted upon by a variety of individuals.

Battelle, John. *The Search: How Google and Its Rivals Rewrote the Rules of Business and Transformed Our Culture.* Rev. ed. London: Nicolas Brealey, 2006. Print. Detailed discussion of rise of Google and its transformative impact on business thinking.

Belfiore, Michael P. *The Department of Mad Scientists: How DARPA Is Remaking Our World, from the Internet to Artificial Limbs.* New York: Harper, 2009. Print. An overview of the history, projects, and applications of DARPA.

Belfiore, Michael. *Rocketeers: How a Visionary Band of Business Leaders, Engineers, and Pilots Is Boldly Privatizing Space.* New York: HarperCollins, 2007. Print. A candid look behind the curtain in the nascent industry of privatized space travel and exploration, and the people whose dreams are helping to make that a reality.

Benkler, Yaochaï. *The Wealth of Networks: How Social Production Transforms Markets and Freedom.* New Haven: Yale UP, 2006. Print. An influential essay on the way social networks allegedly reconfigure the laws of economy.

Bentley, Peter J. *Digitized: The Science of Computers and How It Shapes Our World.* New York: Oxford UP, 2012. Print. A popular book about the origins of modern computers, how they affect our lives today, and what developments are expected in the future, written by a computer scientist and honorary member of the UCL Computer Science Department. Bentley's goal is to show how pervasive a role computers play in the daily lives of most people and how the different aspects of computer science relate to one another.

Bhide, Amar. *The Venturesome Economy: How Innovation Sustains Prosperity in a More Connected*

World. Princeton, NJ: Princeton UP, 2008. Print. Examines the link between U.S. venture capital–backed businesses and the global development of technology in the modern economy as well as the roles of scientists, engineers, entrepreneurs, financiers, consumers, and other key players.

Bollier, David. *Viral Spiral: How the Commoners Built a Digital Republic of Their Own*. New York: New Press, 2008. Print. A history of Creative Commons: its origins and accomplishments in developing flexible licenses to provide limited rights to the public.

Brafman, Ori, and Rod A. Beckstrom. *The Starfish and the Rider: The Unstoppable Power of Leaderless Organizations*. New York: Trade Paperback, 2008. Print. A plea in favor of self-organizing communities enabled by peer-to-peer technologies and social networks.

Brandt, R. L. *The Google Guys: Inside the Brilliant Minds of Google Founders Larry Page and Sergey Brin*. New York: Penguin, 2009. Print. Recounts the history of Page's and Brin's meeting and their decision to form what became Google.

Brandt, Richard L. *One Click: Jeff Bezos and the Rise of Amazon.com*. New York: Penguin, 2011. Print. Detailed examination of the founding and rise of Amazon and of the influence of Bezos on e-commerce. Illustrated.

British Computing Society. *Leaders in Computing*. London: BCS, 2011. Print. A collection of interviews, including a lengthy one with Cerf.

Brun, René, Frederioco Carminati, and Giuliana Galli Carminati, eds. *From the Web to the Grid and Beyond: Computing Paradigms Driven by High-Energy Physics*. New York: Springer, 2012. Print. A scholarly account of the history of experimental high-energy physics (HEP), covering topics such as programming languages, software engineering, large databases, the web, grid and cloud computing, and intellectual property regulations. The article is rich with information but is most accessible to an audience with a basic understanding of physics and computer science.

Bruns, Axel. *Blogs, Wikipedia, Second Life, and Beyond: From Production to Produsage*. New York: Peter Lang, 2008. Print. An examination of collaborative content creation in a variety of environments, including Wikipedia.

Carr, N. *The Shallows: What the Internet Is Doing to Our Brain*. New York: Norton, 2011. Print. A critical look at psychological and neurological effects of Internet usage, including the impact of search engines.

Ceruzzi, Paul E. *Computing: A Concise History*. 2nd ed. Cambridge: MIT, 2012. Print. A broad overview of Internet history, including Cerf's contributions.

Chayko, M. *Portable Communities: The Social Dynamics of Online and Mobile Communications*. Albany: State U of New York P, 2008. Print. Explores how conceptions of community have become redefined in response to social networking, blogging, video sharing, and other web tools.

Christakis, N. A., and J. H. Fowler. *Connected: The Surprising Power of Our Social Networks and How They Shape Our Lives*. Boston: Little, Brown, 2009. Print. Looks at how collaboration and participation in social networking enhance an individual's effectiveness.

Clark, Jim. *Netscape Time: The Making of the Billion Dollar Start-up That Took on Microsoft*. New York: St. Martin's, 1999. Print. Engrossing inside story of how Clark and Andreessen conceived and executed start-up of Netscape and the obstacles they faced competing with Microsoft that ultimately led to demise of the company.

Cross, Mary. *Bloggerati, Twitterati: How Blogs and Twitter are Transforming Popular Culture*. Westport: Praeger, 2011. Print. An examination of the influence of the digital revolution on human behavior, as well as the demographics of the users of different types of Internet services, including blogs and Twitter.

Diaz-Ortiz, Claire, and Biz Stone. *Twitter for Good: Change the World One Tweet at a Time*. San Francisco: Jossey Bass, 2011. Print. Twitter executives reveal the official corporate thinking on how tweeting can be used in the service of worthwhile social change.

Domscheit-Berg, Danial, Tina Klopp, and Jefferson S. Chase. *Inside WikiLeaks: My Time with Julian Assange at the World's Most Dangerous Website*. New York: Crown, 2011. Print. Provides an inside view of the website's evolution and finances as well as its inner workings, including worker tensions, from the point-of-view of a former employee.

Edwards, Douglas. *I'm Feeling Lucky: The Confessions of Google Employee Number 59*. Boston: Houghton, 2011. Print. A unique perspective on Google offered by the company's first director of marketing and brand management.

Fitzpatrick, David. *The Facebook Effect: The Inside Story of the Company That Is Connecting the*

World. New York: Simon, 2010. Print. Corporate history of Facebook from its origins until 2010.

Fox, Richard Logan, and Jennifer Ramos, eds. *iPolitics: Citizens, Elections, and Governing in the New Media Era*. New York: Cambridge UP, 2012. Print. Discusses the impact of social media and political websites on contemporary democracy. Includes illustrations and charts.

Gehani, Nairan. *Bell Labs: Life in the Crown Jewel*. Summit: Silicon, 2003. Print. Insightful firsthand account of Bell Labs and the work environment that existed in the facility.

Giblin, Rebecca. *Code Wars: 10 Years of P2P Software Litigation*. Northampton: Edward Elgar, 2011. Print and e-book. Recounts the legal and technological history of the first decade of the P2P file-sharing era companies.

Goldfayn, Alex L. *Evangelist Marketing: What Apple, Amazon, and Netflix Understand about Their Customers*. Dallas: BenBella, 2012. Print. A look at the marketing techniques of the e-commerce giants.

Goodman, Gail F. *Engagement Marketing: How Small Business Wins in a Socially Connected World*. Hoboken: Wiley, 2012. Print. A definitive small business guide filled with practical advice based on the author's experience helping thousands of small businesses to increase repeat sales through e-mail outreach.

Green, Lelia. *The Internet: An Introduction to New Media*. New York: Berg, 2010. Print. Examines the history of the Internet, its roles in new media, and its emerging future. Explores case studies and new research from around the world to present various aspects of Internet use as a reflection of social, political, and economic circumstances.

Jackson, Eric M. *The PayPal Wars: Battles with eBay, the Media, the Mafia, and the Rest of Planet Earth*. Torrance: World Ahead, 2008. Print and digital. Tells the story of PayPal's history from the view of a former insider, author Eric Jackson.

Jarvis, J. *What Would Google do?* New York: Harper-Collins, 2009. Print. Investigates how Google's business dealings combine the visionary with the ruthless, in an effort to both save the planet and decimate the competition.

Jenkins, Henry. *Confronting the Challenges of Participatory Culture: Media Education for the 21st Century*. Cambridge: MIT, 2009. Print. Examines social media, new forms of creative expression, and their impact on media studies.

Johnson, Brian David. *Screen Future: The Future of Entertainment, Computing, and the Devices We Love*. Santa Clara: Intel Press, 2010. Print. Exploration of the potential future impact of computers on the television and entertainment industries. Covers televisions, phones, cars, and computers as personal entertainment delivery systems.

Kaplan, Saul. *The Business Model Innovation Factory: How to Stay Relevant When the World Is Changing*. New York: Wiley, 2012. Print. Netflix serves as an example of innovation in an existing field; coverage includes the way it triumphed over older, established Blockbuster.

Keen, Andrew. *The Cult of the Amateur: How Blogs, Myspace, YouTube, and the Rest of Today's User-Generated Media Are Destroying Our Economy, Our Culture, and Our Values*. New York: Crown, 2008. Print. Looks at the downside of the social media phenomenon and addresses the negative associations with Myspace regarding privacy and teen safety, fears addressed publicly by Myspace parents, adding to the controversy of the site.

Kelsy, T. *Social Networking Spaces: From Facebook to Twitter and Everything in Between*. New York: Apress, 2010. Print. An introduction to some of the leading social networking websites (including Facebook, YouTube, and Twitter) and explains how to use them for social, business, or academic purposes.

Kirkpatrick, David. *The Facebook Effect: The Inside Story of the Company That Is Connecting the World*. New York: Simon, 2011. Print. A clearly written and straightforward history of Facebook, from its origins as Facemash to its worldwide success, written by a Fortune journalist with the cooperation of Facebook executives.

Klein, Alec. *Stealing Time: Steve Case, Jerry Levin, and the Collapse of AOL Time Warner*. New York: Simon, 2004. Print. The book focuses on the rise and fall of AOL Time Warner, looking at the role various individuals played the companies before, during, and after the merger. Kimsey is one of the individuals whose role is examined.

Knopper, Steve. *Appetite for Self-Destruction: The Spectacular Crash of the Record Industry in the Digital Age*. New York: Simon, 2009. Print. A book-length analysis, written by a contributing editor from Rolling Stone, of the record industry's response to the threat to their business model posed by digital recordings. Knopper argues that the record companies should have made a deal with Napster rather than shutting it down and driving people to other sites.

Lacy, Sarah. *Once You're Lucky, Twice You're Good: The Rebirth of Silicon Valley and the Rise of Web 2.0*. New York: Gotham, 2008. Print. An overview of the renaissance of computer and web entrepreneurs in California's Silicon Valley.

Levy, Steven. *In the Plex: How Google Thinks, Works, and Shapes Our Lives*. New York: Simon, 2011. Print. An inside look at the company culture of Google. The author was given direct access to the major figures in Google; the book is thus based on numerous discussions and interviews with the leading personalities in the company.

Levy, Steven. *The Perfect Thing: How the iPod Shuffles Commerce, Culture, and Coolness Millennia Makeover*. New York: Simon, 2006. Print. Examines the formation of the Apple iPod and provides a broad overview of the development of music on the Internet.

Lih, Andrew. *The Wikipedia Revolution: How a Bunch of Nobodies Created the World's Greatest Encyclopedia*. New York: Hyperion, 2009. Print. The author, a veteran Wikipedian, journalist, and academic, covers the history of Wikipedia from early influences on its original owner to the site's origin in the peer-reviewed Nupedia championed by Larry Sanger to the in-fighting and external critics. He sees Wikipedia's importance as more cultural than technical.

Lima, Manuel. *Visual Complexity: Mapping Patterns of Information*. Princeton: Princeton Architectural Press, 2011. Print. Visualizations of data, including Baran's distributed network.

Livingston, Jessica. *Founders at Work: Stories of Startups' Early Days*. Berkeley: Apress, 2008. Print. A collection of interviews with founders of well-known technology companies, including Levchin and PayPal, about what happened in the very earliest days.

Lowe, Janet. *Google Speaks: Secrets of the World's Greatest Billionaire Entrepreneurs, Sergey Brin and Larry Page*. Hoboken: Wiley, 2009. Print. Popular history of Google and its founders, Brin and Page, written in a conversational style and emphasizing the personalities of the two principal subjects as well as their accomplishments.

Mandiberg, Michael, ed. *The Social Media Reader*. New York: New York UP, 2012. Print. Provides a context for the development of social media on the Internet.

Menn, Joseph. *All the Rave: The Rise and Fall of Shawn Fanning's Napster*. New York: Crown Business, 2003. Print. Provides an account of Napster's evolution and initial demise, addressing John Fanning's behind-the-scenes role in the company and highlighting some of Napster's visionary strides that altered the shape of the music distribution industry and some of the debilitating business decisions that led to the company's downfall.

Mezrich, Ben. *The Accidental Billionaires: The Founding of Facebook; A Tale of Sex, Money, Genius, and Betrayal*. New York: Doubleday, 2009. Print. A popular account of the events leading up to the creation of Facebook, concentrating on the years 2003n}05 and the central "characters": Mark Zuckerberg, Saverin, Parker, and Tyler and Cameron Winklevoss. Mezrich's account of these events is notable for its dramatic retelling of incidents, based on interviews and other sources of information. However, some have called into question the accuracy of the account (which formed the basis for the film The Social Network).

Mitnick, Kevin, and William L. Simon. *Ghost in the Wires: My Adventures as the World's Most Wanted Hacker*. New York: Back Bay, 2012. Print. Mitnick returns to his hacking days to provide an account of his adventures and lessons that may be drawn from them.

Morozov, Evgeny. *The Net Delusion: The Dark Side of Internet Freedom*. New York: PublicAffairs, 2011. Print. An argumentative essay that counterbalances the ideas promoted by Barlow and the EFF.

Palfrey, John, and Urs Gasser. *Born Digital: Understanding the First Generation of Digital Natives*. New York: Basic, 2010. Print. The digital world through the eyes of newborns, and a perspective on a generation gap.

Qualman, Erik. *Socialnomics: How Social Media Transforms the Way We Live and Do Business*. New York: Wiley, 2010. Print. Considers the impact of social media on the business world.

Reagle, Joseph Michael. *Good Faith Collaboration: The Culture of Wikipedia*. Cambridge: MIT, 2010. Print. The book places Wikipedia in the context of other efforts, also fired by new technology, to create a freely shared, universal encyclopedia and analyzes the "good faith collaboration" the author views as Wikipedia's defining characteristic.

Rosenberg, Scott. *Say Everything: How Blogging Began, What It's Becoming, and Why It Matters*. New

York: Broadway, 2010. Print. A history of blogging and of the major blogs, such as Boing Boing, by a journalist and Salon.com cofounder, without the hype, misconceptions, or fast-money tips of most other books.

Rowell, Rebecca. *YouTube: The Company and Its Founders*. Edina: ABDO, 2011. Print. A popular history of YouTube and its founders, written for schools. Provides historical and social context for their lives as well as the innovations of the company.

Salus, Peter H., ed. *The ARPANET Sourcebook: The Unpublished Foundations of the Internet*. New York: Peer to Peer Communications, 2008. Print. Assembles primary sources related to the ARPANET project.

Sennett, Frank. *Groupon's Biggest Deal Ever: The Inside Story of How One Insane Gamble, Tons of Unbelievable Hype, and Millions of Wild Deals Made Billions for One Ballsy Joker*. New York: St. Martin's, 2012. Print. Sensationalist but entertaining, the only book-length treatment of Mason and Groupon, focusing on Mason's idiosyncrasies and Groupon's rapid rise.

Smith, Bob, and Anthony Vlamis. *Do You? Business the Yahoo! Way: Secrets of the World's Most Popular Internet Company*. North Mankato: Capstone, 2000. Print. Written at Yahoo!'s height, this book examines the ten principles that led to the company's success.

Smith, Chris, and Marcie McGrata. *Twitter: Jack Dorsey, Biz Stone, and Evan Williams*. Greensboro: Morgan Reynolds, 2011. Print. Covers the early lives of the three founders of Twitter. Discusses Dorsey's early fascination with city maps and computer programming and the interest Williams and Stone had in blogging that led to their careers. Traces the development of Twitter and the roles each founder played. Aimed at young adults, this source nonetheless contains a wealth of information that anyone interested in Twitter or its founders will find useful.

Stross, R. *Planet Google: One Company's Audacious Plan to Organize Everything We Know*. New York: Free Press, 2009. Print. A look at Google's plans to become a one-stop location for information needs, including its potential to serve as a gatekeeper for data and the potential consequences arising from this dominance.

Tapscott, Don. *Grown Up Digital: How the Net Generation Is Changing Your World*. New York: McGraw-Hill, 2009. Print. A description of the Net Generation, young adults who have grown up in a digital world, based on extensive surveys. Provides insight into their revolutionary use of technology, including their use of professional networking sites such as LinkedIn.

Tewksbury, D., and J. Rittenberg. *News on the Internet: Information and Citizenship in the 21st Century*. New York: Oxford UP, 2012. Print. Examines how news-related Internet sites have altered the process of news gathering, resulting in the segmentation of the news audience.

Wu, Tim. *The Master Switch: The Rise and Fall of Information Empires*. New York: Vintage, 2011. Print. A history of a pattern the author argues information technologies (including telephone, radio, and film) in U.S. history have followed: moving from an open and entrepreneurial environment to one dominated by a few large corporations. The author, a Columbia University professor and senior adviser to the U.S. Federal Trade Commission, argues that the Internet is in danger of following the same course and losing the freedom of its early years to become dominated by one or a few companies.

BIOGRAPHICAL DIRECTORY

The following list briefly summarizes the achievements of the innovators covered in this publication.

A

Jay Adelson: One of the founders and the first chief executive officer (CEO) of the social news website Digg, Jay Adelson started with Netcom, one of the first wide-scale Internet providers, and was among the industry representatives called to testify before the U.S. House of Representatives' Homeland Security Subcommittee on Cybersecurity, Infrastructure Protection, and Security Technologies on the role of the private sector in securing the Internet. After leaving Digg in 2010, he became the CEO of SimpleGeo, Inc., a position he held for less than a year before the company was purchased by Urban Airship. He continues to serve as an adviser for SimpleGeo.

Tom Anderson: The cofounder of Myspace in 2003, Tom Anderson was for years the face of social media, his account being added as a friend by default to any new user on Myspace—making his profile photo possibly the most-viewed face on the Internet, at least in North America, during that time. Although Myspace was neither the first social network nor in the end the biggest success, it was the first success, and introduced most of the general public to the idea of online social networking.

Marc Andreessen: Mark Andreessen led the team that created Mosaic, the first graphical web browser, in the early 1990s, and soon afterward he cofounded Netscape Communications to commercialize this revolutionary innovation, opening the use of the Internet to millions of people around the world. He went on to found companies that pioneered cloud computing, social media, e-commerce, and many other Internet-related applications taken for granted today. He also cofounded Andreessen Horowitz in Silicon Valley, a venture capital firm investing in emerging products that have the potential to transform society through information technology. His opinions and forecasts are widely sought today, and he serves on the boards of a number of major technology companies.

Anonymous: The online network of hactivists known as Anonymous, with thousands of members and no official leadership, is variously viewed as either heroes or cyber criminals and is the best known of all hacking groups. Membership in Anonymous, as in most computer hacking groups, is intentionally loose, with members entering and leaving at will. The group's motto is "We are Anonymous. We are legion. We do not forgive. We do not forget. Expect us." The overall purpose of Anonymous, according to members, is to empower the public.

Marco Arment: During two weeks in 2006, Marco Arment helped David Karp in the creation of the blogging platform Tumblr. By combining the best of online social networking and the Web 2.0 revolution, Arment and Karp were able to provide users with a simple platform for self-expression. Arment's work on Tumblr and his later project Instapaper reflect the developer's desire for efficiency in the Internet age.

Jeff Arnold: Jeff Arnold engineered his knowledge of marketing medical equipment into creating the website WebMD, which became one of the Internet's most often visited sites for medical information. Arnold's goal for WebMD was to make it the link among the different facets of the medical industry, providing consumer access to doctors, pharmacists, drug companies, and insurance companies. After leaving WebMD, Arnold helped found other successful websites, including HowStuffWorks, LidRock, and Sharecare.com.

J. Michael Arrington: J. Michael Arrington is an influential technology blogger and venture capitalist. A former corporate attorney, Arrington has a hard-hitting, take-no-prisoners writing style that has catapulted some Silicon Valley start-ups and sunk others. Although often under fire or a subject of derision for his brash manner and outspokenness, he is nonetheless considered one of the most prominent technology personalities and a major power broker. The companies in which he has invested have for the most part done well, and his buoyancy and knack for honing in on cutting-edge start-ups are major components of that success.

Julian Assange: Australian computer programmer, journalist, publisher, and activist Julian Assange's career has been shaped by his beliefs in transparency and the freedom of information. He entered the computer field as a hacker at age sixteen. After arrest and prosecution, he turned his talents to the rapidly growing Internet, helping the 1993 development of one of Australia's first public Internet service providers, the Suburbia Public Access Network. He also developed a number of free computer software programs. Assange achieved widespread recognition in 2006 as the founder and public spokesman for the website WikiLeaks, which used Internet technology to enter leaked or hacked secret and classified information into the public domain.

B

Mitchell Baker: Answering to the self-chosen title Chief Lizard Wrangler at the Mozilla Foundation and Mozilla Corporation, Mitchell Baker has remained committed to offering open source tools for Internet development. In 2005, Time magazine named Baker on its annual list of 100 Most Influential People.

Paul Baran: Paul Baran's research suggested a distributed network as a strategy for building communications systems that could survive serious infrastructural damage (specifically a nuclear attack), and when the Internet ancestor ARPANET was created, it was with that goal in mind. Baran also developed a key form of data transmission for networks, packet switching, which helped make the Internet feasible.

John Perry Barlow: John Perry Barlow has been one of the most influential political thinkers of the Internet society. Over the course of a career when he has been simultaneously lyricist, lobbyist, essayist, and consultant, he has never ceased to use his communication skills for protecting the constitutional rights of American "netizens." A man of both ideas and action, Barlow helped found the Electronic Frontier Foundation. Widely acclaimed for his visionary insights, he has been a source of inspiration for a generation of political thinkers specializing in new technologies.

Carol A. Bartz: Carol A. Bartz is an American business executive who served as chief executive officer (CEO) of Yahoo, an Internet corporation best known for its web portal and directory of websites, from 2009 to 2011, when she was fired amid a storm of media exchanges. She was among the nation's best paid CEOs, with a compensation package that totaled more than $75 million for her brief tenure at Yahoo! Earlier (1992–2006) she was the CEO of Autodesk, Inc., where more than doubled the company's revenue and transformed it from a little-known creator of computer-aided design software into the world's leading supplier of design software used in buildings, automobiles, and movie animation.

Tim Berners-Lee: Like those of many innovators, Tim Berners-Lee's career has been one of collaboration. Very few, however, can claim such a high degree of individual responsibility for a major accomplishment as he can in developing the World Wide Web. Working as a Fellow at the European Organization for Nuclear Research (Conseille Européen pour la Recherche Nucléaire, or CERN), he created a means by which large amounts of technical and scientific information could be stored, accessed, and freely shared by a large community. This system, which in its early years was used exclusively at CERN, became available on the Internet and has changed nearly every aspect of life in social, economic, political, and cultural spheres of activity.

Garry Betty: Garry Betty's role as chief executive officer (CEO) of EarthLink dramatically transformed the Internet service provider from a floundering start-up to a global telecommunications giant. By embracing new technologies, partnering with the right people, and constantly expanding the company's reach, Betty laid a foundation for the way Internet-based companies did business. Competitive, soft-spoken, but ever-adaptable, he was always a force to be reckoned with, refusing to allow stock prices or his competitors to get the better of his can-do attitude.

Jeff Bezos: Jeff Bezos is the founder and chief executive officer (CEO) of Amazon, among the earliest and most respected Internet entrepreneurs. He turned Amazon into a billion-dollar business that has gone far beyond the books that were its first products. Throughout Amazon's meteoric rise, Bezos has maintained an emphasis on offering a wide selection of products, keeping prices competitive, and ensuring fast delivery. Calling himself a "change junkie," he has never been afraid to take chances and has been guided by his own intuitive grasp of what customers want.

David Bohnett: David Bohnett is an entrepreneur who cofounded the free web hosting service GeoCities, founded the Los Angeles venture capital firm Baroda Ventures, and has been involved in many other online ventures, including OVGuide.com, Wireimage.com, and Xdrive.com. While remaining active as a technology entrepreneur, he has become a noted philanthropist and patron of the arts. His Bohnett Foundation has provided more than $40 million in funding to a variety of arts, educational, and civic programs, as well as gay and lesbian causes.

Andrew Breitbart: Andrew Breitbart was a driving force behind the alternative media movement, which recognized and harnessed the power of the Internet to engage the masses and drive political change. He spent his early career working with Matt Drudge to create one of the world's most influential political news aggregation sites, The Drudge Report, which provides ready and direct access to content from all types of news channels all over the world. Breitbart went on to cofound the equally influential Huffington Post but left almost immediately when it became a forum for the liberal left. In 2005, Breitbart created his own online community for the political right under the umbrella of Breitbart.com. His sites—Breitbart.tv, Big Hollywood, Big Government, Big Journalism, and Big Peace—went beyond directing or hosting media traffic. They also served as channels to present breaking news that challenged what Breitbart believed to be the liberal establishment and leftist popular culture.

Sergey Brin: Sergey Brin cofounded Google, the leading Internet search engine, with Larry Page; the company has since expanded into many other Internet services, including e-mail, cartography, shopping, blogging, and social networking. Brin and Page are also noted for their emphasis on articulating a corporate philosophy based on making the world a better place and helping people to access information freely.

Tina Brown: Tina Brown parlayed a successful career in print media, notably at Vanity Fair and The New Yorker, into leading roles with the website TheDailyBeast.com and Newsweek magazine. Noteworthy for her ability to find content that is wildly popular with the reading public, Brown has sometimes been accused of relying on sensational and low brow material. A member of the Magazine Editors' Hall of Fame, Brown has been able to translate her success in traditional media to new platforms, providing a model for other media conglomerates seeking to make a profit with web-based publications.

Stewart Butterfield: Stewart Butterfield is one of the pioneers of the Canadian technology evolution. His desire for nonviolent online communities that foster communication and sharing is a hallmark of his life's work. After he helped solidify the concept of Web 2.0 and image sharing online, Butterfield returned to the programming life. Whether through his work in online video games or his revolutionary photo-sharing platforms, Butterfield has proven the importance of user-driven content. By providing Flickr users with the site features they need to store and share their images with the world, Butterfield's platform has changed the way people think about photo sharing.

Dries Buytaert: Dries Buytaert created the Drupal open source content management system (CMS) and platform in 2000 while attending university in his native country of Belgium. The system powers approximately 1 million websites across the globe—including such significant and disparate sites as those for the National Aeronautics and Space Administration (NASA), Twitter, and eBay. In 2006, Buytaert cofounded the Drupal Association, a not-for-profit organization dedicated to promoting Drupal. A year later, in 2007, he cofounded Acquia, ranked by Forbes in 2011 as one of the Top 100 Most Promising Companies. Acquia is a for-profit enterprise designed to help companies leverage Drupal's technology, reach, and value through complementary products, services, and support. In 2008, Buytaert cofounded Mollom, a web service that helps sites filter the quality of content contributions and stop website spam.

Owen Byrne: A cofounder of Digg, Owen Byrne was an experienced software engineer who prepared the PHP code for the social news site while assisting Kevin Rose and other partners in organizing the business. He is also a web engineer for GazeHawk, a company that develops eye-tracking services using webcams rather than specialized peripherals, which was purchased by Facebook in March 2012.

C

Robert Cailliau: Robert Cailliau is a Belgian-born engineer and computer scientist who, independently of Tim Berners-Lee, proposed a project to develop a hypertext system at the European Organization for Nuclear Research (Conseille Européen pour la Recherche Nucléaire, or CERN), also known as the European Laboratory for Particle Physics. The project resulted in the World Wide Web. In 1990, Cailliau joined Berners-Lee as a partner in his attempt to win approval for the Berners-Lee proposal. Cailliau rewrote the project proposal, lobbied management for funding, and collaborated with Berners-Lee on papers and presentations. In 1992, Cailliau produced Samba, the first web browser, for the Apple Macintosh. He was instrumental in the push to secure approval of the document that allowed CERN to place the web technology in the public domain in 1993. He is also a founding member and past chairman of the International World Wide Web Conference Committee.

Elisa Camahort Page: Elisa Camahort Page is the groundbreaking chief operating officer (CEO) of BlogHer, one of the largest social networking organizations focused specifically on women. Before cofounding BlogHer in 2005 with Jory Des Jardins and Lisa Stone, Camahort Page ran Worker Bees, a marketing consultancy that integrated social media with corporate marketing strategies. Camahort Page has been influential in encouraging women to take part in technology, to use the Internet for communication, and to create a financially sound model that allows her large-scale blog to thrive.

Steve Case: With America Online (AOL), Steve Case gave new computer users a tool for entering the world of technology. A service provider, social network, and Internet browser, AOL became one of the most respected names in the computing industry. After negotiating the merger of AOL with Time Warner, Case left the company in 2003 to devote his time to Revolution, a venture firm that manages his network of health care and media investments, and to the Case Foundation.

Catherine M. Casserly: Catherine M. Casserly is the chief executive officer (CEO) of Creative Commons, a nonprofit organization with the purpose of simplifying the legal, free exchange of knowledge and culture in the new digital environment created by the Internet. Since 2001, Casserly has been involved with the open source movement. As a program consultant at the William and Flora Hewlett Foundation, she was instrumental in the $1 million grant by that foundation that helped to establish Creative Commons in 2001. She was directing the Open Educational Resources program of the Carnegie Foundation for the Advancement of Teaching when she was elected to the Creative Commons board of directors in 2010. In March 2011, she succeeded Joi Ito as the nonprofit's CEO.

Vinton Cerf: Acknowledged as one of the fathers of the Internet, Vinton Cerf was involved both with the development of the transmission-control protocol/Internet protocol (TCP/IP) used by the Internet and other networks and with the first Internet-compatible commercial e-mail. Additionally, he helped form and eventually chaired the Internet Corporation for Assigned Names and Numbers (ICANN), which coordinates Internet domain names, IP addresses, name servers, and registries, and he has worked as an executive for Google since 2005.

Steven Chen: Steven Chen, a former PayPal employee, cofounded YouTube with his partners Chad Hurley and Jawed Karim in 2005. Since its inception, YouTube has become the most popular video-sharing site on the Internet and the third most popular website in the world, following Google and Facebook. In 2006, Chen sold YouTube to Google and has since founded AVOS Systems, which owns the popular bookmarking site Delicious.com (formerly del.icio.us) and in 2012 was launching a new online magazine publication site, Zeen.com.

David Clark: In the twenty-first century, David Clark is considered one of the Internet's elder statesmen. The former chief protocol architect of the Internet, he headed the Internet Architecture Board for most of the 1980s, overseeing the transitional period after the early days of the Defense Advanced Research Projects Agency (DARPA) and before the inception of the World Wide Web.

James H. Clark: James H. Clark is a legendary Silicon Valley technology innovator and entrepreneur. He used his research on computer graphics as an engineering professor at Stanford University to develop powerful new computer chips to render three-dimensional computer images in real time and thus has been dubbed by some as the "father of computer graphics." He founded

Silicon Graphics, Inc. (SGI) in the early 1980s to commercialize this technology and thereby revolutionized visual production of movies, videos, and scientific imaging. Clark also pioneered the Silicion Valley venture capital model that became the hallmark of the dot-com boom of the late 1990s. Clark went on to invest in a cadre of new web start-ups, such as myCFO, Shutterfly, and Healtheon, which he merged with WebMD in the early 2000s to create one of the most widely visited health information portals on the web.

Bram Cohen: The father of BitTorrent, Bram Cohen developed a peer-to-peer file-sharing protocol (and wrote its first client program in Python), which has since taken up nearly half of the Internet's traffic. What BitTorrent offered was not a single service or site, such as Napster and previous peer-to-peer file-sharing programs, but a protocol to be used by programs to distribute "torrents" of data, bit by bit. Cohen founded BitTorrent, Inc., to continue to support the program, which has become the most successful peer-to-peer file-sharing program. He was recognized in 2005 as an influential business leader, named to Technology Review's TR35 (thirty-five innovators under age thirty-five) and Time magazine's 100 Most Influential People.

Ron Conway: Ron Conway is an angel investor—typically a wealthy individual who invests money (typically amounts from $20,000 up) in high-potential start-up firms, often as a source of initial funding before venture capitalists become involved. He has invested in almost every major Internet start-up since the 1980s, including Google, Facebook, PayPal, and Yelp. He is also well known for saving distressed young companies from certain failure by tapping his extensive network of capital sources. In 2005, Conway left Angel Investors LP, the fund he founded in 1998, to launch SV Angel. SV Angel is a venture capital fund that provides investment support to young companies primarily in the technology sectors that cannot secure funding through traditional investment channels.

Stephen Crocker: Since the 1960s, Steve Crocker has been involved with nearly every major American body overseeing the Internet, including the Advanced Research Projects Agency (ARPA), the Internet Engineering Task Force, the Internet Architecture Board, and the Internet Society. In 2012 he was chair of the board of the Internet Corporation for Assigned Names and Numbers (ICANN). One of the fathers of the Internet, he has received awards for his early work on the general architecture of the Internet, development of the community that has continued to work on networks, and the Request for Comments series, which he assumed was merely a temporary series of notes.

Sky Dayton: Entrepreneur Sky Dayton, at twenty-three, was already the owner of two successful Los Angeles coffeehouses when he founded EarthLink, an Internet service provider, in 1994. A millionaire by age twenty-six, he went on to cofound eCompanies, an Internet start-up incubator; Boingo, a Wi-Fi software and service provider; and Helio, a mobile virtual network operator for the youth market. He is also is a member of the Warren Bennis Leadership Circle of the Center for Public Leadership at the Kennedy School at Harvard University.

Susan L. Decker: Susan L. Decker has served as a role model for women who want to be successful in their careers without giving up the right to have a family. She is best known for her tenure (2000–09) at Yahoo, where she began as chief financial officer and ultimately became president of the company in 2007. During that time, she was the second most highly paid female business executive in the United States. She grew the company's the advertising base, making key acquisitions and focusing on maintaining transparency with Wall Street. When the economic downturn and a takeover bid from Microsoft led to a difficult period for the company, chief executive officer (CEO) Jerry Yang was replaced in 2009 with an external candidate, Carol Bartz, leading to Decker's resignation from Yahoo! in 2009. Her business acumen and her ability to get along well with others have made her a top choice of company heads such as Steve Jobs, Warren Buffet, and Craig R. Barrett when looking for individuals to serve on their boards.

D

Jory Des Jardins: Jory Des Jardins, together with new media entrepreneurs Elisa Camahort Page and Lisa Stone, cofounded BlogHer in 2005. She leads the company's partnership initiatives as president of Strategic Alliances. Her leadership in that capacity has helped BlogHer develop unique and potent strategic relationships that make it easier for women across the globe to communicate and find information and products. Before BlogHer's conferences, publishing platform, and online community, women were only a footnote in the male-dominated blogosphere. Thanks to BlogHer, all tech-saavy women, from social media entrepreneurs to stay-at-home moms, have a voice that can be heard worldwide.

Chris DeWolfe: Chris DeWolfe was the cofounder of the first globally successful social networking site, Myspace. For years it dominated the Internet as the place to be for cyberactive teenagers. It engaged a marketing strategy that took affiliate marketing and social data storage to a new level, largely thanks to DeWolfe, with his background in the world of finance, marketing, and Internet start-ups. He used this experience to assist in the creation of an Internet phenomenon that took the world by storm—so much so that traditional media king Rupert Murdoch bought Myspace. The success of Myspace soldified DeWolfe's place in social networking history, despite Facebook's later dominance.

William Ding: William Ding changed the state of the Chinese Internet industry with the founding and evolution of his company NetEase. When he launched the company in 1997, most of China's immense population did not have easy or affordable access to the Internet. Ding revolutionized the market by creating an online portal that gave anyone in China free access to e-mail and the Internet. NetEase became China's leading Internet portal and community and made Ding one of the world's wealthiest entrepreneurs. With the inclusion in its portfolio of online multiuser computer games, NetEase and Ding continued to blaze trails in China's Internet frontier.

Jack Dorsey: Entrepreneur and computer programmer Jack Dorsey is best known as the creator of Twitter, a microblogging tool that uses messages of 140 characters or fewer to share news and other information with followers. At first disregarded by many as a trivial service for the egotistical, Twitter gained respect as groups and individuals used it as a platform for political, social, and increasingly commercial agendas. Between Twitter and Square, a platform to accept debit or credit-card payments via smart phones, Dorsey has helped generate $10 billion in market value. He has been hailed by the press as a modern Thomas Edison and the next Steve Jobs.

Matt Drudge: Matt Drudge is the creator and editor of the eponymous website The Drudge Report. Although the website is reviled by some, the self-proclaimed anti-government libertarian created one of the more popular sites by offering aggregation of news found elsewhere as well as some original stories. Drudge includes links to sites from across the political spectrum and has developed a reputation for sometimes breaking news stories before large news organizations do so.

E

Eric Eldred: Eric Eldred has been a computer engineer, analyst, and computer systems administrator at various times in his career. His most significant efforts, however, have not been in any technical specialty but in the legal and economic realms, to expand public access and the list of works in the public domain. Running his own organization, Eldritch Press, to make works in the public domain available over the World Wide Web, he has been restricted by the provisions of the Copyright Term Extension Act (also known as the Sonny Bono Act), which extended the time that authors and their estates— both personal and corporate copyrights—are in effect. The result was Eldred's attempt, through the Supreme Court case Eldred v. Ashcroft (2003), to overturn the copyright extensions and challenge the constitutional power of Congress to extend copyrights.

F

Caterina Fake: Caterina Fake developed online communities where people could share art, photography, and writing and chat about common interests. Her Internet start-ups Flickr and Hunch gained the attention of Yahoo! and eBay, earning her millions. Today, Fake is seen as a role model for women interested in Internet entrepreneurship. Her abilities to think outside the box, focus on a goal, and collaborate with others on creative projects have played key roles in her success.

John Fanning: John Fanning is a somewhat controversial figure who is both credited and chastised for his role in the founding and fall of the Internet-based peer-to-peer music-sharing company, Napster. He cofounded the company with his nephew, Shawn Fanning, in 1999. As owner of a 70 percent stake in Napster, John Fanning maintained control of the company as its chief executive officer (CEO) and chairman of the board of directors. At first hailed as a revolutionary new way to distribute music, Napster soon became the target of media and recording industry giants claiming copyright infringement and illegal distribution. Fanning ultimately lost the legal battles and the company but continues to be recognized as an Internet industry pioneer.

Shawn Fanning: Shawn Fanning is a pioneer of peer-to-peer technologies and social networks. After releasing Napster, a revolutionary software application enabling Internet users to exchange music files, he launched various projects aimed at enhancing social interactions on networks. A computer programmer, entrepreneur, and angel investor, he has helped shape the digital society with ventures such as SNOCAP, Rupture, Path.com, and Airtime.

Jake Feinler: Jake Feinler is an Internet and information scientist who worked at the Stanford Research Institute (SRI), where she managed the Network Information Center (NIC) for the Advanced Research Projects Agency Network (ARPANET) and then the Defense Data Nework (DDN), which were the first packet-switching networks that allowed scientists to share resources among universities. Over time, this system evolved into the Internet. Feinler's group was also responsible for the Internet's Domain Name System (DNS). From 1989 to 1996, Feinler worked at the National Aeronautics and Space Administration's Ames Research Center. In 2010, she published a history of the NIC. Feinler was inducted into the Internet Hall of Fame as an Internet "pioneer" in 2012.

Barbara J. Feldman: Barbara J. Feldman is the owner and founder of Surfnetkids.com, Inc., an online publishing company that creates educational content for parents, teachers, families, and children. Feldman created Surfnetkids in 1996 as an archive for her nationally syndicated weekly newspaper advice column Surfing the Net with Kids. Feldman has more than sixty websites, including FreeKidsColoring.com and JokesByKids.com. She is an expert in building audiences for advertising-supported content sites and promoting them for educational uses on the Internet. A former computer consultant and programmer, she is also a newsletter publisher, shareware author, and self-proclaimed "websurfer surpreme." She blogs at barbara.feldman.com.

David Filo: While he was pursuing a Ph.D. in electrical engineering at Stanford University, David Filo cofounded the Internet directory that soon became Yahoo, Inc. Famously working for a salary of only $1 per year, he has retained a technical role and as of 2012 was still Yahoo!'s largest single shareholder. Perennially listed as a billionaire high-tech entrepreneur, he is not fond of publicity and maintains a very private life, working diligently behind the scenes to support the world-renowned business that he cocreated in a trailer in 1994.

Heather Perram Frank: Heather Perram Frank is a writer, editor, blogger, media consultant, and editor-in-chief of USA Today's Weekend magazine. Her experience includes extensive media production at The Huffington Post and at the popular Internet service provider and media production company America Online.

Janus Friis: Janus Friis is the cofounder of two of the Internet's most popular and influential technology products: Kazaa, a file-sharing service designed to operate on the FastTrack protocol, and Skype, an Internet telecommunications suite. Friis maintains an active interest in the ownership of Skype and has also cofounded Joltid, which devleops online marketing technologies, the commercial music network Altnet, and the online music and video-streaming sites Rdio and Vdio.

G

Gail F. Goodman: Gail F. Goodman is chairman, president, and chief executive officer (CEO) of the e-mail marketing company Constant Contact, Inc., based in Waltham, Massachusetts, and founded in 1998. A small business expert and visionary, Goodman revolutionized the way that small businesses and organizations effectively maintain relationships with their customers, clients, and members through e-mail and othering marketing campaigns. Constant Contact provides small businesses with e-mail marketing, event marketing, social media marketing, and online survey tools and has become an industry leader in online marketing, used by more than 450,000 small organizations worldwide and earning more than $174 million in revenue. In 2007, it became a publicly traded company.

Ron Gorodetzky: Ron Gorodetzky was one of the first employees of Digg, hired by founder Kevin Rose to develop much of the code and architecture for the social news-sharing site for which Owen Byrne had written the PHP script. Gorodetzky was instrumental in developing many of the features and site changes that Digg adopted in its early years, as it became one of the most popular sites on the Internet—fifty-fifth in Alexa's

global rankings—and was pursued by larger companies. He remained with the site as it declined (to 215th in Alexa's 2012 ratings) and as a new version was rolled out, before founding the Fflick movie recommendation site, which was purchased by Google.

Brad Greenspan: Considered a "boy wonder" among Internet entrepreneurs, Brad Greenspan started both eUniverse and Myspace. Myspace especially became an exceptional success, but by the time of its $580 million sale to News Corp., Greenspan had left the business after an accounting scandal.

H

Heather Harde: For five years, Heather Harde ran the most successful and most popular technology news site on the Internet. As general manager of the top technology blog on the web, TechCrunch, Harde increased traffic, diversified the brand, and ensured that the blog provided the very latest in technology and start-up news. In her role as vice chairman of a San Francisco–based technology innovation organization, Harde inspires women in technology while having a significant impact on perceptions of media and technology.

Michael S. Hart: Michael S. Hart is best known for his invention of electronic books and for founding Project Gutenberg. With access to substantial computing power at the University of Illinois at Urbana-Champaign and inspired by a free printed copy of the U.S. Declaration of Independence, he began typing the text of the declaration into a computer and transmitting it to other users on July 4, 1971. He added many other public-domain texts to that first one over the next forty years. Project Gutenberg, named for the fifteenth-century German printer Johannes Gutenberg, whose movable-type printing press is considered to have inaugurated the age of print, was the first and largest single collection of free electronic books available on the Internet. Hart also devoted four decades to championing the open source movement, which he helped to start. In 2006, he cofounded the World eBook Fair.

Reed Hastings: Reed Hastings cofounded Netflix, the world's most popular DVD-by-mail service, with Marc Randolph in 1998. Netflix has since transformed the movie rental business: Brick-and-mortar competitors have downsized or gone out of business (although Blockbuster

attempted a similar DVD-by-mail service for a time). Netflix's streaming service on the Internet helped drive the popularity of streaming video, which in turn greatly increased the bandwidth usage of the average Internet customer and drove the need for more robust infrastructure and higher-bandwidth connections. Despite notable missteps, Netflix's success has endured, transforming itself from a well-known novelty to a true force in the entertainment industry to one that has further balkanized the television audience and affected movie ticket sales.

Shani Higgins: After working for a number of investment, software, and publishing firms, Shani Higgins was hired to head day-to-day operations at Technorati, Inc., the company behind the Technorati.com blog search engine. Higgins launched Technorati Media, the world's largest social media advertising network, as well as Technorati's private advertising exchange. She also arranged the company's first content acquisitions, acquiring the blogs and staff of Blogcritics and the Silicon Valley Moms Group. In 2011, she became the company's third chief executive officer (CEO).

Reid Hoffman: Reid Hoffman is a risk taker whose visionary viewpoint has helped shape the way the world does business. From the start, Hoffman knew that he wanted to make a difference on a global scale. He recognized that the Internet was the best means to that end and focused his efforts on employing technology to connect and empower individuals everywhere. He cofounded LinkedIn as a forum for online networking and sharing of information among professionals and would-be entrepreneurs. Today, LinkedIn is the world's largest professional networking site.

Meg Hourihan: Meg Hourihan is the cofounder of Pyra Labs, which created the popular weblog software Blogger, a free web-based tool that introduced a simple means of launching a personal website, the blog. Blogger was later bought by Google. An innovative entrepreneur and pioneer blogger, Hourihan writes the award-winning blog Megnut.com and was one of Technology Review's TR35 ("35 innovators under 35") and one of PC Magazine's People of the Year in 2004. Along with Blogger cocreators Paul Bausch and Matthew Haughey, Hourihan published the book We Blog: Publishing Online with Weblogs in 2002. She frequently speaks on the subject of blogs and young women entrepreneurs.

Tony Hsieh: Internet entrepreneur Tony Hsieh sold his first company, LinkExchange, to Microsoft for $265 million in 1998. He subsequently cofounded Venture Frogs, then joined Zappos. Under his leadership, Zappos has grown to a billion-dollar online shoe retailer that is dedicated to customer service. From a young age, Hsieh has been involved in numerous flourishing companies, which he has inscribed with his own unique business and organizational culture. Hsieh's technical knowledge, creativity, leadership qualities, and entrepreneurial spirit have combined to make him a successful business innovator in today's world.

Arianna Huffington: Alternately known as a "force of nature," "the patron saint of new media," and "the queen of aggregation," Arianna Huffington has helped to redefine news media on the Internet. She cofounded The Huffington Post in 2005 as an alternative to conservative news sites. Regularly offering both original and compiled news and entertainment stories, images, and videos, The Huffington Post continues to draw an increasing number of visitors to its site. Even though her detractors question her transformation from staunch conservative to active liberal, they have been forced to acknowledge Huffington's flair for providing a comfortable place for "Huffsters" to vent their opinions on everything from politics to celebrity antics.

Steve Huffman: Straight out of college, Steve Huffman founded the social news site Reddit with classmate Alexis Ohanian, using seed money from Y Combinator. A competitor to Digg, which began around the same time, Reddit was acquired by Condé Nast Publications while Digg turned down suitors until long after its price had fallen. Huffman left Reddit in 2009, returning to Y Combinator and forming a start-up, the travel search engine Hipmunk.

Chris Hughes: By the age of twenty-five, Chris Hughes was considered a success in the fields of both social networking and political campaigning. Never as interested in the computer side of creating Facebook as the rest of his Harvard friends, Hughes had a special knack for understanding the impact of particular features on users of the social networking site, which earned him the nickname the Empath among his fellow Facebook cofounders. After graduating from Harvard, Hughes devoted his full attention to turning Facebook into the top social networking site in the world. Much more than his friend and cofounder Mark Zuckerberg, who believed the Internet should be used for sharing information, Hughes understood the need for privacy. After leaving Facebook, Hughes expanded his interests to public policy, and he is credited with developing the online campaign, which became a primary source of funding, for Barack Obama's presidential bid in 2008.

Chad Hurley: Chad Hurley cofounded the popular website YouTube, which revolutionized the way many viewed video by allowing users to share their creations online. Although YouTube does not charge users a fee to upload or view videos, it does sell advertising, making it highly profitable. After selling YouTube to Google in 2006, Hurley stayed on as chief executive officer (CEO) through 2010 and has continued to serve as an adviser to the company.

J

Van Jacobson: Although his name lacks the public recognition of many of the giants of the late twentieth and early twenty-first century technology revolution, Van Jacobson played an important role in bringing the World Wide Web to the global public. His work on redesigning the transmission-control protocol (TCP) and expanding its scope was instrumental in providing the means of digital communication that came to be known as the Internet. Jacobson's technology, which involved the development of what is popularly known as Jacobson's algorithms, made it possible for the Internet to continue to expand without collapsing in the late 1980s. His work on networking led him to create diagnostic tools such as traceroute, tcpdump, and pathchar.

Jeff Jaffe: Since entering the information technology industry in 1980, Jeff Jaffe has been a committed researcher and activist. For more than thirty years, his research-guided philosophy has centered on creating an efficient and rapid Internet environment. His skills have caught the attention of numerous worldwide leaders and in 2010 propelled him to a position as chief executive officer (CEO) at the World Wide Web Consortium (W3C).

Xeni Jardin: Digital media commentator Xeni Jardin is a contributor to Wired, a correspondent for National Public Radio (NPR), and a frequent guest commentator on television news broadcasts. She is the coeditor of the blog Boing Boing, as well as a culture journalist with publications in numerous major venues. She also hosts and executive produces Boing Boing Video.

Sandy Jen: Sandy Jen is an entrepreneur who, together with cofounders Seth Sternberg and Elaine Wherry, launched the first web-based instant-messaging product, Meebo Messenger, in September 2005. Meebo represented a revolutionary approach to person-to-person (P2P) communication in the days before social media was a household term. As chief technology officer, Jen drove the company's back-end development and innovation as it continued to launch new products to meet the evolving communication and information needs of users. In June 2012, Jen joined Google's technology team, working on Google+, following that company's acquisition of Meebo.

K

Brewster Kahle: Since the mid-1980s, Brewster Kahle has focused on developing technologies for information discovery and digital libraries. As a digital librarian, he has played a major role in making information easy to find and widely available through the Internet. Kahle is most famous for founding the Internet Archive, a nonprofit digital library with the mission of "universal access to all knowledge." An idealist with focus and discipline, Kahle would like to save a copy of every type of information resource on Earth.

Robert Kahn: Robert Kahn's involvement with AR-PANET and eventually the Internet began at the very start of the ARPANET program in 1968, when he was part of the team at Bolt, Beranek, and Newman that developed the network for the Department of Defense. Eventually joining the Advanced Research Projects Agency (ARPA) in 1973, Kahn headed what was the largest government computer research and development program to that time. Along with Vinton Cerf, Kahn developed the transmission-control protocol/Internet protocol (TCP/IP) in the early 1970s, establishing a means whereby computers on a network (such as ARPANET or the Internet) could communicate with computers on different networks. In addition, he was instrumental in creating open architecture, meaning that information could be accessed openly rather than through programs that were protected as proprietary intellectual property.

Mitchell Kapor: Mitchell Kapor is best known for the design, development, and marketing of the spectacularly successful spreadsheet program Lotus 1-2-3 in the 1980s. He has, however, a string of other accomplishments. He has been a significant force in making the benefits of technology available to a wide range of people, especially minorities. As an entrepreneur, investor, and founder of the Mitchell Kapor Foundation, he has sought to bring educational opportunities to minority students and to minority-owned companies trying to establish themselves in the information technology (IT) field. He has also worked in the areas of open systems development for the Internet, revising outdated copyright protection laws, and creating an effective national technology policy.

Jawed Karim: Jawed Karim was one of the three cofounders of the Internet video-sharing site You-Tube, credited with the initial idea for the site; he also worked on the pioneering Internet commerce site PayPal, which facilitated the exchange of money over the Internet. Although Jawed became a multimillionaire when YouTube was sold to Google, he has largely stayed out of the limelight and later returned to his academic studies, with the goal of becoming a university professor.

David Karp: The founder and chief executive officer (CEO) of Tumblr, David Karp has an estimated net worth of more than $40 million. He was named one of the TR35 ("35 innovators under 35") in the Massachusetts Institute of Technology Technology Review's 2010 TR35 list when he was twenty-four years old.

Jim Kimsey: Entrepreneur and philanthropist Jim Kimsey is best known as a cofounder of America Online, Inc. (AOL). Kimsey served as president and chief executive officer (CEO) of the company during the first decade of the Internet service provider's existence. He was the first chairman of the board of directors, a title he held after he was succeeded as CEO by Steve Case. Kimsey resigned from the board in 1997 to lead the AOL Foundation, a philanthropic organization with AOL backing, until AOL merged with Time Warner. Kimsey is chairman emeritus of AOL and served as chairman of the International Commission on Missing Persons from 2001 to 2011. He continues to be active in various cultural and charitable groups. In 2012, he recorded a privately distributed country-rock album as Verlin Jack.

Michael Kinsley: Michael Kinsley, an American political journalist and pundit, founded Slate, an online magazine that was originally part of Microsoft's Internet presence. Kinsley was twice editor of The New Republic and he served as editor of Harper's and the Washington Monthly and American editor of The Economist. For six years, he was cohost of CNN's Crossfire and earlier was a regular with William Buckley, Jr., on PBS's Firing Line. A longtime contributing writer for Time magazine, Kinsley has also written columns for The Wall Street Journal and The Times of London. He has been a regular columnist for Politico and Bloomberg's View and is author or coauthor of half a dozen books.

Steve Kirsch: For more than thirty years, Steve Kirsch has offered innovation to the information technology industry. As an entrepreneur who constantly strives to create cutting-edge technology, he has provided new devices and software which has assisted both individual users and companies. Furthermore, Kirsch's deep commitment to philanthropy has set an example for others inside and outside the industry.

Peter T. Kirstein: Peter Kirstein was a pioneer in helping to establish the Internet in Europe and led the group that established the first Internet connection between the United States and the United Kingdom. He was first head of the computer science department at University College London and has been involved in many international collaborations over the course of his career.

Leonard Kleinrock: Leonard Kleinrock's contributions to the Internet have been extensive on both the theoretical and practical levels. He has referred to himself as the father of modern data networking, a claim disputed by some. He conducted research into and enhanced the theoretical framework for packet switching, a technology that allows messages to be broken into smaller segments and then reassembled at the point where the message was to be sent. This method would allow faster transmission with the ability to share computer resources most effectively. On a practical level, Kleinrock and his staff at the University of California at Los Angeles (UCLA) supported the creation of the first major network, the Advanced Research Projects Agency Network (ARPANET), developing and implementing its first node at UCLA. He later developed otherideas on how the resulting Internet could be improved and has been an advocate for greater mobility, or what he calls "nomadic computing."

Timothy Koogle: Timothy Koogle was the first president and chief executive officer (CEO) of Yahoo, Inc. He was recruited by investor Mike Moritz of Sequoia Capital to be Yahoo!'s sixth employee. In the company of Stanford Ph.D. dropouts, he was comparatively a wise old sage at forty-five. His folksy and reasoned style guided the company through the first six years of explosive growth on the world stage. In 2001, Koogle was replaced at the helm of Yahoo! by entertainment executive Terry Semel. A mechanic at heart, Koogle then retired to a couple of board seats and the occasional race car seat.

Gary Kremen: Gary Kremen is an Internet and software engineer known for capitalizing on the value of Internet domain names; among the names he has registered are jobs.com, autos.com, and sex.com. His eleven-year battle to reclaim sex.com was highly publicized and established the legal principle that a domain name is property and thus can be stolen, even if the original owner did not pay for it. Kremen also cofounded one of the world's first open source software companies and created a pioneering green power company to encourage the use of solar energy.

L

Max Levchin: Max Levchin is a Ukrainian-born, but primarily American-raised, computer scientist who has used his technology skills and business savvy to become a successful Silicon Valley entrepreneur. As a founder and key driving force behind the online payment-processing company PayPal, in 2002 he helped lead the first successful initial public offering (IPO) of a technology company after the terrorist attacks of September 11, 2001. After selling the post-IPO PayPal to eBay later in 2002, he then founded, invested in, and became chief executive officer (CEO) of Slide, an online service designed to give people an easy way to improve their blogs and personal pages with photo slide shows, videos, and other visual content. After selling Slide to Google in 2010, Levchin founded a company named HVF, which is reported to be an incubator employing tactics similar to those that Levchin used to launch Slide and other companies in which his role was more limited (such as Yelp, whose board includes Levchin).

Robin Li: Robin Li is a Chinese Internet entrepreneur and cofounder, chairman and chief executive officer (CEO) of Baidu, Inc., the Chinese web services company that runs China's most popular search engine and the world's third-largest independent search engine. In 2011, Forbes named him the richest man in China and the ninety-fifth richest in the world, with an estimated worth of $10.2 billion. Li excels at improving

algorithms for search engines; for example, he developed the RankDex site-scoring algorithm for ranking search engine pages, which was awarded a U.S. patent. This technology is used in the Chinese-language search engine Baidu, which Li cofounded in 1999 and which now holds 85 percent of the Chinese market share.

J. C. R. Licklider: Sometimes known as the Johnny Appleseed of twentieth-century computing, J. C. R. Licklider has been credited by various sources as the creator of the Internet, cloud computing, libraries as repostories for information accessed electronically, and e-commerce. Licklider's accomplishments were not based on design and development of system architectures, hardware, or software. Instead, his great contribution was as a visionary, an "idea man," who conceives concepts and then brings them to the attention of those who eventually design and implement his vision. On a more practical level, Licklider's positions in key organizations (particularly the Defense Advanced Research Projects Agency and Bolt, Beranek, and Newman), as a leader of efforts backed by funds that he freely and judiciously applied, went far toward making his visions, including his concept of what is now the Internet, reality.

M

Andrew Mason: Andrew Mason is the founder of Groupon, a Chicago-based Internet company that offers discounted gift certificates that are localized to major markets. The name is a composite of the words group and coupon.

Michael Mauldin: In 1994, Michael Mauldin created the Internet search engine Lycos with three pages of code. A year later, the venture capital company CMGI purchased program and built it into a publicly traded company. Mauldin went on to cofound Conversive (formerly Virtual Personalities, Inc.) in 1997, which creates computer-generated human characters. In 2000, his obsession with robots was initiated by an episode of the television show Battle Bots, and robotics have fascinated him since.

Marissa Mayer: Marissa Mayer is one of the Internet world's most prominent female executives and has attracted considerable attention as the youngest CEO of a Fortune 500 company (Yahoo!) who did not found the company. By June 2012, when she began her tenure at Yahoo, she was best known for her thirteen years with

Google, during which she worked as a product manager, engineer, and designer for a range of services, including Gmail, Google Books, and Google Maps. Her competence and vision enabled her to rise through the ranks to an executive position at Google, and she demonstrated her potential for further growth when, at the age of thirty-seven and pregnant, she struck a blow for women in technology (and in the corporate world generally) by taking the top spot as chief executive officer (CEO) at Yahoo!

Kevin Mitnick: Kevin Mitnick is one of the most famous computer hackers in history. He became fascinated with breaking into mechanical and computer systems at an early age and progressed into hacking the computer networks of large companies, copying their software and reading their records, e-mails, and other private information. Like many other hackers, he was allegedly motivated by intellectual curiosity and the desire to demonstrate to corporate interests that their property was not as safe as they believed and did not wish to benefit materially from his crimes. After having been a convicted criminal and a fugitive, Mitnick has reinvented himself as a computer security specialist particularly well positioned to advise companies on how to repel hackers like him.

Paul Mockapetris: Paul Mockapetris is best known for creating the Domain Name System (DNS), which for twenty years has helped structure the distribution of e-mail messages and Internet communications on multiuser networks. He is also responsible for a number of other Internet-related achievements that have led to his induction into the Internet Hall of Fame and having received numerous awards and distinctions. After a lengthy career in academia, in 1995 he entered the commercial sector to work as chair and chief scientist at Nomunim, Inc., which creates software to assist in DNS applications and is based in Redwood City, California.

Dustin Moskovitz: Dustin Moskovitz is one of the cofounders of Facebook, one of the world's most prominent social media networks and the focus of considerable attention. He left Harvard University after two years majoring in economics in order to move to Palo Alto with Mark Zuckerberg. There they founded the company in 2004, with Moskovitz acting as chief technologist and development strategist. In 2008, he left Facebook to start a new company, Asana, which aimed to provide applications that mirrored in working life what Facebook does for social life. He retains his holding in Facebook and, after the flotation of the company in 2012, was estimated to have a net worth in excess of $5 billion.

Markos Moulitsas: Markos Moulitsas is one of the most influential voices on the Internet, with a community blog, The Daily Kos, that reaches 2 million readers and is a leading site for left-central readers as well as regular columns for traditional media. The Daily Kos has become such an important part of progressive politics that Moulitsas has become incorporated, informally, into the Democratic Party's intelligentsia, and his opinion on potential candidates a valued one. As a proponent of grassroots activism and bottom-up self-organization as a means of effecting political change, Moulitsas aims to promote The Daily Kos as a seamless link between mainstream journalism and citizen journalism. He balances his activities there with work for the mainstream media and his other commercial interests, which include a network of sports blogs.

Elon Musk: Elon Musk used his technology skills and business savvy to become a successful, serial, U.S.-based entrepreneur. Musk's first company, which he cofounded with his brother shortly after leaving the graduate physics program at Stanford University, was called Zip2; it provided online content publishing software for local news organizations and was acquired by Compaq. As a founder and early driving force behind online payment-processing company PayPal, Musk in early 2002 reaped significant financial rewards from PayPal's initial public offering (IPO)—the first successful IPO of a technology company after the U.S. terrorist attacks of September 11, 2001. After eBay acquired the post-IPO PayPal later in 2002, Musk then used the significant wealth he had accumulated from Zip2 and PayPal to cofound, invest in, and become chief executive officer (CEO) of both Space Exploration Technologies (SpaceX) and Tesla Motors.

N

Ashwin Navin: Ashwin Navin cofounded BitTorrent, Inc., in 2004 with brothers Bram and Ross Cohen to maintain and promote the peer-to-peer file-sharing protocol developed by Bram. Navin served as the company's first president, handling business matters, while the Cohens dealt with product development. In 2008, Navin resigned from BitTorrent to focus on other businesses, Flingo and i/o Ventures.

Col Needham: Hewlett-Packard technological engineer Col Needham founded the Internet Movie Database, commonly known by its web address acronym IMDb, in 1990. The searchable entertainment industry database grew from the movie credit lists of Needham and other online film enthusiasts. IMDb had emerged as one of the most popular entertainment websites by the late 1990s, in part driven by its frequent appearance at the top of results returned for movie-related Internet searches. Needham remained with the Internet Movie Database after its 1998 acquisition by online entertainment e-commerce leader Amazon. The Internet Movie Database's growth placed him within the ranks of the leading Internet entrepreneurs. He is among the pioneers of telecommuting to maintain a role as the site's managing director and is also known for his business philosophy, which is centered on the vital importance of the site's visitors' contributions to its success.

Craig Newmark: Craig Newmark founded Craigslist to build a community that could use the Internet as a tool to help others: a simple site that connects people around the world, where they can satisfy basic human needs in finding work, shelter, and relationships in one place. Despite Craigslist's success, Newmark stuck to his core values and remained a "customer service representative" for his own site, using undisclosed profits to fund citizen journalism projects and other causes involving civic participation.

Luke Nosek: Polish-born American Internet entrepreneur Luke Nosek is known for his leading roles in the fields of e-commerce and venture capitalism. He

was a cofounder of the payment and cryptography services company Confinity, which merged with Internet financial services company X.com to form the online financial transactions broker PayPal in 1998. Nosek remained with PayPal until its acquisition by online auction site eBay in 2002. PayPal emerged as one of the leading online payment options both within and outside eBay. Meanwhile, Nosek gained renown as a member of the so-called PayPal Mafia, the group of company leaders who had been together since their early days at the Stanford Review newspaper.

O

Kevin O'Connor: Best known for his founding of DoubleClick, which at its prime was the most successful Internet advertising company in existence, Kevin O'Connor is also an author, a college professor, and an astute investor. He became successful in business immediately after graduating from college and continued to hone his computer and financial skills.

Alexis Ohanian: Alexis Ohanian founded the social news site Reddit with Steve Huffman immediately after the two graduated the University of Virginia. He later joined Huffman's travel search engine start-up, Hipmunk, as well as working as Y Combinator's "Ambassador to the East," mentoring East Coast start-ups.

Pierre Omidyar: Throughout his career as a software engineer at Claris and a developer services engineer for General Magic, Pierre Omidyar's major interest was in online commerce and online auctions. With the establishment of the auction site eBay.com, he brought together buyers and sellers of huge numbers of different products and services. EBay is now the most widely recognized site where buyers and sellers meet, and Omidyar is widely recognized as one of the most innovative and creative Internet entrepreneurs. He and his wife are passionate philanthropists who have donated millions of dollars to social causes.

P

Larry Page: As a codeveloper of the PageRank algorithm, Larry Page provided the tools that led to the creation of Google, Inc., a multinational corporation that provides a variety of Internet-related products and services. Based on the success of its Internet search engine, Google has extended its products to include e-mail, an office productivity suite, social networking tools, and other online productivity software. Page, who serves as chief executive officer (CEO) of Google, is responsible for the operation of the company responsible for the most often visited website on the Internet.

Sean Parker: Sean Parker was the cocreator of the pioneering music file-sharing site Napster, which demonstrated the viability of distributing individual songs over the Internet as MP3 files. The success of Napster helped both artists and users bypass traditional record companies, tapping years of frustration at the music industry, and led

to the creation of the Apple iTunes store, a profitable commercial operation selling individual songs over the Internet. Parker also played a crucial role in the creation of the social networking site Facebook, helping founder Mark Zuckerberg obtain funding; Parker also served as president of Facebook and has been involved with several other web products, including Plaxo and Spotify.

Bob Parsons: Vietnam War veteran Bob Parsons founded the highly successful domain registry website GoDaddy.com. A determined spirit and charitable heart have helped Parsons's endeavor flourish into the multimillion-dollar industry it is today. GoDaddy came into being during the early years of the Web 2.0 evolution and soon became the dominant website registry and hosting service. It has experienced some controversy, however, most of it surrounding its founder, Parsons. His determined nature and ability to capitalize on bad press have made him a major player in the virtual world and an example for those who did not perform well during school and succeeded despite growing up with more disadvantages than advantages. Hard work and persistence despite failure are the hallmarks of Parsons's professional career.

Radia Perlman: Although she dislikes the title, software engineer and inventor Radia Perlman is known as the mother of the Internet for her design of the spanning tree protocol (STP), which has kept the Internet accessible through networking even as it has continued to expand. She also developed TRILL (for Transparent Interconnection of Lots of Links), a more sophisticated protocol that fixed problems with STP. She is also a pioneer in tangible computing and is responsible for the development of link-state routing. In the field

of Internet security, Perlman has developed sabotage-proof networks, certificate revocation, and password protection. She holds more than one hundred patents, approximately half of in conjunction with Sun Microsystems, her longtime employer, and has other patents pending. Her textbooks have become required reading for both students and professionals.

Christopher Poole: Christopher "moot" Poole is the founder of the popular Internet image-sharing board, 4chan.org, and the online image remix site Canvas (URL canv.as). Poole was declared Time magazine's Most Influential Person of 2008 in an online poll. A strong proponent of online anonymity and privacy rights, he speaks at conferences and on panels as an advocate of free online culture.

R

John Rezner: John Rezner was in the right place at the right time in November 1994, when he and his partner, David Bohnett, cofounded GeoCities, which has been called the Internet's "first cybercommunity." Rezner helped guide the company in its revolutionary efforts to give the public a voice in creating the Internet as it was becoming a part of the everyday lives of people around the world. He developed technology that made GeoCities so user-friendly that even those uninitiated in computer technology or web publishing could create their own sites.

Larry Roberts: Of all of the individuals credited as having contributed to the development of the Internet, Larry Roberts was not only present at the creation but also one of the most critical involved. His participation began with the first small-scale and primitive networks at the Massachusetts Institute of Technology's Lincoln Labs in the early to mid-1960s. His interest in and comprehension of J. C. R. Licklider's concept of

an "intergalactic network" informed his eventual role as program manager responsible for all aspects of the management and design of the ARPANET.

Michael Robertson: Long recognized as a groundbreaking entrepreneur and a businessman with a defiant streak, Michael Robertson has pushed the boundaries of the information technology industry. Best known for his creation of MP3.com, Robertson has exhibited a willingness to test the limits of technology, business, and copyright laws, which has placed him at odds with stakeholders both inside and outside the computer industry.

Kevin Rose: Kevin Rose left a career in broadcasting at TechTV to cofound Digg and Revision3, a social news site and web TV developer, respectively. He oversaw Digg's most successful period, founded the short-lived but financially successful Pownce social network, and was eventually hired by Google Ventures.

S

Sheryl Sandberg: Sheryl Sandberg is credited with helping to build Google into the powerhouse it became before moving to Facebook, where she became a major force in expanding both the fortune and the user base of the social networking site. She has risen to the height of her career while raising a family and maintaining a strong base of friendships and promoting women's

issues. When she left Google in 2008, her loss was considered a major setback for Google but a major victory for Mark Zuckerberg and Facebook.

Larry Sanger: Larry Sanger is an American philosophy professor best known as the cofounder of Wikipedia. It was Sanger who gave the online, collaboratively written encyclopedia its name, combining the term wiki, which denoted the server software that allowed users to create and edit web page content on any browser, with pedia, a root of encyclopedia, meaning "education." He was responsible for the day-to-day oversight of Wikipedia until he left the project in 2002 and became a vocal critic of the open source encyclopedia in the years after he severed his connection with the group. Later, he founded Citizendium, another wiki encyclopedia project more strictly regulated and edited than Wikipedia. Sanger also served as executive director of Watch-KnowLearn.org, a directory of free educational videos for students in grades 1 through 12.

Eduardo Saverin: Eduardo Saverin, born to a wealthy Jewish family in Brazil and raised in the United States from age thirteen, is best known as the cocreator, with Mark Zuckerberg, of Facebook (dramatized in the 2010 feature film The Social Network with Andrew Garfield as Saverin). Saverin was friends with Zuckerberg when they were both students at Harvard University, and he was the first investor in Facebook; he later sued Zuckerberg. Saverin has more recently invested in other technology start-ups, including Qwiki and Jumio. His decision to renounce his U.S. citizenship (he remains a citizen of Brazil) and take up residence in Singapore before Facebook's initial public offering (IPO) attracted public scrutiny, many charging that the move was designed to avoid paying U.S. taxes (Singapore has no capital gains tax), but Saverin insists the move was motivated only by his desire to live and work in Singapore.

Marc Seriff: American Internet executive Marc Seriff is known for his technical, entrepreneurial, and investment knowledge and experience with Internet-based start-up companies (commonly known as dot-coms). He was an early employee of the data communications company Telenet Communications, Inc., joining the company in 1974 and helping to develop the first commercially available e-mail. He then worked at several start-up companies, including Digital Music, where in 1981 he helped develop the first downloading service for music. Seriff's most notable achievement was the 1985 cofounding of the Internet service provider Quantum Computer Services with Jim Kimsey and Steve Case. The company was renamed America Online, Inc. (AOL) in 1991. Seriff served as the company's first chief technical officer, after retiring from America Online in 1996.

Dave Sifry: A vocal member of the open source movement, entrepreneur Dave Sifry moved from Linuxcare—his start-up offering Linux consulting and tech support in order to encourage the adoption of Linux by businesses—to Technorati, which began as a blog search tool and added numerous blogs' worth of content and an innovative advertising platform. Technorati has since become the third-largest social media property, after Facebook and Twitter.

Ben Silbermann: Ben Silbermann is cofounder and chief executive officer (CEO) of Pinterest, one of the world's most popular social networks. In 2009, Silbermann, along with Paul Sciarra and Evan Sharp, began working on a site on which people could share collections of things that interested them by electronically pinning images of those things to an interactive virtual bulletin board. Less than three years later, Pinterest had nearly 20 million unique visitors each month and $138 million in funding. The network has been valued as high as $1.5 billion, and by 2012 it was recognized as the fastest-growing social media site, outdistancing both Facebook and Twitter.

Craig Silverstein: As the first employee hired by Google founders Larry Page and Sergey Brin, Craig Silverstein will always have a special place in the history of the organization. Google's rapid rise was greatly assisted by Silverstein's deep computer programming skills and his commitment to providing users of the Google search engine with efficiency, accuracy, and speed.

Russel Simmons: Russel Simmons (not to be confused with hip-hop mogul Russell Simmons) is best known as the cofounder, along with Jeremy Stoppelman, of the social media and review site Yelp. Simmons worked as lead software architect at PayPal during its early days; he also worked at an incubator started by the company's cofounder, Max Levchin. Simmons is interested not only in computer entrepreneurship but also in exploiting the flexibility of the computer and the Internet for educational applications.

Biz Stone: Biz Stone has been called a serial entrepreneur because of his involvement with several enterprises: blogging sites Xanga and Blogger, podcasting company Odeo, and start-up incubator Obvious Corporation. He was a cofounder of the latter two. He is best known as a cofounder of Twitter, the free microblogging service that enables subscribers to send and receive text-based messages of 140 or fewer characters. He served as the company's creative director until 2010. He is also the author of *Blogging: Genius Strategies for Instant Web Content* (2002) and *Who Let the Blogs Out? A Hyperconnected Peek at the World of Weblogs* (2004).

Lisa Stone: Lisa Stone, along with Internet entrepreneurs Elisa Camahort Page and Jory Des Jardins, cofounded BlogHer in 2005 to create opportunities for women bloggers around the world to access and engage in a community dedicated specifically to the interests and information relevant to today's women. Stone serves as the company's chief executive officer (CEO) and was the chief architect behind BlogHer's distributed, diversified media business. She helped grow the company from a grassroots conference into a top-ranked women's community through the development of innovative models to deliver profitable, high-quality online media and to attract and compensate a massive base of new content contributors.

Jeremy Stoppelman: Jeremy R. Stoppelman is one of a new generation of Internet entrepreneurs revolutionizing Internet commerce and opinion sites. Stoppelman learned about Internet commerce while working as a vice president of engineering at the online payment company PayPal. Online auction site eBay bought PayPal while Stoppelman was employed there. With the introduction of Yelp in 2005, Stoppelman and partner Russel Simmons made it possible for customers in the San Francisco area to rate local businesses. Yelp has since gone nationwide, and ventured into public stock trading.

T

Jeff Taylor: Jeff Taylor has been an Internet entrepreneur for most of his life. He invented the job search site Monster.com, the social networking site Eons.com, and the online obituary site Tributes.com. Despite selling Monster early on, he stayed with the company after the sale to develop, implement, and communicate its corporate strategy. He has extensive marketing experience with baby boomers and their changing needs as they grow older. By transforming newspaper sections into online marketplaces, he has changed the landscapes of traditional media and careers; in addition, by aligning online commerce and social networking, Taylor has become one of the most innovative entrepreneurs in today's consumer industry.

Peter Thiel: Peter Thiel is an investor, hedge fund manager, and entrepreneur who cofounded PayPal with Max Levchin. He was the first outside investor in Facebook and has a lengthy record of supporting successful Internet innovators. He has used his substantial personal wealth to fund a range of projects, through the Thiel Foundation and other vehicles, in line with his scientific and libertarian interests. In doing so, he has established a reputation as a leading philanthropist in venture capitalism. These efforts are in part an attempt to prevent what he believes to be a coming catastrophe by developing necessary preventive technology.

Danielle Tiedt: Danielle Tiedt is recognized in the technology industry as a marketing innovator who helped Microsoft Corporation launch and promote many of its successful computer networking and web-related products and services during her fifteen-year tenure with the industry behemoth. She is most closely associated with the roles she played in showcasing MSN and in launching the Bing search engine in 2009. Tiedt was recruited by Bing's main rival, Google, in February 2012 to lead the search engine leader's marketing efforts for the popular online video-sharing service YouTube. She was brought in specifically to devise new and creative ways not only to position YouTube as the primary destination for original video content but also to make it extremely attractive to advertisers so that it will ultimately generate advertising revenue rivaling that traditionally seen in television.

Ray Tomlinson: Ray Tomlinson achieved what became his principal career success in 1971, when he was working on the ARPANET system and devised the means for the world's first network e-mail system. His innovations led to the development of systems that would one day become the Internet.

Gina Trapani: The founder of the Lifehacker blog in 2005, Gina Trapani continued to oversee the blog until 2009. She continues to work as a blogger and tech commentator, cohosting the This Week in Google netcast, and developing Expert Labs' crowdsourcing platform.

Mena Trott: Mena Trott was the president of Six Apart, a company she cofounded with her husband, Ben Trott. Mena was an early blogger, and the Trotts developed

Movable Type, one of the tools within Six Apart, because she was dissatisfied with the blogging software available to her. Mena Trott is sometimes called the "founding mother" of the blog revolution because of the popularity of Six Apart and its tools, including not only

the easy-to-use blogging tool Movable Type but also the blog-hosting service Typepad; these tools made it possible for people with limited technical skills to become involved in blogging.

W

Jimmy Wales: Jimmy Wales, cofounder of Wikipedia, has believed that everyone should have the freedom to access information and the ability to add to our human knowledge base. While Wikipedia operates as a nonprofit organization, Wales has used his background in finance to provide sustainable capital for the free online encyclopedia. Charismatic but controversial, labeled as "benevolent dictator" and "spiritual leader" by his colleagues, Wales is the public face of Wikipedia, spreading the gospel of free access to information while the net worth of Wikipedia grows into hundreds of billions of dollars.

Jay S. Walker: Jay S. Walker is the founder, chairman, and chief executive officer (CEO) of Walker Digital LLC, a developer of new and patentable digital business models. He is the founder of numerous Internet-based start-up companies. Walker's most recognized accomplishment was the founding of the e-commerce site Priceline.com, for which he served as vice chairman until 2001. The site revolutionized both the travel industry and digital commerce in general through its introduction and popularization of buyer-driven commerce, a marketing tool that allows consumers to set their own price for goods and services and be matched with suitable companies. Walker Digital received a patent for the business model in 1998. Walker was the driving force behind Priceline, a pioneer of buyer-driven commerce on the Internet and one of the most successful companies to emerge from the so-called dot-com boom of the late twentieth century.

Neil Clark Warren: Neil Clark Warren is best known as the founder of eHarmony, an online matchmaking service, and as an author of popular articles and books giving relationship and marriage advice. A professional psychologist, Warren has said that he founded eHarmony as an outgrowth of his counseling practice and that his motivation was to help people identify partners with whom they could form a lasting and happy marriage. Warren is the public face of eHarmony: His image appears in many advertisements for the site, and he makes

many media appearances (on more than three thousand radio and television programs, according to the eHarmony website). Warren has also published nine books and hundreds of articles promoting his views on relationships and marriage. Although eHarmony began as a primarily Christian dating site, in 2005 Warren moved away from focus on that particular market and toward appealing to a much broader market; today. eHarmony presents itself (on its website and through advertising) to potential users as similar to many other online dating services.

Jeff Weiner: Internet executive Jeff Weiner began his career at Warner Bros., where he was employed in a variety of roles from 1994 through 2000, helping expand the company's Internet presence. He oversaw the development of Warner Bros. Online in 1996 and served as the new division's vice president. He next cofounded Windsor Digital and was an executive in residence at Accel Partners and Greylock Partners before joining Yahoo! in 2001. His executive experience at Yahoo! included senior vice president of corporate development, senior vice president of search and marketplace, and executive vice president of its Network Division. Weiner left Yahoo! in 2008 to become acting president of the leading global online professional networking company LinkedIn. He took the role of LinkedIn's chief executive officer (CEO) in 2009, helping the company expand its global presence. He is recognized for his skills in management, corporate and product development, and business operations as well as his creativity, marking him as one of the prototypical of Silicon Valley start-up executives.

Tim Westergren: Tim Westergren is a former rock and jazz musician who is best known as the cofounder and chief strategy officer of Pandora, a service that assists users in creating their own radio stations. A record producer with two decades of experience, Westergren is also an award-winning composer and an accomplished pianist and plays the bassoon, drums, and clarinet as well. He has managed artists and scored feature films. In 1999, Westergren and Will Glaser devised the Music Genome Project, a typology for categorizing a piece of music according to almost two thousand traits. The Music Genome Project, which is updated continually, is the base upon which Westergren built Pandora.

Elaine Wherry: Elaine Wherry is one of the cofounders of the social media platform Meebo, created in 2005. She started the company with two other college friends in a California apartment. Meebo was a Web 2.0 company, part of a group of start-ups founded on the concept that the Internet is a platform of information sharing, interoperability, user-centered design, and collaboration on the web. Web 2.0 companies center on user-generated content and include blogs, wikis, and social networking sites. Meebo was a major web-based instant-messaging (IM) system in that, while it was not the first chat service, it quickly became the most popular because it was the most accessible and most convenient, allowing users to bypass software hurdles. Wherry developed Meebo's initial JavaScript framework in 2004. She was integral in creating products such as Meebo Messenger, Meebo Mobile, and the Meebo Bar. She oversees the look and feel of all Meebo products.

Meg Whitman: Meg Whitman is a business leader who has served in executive positions in a variety of companies, from Disney to Hasbro to eBay. Her bid for governor of California in 2010 did not succeed but was quickly followed by invitations to apply her talents

and experience to new ventures, notably as Hewlett-Packard's chief executive officer (CEO) in 2011. Well connected with other corporate leaders, she continues to contribute to American business development, serving on the boards of several major corporations.

Evan Williams: Evan Williams is a computer programmer and entrepreneur from Nebraska who has been involved with two of the Internet's most visited sites: Blogger and Twitter. He has worked at a number of prominent Internet companies on both full-time and contract bases but has become best known as one of the three founders of Twitter, where he continues to work in an executive position, developing strategy. Twitter has hundreds of millions of users and has revolutionized online communications for many of those people. Twitter and tweet have entered the lexicon as verbs familiar to nearly everyone with a mobile phone or computer, and few news, entertainment, and other major corporations do not offer interactive communications with viewers and listeners via their websites and social media pages.

Steve Wolff: Steve Wolff was a seminal figure in the early development of the Internet, particularly through popularizing the network with leading decision makers and helping to make its potential clear. This has led to his classification as one of a small group of people regarded as fathers of the Internet. He was involved with the creation of ARPANET and numerous other important developments in a career lasting more than fifty years.

Y

Jerry Yang: With Stanford University colleague David Filo in 1994, Jerry Yang created a directory of websites located on the Internet that eventually became known as Yahoo! Quickly evolving into one of the leading Internet websites, Yahoo! enjoys some of the highest rates of

traffic of any website, second only to Google as of 2012. Although Yahoo! continues to be highly successful, the failure of its stock price to keep up with that of Google led to a series of new chief executive officer (CEO) s after Yang stepped down in 2009.

Z

Niklas Zennström: Niklas Zennström has been termed one of the leading technology "disrupters." He has leveraged licensing, corporate start-up logistics, ownership, and litigation to disrupt, delay, and disguise information in many technology businesses. With his vision to allow consumers and businesses to interact freely over the Internet, Zennström exploited peer-to-peer

(P2P) networks with his Danish collaborator and business partner Janus Friis. Early on, Zennström used these file-sharing code systems so consumers could download files with Kazaa and later stream music with Rdio. Subsequently, Zennström and Friis were responsible for the development of the Internet video service Skype, which bypassed conventional telecommunications companies to facilitate global Internet communication. A billionaire entrepreneur and visionary, Zennström serves as a role model for many technology start-ups and, along with Friis, invests in the ideas of others through his venture capital company Atomico.

Mark Zuckerberg: Computer programmer and social media visionary Mark Zuckerberg was the motivating force behind the creation of Facebook, which became the top-ranked social networking site in the world. Facebook users sign up with the site to share their lives with selected friends or with the public if they so choose. While still a student at Harvard, Zuckerberg and a group of friends launched the site as a way of connecting students to one another. Continuing to serve as chief executive officer (CEO) while retaining 56.9 percent of Facebook's voting power, Zuckerberg has remained firmly in control of the company, refusing buyout offers, including those from Google, Viacom, and Yahoo! He did allow Microsoft to buy a 1.6 percent interest in the company in 2007. Time magazine named Zuckerberg as its Person of the Year in 2010.

Indexes

Category Index

Company Index

INDEX